THE WORLD'S GREATEST KNIFE BOOK

24th Annual
KNIVES 2004

D0926072

Edited by
Joe Kertzman

KNIVES 2004 STAFF

Joe Kertzman, Editor

Ethel Thulien, Designer
Tom Nelsen, Designer
Patsy Howell, Designer

Editorial Comments and Suggestions

We're always looking for feedback on our books. Please let us know what you like about this edition. If you have suggestions for articles you'd like to see in future editions, please contact

Joe Kertzman/Knives
700 East State St.
Iola, WI 54990
email: kertzmanj@krause.com

The Cover Knives

There's an underlying knife on the cover, or at least it's lying under the rest—the Northwest Tlingit Wolf Dagger by Edward Brandsey. The main feature, aside from a shapely 13-inch, browned O-1 blade, is the mammoth-ivory handle butt with abalone and mother-of-pearl inlays, giving the knife an American Indian flavor. At bottom left is a Brad Duncan one-hand, locking-liner folder sporting a tan G-10 handle, and a 3-1/2-inch 6K Stellite blade fused to 440C. The William B. Ellis fighter above it combines, in a most appealing way, a desert ironwood grip and yellow-brass rivets, guard and sub-hilt. Also noteworthy is the filework, fit and finish. Sticking out its steely tongue is Philip Booth's scale-release switchblade that showcases a coral handle, copper liners that have been hammered, antiqued and shaped into a dragon-like body, and mokume bolsters carved into a dragon's head. A crocodile and flamingos share the spotlight on a Stephen Mackrill knife (top) parading color scrimshaw on a hippo tooth handle, and a raindrop-damascus blade. The overall theme is beautiful custom knives, and the mix shows how diverse the genre has gotten.

Published by

 **krause publications**
An F&W Publications Company

700 East State Street • Iola, WI 54990-0001
715-445-2214 • 888-457-2873
www.krause.com

Please call or write for our free catalog of publications.
Our toll-free number to place an order or obtain a free catalog is 800-258-0929
or please use our regular business telephone 715-445-2214.

Library of Congress Catalog Number: 80-67744

ISBN: 0-87349-687-6

INTRODUCTION

Words and phrases most knifemakers don't know, don't care to know or choose not to know: 401(k) plan; 40-hour work week; voice mail; casual Friday; punch the clock; pension plan; conference call; secretary; corporate bonus; cost-of-living raise; retirement benefits; glass ceiling; cubicle; chief executive officer; 5 o'clock shadow; corporate ladder; sales meeting; boss; brown-noser; car-pool; water cooler gossip; lunch hour; daycare; office pool; power nap; power lunch; and power broker.

Don't get me wrong. Knifemakers work. They slave. Most pay their bills, taxes and debts to society, have children, set schedules, meet deadlines, achieve goals, do finances and, if lucky, set a little money aside for a rainy day. They all know the meaning of the term "sweat equity." They live and breathe their work. They depend on their own hands, minds, tools, machinery, skills, determination and dedication to make a living, to earn a buck.

When asked why they don't join the nine-to-five crowd, most knifemakers say they do not want to work for someone else. They gain satisfaction from making something from nothing. They enjoy taking a piece of steel and forging a blade. They take pride in fashioning a finished knife from nothing but raw materials. They build and create. There is an end product they can hold, admire and call their own. They work at their own pace, set their own hours and evaluate their own output. Knifemakers are the planners, designers, fabricators, salesmen and saleswomen, marketers, promoters, representatives, accountants, clerks, packagers, shippers and janitorial staff. Responsibility is ultimately theirs. They take the credit and the blame. Knifemakers answer to no one but themselves. It's the way of the craftsman in America and abroad.

So, with no "incentive programs" or "bonus initiatives," why would anyone expect a quality knife to come from the hands of these self-employed shop junkies, these society dropouts, self-indulgers, mad scientists, whacky inventors, system shunners and self-proclaimed innovators? Why would we trust anything built from scrap with no molds, set tolerances, quality control measures or diagnostics? Knife enthusiasts, collectors, users and general "nuts" would have it no other way. We love these knife guys! Can you think of another industry where there are more people making something by hand than there are those running machines to output similar products?

There's nothing wrong with factory and production knives. Many of the knifemakers in this industry collaborate with factories on new blades and knife models. It's just that no machine can make knives as beautiful as those inside the pages of *Knives 2004*, not even the most well-oiled, technologically advanced, power-packed, mega-memory, super machines in the universe. Nope, it takes five-to-10 good fingers, a hand or two, some brawn, imagination, time, patience and skill to craft knives this beautiful to the eye.

As a bonus, the editor has taken the liberty of hiring some of the most skilled knife writers to pen a few good stories for your reading pleasure. Lance Strong invites you along on a shop tour to peruse retooled Ruana knives, the edged results of a knifemaking business passed down to the sons of the late, great blade builder Rudy Ruana. John Lewis Jensen takes you to visit Meier the Steel Magician— Daryl Meier, that is, forger of dazzling damascus billets for blades. Dexter Ewing introduces you to "mid-tech" knives. Attorney at Law Evan Nappen reveals the Most Illegal Knife in America, and Mike Haskew unveils the Mount Everest of Knifemaking. You'll Swing Low to a Sweet Chopper and sing the Swan Song of the Balisong. There's even a tribute to Bill Moran between book covers, and a comparison of horn and stag knife handles.

Read about the hottest trends, state-of-the-art processes, knife embellishments and all that's sharp in the handmade and factory realms.

Who needs a day job? Keep those office memos, lunch meetings, business trips and bonus plans. Let's "get busy" with some handmade knives.

Joe Kertzman

Knives 2004
CONTENTS

WOODEN SWORD AWARD 2004

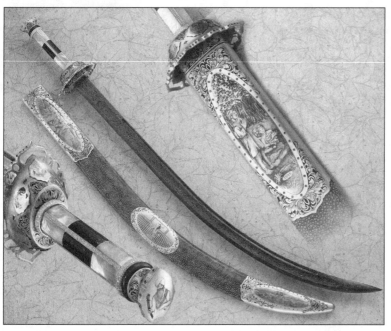

Occasionally a knife or sword surfaces that someone poured his or her heart into, creating a functional, edged objet d'art. Jot Singh Khalsa fashioned such a sword for a man who has been a teacher and an inspiration to him, a man regarded, according to Khalsa, as the "Pope" of the Sikh religion in the West. The sword Jot created is just as inspirational to blade enthusiasts as the teacher has been to his students. It showcases 20 carats of diamonds set into 18k gold, a lapis-lazuli and mother-of-pearl handle, a swooping and "sweep-me-off-my-feeting" Devin Thomas stainless damascus blade, ruby inlays and gold engraving by Julie and Buster Warenski depicting scenes from the "Pope's" life. Much of the scabbard was fashioned by Vince Evans, but the sword is Jot's original design. It is the design and the resulting "sword smorgasbord" that warrant the presentation of the Wooden Sword Award to Jot Singh Khalsa. For a larger picture of the sword, see the "Super-Sized Steel" section of "Trends." (Coop photo)

Living the Ruana Knife Legacy

"Old-school" Ruana knives have become "new-school" lessons in quality craftsmanship

The old guard and new guard of Ruana Knife Works include the late Rudy Ruana (left) and his able predecessors in the knife business, from left at photo on right, Mark Hangas, Vic Hangas and Mike Hangas. Vic holds the Ruana 60th Anniversary Limited Edition Bowie.

By Lance Strong

ELEVEN YEARS AGO, when I wrote an article about knifemaker Rudy Ruana for "Knives '93," I was concerned about whether the quality and reputation of Ruana knives would hold up for the long term. Yet, despite the fact that Rudy had died seven years earlier, in April of 1986, I had every reason to believe the company would continue a storied tradition of building sturdy knives.

Rudy's son-in-law, Vic Hangas, had been with Rudy since 1964 and took over company operations from him in 1983. That's 19 years of working side-by-side with the old man and putting his own touch on virtually every Ruana knife to leave the shop during that time. Ruana knives are still handcrafted in the small shop where Rudy began forging out blades 65 years ago.

I had briefly owned one of the "new school" Ruana knives, with updated stamps on both the alumi-

New for 2003 is a reproduction of a Lewis and Clark knife called the "Ruana Explorer," and the author was treated to a look at the prototype (pictured) before the logo (inset) was even stamped into the blade.

num-alloy handle and leather sheath. Though parading a somewhat better finish than early models, the new knife looked and felt like any of my old Ruanas. When I put it to my ever-present Norton 8-inch soft Arkansas sharpening stone, the hammer-forged, high-carbon-steel blade felt the same as previous edges. I didn't keep that knife long. My alligator-hunting guide, Gary Nunez of Abita Springs, Louisiana, took a real hankering to it, and I left it with him as thanks for a fun and successful hunt. At the time, it skinned and butchered six gators and I have no idea how many since.

I've witnessed businesses built by fathers who raised their children in them, leaving the companies in the care of who they believed to be able offspring, only to have the enterprises run poorly and go down the drain in a few years. I certainly didn't want that to happen to Ruana Knives, nor did I want to see any major changes to an already successful product line and knife design. I'd heard the Ruana Knife Works business was booming, even more than in the past, from my Montana friends, so in the summer of 2002, I decided to drive once again to Bonner, Montana and see what was what.

The shop seemed to have a new coat of paint and a couple of other improvements, but was basically the same—so far, so good. When my wife and I entered the building, it was customer friendly, with a service counter and space behind it,

and the ubiquitous elk rack hanging on the wall. The work area was off to the right in another room, and greeting us was a smiling and cheerful Mike Hangas, Vic's son.

Mike put me at ease, opening a color catalog (what would Rudy think!) and hauling out finished knives—some to be shipped to customers, and a few others available for immediate sale. It became apparent that the blade grinds were some of the finest I'd seen on any knife, anywhere, made by anyone. In viewing clean, neat lines with no pits, holes or bad bevels, I was falling in love.

"My brother, Mark, can really grind a fine blade," Mike stated proudly. Indeed he can. Mark has been with the business since 1976, so he, too, worked with Rudy until the elder retired, in 1983, at 80 years of age. Though he's somewhat self-effacing, Mike, who joined in 1984, is also a critical part of the solid triangle that makes up Ruana Knife Works, Inc. He processes orders, meets the occasional client who walks through the door, and handles the computer correspondence.

The day of my visit, Mark and Vic cheerfully stopped their work for introductions, some quick snapshots at my request and an interview. As they were cleaning up to go fishing for the rest of the day, I made arrangements to revisit in a few weeks.

Sadly, in the interim, there was a death in the family of Mark's wife, so he was not available when

I returned to the shop. I asked Mike how many knives his dad, Vic, had made with Rudy. The number came to about 30,000. I was astounded! Mike double-checked his figures, and the simple math of knives per month, and then year, multiplied by the resulting number of years proved the figure to be correct. I thought, "so much for wondering if Vic had sufficient hands-on experience working with Rudy."

Knife Coveting

A customer was at the Ruana shop looking at a model 20 B Skinner with a finger-grip handle—a knife I covet but do not own. The finger grooves fit my hand well, unlike the old Randall models I also like so much. With his permission, I checked out the grind, fit and finish, and found them above reproach. I was handed a model 22 Hatchet, also featuring standard finger grooves, and it proved to be more balanced than my old Rudy-made model.

"It's a little smaller but with better balance and a heavier head," Mike told us. I'd add that the handle is significantly more ergonomic in design and, like the 20 B Skinner (the company's signature knife), seems custom fit to my hand. I didn't want to put it down. As it turns out, the customer didn't, either, and took a set of the knives home with him.

While it's not a good idea to store non-stainless knives in leather sheaths, you can get away with it in dry climates if—and that's a big if—the leather is properly vegetable tanned. I can think of at least nine Ruana knife owners who live in low-humidity states, and none of them have had problems with rust from the company's sheaths. (Don't store your knife in the sheath if it's wet, however.)

The new sheaths seem to be made of even higher-quality leather, but Mike notes that it's still leather tanned by the Muir and McDonald Co., as were original Ruana knife sheaths. A tanning recipe from 1863 calls for bark of Douglas fir trees and hemlock—the primary reason the leather doesn't attack the blade steel. The hides are free from the barbed-wire scars I've become accustomed to, and

The stages of development of a Ruana knife are portrayed in this telling photo, from a billet of steel (top left) to a finished four-finger hunter (bottom right).

Although Ruana bowies are built to be used, they have become increasingly popular as collector items. Many knife collectors consider bowies works of art.

apparently come from dairy cattle of the Tillamook, Oregon region.

If it becomes necessary to store a knife in the sheath, it's a good idea is to coat the blade with a thin film of Rust Free, available from A. G. Russell Knives. A food-grade type of silicone, Rust Free does not perpetrate the same ill effects as gun oil does on meat or leather.

Rivets are now neater and much smaller, and made from brass rather than the old-standby copper or short-lived aluminum Rudy used, a change made in 1996 or 1997. A slight change to the logo stamp on the sheath was implemented in 1984. American elk stag continues to be employed for the dovetailed inserts on the knife handles.

"Our elk antlers come mostly from Montana, Idaho and Wyoming," Mike told me, "and we will never knowingly buy game-farm antlers." In fact, dry elk sheds are preferred over green antlers that take a year to dry, thus lengthening the production time, and there is no question of the legality of sheds.

Another recycling aspect concerns the aluminum alloy used in the handle stock of most knife models. I knew it wasn't pure aluminum, as that is too light and soft, and would blacken the knife user's hand. What I didn't know is that Ruana aluminum has always been made from scrap piston heads and other sources, including aluminum alloy wheels. With that information, I cut a glance at the spare tire on our new Jeep Liberty waiting outside. (Gee, I don't know, honey, do you think someone stole the spare during the night? Not to worry, I have a great matching pair of Ruana Skinners for us. I call this model the "Liberty.")

Vic interrupted my daydream when he entered the room to work on handles, showing me various woods, as well as Micarta®, used on the Steelhead models and some of the Custom Brass offerings. The latter are round-handled, full-tang knives, finely finished and preferred by many users. During my earlier visit, my wife spotted the 60th Anniversary Limited Edition Bowie. It debuted in 1998, a design involving a 1/8-inch, hammer-forged blade, with 100 limited edition and serial-numbered pieces in the line. The blade is engraved for the occasion, and the handle is a combination of elk antler, stained curly maple, Micarta and brass spacers. The bowie balances superbly in the hand, though most owners will likely be content to show it off in optional glass-door cases of walnut, oak or cherry. There are three choices of color for the felt backdrops in the display cases.

New for 2003 is a reproduction of a Lewis and Clark knife called the "Ruana Explorer," and I was treated to a look at the prototype. I believe it's modeled after trade knives carried on the expedition and, as such, does not have a full tang, but instead the blade is securely steel-pinned into the crown-stag handle. The original grips were wood, but Vic and sons wanted to use something nicer. The 6-1/2-inch blade is marked with a special logo and serial number.

Sentimental Stag Grips

If they wish, customers can supply their own crown stag, assuming it's the right size, for a personal and sentimental handle. The Ruana Explorer, with its quality leather sheath, retails in the $450-$500 range, and a portion of the purchase price is donated to the Travelers' Rest State Park program (see www.travelersrest.org). Again, the

Modern Ruana sheaths are sent to the Muir and McDonald Co. tannery, as they have always been. A tanning recipe from 1863 calls for bark of Douglas fir trees and hemlock—the primary reason the leather doesn't attack the blade steel. The hides are free from the barbed-wire scars the author has become accustomed to, and apparently come from dairy cattle of the Tillamook, Oregon region.

Above: Ruana knives, with antler handle slabs pinned in place, are ready for final polishing.

Right: Vic Hangas of Ruana Knife Works grinds a matched pair of elk-antler handle inserts.

Finished Ruana blades, with handles cast in place, await elk-antler grip inserts.

all-important blade-to-handle balance is superb, and I requested my name to be put on the waiting list for an Explorer knife.

So, how do the new Ruana knives stack up? They are definitely better than their predecessors! Fit, finish and ergonomics are vastly improved, while still retaining the hammer forging and famous tempering. I'm fussy about my steel, having used blades in climates from deserts to jungles, and from mountains to marshes, for many decades. A blade has to work right. Speaking of steel, the Hangas boys still use 1095 or its equivalent for small knives, and 5160 chrome-molybdenum for the extensive line of larger bowies.

These are not whiz-bang stainless steels, but tried-and-true, clean, high-carbon steels that will perform as necessary for generations to come, and with little care. The secret is in the properly hammer-forged and hardened steel, as opposed to overly hard, exotic blades that are brittle and nearly impossible to sharpen in the field.

My concern about whether the quality and reputation of Ruana knives would hold up for the long term was unwarranted and proved to be just plain false. The company certainly does continue a storied tradition of building sturdy knives—and *good* old-fashioned knives at that! ●

For more information on quality Ruana knives, contact Ruana Knife Works, Inc., P.O. Box 520, Bonner, MT 59823, www.ruanaknives.com. Because it's a three-man shop, the Hangas's have requested that readers please write or email them only. The time saved will be reflected in the speed orders are processed. A free color catalog tells the entire knife story, and also showcases Montana-made leather sheaths, sharpeners and clothing items. Walk-ins at the shop are welcome, and there is often a limited selection of knives on hand for immediate purchase. Please remember, though, it's a tiny shop where time is important.

Experience Sword Art— Korean Style

Master Kim's focus narrows as he changes from polite master to precise and intense warrior

By Greg Bean

IN THE HANDS of a master, the Asian sword is not only a weapon, but an instrument of meditation and personal development. In the hands of a smith, it is a work of art. Korean Master M.K. Kim, with his *jin gum* (a sword similar to a katana) in hand, personifies the mix of serenity and lethality emblematic of Asian martial arts, and his weapon reflects over a thousand years of design and refinement.

His *dojang* (fencing school) is equipped with mirrors on one wall, a padded floor, punching bags and a weight room. Students from 5-to-50 years old, punch, block, kick and brandish swords. With traditional Korean music playing in the background, the atmosphere blends coaching and aesthetics, dance studio and boxing gym. Master Kim balances these elements with grace and ease.

When Master Kim, president of the Southeast United States World Haidong Gumdo Federation, demonstrates a cutting test, his focus crystallizes as he changes seamlessly from a polite, encouraging master to a precise and intense warrior. Bamboo approximates the density of bone, and a clean cut like this reveals a skilled hand at the sword.

Haidong gumdo, Korea's venerable sword art, traces its roots to the 3rd century kingdom of Koguryo, one of the three primary historical dynasties. While not as well known as tae kwon do and *tang soo*, haidong gumdo is a growing art, with 150 schools in the United States and schools in more than 20 countries worldwide. Master Kim, president of the Southeast United States World Haidong Gumdo Federation, oversees the certification and instruction for the southeast, one of the four regions of the country.

Rolled mats simulate the resistance of combat or duel targets. Demonstrating a follow through that would impress Tiger Woods, this mid-section cut would have gutted a 3rd-century warrior, even through armor.

With his focus as sharp as his weapon, Master Kim surgically removes the portion of a rolled mat that is just about head height. Ouch!

A formal salute pose, honoring one's opponent, is an essential part of Korea's venerable sword art *haidong gumdo*.

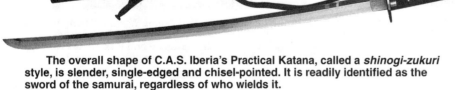

The overall shape of C.A.S. Iberia's Practical Katana, called a *shinogi-zukuri* style, is slender, single-edged and chisel-pointed. It is readily identified as the sword of the samurai, regardless of who wields it.

reflected by the respect and reverence his students show him.

For centuries, the sword art of *jangbaekryu*, attributed to Korean Gen. Yu Yu, was the accepted form of warfare. As firearms replaced edged weapons, sword arts continued as a means for discipline and physical development. The warrior class developed by Gen. Yu Yu—*the samurang*—dominated the Korean peninsula between the 3rd and 7th centuries.

As their dynasty passed, the samurang faded from view. Some ended their own lives, and others migrated to Japan where, according to Master Kim, they were the seminal influence for the samurai. Some samurang fled to the mountain regions outside the mainstream where jangbaekryu passed from man to man in relative obscurity until the last quarter of the 20th century.

Master Kim's credentials include membership in the Korean National Army demonstration team, as well as being crowned the 1989 Korean tang soo do champion and the 1990 tang soo do world champion. Though retired from competition, world champions having little else to win, he is still a dedicated practitioner of the martial arts he teaches—tae kwon do, tang soo do and haidong gumdo. As a devotee of haidong gumdo, he sustains his skills through teaching forms, sparring and cutting, the prime showcase for one's skills.

With 50 haidong gumdo students at his Charlotte, North Carolina, dojang, Master Kim, born in Korea and a U.S. resident for 15 years, travels often to teach seminars around the country and takes

his students to Korea for the bi-annual world championships. With a powerful build and the politeness of a diplomat, Master Kim's love of the arts shows in the humor with which he teaches children, and is

Just as tae kwon do uses flying techniques, so does haidong gumdo. Leaps and spins train a warrior to fight on uneven surfaces or while in pursuit.

Demonstrating a cutting test, Master Kim's focus crystallized as he changed seamlessly from a polite, encouraging master to a precise and intense warrior. With his sword in hand and a target in front of him, there is no mistaking haidong gumdo is a deadly art.

Cutting media include rolled reed mats, bamboo, hanging or suspended paper, and thrown fruit. Rolled mats approximate the density of flesh, and bamboo the density of bone, both simulating the resistance of the targets of combat or a duel.

Concentration and skill are needed to make the cuts cleanly. Lacking either of these traits, and the martial arts practitioner shreds the materials. Paper, from rice paper to newsprint, is attached to a support and hung by its own weight. The goal is to cut the paper cleanly rather than tearing it. Cutting fruit thrown in the air is another test. From a ready position with his sword in its scabbard, Master Kim would first throw the fruit, and then draw his sword, wait, watch and swing, hopefully cleaving the fruit.

The Quest for Sharpened Steel

Gumdo practitioners train with several types of swords, from bamboo-bladed pieces to live steel. Beginners start with a *mok cum*, a wooden sword. After six months of study, a student advances to a *ka cum*, a blunt-edged steel sword. Attaining the black belt, a two-year process, earns the right to use a sharpened steel sword, a jin gum. Once sufficiently trained, students spar with the *jok do*, a bamboo sword. The jok do, with splits along its length, provides cushioning and give to the blows.

The first haidong gumdo lessons teach the basic cuts, including the straight, angular, lateral and diagonal cut. Once skilled at cutting, footwork and combinations of footwork and cutting are added to simulate combat against one or more opponents.

Cuts are first practiced from a training stance called *gima gyunjukse*, resembling a horse-riding stance. The student makes stationary cuts at an opponent directly in front of him. The next fundamental stance, the *daedo gyunjukse*, resembling a traditional front stance, adds mobility to the training.

Forms are a series of stylized movements used in combat. Aside from the cuts and blocks, such feats as dodging, spinning, leaping and rolling on the ground are incorporated into the sword maneuvers.

Two and three people train using the jok do with quite a bit of blade contact, sometimes for extended lengths of time, adding conditioning, speed and muscle memory to the movements.

Haidong gumdo emphasizes drawing the sword smoothly and rapidly. From its resting position, with the scabbard turned and adjusted to parallel to the ground, the sword is drawn, raised above the head and lowered to the front of the body with the tip at about eye level. The top hand encircles the grip at

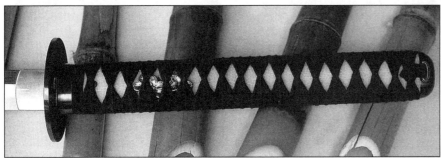

A braid, or *ito*, defines the two-handed grip of C.A.S. Iberia's Practical Katana, and is wrapped to leave diamond-shaped openings that reveal the stingray skin underneath. A close-up unveils the fine detail of the ito, the *menuki* (handle ornament) and the ray skin.

Master Kim spars with one of his students with a *jok do*, the bamboo facsimile of a *jin gum* sword used for sparring.

hand's length from the guard, while the lower hand anchors the sword at its end.

The sharpened jin gum steel sword comes in two styles and three lengths. The *sam koc do* has a lighter blade and is used for cutting straw mats, suspended paper and objects such as fruit thrown in the air. The *yook koc do* has a heavier blade, and while it can be used for cutting the lighter materials, it is preferred for severing heavier objects, such as bamboo.

Of the three lengths, the longest, the *chang do,* was initially built as a military weapon and worn openly. The shortest, the *so do,* was a covert weapon and could be concealed in the sleeves of the traditional, flowing clothing. The medium-length sword, *ye do,* seems to have more general purpose, perhaps even as a civilian arm.

The debate between the Korean, Japanese and Chinese on their martial arts, weapons and history will go on forever. At the least, both samurang and samurai were warrior classes, with honor codes that placed duty and loyalty above their own lives. Both are identified with their sword art and its traditions. The Japanese swords are the most widely known, however, and certainly represent a peak of form and function. Their history is also well documented.

The katana is attributed to Amakuni, an 8th-century sword smith dismayed to see so many warriors' blades breaking. He developed the long, curved, folded-steel, single-edged sword wielded with a two-hand grip that has come to be associated with the samurai. After 500 years of refinement, the 13th-century smiths are thought

by many to be the crest of the Japanese sword makers. Muramasa and Masamune are mentioned as the finest, with Masume swords compared to Stradivarius violins, and just as rare.

The Rembrandts of Swords

The surviving swords from these gifted makers are treated with the reverence of old paintings and would no more be used in sparring than a Rembrandt would be painted over as an exercise in brush-stroke techniques. For the modern warrior, there are alternatives to using ancient swords.

Martial artists frequently practice hand and foot training using staff and cane, and various edged weapons, including the sword. Typically, they are users, not collectors.

The practitioner's needs differ from those of the collector. A collector prowls for documented, historical pieces, much as an art or violin collector would. The practitioner's needs are more pragmatic; he or she seeks a weapon for use, not a display case. As such, the modern swordsman may not want the role of a museum curator, nor pay the price for a museum piece.

C.A.S. Iberia recognized the need of the sword artist for a decent, working sword. Towards that end, Hanwei, C.A.S.'s premier product line, combined a high-quality blade with modern manufacturing and materials. The Practical Katana emerged as a safe, durable katana with superb performance and an attractive price. This katana is C.A.S.'s biggest seller, demonstrating the soundness of the company's concept.

The most critical part of any sword, the blade, is homogenous, straight-forged, high-carbon steel, made to the same quality standards as C.A.S. Iberia's high-end blades. The blade is differentially tempered, meaning the edge is hard and the blade spine is softer and more flexible. The edge of the Practical Katana reaches 60Rc on the Rockwell Hardness Scale, and the spine measures 40Rc. This combination yields a sharp, hard

Hitting a small, moving object, in this instance an orange, is one of the most difficult of maneuvers. Low flying birds beware.

A close-up of the tip of the C.A.S. Iberia Practical Katana reveals the *hamon* (temper line) and the planes of the blade as they converge at the tip, the *kissaki*. This style of *kissaki* is of medium grind referred to as a *chu*.

edge, and a durable, shock-absorbing back.

The signature of the tempering, the *hamon*, is a subtle temper line differentiating the two degrees of hardness. The hamon of a custom piece can be intricate and beautiful, only bound by the imagination and technique of the blade maker. An ornate hamon, however impressive, does not enhance performance, but does enhance the price. The Practical Katana's hamon is a straight line, and its tempering is a manufacturing rather than aesthetic process.

Hanwei innovated a more secure, less orthodox way to fix the blade to the *tsuka*, or grip. Traditionally, a partial tang is held in place by a bamboo peg and needs

periodic maintenance, a task requiring skill and knowledge to refit correctly and safely. The Practical Katana has a hook-shaped notch in the tang, which matches a duplicate shape in the handle, and has a lug placed in the notch to further stabilize the blade. Besides the safety benefit of a blade that won't come loose when slinging steel in the dojo or dojang, the fixed blade also insures the *tsuba*, or guard, stays tight.

The tsuba has practical and decorative purposes. Tsubas approach fine art to connoisseurs, with designs as varied, beautiful and appreciated as watercolor landscapes. Collectors of tsubas will dispense with the katana and show their prizes in display cases. Of

course, an intricate, individually crafted tsuba neither adds protection nor moderates the cost. The Practical Katana's tsuba will not win prizes for beauty but will keep the modern samurang's or samurai's hands off his or her own blades.

Carving the *saya*, or scabbard, for each uniquely shaped blade is a significant cost for custom katanas. Classically, a craftsman shaped a saya to match the particular curve of each blade. The arc of a forged blade forms during the heat-treating and quenching process and varies with the profile of the cross-section and its taper through the length of the blade.

Hanwei forge developed techniques to forge the blades with uniform cross-sections, a technological feat in itself for blades employing so much hand production. The cross-sections yield standardized curves, allowing mass-production instead of hand production. Hanwei modernized further by using synthetic ray skin on the grip, and cotton for the wrapping instead of silk. The look and feel is the same, but the modern materials yield a welcome savings.

Before corporations took over the world, a series of hereditary craftsmen each contributed their specialty. Blade makers, polishers, tsuba, tsuka and saya makers spent years learning their jealously guarded crafts and produced legendary katanas at legendary prices. Guilds, ancestral specialties, secret techniques and mystic rituals have given way to metallurgy, research and development, quality control, and coordinated manufacturing. As a result, the customer benefits.

Worldwide communications and commerce foster productive unions of technology and tradition between any number of regions, cultures or countries. Swedish steel is used in German cars built in South Carolina. Celtic art is incorporated into tattoos, a Pacific islands invention, and displayed by college students in every community in America. Martial artists combine differing national forms to yield hybrid results taught in studios worldwide. C.A.S Iberia, an international company with a Spanish name, distributes Japanese-style swords forged in China and swung by Scots Highlanders, Korean masters and American practitioners. It is surely a win-win situation for all. ●

Advanced forms of haidong gumdo train fighters for multiple opponents, though when using live steel, the students do not follow through with their cuts.

Bill Moran Embodies the True Knife Craftsman

American craftsmanship is not dead— it lives on in the knives of Bill Moran

By
Dominique Beaucant

ONE FLIP THROUGH the pages of this book, and it becomes obvious that the age of the craftsman in America is not dead. It neither died with our grandfathers, nor with their fathers before them, but it has diminished to a great extent in this country. Much of the quality workmanship the United States once enjoyed has given way to modern equipment, machines and assembly line methods of manufacture. There is surely something missing in modern craftsmanship.

Most people of this generation will likely never know the beautiful handwork that once prevailed in our nation, back when there were only skill and raw materials with which to produce items of one's needs and desires. Once in a great while can a glimpse into the past be revealed by means of someone who turns out the best possible product through a great sacrifice of time and outpouring of talent.

This small, flower-and-fern-bordered shop looks innocuous, but inside some of the finest and deadliest blades imagined are made. It's Bill Moran's knife shop in Middletown, Md., located along historic Route 40A. If you drive by without knowing what magic takes place inside, you've missed the experience of a lifetime. Over the years, countless visitors have stopped by Bill's shop to have one of their old hunting, skinning or fighting knives sharpened, or to see a masterpiece in progress. And yes, after so many years, the large, wooden bowie knife still hangs above the shop's entrance!

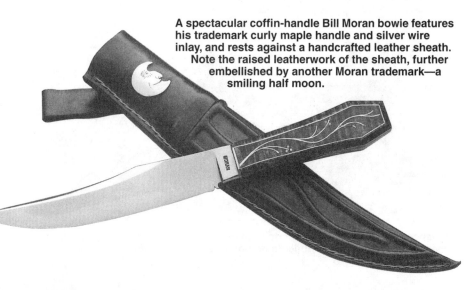

A spectacular coffin-handle Bill Moran bowie features his trademark curly maple handle and silver wire inlay, and rests against a handcrafted leather sheath. Note the raised leatherwork of the sheath, further embellished by another Moran trademark—a smiling half moon.

Such is the case for the past six decades in the shop of William "Bill" Moran Jr. Through him, a door opens to the way a real craftsman turns his skills into breathtaking beauty. In front of Moran's shop, one mile east of historic Route 40-A in Middletown, Md., hangs a sign that is foreign to most non-knife enthusiasts—a huge wooden bowie knife suspended from two poles above the shop's entrance. Such overhead signs these days are reserved for ranches, museums or western movies, along with similar placards proclaiming a craftsman to be a "wheelwright" or some other long-dead trade.

Moran's welcome guidepost means just what it implies—a bladesmith works his magic on the other side of the entryway. The small, flower-and-fern-bordered shop looks innocuous, but inside some of the finest and deadliest blades imagined are forged and finished. If you drive by without knowing what magic takes place inside, you've missed the experience of a lifetime.

Over the years, countless visitors have stopped by Bill's shop to have one of their old hunting, skinning or fighting knives sharpened, or to see a masterpiece in progress. From the heart of Moran's forge come some of the world's best knives; these are more than just knives—they are pieces of artistic beauty that speak of the skill and care of their maker.

The 78-year-old Moran has had a love for knives since his childhood. Bill's first attempt at making knives was at 10 years of age when he took one of his father's old rusty saw blades and shaped it into a crude knife blade. At that time, Bill lived with his parents on a 150-acre dairy farm, called "Gayfield," in the small village of Lime Kiln, Md. There is quite an interesting story behind the farm.

The history of the land on which the house and farm were built dates back a long way, as Bill's father was the third owner. The first owner was Charles Caroll, whose land was granted to him by England before the Revolutionary War. The plot extended all the way to the Potomac River. Some might recognize Caroll as one of the great men who penned their names on the original Declaration of Independence.

The relatively large land plot was sold to the Rohrback family, and Moran's father acquired it in 1924. In 1961, it was again sold, this time by Bill, to Roscoe Bartlett. Bartlett still owns the land and has been a prominent

Bill Moran's Texas Sesquicentennial Bowie showcases a handle inlaid with silver wire to form copies of actual cattle brands.

U.S. congressman for many years. In 1959, Bill moved to his present house in Maryland.

Although chores on the old farm took most of the young Moran's time, he managed to pursue his passion and soon built himself a small blacksmith shop in the back of his father's barn. There, he spent most of his free time experiment-ing with steel and learning how to make knives. Bill recalled the result of his first knifemaking attempt, admitting, "It wasn't too pretty and far from being well made." Regardless, it was the first Moran knife, and Bill added, "In a way, I'm happy that none of the early blades were stamped [with his name]."

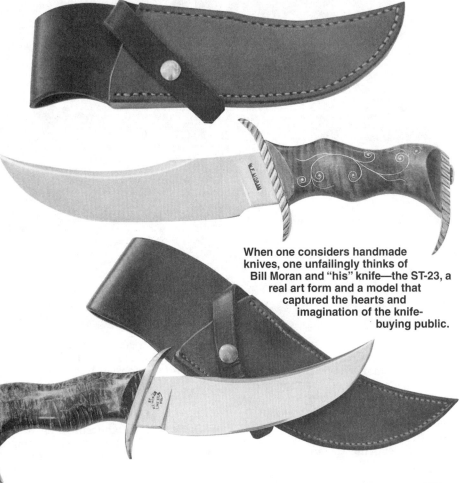

When one considers handmade knives, one unfailingly thinks of Bill Moran and "his" knife—the ST-23, a real art form and a model that captured the hearts and imagination of the knife-buying public.

Bill Moran gestures while explaining the process of starting a coal fire. A lifetime of forging has permitted him to build, by hand, every kind of tool imaginable for fashioning knives. For over 62 years, he has been forging red-hot steel into knives now recognized as the best in the world. At 78 years young, he continues to do it all by hand, forging, hammering, grinding, quenching, honing and finishing blades, and handcrafting knives and sheaths from start to finish. The quenching process can warp a forged blade during cool-down, but a few minutes in a vise straightens it right out. Making sure everything is in order, Bill seems satisfied with the forged blade as he checks for any imperfections.

Bill says, "In those days, I couldn't find a decent knife." So, he set out to make a better knife himself. After years of practice, every knife Moran turned out was snapped up, and orders began to come. He did much reading on the matter of knifemaking and found that, by copying the same methods used by 16th-century bladesmiths, he could produce a blade far superior to anything readily purchased.

Moran Takes Up the Hammer

Some believe bladesmithing was all but a dead art in America when Moran took up the hammer. Today, Moran represents the utmost in skill, talent and genuine leadership in the cutlery industry. He has been making knives full time since 1959, and has been recognized by his peers to be one of the finest practitioners of his craft. The Moran emblem has become legendary, and the Moran knife has emerged as a treasure for those fortunate enough to own one.

As Bogart films are to movie buffs, a Moran knife is an object of veneration among outdoorsmen and knife collectors. His knives are in greater demand than ever, for they have become the most coveted blades in the market. Prices for Moran knives have reached dizzying heights in the past few years, as evidenced by the fact that each Moran knife could immediately sell for a much higher price upon receiving it than what was paid for it seconds ago. It is also fair to say that today's investors will see more appreciation over the years. Outdoorsmen, sportsmen, military personnel and knife collectors have developed an insatiable appetite for Moran knives.

Like the young Moran who began to fashion the high quality knives upon which his reputation has grown, the matured Moran has never lost his enthusiasm for making them. Moran never quite advertised his work. As opposed to other makers of that era, his fame spread by word of mouth. As he pointed out, his big break came when Harold Peterson included Moran's work in the now classic knife book "American Knives—The First History and Collector's Guide," printed in 1958.

In 1960, Bill decided to build his own shop at its present location and erected a 20x40-foot building where he could devote all his time to the art he loves. In his shop, he designed and built a stone forge like the ones used in the 18th century. Among other equipment in his shop are numerous grinders, polishing wheels, anvils, vises and woodworking tools, many of which were made by Moran. Of particular interest is a 500-pound grinding stone that was brought into this country more than a century-and-a-half ago, and which Bill used extensively in the 1950s.

The actual process of making a knife blade is a long and tedious operation. In order that Moran could be assured of building the best quality knife, decades ago, he sent specifications to the manufacturers of Bethlehem Steel Co. Bill said, "They went out of their way to make sure I got exactly the steel I required by having their metallurgists analyze, experiment and find the right properties to fit my needs."

Today, our country is noted for producing the finest steel, much of which is far superior to the imported steels that Moran has seen. Beginning his daily operation with the highest-quality steel available, the first step is to emerge a bar of it in a red-hot coal

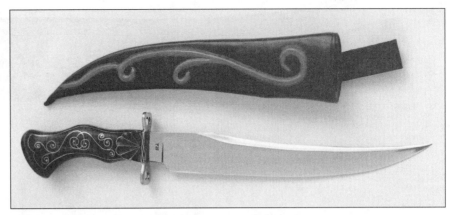

This is none other than the Bill Moran ST-24, a knife that has received praise among knifemakers, enthusiasts and collectors the world over. This particular model could be the most desired fighting knife in existence today.

forge so that it can be rough shaped on an anvil.

Unlike production methods, where many blades are stamped out, forging and hammering causes the steel to take on a new degree of hardness that many believe could not otherwise be realized. Taking the utmost care to shape the blade, the operation melds the bar of steel into somewhat of a crude shape, even though Moran insists his blades are forged until they are 90 percent of the actual desired shape. Now begins the process of grinding, which alone incorporates five separate operations.

"You must forge thick and grind thin," related Moran. The next operation completely separates the Moran knife from any other known—the tempering and hardening processes. At the beginning of his career, and until only decades ago, Bill was the only domestic smith known [to the author] practicing the ancient methods of hand tempering blades.

Hardening and tempering processes are the keys to a fine steel blade. "At the beginning, my biggest problem was the lack of instructions on heat treating steel," Bill said, "and not even the local blacksmiths understood the finer points and techniques of the heat-treating process." With no one to offer guidance, the young bladesmith's school of hard knocks was actually a school of countless hammer blows. It was only natural that he turned out some culls in the pro-

cess of learning the art of the forged blade.

Within the Steel Structure

What makes modern Moran knives so special? He said, in order to obtain a good blade, it must be tempered to at least four different levels of hardness. Of course, Moran's blades are forged, but more than that, they're forged and tempered by the hand of a master. A number of differences exist between a blade shaped through stock-removal methods and one that is forged. The molecular structure of a forged blade is different from commercially heat-treated blade billets, and Moran believes such molecular makeup lends greater strength to the steel.

The steel molecules along the cutting edge of a Moran-forged blade are compressed much tighter than those on the spine of the blade, and the increased density enhances its ability to hold an edge. The grain structure of the steel following the blade curve remains consistent until it reaches the point. On some less-than-perfect blades born from steel stock, high-stress areas near their tangs result from cutting across the grain with a hacksaw or band saw. On a properly forged blade, the tang is fully annealed for maximum tensile strength, protecting from breakage an area that can be one of the stock-removal blade's weakest points.

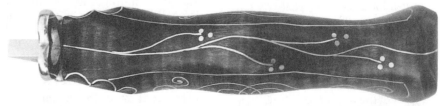

A close-up of a typical Bill Moran knife handle allows a view of his detailed silver wire inlay work.

This elaborate and classic Bill Moran rendition of a bowie knife is complemented by intricate raised motif on a wood-lined sheath.

While a modern stock-removal blade is generally hardened in a furnace that heats the whole blade to the same temperature, a skilled bladesmith can vary the temperatures on several spots of his blade, a process known as "differentially heat treating."

Done by the trained hand and eye of an experienced bladesmith, like Moran, the steel is heated and observed for colors as the temperature rises and falls, resulting in a blade that exhibits more than one level of hardness. This is simply not possible to achieve in a commercial heat-treating oven. A blade forged and tempered in this manner is nearly impossible to break using man's strength alone.

While these qualities can make a forged blade much more durable than commercial ones, I should point out that this is true only for an experienced smith and depends also on who's doing the forging. Many of those so-called forged blades are not equally made, and I have tested, over the years, blades made using stock-removal methods that surpassed those that were forged. To properly forge a blade takes great skill and a vast knowledge of steel and heat ranges.

It takes years of practice for the average bladesmith to perfect the methods of shaping a bar of steel with a hammer. When it comes to grinding a forged blade, much practice and ability is also required, since a forged blade is never perfectly flat, as would be a good bar of steel intended for stock-removal blade shaping. Rather than producing blades that are hard and non-springy, Moran's products are designed to have great resilience in support of the hardened cutting edge.

The point of a knife's blade is another high-stress area, receiving more abuse than perhaps any other part of the blade. The temperature must be drawn to achieve a blade so tough, it will not break. To lend added strength to the point area, a Moran forged blade is put into service with its tip just slightly softer than the cutting edge.

The main cutting edge on a Moran knife is tempered to suit the intended use of the knife, however it is needed, instead of the hardness and temper being the same at all points on the cutting edge. Only through this hand tempering process can all the best qualities of a piece of steel be realized.

The next operation is to finish-grind and polish the blade. Moran uses six different polishing operations to bring the now-hard steel to a mirror-like finish. The blade, now complete, is ready for a handle. Here again, Moran incorporates beauty and endurance in choosing the material for the handles.

Using exotic woods, most of which must be imported from around the world, he shapes, fastens and finishes the wood in harmony with the graceful lines of the steel. A trademark of a Moran knife is a stunning curly-maple handle inlaid with silver wire. Curly maple has no natural enemies and, therefore, is almost completely free of maintenance. As on his trademark knife handles, Moran inlays most curly maple sheaths he fashions with silver wire. He said he hasn't found another type of wood for inlay scroll like high-quality maple. Of course, Bill has also used Brazilian rosewood, ebony, curly oak and walnut for the handles, along with the popular India Sambar stag.

Honed to Perfection

The final step in the entailed operation is the all-important sharpening process. This is the true test of a good knife's blade. It may be beautiful, but will it cut? Bill can show you knife blades he has forged that cut into solid pieces of hickory nearly a hundred times and still shave hair like a razor.

For more than two decades, most Moran knives have come with wood-lined sheaths covered in fine leather. Although most knifemakers offer sheaths with their knives, few of the artisans are captivated with leatherwork. Each sheath provided with a Moran knife exhibits leatherwork or some other form of ornamentation, another example of how Moran takes an existing form and improves it.

As in the old days, Bill hand shapes leather to fit each particular blade, and sews the leather pieces together to form a custom sheath. With a final polishing of all parts of the knife, the job is complete. A now beautiful work of the cutler's art speaks of care and skill. Many of Bill's knives and sheaths have taken up to a month each to produce. This process cannot be rushed, for each step demands the utmost in care and accuracy to be worthy of the Moran emblem.

Bill Moran has sold knives to some of our nation's most prominent people, but he has always refused to use these names as selling factors for his knives. It is known as fact, though, that some of our Army Special Forces carry Moran knives.

In Bill Moran can be found one of the few remaining true craftsmen. Modern methods are not to be condemned, for it is upon these methods that our nation is built, but you can't help but appreciate the beauty of the hand-forged blade. Moran has spent almost all of his life promoting handmade forged knives and it can be said, without the slightest room for argument, that he has succeeded. ●

THE SWAN SONG OF THE BALISONG

Steeped in history, the balisong, or butterfly knife, is still the best-kept secret in knife collecting

By Richard D. White

All photos by Richard D. White

THE WORD "BALISONG" has an almost pastoral or tropical connotation to it. One might think that it is somehow connected to the group of Bali islands that dot the South Pacific. Although the balisong knife can trace its roots to the Philippine Islands, the word "balisong," meaning "broken horn," or its modern description as a "butterfly knife," hardly evokes the ingenious design or effectiveness of the storied, island fighting knife.

Today, the term "Bali-Song" is trademarked by Benchmade Knife Co. Whether designated a "balisong" or "butterfly knife," such an edged tool or weapon is an innovative folding knife with a split and hinged handle. The hinged handle halves pivot from the blade tang and most often lock together when the knife is open and the grips are in line with the blade.

When the handle halves are unlocked, they are easily, and often swiftly, swung out and up, spread-

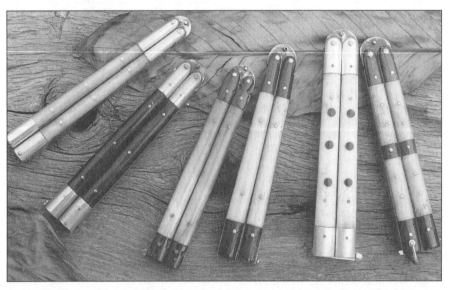

Pictured is an outstanding collection of World War II Filipino balisong knives. The variety of handle materials is clearly evident, with most incorporating bone and water buffalo horn grips. Aluminum and brass are also popular components, with much of the raw materials scavenged from downed aircraft.

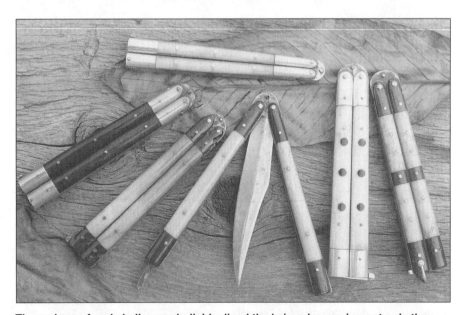

The makers of early balisongs individualized the knives by varying not only the handle material, but also the use of inlay material, and by using dark horn as grip spacers, the latter exemplified by the knife on the far right. Some bolsters are brass, and some aluminum. The top example is handled in Plexiglas, probably from an aircraft cockpit.

eagle like, up and around 180 degrees until they meet again, completely encompassing, hiding and securing the blade. In that closed position, the handle halves of most butterfly knives can be locked together again.

With the handle locked in the "open" position, the folder is transformed into a significant fixed-blade knife with tremendous fighting potential. In a partially opened position, the two handles of this knife resemble the wings of a butterfly. In fact, the derivation "broken horn" most likely refers to the handle material traditionally employed on butterfly knives—the horn of the water buffalo.

Closely associated with the Batangas province in the Philippines, the butterfly knife traces its origins to the early days of cutlery history. Some researchers have dated it as far back as 800 A.D. More commonly, its Philippine origins date to around 900 A.D., and some recent research indicates, much to the surprise of some, that the butterfly knife actually originated in France, perhaps as early as 1600.

Early German examples can frequently be found bearing the stamping "DRGM" and a patent number. The letters "DRGM" designate such knives as "German Empire Utility Designs," a blade stamp used by a Deutsch manufacturer in and around World War I and World War II. A picture of a charging bull, the company's sym-

bol, appears on the reverse side of each blade. Generally, examples found with these stamps are all metal, and are engraved with metric rule marks along both of the folding handle sides.

A second German example bore the stamping "Bontgen & Sabin's," a second innovative knife company, and one that was granted an English patent on the folding balisong mechanism as early as the 1880s. Bontgen & Sobin's examples also bear the words "MADRID" and "METER," almost totally hidden by the handle mechanism. Still another example, a small metal butterfly knife, bears the tang stamping "LEDERER IMPORT COMPANY, GERMANY," and advertises "The German American Trust Company, Denver."

Given its European roots, the butterfly knife's association with Filipinos is somewhat confusing until one realizes that the Philippines were once a colony of Spain, and the balisong was certainly introduced to the Filipino peasants by merchants or sailors. Almost immediately, the somewhat simple but innovative folding knife design became popular among the native people.

Steel Specialization

Once introduced into the Philippines, production of the butterfly knife became one of the major cottage industries on the islands, gen-

erally centering in and near the Batangas province in the North. In this area, different families developed specialties in fashioning the butterfly knife's various parts. One family would serve as blacksmiths, forging and forming the steel used in the blades. Another family cut out the buffalo horn, and their neighbors would measure, cut and form the brass housing for the bodies of butterfly knives. Still other families assembled the various parts, cut the latches, pinned the handle material to the bodies and finished the final weapons.

The balisong and other handmade Pacific weapons were integrated into various martial arts and used in coordination with intricate body moves. Despite its regional popularity, the balisong was destined to remain in relative obscurity until World War II and the subsequent occupation of the Philippines by the U.S. military.

The story of the Japanese occupation of the Philippines, and its later emancipation by Gen. Douglas MacArthur, is well documented, but worth repeating. In July of 1941, approximately 16,000 Americans and 12,000 Philippine Scouts were stationed in the Philippine Islands, an American territory and significant outpost in the South Pacific.

In December of 1941, after the bombing of Pearl Harbor, the Japanese landed a major military force in Lingayen Gulf on the island of Luzon. They surrounded the native

The photo illustrates three views of the butterfly knife—in the closed position, partially open to show the butterfly-wing-like handle halves that give the knife its name, and in the fully open position with the latch in place. The rivets that hold the handle material in place were almost always made of copper wire, most likely from downed military aircraft.

population and occupied the capital of Manila, all by January of 1942.

On March 11, 1942, after President Franklin D. Roosevelt evaluated the significant takeover of the Philippines by the Japanese, he made the decision to have MacArthur, along with his wife and young son, evacuated by PT boat. The purpose was to get MacArthur to Australia to command Allied ground forces in the South Pacific and organize the defense of remaining Allied areas.

MacArthur reluctantly left the Philippines and headed for Australia, leaving behind thousands of American soldiers and Filipino fighters to fend for themselves. MacArthur, as he was leaving, promised the Filipinos that he would someday return.

The Japanese advanced on the Philippine island of Luzon, squeezing American and Filipino troops into a defensive perimeter on the Bataan Peninsula. By April of 1942, 76,000 American and Filipino defenders found themselves surrounded by Japanese, completely out of food, munitions, shoes and medical supplies, and were forced to surrender to the Japanese. The surrender of American troops on Bataan was the largest mass capitulation of U.S. soldiers in our nation's history.

After Bataan fell, some Allied forces held out for another month on the fortress island of Corregidor at the mouth of Manila Bay. Of the 70,000 Allied troops who began the Bataan Death March, about 7,000 died during the ordeal.

It was not until October 20, 1944, that MacArthur fulfilled his promise to return to the Philippines and liberate it from the Japanese who held it for so many years. The combined total casualties resulting from the overall defense of the Philippine Islands added up to over 1,000,000 Filipinos, including civilian casualties, 60,628 Americans and more than 300,000 Japanese.

Because of the significant numbers of American servicemen who fought in the Philippines, and the close relationship that existed between the American soldiers and the Filipino freedom fighters, the concealed fighting knife known as the "butterfly knife," or "balisong," became quite popular with the American soldiers. The balisong was one of the most popular items taken from the Philippines by American soldiers who were stationed and fought in the islands. Numerous examples of this native folding knife made their way back to the United States.

An examination of the knife itself reveals some significant characteristics. Traditional balisongs are almost always just over 5 inches in length, in the closed position, and can reach nearly 10 inches long when open. The two sides of the knife are hollow, usually made of brass, and are shaped like three-sided channels or troughs. When the knife handles are closed around the blades, the hollow channels completely encompass and hide the sharpened steel.

Blades of the Balisongs

The blades of wartime balisongs are quite distinctive, with nearly every butterfly knife showcasing an extremely long, slender clip-style master blade ending, at the butt end, in a rounded pivot point, and with a stop pin embedded in the pivot. The blades often exhibit saber-style grinds running the entire lengths of steel, and are generally hollow ground. For those familiar with grinding, the ability to accurately hollow grind a blade

The blade style of most balisong knives is a slim, clip point, and is usually hollow ground the length of the blade. Other blades are closer to spear points with large, upper false edges.

freehand, and match the grind on both sides of the blade, is a significant feat, one which has been mastered by the Filipino craftsmen.

Today, there is still exists significant balisong production in the Philippines, accomplished by individual families who have continued to work in a cottage industry setting. However, those balisongs that can be traced back to the World War II era are especially collectible and are generally identified by examining the materials that make up the fighting knives.

Because early butterfly knives, by necessity, were made using indigenous resources, the Filipinos soon discovered that the best high-grade materials could be found scattered around in the jungle. Blade steel came from wing struts and other parts of downed aircraft that crashed during the American-Japanese conflict. The steel in these planes proved to be of the highest quality, and could be forged into balisong blades.

Copper wiring found throughout the planes was employed as pinning material for anchoring the sides of the knives, and some of the handle scales were fashioned from Plexiglas cockpit covers. The aircraft cockpits were frequently tinted in various shades, giving variety to the balisongs. The bolsters of butterfly knives are largely aluminum, a material found in great abundance scattered throughout the wreckage of downed aircraft. Aluminum was also integrated into the latches that held the two handles together. Brass from ammo shells made for similarly strong balisong latches.

Many of the most beautiful balisongs parade handles of black water buffalo horn, white water buffalo horn, or a combination of both. In some cases, ivory or bone was used in place of horn. As individual as they are common, balisongs were decorated by village craftsmen who used special combinations of marks to indicate the makers of the concealed knives. Sometimes the marks, usually a series of small, drilled indentations in the latch portions of the knives, were color coded as individual signatures.

In the past several years, there has been a significant increase in the popularity of all forms and types of military knives. Prices for not only production knives, but also handmade knives, have literally skyrocketed. The popularity is due, in part, to the recognition of the role played by combat knives in the successes of the American military.

Other factors have attributed to the popularity of military knives as serious collectibles, including the increased documentation of the histories connected with individual pieces, the publication of several outstanding books on military

A close-up of the latching mechanisms of three Filipino balisongs illustrates how the craftsmen who made them decorated each with a series of dimples, special filework, or a series of colored dots inset into the brass or aluminum latches. The decoration was a way of showing ownership, and colors were generally red and green.

Balisongs, although generally attributed to the Philippines, are thought by some to have originated in Europe. Here are two German examples with metal grips scribed in ruler markings. Both have flat-ground blades and metal latches.

A group of balisongs is arranged with another traditional Filipino fighting/utility knife. The large knife is called a "bolo," or "moro," a design that was the inspiration for the American military bolo knives.

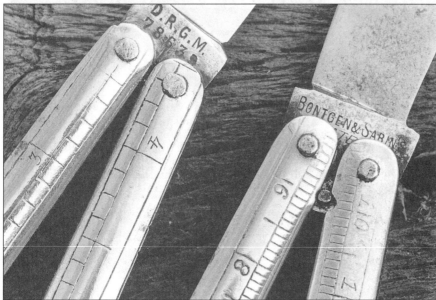

Blade tang stamps found on German balisongs include "D.R.G.M.," designating the knife as a German Empire Utility Design. Such models also showcase what is generally accepted as patent numbers. The second balisong is stamped "Bontgen and Sabins," a tang mark dating back as early as the 1880s.

A metal knife like most German balisongs, the handle of this one is stamped "The German American Trust Co., Denver." The tang stamping reads "The Lederer Import Co., Germany."

knives, and the desire of former military personnel to capture a piece of history by purchasing the important artifacts.

Of special interest in the last year, or so, has been the rise in the popularity of "theater knives"—combat knives custom made by soldiers in various theaters of action, generally the Pacific Theater. The handmade or modified-production knives have become one of the hottest collecting categories in recent years, with prices for outstanding models presently topping out in the hundreds of dollars.

Until recently, the handmade folding knife known as the "balisong" has generally gone unnoticed by collectors. The exception being cutlery companies, like Benchmade Knife Co., that have continued the balisong tradition through the manufacture of modern incarnations with updated materials and steels. In the estimation of several serious collectors and cutlery historians, the World War II balisong is potentially destined to capture a significant second look as military historians and collectors begin to understand the role of handmade knives in the wartime conditions that existed in the Philippine Islands.

It is not too late to get in on the excitement associated with finding one of the unique folding knives. Compared to the prices presently realized for unique World War II theater knives, balisongs continue to be a real bargain, in the $45-$95 range, for unusual examples. ●

The Mount Everest of Knifemaking

The integral knife is the ultimate challenge for any knifemaker, and the most solid of knives to carry

By Mike Haskew

IN EVERY INSTANCE, the making of a custom knife is an exercise in problem solving, of overcoming obstacles to craft the most unblemished, beautiful and useful edged tool possible. Through this process, the knifemaker gains a great measure of satisfaction and joy in his work.

In the modern era, a relative few custom knifemakers have chosen to take on the challenge of the integral. Those who have done so will say that the integral knife is simultaneously the cause of major headaches and the source of some of their biggest smiles.

"It's one of the most difficult ways to make a knife there is," admitted Edmund Davidson. "Still, if it weren't for integrals, I probably would not be

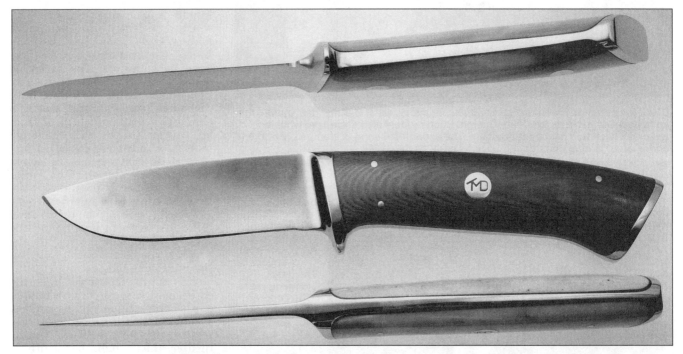

Ted Dowell, the acknowledged father of the modern integral explained, "It is a knife carved out of one piece of steel, with an integral hilt only, or a hilt with a cap." Dowell's Integral Hilt and Cap Knife is available in three blade sizes and involves a tapered tang. Grinding and tapering the tang, he said, is much more difficult with an integral knife than on a conventional full-tang knife or on a regular integral-hilt model because of the end or butt cap.

making knives. You have to have machinist skills and the right equipment—a band saw, for example, rather than a bench saw."

While individual makers of integral knives employ processes that work for them, there is general agreement on exactly what constitutes an integral knife. Ted Dowell, the acknowledged father of the modern integral explained, "It is a knife carved out of one piece of steel, with an integral hilt only, or a hilt with a cap."

Davidson agrees. "The integral, by the definition I take out of the dictionary, is a complete unit," he reasons. "All of the knife hardware, the guard, butt cap, handle, tang and blade are completed out of one bar of steel. In other words, you don't add those. You fashion them out of a single steel bar."

Dowell, who was the first to make a knife with both an integral hilt and cap, acknowledged that the late G.W. Stone fashioned an integral-hilt hunting knife, which Stone called the "Diana." Dowell, however, had not seen Stone's knife before embarking on his own integral endeavor.

"My dad had come down to Boston from Nova Scotia and worked for a short time as an auto mechanic. Among his tools was a screwdriver, and that screwdriver basically had an integral hilt. That is where I got the idea for the integral knife," Dowell related.

A student of integral-knife history, Dowell points out that the idea has been traced back as far as the Vikings, who were known to fashion an integral-style knife called the "scramasax," with a blade measuring between 12 and 17 inches in length. Samples of these have been recovered, but after being buried, their wood, bone or stag handles rotted away, leaving the integral core. According to Davidson, during the late-19th and early-20th centuries, German artisans drop forged integral cutlery.

The rejuvenation of the integral began in the early 1970s with Dowell, as well as with Billy Mace Imel, who followed Dowell's lead. Davidson was introduced to integral-knife construction during that period via photographs that appeared in gun publications.

"T.M. [Ted] Dowell had done some integrals, and he was the man," remembered Edmund. "Shortly after that, I saw some of Billy Mace Imel's work and something said to me that this was the way to make a knife. And it wasn't something everybody was practicing, by any means."

Today, more knifemakers are trying their hands at integrals in North and South America, and in Europe. These craftsmen include Fanie LaGrange, Ricardo Vilar, Reinhard Tschager, J.W. Townsend, Ludwig Fruhmann, Wendell Barnes, Thomas Haslinger, Ricardo Velarde, and Dietmar Kressler, among others.

All the Integral Parts

Most of these craftsmen use stock-removal methods of building integral knives rather than forging, and as with knifemaking in general, a variety of blade steels and handle materials are employed for integrals.

Haslinger prefers BG-42 for its corrosion resistance and ductility, while also using stainless damascus, CPM S30V and CPM S60V. Dowell and Davidson use BG-42, but the mainstay of Dowell's production is in D-2. He also endorses Vascowear for its edge-holding capability. Davidson likes A-2 and 440C but has sworn off CPM 420V after making only three pieces because of the difficulty in cutting, grinding, buffing and honing it.

Handle materials range from exotic and stabilized woods to Micarta® and Velarde's choices of walrus and mammoth ivory. Haslinger works with stone, such as jasper, charoite and sodalite, fossilized dinosaur bone, ivory and stabilized wood, sometimes accented with gold or silver wire wrap.

The true test to the maker of integral knives lies in patience and perseverance. The process is labor intensive and exhausting to the extent that a single maker cannot achieve the production of large quantities of truly handmade integral knives.

Knifemaker Edmund Davidson was introduced to integral-knife construction via photographs that appeared in gun publications. "T.M. [Ted] Dowell had done some integrals, and he was the man," remembered Edmund. "Shortly after that, I saw some of Billy Mace Imel's work and something said to me that this was the way to make a knife." Davidson's modern integrals, like this highly embellished piece, are well regarded by a bevy of collectors today. (PointSeven photo)

The amount of filework required is tremendous. Dowell might make 15 integral knives in a year, and Davidson fashions closer to 20 pieces annually. Velarde, who has made integrals exclusively since 1998, is on the upper end of productivity, at 50 knives yearly.

"I have always tried to figure the time element out and have never been successful," explained Dowell, who has now limited his knife orders to featherweight, lightweight and integral hilt-and-cap designs. "I used to machine about four integrals at a time, and that would take two days. Then, to grind, finish and heat treat them, you are looking at a little over a week, probably 10 days to do four

integrals. The heat treating alone takes a full day. Of course, that was when I was young. Now, I'm lucky if I can heat treat one and finish it up in about two weeks."

Velarde apprenticed under, worked with and learned from Steve Johnson for three years, and was introduced to Kressler's integrals during that time. It was Johnson who encouraged Velarde to explore the integral fully by apprenticing under Kressler.

"I worked with Dietmar for many hours every day," Ricardo recalled. "Right away, I realized that the work was completely different. I was excited to see the tools he used to make these extremely symmetrical knives."

"There was a band saw, a grinder, a drill press and probably 400 files," Ricardo continued. "Let's say you make a mistake on the guard of a regular fixed-blade knife. You can take it off and put another one on. There is no second chance with an integral. It takes a lot of practice to be able to keep the flat area in front of the guard with sharp edges, and if you don't have the necessary skills, you will round the edges and ruin the knife. This is why some makers of integral knives avoid having this type of flat and square area ahead of the guard, and opt for a large radius."

Not only does the making of an integral take practice and skill, it also requires some muscle and brawn. "I've made integrals since 1987, and my hands are really feeling the effects," Davidson said. "It's hard on the body doing all the gripping, grinding, sanding and filing by hand. It takes about five times longer to make a basic integral as it does a standard hunting knife."

Davidson has actually made integral Japanese-style wakizashi swords, one of which has an overall length of 23 inches and a blade just under 15 inches. It is 1 inch thick and 3 inches wide. The initial bar of steel that Davidson wrestled and worked weighed 20 pounds.

According to Dowell, the process of making an integral involves a number of steps that vary greatly from the construction of a standard fixed-blade knife. Working to minute detail on a two-sided object, and trying to match the sides perfectly, is a tall order that requires a thorough assessment of risks.

Hollow Out the Middle

"The number one thing with an integral is that you can't put it on a platen, which is what you would do with a normal knife, because you would grind away too much material," explained Dowell, a founding member of The Knifemakers' Guild, and one who organized the first all-custom-knife show ever in the United States, held in Kansas City in 1975. "You've got to come in from the side, and what I usually try to do is hollow out the middle as best I can. After that, it is mostly hand filing."

Usually starting with 5/8-inch stock, Velarde mills the area where the guard will go and then roughly shapes the handle. "That removes the bulk of the metal," he commented, "and then you get down pretty much to filework. You can use a caliper on the back of the guard, and I can usually tell that things are

Reinhard Tschager's full integral parades a mammoth-ivory handle and gold inlay and engraving of the Chrysler building. It is also inset with diamonds, blue sapphires and amber.

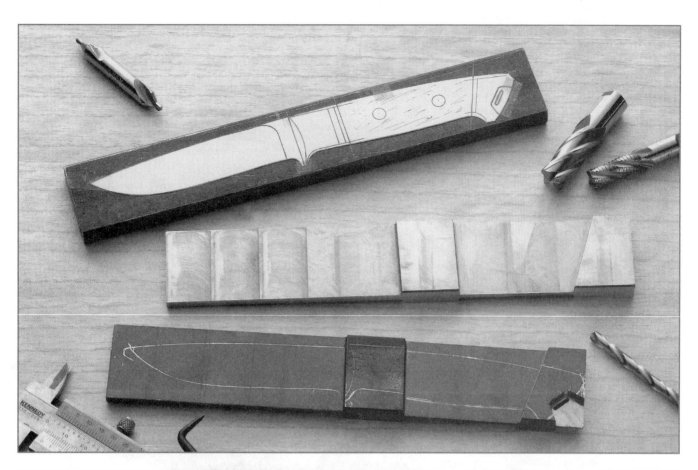

Knifemaker Ricardo Velarde provides an insight into the process of making a knife of integral construction. At top in the first photo is a drawing approved by one of Velarde's knife customers. Below it is a piece of steel that he has started to mill into a blade, and lastly in that photo is a scribed outline of the knife on the steel. From top to bottom in the next photo are the cutout knife, a hollow-ground blade and a shaped guard and pommel, and finally a finished Full Integral Classic Hunter with a stag grip. (PointSeven photos)

lined up because I have developed an eye from looking at it. You still measure, and I do a lot of that. With files, you can fix things and get close to a finished shape."

Davidson remembers taking off on his own voyage of discovery when he started with integral knives. His basis was a functional understanding of milling

machine operations, and from there he created a clamp and a method of setting up an indicator to make his depth of cut for the blade and handle thickness uniform. Afterward, hours of work with the band saw and grinder followed. He uses no CNC (Computer Numerically Controlled) machining equipment, preferring to employ manual mills in his shop.

One interesting integral twist, which is usually saved for last on a standard knife, is the completion of any engraving or inlays in handle material prior to heat treating.

"The integral can present special challenges, particularly during heat treating," said Haslinger, who does that procedure himself. "If you use inlays in the handle, guard or butt cap, then you have to deal with heat treating in different cross sections, and this can cause distortions."

Davidson related, "Engraving is where integral construction is opposite from regular construction. The engraving on an integral has to be done prior to any heat treating. That piece of steel has to be 100 percent fashioned and finished because once it is heat treated, an engraving bit will only scratch it. When the blade goes to heat treating, you have to make sure that every scratch or mark is out of that steel because, if you think it is hard to get marks out of steel that has been annealed, wait until it is heat treated. You have to envision the completed knife prior to heat treating."

The ability to use the mind's eye to see a finished knife before the

real thing is even begun provides a distinct advantage to the integral maker. This process can eliminate a number of mistakes before they are made, and that single mistake could bring hours of work to no production.

"Before I even start out to make an integral in the shop, I actually do a full-scale drawing of the details, and it helps with the overall design of the knife," added Haslinger. "I might spend up to three hours with a drawing and post it somewhere in the house so I can look at it constantly. I find you have to be able to make materials flow with the overall design and balance. For a knife to be aesthetically pleasing is a challenge in itself."

Those who buy integral knives are often collectors or those who intend to put a solid piece of cutlery to work. In either case, the men who make them believe their customers appreciate the extra effort that goes into making a top-quality integral. Haslinger's integrals, primarily daggers, begin at

$900, while Davidson, who has more than 100 integral models, will part with a "plain Jane" for around $650. His more expensive pieces top $1,000. Dowell's featherweights and lightweights begin at around $200 to $250, compared to his integrals, which bring about $1,200.

"Look at the knife," said Velarde, whose integral hunters and fighting knives range in price from $1,600 to $2,500. "Nothing is ever going to fall off it. There are no gaps between the guard and the tang or soldered joints that are bad. It is a solid piece. The guys who know about integrals do appreciate them, but many people don't have any idea what an integral is. So, sometimes I take pieces of work in progress to [knife] shows to give them an idea of what is happening."

Those who have already developed an affinity for the integral knife know what they are seeing. They may, in fact, be holding the ultimate—the Mount Everest of knifemaking—in their hands. ●

Swing Low Sweet Chopper!

Light axes and hatchets survive the encroachment of chain saws and power tools

By Rod Halvorsen

SUCH A FANTASTIC invention is the axe—one of mankind's greatest edged tools. For millennia, it has been used to advance and develop cultures all over the world. In land clearing, home construction, furniture making and hearth tending, the axe knows no equal. Its shape and form has been continuously refined and redefined, with a progressive level of specialization culminating in the late 19th century. Coopers, boat makers, cabinetmakers, homebuilders, roofers, fishermen, firemen and, of course, woodsmen and loggers all possessed their own unique and favored designs.

A few of the more specialized forms still exist, but rapidly, within about a 60-year period beginning in the early 1900s, the axe fell from grace. Where an axe was once the preferred tool of tradesmen and loggers, power tools speedily trumped its cutting abilities. The trades experienced a takeover by power saws, mortising and milling machines and, in the woods, the chainsaw made the axe nearly obsolete.

Nowhere is the demise of the axe more apparent than in the logging industry. Living, as I do, in logging country, I see the poor axe relegated to use as a maul for setting felling wedges, its edge rarely called to duty. Fortunately for the axe and its makers, there are still quite a few folks who need and appreciate the old chopper. Some groups include hikers, hunters, campers and backpackers who continue to demand quality hatchets and light axes.

Shelter and fire making are made easier with the axe, as is post and peg pounding, and butchering game. Aficionados of the outdoors demand portable and efficient axes. To them, weight and size must be kept to a minimum. Those search-

With its steep edge grind, the Collins 2-1/4-pound Single Bit made a compact and efficient firewood splitter but was somewhat unwieldy for limbing and general camp use.

Effective at notching and bucking poles, the German Helko American claw Hatchet with Nail Puller also makes a useful combination tool for game blind and deer stand construction.

After several others failed, Gerber's Splitting Axe didn't hesitate a bit on its way through this big chunk of fir.

ing for just the right light axe should take heart. There are many excellent designs available.

The many who value portability in their cutting tools should welcome the large selection of light axes and hatchets I assembled herein, arbitrarily setting an upper limit of about 2 lbs. for head weight. One of the first features any buyer will immediately notice is the sharpness of the factory edge. In order to make some comparisons, I have contrived an informal grading system. The range of factory edge sharpness on my samples was so wide, I felt some comparative scale seemed to be in order.

Graded Edges

Any axe that was absolutely shaving sharp right out of the box was given an "A++" grade. If the axe was sharp but just wasn't quite hair-popping sharp, it got an "A+." An axe with a highly useful edge requiring no sharpening for skinning and general utility work was assigned an "A" or "A-." Those requiring just a touchup with a stone before commencing operations received a "B+." If a file was needed to start the sharpening, the axe graded "B" or "B-." Any axe that required extensive filing or grinding, or needed the edge angle changed to enable it to be used for efficient limbing work got a "C." For axes graded "C," I usually found I needed to utilize a belt grinder, files and stones to achieve a truly shaving-sharp edge.

It should be said that a "dull," or non-sharp, factory edge does not necessarily mean a poor quality axe. Factories ship their axes to many different customers. Some end users might want to put a specific edge on the tool. An axe possessing extra "meat" (steel) behind the edge allows the customer to grind to his specific taste.

In addition, a fine factory edge may not be a benefit for all work. For example, grubbing use near or in the ground will quickly make a mess out of a thin razor edge of any quality. Thus, the grading scale should not be thought of as a measure of "from better to worse," but rather as a means by which a buyer might have some idea about the fineness of edges available.

Once graded, and before heading to the woods and game pole, all axes except for the Collins 2-1/4-inch Single Bit were brought up to hair-shaving sharp edges.

With the exception of those sheaths accompanying the Gerber Camp Axe and Back-Paxe, none of the hand axes or hatchets came with scabbards I would trust for

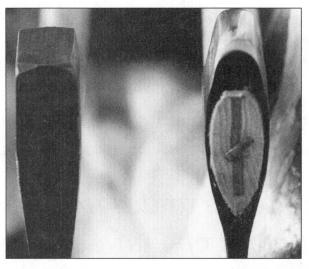

It's the shape that makes it possible! The Skinning Poll on Gransfors Bruks' Hunters Axe (right) is tapered and polished to enable it to slide between hide and carcass. The Gransfors Bruks axe is compared to the common square poll type as found on the fine Snow and Nealley Penobscot Bay Kindling Axe (left).

belt carry. All arrived with some form of edge protector. No axe should ever be carried without a sturdy edge guard!

Buck Knives is a company familiar to all devotees of outdoors activities, and Buck has done itself proud with the Camp Axe. Employing a permanently fixed synthetic handle and rust-resistant head finish, it should find favor with any who camp, hike or hunt in moist, humid environments. Weighing in at 19 ounces, and with an overall length of 1 foot, it is compact and handy.

The Camp Axe head is forged in Taiwan from 1045 steel, and the hardness specification is 43-45Rc on the Rockwell Hardness Scale. Balance is good, and with an "A-" edge, it is useable directly out of the box. One unusual feature is a hole in the head, which enables the user to simply hang the axe on a nail when not in use. The factory edge protector is second to none. Made of hard plastic, it snaps on and is secured by a stout web strap.

India Head Quartering?

Machete and military blade collectors will certainly recognize the Collins name. Now owned by Mann Edge Tool Co., Collins Axe makes a wide variety of traditionally designed wood and metal axes. Heads on the 1-1/4-pound Camp Axe and the 2-1/4-pound Single Bit are manufactured in India from 1045 steel, while the Hudson Bay head is forged in the United States of 1060. Hardness of all models is specified at 45-58Rc.

I graded the Hudson Bay factory edge a "B-," with the other two tagged as "C's." The Camp Axe is a traditional Boy Scout-type hatchet, and at 13 inches overall, is compact enough for a rucksack. A couple inches longer, the Single Bit is stout and heavy for its length. With a short handle, relatively heavy head

Exceptionally handy, the Outdoor Edge Pack Axe halved this mutton carcass with no trouble at all.

and steep factory edge grind, I found it most useful for splitting firewood, a chore it seemed to relish.

All handles are milled from American Hickory. Unfortunately, the heads on both the Single Bit and Hudson Bay axes loosened and actually slid about half way off during testing. Removing them, I found substantial gaps between the wood and the heads. Once refitted with release agent on the heads and bedded in JB-Weld, I experienced no additional problems. In fact, the Hudson Bay axe has become a favorite of mine.

With a 1-1/2-pound head and an overall length of 26-3/4 inches, the Hudson Bay is comfortably strapped to a pack. Its tried-and-true design combines an efficient head with a

Vaughn's and Gransfors Bruks' truly diminutive hand axes aren't just cute. They are performers!!

fairly stout "poll" (blunt or flat head opposite the edge), providing such balance, it seems to simply float in use. As an all-round utility axe, I have found it hard to beat.

Illinois-based Estwing Manufacturing Co. has been making all-steel hand axes for many years. Outfitted with a comfortable stacked-leather handle, the Estwing Sportsmans Axe's factory edge received an "A" grade. The 26-inch, steel-tube-handled Campers Axe edge received a "B," and while steel type and hardness specs are manufacturer's secrets, both of the models tested performed superbly.

Balance of both is quite good, and construction is sturdy in the extreme. The synthetic rubber handle on the Campers Axe absorbed vibration and provided excellent grasp even when hands were wet. At 13 inches overall, the Sportmans Axe is small enough for belt carry, and both head designs feature strong and serviceable polls for pounding tent pegs and the like.

Gerber Legendary Blades is known for manufacturing superb knives, and its trio of Finnish-made axes is in keeping with that sterling reputation! Hearkening back several thousand years, the head-in-haft construction is modernized with a hollow, polyamide-fiberglass handle.

Integrating extreme weight-forward balance, all three Gerber models displaced material during tough "bucking" (fast swinging) work noticeably faster than any other axe tested. Differentially heat-treated, the edges are specially hardened to stay sharp, while the polls are tempered to allow them to be used for pounding.

At 8-3/4 inches overall, the little Back-Paxe was the shortest hand axe tested, but in spite of its rather stubby appearance, it proved the equal of many much-larger models. The 17-1/2-inches-long Camp Axe provided yet more leverage, and at

28 inches in length, both the XL and Splitting Axes allowed for truly rapid and strain-free bucking and splitting work.

The Splitting Axe is so outstanding in performance, it warrants special mention. Common to many splitting axes or mauls, it features integral, tapered lugs flaring out from the sides of the head. These lugs provide increased width for splitting chunks of firewood. The rest of the blade of the Splitting Axe is of a pure felling type. This combination makes for a truly universal tool capable of being used for bucking and splitting chores. I can't imagine a better all-purpose chopping tool for the backcountry camper than the Gerber Splitting Axe. Factory edges of the Gerbers varied just a little, with the Back-Paxe rating an "A," and the others each a "B+."

Swoon Blade

Traditionalists will swoon over the remarkable, handmade products of Sweden's Gransfors Bruks.

Truly unique in today's world of investment casting and CNC (computer numerically controlled) mass production, each axe is stamped with the initials of the Swedish smith who forged it. With a sturdy and well-fitted American Hickory handle, each axe reflects the company's awareness of its 100-year history of individual craftsmanship.

Recognizing the reality that its products will primarily service hunters, campers and backpackers, Gransfors Bruks has ground the axes with almost surgical edges designed for small timber cutting, limbing and butchering. Indeed, a hunter could easily leave his knife home and still get by nicely with any one of the three models I tested.

Because of the relatively high hardness specification of 57Rc, and because the edges are so finely sharpened, rough work near the ground or around rocks should be avoided lest severe damage occurs.

Skinning of small and large game was nicely accomplished with all three. The Hunters Axe certainly lived up to its name, with the specially designed Flay Poll (skinner) proving itself to be no gimmick! During skinning of butcher lambs, mutton and deer, the Flay Poll proved a timesaver, and this axe has forced

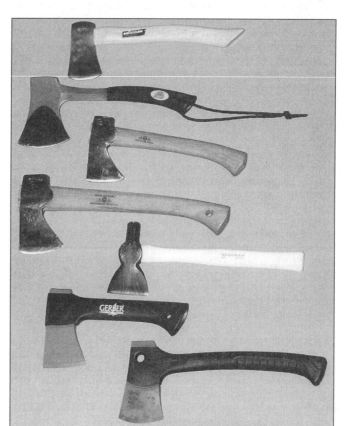

Top-to-bottom are a Vaughn Sub Zero Hand Axe, the Outdoor Edge Pack Axe, a Gransfors Bruks Mini, the Gransfors Bruks Wildlife Hatchet, Vaughn Oyster Hatchet, Gerber Back-Paxe and Buck Camp Axe.

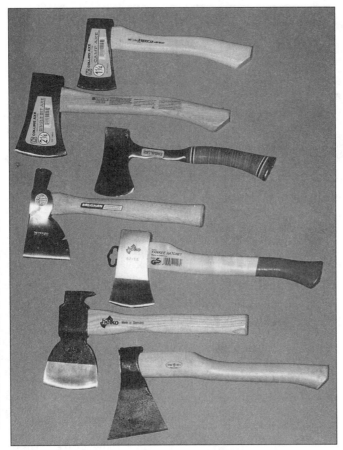

An impressive selection of hatches includes, from top, the Collins Camp Axe, a Collins 2-1/4 Single bit, an Estwing Sportsmans Axe, a Vaughn Half Hatchet, one Helko Yankee Hatchet, a Helko American Claw Hatchet with Nail Puller and a Sovietski Compact Siberian Woodsman Axe.

me to rethink my old, routine skinning methods! As an additional feature, the handle is roughed up where grasped by the strong hand, providing increased purchase even when the palm is covered in blood or fat.

The 10-1/2-inch Mini weighs 11 ounces and combines most of the usefulness of a jackknife with legitimate chopping capability. The 13-3/4-inch Wildlife Hatchet, with a 1-pound head, steps up performance while still remaining compact enough for a large pocket. At 18-3/4 inches in length, the incomparable Hunters Axe allows for tremendous leverage when heavy limbing or bucking work needs doing. Because of its long, well-shaped handle, the 1-1/2-pound head feels much lighter than it is.

The German firm of Helko-Werk has been making cutting tools for over 150 years. The three I tested demonstrate excellent manufacturing technique. All are forged from German C45 steel and hardness rated at 47-55Rc.

The Yankee Hatchet, with a 1-1/2-pound head, would be right at home in any campsite or hunting lodge. With a "C" factory edge, it needed sharpening before it was suitable for limbing and bucking. However, its edge held well, and balance was excellent. At 15 inches overall, it is a bit long for belt carry, but wouldn't get in the way on a pack frame.

The Helko-Werk American Claw Hatchet with Nail Puller possesses a 2-pound head with straight edge and hammer poll. Both 16d and 20d nails were easily driven into and pulled out of dimensional lumber using the hatchet. This one came from the factory with a "C" edge, but after sharpening, would serve well as a handy multi-purpose tool for construction of hunting blinds or tree stands.

German engineers are known for their innovative thinking, and nowhere is this displayed more clearly than in Helko-Werk's current series of Vario 2000 axes. Heads on the axes can be easily replaced, or different styles selected and fitted on the same handles. Two bolts pass from the heads through the hickory hafts, with aluminum washers backing them up on the poll sides.

Company literature warns that the polls must not be used for hammering, and using the axes for splitting, or twisting of the handles when the heads are embedded in wood are prohibited due to the stress such activities places on the handles where the bolt holes are located. Obviously, these restrictions limit the use of the tools substantially, but after sharpening the "B-" factory edge of one such axe, I found it to limb and buck quite well. At 17-3/4 inches overall, this one is too much for belt carry, but if the use restrictions aren't a cause for

worry, its good chopping capabilities would be a boon to the camper.

From Haft to Head

Outdoor Edge Cutlery's 11-inch Pack Axe is a portable hatchet ideal for riding on a belt or in a small day pack. With haft and head forged from one piece of 1050 steel, it arrived with a "B-" factory edge. Once sharpened, this one turned out to be quite a performer. For limbing and bucking small lengths of campfire wood, it was well balanced and bit deeply without undue binding. The Kraton® grip prevented hand slippage, even when wet, and provided the most secure grip of all the hand axes tested during butchering chores. A well-designed edge guard, or scabbard of sorts, fully encases the head, closing with a hard snap.

Snow & Nealley has been manufacturing cutting tools in Maine since 1864. The company has ample experience manufacturing a varied line of high quality axes, and the workmanship shows in the Penobscot Bay Kindling Axe. Hardened to 53-58Rc, the traditional Hudson Bay-style 1-3/4-pound head is forged from Pennsylvania-smelted 1060 steel.

The axe was shipped with a "B" edge and a fine leather sheath/edge guard. I found this axe to be heavy enough for rough bucking chores and yet light enough for one-hand limbing of small-diameter shelter poles. In addition, the blade maintains enough material behind the edge to split campfire wood with aplomb.

One outstanding feature of the Kindling Axe is the large knob present on the end of the hickory handle. Initially, this bulbous addition appears odd, yet during use, it proves its worth and makes me wonder why it is not present on other axes of this type. Filling the hand as it does, it eliminates hot spots and allows all fingers secure purchase. Comfort and control are the result.

Sovietski Collection offers a line of traditionally designed and manufactured axes. Two of the smaller hand axes were obtained for testing. Both designs hearken back to axes produced centuries ago. These styles have been passed down through generations and continue to be popular in Russia. Forged from "instrument grade" steel, they reach a Rockwell hardness rating of 50-53Rc. Handles appear to be beech wood, and though the surface area of the haft at the head is not large, neither have loosened in spite of some vigorous work.

The 1-3/4-pound head of the Compact Siberian Woodsman is fan or

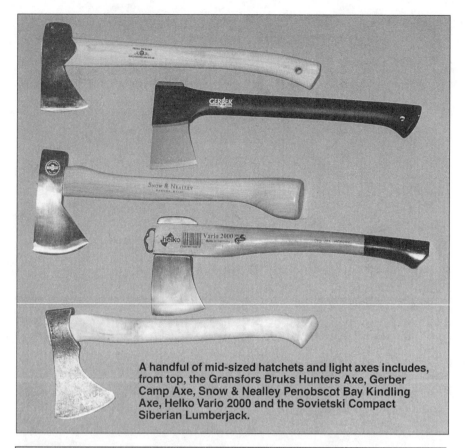

A handful of mid-sized hatchets and light axes includes, from top, the Gransfors Bruks Hunters Axe, Gerber Camp Axe, Snow & Nealley Penobscot Bay Kindling Axe, Helko Vario 2000 and the Sovietski Compact Siberian Lumberjack.

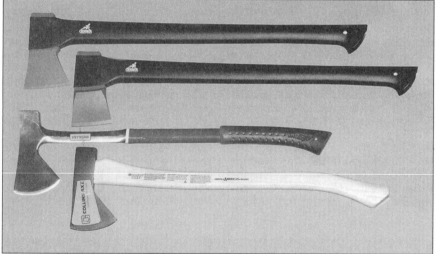

On the lengthier side are the (from top) Gerber XL Axe, Gerber Splitting Axe, Estwing Campers Axe and Collins Hudson Bay Axe.

triangle shaped. I graded the superbly ground straight edge an "A+." The straight edge performed especially well during butchering work. It held close to the bone when cleaving carcasses, and with a cutting block underneath, it could be used quite effectively to dice meat. With an overall length of 15-1/4 inches, this places it at about the upper end of comfortable belt carry for me, though it would present no difficulties being carried in or strapped to the side of a pack.

The Compact Siberian Lumberjack evokes images of Viking long ships and pillaged villages, but I am assured this is a style still used for camp and home chores in Russia.

Continued use gave me growing confidence that, over time, various chopping skills with the Compact Siberian Lumberjack would become second nature. With an "A" graded edge, the blade shape encouraged it to be worn on a belt, though a sturdy sheath should be used to ensure safety. At 17-1/2 inches in length, comfortable carry means it should be strapped to a pack.

While I favored the Compact Woodsman, the quality of both is excellent, and I found both to be of great utility. No doubt, collectors will find their unique shape and history to be of particular interest.

Vaughn Manufacturing Co. has become one of the foremost designers and manufacturers of quality striking and cutting hand tools. All the Vaughn axes I tested are forged from 1080 high carbon steel, hardened at 40-60Rc. Handles are American Hickory and all edges received a "B" grade.

While the origin of the Half Hatchet can be found in the building trades, it performed well as a compact utility tool for camp and woods use. A nail-pulling notch is provided on the blade, and it will easily accommodate 8d headed nails, though 16d nails were just thick enough in diameter that they tended to slip out. Driving nails was a snap. With its 22-ounce head and short, 13-inch overall length, belt carry in a scabbard would present no problems.

The 12-inch Vaughn Oyster Hatchet possesses a hammerhead and straight blade. Though light in weight, this little chopper performed limbing and small bucking chores well. Nails up to and including 20d size were easily driven in kiln-dried dimensional lumber, and the hammerhead is just large enough to pound tent pegs in tough ground. A backpacker seeking a compact chopping companion should take a long look at this one.

Shrunken Head

Vaughn's tiny Sub-Zero looks for all the world like a shrunk-down falling axe. First impressions are that it is but a toy. In this case, such first impressions are wrong! The little Sub-Zero is absolutely pocket sized, but I found no difficulty getting through 150-pound sheep carcasses with it. This is something I can't do with most heavy hunting knives.

With an 8-ounce head, total weight is less than a pound, and at 10-1/2 inches overall, just a bit of the handle sticks out of the back pocket of a pair of jeans! While heavy bucking jobs are certainly beyond its ability, the Sub-Zero is fully capable of cutting both emergency shelter poles and small lengths of firewood for a stranded hunter or hiker.

While power tools have certainly signaled the demise of many of the specialized axes of past centuries, outdoors enthusiasts should take heart in the knowledge that many superb chopping tools are available for their use. Let's hope this state of affairs continues for a long time to come!　●

Meier

the Steel Magician

Daryl Meier lays the hammer down when it comes to forging dazzling damascus billets for blades

By John Lewis Jensen

DARYL MEIER MADE the first billet of pattern-welded steel, or damascus, I ever used, and I continue to integrate his steel into the majority of my knife blades. I have worked closely with Daryl since 1995. He was at the forefront of the damascus re-insurgence in the early 1970s, and has gone on to influence and teach many of today's prominent damascus makers.

Damascus is a layered composite of steels and, sometimes, pure nickel, with a visible pattern that is continuous throughout the entire structure of the material. It is not just a surface pattern applied to metal. It embodies an age-old process that is commonly achieved through stacking different grades of steel in alternating layers and forge-welding them together.

There are endless possibilities on how to further manipulate the knife-blade material to produce various patterns. Some damascus patterns will change as you cut blade shapes from the initial bars or billets, and the changes will become more dramatic as you get closer to the core of the pattern-welded steel. Certain patterns will become tighter and more intricate, while others will appear looser.

Mosaic patterns will change little, if any, when roughing out a blade shape. "Random" pattern, for example, will produce concentric lines that mimic whatever shape you cut into it. A "twist" pattern can result in star-like shapes, depending on how you section it.

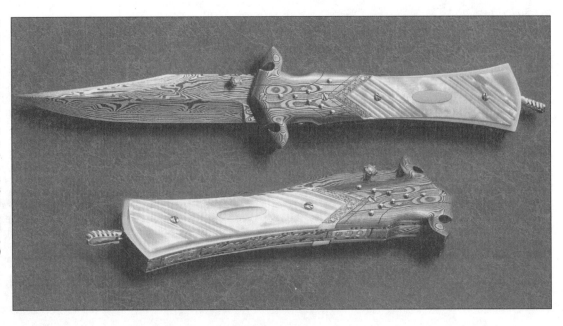

A gorgeous George Dailey folding bowie exhibits a Daryl Meier San Mai-style blade with Turkish-twist-pattern damascus on the outside and a random-pattern-damascus core. The bolster is Meier's vertical-ladder-pattern damascus. The knife also sports a carved mother-of-pearl handle, gold and diamond inlays, a gold bail and titanium liners. (PointSeven photo)

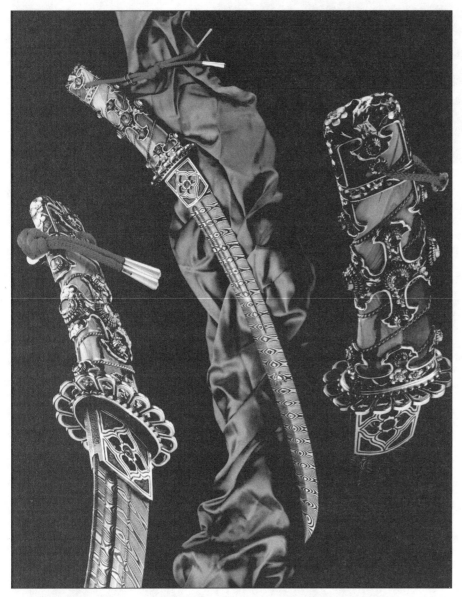

Paul Jarvis's highly embellished, upswept, Persian-style fixed blade features a low-layer Daryl Meier twist-damascus blade. The eye-popping damascus pattern is complemented by carved sterling silver fittings, a fossil-ivory grip and gold and gemstone inlays.

I had to work with damascus! I researched the material, and my pursuit and investigation led me to one man—Daryl Meier.

Daryl's passion for pattern-welded steel further fueled mine. Of course, there were many people selling damascus to knifemakers, and there have been many who have achieved prominence and recognition for their damascus since. Still, Daryl was one of the few who strictly provided the steel for others on a full-time basis, and he was the first to do this within the knife-making community. This, along with his reputation, impressed me.

My philosophy has always been, "If someone else can do it better, then let them." Daryl has a similar philosophy: "I'll do for you what I do best, so you can do what you do best!" This is why I use Meier steel for my knives—he can make it better than I could probably ever aspire to manipulate the blade material.

My main concerns when I formally investigated pattern-welded steel had to do with its cost and the rumors of weld flaws. The thought of spending a significant amount money, and investing all the time it takes to profile and grind one of my blades, and then possibly discover a crack or weld flaw deep within it made me nervous. Everyone I talked to about these concerns reassured me in regards to Meier's damascus.

Daryl was born on a farm, in 1940, in Randolph County, Ill. From an early age, he was interested in making things and developed a need to create. His first real hands-on experience was in repairing muzzle-loading guns. There were no parts available, so he had to make them himself.

The "ladder" and "raindrop" patterns, when cut into, will become softer or looser, yet otherwise look the same as they do uncut.

The "Turkish twist" pattern reveals rows of intricate stars and swirls, with variations of the shapes depending on how many layers the initial billet had. Low layers will produce loose, bold patterns, while high layers will produce tight patterns. These are the basic building blocks of damascus. From there, virtually anything can be achieved.

I became interested in building knives while pursuing a degree in jewelry making and metal smithing at the Rhode Island School of Design. As I was introduced to pattern-welded steel, I became incredibly fascinated with it.

Knifemaker Bud Nealy employed Daryl Meier ladder-pattern damascus for the blade and bolster of his Persian bowie, which also sports a sambar-stag handle. (Weyer photo)

The Hoover Forge?

"I did try to make a gun part by blacksmithing in the backyard when I was around 13 years old," he says. "I dug a hole with a trench running off to one side in the yard, borrowed my mom's vacuum cleaner, put a tube of some sort into the trench, then hooked the vacuum cleaner to the other end. I

A prime example of one of Virgil England's fantasy knives showcases a creatively carved Daryl Meier random-pattern-damascus blade, and a bronze-and-wood handle.

made a fire in the hole, used the vacuum as a blower, heated some steel and probably used a regular claw hammer to try and forge it. Of course, it didn't work, but I tried."

Daryl's family eventually moved from the farm into town. In those days, there were still practicing blacksmiths in the area. Daryl visited them in his early years and, as he explains, "I was interested in what they were doing, though I did not pursue it as a vocation until way into my adulthood."

After high school, Daryl went on to college where he received a bachelor's degree in mathematics with a minor in zoology. Meier embarked on blacksmithing as a hobby, went back to school to undertake a master's degree in education and became a vocational instructor in the field of blacksmithing. "I eventually got involved in pattern-welded steel and specialized in it," he remarks.

When I first contacted Daryl about damascus, I picked his brain for hours. He explained his beginnings in the field, saying, "It was at a gathering of blacksmiths in Lumpkin, Georgia, in 1973, that I first observed a demonstration by Ivan Bailey on the basics of making pattern-welded steel. That marked the start of my fascination with the making of this mystic material."

It was also in 1973 that knifemaker Bill Moran first exhibited handmade damascus knives at The Knifemakers' Guild Show in Kansas City, Mo.

I soon discovered that Daryl is one of the few who has the equipment necessary and the ability to properly heat and weld large and wide billets. This turned out

to be an important consideration in my work. My knife designs are different from the norm and often require the use of wider billets.

These same concerns and more are what led knifemaker Virgil England to work with Meier Steel. As Virgil explains, "Daryl can make anything. It's only a matter of what you're willing to spend. I don't challenge him because I don't have him make any real bizarre patterns for me. I'm doing weird sizes and shapes [rather than odd damascus patterns].

"When you try making a pattern to fit a certain size or shape," Virgil continues, "sometimes you have to do it a few times. With my outsized or odd-shaped knives, it is not cost effective for me to do fancy patterns. So, I work with 'random' pattern 99 percent of the time. I am more interested in the structural integrity of the material rather than how cool the pattern is."

Virgil also comments on Daryl's working methodology, remarking, "When he goes

to build a pattern, he sees the whole picture to begin with, and then he works out how to arrive at that end spot. He can visualize the contours of the finished piece of metal before it is done, so, when it is flattened out, you understand that the high and low spots are exactly where he planned them to be."

Virgil speaks about his early history with Daryl. "I had originally run into Daryl's damascus around 1977, whenever The Knifemakers' Guild Show first moved to Dallas," Virgil remembers. "He had damascus for sale, which freaked everyone out. He was making incredible damascus and was starting to use a wire EDM [Electrical Discharge Machine] to assist in the bizarre patterns. It was revolutionary."

For his Virtual Velocity knife, knifemaker John Lewis Jensen marries a hot-blued Daryl Meier ladder-pattern blade with a Meier random-pattern bolster and Meier's Turkish-twist damascus pattern for a secondary bolster.

Work Speaks for Itself

"Daryl is an intellectual; he is not a salesman or a self-promoter," Virgil says. "He has always shown up expecting the quality of his work to speak for itself. Working with Daryl, for me, has been good because he visualizes well over the phone. He has absolutely no limit on what he will try on a piece of steel. I use Daryl exclusively, and the reason is consistency. His accuracy is so incredible."

Daryl has been making pattern-welded steel, serving the knife and sword industry, for over 25 years. The composition of Meier Steel is a mix of 1095 and A203E for the majority of the steel produced, as well as W-2, 15n20 and pure nickel. Five different patterns are always available. These include random, twist, ladder and the fancier Turkish twist. He also offers the awesome mosaic "Calico Rose," which he developed. Limited editions and special patterns are available "as the need arises and the mood permits," he says.

He also does some custom one-of-a-kind patterns to customer specifications. I have been working with Daryl on clad steel, or San Mai, projects. This steel is similar in organization to a three-layer sandwich, with the core being one steel or pattern, and different steels or patterns for the outside. The process produces a great effect. As you grind into the billet, you end up with a distinct pattern running parallel to the edge, and above that, you have the outside pattern. It is a great option if you have particular requirements for your blade edge, all the while maintaining a beautiful pattern on the rest of the blade, or you can have two contrasting patterns on the same blade!

Daryl states, "My steel can be made into any of a variety of patterns. I work with many bladesmiths and collectors in selecting a pattern, basically helping people create their dream knife or sword."

Daryl further explains, "Meier Steel has been used mostly for knife blades, in which the requirements are not only for performance, but also for beauty, character and mystique. There is no limit on possible uses."

About his repertoire, he adds, "This is what my business is about—the artistic beautification of steel. Pattern-welded steel truly brings an added aesthetic dimension that makes a knife or sword even more interesting, setting it apart as a one-of-a-kind work of art."

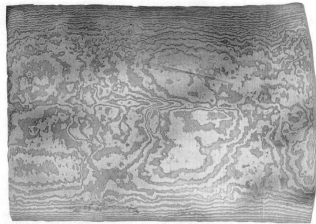

Close-up photographs of billets of Daryl Meier damascus are clear examples of patterns the damascus-maker offers. From top are a random-pattern damascus billet, ladder-pattern steel, a twist-pattern billet, a center-twist-pattern steel billet and an example of waffle pattern.

Daryl explains his love and interest of the material and the process of making it. "What interests me is the creative opportunity with the patterning, which also involves, to a degree, the mechanical properties of putting two different materials together and the resulting advantage the composite would have," he notes. "My main interest is in the patterns. I see it as an open field. We've just barely scratched the surface.

"I use a hand hammer and an anvil to do some forge welding on things like the Turkish pattern," he explains. "I use a power hammer for the main billet setup, taking this billet up to as many layers as is necessary for the project. Take the Turkish Twist pattern as an example. I'll start with a billet and weld it in the power hammer, draw it out, stack it and weld it again. Then, using the power hammer, I will take it down to a particular size. After that, I twist it, and then I go to my hand hammer and anvil to do the welding of the bars."

Daryl continues on with pride about his larger equipment, saying, "The power hammer that I have is a 3B Nazel self-contained air hammer. It was built around 1925. It is a 10-horsepower machine, and it's fabulous! It's rated as a 400-pound hammer, which was the predecessor to the self-contained air hammer.

"I also have a homemade hydraulic press that I use to weld some of the mosaic patterns and to do special shaping," Daryl continues. "I own what is called a laboratory rolling mill. It's big for a blacksmith's shop, but it's a toy as far as rolling mills are concerned. It was built originally for Ford Motor Co. in 1953, and it's powered with a 50-horsepower motor.

"I primarily use it to do any of the clad steel, the material that is like a sandwich, with a core and two outside pieces," Daryl says. "The first of that type of stuff was done under the power hammer, but the rolling mill is so much nicer for that because it is so precise in terms of uniformity of the layers."

Clamp, Crank, Grab and Twist

Daryl finishes up with a brief explanation of one of the other most-often used tools in his shop. "I also use a homemade twisting devise, which is hand powered," he relates. "Essentially, it is a section of I-beam with legs on it. It's got a sliding pipe vise on it, and I take a hot piece of steel, stick it in the vice and clamp it down. I grab the free end of it with a handle made from a vice grip. I then crank the stuff and twist it. I use that to make the single-bar-twist pattern and the stock for Turkish twist. Those are the main machines for hot work."

While Meier Steel is a business that primarily provides custom knifemakers and other artisans with pattern-welded steel, Daryl has used his steel for his own special projects from time to time. One particular noteworthy endeavor was back in 1990, when then governor of Illinois, Jim Thompson, commissioned Daryl to make and present a special knife for former U.S. President George Bush. Daryl says he chose a mid-19th-century bowie knife design for this commission because it is "the American knife."

"I tried to depict a scene in the blade that would remind [the former] President Bush of his view during the inaugural parade," Daryl explains. A pattern was forged into the steel depicting 13 waving flags along the length of the blade, each representing one of the original 13 colonies. The flags in the steel all have 50 stars in five rows of six, and four rows of five. All stars have five points. There is a banner running the length of the blade, on both sides, that reads "U.S.A." Remember, this is damascus, so the pattern runs all the

Daryl Meier has forged damascus for his own special projects from time to time. One particular noteworthy endeavor was back in 1990, when he was commissioned to make and present a special knife for former U.S. President George Bush. Daryl says he chose a mid-19th-century bowie knife design for this commission because it is "the American knife." "I tried to depict a scene in the blade that would remind [the former] President Bush of his view during the inaugural parade," Daryl explains. A pattern was forged into the steel depicting 13 waving flags along the length of the blade, each representing one of the original 13 colonies. The flags in the steel all have 50 stars in five rows of six, and four rows of five. All stars have five points. There is a banner running the length of the blade, on both sides, that reads "U.S.A."

way through the material. This is an incredible feat of forging.

The work that Daryl has done is certainly the bedrock of steel manipulation today. Daryl has done an incredible amount of work piecing information together, spending time on the science, metallurgy, and history of damascus.

There was some early information written in obscure journals and, since Daryl does read German, he was able to translate some of that not only into English, but also into modern scientific terms that we would understand. He then put it into a format that was read-

able and accessible to the general public. It was published in Dona Meilach's book "Decorative and Sculptural Ironwork." Daryl used hardcore science, then translated it into layman's terms that anyone could pick up and understand. The information given in the book on patterned steel was remarkable, and word spread internationally.

"As far as the future of where this material is going, in terms of my own work, I have some ideas," Daryl says. "In terms of the aesthetic stuff, I'm still working on some questions, problems, concepts and ideas that I've been playing with for over 20 years. I'm looking at new ways of pattern manipulation. Using the technique employed in developing ladder pattern, I'm trying to get into imagery that works differently than the mosaic method."

Daryl elaborates, "I'm interested in the optical effect, known as 'Chatoyancy,' which is a phenomenon similar to that of a holographic image. You see something that's really not there. This is seen in a

ladder pattern, particularly if you etch it sufficiently to create topography, then you re-polish it. In different angles of incident lighting, it appears that the surface undulates. Taking that to the next step, what if you could create an image of an indi-

Daryl Meier damascus seems to dance across the carved blade and scalloped bolsters of a Ken Steigerwalt folder. (PointSeven photo)

vidual's face using that same basic concept? Under certain lighting conditions, you'll have a holographic-like image of a human face that would appear only if you turned the steel in the correct lighting."

That's one direction that he's going, and another direction is toward exotic mixtures of materials, particularly dealing with the mechanical properties that are concerns in the knife world. "I welded some diamond particles in Eutectic steel 10-12 years ago, and I would like to pursue that," Daryl comments. "I think there is some potential there in terms of edge holding, aggressive cutting, that sort of thing."

What has continually struck me over the years about Meier Steel is how easy it is to work and use, from cutting, grinding, carving, heat treating and etching, all steps have been simple and problem free. I always look forward to using it. Etching is the final step to reveal the pattern to its full potential. I don't think anything etches quite as easily as Meier Steel.

Knifemaker Paul Jarvis, who uses Meier Steel almost

exclusively, has developed deep etching this material to nearly an art in itself. Paul says, "I've been using his stuff 10, maybe 15 years. I use his stuff because I know that I can depend on it. He'll make me anything I want, relatively quickly."

I remember the first time I saw Paul's work and what he had achieved with the damascus. The etching was so deep that I thought he had hand carved the recesses of the pattern. They were literally 1/16-inch-or-more deep! This also caused the edge of the blade to develop serrations. Even with this style of deep etching, the contrast keeps sharp and dramatic, never muddy or blurry.

Throughout this article, Daryl's humble character is evident. He is extremely gifted and talented, and is always ready and willingly to share what he knows in a wonderfully simple and concise manner. Daryl has not gotten the credit or accolades he deserves. I certainly hope that the information presented here helps to alleviate that. ●

John Lewis Jensen's Stallion Talon sports a San Mai-style Daryl Meier damascus blade, basically a high-contrast Turkish-twist pattern on the outside, and a CPM 440V core. Jensen employed Meier's ladder-pattern damascus for the bolsters, and complemented the steel with a fossil-walrus-ivory handle, and gold and gemstone inlays.

Sheep Horn Horns In On Stag

Sheep horn is a good alternative to the currently-illegal-to-export India sambar stag so popular on domestic knife handles

By Jack Collins

I HAVE ALWAYS loved stag-handled knives. All of my friends know, "Collins is a sucker for a good looking piece of stag." I believe this fascination with stag began when I was about 7 or 8 years old. I went to the grocery store with my grandmother and, for some reason, I was sent to wait in the car while she completed her shopping (probably because I was not behaving appropriately).

While I was cooling my heels in her car, a young man came out of the hardware store next door. He sat in his own car and examined his newly purchased knife, leaving the car door open, and I looked on enviously. It was a fixed blade knife with a 4- or 5-inch blade and a leather sheath. It had a stag handle and, if memory serves me right, a full tang. I have no idea who made the knife or what price the young man paid for it, but it was wonderful! I vowed then and there (if 8 year olds can vow) that some day I would have a knife "just like that."

These straight knives by (left to right) Ricky Fowler, two from Ron Frazier, Ruana Knives, Muela of Spain and two from Wayne Hendrix all support a staggering variety of stag grips.

My appreciation for stag has never wavered. I have learned in the intervening 62 years that the best stag is sambar stag from India. For years, the East Indian antlers were collected as sheds and sold for the express purpose of providing handles for knives. This particular antler seems to yield the most pleasing surface texture, with a degree of roughness that allows the user to grasp the knife handle with confidence and comfort, a combination that few other materials offer.

Stag is also said to be a "warm" material. I'm not sure just what that means, since I am convinced that stag assumes the temperature of its environment, just like most other materials. I believe it does not have the capacity to draw heat from a contacting surface as quickly as does steel, for example, so perhaps that is what "warm" means in this context. I considered leaving a knife outdoors overnight and sticking my tongue on it in the morning to test this theory, but decided that the theory alone was sufficient. Stag just seems right on a knife.

It's obvious the fascination I have with stag is directly related to that long ago day in the grocery store parking lot, but the connective emotion does not seem to be uniquely mine. As a testament to the universal appeal of stag, witness the lengths to which some manufacturers go to make other materials appear to be stag. Bone is picked, carved, scorched and otherwise treated to create the stag look. And of course, there is always ersatz stag made of some sort of plastic with varying degrees of quality.

Most knifemakers will tell you that stag-handled knives draw the most customer interest when displayed on their tables. Some blade builders have made a name for themselves, not alone by the excellence of their knives, but also for their use of stag handles. Current makers who come immediately to mind include Ron Frazier, Pat Tomes, George Herron and Wayne Hendrix, to name but a few.

There is a fly in that ointment, however. The government of India has banned the export of sambar stag antlers. As in so many instances, greed has reared its ugly head. Some couldn't wait for the antlers to be shed and solved that little dilemma by the simple, but highly illegal, expedient of killing the deer! This has led to the ban, which will, I hope, allow the sambar deer to recover to the point where the ban will be lifted for the gathering of some controlled amount of shed antler.

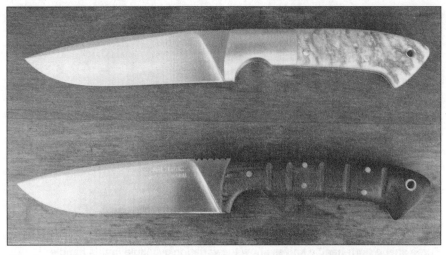

Two Jones Knives fixed blades include "The Only Knife You'll Ever Need" (bottom) and "The Only Knife You'll Ever Need—Elegant Model" (with sheep horn handle). The bottom knife is touted as the answer to any cutting need one might encounter in the wild. The top knife is equally functional, but look how the use of sheep horn sets it apart. Beautiful!

Ed Fowler is probably the foremost proponent of sheep horn for knife handles. Shown here is Ed's Yearling Pronghorn model.

Until then, the cost of stag knife handle material has risen to the point that many makers do not include it on knives unless a customer specifies stag in ordering a knife. Known for stag-handle pocketknives and straight knives, Case (W.R. Case & Sons Cutlery Co.) no longer offers the grip material on knives in its catalog, but instead substitutes mother-of-pearl, abalone and other natural, exquisite and expensive materials.

Similar antler material to stag has been and continues to be integrated into knife handles, but nothing seems to have won the following that sambar stag has for all these many years. I have read that other antler material has a core that is

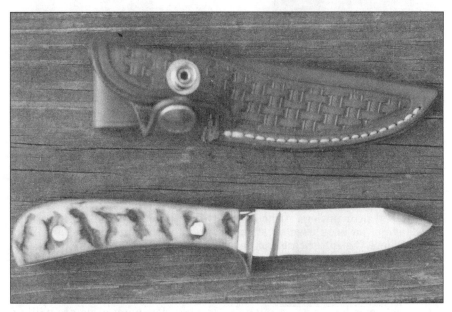

Jim Ragsdale made this drop-point blade and handled it with sheep horn, complementing it with red liners. The knife will do perfectly for cleaning deer.

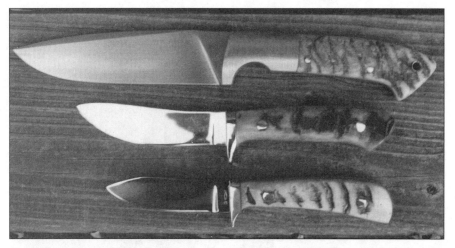

Three sheep-horn-handle knives show the variation available in this handle material, all different, all pleasing. From top are edged tools from Jones Knives, Woodrow Walker and Jim Ragsdale.

Stag performs and looks equally as good on folding knives as it does on fixed blades. From left are folding knives from Sheffield, two from Case, Coleman, another Case pocketknife and Fox 'n' Hound.

The author performed unscientific tests on two sheep horn knife-handle slabs (left) and two stag slabs, trying to determine which, if either, type of natural grip materials would break when hit with equal pressure by the same hammer.

less dense, thus not as suitable for knife handles. Certainly this is true of whitetail deer antlers. Although they have often been used on stick tangs, where the softer core can be drilled out, whitetail antlers are not often employed where slab handles are desired.

Few antlers have the requisite diameter to allow cutting slabs from the circumference. Coupled with the difficulty of securing an antler straight enough to provide sufficient length, the lack of widespread use is understandable. And in most states, the selling of locally taken wildlife parts is illegal. So if you want to use whitetail antler for a knife handle, you must first kill a large buck, and then destroy the trophy! Not many of us are willing to do that.

Not Sheepish About Sheep Horn

What's a sucker for stag to do? I suggest a suitable alternative can be found in sheep horn. Yes, it is actually horn taken from the male of the ovine species. Many of us are in the habit of referring to the antlers of deer, whether whitetail or mule, as "horns," but that is just a colloquialism. Antlers are shed every year, but horns just continue to grow.

I first became aware of sheep horn as a viable material for knife handles through correspondence with Ed Fowler, a knifemaker from Riverton, Wyo., who writes for *BLADE Magazine®*. I asked my share of questions about sheep horn before I ordered a knife from Ed. "Is it brittle?" I inquired. "No," he answered. "Will it stain if it gets blood on it?" I continued. "No," he insisted. All the answers I needed to hear. In his most recent brochure, Ed states, "I will use any material for handles, as long as it comes from the head of a sheep." He further states, "When dropped, it bounces. When wet, it is not slick." That sounds good, doesn't it? Sheep horn also has a pleasing surface texture. Is it "warm?" You decide. For myself, I think it feels just as good as stag.

As compared to past knife shows, I noticed an increased number of sheep-horn-handle knives at the 2002 BLADE Show in Atlanta. I bought two knives for myself, and two as gifts for my hunting buddies, all with sheep-horn slab handles. We like them, but I began to wonder just how the grips would stack up against stag, the material of our dreams.

Not having access to a modern testing lab, I concocted a test to satisfy my own curiosity. The testing apparatus, illustrated in a photo within this story, was made from tools and materials I happened to have available. While not giving quantifiable results, the simple, crude testing arrangement does allow consistency and reproducibility. In short, while I cannot measure the force applied to each sample, I can insure that the same force is applied to each sample. Thus, I can know whether or not the same force will produce the same effect on two different materials, namely, stag and sheep horn.

I used three hammers weighing 10 ounces, 18 ounces, and 26 ounces, with heads weighing 1/2 pound, 1 pound and 1 1/2 pounds, respectively, dropping them in a controlled fashion on the samples of stag and horn.

Crude but effective, the author's experiment involved the hitting of sheep-horn- and stag-knife-handle slabs with a hammer, using identical force on each, to see if either would break under the hammer blows. The hammer shown has a 24-ounce head, and the test sample in place is stag.

By causing the hammers to pivot around a steel rod and allowing them to fall freely, I removed any variable that might have been introduced by my providing the impetus for the blows.

Frankly, I expected to show that the horn would withstand a blow that shattered, or at least cracked, the stag. Starting with the lightest hammer, I bounced it off of each sample in turn. No discernable damage occurred to either material. In using the next-size hammer, and permitting it to freefall onto stag and horn handle slabs, I was left with the same result—no damage to either grip. Okay, get out the big guns (a larger hammer). Guess what? I had the same result. I couldn't bust any sample when laid flat.

I repeated this process with the samples standing on edge. This time, I'd break the handle material. Wrong! I could just barely discern a minor dent in the edge of one piece of stag. I can feel it with my fingernail but I could not clearly photograph it. Similarly, there is a small chip in one piece of sheep horn, on the edge, where there occurs a natural seam. This chip occurred at a sharp corner that would never be allowed to remain on a using knife handle. I emphasize that these minor damages only occurred on one sample of each material. On the other samples, there simply isn't any damage.

There is no difference at these levels of stress! Sheep horn is just as good as stag for my money. Oh, yeah, money. The samples I used were purchased from a supplier of knifemaking material. I paid $18 for the stag and $10 for the sheep horn. As the use of sheep horn rises, it is reasonable to expect the price to come down, while the price of stag can only continue to rise, unless the government of India can see a change in the population of the sambar deer herd.

Please note that my results are not meant to be proof that all sheep horn is the equivalent of all stag in terms of ability to withstand impact stress. I am certain that if one were to pursue this matter to a conclusion, one would find that there is some stress that, when applied to these materials, would, indeed cause failure. That probably would not occur at the same point for each material, so yes, one could prove to be ultimately stronger than the other.

What I have shown, to my own satisfaction, is that either will withstand any reasonable stress to which they may be subjected during normal usage. My prejudice tells me that the stag is more brittle than the sheep horn, but I cannot support that bias with facts, so I must treat it as just that, bias. Also, be aware that neither sheep horn nor stag is a homogeneous material and that these test results

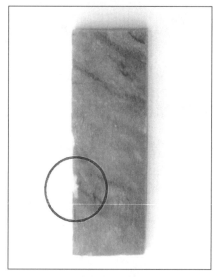

The only discernable damage to any of the four stag and sheep-horn handle samples was this minor chip from one edge of the sheep horn. Damage to stag was too minute to measure.

cannot be extrapolated to all samples. It is also obvious that one cannot destructively test all material prior to use, but I suggest that this simple test procedure is indicative of the ability to withstand stress.

So what does all this prove? For me, and I hope for you, it means that, should we be forced to forego stag-handled knives, we will not be severely inconvenienced by using sheep horn. We may, in fact, find that it's an improvement. I like it, but I still love stag. ●

SURVIVAL
The Ultimate

Over a period of a couple of months, five people—two women and three men—used the knives in this article for all daily tasks

By James Ayres

WE LIVE IN tumultuous times. Daily, we watch newspapers, television and the Internet for news of disasters, plane crashes, terrorist attacks, earthquakes and civil disturbances. Once upon a time, many Americans regarded these events as something that happened far away, often in other countries with strange sounding names. Now we all know that cataclysmic events can, and do, happen anytime and any place. This knowledge has caused increased anxiety for many of us. It has manifested in many ways, one of which is an attempt by people to be more prepared for emergencies.

I have served in the military as a paratrooper, and with a special operations outfit. I also trained

Survival knives tested for this article include, from top, the Bud Nealy Pesh Kabz, Benchmade Nimravus, Cold Steel Lloyd Pendleton Hunter, Ontario TAC, a Trace Rinaldi handmade knife and a Busse Combat fixed blade.

with and worked for a federal government agency in high-threat areas. I have lived and worked in places where violent death was an everyday event. From that experi-

ence, I have learned a few things that might be of use to others.

Serenity can only come from inner peace. Confidence to cope with extraordinary events comes

KNIVES
Civilian Tools

Some of the author's favorite survival pieces are, from top, the Spyderco Bob Lum Tanto, Spyderco Fred Perrin Bowie, Chris Reeve Shadow III, Chris Reeve Mountaineer, Fallkniven F1 and Fallkniven H1.

the kids to the park? No is the resounding answer.

In our everyday lives, we do not have the duties of a special operator, a police officer or a combat soldier. Therefore, we do not need their skills and equipment. As a civilian, you are not expected to quell a civil disturbance, put out a high-rise fire or engage criminals in a firefight. There are others whose duty and honor it is to deal with those threats. You might want to be prepared to lend a hand if asked by one of the professionals who guard us, but it is not your primary responsibility.

As a civilian, it is your duty to get yourself, your family and others who you are able to help to safety. To accomplish this, you need a few skills, some common sense. You might also need a basic tool. You could definitely use an everyday survival knife.

There is an old saying: "The best survival knife is the one you have with you when you need to survive." There is considerable wisdom in that old saying, but it begs the question of what is the best knife to have with you. Let's take it a little further. No one knows when an emergency is going to happen. If they did, they could arrange to be absent. Therefore, since we cannot predict when we will need a knife in an emergency, a survival knife must be small enough, handy enough, to carry at all times.

Further, since we cannot predict the nature of the emergency, the survival knife must be one that can be relied upon to perform a wide range of extreme tasks reasonably well. This paragon of knife must be useful for everyday chores. If it is not, it will sooner or later be left behind. Special use gear of any kind tends to be left behind. The knife must be versatile, because it is likely to be the only tool of any kind you have when events conspire to put you in harm's way.

How Big Is Too Big?

A medium-sized knife, one with a 6- to7-inch blade, is a good compromise between performance and function. Big bowies or choppers will make quick work of many jobs, but are too big for most people to carry every day (not counting Crocodile Dundee and knifemaker Bill Bagwell.) The problem with the medium-sized knife is the same as the hindrance associated with a bowie: it's too big to tote daily. Active-duty military personnel can, and do, carry such knives regularly. But for civilians, the medium-sized knife is cumbersome.

with skills and experience. But it also helps to have a basic emergency tool, along with the knowledge of how to use it. Be prepared.

How can we be prepared?

Must we acquire the skills of a Delta Force operator in order to be secure in our own towns? Should

we burden ourselves like combat soldiers? Do we need to drive monster trucks or sport utility vehicles loaded with radios, water, emergency rations, sleeping bags, a field hospital, a GPS, a SATCOM phone and weapons of mass destruction in order to drive to work or take

Also, in many places, it is illegal. Even in places where it is not illegal, the 6-to-7-inch blade has a high "freak out" factor among the general population. In our culture, it isn't generally acceptable to carry such a knife daily. Remember that we are talking about a knife that you will carry at all times and places, except, of course, in secure areas, such as airports.

A 4-inch blade is about all most of us can manage on a regular basis. For most people and places, a 4-inch blade is within the bounds of social acceptability. In many places, 4 inches is the legal limit for a fixed blade. Of course, in some communities, Los Angeles for example, any kind of fixed blade is forbidden, and in some rarified areas of Los Angeles, many people would regard you as some kind of nut to even carry a Swiss Army knife. But L.A. and Hollywood are not the world.

There are some terrific folders on the market today. Some of them can perform amazing feats, feats never before managed by folders. But a folder is not your best choice for an everyday survival knife. No matter how tough a folder might be, it still folds. No folder can be relied upon to pry open a jammed door in an earthquake-damaged building, or to rip and twist through the sheet metal of a wrecked car.

In the heat and confusion of an emergency, you cannot count on being able to carefully place the blade so that it is not stressed too much. You must have a simple, tough knife that you can access quickly with either hand (one or the other may be injured) and count on it to rip open the skin of a burning plane, or pry open a stuck elevator door in a fire.

An everyday survival knife is one that is with you at all times. You put it on in the morning with your clothing. It's similar to your wallet, watch and keys, just part of your daily dress. So what we need is a tough fixed-blade knife, with about a 4-inch blade. It's better yet if the handle is not too large. Four inches is fine for a handle if you know how to hold it, and 8 inches or less overall is easy to carry. In fact an 8-inch-overall fixed blade can disappear in the pocket of a pair of khakis. In this instance, bigger is not better.

For this article, we tested a wide variety of small fixed-blade knives, both custom and factory, to find a reliable selection. Over a period of a couple of months, five people—two women and three men—used these knives for all daily tasks that could be done with knives. We carried them constantly. Some members of the group were experienced knife users; others were not. Some of the most difficult tests, such as driving the blades into the hood of a Honda to simulate escaping from a wrecked car, were performed by the women. A young woman with no previous experience was able to make a foot-long cut in the car by using her shoe as a baton. The idea was to see if these tools could serve everyone, not just the young, strong and experienced.

We pried open locked doors, chipped away mortar to pull bricks from a wall, and then used those bricks to pound the knives through wood and stucco to simulate escaping from a burning building. All of the knives in this article performed these extreme tasks with minimum damage or no damage. There are many knives in addition to those that were tested that could per-

form equally well, but space doesn't permit us to test them all.

If you are serious about needing a survival knife, and the one you are interested in doesn't appear in this article, ask the maker if his knife will stand up to this usage. If he says yes, then try it yourself. If it works, carry it with confidence. If it fails, call the maker. The makers of the knives in this article, without exception, each said, "Have at it. If the knife fails, I will replace it."

But do not try to cut through a car body with a finely crafted gen-

Small as it may be, the Chris Reeve Shadow III was able to split a 2x4, in addition to withstanding much more use and abuse in the field.

The Fallkniven H1 survived a stab into a car hood in good shape.

tleman's knife and then complain when it breaks. Use some common sense. This kind of treatment is abuse, you might say. Indeed, many makers will say so. They will tell you at length that you should never, never use one of their fine cutting instruments for such tasks, that their knives were not designed for this, that you should use the proper tool for the job. If a maker tells you this, heed his or her advice. Do not rely on such knives for extreme purposes. But if a maker calls his knife a "survival knife" or a "combat knife" or some such label, then it should do the job it is advertised to do. If a maker tells you that he makes a survival knife but you can't use it to survive with, well, sorry folks, someone is missing the point.

Survival Means Knife Abuse

Try telling a father that he shouldn't use his custom survival knife to cut and pry his son out of a wrecked car. Tell a climber he shouldn't use his knife as a piton to arrest his fall from a rock face. Tell the fireman who cut into the side of a steel container with his folder, when he had no other tool available to save a trapped woman, that he shouldn't abuse his knife. This kind of fussiness won't do when destiny comes calling. We carry our knives for many reasons, but if we can't rely on them in emergencies, we need to know it.

Therefore, here are a dozen knives you can count on when the tide is running against you, when

fortune is smiling on someone else, when the building is burning around you. These knives might not save your life, but with some determination and luck, they might. Fortune helps those who help themselves.

Benchmade Nimravus

This is a well-designed spear point that is reminiscent of what used to be called boot knives. This is a good thing. Some of the old boot knives have yet to be surpassed. The grip is secure and allowed the knife to be stabbed into the hood of a Honda without slipping. The edge did take a pretty deep ding in it from being pounded through sheet metal, but that did not hinder its continued use. The Nimravus is a good all-around user.

Chris Reeve Mountaineer and Shadow III

Both of these tiny knives are tough. They are tough far beyond reasonableness. They cut well, and they do not break, even under extreme duress. Each is made from one piece of A-2 tool steel well known for toughness, but I suspect Chris knows more about metallurgy than just the choice of steel would indicate. The small handles on these knives are an advantage, rather then a problem, as some have said. If you cup the handle so that the butt lines up to the base of your palm, you have a very secure grip, one that allows you to thrust without fear of slippage. Both also have hollow handles. These small survival knives define the genre.

Fallkniven F1 and H1

Clean, contemporary design characterizes the entire Fallkniven product line. Fallkniven knives are tough and handsome. We tested the A1 and the H1. Both have blades of about 4 inches. These are full-tang knives with a bit of the tangs exposed at the butts, a good touch, one that allows for pounding on the butt ends without damage. And we did pound on them. We drove them through wood, stucco walls and an auto body. Both came through with no perceptible damage. The convex grinds and good edge geometry make these little gems superior cutting instruments and provide great strength.

Spyderco Knives

The Bob Lum Tanto has a well-supported point and fine balance. It worked better for kitchen chores

The Trace Rinaldi handmade knife was forced through a car hood with a baton and came out none the worse for wear. In fact, it was ripped through sheet metal, pounded into a brick wall and just plain abused. There was nothing more than a few waves in the edge from all this.

The grip of the Benchmade Nimravus is secure and allowed the knife to be stabbed into the hood of a Honda without slipping.

than I thought it would. It also pierced the auto body with no damage whatever. After quite a bit of ripping and tearing through auto bodies, wood and stucco, it was dull but still working. This handy little tanto has a full, tapered tang and showed no ill effects from being pounded through sheet metal, using a 2x4, by Mike Hernandez, a former ball player who weighs about 250 pounds and did not hold back.

The Fred Perrin design is probably my favorite Spyderco fixed blade. Mr. Perrin's interpretation of the classic bowie pattern is true to the original in spirit, but it is in every sense a modern knife, made for today's world. At 5 inches, it is a bit long for this category of knife, but it is so clean in execution, so fine in balance, that I could not leave it out. The handle is molded to ergonomic perfection, but it is not a full tang. Therefore, I could not bring myself to pound on the butt for fear of destroying the handle. Of course, in an actual emergency, I would do just that. We did baton the blade on its spine and there was no significant damage. Flat grind, good edge geometry, it is a great cutter.

Trace Rinaldi Custom

With its dropped edge, this design looks like a finely made kitchen knife. It performs like one in the kitchen also, probably the best of the bunch for food prep.

However, don't be fooled by its appearance. This baby is a wolf in sheep's clothing. It has a full tang, and with Trace's permission and reassurance, we ripped through sheet metal, hammered it through the long suffering Honda, pounded it into a brick wall and just plain got on it. I don't know what's going on with this CPM-3V steel, but there was nothing more than a few waves in the edge from all this. Flat grind, good cutter, it is tough beyond expectations.

Ontario TAK

This knife looks tough. It is tough. It is a little large for our purposes, but still within the parameters of the concept. The TAK is not a pretty knife. It is a solid working knife at a great price. The TAK's rough-hewn appearance makes it look out of place in the kitchen, but it has a flat grind that allows it to perform like a mini-chef's knife. One of my testers is a big guy with big hands, and he spends a lot of time outdoors. This was his preferred choice. It is a good knife at a great price, and it will dress out a Honda with no problem.

Busse

Busse has the reputation of making tough knives. That reputation is well deserved. The Busse fixed blade tested in the field is similar to the TAK, in that it has a rough appearance. It looks like the

kind of knife a knuckle dragger would carry. Being a knuckle dragger, I have some idea of what they (we) like. Whereas the Perrin is the kind of knife James Bond would carry, if he carried a knife. The Busse performed pretty much the way it looked, smashing through brick walls and forcing its way through plywood and stucco with minimal edge deformation.

Cold Steel

The Pendleton Hunter looks like an ordinary drop-point hunter. It is reasonably priced, as are all of Cold Steel's products. But this knife will serve for a great deal more than zipping off the hide of your next buck. If you need to pry open a door to get out of an earthquake-damaged house, this little hunter will do the job. I don't know how Cold Steel provides this kind of performance for such a modest price.

Bud Nealy

This custom maker is well known for his innovative carrying systems and for his small fixed blades. Bud's Pesh Kabz looks delicate, almost like a toy, or a lady's knife. The first time we drove this tiny blade into a car body, we did so in fear that we would destroy it. The fear was unfounded. After the first cut into car steel, the Pesh Kabz emerged with no damage whatever. After two or three times of being driven into the car body

The Bud Nealy Pesh Kabz was forced through a car hood by hitting the back of the blade with a shoe. The first time the relatively short blade was driven into a car body, the fear was that it would be destroyed. The fear was unfounded. After the first cut into car steel, the Pesh Kabz emerged with no damage whatever. After two or three times of being driven into the car body with a 2x4, it still looked like new. It became a challenge to see if the author and friends could put a ding in the point. It never happened.

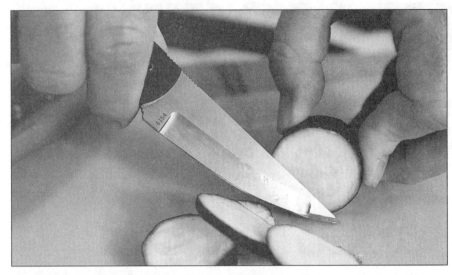

After all the abuse the Bud Nealy Pesh Kabz took in testing, the edge was still sharp enough to cut paper. It also sliced fish (and zucchini, here) like a sushi knife.

With a flat-ground CPM 3V blade, the Trace Rinaldi fixed blade is a good cutter and tough beyond expectations.

The Chris Reeve Mountaineer is fashioned from one piece of A-2 tool steel well known for toughness, but the author suspects Chris knows more about metallurgy than just the choice of steel would indicate. The small handle on the knife is an advantage, rather then a problem, as some have said. If you cup the handle so that the butt lines up to the base of your palm, you have a very secure grip.

with a 2x4, it still looked like new. It became a challenge to see if we could put a ding in the point. It never happened. After all the pounding and all the "What the #@!%" comments, the edge was still sharp enough to cut paper. It also slices fish like a sushi knife. It is so lightweight you forget you are carrying it, truly an everyday knife. Use it once and you will not forget that you have a reliable knife.

Sheath 'Em If You've Got 'Em

Sheaths and carrying systems have evolved a great deal in the past few years. But I'm not convinced that the evolution has been for the best in all cases. The old boot knife sheath commonly had a spring clip to attach it to your boot, a waistband or wherever you wanted to tuck it away.

Sal Glesser put a spring clip on a pocketknife and revolutionized the way we carry folders. If a clip works for a folder, what's wrong with putting a clip on a sheath for a fixed blade? Many of the ingenious solutions to fixed-blade carry are answers to problems that have already been solved.

An everyday carry knife needs to be carried every day, regardless of your attire. A sheath with a belt loop is useless if you leave the house in running shorts. How do you attach a fixed blade to your gi pants if you wear them on the way to the dojo? Are you sure that you will not need your everyday knife while jogging or wearing your board shorts?

None of us have a crystal ball to predict the future. That's the point of the everyday survival knife. All of the good and reliable knives we tested have pretty good sheaths, yet few of them have all-purpose attachment methods. Makers, please, make us a sheath with a clip.

We have reviewed some great knives. But the best of knives won't save us. Knives are inanimate objects; they will do nothing on their own. We must have the will and the purpose to overcome what life brings to us in order to survive. If you are reading this, you have done pretty well so far. Still breathing, aren't you? Don't worry if you don't have the skills of some mythical hero. Most heroic deeds are done by ordinary people. If disaster comes into your life, don't be surprised. Nothing is more common than disaster. Take heart, and set your purpose. You will prevail. ●

THE MOST ILLEGAL KNIFE IN AMERICA

> *Before legislatures "go ballistic," we should educate and organize to protect our knife rights*

By Evan F. Nappen,
Attorney at Law

"¿**C**OMO ESTA?" ASKS Arnold Schwarzenegger in the 1985 movie "Commando," as he fires a ballistic knife into the chest of a bad guy, which amazingly causes immediate death. Hollywood never misses a chance to help fuel a misguided weapons ban, and the ballistic knife was no exception. In May of 1986, Francis Ford Coppola's son and Ryan O'Neal's son were in an automobile accident in which Coppola's son died. O'Neal's son was charged with reckless driving and possession of a ballistic knife. Hollywood elitism and hypocrisy is nothing new.

What made the ballistic knife so frightening to career politicians, media talking heads and assorted *hoplophobes* (those who irrationally fear weapons) is that it's a knife that shoots! A ballistic knife is essentially a blade attached to a hollow handle that fits inside of another outer hollow handle, which contains a coil spring. The coil spring compresses inside the handle, and a latch holds the knife blade down against the spring pressure. When the latch is released, the knife and attached inner handle launch and "go ballistic."

Politically, the ballistic knife helped fill the gap between guns and knives. It enabled knife haters to join ranks with gun haters and both had a common, new, inanimate object to wail and screech about.

Sure enough, one year after "Commando" was released, the Ballistic Knife Prohibition Act of 1986 was signed into Federal Law by then Republican President Ronald Reagan, as part of the Anti-Drug Abuse Act of 1986.

▼A coil spring compresses inside the handle of a ballistic knife, and a latch holds the knife blade down against the spring pressure.

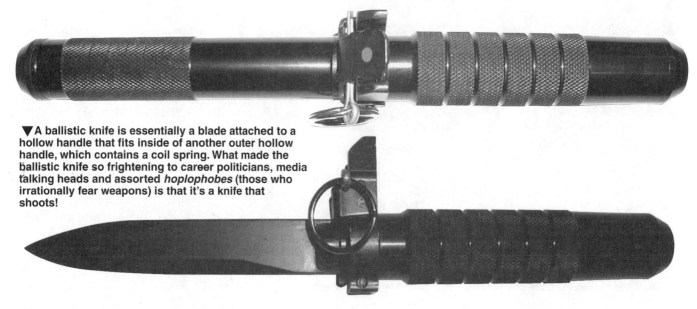

▼A ballistic knife is essentially a blade attached to a hollow handle that fits inside of another outer hollow handle, which contains a coil spring. What made the ballistic knife so frightening to career politicians, media talking heads and assorted *hoplophobes* (those who irrationally fear weapons) is that it's a knife that shoots!

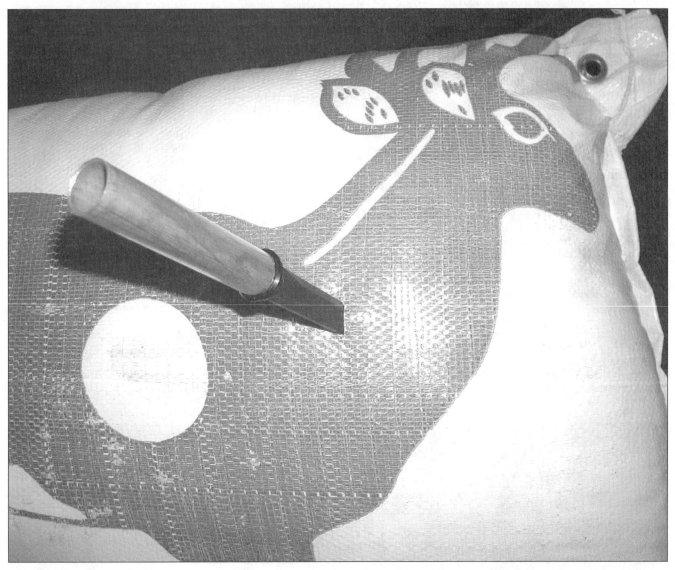

A knife can be thrown with substantially more power and accuracy than can be achieved by firing a ballistic knife. This fact alone makes the ballistic knife ban patently absurd and useless.

In addition to the ballistic knife being slandered and falsely linked to drug abuse, this was the newest national attack on knives since the 1958 Federal Switchblades Laws. Republican Sen. Alfonse M. D'Amato held a news conference pushing for and spinning the proposed ban. He announced that a ballistic knife "is a favored weapon used by drug dealers." He further proclaimed, "Ballistic knives are at least as dangerous as switchblade knives that have been banned since 1958."

The hype surrounding ballistic knives did not help matters. The knives were advertised for sale in Soldier of Fortune Magazine with the pitch "The Commies Had It. We Stole It. Now You Can Buy It!!!!" Ballistic knives were advertised as being able to "kill swiftly and silently." Sen. D'Amato claimed a ballistic knife to be a "dangerous weapon, a terrorist weapon." He further declared, "Ballistic knives have no legitimate sporting purpose. They are sought by professional criminals because they are easily concealed and capable of penetrating a policeman's bullet-proof vest."

Democratic Rep. Mario Biaggi (a well known anti-gun politician and a sponsor of the so called "Cop-Killer Bullet Ban") appeared at a news conference and asserted that ballistic knives were the "latest in cop-killer technology," and that the ballistic knife can "...fire its blade like a bullet" and "penetrate police bullet resistant vests." He stated he had bought his ballistic knife via mail order from the Florida Knife Corp. by putting the $79.95 on his

When the latch of a ballistic knife is released, the knife and attached inner handle launch and "go ballistic."

credit card. Biaggi stated, "…there were no questions asked. I could have been anybody. The ballistic knife is totally accessible to anyone who wants it." At the news conference, the typical "dog and pony show" was conducted by a New York police officer who fired a ballistic knife from 30 feet at a silhouette target of a person.

Of course, there were no known cases at that time of anybody ever being killed by a ballistic knife, no less any reported cases of a police officer being shot at by a "drug dealer or terrorist" (or anyone else for that matter) with a ballistic knife. Furthermore, I could not find any Gallop Poll taken of drug dealers inquiring as to whether a ballistic knife was their "preferred weapon" of the 1980s, but somehow I doubt it considering the ready availability of cheaper and more effective black market firearms.

The Florida Knife Corp. issued a statement that their ballistic knives do NOT penetrate bulletproof vests, but noted that any ice pick could penetrate a bulletproof vest. Bulletproof vests are NOT ice pick proof, however banning ice picks is not as politically correct or headline grabbing. A ballistic knife has as much "sporting purpose" as any throwing knife. Since when is the "sporting purpose test" applied to knives, anyway? What sporting purpose does an 8-inch chef's knife have? Then again, why should facts get in the way of a feel-good knife ban?

The ballistic knife is also known as the K96 knife, the Spetznaz knife, the KGB knife, the Pillum ballistic knife, the Springblade knife, the Spy knife, the Special Forces knife, the Florida knife, the Bloody Mary knife and the Flying Dutchman knife. That's a lot of names for one knife! Some claim that the knife was developed for the KGB. Others claim it was made for the Soviet special forces, called the "Spetznaz." All seem to agree that the ballistic knife design is Russian in origin. With enough vodka, anything is possible.

Federal Law defines a ballistic knife as follows:

United States Code, Title 15 Section 1245

(d) "Ballistic knife" defined.

As used in this section, the term "ballistic knife" means a knife with a detachable blade that is propelled by a spring-operated mechanism.

Pub. L. 85-623, Sec. 7, Oct. 27, 1986. Amended Nov. 18, 1988.

My question: Which one of the following weapons is legally impossible for an average law-abiding citizen to lawfully acquire in interstate commerce under Federal Law?

1. Live hand grenade
2. Suppressed (silenced) .22 pistol
3. Short-barrel (sawed off) shotgun
4. An USI submachine gun
5. Browning .50 M2 machine gun

Of course, knives—any knives, not ballistic knives—can always be thrown. There are many books that deal with the subject of knife throwing for both fun and combat.

6. Howitzer
7. Ballistic knife

You guessed it! A ballistic knife is utterly impossible for an average law-abiding citizen to lawfully acquire in interstate commerce. All of the other items listed are heavily regulated by Federal Law, but are technically obtainable with the proper paperwork, investigation and approval by the Federal Government.

Federal Law prohibits a ballistic knife as follows:

United States Code, Title 15 Section 1245

(a) Prohibition and penalties for possession, manufacture, sale, or importation.

Whoever in or affecting interstate commerce, within any Territory or possession of the United States, within Indian country (as defined in section 1151 of title 18), or within the special maritime and territorial jurisdiction of the United States (as defined in section 7 of title 18), knowingly possesses, manufactures, sells, or imports a ballistic knife shall be fined as provided in title 18, or imprisoned not more than 10 years, or both.

(b) Prohibition and penalties for possession or use during commission of Federal crime of violence.

Whoever possesses or uses a ballistic knife in the commission of a Federal crime of violence shall be fined as provided in title 18, or imprisoned not less than five years and not more than 10 years, or both.

(c) Exceptions.

The exceptions provided in paragraphs (1), (2), and (3) of section 1244 of this title with respect to switchblade knives shall apply to ballistic knives under subsection (a) of this section.

Pub. L. 85-623, Sec. 7, Oct. 27, 1986. Amended Nov. 18, 1988.

The exceptions under Federal Law for ballistic knives are as follows:

United States Code, Title 15 Section 1244

(1) any common carrier or contract carrier, with respect to any switchblade knife shipped, transported, or delivered for shipment in interstate commerce in the ordinary course of business;

The exceptions under Federal Law prohibiting ballistic knives include "the manufacture, sale, transportation, distribution, possession, or introduction into interstate commerce, of switchblade knives pursuant to contract with the Armed Forces; and the Armed Forces or any member or employee thereof acting in the performance of his duty."

(2) the manufacture, sale, transportation, distribution, possession, or introduction into interstate commerce, of switchblade knives pursuant to contract with the Armed Forces;

(3) the Armed Forces or any member or employee thereof acting in the performance of his duty; or

Pub. L. 85-623, Sec. 7, Oct. 27, 1986. Amended Nov. 18, 1988.

The Federal Law on ballistic knives is very similar to Federal Law on switchblades, except that the switchblade law exception for "the possession, and transportation upon his person, of any switchblade knife with a blade three inches or less in length by any individual who has only one arm" does not apply to ballistic knives. One-armed individuals are forced by Federal Law to have to throw their knives by hand just like everyone else!

There are many books that deal with the subject of knife throwing for both fun and combat. A knife can be thrown with substantially more power and accuracy than can be achieved by firing a ballistic knife. This fact alone makes the ballistic knife ban patently absurd and useless. Any decent fixed blade knife can be thrown (although throwing your handmade, damascus, ivory-handled bowie is not recommended). But why should facts and logic stand in the way of any headline-grabbing politician pushing a weapons ban and holding news conferences? Even Arnold Schwarzenegger, in "Commando," first dispatches two bad guys at the

Bows and crossbows can all shoot broadhead arrows. Broadheads are and/or contain razor sharp knife blades. Is a compound bow with a broadhead arrow a "weapon or other device capable of lethal use and which can propel a knife blade?" Of course it is! Sure, it was not the intent of the New Jersey Legislature to ban archery and bow hunting, but it was not the intent of the Florida Legislature to ban switchblades/automatics, either, and yet the Darynani court did just that!

same time by THROWING two knives at them before he resorts to utilizing his ballistic knife on a third antagonist.

Okay, the law is ridiculous, so what's the problem? Who needs to own a ballistic knife anyway, right? Well, here is the problem: the ballistic knife ban is a KNIFE BAN, and just because it isn't your ox being gored does not mean you should ignore it. This ban paves

the way for more knife bans. The politicians see our knife rights as "easy pickin's." They can look like they are doing something about crime, terrorism or drug dealing, when in reality it's just another hit on our knife rights.

Ballistic knife bans lay the groundwork for further knife bans and for activist courts to be judicially dishonest and to prohibit other lawful knives and weapons that are not ballistic knives. Don't believe it? Then you have obviously not read State of Florida, Appellant, v. Pariya Darynani, Appellee, 4th District, Case No. 4D99-4172. In this case, the Florida Court banned formerly lawful automatic/switchblade knives under the guise of Florida's ballistic knife ban. The case is a classic example of anti-knife bias and the abuse of our knife rights that a wrongful knife ban can cause.

New Jersey's ballistic knife ban has even more potential for abuse. The New Jersey ballistic knife ban was signed into law by then Republican Gov. Thomas Kean, who stated, "We have to restrict the flow of knives that serve no useful or lawful purpose." If the "bunny hug-

gers" wanted to push it, New Jersey's ballistic knife law is so overbroad that archery and bow hunting are threatened and could be banned.

New Jersey Law defines a ballistic knife as follows:

Chapter 39 Of New Jersey Criminal Code

Firearms And Weapons 2C: 39-1.

u. "Ballistic knife" means any weapon or other device capable of lethal use and which can propel a knife blade.

Bows and crossbows can all shoot broadhead arrows. Broadheads are and/or contain razor-sharp knife blades. Is a compound bow with a broadhead arrow a "weapon or other device capable of lethal use and which can propel a knife blade?" Of course it is! Sure, it was not the intent of the New Jersey Legislature to ban archery and bow hunting, but it was not the intent of the Florida Legislature to ban switchblades/automatics, either, and yet the Darynani court did just that!

Unfortunately, knife aficionados were not organized, prepared or ready for the ballistic knife fight in the mid-1980s. We were never warned about the future effect and ramifications of ballistic knife bans on our knife rights. We dramatically lost on the ballistic knife issue and are now paying a price. It is time to organize, educate and not repeat our mistakes. ¿Comprende? ●

TRENDS

There's a suddenly popular knife style in the industry, a pattern that has been in existence for ages, but one that has been reincarnated in many forms lately—the *Karambit*. You'll see a few examples of Karambits in the "Biting Blades," section of "Trends," models designed by Liong Mah and fashioned by knifemakers Jeff Hall, Brad Duncan, Mike Snody and Rob Simonich. Each of four *karambit* knives is an interpretation of an ancient Javanese fixed blade, the form of which emulates a tiger's claw.

According to Ernest Emerson of Emerson Knives, martial artists have used generic karambits extensively for years, and the popularity of the knife style in the self-defense community is spreading to blade enthusiasts in general. The karambit-style knife is becoming trendy.

Some modern versions are actually folding knives, and others borrow a few key aspects of ancient Javanese karambits but do not hold true to the exact form. There is even a Karambit.com website, touted as "the internationally recognized authority and official site of the Karambit Utility Knife."

Is it American ingenuity that gives birth to trends? Is it capitalism at its best? Or, could it be that knifemakers, and particularly creative, intuitive, opportunistic and ingenious builders of edged tools, have the wherewithal to recognize a tempting design and revamp it to incorporate their own styles and signature design elements? Is it just craftiness? Whatever the cause of a trend, there is never a lack of knife trends, particularly in the custom, or handmade, end of the blade community.

Handcrafting an edged tool or weapon is a non-exacting science, one that is open to interpretation. It is an art form often passed down from generation to generation, father to son, grandfather to grandson or master to student. To build a bladed instrument so clean, so smooth, sharp, strong and stately that others not only want to hold, use, covet and caress it, but also to copy and emulate it, is to create a trend. With thousands of knifemakers building a plethora of blades by hand, there are bound to be a few stellar examples that make all the hammers stop pounding, the grinders stop grinding and the drills stop drilling long enough for jaws to drop and knife forms to suddenly change. Thus, trends are born.

Joe Kertzman

Long-Necked Grips

GIVE BLADE MAKERS enough time and they'll find giraffe bone suitable for the fashioning of knife handles. Now, I'm not totally inane, but how exactly does one go shopping for just the right bone of giraffe? "Well, it's a nice specimen, but it's a little too narrow at that end, and there's too much marrow in this section." Do mail-order houses stock giraffe bone, keeping the long-legged skeletal remains on shelves waiting for customers to snatch them up like day-old bread? And how does one go about shipping a giraffe bone? Does the UPS man ring the bell of the modern-day Fred Flintstone residence with a 6-foot bone wrapped in brown paper? I mean, that's one tall order!

I'm sure the place to shop would be the tables of knife-supply companies at trade shows (as long as 12-foot tables are available), or through the anything-you-could-wish-for worldwide Web, but still, giraffe bone-handled knives? Come on, people, isn't anything sacred? One minute the dumb, lanky creatures are nibbling on tree leaves at the San Diego Zoo and, once old age catches up with them, their leg bones are shipped to the nearest knifemaker. Or, maybe it's not even the leg bone of the giraffe that makes the best knife handle. It could be a neck bone, a shoulder blade or a collar bone.

One thing is for certain. There are more long-necked knife grips gracing knife-show tables right now than, say, 10, 15, 20 minutes ago when stag or cow bone did the trick. All "ribbing" aside, what giraffe bone represents is the vast array of exotic materials available to knifemakers, and the "lengths" makers of edged tools and weapons go to bring their customers the best, most impressive, gorgeous knives possible. They are willing to stick their necks out, so to speak.

Joe Kertzman

▼DUSTY MOULTON: You've got to admit, the bones from the long-necked beasts make for some eye-popping patterns.

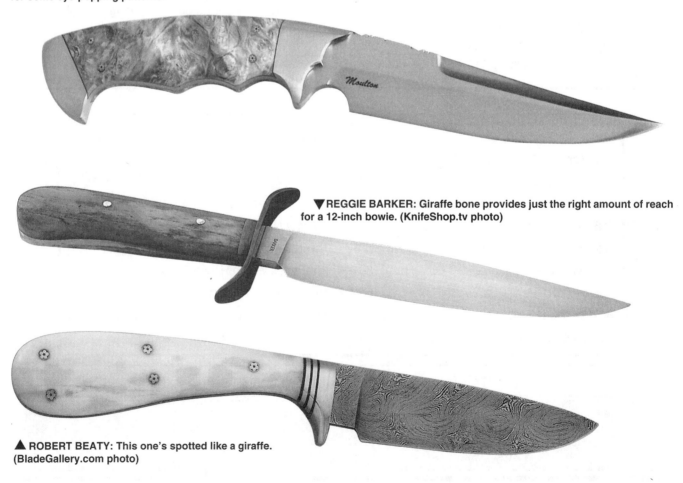

▼REGGIE BARKER: Giraffe bone provides just the right amount of reach for a 12-inch bowie. (KnifeShop.tv photo)

▲ ROBERT BEATY: This one's spotted like a giraffe. (BladeGallery.com photo)

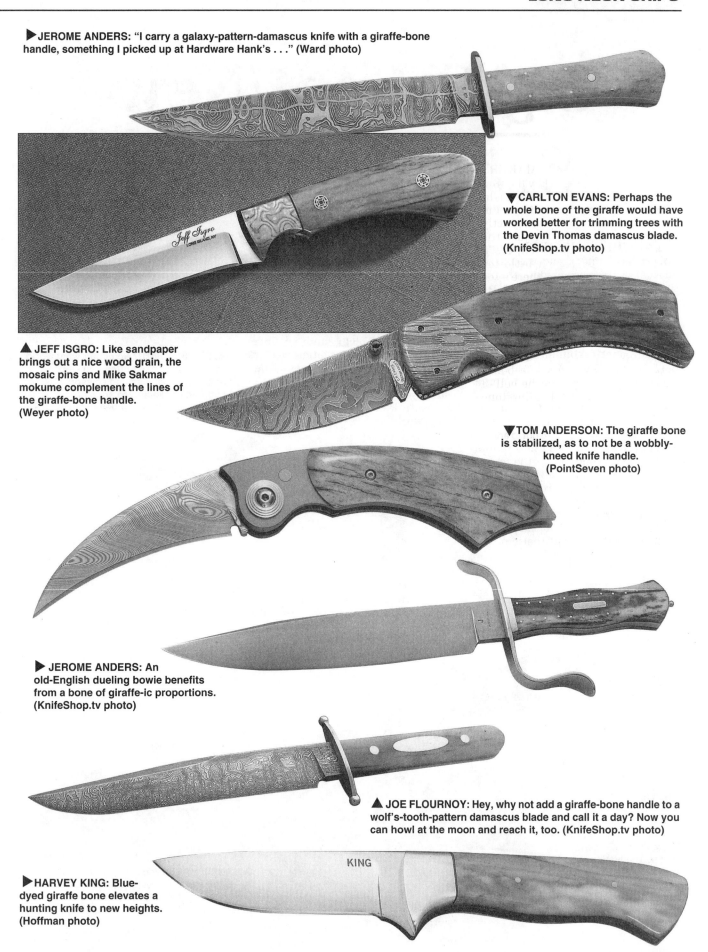

▶JEROME ANDERS: "I carry a galaxy-pattern-damascus knife with a giraffe-bone handle, something I picked up at Hardware Hank's . . ." (Ward photo)

▼CARLTON EVANS: Perhaps the whole bone of the giraffe would have worked better for trimming trees with the Devin Thomas damascus blade. (KnifeShop.tv photo)

▲ JEFF ISGRO: Like sandpaper brings out a nice wood grain, the mosaic pins and Mike Sakmar mokume complement the lines of the giraffe-bone handle. (Weyer photo)

▼TOM ANDERSON: The giraffe bone is stabilized, as to not be a wobbly-kneed knife handle. (PointSeven photo)

▶JEROME ANDERS: An old-English dueling bowie benefits from a bone of giraffe-ic proportions. (KnifeShop.tv photo)

▲ JOE FLOURNOY: Hey, why not add a giraffe-bone handle to a wolf's-tooth-pattern damascus blade and call it a day? Now you can howl at the moon and reach it, too. (KnifeShop.tv photo)

▶HARVEY KING: Blue-dyed giraffe bone elevates a hunting knife to new heights. (Hoffman photo)

Old-School/New-School Folders

NOWHERE IS THE change knives have undergone during the past 50 years more evident than in the knives that fold. Let's take a trip, a trip to a place where bone, especially jigged bone, is powerfully plentiful. It's a land where being heavy is socially acceptable. Wood is an ever-bountiful building material, not a controlled natural resource. Steel isn't stainless. Bolsters serve as more than dormitory cushions and pillows. No one frets about breaking a fingernail opening a knife blade. In this netherworld, pocketknives are put into pants pockets. Everyone knows the purpose of a spay blade, and bloodletting blades are for letting blood.

Come along on another journey. On this flight of fancy, folders practically float in the hand on titanium wings. Weighing a few ounces is ideal. Aluminum is harvested like corn or wheat. Steel is not only stainless, but coated, colored and bead blasted. In this universally modernistic universe, a fingernail never touches a knife blade. Clips are for hanging knives from clothing. Computer, or Y2K, knives are employed to fix computers and, at one time, to prevent Y2K from destroying the world.

Between the two worlds are years of technology and advancements, yet some energetic travelers enjoy visiting both places. They shuttle back and forth between "lands of odds" like commuters on an Amtrak or elevated train. These otherworldly folks carry knives with features common to both places. They tend to borrow from each culture, and that is just as commendable as planting one's roots and remaining steadfast and true to a single world.

Joe Kertzman

◄ **PHILIP BOOTH: No matter what world you're from, it isn't often you see damascus nail files and scissors. The cunning pocketknives are bladed, bolstered, buffed and beautified.**
(Weyer photo)

▲ **GARY CROWDER: Other than the John Fitch damascus blade and fancy file work, this is basically an old-school folder. The blades must be manually pulled out from within the sheep-horn handle, yet in this case, it is a pleasure to do so.**
(Ward photo)

▲ **KANSEI MATSUNO: All "new school" is the damascus and mother-of-pearl, one-hand-opening, locking-liner folder with thumb stud and smooth pivoting action.**

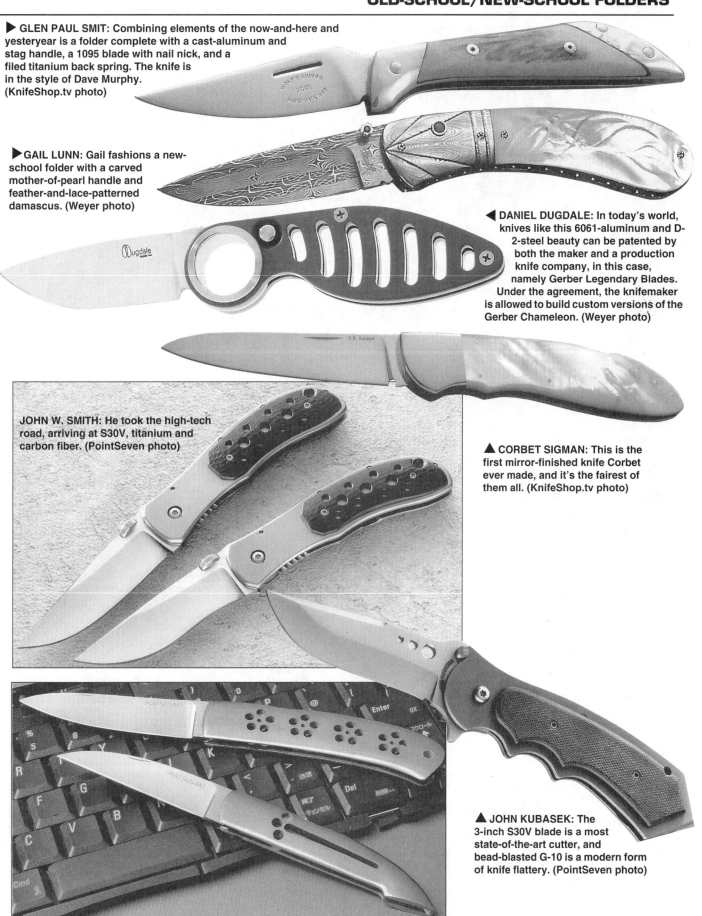

▶ GLEN PAUL SMIT: Combining elements of the now-and-here and yesteryear is a folder complete with a cast-aluminum and stag handle, a 1095 blade with nail nick, and a filed titanium back spring. The knife is in the style of Dave Murphy. (KnifeShop.tv photo)

▶ GAIL LUNN: Gail fashions a new-school folder with a carved mother-of-pearl handle and feather-and-lace-patterned damascus. (Weyer photo)

◀ DANIEL DUGDALE: In today's world, knives like this 6061-aluminum and D-2-steel beauty can be patented by both the maker and a production knife company, in this case, namely Gerber Legendary Blades. Under the agreement, the knifemaker is allowed to build custom versions of the Gerber Chameleon. (Weyer photo)

JOHN W. SMITH: He took the high-tech road, arriving at S30V, titanium and carbon fiber. (PointSeven photo)

▲ CORBET SIGMAN: This is the first mirror-finished knife Corbet ever made, and it's the fairest of them all. (KnifeShop.tv photo)

▲ JOHN KUBASEK: The 3-inch S30V blade is a most state-of-the-art cutter, and bead-blasted G-10 is a modern form of knife flattery. (PointSeven photo)

▲ TAKESHI MATSUSAKI: Futuristic titanium handles meet old-world knife blades.

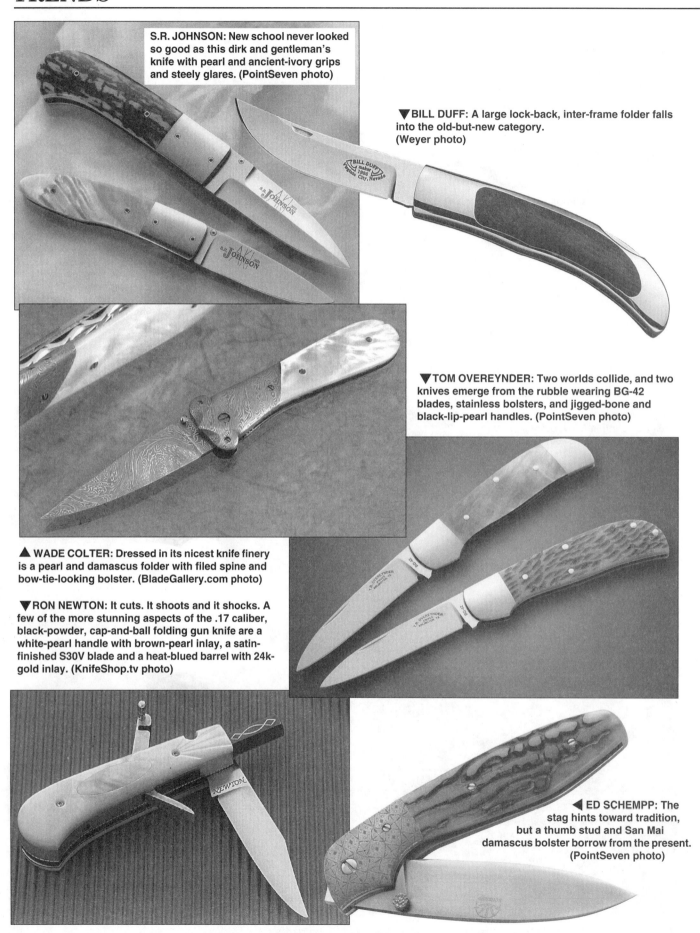

S.R. JOHNSON: New school never looked so good as this dirk and gentleman's knife with pearl and ancient-ivory grips and steely glares. (PointSeven photo)

▼**BILL DUFF:** A large lock-back, inter-frame folder falls into the old-but-new category. (Weyer photo)

▼**TOM OVEREYNDER:** Two worlds collide, and two knives emerge from the rubble wearing BG-42 blades, stainless bolsters, and jigged-bone and black-lip-pearl handles. (PointSeven photo)

▲ **WADE COLTER:** Dressed in its nicest knife finery is a pearl and damascus folder with filed spine and bow-tie-looking bolster. (BladeGallery.com photo)

▼**RON NEWTON:** It cuts. It shoots and it shocks. A few of the more stunning aspects of the .17 caliber, black-powder, cap-and-ball folding gun knife are a white-pearl handle with brown-pearl inlay, a satin-finished S30V blade and a heat-blued barrel with 24k-gold inlay. (KnifeShop.tv photo)

◄**ED SCHEMPP:** The stag hints toward tradition, but a thumb stud and San Mai damascus bolster borrow from the present. (PointSeven photo)

CHARLES BENNICA: The state-of-the-art folder comes with three tools and can be completely disassembled. (Simon photo)

DAN BURKE: They don't build gardener's knives like this anymore . . . well, Dan still does. (PointSeven photo)

▼**BERTIE RIETVELD:** The traditional knife pattern has a colored stainless-damascus blade, a Picasso-stone handle, and anodized-titanium bolsters with a Stanhope lens planted in the center.

▶**JIM HAMMOND:** Of new-world order is a flip-open folder adorned with a sculpted-green-linen-Micarta® handle, a satin-finished 440C blade and titanium liners and springs. (Weyer photo)

▶**TOM WATSON:** White pearl is planted in just the right spots to contrast perfectly with the almost-black Mike Norris damascus blade and bolsters. It's either learned or instinctual art, but either way, it's good! (Hoffman photo)

▲ **TAKESHI MATSUSAKI:** Don't worry, new-school followers, the tortoise shell handle is imitation.

▲ **J.B. MOORE:** It's not retro, it's classic. (KnifeShop.tv photo)

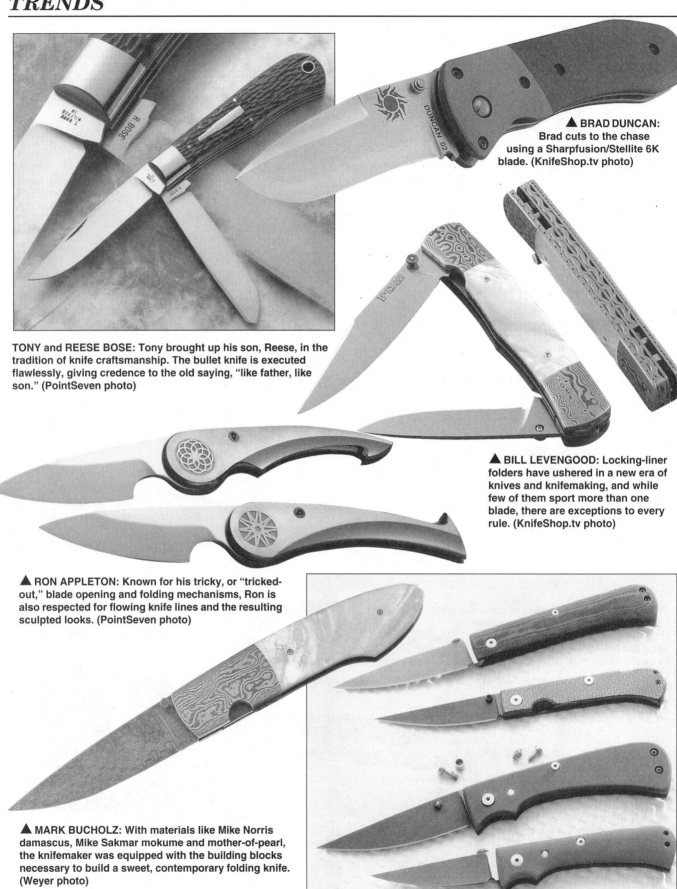

TONY and REESE BOSE: Tony brought up his son, Reese, in the tradition of knife craftsmanship. The bullet knife is executed flawlessly, giving credence to the old saying, "like father, like son." (PointSeven photo)

▲ BRAD DUNCAN: Brad cuts to the chase using a Sharpfusion/Stellite 6K blade. (KnifeShop.tv photo)

▲ BILL LEVENGOOD: Locking-liner folders have ushered in a new era of knives and knifemaking, and while few of them sport more than one blade, there are exceptions to every rule. (KnifeShop.tv photo)

▲ RON APPLETON: Known for his tricky, or "tricked-out," blade opening and folding mechanisms, Ron is also respected for flowing knife lines and the resulting sculpted looks. (PointSeven photo)

▲ MARK BUCHOLZ: With materials like Mike Norris damascus, Mike Sakmar mokume and mother-of-pearl, the knifemaker was equipped with the building blocks necessary to build a sweet, contemporary folding knife. (Weyer photo)

PAUL FOX: Paul's third-generation tactical folders are the latest of progressively better, lighter, faster knives that are easy to carry and access. (PointSeven photo)

▶TOM ANDERSON: High-tech cutting gadgetry can be so cool. (PointSeven photo)

▶JOE KIOUS: Sandwiching gold-lip pearl between damascus bolsters is a veteran move, alright. The blade is damascus by Gary House, another wily veteran. (PointSeven photo)

▲ CARLTON EVANS: This cow-bone-handle folder kicks some derriere. (KnifeShop.tv photo)

LOYD MCCONNELL: A lightweight locking-liner folder dons a stag grip for old time's sake. (PointSeven photo)

▲ JIM MAGEE: Early-day wharncliffe folders never came with damascus blades and titanium bolsters. (Ward photo)

RICK NOWLAND: Retro and rocket-solid are two modern versions of multi- and single-blade folders with dyed-bone handles. (Weyer photo)

▼STEVE SKIFF: Representative of new wave folding knives is a one-hand folder with filed blade and titanium bolsters. (PointSeven photo)

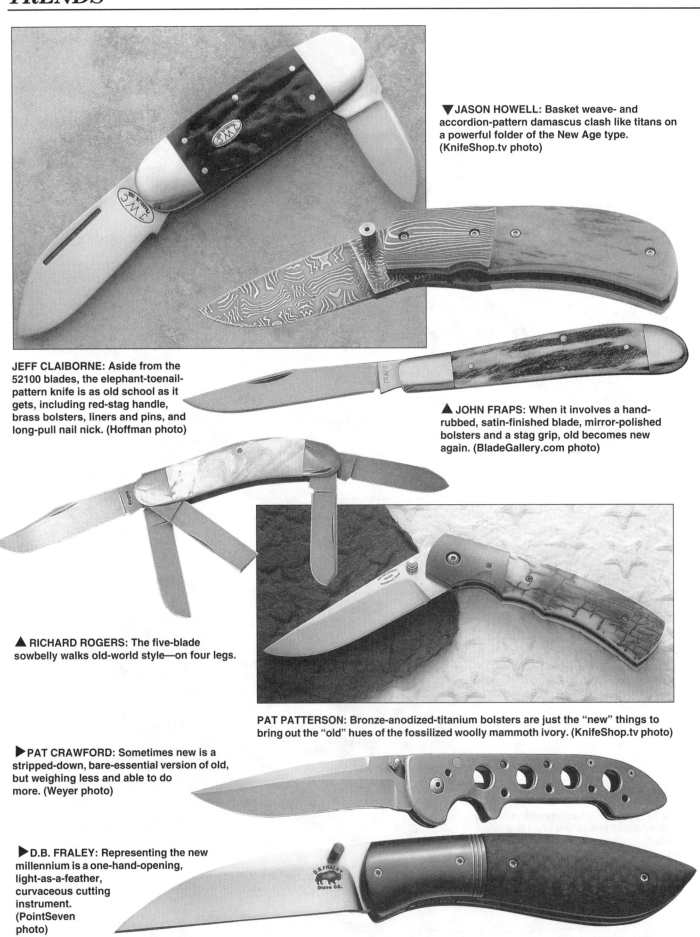

▼ JASON HOWELL: Basket weave- and accordion-pattern damascus clash like titans on a powerful folder of the New Age type. (KnifeShop.tv photo)

JEFF CLAIBORNE: Aside from the 52100 blades, the elephant-toenail-pattern knife is as old school as it gets, including red-stag handle, brass bolsters, liners and pins, and long-pull nail nick. (Hoffman photo)

▲ JOHN FRAPS: When it involves a hand-rubbed, satin-finished blade, mirror-polished bolsters and a stag grip, old becomes new again. (BladeGallery.com photo)

▲ RICHARD ROGERS: The five-blade sowbelly walks old-world style—on four legs.

PAT PATTERSON: Bronze-anodized-titanium bolsters are just the "new" things to bring out the "old" hues of the fossilized woolly mammoth ivory. (KnifeShop.tv photo)

► PAT CRAWFORD: Sometimes new is a stripped-down, bare-essential version of old, but weighing less and able to do more. (Weyer photo)

► D.B. FRALEY: Representing the new millennium is a one-hand-opening, light-as-a-feather, curvaceous cutting instrument. (PointSeven photo)

Biting Blades

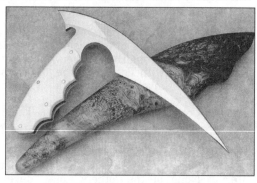

LIONG MAH DESIGNS: The designer terms them "Ancient Soul Knives," but knife-savvy folks might recognize them as Karambit-style knives, both fixed and folding, and fashioned by, from top, knifemakers Mike Snody, Brad Duncan, Jeff Hall and Rob Simonich. (PointSeven photo)

STAN MCKIERNAN: He was just sitting there seething when he decided to go scything. Who would have thought to build a California buckeye burl sheath for the resulting scythe? (Hoffman photo)

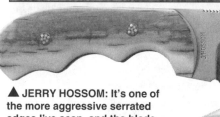

REESE WEILAND: This "Prince of Dragons" actually has teeth with which to bite. Devin Thomas gets credit for the damascus steel, but not in the form it ended up in, and Bob Eggerling forged the bolster damascus. (PointSeven photo)

JERRY HOSSOM: It's one of the more aggressive serrated edges I've seen, and the blade comes to a pretty prickly point. (Hoffman photo)

TODD BEGG: The S30V "Scar Maker" integral knife with damascus grip is ready to tear into a juicy hamburger, hopefully. (BladeGallery.com photo)

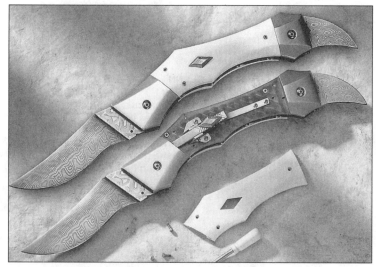

CHARLES KAIN: Ammut was an Egyptian demoness residing in the Halls of Maat. Maat would judge the newly deceased and, should their hearts be too heavy, Ammut would devour their souls. Ammut, the knife, carries a blued-damascus blade with a unique pattern representing Egyptian drapery design.

PHILIP BOOTH: The handles are removable, but the blades of the scale-release automatic are more like permanent teeth. (Weyer photo)

Tantalizing Timascus

I**T IS FUN**, heartening and rewarding when people have a vision and they see it through to fruition. Such is the case with Timascus. The three players involved with its invention are knifemakers Tom Ferry, Bill Cottrell and Chuck Bybee. They deserve all the credit. But it must be said that other knifemakers across the globe envisioned a non-magnetic, lightweight damascus-like material. None of the "others," of course, combined two or more titanium alloys, laminating and patterning them to resemble damascus.

The damascus-looking Timascus is often heated or laminated, and because each type of titanium alloy colors differently, a rainbow of hues is achieved. As Chuck Bybee says, "The boundaries seem limitless." Though the material's current use is reserved for knife "furniture," such as handle scales, guards, bolsters and butt caps, the trio of knifemakers is in the process of developing blade material based on Timascus and other variations of alloys used in Timascus. Knowing these three, it's

only a matter of time before knife blades will resemble rainbow-colored candy canes.

Some people would say that coming up with new knife materials and patterns is like reinventing the wheel, but no wheels I've seen have ever resembled Timascus, and within the knife framework are endless possibilities. I haven't seen a Timascus bowie, sword, push dagger or kukri, but only time will tell!

Joe Kertzman

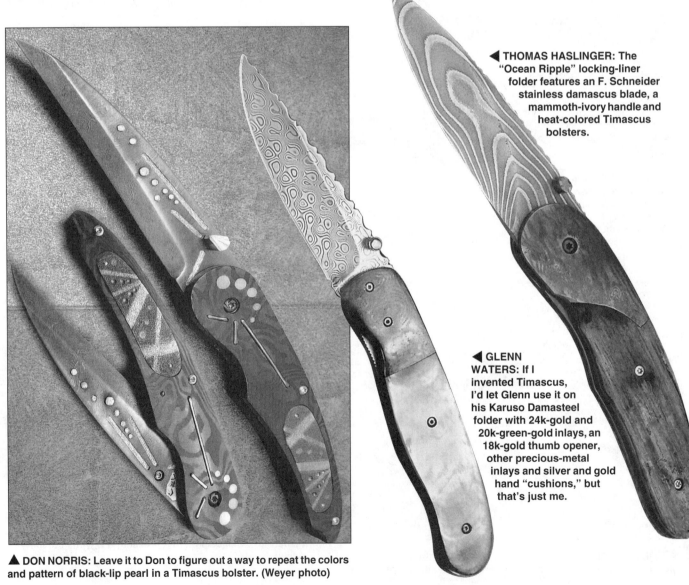

◀ **THOMAS HASLINGER: The "Ocean Ripple" locking-liner folder features an F. Schneider stainless damascus blade, a mammoth-ivory handle and heat-colored Timascus bolsters.**

◀ **GLENN WATERS: If I invented Timascus, I'd let Glenn use it on his Karuso Damasteel folder with 24k-gold and 20k-green-gold inlays, an 18k-gold thumb opener, other precious-metal inlays and silver and gold hand "cushions," but that's just me.**

▲ **DON NORRIS: Leave it to Don to figure out a way to repeat the colors and pattern of black-lip pearl in a Timascus bolster. (Weyer photo)**

▲ JOHN FRAPS: A blue-eyed woolly mammoth handle gets an eyeful from a Timascus bolster and a Mike Norris raindrop-pattern damascus blade. (BladeGallery.com photo)

▲ TOM MAYO, PHIL BOGUSZEWSKI and ROGER DOLE: The many faces of Timascus are illustrated by four folders that incorporate the breakthrough material into their makeup. (BladeGallery.com photo)

▶TED MOORE: Hot-blued Robert Eggerling damascus meets Timascus and likes what it sees. (PointSeven photo)

▶TOM FERRY: To test its mettle, Timascus is butted up against spider-web-pattern damascus, and it fairs quite well, actually. The Timascus handle scales are carved and textured. (BladeGallery.com photo)

◀ JOHN FRAPS: The blue-and-bronze, heat-colored Timascus bolster starkly contrasts a white pearl handle and an ATS-34 blade. (BladeGallery.com photo)

▶TOM FERRY: The Timascus presentation dirk is a presentation in and of itself. (BladeGallery.com photo)

A Burly Bunch of Knives

THE SOIL IS so moist it holds the same characteristics as quicksand. When you step in it, you tend to sink into its lush embodiment. It is so fertile, sprouts peak through its surface. The cells multiply and grow. Photosynthesis takes over in a natural realm. Green is a sign of growth.

▼**ROBERT BEATY:** Insight into why the knifemaker chose California buckeye burl, and the reasoning behind sculpturing the brass and mirror polishing the steel, is gained upon first glance.

An outer shell, the bark, forms and sinewy tissues take root. Upward and outward, fueled by sun, oxygen and water. Cool, fresh water begins life. More pulp, strands, gnarly tissue, knots, fiber, grain and offshoots emerge, come together and form a union. A tree is set free.

Miraculous enough in and of itself, but the woody being has cousins, friends, neighbors and natural enemies. They create a tapestry and canopy. There are bunches of the things, communities, forests full of all that's grand and gargantuan. Existing and coexisting are reds, browns, yellows, beiges, whites and blacks. Together they form wooded territories, lands and colonies.

Along comes a lumberjack. In step the homemaker, the builder, surveyor, planner, conservationist, developer, forester and clearer. Eventually the wood is for sale, on free market, available, quantified, cut and controlled. Knifemakers, among others, need it, or think they do.

They want the wood, value its figure, grain structure, aesthetics, beauty and even its blemishes,

ROBERT DODD: The finest cuts of black ash, ironwood and amboyna were reserved for a trio of splintering fixed blades. (PointSeven photo)

▲ **BOB LAY:** Sheep horn and afzelia wood were lying side-by-side in the prairie, when along came Bob the knife builder. (BladeGallery.com photo)

marks, knots and gnarls. They sand it, polish it, treat it and stabilize it. They bring out its internal pattern and prettiness.

They wrap hands around it and call it good. They see it for what it's worth and relish its properties and natural quality. They want to hold it. They preserve what began as a sprout and save the growth that has become wood, for wood is sacred. Its properties are protected, not by laws, but by natural progression and the law of Mother Nature. Its skin is dry, hard, rough and smooth. It exhibits and holds a couple of the same characteristics as quicksand. When you feel it and experience its raw beauty, you tend to be taken in by it, to sink into its lush embodiment and become lost.

Joe Kertzman

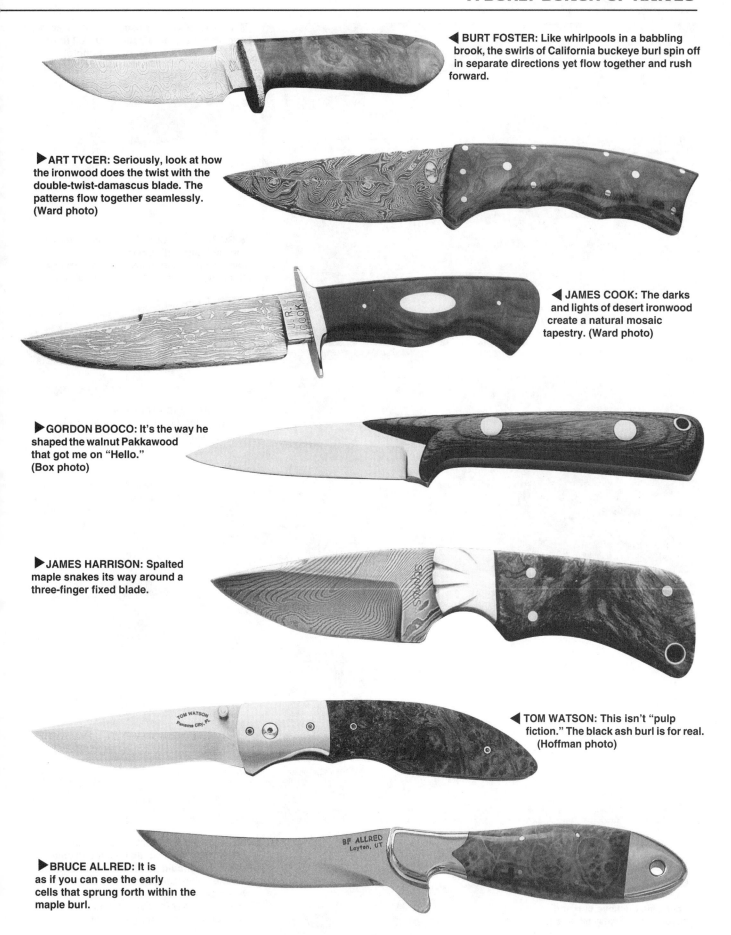

◀ BURT FOSTER: Like whirlpools in a babbling brook, the swirls of California buckeye burl spin off in separate directions yet flow together and rush forward.

▶ ART TYCER: Seriously, look at how the ironwood does the twist with the double-twist-damascus blade. The patterns flow together seamlessly. (Ward photo)

◀ JAMES COOK: The darks and lights of desert ironwood create a natural mosaic tapestry. (Ward photo)

▶ GORDON BOOCO: It's the way he shaped the walnut Pakkawood that got me on "Hello." (Box photo)

▶ JAMES HARRISON: Spalted maple snakes its way around a three-finger fixed blade.

◀ TOM WATSON: This isn't "pulp fiction." The black ash burl is for real. (Hoffman photo)

▶ BRUCE ALLRED: It is as if you can see the early cells that sprung forth within the maple burl.

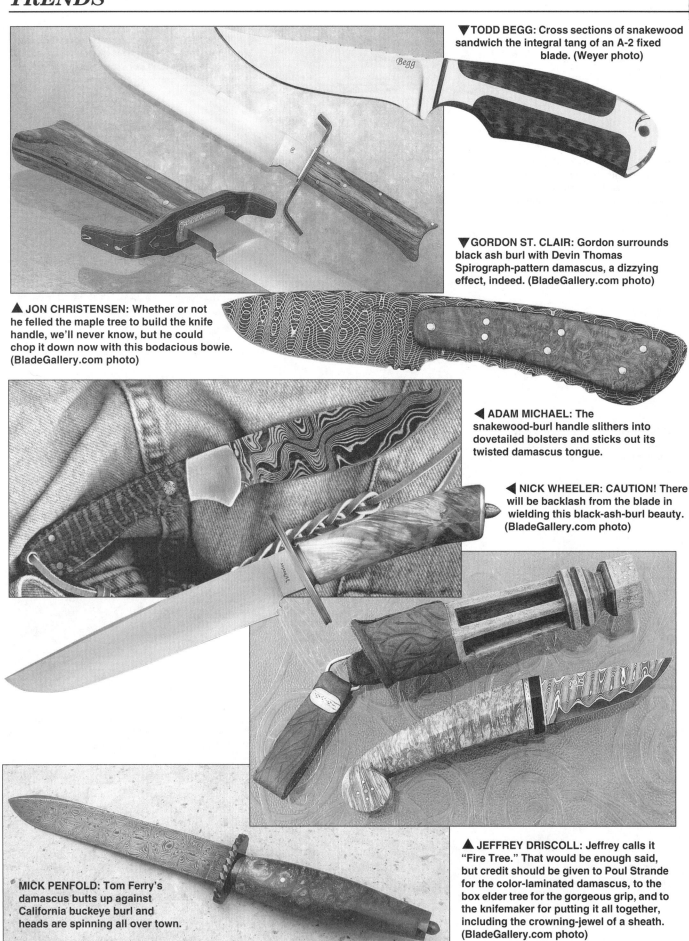

▼TODD BEGG: Cross sections of snakewood sandwich the integral tang of an A-2 fixed blade. (Weyer photo)

▲ JON CHRISTENSEN: Whether or not he felled the maple tree to build the knife handle, we'll never know, but he could chop it down now with this bodacious bowie. (BladeGallery.com photo)

▼GORDON ST. CLAIR: Gordon surrounds black ash burl with Devin Thomas Spirograph-pattern damascus, a dizzying effect, indeed. (BladeGallery.com photo)

◄ ADAM MICHAEL: The snakewood-burl handle slithers into dovetailed bolsters and sticks out its twisted damascus tongue.

◄ NICK WHEELER: CAUTION! There will be backlash from the blade in wielding this black-ash-burl beauty. (BladeGallery.com photo)

▲ JEFFREY DRISCOLL: Jeffrey calls it "Fire Tree." That would be enough said, but credit should be given to Poul Strande for the color-laminated damascus, to the box elder tree for the gorgeous grip, and to the knifemaker for putting it all together, including the crowning-jewel of a sheath. (BladeGallery.com photo)

MICK PENFOLD: Tom Ferry's damascus butts up against California buckeye burl and heads are spinning all over town.

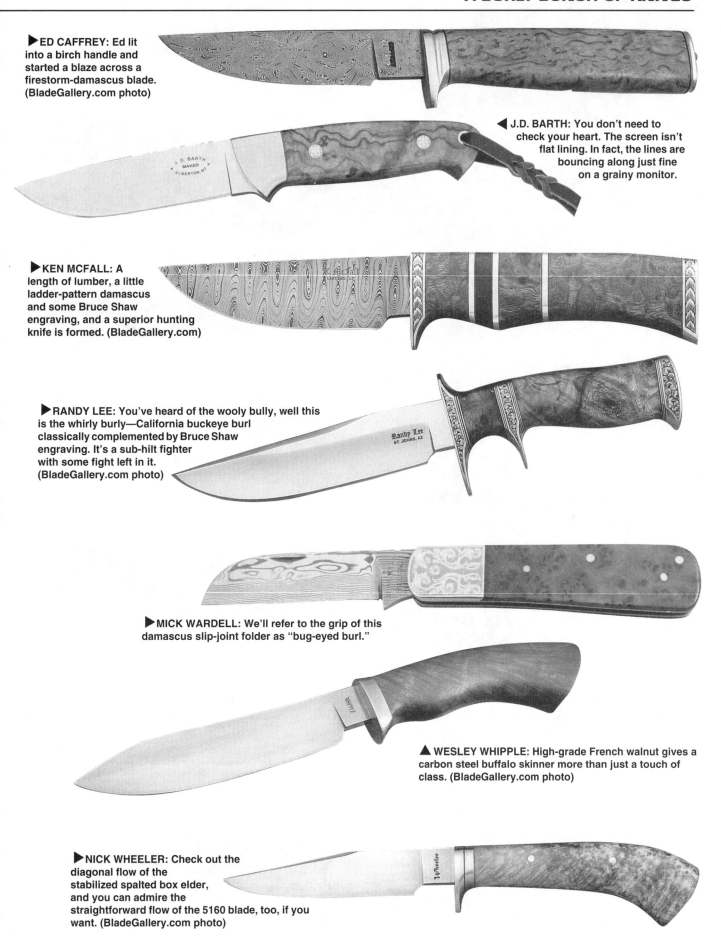

▶ED CAFFREY: Ed lit into a birch handle and started a blaze across a firestorm-damascus blade. (BladeGallery.com photo)

◀J.D. BARTH: You don't need to check your heart. The screen isn't flat lining. In fact, the lines are bouncing along just fine on a grainy monitor.

▶KEN MCFALL: A length of lumber, a little ladder-pattern damascus and some Bruce Shaw engraving, and a superior hunting knife is formed. (BladeGallery.com)

▶RANDY LEE: You've heard of the wooly bully, well this is the whirly burly—California buckeye burl classically complemented by Bruce Shaw engraving. It's a sub-hilt fighter with some fight left in it. (BladeGallery.com photo)

▶MICK WARDELL: We'll refer to the grip of this damascus slip-joint folder as "bug-eyed burl."

▲ WESLEY WHIPPLE: High-grade French walnut gives a carbon steel buffalo skinner more than just a touch of class. (BladeGallery.com photo)

▶NICK WHEELER: Check out the diagonal flow of the stabilized spalted box elder, and you can admire the straightforward flow of the 5160 blade, too, if you want. (BladeGallery.com photo)

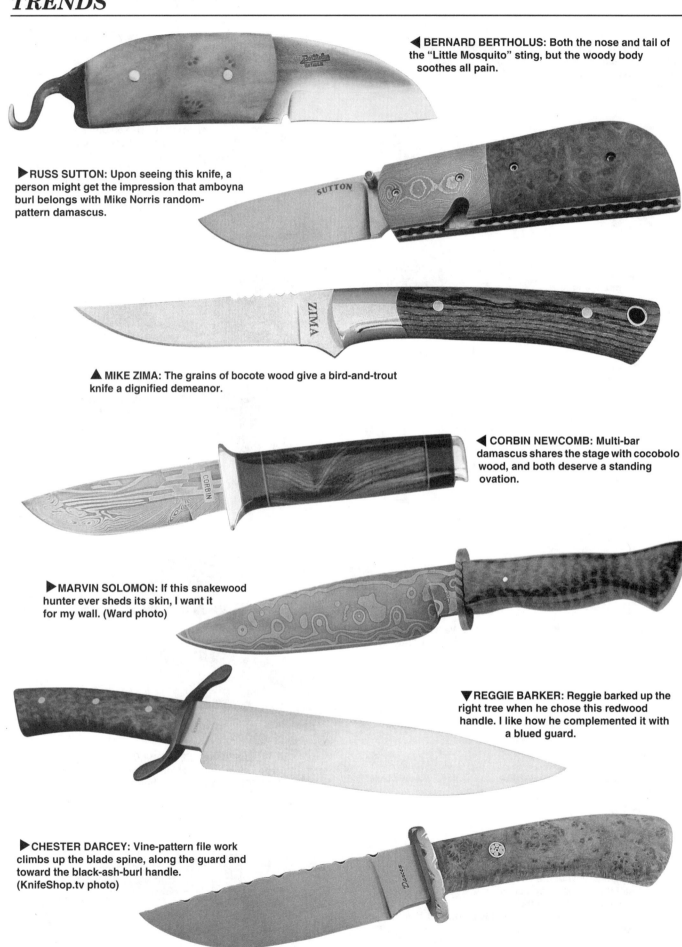

◀ **BERNARD BERTHOLUS:** Both the nose and tail of the "Little Mosquito" sting, but the woody body soothes all pain.

▶ **RUSS SUTTON:** Upon seeing this knife, a person might get the impression that amboyna burl belongs with Mike Norris random-pattern damascus.

▲ **MIKE ZIMA:** The grains of bocote wood give a bird-and-trout knife a dignified demeanor.

◀ **CORBIN NEWCOMB:** Multi-bar damascus shares the stage with cocobolo wood, and both deserve a standing ovation.

▶ **MARVIN SOLOMON:** If this snakewood hunter ever sheds its skin, I want it for my wall. (Ward photo)

▼ **REGGIE BARKER:** Reggie barked up the right tree when he chose this redwood handle. I like how he complemented it with a blued guard.

▶ **CHESTER DARCEY:** Vine-pattern file work climbs up the blade spine, along the guard and toward the black-ash-burl handle. (KnifeShop.tv photo)

▶ **DANIEL CANNADY:** The blemishes, the knots of the California buckeye burl, are what give it character. (Hoffman photo)

◀ **HARVEY KING:** He calls the knife "Whitetail," perhaps for the way the brown burl handle of the hunting knife moves through the woods with a white, steely tail behind it. (Hoffman photo)

▶ **BILL BEHNKE:** It's called "curly maple burl" for good reason. (Weyer photo)

▲ **JERRY DURAN:** Logic called for a bird's-eye maple grip in fashioning a bird and trout knife. (Goffe photo)

▶ **JAMES SHAVER II:** Any more raindrop damascus, and the cocobolo will sprout new growth.

◀ **GUY HIELSCHER:** A stabilized gold-and-red maple handle is married with a brass guard and nickel-and-steel damascus for complete bladed bliss. (Hoffman photo)

▶ **BRETT LAPLANTE:** Take this one into the woods and yell "Timber!"

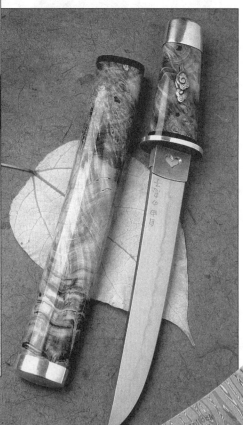

▲ **TOM BOYES:** One might think that snakewood, mokume and mosaic pins would be too much, but the maker pulls the combination off successfully.

◀ **SCOTT SLOBODIAN:** He calls it the "Whirlwind," and it whips right through you. (Slobodian photo)

▲ **PAT PATTERSON:** A "llano" is an open grassy plain in Spanish America and the southwestern United States, the latter being where the maker lives. Perhaps the California buckeye wood handles of the Llano and Llano Sidekick remind him of such a place near his home. (KnifeShop.tv)

▲ **WALLY POLLOCK:** An amboyna burl handle and ladder-pattern-damascus blade might have been too much, but an Asian Ram bolster ties it all together. (KnifeShop.tv photo)

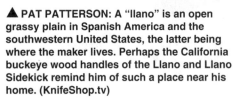

DAVE KAUFFMAN: There are tracks on the blades and plenty of movement along both handles. (PointSeven photo)

▼ **JOHN A. JONES:** The copper collar is the only thing holding this one down.

▲ **PAOLO SCORDIA:** It looks like a snake in the grass, doesn't it?

How the West Was Won

SURE THERE WAS fighting, but that is not how the West was won. Of course famine, suffering, death and disease reared their ugly heads. Just as likely, a few fortunes were won. Camps were set up. Boundaries were drawn. Settlements rose up from the dirt. In other words, milestones were created. People raised families on virgin soil where only deer and buffalo had roamed. It is impossible to pinpoint one single event, one group of people, one contributing factor that shaped the West. Yes, cowboys fought Indians. Wagon trains took slow, bumpy, treacherous roads west. People rode horseback for

thousands of miles. None of it, alone, won the West.

Now, brute strength, determination, belief in a better way of life, motherly and fatherly instincts, bravery, heroism, the will to succeed, the drive to survive, prayer, courage and a little insanity. That's how the West was won. Man couldn't do it alone. He needed other people and he needed tools. Blacksmiths were godsends. Man's oldest tool—the knife—was employed as often as hammers and nails, needles and thread, saws and wood, horses and carts. Edged steel and heavy hammers helped build many a village.

The way the West was won has not been forgotten. It is ingrained into our souls. Close your eyes and picture an Old West town. Imagine Indians doing a war dance around a fire. Follow the wagon trains West. Smell the sweat-soaked buckskin. Hear the babbling brook. Taste the jerky. Use the knife. Feel it in your hand. Set the edge to a buffalo hide. Can you feel the blade bite? That's how the West was won—one move at a time, a time when there was nothing artificial to spoil the wild and untamed, absolutely nothing that could get in the way of man's will.

Joe Kertzman

▼MIKE MANN: The Natchez Bowie is hand-forged from 5160 steel, born from brute strength and symbolic of how the greatest nation in the world came to be. (BladeGallery.com photo)

▼RODRIGO SFREDDO: This is how Rodrigo makes a friction folder, handled in India Sambar stag with a damascus blade and fittings. No friction there, Rodrigo, just a lot of smooth action.

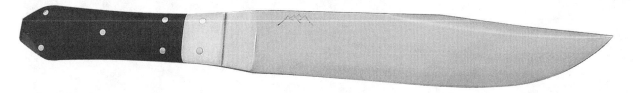

▶GIB GUIGNARD: The rifleman's knife is as rustic and romantic as a frontier couple sharing a tin cup of well water. (BladeGallery.com photo)

▲ DAVID ANDERS: "Evenin' Marshall, can I help you or are you just passin' through?"

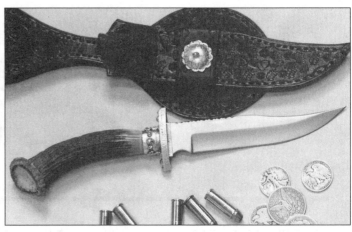

▲ MICHAEL WATTELET: The Cowboy bowie rides high on the hip and is there at the sound of a tripped trigger.

▲ GLENN MARSHALL: The one-of-a-kind mountain man hunter has a deer antler handle and a long clip-point blade, just like a one-of-a-kind mountain man hunter should.

◀ ROBERT ROSSDEUTSCHER: Primitive-style folders are often outfitted with forged back springs, brass tacks, stag handles and high-carbon steel blades, like this one, for instance.

▼ RON HEMBROOK: It has to be more difficult to flint steel than stone. The turquoise, stag and wood are nice touches.

▲ DANIEL WINKLER: Native American styling is evident in the primitive knife of maple, rawhide and file steel. (PointSeven photo)

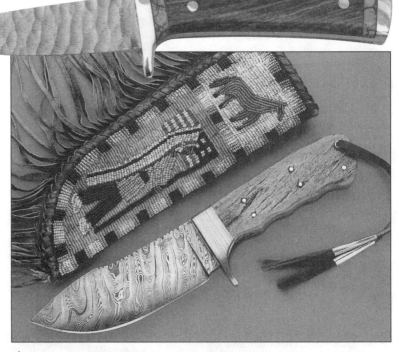

▲ MARK NEVLING: Here's a buffalo skinner in mammoth bone and 320-layer accordion-twist damascus. I can hear the accordions and foot stomping now, and see the hoop skirts twirling under the moonlight. The beaded sheath is breathtaking and proof of an artist at work, namely a Lakota Sioux who made it approximately 40 years ago. It doesn't get any more "West" than that! (Ward photo)

BUSTER WARENSKI: This one sings of California gold rush days and tells tales of the earth, the ores and the treasures that they held. (PointSeven photo)

▲ **JIM SORNBERGER:** Ah, there was gold in the West, and stone and steel and men who knew how to combine elements to fight the elements. It's a Michael Price style dagger with engraved gold and a stone called "gold quartz." (BladeGallery.com photo)

▼ **TOM FERRY:** The 1084 carbon steel is forge welded to shape and given a hand rubbed finish, complemented by a sculpted and stabilized pink myrtle grip and left unsheathed for the time being. (BladeGallery.com photo)

▲ **JAY HENDRICKSON:** A Southwest Clip Point includes a curly maple handle and fine silver inlay, a combination like only a western artisan could dream up under a setting sun . . . on the Great Plains. (BladeGallery.com photo)

◄ **RICHARD MIZE:** A file, some antler, copper rivets and a little ingenuity goes a long way. Westward ho!

► **MIKE WILLIAMS:** Named "Cimarron," the bowie is built with 288 layers of river-pattern damascus, a fossil-walrus-tusk handle and a damascus guard, ferrule and butt cap. It's the stuff of legends. (BladeGallery.com photo)

◄ **CHUCK PATRICK:** It's cable steel, stag and leather, and tough as a Texas longhorn.

Tusk Masters

BIG, HAIRY, ELEPHANT-LIKE creatures called "mammoths," or "woolly mammoths" (further north), lived and roamed tens-of-thousands of years ago in North America, Europe and Asia. Modern knifemakers, some of them also big and hairy, use the remaining, excavated long-upward-curving tusks from the extinct creatures to their own advantage, employing pieces of ancient ivory as knife handles.

Mastodon is an extinct mammal of the genus Mammut, a creature resembling the elephant but larger,

and differing from it and the mammoth mainly in the structure of its teeth. Mastodon ivory is also a current, popular knife handle choice, as is ancient elephant ivory and fossilized walrus ivory. So much for resting in peace—these big, hairy beasts rest in pieces.

As you can imagine, after witnessing your own teeth yellow and decay with age, becoming more brittle, grainy, cracked and even split, ancient ivory of any kind is highly figured, patterned and colorful. Much of it looks like tree bark,

thus the name "bark-mammoth-ivory," and other samples are blue, green, yellow, brown, beige, black, orange, or combinations of those colors and more. Decomposition can be a good thing. Or, maybe the life spans of the giants were so long, their tusks looked that way naturally. Regardless, ancient ivory makes for some mammoth knife handles, gorgeous in their own right, even when you do consider their beastly beginnings.

Joe Kertzman

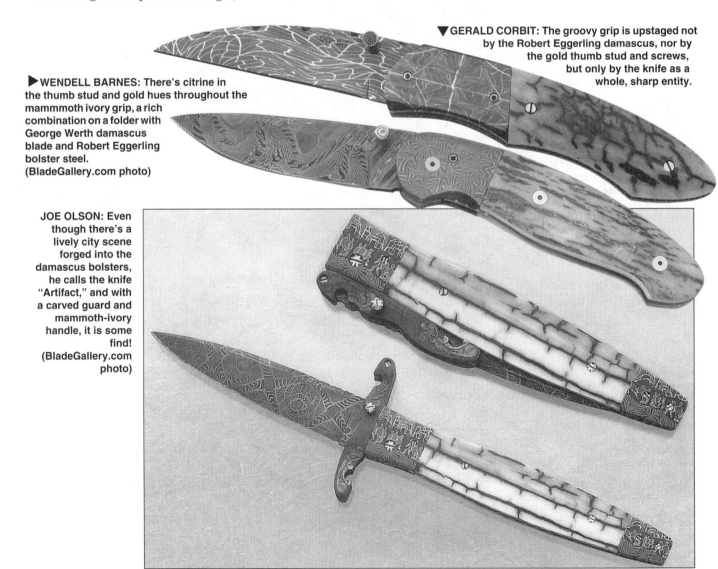

▶ **WENDELL BARNES:** There's citrine in the thumb stud and gold hues throughout the mammmoth ivory grip, a rich combination on a folder with George Werth damascus blade and Robert Eggerling bolster steel. (BladeGallery.com photo)

▼ **GERALD CORBIT:** The groovy grip is upstaged not by the Robert Eggerling damascus, nor by the gold thumb stud and screws, but only by the knife as a whole, sharp entity.

JOE OLSON: Even though there's a lively city scene forged into the damascus bolsters, he calls the knife "Artifact," and with a carved guard and mammoth-ivory handle, it is some find! (BladeGallery.com photo)

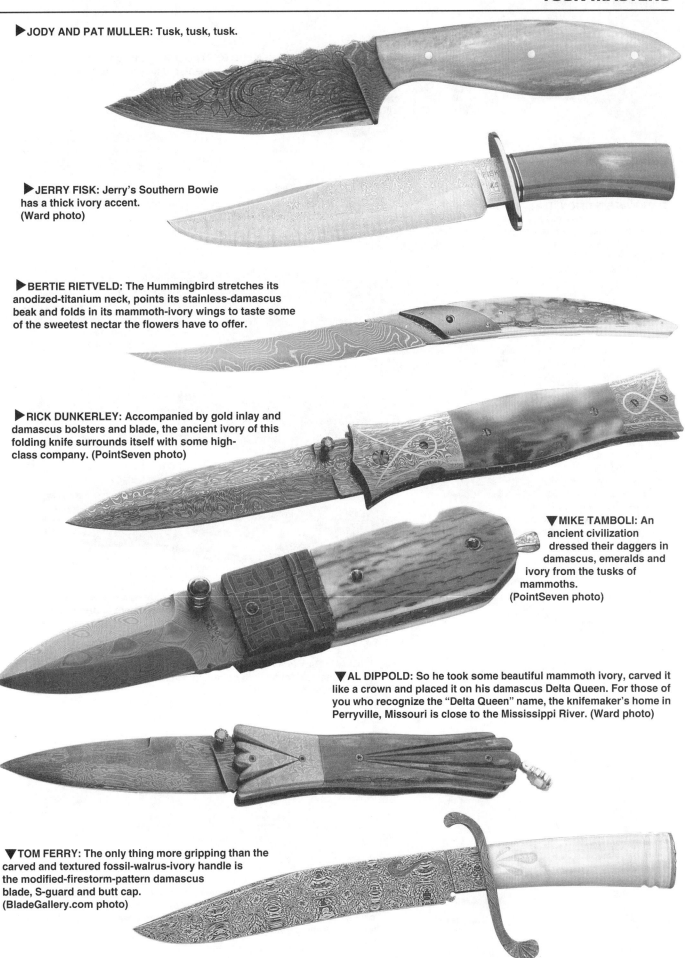

▶JODY AND PAT MULLER: Tusk, tusk, tusk.

▶JERRY FISK: Jerry's Southern Bowie has a thick ivory accent. (Ward photo)

▶BERTIE RIETVELD: The Hummingbird stretches its anodized-titanium neck, points its stainless-damascus beak and folds in its mammoth-ivory wings to taste some of the sweetest nectar the flowers have to offer.

▶RICK DUNKERLEY: Accompanied by gold inlay and damascus bolsters and blade, the ancient ivory of this folding knife surrounds itself with some high-class company. (PointSeven photo)

▼MIKE TAMBOLI: An ancient civilization dressed their daggers in damascus, emeralds and ivory from the tusks of mammoths. (PointSeven photo)

▼AL DIPPOLD: So he took some beautiful mammoth ivory, carved it like a crown and placed it on his damascus Delta Queen. For those of you who recognize the "Delta Queen" name, the knifemaker's home in Perryville, Missouri is close to the Mississippi River. (Ward photo)

▼TOM FERRY: The only thing more gripping than the carved and textured fossil-walrus-ivory handle is the modified-firestorm-pattern damascus blade, S-guard and butt cap. (BladeGallery.com photo)

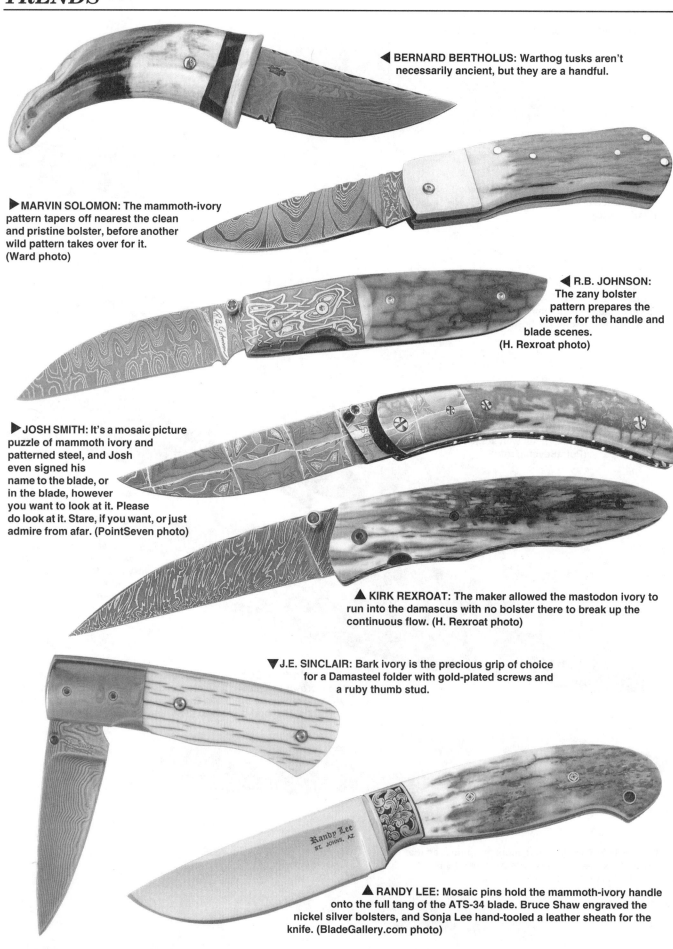

◄ BERNARD BERTHOLUS: Warthog tusks aren't necessarily ancient, but they are a handful.

► MARVIN SOLOMON: The mammoth-ivory pattern tapers off nearest the clean and pristine bolster, before another wild pattern takes over for it. (Ward photo)

◄ R.B. JOHNSON: The zany bolster pattern prepares the viewer for the handle and blade scenes. (H. Rexroat photo)

► JOSH SMITH: It's a mosaic picture puzzle of mammoth ivory and patterned steel, and Josh even signed his name to the blade, or in the blade, however you want to look at it. Please do look at it. Stare, if you want, or just admire from afar. (PointSeven photo)

▲ KIRK REXROAT: The maker allowed the mastodon ivory to run into the damascus with no bolster there to break up the continuous flow. (H. Rexroat photo)

▼ J.E. SINCLAIR: Bark ivory is the precious grip of choice for a Damasteel folder with gold-plated screws and a ruby thumb stud.

▲ RANDY LEE: Mosaic pins hold the mammoth-ivory handle onto the full tang of the ATS-34 blade. Bruce Shaw engraved the nickel silver bolsters, and Sonja Lee hand-tooled a leather sheath for the knife. (BladeGallery.com photo)

▶STEVE HILL: The stunning mammoth-ivory handle sent shock waves through the Steve Schwarzer mosaic-damascus bolsters and a ripple effect across the Robert Eggerling Turkish damascus blade.

▶CHRIS BOWLES: The mammoth-ivory and damascus hunter could down a saber-toothed tiger in no time flat. (Ward photo)

▶HARVEY DEAN: Now, every time Harvey sees a walrus in a zoo, he thinks, "Wow, those tusks would make some spectacular knife handles." He complements this particular tusk the walrus was done using with a mosaic-damascus blade and a stainless steel guard. (KnifeShop.tv photo)

▶ZAZA REVISHVILI: What stimulates the senses more, the fragmented lines of the mammoth ivory, the whirling waves of the damascus, or the concentric rings and balls of the bolster? (PointSeven photo)

▶J.D. BARTH: The veins of the mammoth-ivory handle are like a roadmap leading back to a time before the woolly beast was extinct.

▶MIKE IRIE: Perhaps the mammoth that gave up part of its tusk for the good of the knife handle once did a little dance right there where you are standing or sitting. (Weyer photo)

▶PAT PATTERSON: Here's a case where its bite is worse than its bark. (KnifeShop.tv photo)

▶ED CHAVAR: Out of respect, Ed left the warthog tusk intact. (Weyer photo)

▼WADE COLTER: The milky-white ancient walrus ivory with chocolate-brown swirls speaks to the ice cream sundae lover in all of us. Wade forged and etched the damascus blade, and sculpted the damascus bolsters, giving the knife its just desserts. (BladeGallery.com photo)

◀JERRY MCCLURE: The mastodon ivory is the bark and the root from which the leaf, or scroll, engraving sprouts, flowering into rose-pattern damascus. (Weyer photo)

▶RUSS SUTTON: A mammoth roams to the edge of the mosaic forest and looks out over the trails of damascus that stretch out before him. Devin Thomas forged the damascus trail.

▼J.W. RANDALL: The knifemaker honors the ancient ivory's origins with a pachyderm-like handle inlay and mammoth shapes marching across the powder-damascus blade. (PointSeven photo)

▶GEORGE TICHBOURNE: Mammoth ivory scales mix well with a Damasteel bolster and a Stellite 6K blade.

▶JASON HOWELL: A "tusk brush" might have prevented the cavities in the mammoth ivory, but then we wouldn't benefit from such a comely knife handle. (KnifeShop.tv photo)

▶JARRELL LAMBERT: Here's an ivory hunter that doesn't hunt ivory. (Ward photo)

▶RICK FRIGAULT:
To bring out its finest features, the Siberian bark mastodon ivory just needed a little shaping, some polishing and a final pinning to a full-tang, fishbone-pattern Damasteel blade.

◀ART TYCER: The slight cracks and subtle pattern of ancient walrus ivory give character to an already interesting twist-damascus fixed blade. (Ward photo)

▶DON MAXWELL: With blue meteorite bolsters, Don brought out the blue hues of the fossil mastodon ivory. The 3 5/8-inch blade is Robert Eggerling damascus.

▶DON HANSON III:
You've heard of pink elephants and purple dinosaurs? Well, the handle of Don's double-bolster slip joint is orange walrus ivory.

▶PETE FORTHOFER:
For a totally behemoth knife theme, Forthofer provides a sharkskin sheath with his mammoth-ivory-handle fixed blade.

JOHN FITCH: Tusk Master John enlisted mastodon ivory to complete a 15-inch bowie with a ladder-pattern-damascus blade. (Ward photo)

Super-Sized Steel

THE BIGGER THE canvas, the more room for mistakes. We've all seen the silly commercials and television or movie comedies where the artist, whether a billboard artist, a mural painter or the guy stenciling the team name in the end zone of a football field, makes a mistake just as he or she is nearing completion of the daunting task, effectively ruining hours of tedious work. It happens to knife and sword makers, too. Ask such a craftsman how many pounds of steel he's scrapped.

If the craftsmen of the super-sized steel on this and the following page made any mistakes, you'd be hard pressed to find them. Give them credit for even attempting to take such long lengths of steel and turn them into clean, smooth, stylish weapons.

You could take any one of these pieces home to your girlfriend or wife and, unlike that eight-point buck you brought home last hunting sea-son, you'd get little-to-no resistance when asking her if you could hang it on the living room wall. There isn't anything about these pieces that screams "bachelor pad furnishings." These are classically designed, well-finished, stylishly eclectic, tastefully completed and handcrafted conversation pieces. You could invite guests over for dinner, cocktails and a tour of your "sword and dagger room" to see if there's anything they'd like to pick out and take home with them as a party favor. Well, maybe they could borrow it for a couple months. It's not a bad idea, is it? We could expand the markets for super-sized swords, daggers and sword canes. For now, let's take aim at the pieces at hand and begin by creating demand for such highly fashioned, fierce fighting weapons. We'll worry about the parties and receptions at a later date.

Joe Kertzman

▲ DANIEL WATSON: The founder of the Angel Sword Corp., Daniel is fast becoming known for such heavenly bodies as this 40-inch sword with bone handle and tightly-patterned Techno-Wootz blade. (PointSeven photo)

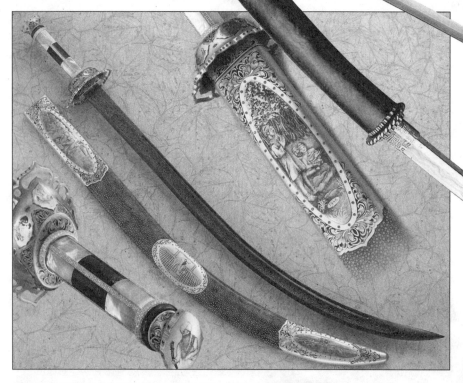

JOT SINGH KHALSA: When Jot called it "one rather unique sword," it was the understatement of the year. Among the features too numerous to mention are a Devin Thomas stainless-damascus blade in a most fanciful, upturning pattern, 20 carats of diamonds in 18k gold, a lapis-lazuli and mother-of-pearl handle, rubies, Julie and Buster Warenski engraving, and decorating depicting scenes from the life of a man Jot considers the "Pope" of the Sikh religion in the West. (Coop photo)

▲ RAY ENNIS: A walnut and damascus Japanese wakizashi is a wall hanger, for sure, but it would also prove attractive to samurai swordsmen for more practical purposes. (Weyer photo)

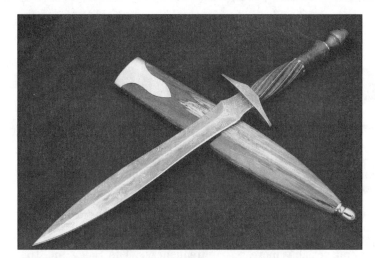

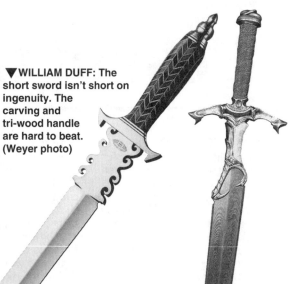

▼WILLIAM DUFF: The short sword isn't short on ingenuity. The carving and tri-wood handle are hard to beat. (Weyer photo)

STAN MCKIERNAN: Should we start with the handle, blade or sheath? Let's just admire and leave the descriptions to the imagination.

►VIRGIL ENGLAND: The one-and-a-half-hand sword incorporates all-damascus components forged to shape, some bronze, a little leather, a smidge of stingray skin, a pinch of stellar sea cow bone and a lot of imagination, talent and foresight.

DAVID GOLDBERG: Put your hand in the handprint of the man who built one of the coolest sword canes cutting. (PointSeven photo)

BRYAN COURTOIS: Crossing swords has never been so much fun. There should be a yellow, diamond-shaped sign that reads "Sword Crossing." Seriously, they're well-crafted 440C stainless swords with great guards and handles, and sufficient sweat and tears.

DAVID GOLDBERG: We've seen similar Japanese pieces, but how often have we contemplated how long it takes to forge such a clean 30-1/2-inch blade, carve the guard, wrap the handle and fashion the saya (sheath)? (PointSeven photo)

Best of the Bowies

THEY KEEP COMING back to the watering hole. They return for more. No matter how diversified they get, no matter how many patterns they make, and regardless of how fancy, fantastic or futuristic their designs, knifemakers always revert back to building bowies. Just about every knifemaker in the world—and going by the directory section of this book, there are thousands—makes, or has made, at least one bowie knife. How can al-

▶ **CAMERON HOUSE: It is hand rubbed, satin finished and oh-so-sexy. (BladeGallery.com photo)**

individually minded knifemakers agree on one pattern, one design, a single type of knife?

Maybe the entire knifemaking community got together and decided that, as an initiation into their cutting club, they'd each build at least one bowie knife and possibly more. Perhaps they did it just for fun to see if anyone would notice.

More likely, the truth runs deeper. There is a style of knife, a big, biting, burly, beast of a knife that holds power, strength and resolve. It speaks to the inner souls

of those who believe in American heritage, freedom and liberty. The handle is the size of a man's hand. The guard flares out across thumb and forefinger, and the deep blade extends outward and up, toward demons, gods, enemies, evil and righteousness. The edge of the long, clipped blade catches a ray of sunlight, gleams, glistens and shoots it back into the eye of anyone who dares approach it.

The bowie blade is to modern America and the world at large what the sword has

always been to emperors, knights, kings, warriors, renegades, lords and crusaders. It speaks of Col. James Bowie, a fearless freedom fighter who brawled hand-to-hand, fist-to-fist, blade-to-gunpoint with the upper and lower crust, commoners and landlords, leaders and followers, generals and foot soldiers. It is he who the bowie is named after, and the grit is still there, deep in the blade with the blood, bone and guts. It's that gruesome and gallant makeup that defines the bowie knife. Everything else is just window dressing.

Thirst for the bowie knife is increasing, not subsiding. It has not been quenched. They keep coming back to the watering hole for one more drink of everything bowie.

Joe Kertzman

JERRY FISK: He Jerry-rigged a stunning Searles-style bowie with 284-layer, ladder-pattern damascus, an antiqued-elephant-ivory grip and a clamshell guard. (KnifeShop.tv photo)

▶ **JEROME ANDERS: Here's a Full Dress Bowie that's fully dressed in ancient ivory, nickel silver and a dueling S-guard. (KnifeShop.tv photo)**

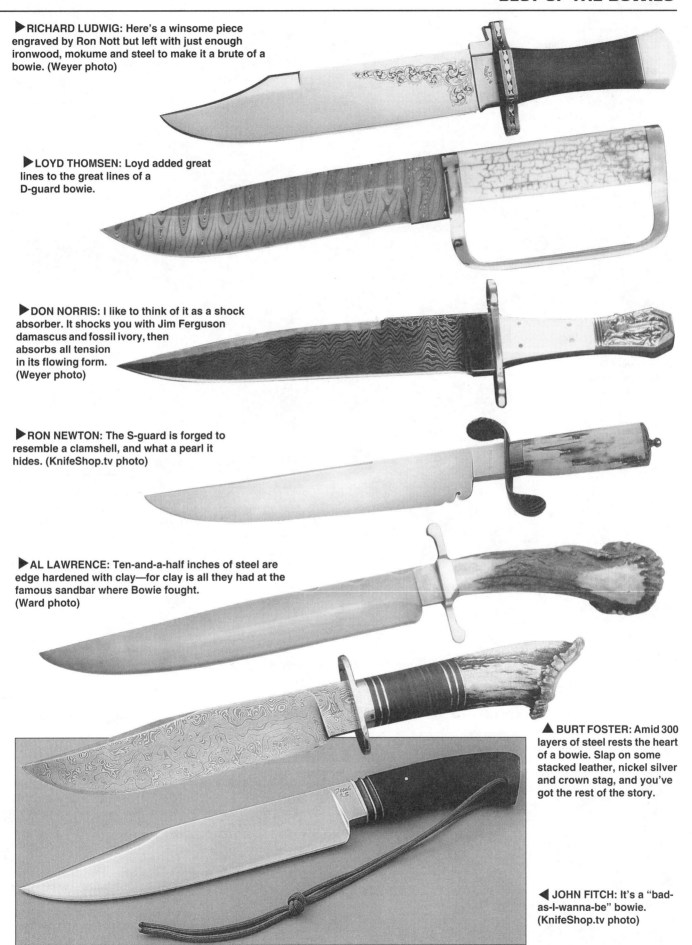

▶ **RICHARD LUDWIG:** Here's a winsome piece engraved by Ron Nott but left with just enough ironwood, mokume and steel to make it a brute of a bowie. (Weyer photo)

▶ **LOYD THOMSEN:** Loyd added great lines to the great lines of a D-guard bowie.

▶ **DON NORRIS:** I like to think of it as a shock absorber. It shocks you with Jim Ferguson damascus and fossil ivory, then absorbs all tension in its flowing form. (Weyer photo)

▶ **RON NEWTON:** The S-guard is forged to resemble a clamshell, and what a pearl it hides. (KnifeShop.tv photo)

▶ **AL LAWRENCE:** Ten-and-a-half inches of steel are edge hardened with clay—for clay is all they had at the famous sandbar where Bowie fought. (Ward photo)

▲ **BURT FOSTER:** Amid 300 layers of steel rests the heart of a bowie. Slap on some stacked leather, nickel silver and crown stag, and you've got the rest of the story.

◀ **JOHN FITCH:** It's a "bad-as-I-wanna-be" bowie. (KnifeShop.tv photo)

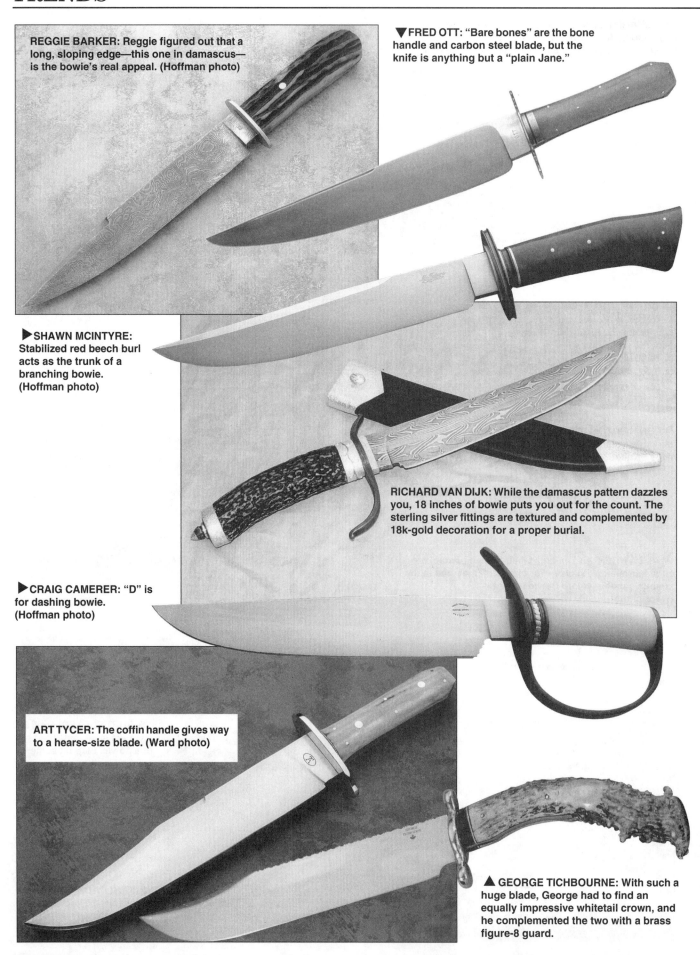

REGGIE BARKER: Reggie figured out that a long, sloping edge—this one in damascus—is the bowie's real appeal. (Hoffman photo)

▼FRED OTT: "Bare bones" are the bone handle and carbon steel blade, but the knife is anything but a "plain Jane."

▶SHAWN MCINTYRE: Stabilized red beech burl acts as the trunk of a branching bowie. (Hoffman photo)

RICHARD VAN DIJK: While the damascus pattern dazzles you, 18 inches of bowie puts you out for the count. The sterling silver fittings are textured and complemented by 18k-gold decoration for a proper burial.

▶CRAIG CAMERER: "D" is for dashing bowie. (Hoffman photo)

ART TYCER: The coffin handle gives way to a hearse-size blade. (Ward photo)

▲ GEORGE TICHBOURNE: With such a huge blade, George had to find an equally impressive whitetail crown, and he complemented the two with a brass figure-8 guard.

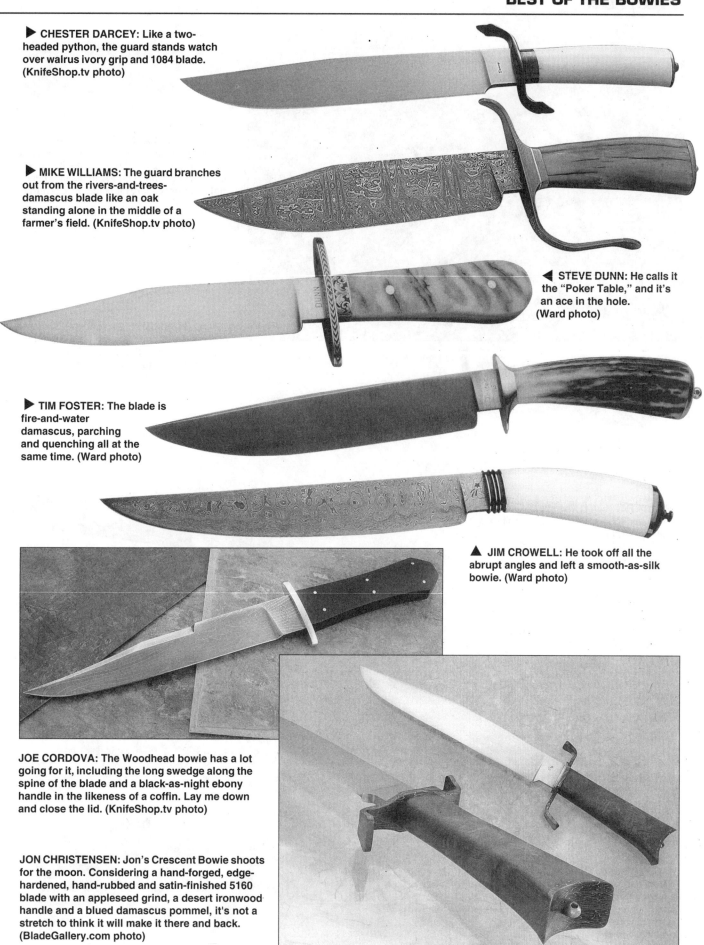

▶ **CHESTER DARCEY:** Like a two-headed python, the guard stands watch over walrus ivory grip and 1084 blade. (KnifeShop.tv photo)

▶ **MIKE WILLIAMS:** The guard branches out from the rivers-and-trees-damascus blade like an oak standing alone in the middle of a farmer's field. (KnifeShop.tv photo)

◀ **STEVE DUNN:** He calls it the "Poker Table," and it's an ace in the hole. (Ward photo)

▶ **TIM FOSTER:** The blade is fire-and-water damascus, parching and quenching all at the same time. (Ward photo)

▲ **JIM CROWELL:** He took off all the abrupt angles and left a smooth-as-silk bowie. (Ward photo)

JOE CORDOVA: The Woodhead bowie has a lot going for it, including the long swedge along the spine of the blade and a black-as-night ebony handle in the likeness of a coffin. Lay me down and close the lid. (KnifeShop.tv photo)

JON CHRISTENSEN: Jon's Crescent Bowie shoots for the moon. Considering a hand-forged, edge-hardened, hand-rubbed and satin-finished 5160 blade with an appleseed grind, a desert ironwood handle and a blued damascus pommel, it's not a stretch to think it will make it there and back. (BladeGallery.com photo)

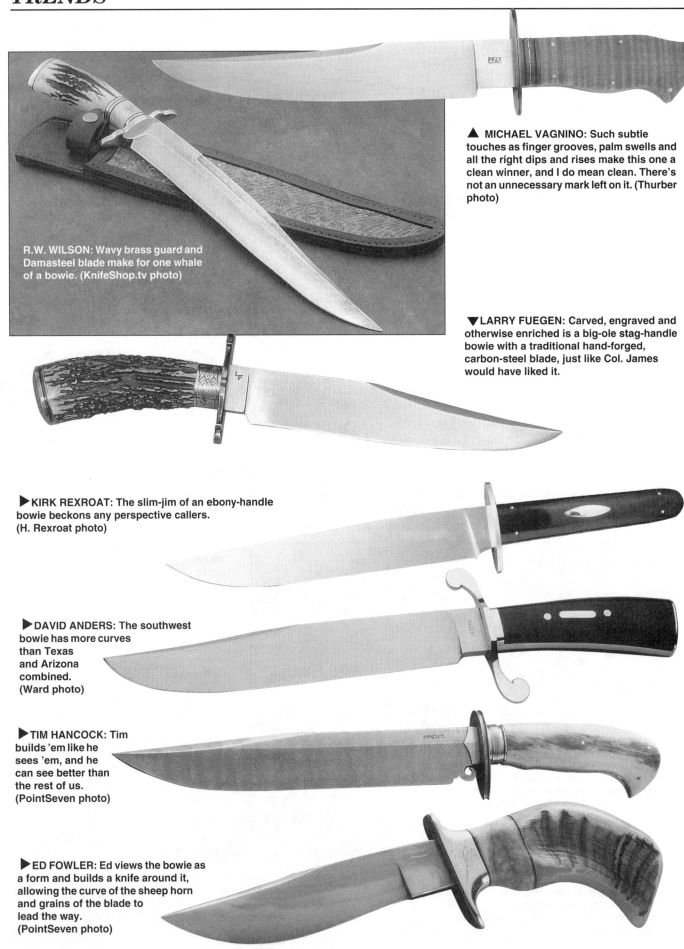

R.W. WILSON: Wavy brass guard and Damasteel blade make for one whale of a bowie. (KnifeShop.tv photo)

▲ MICHAEL VAGNINO: Such subtle touches as finger grooves, palm swells and all the right dips and rises make this one a clean winner, and I do mean clean. There's not an unnecessary mark left on it. (Thurber photo)

▼LARRY FUEGEN: Carved, engraved and otherwise enriched is a big-ole stag-handle bowie with a traditional hand-forged, carbon-steel blade, just like Col. James would have liked it.

►KIRK REXROAT: The slim-jim of an ebony-handle bowie beckons any perspective callers. (H. Rexroat photo)

►DAVID ANDERS: The southwest bowie has more curves than Texas and Arizona combined. (Ward photo)

►TIM HANCOCK: Tim builds 'em like he sees 'em, and he can see better than the rest of us. (PointSeven photo)

►ED FOWLER: Ed views the bowie as a form and builds a knife around it, allowing the curve of the sheep horn and grains of the blade to lead the way. (PointSeven photo)

▼ JAMES COOK: The oval guard and oval handle shield put into focus the overall shape of steely blade and ironwood grip. (KnifeShop.tv photo)

JIM WALKER: Trace a line from the nickel-silver pommel, along the stag grip and the spine of the damascus blade, and you have a perfect curve that rises up ever-so-slightly at the tip. (KnifeShop.tv photo)

▶J.W. RANDALL: The fossil walrus tooth of the handle doesn't look like it could bite nearly as hard as the long, damascus blade. (KnifeShop.tv photo)

▲ WALKER, WILLIAMS, RANDALL, PETE, RUTH and FITCH: And if it took a half-dozen more knifemakers to build a bowie this beautiful, it would be well worth it. (Ward photo)

▲ BRETT GATLIN: The Gatlin bowie is dressed in stag. (Ward photo)

▶SHINICHI KATO: Stag is really nature's grip and the D-Guard is nature's way of telling you that the blade might bite.

▲ MICK PENFOLD: The groovy file work applied to the guard and the Jim Ferguson damascus blade are far more pronounced than the natural texture of the water-buffalo-horn handle.

Heads and Hafts Above the Rest

▼**LONNIE HANSEN:** When hefted by its African black-wood haft, the head is raised to eye level and the damascus is studied as much for the pattern as its carved form. (BladeGallery.com photo)

▼**J.W. RANDALL:** It is what it is—a hand forged spike hawk with maple handle and a proud demeanor.

◀**KEVIN HARVEY:** Most people saw Mel Gibson in "The Patriot," but Kevin saw the tomahawk he carried, went home and built himself a replica. All he had was a hammerhead, so he hand forged and hand filed the "hawk" from that. The shaft is ash and the scrolls are burned into the wood. (Louw photo)

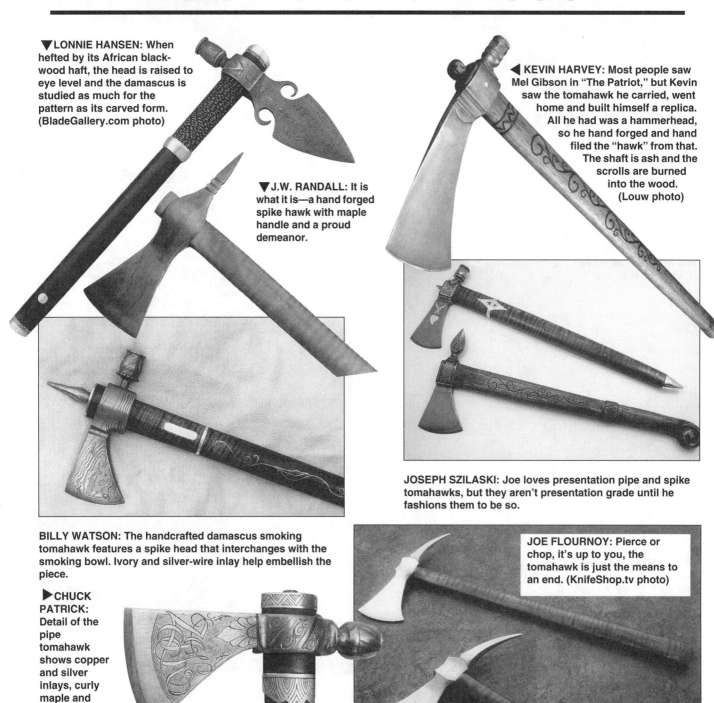

JOSEPH SZILASKI: Joe loves presentation pipe and spike tomahawks, but they aren't presentation grade until he fashions them to be so.

BILLY WATSON: The handcrafted damascus smoking tomahawk features a spike head that interchanges with the smoking bowl. Ivory and silver-wire inlay help embellish the piece.

▶**CHUCK PATRICK:** Detail of the pipe tomahawk shows copper and silver inlays, curly maple and engraving by Tom Patterson.

JOE FLOURNOY: Pierce or chop, it's up to you, the tomahawk is just the means to an end. (KnifeShop.tv photo)

Re-mastered Knives?

THEY LOOK, FEEL and cut like the originals. Some even smell, taste and, when flicked or rapped with fingernails, sound like earlier models. It's not a digital surround sound like a remastered Elvis Presley recording on compact disc, nor is it a fresh-from-the factory smell, or a slices-like-a-razorblade cut. The taste isn't clean. The feel isn't new. These are re-mastered knives. They are handcrafted in ways similar to those of the masters.

Who are the masters, and how did they become "masters of their trade?" Well, first, knifemaking is a trade. It's a learned trade. In many cultures, the crafts of forging blades, grinding blade steel, blade polishing and outfitting knives with proper handles are passed down from generation to generation, from master to apprentice. These are perfected arts that can only be accomplished with human

hands. An owner of a knife company recently admitted that one of the main reasons his gentleman's folding knives are so popular, and fetching high dollar, is that the blades are hand finished and polished to a beautiful sheen, something, he said, that can not be accomplished by a machine.

The masters of the past, whether from England, Japan, Germany, the United States, Finland, Sweden or elsewhere, became the best at what they did. Somehow, word of their skills spread. Their work was appreciated, studied, demanded and, now, emulated.

For some, it was the style of their knives that struck chords and played with people's desires to buy them. Others excelled at forging the finest blade steel, grinding and putting edges on blades, heat treating, engraving, inlaying precious jewels, carving, etch-

ing, or making a knife balance and feel good in the hand. Some exhibited perfect fit and finish. For others, it was a combination of all or some of the above that made them masters of their craft.

Today, the masters are honored with replicas of their work. Some of the masters might take offense to such forgery, but the vast majority of them are probably dancing with joy, wherever they may be. They realize that to copy is the greatest form of flattery. Though there is a modern knifemaker re-mastering each one of their knives, there can only be one, true, original master for every style of knife. The masters rest easy knowing that their work was worth repeating. They smile at the compliments, voice their approval and nod knowingly, like only masters can.

Joe Kertzman

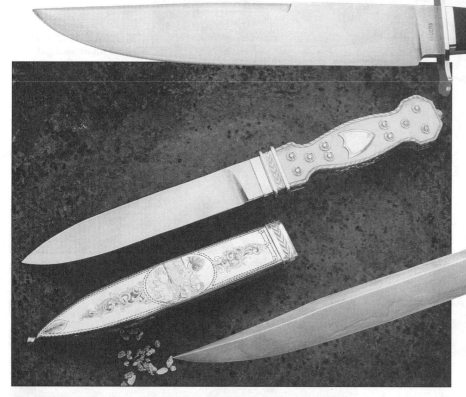

▲ DAVID ANDERS: Like stars in the night sky, handmade pins highlight the black-wood handle of a Sheffield-style bowie. (Ward photo)

▲ HARVEY DEAN: Reaching out to grab you is a sharp replica of an antique bowie, bold in its subtle but stunning clip-point blade, gold guard and throat, and ivory handle. The dog-bone-style handle with gold studs is as heavenly as the original knifemaker. (KnifeShop.tv photo)

JIM SORNBERGER: In early-day San Francisco, any '49er worth his weight in gold wore a dress bowie with an ivory handle literally wrapped in gold, a gold guard, gold rivet studs and a golden shield.

◀ **LUCIANO OLIVEIRA DORNELES:** The Brazilian knifemaker reproduced a Bill Moran ST-24 by looking at a picture of the knife, and the remake weighs the same as the original. (Beaucant photo)

▼ **DOUG NOREN:** If knifemakers didn't emulate the masters of the craft who came before them, they wouldn't often get the chance to silver plate a bronze guard, or combine ivory with briarwood for a handle. This one's in the style of Joseph Rodgers & Sons.

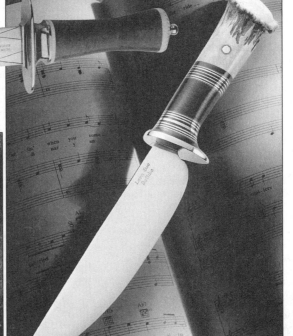

▲ **RON NEWTON:** Early knifemakers didn't have the tools of the trade known now, and engraving was not nearly as advanced. But it sure was cool, and the handle checkering and carving wasn't too bad, either. This one is like Samuel Bell made them, maybe, dare say I, better. (PointSeven photo)

◀ **LORA SUE BETHKE:** You'd think we'd get enough of William Scagel style knives. You'd think. (PointSeven photo)

STEVEN RAPP: Steven seems to have an exclusive on wrapped gold quartz handles in the Michael Price dagger style, or maybe he's the only one willing to try it. Julie Warenski engraved the pretty piece. (PointSeven photo)

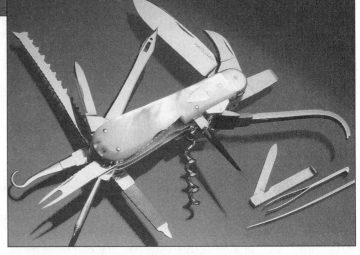

TAKESHI MATSUSAKI: A Joseph Rodgers Sport Knife puts the sport back in knifemaking. This one is an Olympic event.

▼DR. JIM LUCIE: Sometimes it seems as though Jim has been making William Scagel replicas for nearly as long as Scagel made originals, and it shows through in the workmanship. (PointSeven photo)

▼JOSEPH SZILASKI: There were only 12 of the original William Scagel knives of this style known to have been made, so Szilaski makes it an even baker's dozen.

▲ HIDEKI HAYASHIDA: A dagger in the style of Michael Price is engraved grandly by Simon Lytton. Engraving and snake wood are such an energetic combination. (BladeGallery.com photo)

▲ AL DIPPOLD: Al appreciates how Sheffield, England knifemakers fashioned their folders, so he did one up pretty like. (PointSeven photo)

▶DOUG NOREN: Did George Wostenholm really make Sheffield bowies this clean and curvaceous? (Ward photo)

◀ROBERT APPLEBY: Hand forged from a file, the William Scagel style knife features a mirror-polished and convex-ground blade, a brass guard and a brass, Bubinga wood, stacked-leather, black-Micarta® and elk antler handle, all within 12 inches.

▶ED SCHEMPP: The maker's modernized version of a Green River knife is actually a locking-liner folder involving a San Mai damascus blade, a stag handle and a Devin Thomas mokume bolster. (BladeGallery.com photo)

CHARLES WEISS: Black jade bulges the handle out like a sore thumb, but Jerry Rados damascus sooths it, and engraving heals the Michael Price style dagger completely. (PointSeven photo)

▼**ETORE BERTUZZI:** Ron Lake, who's alive and well, will appreciate this tribute to him and his inter-frame folders, this one with an ATS-34 blade, aluminum grip and Galolite handle insert.

▼**RON WELLING:** In his death, William Scagel has more followers than apostles who are living and breathing. (Weyer photo)

▶**EDMUND DAVIDSON:** Forged to perfection is the Loveless Big Bear integral with eye-popping desert ironwood handle. (PointSeven photo)

▲ **RICHARD WRIGHT:** The original design of the ambidextrous bolster-release switchblade dates back to 19th-century Sheffield, England. The forged-to-shape blade is Jerry Rados Turkish damascus, and the front and rear bolsters are made from an Ithaca 10ga damascus shotgun barrel.

▲ **MICK PENFOLD:** If the original Samuel Bell bowie was anything like this, it's no wonder Mick replicated it, his with nickel silver fittings engraved by Jim Whitehead.

BUSTER WARENSKI: The sugalite on the handle seems to bulge out like fluffy pillows from silver cases. Julie Warenski added her soft touch of gorgeous engraving to a Michael Price style dagger. (PointSeven photo)

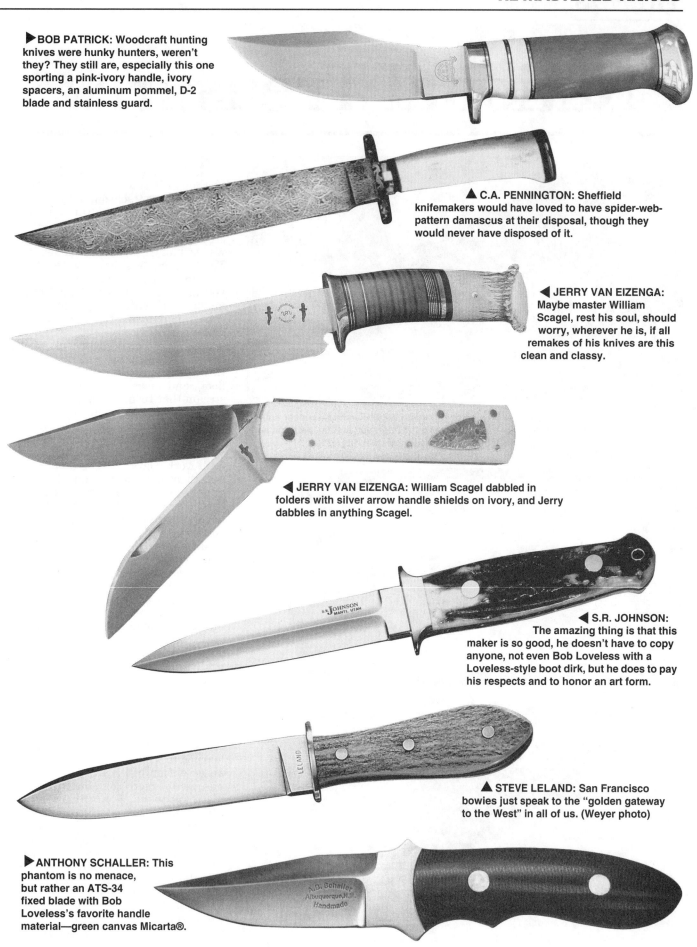

▶BOB PATRICK: Woodcraft hunting knives were hunky hunters, weren't they? They still are, especially this one sporting a pink-ivory handle, ivory spacers, an aluminum pommel, D-2 blade and stainless guard.

▲C.A. PENNINGTON: Sheffield knifemakers would have loved to have spider-web-pattern damascus at their disposal, though they would never have disposed of it.

◀JERRY VAN EIZENGA: Maybe master William Scagel, rest his soul, should worry, wherever he is, if all remakes of his knives are this clean and classy.

◀JERRY VAN EIZENGA: William Scagel dabbled in folders with silver arrow handle shields on ivory, and Jerry dabbles in anything Scagel.

◀S.R. JOHNSON: The amazing thing is that this maker is so good, he doesn't have to copy anyone, not even Bob Loveless with a Loveless-style boot dirk, but he does to pay his respects and to honor an art form.

▲STEVE LELAND: San Francisco bowies just speak to the "golden gateway to the West" in all of us. (Weyer photo)

▶ANTHONY SCHALLER: This phantom is no menace, but rather an ATS-34 fixed blade with Bob Loveless's favorite handle material—green canvas Micarta®.

National Treasures

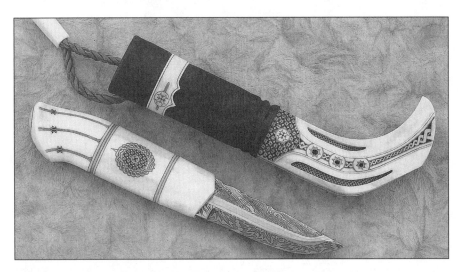

JONNY WALKER NILSSON: The first step involved drying naturally shed reindeer antler one-to-two years for the handle, then its surface was hand engraved in Sami patterns and complemented by a composite-damascus blade forged by Mattias Styrefors. (BladeGallery.com photo)

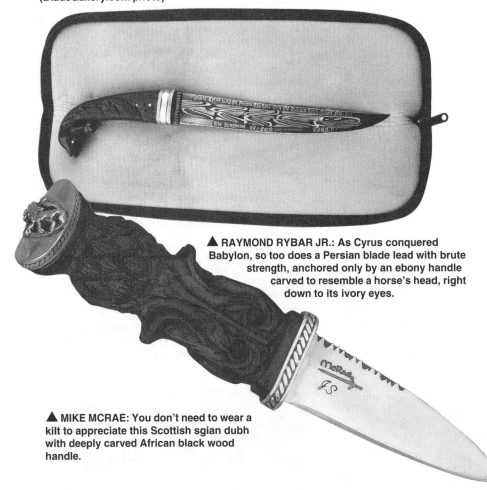

▲ **RAYMOND RYBAR JR.:** As Cyrus conquered Babylon, so too does a Persian blade lead with brute strength, anchored only by an ebony handle carved to resemble a horse's head, right down to its ivory eyes.

▲ **MIKE MCRAE:** You don't need to wear a kilt to appreciate this Scottish sgian dubh with deeply carved African black wood handle.

THE THATCHED ROOF looks as though it leaks like a sieve, but during the wet season, not a droplet of water seeps through it. Inside, a shaggy haired gent crouches down, bare feet giving way to hairy legs and khaki shorts. The handmade shirt is soiled, but the smile is genuine as he shows you his prized possession, a handmade kukri with a length of blade that would make the Toro dealer green with envy.

The 10-foot grinding wheels turn freely, each on a log axis, spinning through open sections of the wooden floor and swishing through the stream that turns them below. Men lay on boards grinding blades. As odd as it sounds, their horizontal positions on hard surfaces might just be the most comfortable for such work. Days are long and hard, but their craft is building blades, and it's an honorable profession.

The browned skin of the Japanese sword smith is wet with perspiration. It's dirty work, but tradition dictates the wearing of white clothing during forging demonstrations. The heavy pounding and hot fire take their toll, but the master has solved the mystery of homogenous grain structure, clay hardening, edge quenching, differential tempering, shaping and otherwise manipulating steel. The pride shows in his work.

Guiding hunters through thickets of grass that slice skin as quickly as the machete he holds is an Afrikaner who knows the terrain as a commuter knows the cross streets by name. He has learned to wield a blade as if it was an extension of his bony arm, and has used it more than once to save his paper-thin skin. Sharpening the lengthy edge is second nature, and hanging it from its designated peg is an afterthought at day's end, when the moon rises and the orange orb of a sun sets over the hazy horizon.

Scenes like these are where true blades are born, their origins as important as their cut.

Joe Kertzman

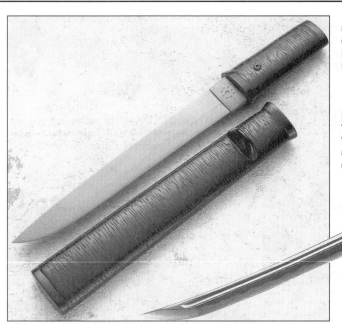

◀ STEVE SCHWARZER: Adopting the Japanese style takes a humble knifemaker who gives up his own pride and bows to the masters before him. Steve immerses himself in the craft, outputting his own masterful bladed creations. (PointSeven photo)

▶ DAVID SCHLUETER: In carving the lace-wood handle and forging the two-foot blade, the maker's mind was thousands of years back and continents away. (Scherzi photo)

▼ RICHARD VAN DIJK: The Mediterranean gent's knife has a flair all its own, and just as pronounced as the carved sterling fittings, damascus blade and black-as-night ebony handle.

▼ TAS KERLEY: It's one sharp curve. Proceed with caution.

▲ DAVID GOLDBERG: The "Gin Hou" (Silver Wasp) stings us with a high-grade iron-and-steel blade, solid-sterling-silver fittings, and a padauk wood handle covered in sting ray skin. (PointSeven photo)

SCOTT SLOBODIAN: The maker must live and breathe the Japanese culture in order to capture its essence as thoroughly as the "Sacred" model does. Skillfully carved copper fittings adorn the leather-wrapped stingray-skin handle. The blade's temper line waves like a Japanese flag in high winds. (Slobodian photo)

▲ STAN MCKIERNAN: If Malaysian gentlemen are fortunate enough to carry knives like this, the country is sounding better all the time. The red-coral and redwood burl handle is a work of art, and the blade sends shivers down the spine (its own and mine).

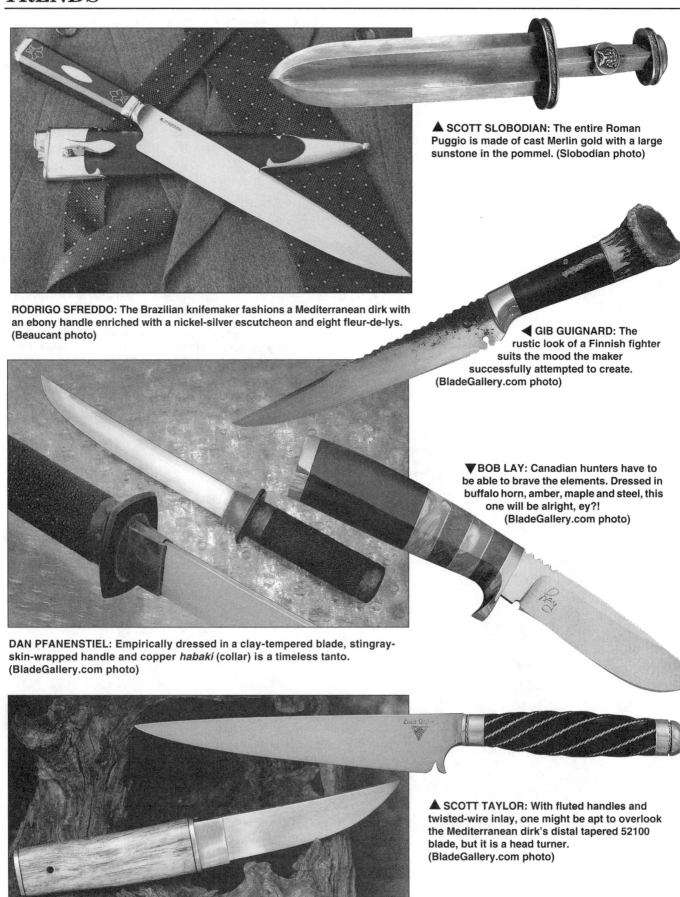

▲ SCOTT SLOBODIAN: The entire Roman Puggio is made of cast Merlin gold with a large sunstone in the pommel. (Slobodian photo)

RODRIGO SFREDDO: The Brazilian knifemaker fashions a Mediterranean dirk with an ebony handle enriched with a nickel-silver escutcheon and eight fleur-de-lys. (Beaucant photo)

◄ GIB GUIGNARD: The rustic look of a Finnish fighter suits the mood the maker successfully attempted to create. (BladeGallery.com photo)

▼ BOB LAY: Canadian hunters have to be able to brave the elements. Dressed in buffalo horn, amber, maple and steel, this one will be alright, ey?! (BladeGallery.com photo)

DAN PFANENSTIEL: Empirically dressed in a clay-tempered blade, stingray-skin-wrapped handle and copper *habaki* (collar) is a timeless tanto. (BladeGallery.com photo)

▲ SCOTT TAYLOR: With fluted handles and twisted-wire inlay, one might be apt to overlook the Mediterranean dirk's distal tapered 52100 blade, but it is a head turner. (BladeGallery.com photo)

AKIHISA KAWASAKI: The tanto looks like a simple design, and looks are as deceiving as the twinkling eyes of opposing forces.

▲ RICHARD LARSON: Warriors find solace not in the violence attributed to them, but in the peace of mind such sharp masterpieces bring to them.

▲ DAVID SCHLUETER: Nothing was left off this wakizashi, not the foot-and-a-half blade with distinct temper line, not the stingray-skin panels, the traditional lacing, handle charms, polished copper or the textured, hammer-finished steel guard. (Scherzi photo)

▶ED SCHEMPP: The blade and bolster of the "Celtic Dichotomy" are radial-braided Celtic Knots & Crosses pattern damascus. That's one way to get a point across. (BladeGallery.com photo)

STAN MCKIERNAN: Muscles bulge as a bent arm retrieves the blade from within its wooden saya (sheath) as quietly as a whisper and with the purpose of a samurai swordsman. (Ward photo)

◀JOSEPH SZILASKI: Forged D-2 steel and a Wenge wood handle are one thing, but finished to silky-smooth surface textures and highly polished until both gleam is another story. Brass collar and stainless guard complete the package.

▶ANDERS HOGSTROM: The blade of the Kwaiken is clay tempered in a traditional Japanese manner, and both bevels of the double-edged steel are honed to hair-splitting sharpness. (BladeGallery.com photo)

▶J.P. HIGGINS and TOM STERLING: "I'll flint knap an obsidian blade, and you build a handle that borrows both Japanese and Celtic design features." (BladeGallery.com photo)

Upswept Edges

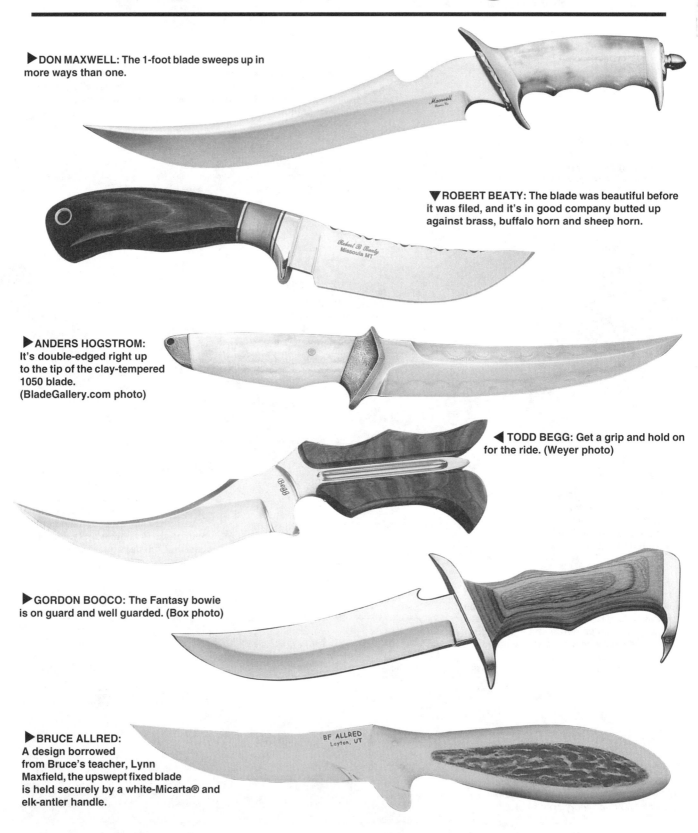

▶**DON MAXWELL:** The 1-foot blade sweeps up in more ways than one.

▼**ROBERT BEATY:** The blade was beautiful before it was filed, and it's in good company butted up against brass, buffalo horn and sheep horn.

▶**ANDERS HOGSTROM:** It's double-edged right up to the tip of the clay-tempered 1050 blade. (BladeGallery.com photo)

◀**TODD BEGG:** Get a grip and hold on for the ride. (Weyer photo)

▶**GORDON BOOCO:** The Fantasy bowie is on guard and well guarded. (Box photo)

▶**BRUCE ALLRED:** A design borrowed from Bruce's teacher, Lynn Maxfield, the upswept fixed blade is held securely by a white-Micarta® and elk-antler handle.

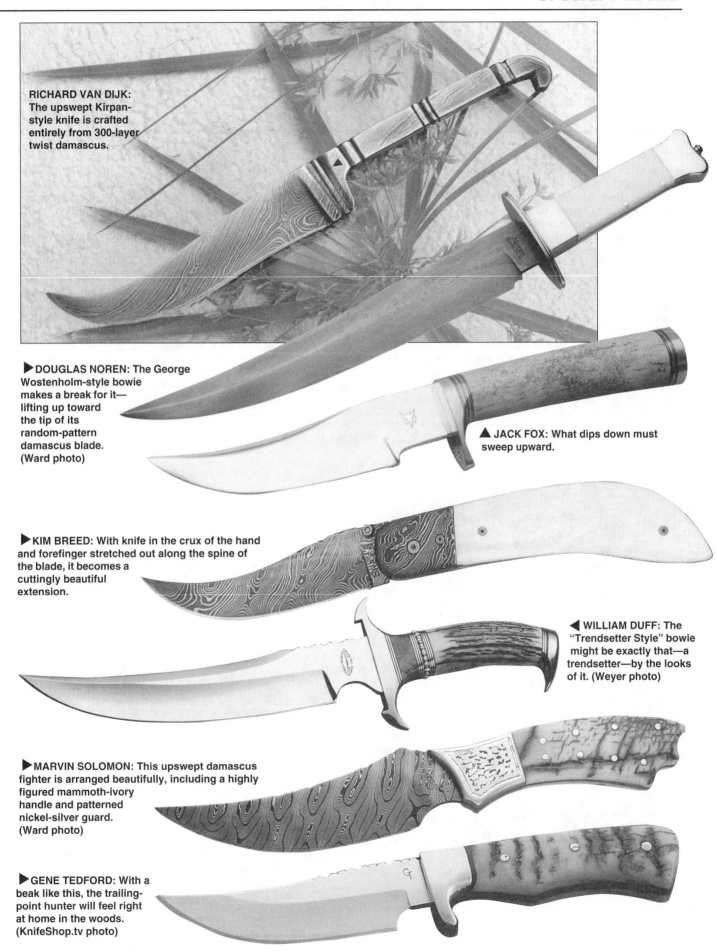

RICHARD VAN DIJK: The upswept Kirpan-style knife is crafted entirely from 300-layer twist damascus.

▶**DOUGLAS NOREN:** The George Wostenholm-style bowie makes a break for it—lifting up toward the tip of its random-pattern damascus blade. (Ward photo)

▲ **JACK FOX:** What dips down must sweep upward.

▶**KIM BREED:** With knife in the crux of the hand and forefinger stretched out along the spine of the blade, it becomes a cuttingly beautiful extension.

◀ **WILLIAM DUFF:** The "Trendsetter Style" bowie might be exactly that—a trendsetter—by the looks of it. (Weyer photo)

▶**MARVIN SOLOMON:** This upswept damascus fighter is arranged beautifully, including a highly figured mammoth-ivory handle and patterned nickel-silver guard. (Ward photo)

▶**GENE TEDFORD:** With a beak like this, the trailing-point hunter will feel right at home in the woods. (KnifeShop.tv photo)

Prize Fighters

THEY KNOW HOW to make them sting, don't they? Ouch. It hurts to look at them. Long, lean and mean are these prizefighting machines. You get choked up thinking about choking up on one of them. The forms are so similar yet individualized. It is as if knifemakers know what a fighting knife is supposed to look like and work until they achieve that familiar form, then they make it their own. Fighting knives are easy to pick out of a group. It's like picking the bully out from a group of otherwise angelic, clean-cut kids, or picking the naughty girl out from a group of proper young ladies, or the cop out from a criminal lineup, or the peace activist out from a crowd of skinheads.

The fighting knife exudes purpose in design. It is a deadly looking piece. It's often ramrod straight, curved like a shark's tooth or bent down like a fang. The grip is meant for both purchase and movement. The point is penetrating. The grinds are as exact, as long and as stunningly purposeful as the blade itself.

And since purpose is such an important factor of fighting knives, it's best to get it out in the open and out of the way. The purpose of the knife is well defined. There's no sense in mincing words or being mealy-mouthed about it. They were originally meant for fighting an enemy, whether human or beast. But we don't fight that way anymore, nor do we wage wars the way we used to wage them, or go out looking for a fight with bow and arrow or blowgun. No, times do change, usually for the better.

A fighting knife is a raw, untamed form, and few-to-none of them are ever used for fighting. They're used in our minds. The hand extends outward, the arm arches up and outward, the wrist snaps, the enemy aliens fall one by one. You crouch, leap, charge and circle. Arms go back up like winged extensions and you strut like a goose. Fighting knives do that—make you king of the world for a day, of your own world, a prize fighter blowing kisses into the crowd. Ah, the glory of it all.

Joe Kertzman

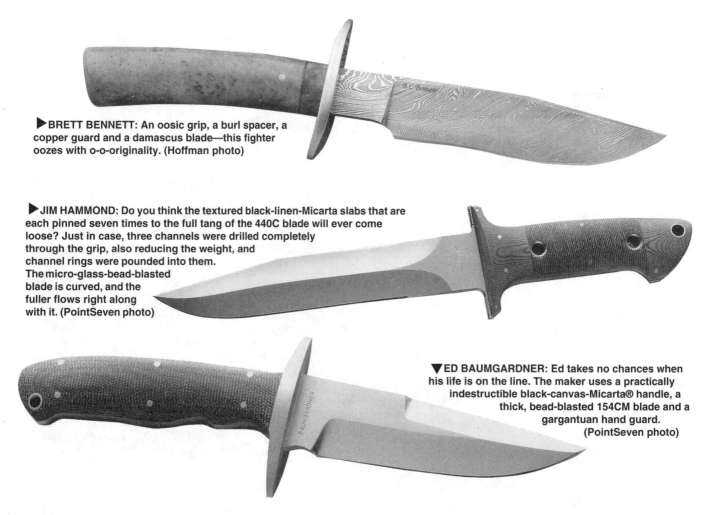

▶**BRETT BENNETT:** An oosic grip, a burl spacer, a copper guard and a damascus blade—this fighter oozes with o-o-originality. (Hoffman photo)

▶**JIM HAMMOND:** Do you think the textured black-linen-Micarta slabs that are each pinned seven times to the full tang of the 440C blade will ever come loose? Just in case, three channels were drilled completely through the grip, also reducing the weight, and channel rings were pounded into them. The micro-glass-bead-blasted blade is curved, and the fuller flows right along with it. (PointSeven photo)

▼**ED BAUMGARDNER:** Ed takes no chances when his life is on the line. The maker uses a practically indestructible black-canvas-Micarta® handle, a thick, bead-blasted 154CM blade and a gargantuan hand guard. (PointSeven photo)

▼MICHAEL MCCLURE: There's a line, a fuller, as it is called, running lengthwise down the center of the blade where the two blade geometries, or grinds, meet. It is also where the maker's own damascus pattern converges. Tell me the design isn't planned and purposeful. (PointSeven photo)

▼EDMUND DAVIDSON: Edmund lets loose a lot of steel within this integral fighter. Single-billet steel components consist of a 4 1/2-inch A-2 blade, a sub-hilt, or double finger guard, pommel and full tang. It's a mighty, mighty boss blade. (PointSeven photo)

▶DEAN LANER: One of them is cleaner and meaner than the next. The grinds are perfect, the finish fine and the fit, well, they look to fit like prize-fighting gloves. (PointSeven photo)

▼JOHN FITCH: The clip-point fighter is reminiscent of the knife that old scrapper, Col. James Bowie, used. (KnifeShop.tv photo)

◀WILLIAM ENGLE: It's sharp and there's a lot to sharpen.

▶GENE TEDFORD: Gene doesn't believe in getting up close and personal with the enemy, so the fighting bowie is over a foot long. (KnifeShop.tv photo)

◀SHIVA KI: "Spirit Blade" features a ferocious style, and a handle of cocobolo, anaconda skin and Japanese silk wrap. The Spirit moves. (Beaucant photo)

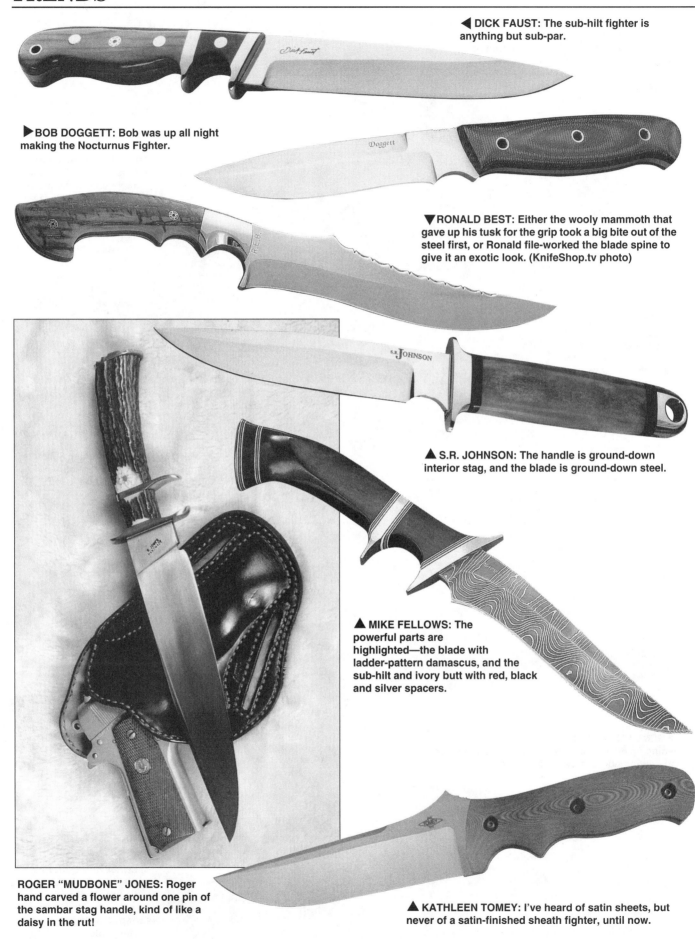

◀ **DICK FAUST:** The sub-hilt fighter is anything but sub-par.

▶**BOB DOGGETT:** Bob was up all night making the Nocturnus Fighter.

▼**RONALD BEST:** Either the wooly mammoth that gave up his tusk for the grip took a big bite out of the steel first, or Ronald file-worked the blade spine to give it an exotic look. (KnifeShop.tv photo)

▲ **S.R. JOHNSON:** The handle is ground-down interior stag, and the blade is ground-down steel.

▲ **MIKE FELLOWS:** The powerful parts are highlighted—the blade with ladder-pattern damascus, and the sub-hilt and ivory butt with red, black and silver spacers.

ROGER "MUDBONE" JONES: Roger hand carved a flower around one pin of the sambar stag handle, kind of like a daisy in the rut!

▲ **KATHLEEN TOMEY:** I've heard of satin sheets, but never of a satin-finished sheath fighter, until now.

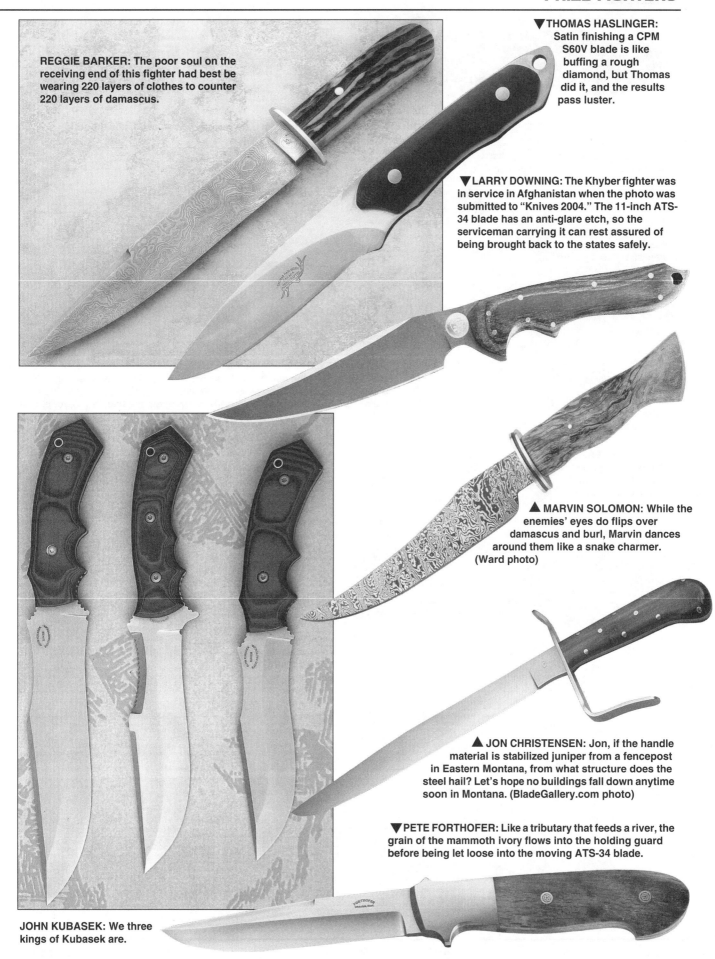

REGGIE BARKER: The poor soul on the receiving end of this fighter had best be wearing 220 layers of clothes to counter 220 layers of damascus.

▼**THOMAS HASLINGER:** Satin finishing a CPM S60V blade is like buffing a rough diamond, but Thomas did it, and the results pass luster.

▼**LARRY DOWNING:** The Khyber fighter was in service in Afghanistan when the photo was submitted to "Knives 2004." The 11-inch ATS-34 blade has an anti-glare etch, so the serviceman carrying it can rest assured of being brought back to the states safely.

▲**MARVIN SOLOMON:** While the enemies' eyes do flips over damascus and burl, Marvin dances around them like a snake charmer. (Ward photo)

▲**JON CHRISTENSEN:** Jon, if the handle material is stabilized juniper from a fencepost in Eastern Montana, from what structure does the steel hail? Let's hope no buildings fall down anytime soon in Montana. (BladeGallery.com photo)

▼**PETE FORTHOFER:** Like a tributary that feeds a river, the grain of the mammoth ivory flows into the holding guard before being let loose into the moving ATS-34 blade.

JOHN KUBASEK: We three kings of Kubasek are.

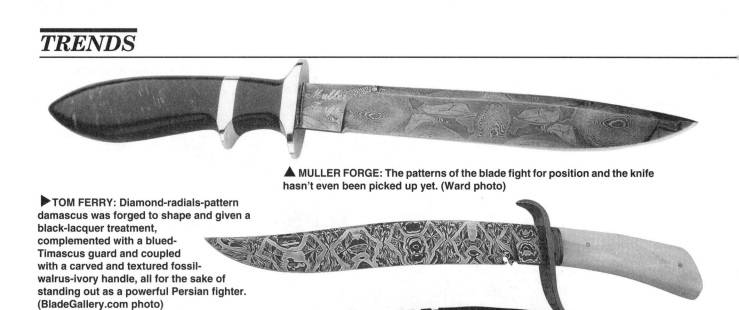

▲ MULLER FORGE: The patterns of the blade fight for position and the knife hasn't even been picked up yet. (Ward photo)

▶ TOM FERRY: Diamond-radials-pattern damascus was forged to shape and given a black-lacquer treatment, complemented with a blued-Timascus guard and coupled with a carved and textured fossil-walrus-ivory handle, all for the sake of standing out as a powerful Persian fighter. (BladeGallery.com photo)

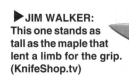

▲ DAN GRAY: The black-Micarta handle appears as if it is filed, or checkered, near the spine, but those are mosaic pins with brass inlays to complement other domed nickel-silver pins. For good measure, the blade is hollow ground and nitrogen soaked—to bring out the flavor? (Weyer photo)

▶ JIM WALKER: This one stands as tall as the maple that lent a limb for the grip. (KnifeShop.tv)

▲ ART TYCER: Did he mean to repeat the oval grain structure of the buckeye burl in the damascus? (Ward photo)

▶ DAVID ANDERS: The stabilized-maple handle slabs of this long damascus fighter are made even more stable with 16 domed pins on each side.

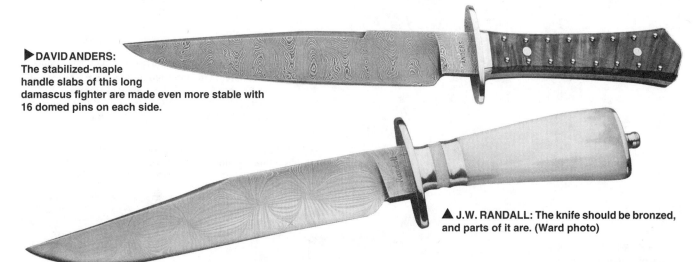

▲ J.W. RANDALL: The knife should be bronzed, and parts of it are. (Ward photo)

Gnarly Neck Knives

▲ **J. and TESS NEILSON:** Even more intriguing than the 2-inch cable-damascus blade and Chechan wood handle is the open-frame magnetic neck sheath. The magnet is rated to 7 pounds, so pull hard.

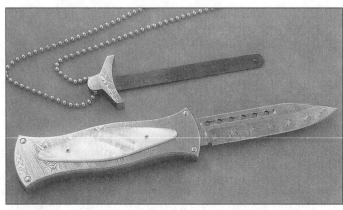

▲ **JOHN KUBASEK:** This is the first custom knife that incorporates the patented Rip Cord mechanism first employed by Phantom Knives. With the Damasteel blade lying flush against the Popsicle-stick-like extension of the sheath, and both stick and blade pushed back into the knife handle, a yank downward on the grip makes the stick pull against the blade and pop it out of the handle. (KnifeShop.tv photo)

▶ **LARRY RAMEY:** A tug on the lanyard or the textured G-10 handle would extract the blade from its Kydex® neck sheath and reveal the powerful damascus blade pattern.

RAY KIRK: Here's a long, thin neck knife to be strung around and hung from long, gangly necks. (Ward photo)

STEVE HILL: This neck knife is so pleasant looking, with pearly handle and upscale Robert Eggerling Turkish damascus blade, no one would think twice about admiring it, even if yanked abruptly out of its sheath in one swift motion.

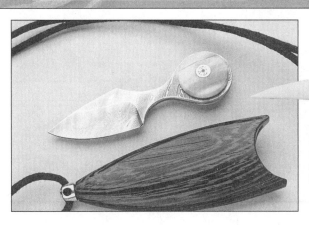

◀ **STAN MCKIERNAN:** Last year's neck knives didn't have high-carbon damascus blades, fossil-walrus-ivory grips and leather-lined Wenge wood sheaths. (Ward photo)

▲ **GLEN SMIT:** The "Fang" might hang a little too close to the neck for non-vampire types.

The Hunt Is On

BRRRR!! IT'S COLD. Look at that mist. I can see my breath. H-u-u-u-u-hhhhh . . . yes, it's c-o-o-l-d! The coffee tastes so good, but if I keep drinking this stuff, I'm going to be answering the call all day. Gosh, I love fall. The pines smell good, and the birds . . . listen to 'em. The little balls of feather almost put me in a good mood. Haha! I can't let these guys know that or they'll think I've lost my cool. Look at those softies. They aren't even up yet, and it's . . . oh, my, it's only 4 o'clock. What am I doing up already? I must be crazy. They're probably hung over . . .

man, it was fun playing cards last night. These wool socks put me in the hunting mood, and I love the way they feel. I wish I could hunt all the time. I'm at my best in the woods, like the king of the natural world. It's as if I was meant to do this. I can't even imagine what it's like not to hunt, not to know, like some unfortunate people, how this feels. I've always liked this hat. Man, I sure did miss these gloves. I love the musty smell. Speaking of which, I've got the gun oiled, and it's sighted. It's sighted, and I'm a huntin' fool. The knife . . .

yeah, the knife. Feel that sucker. It's like it belongs in my hand. When I snap that puppy back in its sheath, ahhh, there we go. Old Man Smith did a good job on that leather. It's stiff, and it smells, ohh, so good. Strap it on my belt, and I'm ready. Am I ever ready. Where are they??? It's only 4 o'clock. Maybe I'm a fool but it sure feels right. Yeah, it feels right to me!

Joe Kertzman

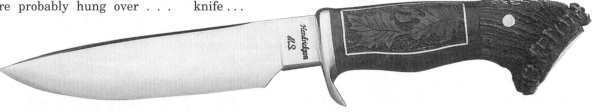

▲ **JAY HENDRICKSON:** His own style—that's what Jay has, and it involves maple-leaf carving in curly maple, classic patterning to be remembered. (BladeGallery.com photo)

▲ **BOB LAY:** The grip won't slip, but if it does, the guard is hard, and the thumb grooves behoove you to choke up on them. Check out the basket weave engraving by Kenneth Warren. (BladeGallery.com photo)

R.W. WILSON: These hunters pounce better than the hunted. (KnifeShop.tv photo)

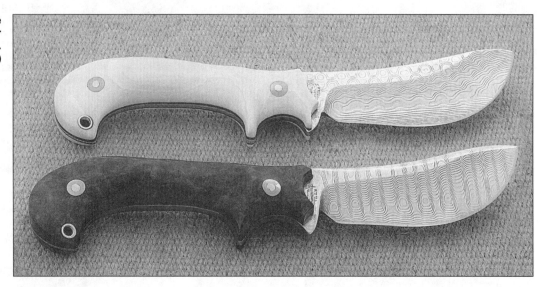

▶**SCOTT TAYLOR:** This knife could slit, gut, skin, quarter, dress, clean and butter the bread. (KnifeShop.tv photo)

◀**JERRY HENDRIX:** The engraving and mosaic pins, along with the maker's name in wispy type, fancy this one up just a bit. Otherwise, the white Micarta® is clean, and Tom McArdle gets credit for the engraving.

▶**BURT FOSTER:** Everything about this knife is smooth. There's no discernable grind line. There's hardly even a seam between the damascus and oosic. And everything is rounded.

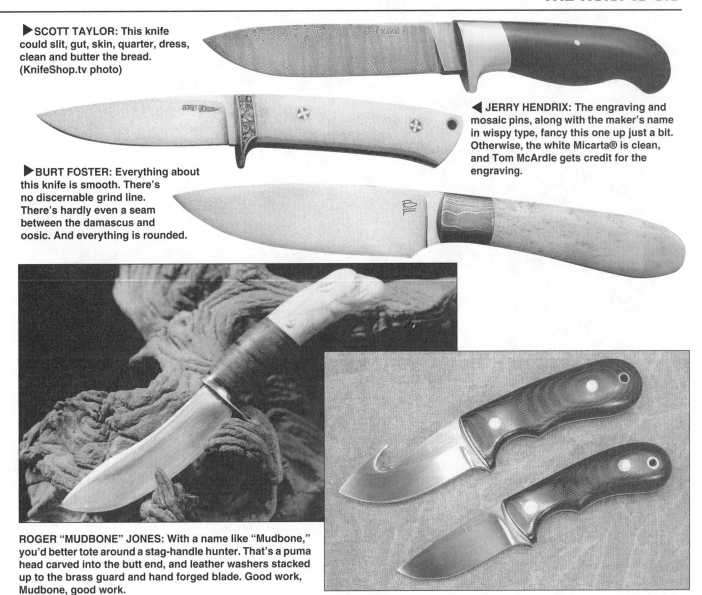

ROGER "MUDBONE" JONES: With a name like "Mudbone," you'd better tote around a stag-handle hunter. That's a puma head carved into the butt end, and leather washers stacked up to the brass guard and hand forged blade. Good work, Mudbone, good work.

BILL LEVENGOOD: Two swell Palm Swell Hunters parade green-and-black Micarta grips and CPM S30V blades. Who says you can't achieve a fine blade finish with CPM S30V?

▼**STEVE NOLEN:** Outstanding in the field are a pair of hunters with some of the prettiest bird's-eye-maple handles one ever did lay eyes on. (Hoffman photo)

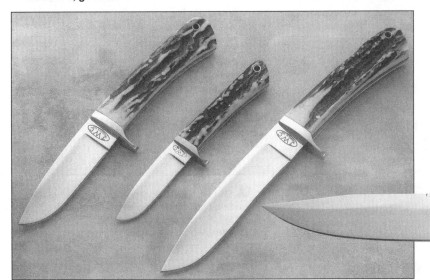

JEFF CLAIBORNE: Forged, fit and fine are three hunters in assorted sizes. (Hoffman photo)

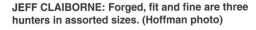

◀ **GARY RODEWALD:** There you are in a tree stand playing with your knife and the deer walks by undetected. (BladeGallery.com photo)

JAY MAINES: The Hunter's Ulu is a lulu.

▲ **GUY HIELSCHER:** The knifemaker tried to stabilize the Afzalia burl, but it partnered up with damascus and overwhelmed him. (Hoffman photo)

▼ **JOHN PARKS:** It's all in the details—matching the brass bolster and tacks, polishing the bone grip and hand rubbing the blade. (KnifeShop.tv photo)

▲ **JOHN HUTCHESON IV:** Sometimes the obvious knife style is the one that hits you right between the eyes. (Hoffman photo)

▲ **GIB GUIGNARD:** Sterling silver and stag bode well for a hunter, and a hand-rubbed ATS-34 blade has to be a good omen. (BladeGallery.com photo)

ROBERT BEATY: The handle is first-cut Rocky Mountain big horn with turquoise spacers and red liners. And there's also a fileworked ATS-34 blade, a leather sheath and some other work the maker put into it. (BladeGallery.com photo)

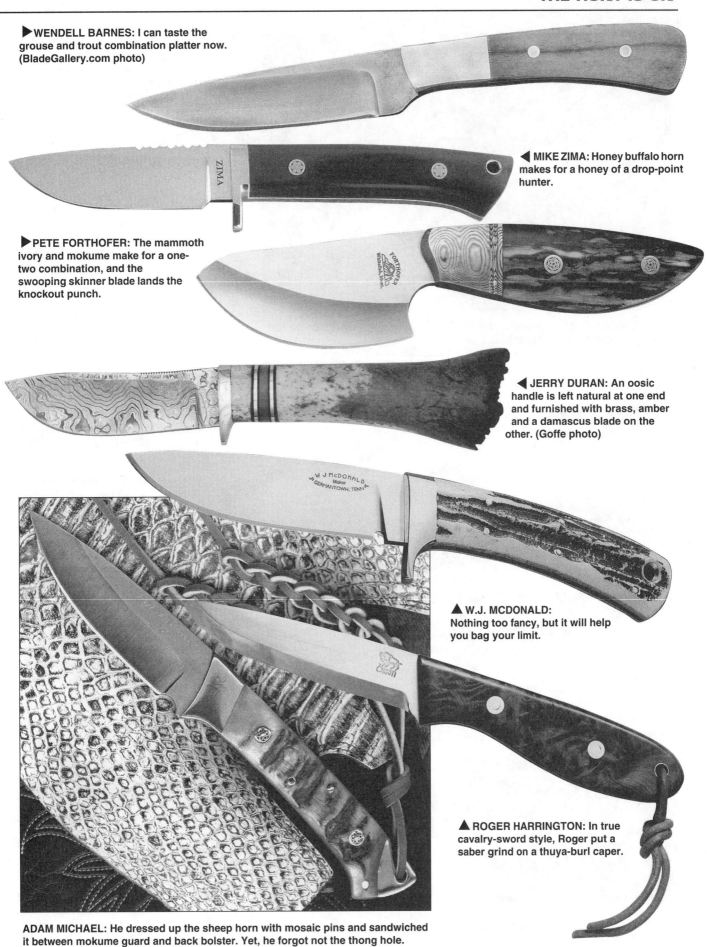

►WENDELL BARNES: I can taste the grouse and trout combination platter now. (BladeGallery.com photo)

◄MIKE ZIMA: Honey buffalo horn makes for a honey of a drop-point hunter.

►PETE FORTHOFER: The mammoth ivory and mokume make for a one-two combination, and the swooping skinner blade lands the knockout punch.

◄JERRY DURAN: An oosic handle is left natural at one end and furnished with brass, amber and a damascus blade on the other. (Goffe photo)

▲W.J. MCDONALD: Nothing too fancy, but it will help you bag your limit.

▲ROGER HARRINGTON: In true cavalry-sword style, Roger put a saber grind on a thuya-burl caper.

ADAM MICHAEL: He dressed up the sheep horn with mosaic pins and sandwiched it between mokume guard and back bolster. Yet, he forgot not the thong hole.

DICK FAUST: Years of experience is the only thing that can teach a knifemaker how to design a small skinner as effectively as Dick has executed this one.

LOYD THOMSEN: The materials on this one are stunning, and almost hide the fact that it is an excellent hunting knife design.

ED WALLACE: The hunt is on with leather, stag and steel. (KnifeShop.tv photo)

J.P. HOLMES: For the "sea hunter," it's an interesting choked-up style with dip-down blade for filleting without fatiguing. Red Micarta, pheasant wood and koa are the trio of handle materials, and the 420V blade has medium flex. (BladeGallery.com photo)

MULLER FORGE: Look close enough and one discovers redwood on either side of the stacked leather. (Ward photo)

JON CHRISTENSEN: You won't get any slivers from the smooth cocobolo grip, or any nicks on the edge-hardened 5160 blade. So, fear not, good hunter. (BladeGallery.com photo)

MIKE THOUROT: A choked-up skinner with snappy brass guard and pins gets you feeling all choked up inside. (Weyer photo)

▶ **GENE OSBORN:** Gene left tracks on the damascus blade to get himself in a hunting mood. (KnifeShop.tv photo)

◀ **HARVEY DEAN:** Harvey put a stainless escutcheon on the stag handle and a little elbow grease on the 384-layer-damascus blade. (KnifeShop.tv photo)

◀ **JOHN SCHMIDT:** That's a highly figured mammoth ivory handle, not stag, and to go with it, a mammoth-ivory fob dangling from the leather lanyard. (KnifeShop.tv photo)

▲ **PHIL THAM:** It has more curves than the Indy 500, but just enough to be a capable caper. (KnifeShop.tv photo)

◀ **JOHN YOUNG:** We all love a close-knit hunting family. (Weyer photo)

▼ **TOM LEWIS:** The damascus duo is headed to the bat cave for a rendezvous with any joker that gets in their way.

JOHN FITCH: The stag came from the woods and it's going right back in. (KnifeShop.tv photo)

Fantasies Worth Having

WHAT WOULD IT be like to be muscle bound, to have no flab, to have rough features, but good looks, to have long hair and bulging biceps, to be able to outfight and outsmart anyone who tried to cross you, to look good in rags, to have more power in your arms and legs than most wild animals, to be able to survive in the wilderness, to be wild, to be totally self-sufficient, a modern-day warrior or gladiator? What knife would such a character straight out of an adventure flick carry? How would the individual hold it, sheath it, sharpen it and use it? What types of animals would he hunt, field dress and clean? With that much power would you, yourself, be good or evil?

Fantasizing is a fun little game to play when you're the main character of imagination run rampant. When you meet knifemakers who fashion, not build or make, but fashion, fantasy knives, you wonder to yourself, "What kind of a person dreams up such extraordinary designs?" Fantasy knives worth having are often created by seemingly normal, well-adjusted, happy, businesslike folk, almost human, it seems. But their dreamlike states, oh, these are creative types who have enough self-awareness, self-esteem and reliance to allow their imaginations to run wild. They form knives so abstract, so absurd, distracting, attracting, fetching, fantastic, phenomenal and whimsical, they're mesmerizing.

Holding one of these bladed bastions, one fantasizes about running over barren land, fighting enemies at every turn, searching, searching for something, for that utopia where vegetation is lush, the rain refreshes the earth, the stars shine bright in the night sky, the sun rises a bright orange and sets a deep red, where women and men intermingle, and your sweetheart steels your attention and brings excitement back into your life. Where would such a place be? Perhaps the knives will guide us there. It's a fantasy worth having.

Joe Kertzman

◀ **MAX BERGER:** When Max orders blade steel from the supply store, it's not 1-inch bar stock, it's entire sheets that he can cut away, pound, grind, carve, saw, radius, shape, polish, hone and handle. (Weyer photo)

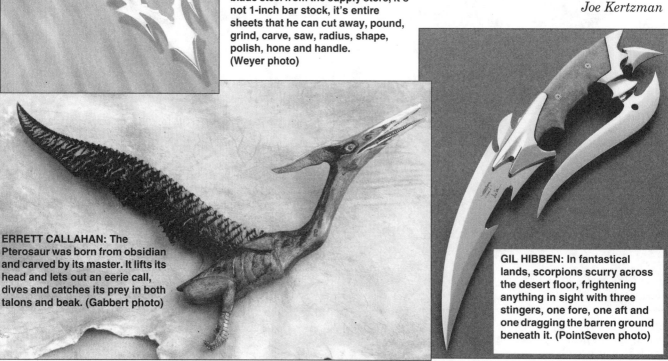

ERRETT CALLAHAN: The Pterosaur was born from obsidian and carved by its master. It lifts its head and lets out an eerie call, dives and catches its prey in both talons and beak. (Gabbert photo)

GIL HIBBEN: In fantastical lands, scorpions scurry across the desert floor, frightening anything in sight with three stingers, one fore, one aft and one dragging the barren ground beneath it. (PointSeven photo)

VIRGIL ENGLAND: In one, swift motion, he retrieved the length of tapered blade from alongside his shin, thrust it forward and pierced the armor of his attacker.

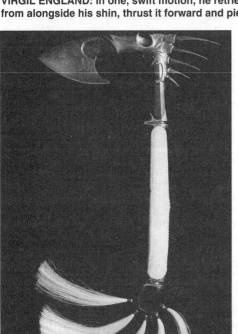

▶WILLY B. ELLIS: Thor's Revenge is a push dagger that can be pushed in many directions, not just down. The blades are by Robert Eggerling and Thunder Forge, and the knife is a slashing good time.

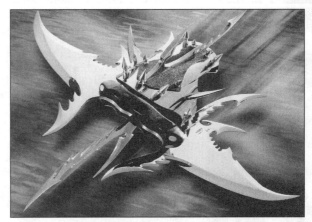

◀GIL HIBBEN: The steel Stingray was anything but an aquatic animal. The beast flew through the air with ferocious speed and evil intentions. Blood dripped from its talons as it ripped through anything in its path. Paul Ehlers designed the monster. (PointSeven photo)

VIRGIL ENGLAND: It screams like a banshee and its pointed head can turn and strike in any direction.

▶J.P. HIGGINS and TOM STERLING: The Dagger of the Sun is a weapon of the gods, made from rainbow obsidian in the form of a leaf and sent sailing through the air with deadly accuracy. (BladeGallery.com photo)

▶JOHN ETZLER: It looks a little less shocking, but don't be fooled. The Devil's Finger points downward like an arthritic digit, yet it pierces and slashes like the legendary pitchfork itself. (PointSeven photo)

▶JOHN LEWIS JENSEN: The deep-etched, jewel-encrusted weapon sparkled in the sun and sent rays of blue, purple, bronze and red shooting back into the sky. Damascus patterning danced across the blade, and he could not tell if it was real or Virtual Velocity.

Those Dastardly Daggers

THE ART DAGGER is one that is fashioned in a spirited, creative way. The original purpose of the push dagger was to be pushed into the enemy's sternum like a wooden stake into the heart of a vampire. The ceremonial dagger also brings forth images of human sacrifice, war, pomp, splendor, festivity, ferociousness, celebration and death.

The Celtic leg dagger was worn concealed on the side of a Scott's calf muscle, bulging out just enough for fast deployment of the handle and blade. Gypsy daggers bring to mind flowing, flowery clothing, bait-and-switch games, thievery, dance, illusion, shadowy figures and showmanship. Such are the romantic, dark, evil and exotic faces of the dagger.

Speaking of faces, daggers have at least two and sometimes four, distinct blade facets. Double-edged steel shoots straight out from handle and directly to a point with few curves between. The sides run parallel momentarily before tapering evenly to a centered blade tip. The blade is thick in the middle and razor sharp along both edges.

The dastardly dagger slips into its equally demonic sheath with the silence of a snake in tall grasses. Both slither and stab with pointed tongues. They lap at the wicked side of the world. They are powerful, lightening fast and as sinfully delicious as chocolate-covered cherries.

The allure is easy, and it's often such weakness that brings one to his or her demise. Immediately before releasing a last, desperate gasp, one looks up the piercing blade to the hand that controls the edge, stares sin in the eye and spits in the face of evil. Goodness reigns once again, because there aren't enough daggers to undo decency, no matter how dastardly they tend to be.

Joe Kertzman

GORDON BOOCO: This dagger, with imitation-white-pearl handle, was made from a blueprint drawn by a customer. From the cunning mind of the customer comes double-edged danger as only a dagger could bring it. (Box photo)

◀ RICHARD WRIGHT: Can you hear the folding blade of the automatic dagger snap into place? (KnifeShop.tv photo)

▲ DWIGHT TOWELL: Though a dagger design is inherently straightforward, this one uses more forms than a divorce lawyer and is just as deceptively sinister. Engraving, gold and mammoth ivory could go before a court of appeals.

▼NICK WHEELER: Nick's Bow Tie dagger is dressed in a BG-42 blade and a Hawaiian curly-koa-wood handle for a night on the town and possibly some steel flashing if an opportunity arises. (BladeGallery.com photo)

THOMAS HASLINGER: He carved out the perfect stabilized-maple-burl grip, filed a flaring F. Schneider stainless-damascus guard and ground a superior CPM S60V blade.

◀SCOTT SLOBODIAN: The powder steel blade of the Gypsy dagger somehow depicts the chaotic state in which a gypsy's dagger might find itself entangled.

▶ANDERS HOGSTROM: This strapping, young Celtic leg dagger dons an ostrich-leather cover over a wood handle, a grayed and textured sterling silver guard and a clay-tempered 1050 blade. Strap one on, young lad. (BladeGallery.com photo)

GENE LORO: Quillon daggers with damascus blades line up like soldiers standing at attention. (Hoffman photo)

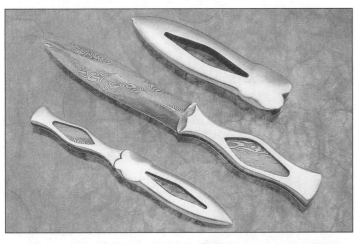

AUDRA DRAPER: The damascus and nickel-silver dagger by Audra Draper is a window to another world. (BladeGallery.com photo)

◀TOM FERRY: It would probably be less painful to die by the Blue Plague dagger than by the bubonic plague. This modern warrior employs a biohazard-pattern mosaic-damascus blade, a Timascus grip with pearl window frames on each side, and a forked butt for backward plaguing. (BladeGallery.com photo)

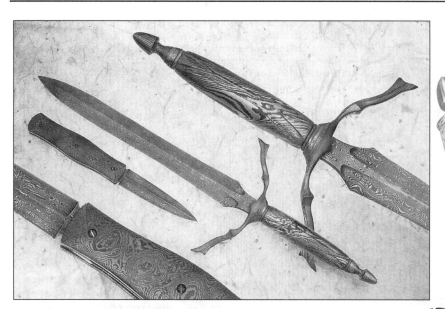

NICK WHEELER and TOM FERRY: Two Timascus and damascus daggers do double the damage. (BladeGallery.com photo)

◀ J.W. MCFARLIN: This one spirals and plunges. The cherry burl handle is fluted and festooned with silver wire inlay. (Weyer photo)

▶ DANIEL WATSON: The wire-wrapped handle and Techno-Wootz blade are such that gladiators and knights would have welcomed such a daring dagger. (Weyer photo)

▶ JOHN WALKER: It's a darling dagger with charming Tanya Van Hoy engraving, three sterling wire wraps, a stellar sea cow handle and a bite that will send you home sobbing.

RAYMOND RYBAR JR.: The push dagger carved with serpent and skull is actually biblical in nature and a testament to the maker's abilities.

▲ KEVIN HARVEY: The stepped, integral bolster is set with four rubies. Jeweler Frances Farrell added 14k gold touches, and Helene Van Wyk engraved the plush dagger of push. (Louw photo)

▲ LOYD THOMSEN: This is one dizzying dagger.

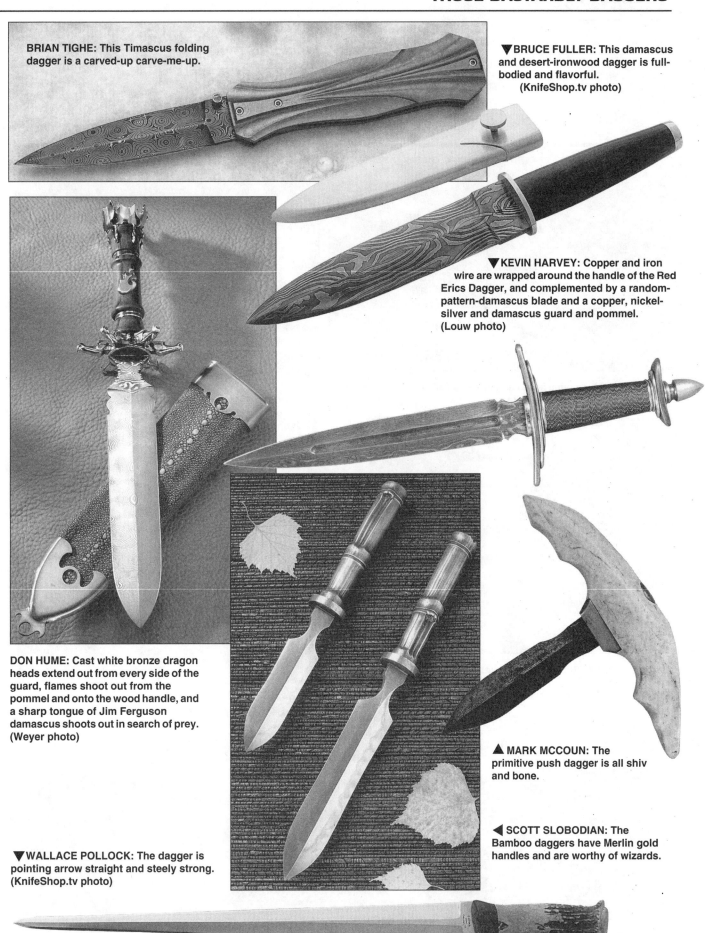

BRIAN TIGHE: This Timascus folding dagger is a carved-up carve-me-up.

▼**BRUCE FULLER:** This damascus and desert-ironwood dagger is full-bodied and flavorful. (KnifeShop.tv photo)

▼**KEVIN HARVEY:** Copper and iron wire are wrapped around the handle of the Red Erics Dagger, and complemented by a random-pattern-damascus blade and a copper, nickel-silver and damascus guard and pommel. (Louw photo)

DON HUME: Cast white bronze dragon heads extend out from every side of the guard, flames shoot out from the pommel and onto the wood handle, and a sharp tongue of Jim Ferguson damascus shoots out in search of prey. (Weyer photo)

▲ **MARK MCCOUN:** The primitive push dagger is all shiv and bone.

◄ **SCOTT SLOBODIAN:** The Bamboo daggers have Merlin gold handles and are worthy of wizards.

▼**WALLACE POLLOCK:** The dagger is pointing arrow straight and steely strong. (KnifeShop.tv photo)

Tiny Tips

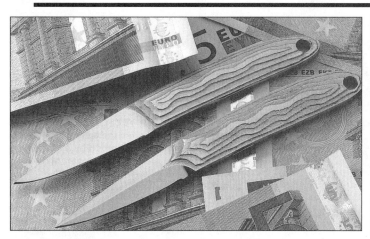

▲ KOUJI HARA: Carving knife handles this small, to this degree, is nothing other than a labor of love.

▲ EARL WITSAMAN: Earl had the good fortune of completing three fixed blades in Devin Thomas damascus (twist, shark's tooth and ladder patterns.) (Weyer photo)

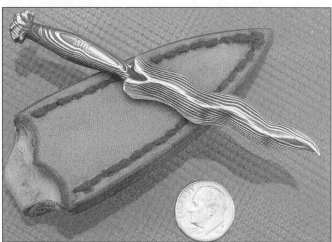

▲ AUDRA DRAPER: It might be a "wittle wavy bwade," but the one-piece, forged, etched and sculpted miniature kris dagger is "a wot of bwade." (BladeGallery.com photo)

▲ LARRY MENSCH: Larry claims these are, "Damasteel minis to help George Washington protect our country. God bless America."

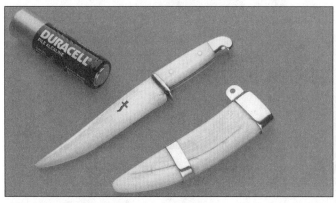

▲ DOUGLAS NOREN: The Scagel String Cutter might be cute, but it isn't cuddly. (Ward photo)

▲ LLOYD "PETE" PETERSON: Diminutive damascus is no less impressive than full-size steel.

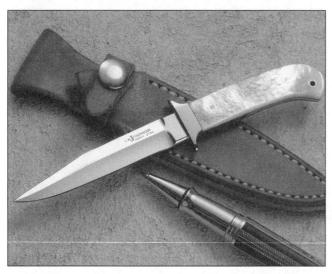

S.R. JOHNSON: The miniature boot knife and sheath could only be properly worn by an elf.

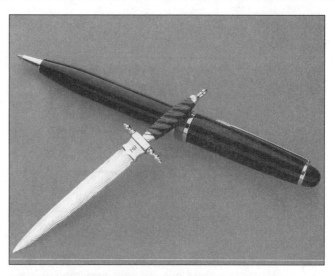

GEORGE ZIMMERMAN: Fluting the handle and carving the guard of the miniature dagger must have been a gargantuan undertaking. (Ward photo)

RON HEMBROOK: Ron says this is "The big and small of it."

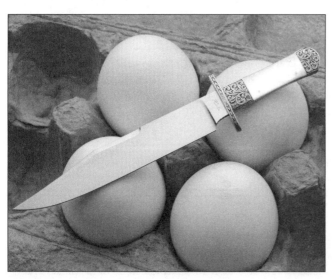

LORA SUE BETHKE: This tiny tip is handled with an antler tip. (Ward photo)

FRED CARTER: With a little egging on, Fred completed a 4-inch bowie featuring a 4-inch, flat-ground, satin-finished blade, a 416 stainless steel guard and a mother-of-pearl handle. It also showcases relief-engraved scroll.

CHARLES BENNICA: As small as a cigarette, the miniature cutter is a full integral, one of the most difficult knife styles to make in full size, and nearly impossible to handcraft in miniature.

STATE OF THE ART

Most of us can close our eyes and imagine breathtaking vistas, mountainous terrain, an unspoiled valley, a rushing waterfall, or even a beautiful girl, handsome guy or a playful puppy. If you have kids, sometimes you can see their faces when daydreaming or reminiscing. Imagine having the ability to paint those images, or better yet, to take needle and ink and to, dot by dot, create such a scene beneath the pores of ivory. Can most of us even fathom possessing the skills necessary to engrave flowers using hand files and engravers, or to cut grooves in steel until they resemble scrolls, flowers, faces or scenery?

When you see a sculpture outside a museum, do you say, like most of us untrained onlookers, "That's different," or "Hmmm. Interesting?" Or, are you one of those chosen few who remark, "I could do that," or "I would have done it differently?" As fate would have it, a minority of blade enthusiasts are blessed with the abilities to inlay gold until it highlights just the right parts of a knife, or to forge damascus until the patterns evoke a range of emotions from those who gaze upon it. Carving shapes that actually resemble real objects or fantastical places and beings is a craft reserved for the most creative individuals.

The "State of the Art" section of "Knives 2004" not only gives an overview of the developments in knife art, it actually represents a state of evolvement. In looking at the objects of blade art, try to imagine being the artist. As does a therapist, attempt to get into the heads of the artists. What were they fantasizing about, what were they thinking when they blended cutlery with an artist's canvas? Were their minds separated from their bodies? Did their creative beings emerge? Could they have retained complete control of all senses and still formed something so fascinating?

Maybe art appreciation involves letting go of all preconceived notions and inhibitions. Break loose of all that confines you and paint those vistas, mountains, valleys, pretty faces and playful puppies with your own needles and ink. Tread where the artist dared go and delve into their very being. Now you've entered your own artistic state and can better appreciate all that passes before you.

Joe Kertzman

Needle-and-Inked Knives

WHY DO IT? The knife doesn't cut any better with a white tiger scrimshawed on the handle. The wrinkled face of an elderly Native American won't give the blade more rope-cutting power. When done well by an imaginative artist, scrimshaw is just as fabulous on an ivory-inlaid keepsake box or ivory tabletop as it is on a knife handle. Tabletops and keepsake boxes are bigger, so there's more "canvas" for the artists' renditions. Pistol grips are good places for the needles and ink of talented scrimshanders. Here's one, how about scrimming the keys of a piano? Well, maybe that's going a bit far, though it's probably been done. In fact, I read once that there is a certain African tribe that not only needle-and-inks their own teeth but also carves them. Ouch!

Why knife handles? It goes back to the pistol grips. Pistols with ivory or pearl grips are some of the most coveted, collected and strikingly handsome of all short firearms. The same can be said for knives with pearl or ivory grips. If ivory is the flavor of the day, then scrimshaw is the embellishment of choice. The most discerning knife collectors gather around scrimmed-ivory grips and inspect the pictures, the stories told underneath the pores of the ivory. They read colorful dots until they understand the artist's intentions and frame of mind.

It is often said that a well-worn knife can tell stories. Well, even before the ink is dry on a freshly scrimmed knife handle, it tells many stories. Sometimes, not only are the dots of the scrim, itself, connected, but the blade steel, guard and bolster material, handle and other knife "furniture" are tied together by a scrimshawed scene. Each knife handle in this section speaks volumes—about the knife-maker, about the collector and, especially, about the needle-and-ink artist who revealed an intimate part of his or herself, who poured his or her heart out onto the grip of an edged tool or weapon.

Joe Kertzman

▼**TINA HANSON: For those who didn't recognize the knife by Don Hanson III as a sunfish pattern, Tina scrimshawed a little hint on the mammoth-ivory handle scales. (PointSeven photo)**

▼**JOHN STAHL: Belt buckles make fabulous places for artists to showcase their work. Of course, if a knife blade happens to pop out of one end of the buckle, it's all the better. The knife is by John Kubasek. (KnifeShop.tv photo)**

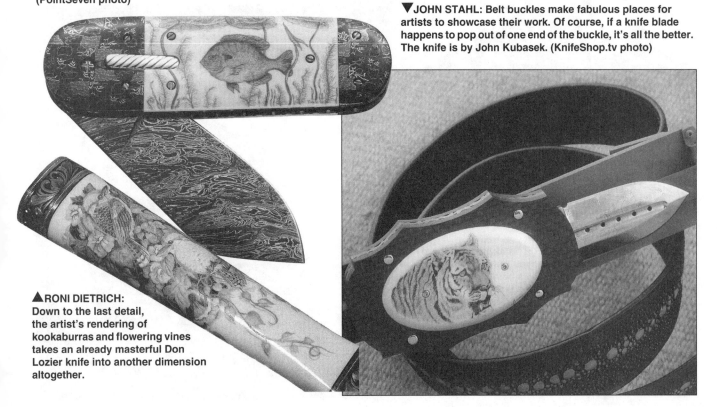

▲**RONI DIETRICH: Down to the last detail, the artist's rendering of kookaburras and flowering vines takes an already masterful Don Lozier knife into another dimension altogether.**

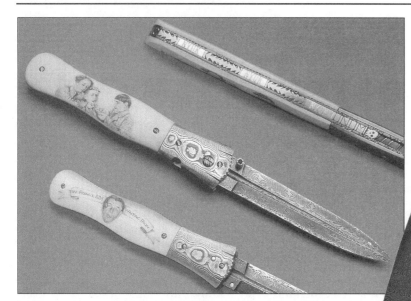

HILTON PURVIS: Tiger scrimshaw on an Owen Wood hunting knife is part of a "Big Five Cats" (lion, tiger, leopard, cheetah and jaguar) set of knives, all going to one collector, but crafted by five South African knifemakers.

LINDA KARST STONE: Oosic and amber spacers on a Randy Lee dagger emulate the fur tones of a scrimshawed jaguar, and the blade mimics the big cat's teeth. (BladeGallery.com photo)

LORI RISTINEN: This Steve Hill knife was commissioned by a customer who the maker claims is the biggest Three Stooges collector in the West, a gentleman who also happens to be a dentist. Open wide, nyuk, nyuk! (Freiburg photo)

J.D. CLAY: He made the deer jump, and he fashioned the knife, too.

LINDA KARST STONE: It's the wildest horse on the most untamed Daniel Winkler knife most of us have ever had the privilege of seeing. (PointSeven photo)

JESSE GHERE: Think of the wrinkled skin of a pachyderm and you'll know why knifemaker Jerry McClure chose this particular mosaic-damascus pattern for the bolster of a folder with elephant scrimshaw. (KnifeShop.tv photo)

SANDRA BRADY: George Herron made one knife yearly from 1997 to present (but two in 2002) and he was honored to have Sandra scrim each with an outdoor scene like only she can depict. (Weyer photo)

▲RICK BOWLES: His vision of the Native warrior came long before he scrimshawed it on a Gary Randall bowie. (BladeGallery.com photo)

▶RICHARD "HUTCH" HUTCHINGS: Barbarianism is alive and well, even in the civilized world, thanks to the minds of knifemaker Gil Hibben and his favorite scrimshaw artist. (PointSeven photo)

◀JOHN STAHL: The falcon perches, eyes searching, on the handle of a Howard Hitchmough folder.

◀JUAN LONEWOLF: Old "Eagle-Eye Lonewolf" did it again.

◀SHARON GRACE: Black stipple on warthog ivory results in an African wild dog, and knifemaker Arno Bernard knows he barked up the right tree with Sharon as his scrim artist.

▶BARBARA ROBERTS: How do knifemakers like Jack Roberts "just happen" to marry incredibly talented scrimshaw artists? It seems like you could reach out and touch the face of the Native American.

▶CHRISTIAN: The artwork takes us back to the days of the proud Mohawks (the Native Americans and their hairstyles). The folding knife is by Gary Headrick.

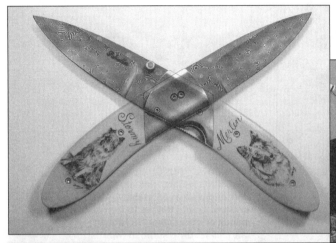

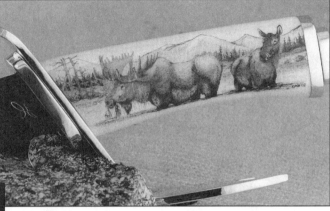

SANDRA BRADY: Knifemaker Anthony Schaller says Merlin and Stormy are best friends. I have a feeling they have a friend in Anthony, too.

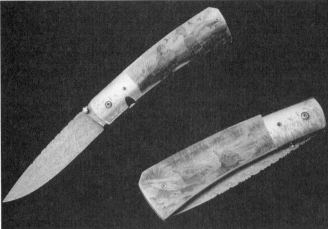

KRISTEN BARNDT: A moose pair is brought to life on the alternate-ivory grip of a 16-inch bowie by Larry Mensch.

BARBARA ROBERTS: Fatigue, consternation and stubborn pride are written all over the face of the cowboy riding the handle of a Jack Roberts drop-point hunting knife.

MICK WARDELL: You have to wonder if, when done posing for the scrimshaw artist, the bullmastiff ate the bone handle of the knife.

KIRK REXROAT: It's as foggy as duck (or turtle) soup out there, but the talent of the scrimshander is clear. (H. Rexroat photo)

JACK FOX: The scrimshaw artist who took pen and ink to a whale tooth is unknown, but Jack bladed and befriended the toothy extraction.

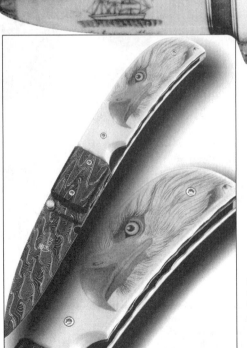

MIRELLA PACHI: Mammoth ivory is graced by another one of God's greatest creations. Francesco Pachi fashioned the knife with blued-damascus blade and mosaic-damascus bolsters.

◄LINDA KARST STONE: The woodsy retreat is brought to the forefront on an Edmund Davidson integral. (PointSeven photo)

▲▼BILL OLSON: Bill scrimmed a Native American in full headdress on one side of a Richard Orton knife and an eagle in flight on the other side. It's a Jim Ferguson droplet-pattern-damascus blade.

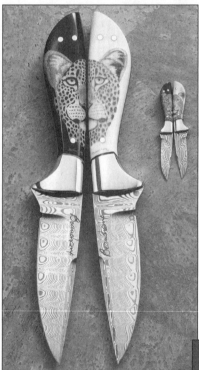

MARY MUELLER: A large bear roams the highlands and is framed by Jim White engraving. The grooved and groovy Bear Bowie is from the hands of skilled Alaskan knifemaker Russ Kommer. (BladeGallery.com photo)

◄GAETAN BEAUCHAMP: Mammoth ivory and water buffalo horn are two handle choices, but you have to buy both knives to get the whole story. (PointSeven photo)

◄SUSAN COLVIN: A strapping young buck stares out from the handle of a knife made by the strapping young Dick Atkinson.

►SHARON GRACE: Of birds, flowers and beautiful girls is the "Nouveau" knife, part of a set and made by Sharon's dad, William Burger.

▲SANDRA BRADY: There's more wild game on the woolly-mammoth-ivory handles of a set of Larry Downing steak knives than you can shake a sharp stick at. (Weyer photo)

Lacy Inlays

THOSE FAMILAR WITH the finest knifemakers in the world, both past and present—anyone from Samuel Bell and Michael Price to Bill Moran, Dwight Towell, Jay Hendrickson and Michael Walker—are also familiar with silver, gold, twisted-wire, pique, domed-pin and other knife-handle inlay techniques. Lacy silver wire inlaid into an African blackwood handle is rather like a gemstone set in gold. Tasteful and well-executed inlays can mean the difference between high-quality custom knives and extraordinary collector's pieces.

Inlay adds a touch of class, and as much as we'd like to think that the old caste system of dividing people and objects into classes—like wealthy folk, the rich, middle class, lower class and poor—is obsolete, let's face it, there is still a first-class seating section on airplanes, and there are still those who can afford the finer things in life and, sadly, those who can't. But having class, being classy, isn't always about money. Some of the poorest people in the world have more class in their pinkie fingers than many of the richest. No, class is about style and grace.

The tendency toward style, grace and subtle elegance is either learned or innate, but the ability to richly embellish objects like knives is a gift. Those knifemakers who treasure their gifts and use them wisely, to their full extent, ever pushing the envelope of creativity, fashion some of the finest knives in existence. Lacy inlays set into the grains of wood, below the porous surface of ivory or within the grain structure of low-carbon steel set new standards for knives. It's that extra touch of class, the attention to detail, the underlying current below the surface that defines lacy inlays. After all, it's what's inside that counts!

Joe Kertzman

◀ GLENN WATERS: On front of a stainless-damascus handle are two rabbits sitting under the rushes and next to a small stream, watching the moon. The rushes are 24k-gold inlays. On the back is a Japanese water bird in a stream with bamboo. The bamboo shoots are also gold of the 24k variety.

▼ KEN DURHAM: A little vine wends its up an African blackwood grip and sprouts flowers despite its dark environment. (Hoffman photo)

▶ HARUMI HIRAYAMA: A blast of wind and . . . where are all the petals and butterflies flying?

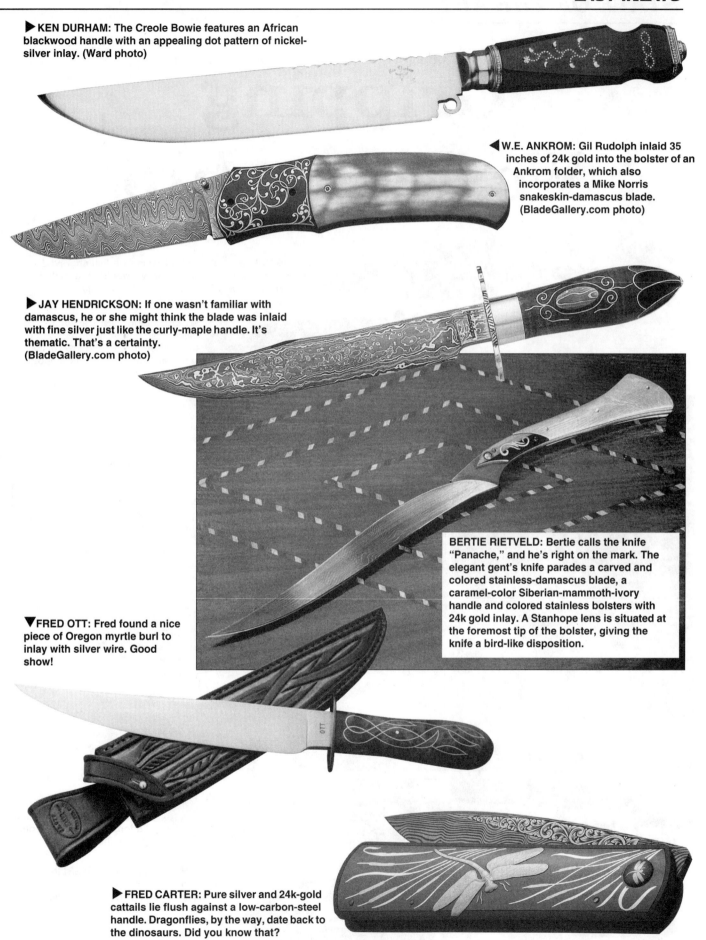

▶KEN DURHAM: The Creole Bowie features an African blackwood handle with an appealing dot pattern of nickel-silver inlay. (Ward photo)

◀W.E. ANKROM: Gil Rudolph inlaid 35 inches of 24k gold into the bolster of an Ankrom folder, which also incorporates a Mike Norris snakeskin-damascus blade. (BladeGallery.com photo)

▶JAY HENDRICKSON: If one wasn't familiar with damascus, he or she might think the blade was inlaid with fine silver just like the curly-maple handle. It's thematic. That's a certainty. (BladeGallery.com photo)

BERTIE RIETVELD: Bertie calls the knife "Panache," and he's right on the mark. The elegant gent's knife parades a carved and colored stainless-damascus blade, a caramel-color Siberian-mammoth-ivory handle and colored stainless bolsters with 24k gold inlay. A Stanhope lens is situated at the foremost tip of the bolster, giving the knife a bird-like disposition.

▼FRED OTT: Fred found a nice piece of Oregon myrtle burl to inlay with silver wire. Good show!

▶FRED CARTER: Pure silver and 24k-gold cattails lie flush against a low-carbon-steel handle. Dragonflies, by the way, date back to the dinosaurs. Did you know that?

Gripping Workmanship

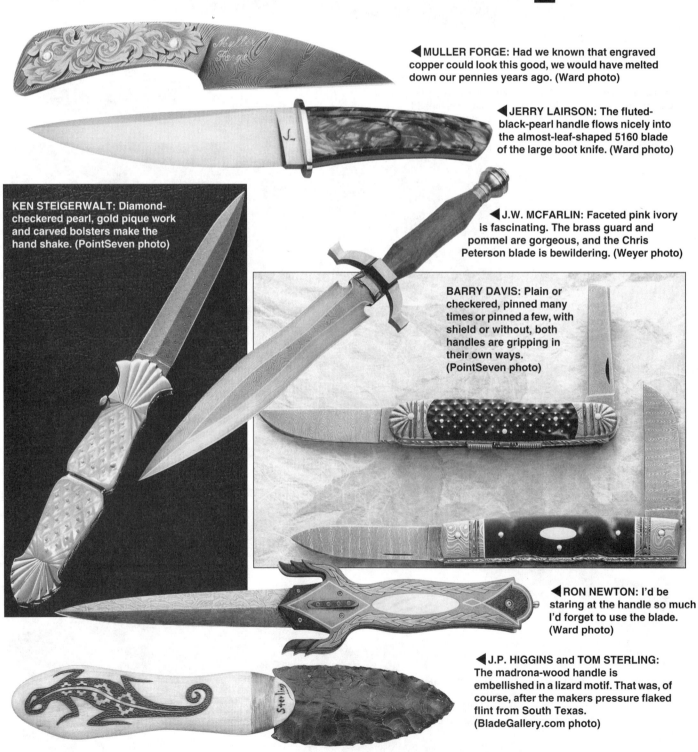

◀MULLER FORGE: Had we known that engraved copper could look this good, we would have melted down our pennies years ago. (Ward photo)

◀JERRY LAIRSON: The fluted-black-pearl handle flows nicely into the almost-leaf-shaped 5160 blade of the large boot knife. (Ward photo)

KEN STEIGERWALT: Diamond-checkered pearl, gold pique work and carved bolsters make the hand shake. (PointSeven photo)

◀J.W. MCFARLIN: Faceted pink ivory is fascinating. The brass guard and pommel are gorgeous, and the Chris Peterson blade is bewildering. (Weyer photo)

BARRY DAVIS: Plain or checkered, pinned many times or pinned a few, with shield or without, both handles are gripping in their own ways. (PointSeven photo)

◀RON NEWTON: I'd be staring at the handle so much I'd forget to use the blade. (Ward photo)

◀J.P. HIGGINS and TOM STERLING: The madrona-wood handle is embellished in a lizard motif. That was, of course, after the makers pressure flaked flint from South Texas. (BladeGallery.com photo)

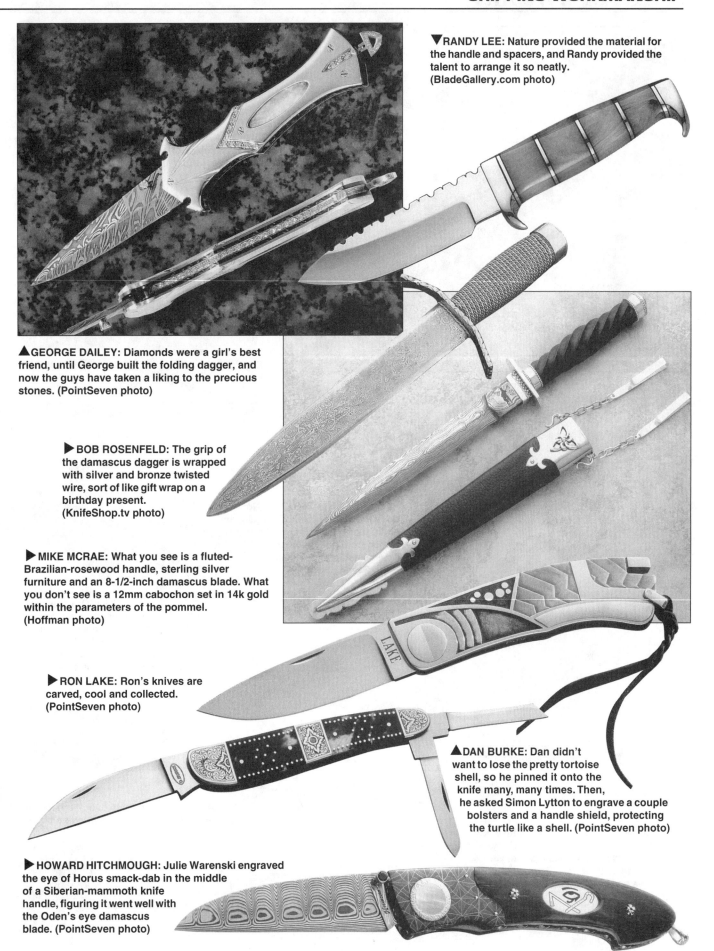

▼RANDY LEE: Nature provided the material for the handle and spacers, and Randy provided the talent to arrange it so neatly. (BladeGallery.com photo)

▲GEORGE DAILEY: Diamonds were a girl's best friend, until George built the folding dagger, and now the guys have taken a liking to the precious stones. (PointSeven photo)

►BOB ROSENFELD: The grip of the damascus dagger is wrapped with silver and bronze twisted wire, sort of like gift wrap on a birthday present. (KnifeShop.tv photo)

►MIKE MCRAE: What you see is a fluted-Brazilian-rosewood handle, sterling silver furniture and an 8-1/2-inch damascus blade. What you don't see is a 12mm cabochon set in 14k gold within the parameters of the pommel. (Hoffman photo)

►RON LAKE: Ron's knives are carved, cool and collected. (PointSeven photo)

▲DAN BURKE: Dan didn't want to lose the pretty tortoise shell, so he pinned it onto the knife many, many times. Then, he asked Simon Lytton to engrave a couple bolsters and a handle shield, protecting the turtle like a shell. (PointSeven photo)

►HOWARD HITCHMOUGH: Julie Warenski engraved the eye of Horus smack-dab in the middle of a Siberian-mammoth knife handle, figuring it went well with the Oden's eye damascus blade. (PointSeven photo)

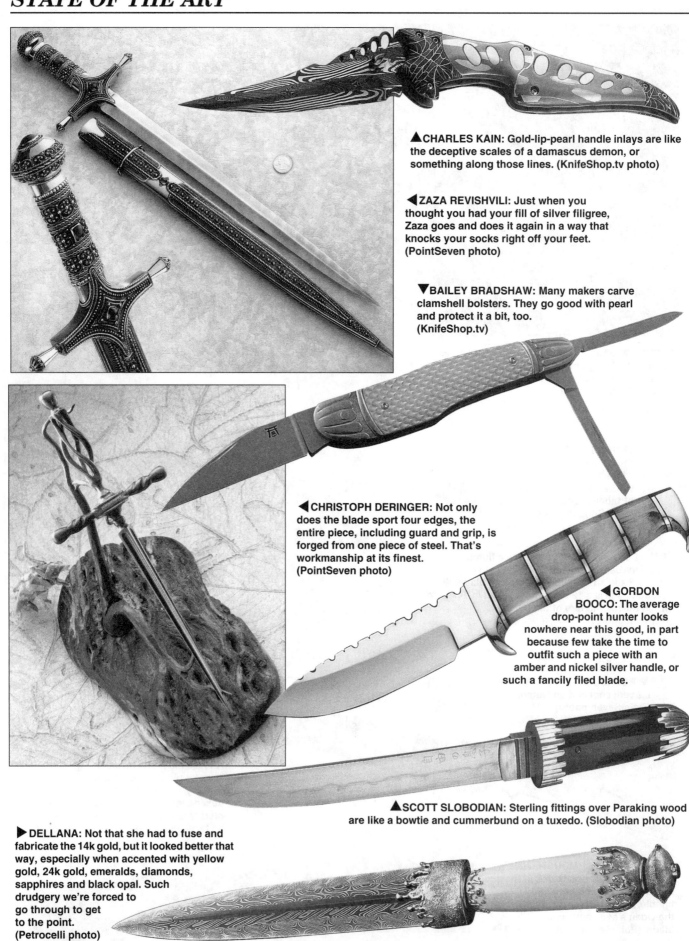

CHARLES KAIN: Gold-lip-pearl handle inlays are like the deceptive scales of a damascus demon, or something along those lines. (KnifeShop.tv photo)

ZAZA REVISHVILI: Just when you thought you had your fill of silver filigree, Zaza goes and does it again in a way that knocks your socks right off your feet. (PointSeven photo)

BAILEY BRADSHAW: Many makers carve clamshell bolsters. They go good with pearl and protect it a bit, too. (KnifeShop.tv)

CHRISTOPH DERINGER: Not only does the blade sport four edges, the entire piece, including guard and grip, is forged from one piece of steel. That's workmanship at its finest. (PointSeven photo)

GORDON BOOCO: The average drop-point hunter looks nowhere near this good, in part because few take the time to outfit such a piece with an amber and nickel silver handle, or such a fancily filed blade.

SCOTT SLOBODIAN: Sterling fittings over Paraking wood are like a bowtie and cummerbund on a tuxedo. (Slobodian photo)

DELLANA: Not that she had to fuse and fabricate the 14k gold, but it looked better that way, especially when accented with yellow gold, 24k gold, emeralds, diamonds, sapphires and black opal. Such drudgery we're forced to go through to get to the point. (Petrocelli photo)

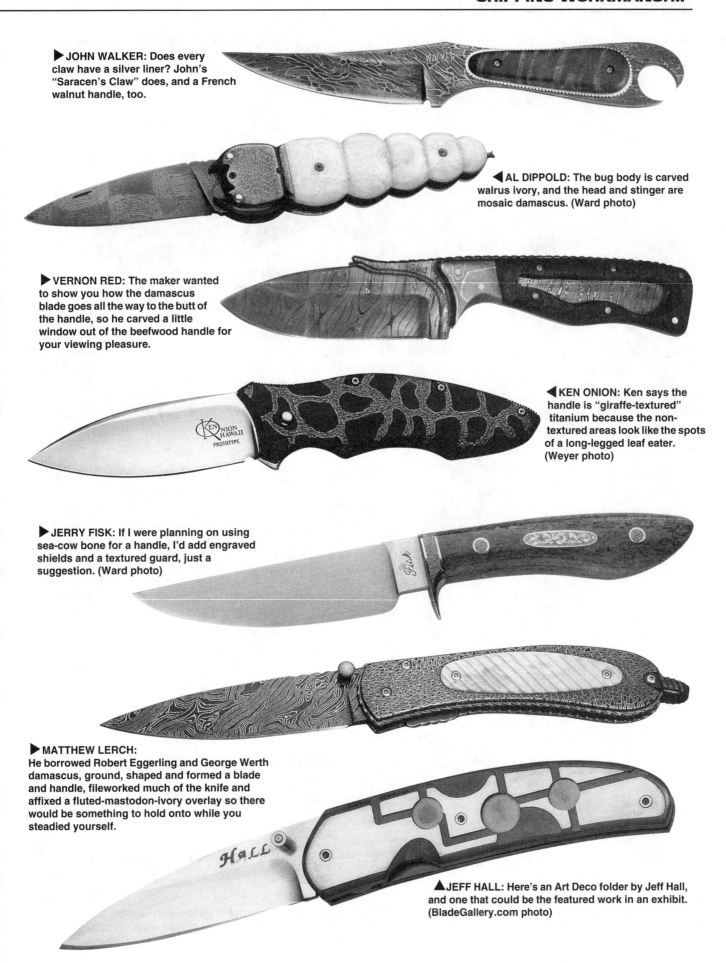

►JOHN WALKER: Does every claw have a silver liner? John's "Saracen's Claw" does, and a French walnut handle, too.

◄AL DIPPOLD: The bug body is carved walrus ivory, and the head and stinger are mosaic damascus. (Ward photo)

►VERNON RED: The maker wanted to show you how the damascus blade goes all the way to the butt of the handle, so he carved a little window out of the beefwood handle for your viewing pleasure.

◄KEN ONION: Ken says the handle is "giraffe-textured" titanium because the non-textured areas look like the spots of a long-legged leaf eater. (Weyer photo)

►JERRY FISK: If I were planning on using sea-cow bone for a handle, I'd add engraved shields and a textured guard, just a suggestion. (Ward photo)

►MATTHEW LERCH: He borrowed Robert Eggerling and George Werth damascus, ground, shaped and formed a blade and handle, fileworked much of the knife and affixed a fluted-mastodon-ivory overlay so there would be something to hold onto while you steadied yourself.

▲JEFF HALL: Here's an Art Deco folder by Jeff Hall, and one that could be the featured work in an exhibit. (BladeGallery.com photo)

RICHARD BROWNE: Well, ladies, you've been waiting for your knight in shining armor. Here he is. Don't blow it. (PointSeven photo)

GEORGE DAILEY: The boot has damascus lowers, carved uppers and gold-and-diamond spurs. (PointSeven photo)

MARVIN SOLOMON: It would have been a nice damascus fixed blade with a plain Micarta® handle, but the inlay takes it up a notch. (Ward photo)

DERYK MUNROE: Some people see things the rest of us never dream about, unless those with clairvoyant tendencies are able to create what they see, then we can all enjoy it. Thanks, Deryk. (PointSeven photo)

STEPHEN OLSZEWSKI: The girl Stephen knows is so beautiful, he immortalized her in solid 14k gold, showered her with carved-pearl flowers and gave her a diamond to make it official.

BOB LAY: Quite a few old-school knives had stacked-leather-washer handles. Now we do it with buffalo horn, amber and green maple. Who says the world isn't a better place? (BladeGallery.com photo)

PAUL JARVIS: Antique butterfly knives don't have Daryl Meier damascus blades with integral spiked guards, maple burl handles, bronze bolsters or red garnets. (PointSeven photo)

◀BARRY GALLAGHER: Something told Barry that mokume side plates would go well with the mosaic-damascus blade, and that, if he overlaid the mokume with tortoise shell and inset it with a few tiger eyes, it would result in a thematic composition of color and texture. Something told him that. (PointSeven photo)

▼BILL KELLER: Not just pearl inlays, but checkered pearl inlays, not just damascus, but filed damascus, not just gold, but carved gold, not just a knife, it's a slice-me and dice-me masterpiece of steel. (KnifeShop.tv photo)

▲BOB PATRICK: The integral D-2 blade and ferrule give the pink ivory the edge it needs.

▲FRANS VAN ELDIK: The front half of the handle is Russian mammoth ivory, and the back half is Alaskan mammoth ivory. So, something crossed the Bering Strait, and a sub-hilt fighter of Guido Wilbert damascus is the better for it. Daniel Matagne inlaid the gold. (Van Tien Hoven photo)

▲MICHAEL VAGNINO: If the Quillion dagger has a black and silver blade, you might as well give it a black and silver grip. (Thurber photo)

▼RICHARD HEHN: He either found a piece of mammoth ivory with a spectacular crack down the middle, or he carved it that way.

▲DON NORRIS and TODD KOPP: Only fluted fossil ivory, blued-steel fittings and twisted-wire wrap could measure up to such a spectacular damascus blade. (PointSeven photo)

Carve 'Em Up, Sculpt 'Em Down

IT ALL STARTS when you're a child and you learn to stay inside the lines coloring with crayons. Then, there are the art classes in grade school and high school, eventually a couple college courses and, "voila," you're an artist. You can carve dragonheads in deer stag, mermaids in pearl and elephants in ivory. Next, the city council votes to have you sculpt a Viking for the front lawn of the town hall, and local philanthropists beckon you to design their office buildings and mansion entryways.

Or, you never learn to color inside the lines, you do what you can to get through art classes and fail miserably trying to draw a portrait to impress your sweetheart.

Upon contemplation, it is amazing how many knifemakers are able to carve, sculpt, draw, design, engrave, etch, scrimshaw and inlay fantastic forms. The craftsmen with the ability to envision, design, shape and fashion both working and pleasing knives must have some sense of form and function, some artistic tendencies, anyway. There are those knifemakers who have a basic understanding of form, and those who excel at making lines flow, shapes emerge and beings take form.

It is the latter group of talented artisans with a flair for the fantastic that we showcase herein. It is their work that surpasses the institutional artist who knows the difference between baroque and impressionism. No, instead, the folks who practice knife art, some with formal training, and others from the institute of hard knocks, understand the difference between "broke" and "impressive."

Joe Kertzman

◄**TAYLOR PALMER:** Two sides of a knife give multiple insights into the military life of Pvt. Calvin Atwood, USMC, all in carved bronze, all inside a blade.

STEPHEN OLSZEWSKI: King Arthur and Guinevere overlook their courts of cut.

▲**BARRY GALLAGHER:** Carved bolsters and pearl, heat-blued dragonflies-pattern damascus, a "gold-nugget-textured" steel back strap—it's all in a day's work in the knife shop, or shall we call it a studio? (BladeGallery.com photo)

◀**LLOYD PENDLETON:** Blades of a feather flock together. (PointSeven photo)

▼**MATTHEW LERCH:** Carved mother-of-pearl puts a face to the knife, and Damasteel gives it a little spine.

▶**HARUMI HIRAYAMA:** Any dinner guest would be on cloud nine with this billowy kitchen knife grip—carved from a thick piece of mother of pearl—at hand.

▶**TAI GOO:** The act of beautifying a knife handle often coincides with making it functional. The blade is wootz steel, and, as for the grip, lignum vitae.

▶**RICK DUNKERLEY:** Textured and carved pearl is gripping in more ways than one. (PointSeven photo)

▶**GAIL LUNN:** A gilded frog straddles a carved-bone lily pad, honing his fly-catching skills.

◀**JOSEPH SZILASKI:** "Steel, ivory, heck, I'll carve it all. It's no sweat off my beak."

▶**SCOTT SLOBODIAN:** Dynasties were built upon Chinese-style knives like this. The dragon-skin damascus is accompanied by an intricately carved stag-horn handle of dragon proportions. (Slobodian takes his own pictures, too. Go figure.)

▶**LARRY FUEGEN:** One would not work without the others, not the carved-mammoth-ivory handle, the carved ladder-pattern-damascus blade or the engraved sterling-silver band.

▶**STEVE JERNIGAN:** Deeply carved are stainless damascus and black-lip pearl. The wavy lines encircle the frame and blade, ingraining themselves into the memory banks of all who bear witness. (PointSeven photo)

▼**JODY and PAT MULLER:** Hand-carved blackwood finds itself in the company of a composite damascus blade.

◀**DONALD VOGT:** Carved is the Devin Thomas damascus blade, the Robert Eggerling damascus bolsters, the mother-of-pearl handle, the knife, actually, and the medium is sharp, so, so sharp.

▲**RICHARD WRIGHT:** Front and rear bolsters are made from sterling silver and are carved in a fluted design, with leaves on the front bolster.

◀**LARRY LUNN:** A sculpted mother-of-pearl handle blossoms in the limelight.

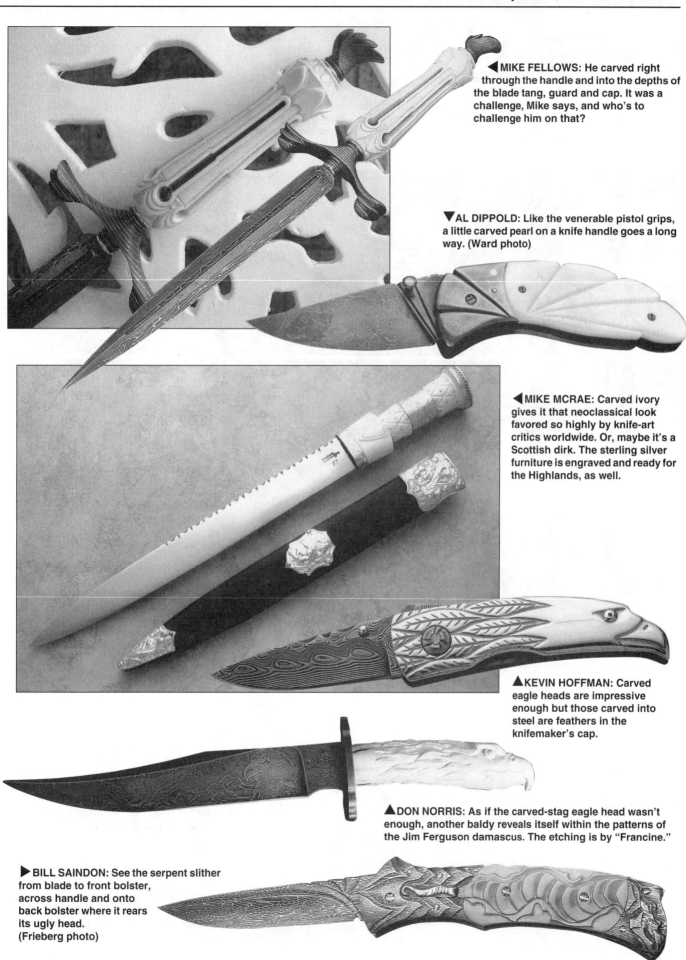

◄MIKE FELLOWS: He carved right through the handle and into the depths of the blade tang, guard and cap. It was a challenge, Mike says, and who's to challenge him on that?

▼AL DIPPOLD: Like the venerable pistol grips, a little carved pearl on a knife handle goes a long way. (Ward photo)

◄MIKE MCRAE: Carved ivory gives it that neoclassical look favored so highly by knife-art critics worldwide. Or, maybe it's a Scottish dirk. The sterling silver furniture is engraved and ready for the Highlands, as well.

▲KEVIN HOFFMAN: Carved eagle heads are impressive enough but those carved into steel are feathers in the knifemaker's cap.

▲DON NORRIS: As if the carved-stag eagle head wasn't enough, another baldy reveals itself within the patterns of the Jim Ferguson damascus. The etching is by "Francine."

▶BILL SAINDON: See the serpent slither from blade to front bolster, across handle and onto back bolster where it rears its ugly head. (Frieberg photo)

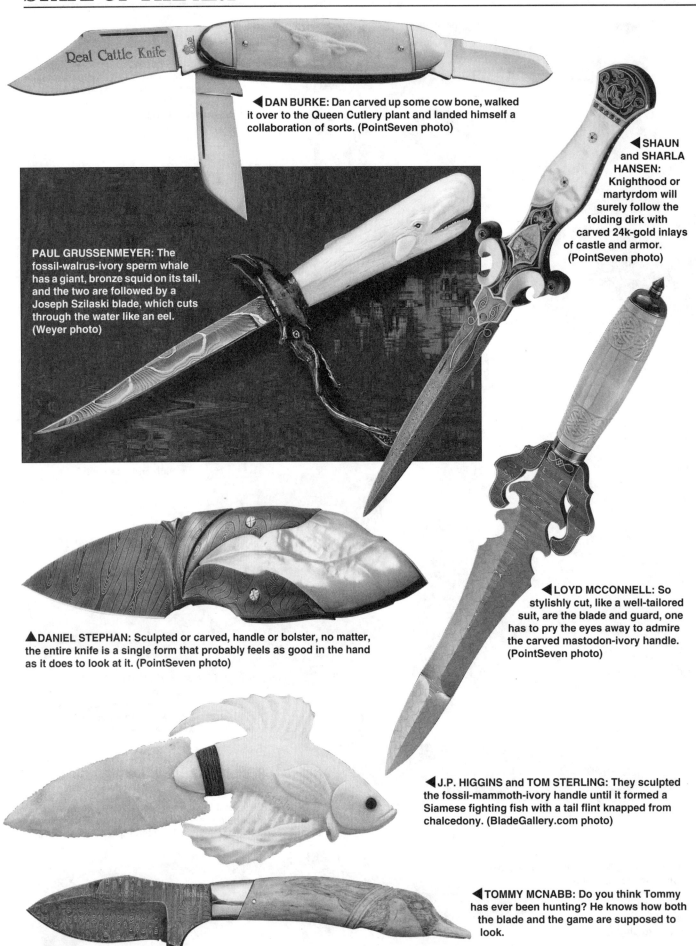

DAN BURKE: Dan carved up some cow bone, walked it over to the Queen Cutlery plant and landed himself a collaboration of sorts. (PointSeven photo)

SHAUN and SHARLA HANSEN: Knighthood or martyrdom will surely follow the folding dirk with carved 24k-gold inlays of castle and armor. (PointSeven photo)

PAUL GRUSSENMEYER: The fossil-walrus-ivory sperm whale has a giant, bronze squid on its tail, and the two are followed by a Joseph Szilaski blade, which cuts through the water like an eel. (Weyer photo)

DANIEL STEPHAN: Sculpted or carved, handle or bolster, no matter, the entire knife is a single form that probably feels as good in the hand as it does to look at it. (PointSeven photo)

LOYD MCCONNELL: So stylishly cut, like a well-tailored suit, are the blade and guard, one has to pry the eyes away to admire the carved mastodon-ivory handle. (PointSeven photo)

J.P. HIGGINS and TOM STERLING: They sculpted the fossil-mammoth-ivory handle until it formed a Siamese fighting fish with a tail flint knapped from chalcedony. (BladeGallery.com photo)

TOMMY MCNABB: Do you think Tommy has ever been hunting? He knows how both the blade and the game are supposed to look.

The Color Guard

Here's something as deep as the bluest ocean and as perplex as the most vivid of rainbows. I once heard this little tidbit from a semi-reliable source, but to be accurate, I took a minute to research it and uncover the truth. Sure enough, Merriam Webster's Collegiate Dictionary, Tenth Edition defines color as a "phenomenon" of light, or a visual "perception" that enables one to differentiate otherwise identical objects. You see, or wait, I guess you don't see, but anyway, color has more to do with the way light hits things and the way we observe the reflecting light than the actual hue of the objects themselves. It is perceived. It is a phenomenon (or an observable object known through the senses.) How do you like those apples? Seeing stars, are you? Did someone turn out the lights? Are you in a purple haze? Feel like you are fumbling through the dark?

That's understandable, just take a good look at the most colorful knives in the world, and you'll be back to your senses in no time. Your focus will slowly readjust; it will sharpen, if you will, and you'll be seeing the colors for what they really are, or at least for how you perceive them to be. Regardless, have at it, and remember that the objects in the book are closer to true colors than they appear.

Joe Kertzman

DEVIN THOMAS: *The damascus blade is a perfect complement to the titanium frame and Tiger Iron inserts on this beautiful locking-liner folder from Melvin Nishiuchi. (Michael Fong photo)*

◄ **W.J. MCDONALD**: *Maybe next time the maker will choose a handle with a little color for his Loveless-style drop-point hunter. It's stabilized maple burl dyed blue, by the way.*

▲ **D'ALTON HOLDER**: *The mastodon-tooth handle is the color of a saber-toothed tiger. (PointSeven photo)*

DON HANSON III: *Where ▶ Don got the 18k red gold that he carved into bolsters, or the green, purple and pink black-lip pearl he employed as a handle, no one knows, but I think he has a secret stash hidden somewhere.*

RICK DUNKERLEY: ▶
Grape juice anyone?
(PointSeven photo)

ETORE BERTUZZI: *This* ▶
replica of a Ron Lake inte-
gral deserves mention for
its swell random-pattern-
damascus blade and
equally fetching lapis han-
dle inlay.

BARRY GALLAGHER: *Abuzz with action* ▼
is the Green Hornet Folder, swarming
with a winged ladder-pattern-damas-
cus handle, paua-shell inlays, 14
emeralds and a hornet-pattern
mosaic-damascus stinger.
(BladeGallery.com
photo)

▶ **MARVIN SOLOMON:** *It's*
green malachite and damascus,
and you'd better do what
Solomon says. (Ward photo)

JOE CORDOVA: *It might* ▶
be imitation tortoise shell, but
any sea turtle worth its salt
would proudly don the same
colors. (KnifeShop.tv photo)

DWIGHT TOWELL: *A royal purple Charoite stone is crowned with engraving and raised 24k gold.*

MICHAEL WALKER: ▶
Flames shoot across the "zippered" damascus blade, a gold star blazes on the bolster, and gold-inlaid titanium sends a knife into orbit. (PointSeven photo)

JERRY MCCLURE: *With blue-* ▶ *mastodon-ivory handle, blue-anodized-titanium liners and a sapphire thumb stud, it's definitely a boy's toy. (Klosson photo)*

MILTON CHOATE: *The red-and-black Micarta®, yellow amber and green Corian represent the colors of the Vietnam In Country Service Ribbon.* ▼

KEVIN HARVEY: *These* ▲ *are the colors you get when you hot gun blue bubble-and-squeak-pattern damascus. Perhaps the name of the damascus is derived from the fact that these are the same colors you get when bubble gum sticks to the bottom of your shoe. (Louw photo)*

◀ **JACK LEVIN:** *Decorated in the late baroque style, the fluted blade is carved from Swedish damascus, including all profiles resembling the outlines of old armor. Chris Meyer and Ron Nott engraved the Roman-type folding dagger, and when the blade is opened, it activates a switch knuckle shield, which simultaneously shoots open into the vertical position. (PointSeven photo)*

CORBET SIGMAN: Who ▶ says pink isn't a good color for a knife? (KnifeShop.tv photo)

GLENN WATERS: The "Aoi Cho" ▶ (Blue Butterfly) knife never flutters, or falters, once! It just flits and dances.

JIM SORNBERGER: The color-engraved tiger looks real against a blue-green background with amber ◀ waves of grass.

RUSS KOMMER: Blue ▶ zebras walk out of the green forest (black-lip pearl) and across the Gerome Weinand damascus blade and bolsters. (PointSeven photo)

MARK STEINBRECHER: A ▶ pair of double-action folding daggers showcase carved elephant ivory handles overlaid with gold twisted wire, Robert Eggerling damascus blades and bolsters, and malachite inlays. (PointSeven photo)

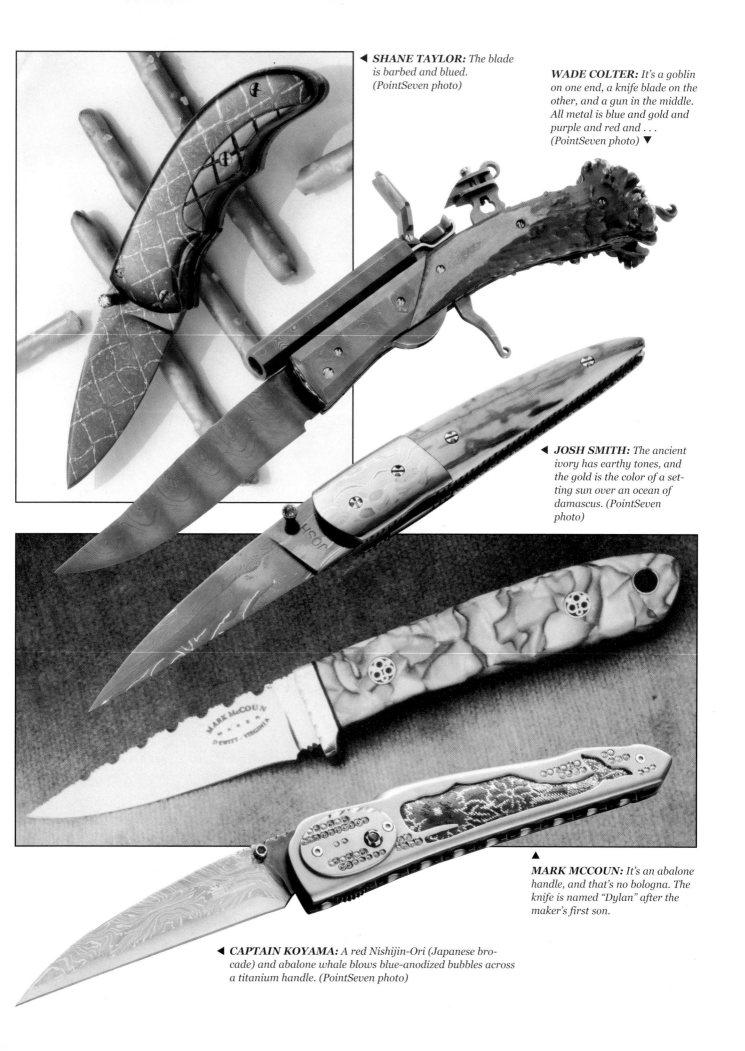

SHANE TAYLOR: The blade is barbed and blued. (PointSeven photo) ◄

WADE COLTER: It's a goblin on one end, a knife blade on the other, and a gun in the middle. All metal is blue and gold and purple and red and . . . (PointSeven photo) ▼

◄ **JOSH SMITH:** The ancient ivory has earthy tones, and the gold is the color of a setting sun over an ocean of damascus. (PointSeven photo)

▲ **MARK MCCOUN:** It's an abalone handle, and that's no bologna. The knife is named "Dylan" after the maker's first son.

◄ **CAPTAIN KOYAMA:** A red Nishijin-Ori (Japanese brocade) and abalone whale blows blue-anodized bubbles across a titanium handle. (PointSeven photo)

JOE CORDOVA: *First Betsy Ross did it with needle and thread, and now Joe does it with beads. (KnifeShop.tv photo)* ▶

◀ **JEFF HALL:** *The "Mean Streak" features "eroded" G-10 handle scales with "worm holes," and blue-gray camouflage-titanium handle liners with a matching pocket clip. (PointSeven photo)*

LYNN MAXFIELD: *The Kitty Paw knife doesn't spit up any hairballs, but it has a reconstituted malachite handle (and an emerald thumb button.)* ▶

STEVE HILL: *Steve says the colors in* ▶ *the mammoth ivory remind him of an aerial view of Florida, hence the title of the knife—"Gator Country." That's a cool alligator carved into Steve Schwarzer's swampy water-pattern-damascus bolster, too. Robert Eggerling can be credited for the blade steel.*

OWEN WOOD: *A thorn bush grows toward a thorny blade. (PointSeven photo)*

DRAPER FAMILY (MELISSA, AUDRA AND MIKE): *A synthetic abalone handle was just the thing for Melissa's knife, looking much like sparkly wrapping paper for a gifted child. (BladeGallery.com photo)* ▶

JOHN LEWIS JENSEN: *John* ▲ *claims the "Succubus" knife is named after those lascivious female spirits that seduce men in their sleep, adding that it is a sensual, elegant and extreme folder seeming to be stalking or creeping, possibly a feline-type creature frozen in its prowl.*

CHARLES KAIN: *A rock-and-roll band named the "Scorpions" once said it was "love at first sting." (KnifeShop.tv photo)* ▶

GERALD CORBIT: *Color scrimshaw by Gary Williams meets engraving by Chris Meyer head-on in a showdown of the big cats.* ▲

TOM FERRY: *The Timascus handle is carved to give the appearance of flames spreading across an already blue-flame-hot knife. The blade is Talonite. (BladeGallery.com photo)* ▲

KEVIN HOFFMAN: *We know the kokapelli isn't singing acappella.* ▶

▲ **BOB APPLEBY:** *It's ice blue and it has a steely glare.*

◀ **JOT SINGH KHALSA:** *This one makes us all green with envy. (Coop photo)*

◀ **SCOTT SLOBODIAN:** *Dyed, tiger-striped maple makes us all see red.*

PETE FORTHOFER: *I guess it shouldn't be surprising how something buried under the earth for thousands of years, like mammoth ivory, takes on such earthy tones.*

◀ **PETER MARTIN:** *The fantasy bug knife is a beetle with slip-joint wing blades of powdered-mosaic-damascus steel. The body is apple coral, black-lip pearl and mammoth tooth, and the bug has opal eyes.*

Some Dynamite Damascus

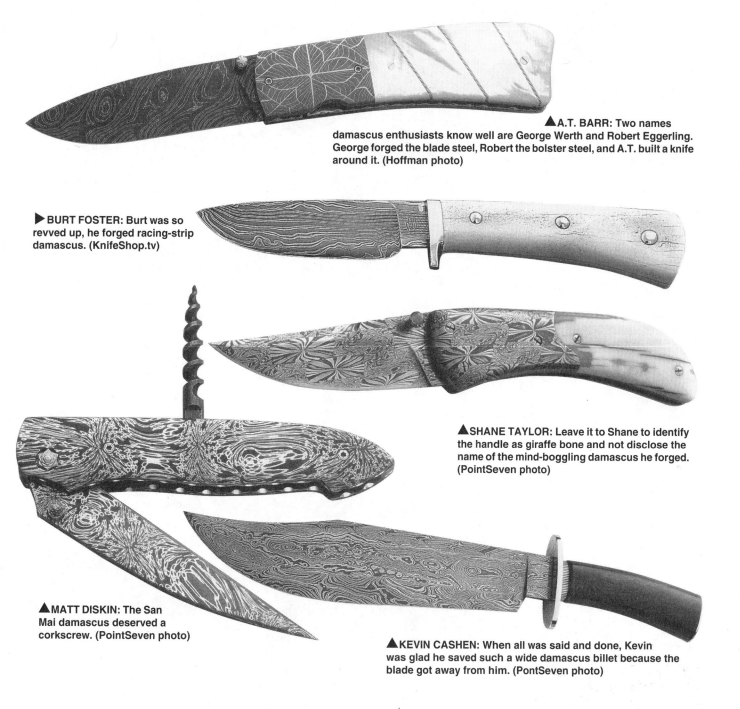

▲**A.T. BARR:** Two names damascus enthusiasts know well are George Werth and Robert Eggerling. George forged the blade steel, Robert the bolster steel, and A.T. built a knife around it. (Hoffman photo)

▶**BURT FOSTER:** Burt was so revved up, he forged racing-strip damascus. (KnifeShop.tv)

▲**SHANE TAYLOR:** Leave it to Shane to identify the handle as giraffe bone and not disclose the name of the mind-boggling damascus he forged. (PointSeven photo)

▲**MATT DISKIN:** The San Mai damascus deserved a corkscrew. (PointSeven photo)

▲**KEVIN CASHEN:** When all was said and done, Kevin was glad he saved such a wide damascus billet because the blade got away from him. (PontSeven photo)

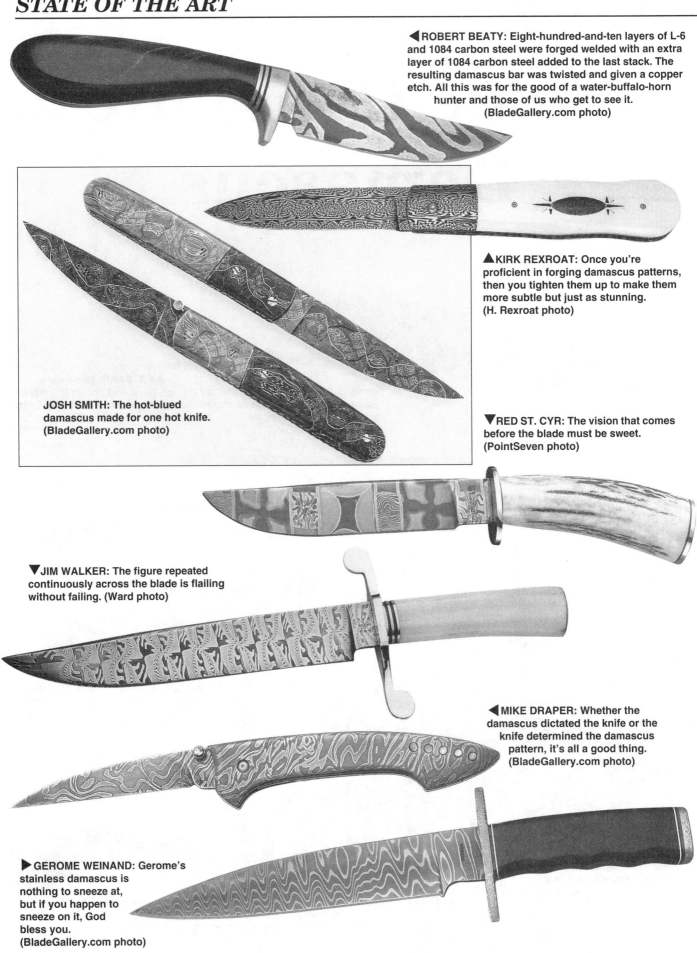

◀ROBERT BEATY: Eight-hundred-and-ten layers of L-6 and 1084 carbon steel were forged welded with an extra layer of 1084 carbon steel added to the last stack. The resulting damascus bar was twisted and given a copper etch. All this was for the good of a water-buffalo-horn hunter and those of us who get to see it. (BladeGallery.com photo)

JOSH SMITH: The hot-blued damascus made for one hot knife. (BladeGallery.com photo)

▲KIRK REXROAT: Once you're proficient in forging damascus patterns, then you tighten them up to make them more subtle but just as stunning. (H. Rexroat photo)

▼RED ST. CYR: The vision that comes before the blade must be sweet. (PointSeven photo)

▼JIM WALKER: The figure repeated continuously across the blade is flailing without failing. (Ward photo)

◀MIKE DRAPER: Whether the damascus dictated the knife or the knife determined the damascus pattern, it's all a good thing. (BladeGallery.com photo)

▶GEROME WEINAND: Gerome's stainless damascus is nothing to sneeze at, but if you happen to sneeze on it, God bless you. (BladeGallery.com photo)

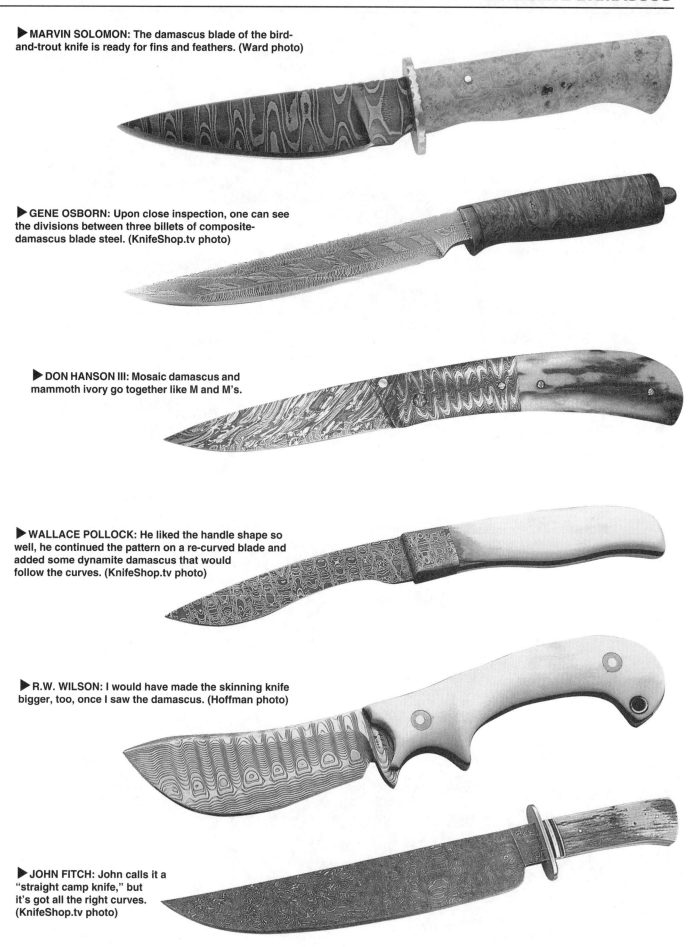

▶ MARVIN SOLOMON: The damascus blade of the bird-and-trout knife is ready for fins and feathers. (Ward photo)

▶ GENE OSBORN: Upon close inspection, one can see the divisions between three billets of composite-damascus blade steel. (KnifeShop.tv photo)

▶ DON HANSON III: Mosaic damascus and mammoth ivory go together like M and M's.

▶ WALLACE POLLOCK: He liked the handle shape so well, he continued the pattern on a re-curved blade and added some dynamite damascus that would follow the curves. (KnifeShop.tv photo)

▶ R.W. WILSON: I would have made the skinning knife bigger, too, once I saw the damascus. (Hoffman photo)

▶ JOHN FITCH: John calls it a "straight camp knife," but it's got all the right curves. (KnifeShop.tv photo)

◄MELVIN NISHIUCHI: The raindrop-pattern damascus by Devin Thomas has a pooling effect with the labradorite stone handle. (Fong photo)

►KIRK REXROAT: Old-school mosaic damascus had thick lines and resulting boxy patterns, but not the new stuff. Strut it, Kirk. (BladeGallery.com photo)

▲BRUCE BUMP: This leading champion of a cause is aptly named "Paladin." (BladeGallery.com photo)

►BILL BUXTON: Bill Buxton's fighter shows off radial-pattern damascus. (Hoffman photo)

►CLIFF PARKER: A zigzag damascus pattern resembles lightening bolts exploding across blade and bolsters, and it's just as electrifying, too. (BladeGallery.com photo)

◄LARRY LUNN: Such a clean, pearl-handle automatic dagger deserves a network of subtle lines. Larry gives credit for the damascus to Robert Eggerling. (Weyer photo)

◄BOB DOGGETT: Damasteel is a perfect fit for a Bob Loveless-style boot knife. (Hoffman photo)

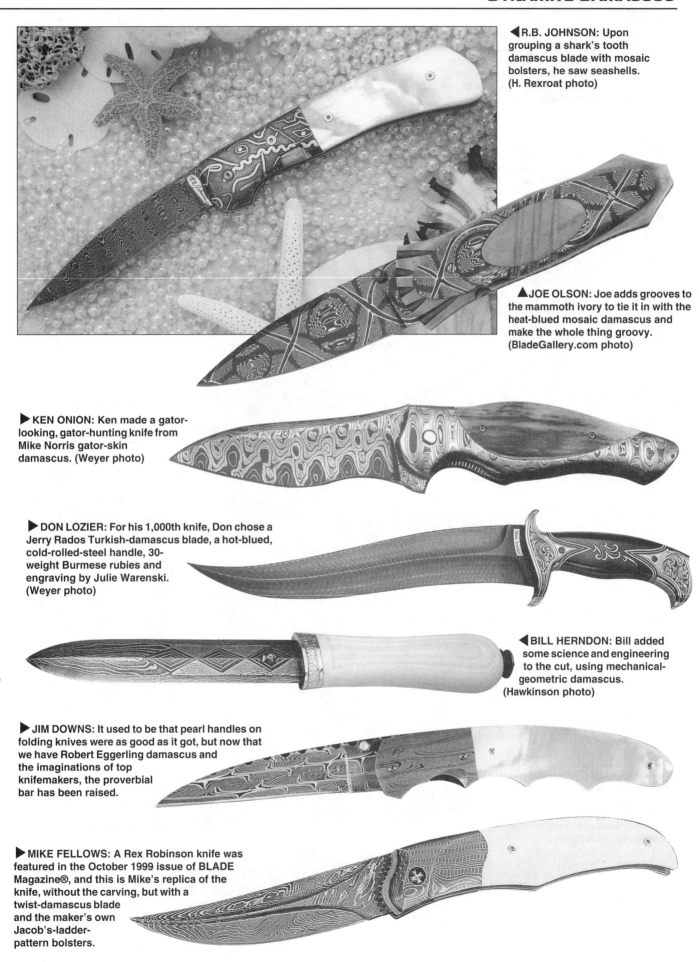

◀R.B. JOHNSON: Upon grouping a shark's tooth damascus blade with mosaic bolsters, he saw seashells. (H. Rexroat photo)

▲JOE OLSON: Joe adds grooves to the mammoth ivory to tie it in with the heat-blued mosaic damascus and make the whole thing groovy. (BladeGallery.com photo)

▶KEN ONION: Ken made a gator-looking, gator-hunting knife from Mike Norris gator-skin damascus. (Weyer photo)

▶DON LOZIER: For his 1,000th knife, Don chose a Jerry Rados Turkish-damascus blade, a hot-blued, cold-rolled-steel handle, 30-weight Burmese rubies and engraving by Julie Warenski. (Weyer photo)

◀BILL HERNDON: Bill added some science and engineering to the cut, using mechanical-geometric damascus. (Hawkinson photo)

▶JIM DOWNS: It used to be that pearl handles on folding knives were as good as it got, but now that we have Robert Eggerling damascus and the imaginations of top knifemakers, the proverbial bar has been raised.

▶MIKE FELLOWS: A Rex Robinson knife was featured in the October 1999 issue of BLADE Magazine®, and this is Mike's replica of the knife, without the carving, but with a twist-damascus blade and the maker's own Jacob's-ladder-pattern bolsters.

►**GERALD CORBIT:** Who says dots and stripes don't match? Robert Eggerling provided the bolster steel, and Harry Limings engraved the gold inlays on the back spacer.

▼**REINHARD TSCHAGER:** The A. Mlach mosaic-damascus blade actually emulates the mosaic tiles, photographs and patchwork quilts of which many folks are familiar.

▼**OWEN WOOD:** The titanium bolsters and damascus blade are a dynamic duo. (PointSeven photo)

►**SCOTT TAYLOR:** Gold wire inlay on a fluted ivory handle is a smashing success, and even more so when it leads into career-changing 10-inch random-pattern damascus blade and guard. (KnifeShop.tv photo)

◄**RICHARD EPTING:** He hailed from Damascus and carried a forged folder he opened with one hand. (KnifeShop.tv)

►**BARRY GALLAGHER:** Heat rolled radials and rods pull up to a mosaic-damascus bolster before switching gears into a dovetailed, sculpted-fossil-ivory grip. (BladeGallery.com photo)

◄**D.B. FRALEY:** Are they faces, ghosts, cells or eggs in an incubator? It's fun to guess, isn't it? Devin Thomas, who forged the damascus, could probably tell us. (PointSeven photo)

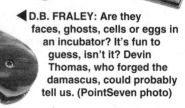

▶TOM FERRY: The Persian folder arches its back and lets its damascus roar. (Weyer photo)

▲DAN BURKE: The blued-damascus blades and bolsters of a dogleg jackknife are the epitome of an epiphany. (PointSeven photo)

▶TODD BEGG: This one is damascus to the core. (BladeGallery.com photo)

◀JAMES LUMAN: Ethiopian-cross damascus makes a hunter a bit more respectable. (BladeGallery.com photo)

◀BRUCE FULLER: Do you ever get the feeling that those forging random-pattern damascus aren't always doing it so randomly? (KnifeShop.tv photo)

▶RICK EATON: Mosaic damascus flexes its muscles and bulges out the knife handle a bit. (PointSeven photo)

◀DENNIS FRIEDLY: Step One: Use Robert Eggerling ladder-pattern damascus. (BladeGallery.com photo)

Fitted Sheaths

▶KENNY ROWE: The ray skin inlay is plum colored and plum pretty.

▲LOYD THOMSEN: Loyd likes his knives enough to tuck them in and secure them with a snap.

◀JOE KEESLAR: The western-style loop sheath walks tall and wears a badge.

▼DAVE COLE: The cobra skin acts as a hood over the pointed head of a fixed blade.

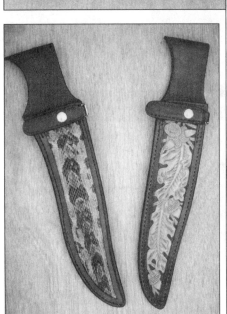

▲KENNY ROWE: One rattles like a snake and the other shakes like a leaf.

▲ROGER and TERESA JONES: Handcrafted, raised-leather panels are held together with Spanish braid and handmade studs.

▲KENNY ROWE: Not one to toot his own horn, Kenny lets the hand-tooled elephant trumpet the sheath.

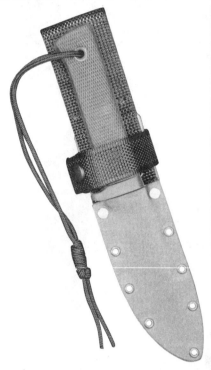

▲SCOTT HENDRYX: The hunter belt sheath is designed specifically for skinning knives and other hunting blades in the 5-inch and shorter range.

RICK BRUNER: After stitching the sheath shut, Rick gave up the thimble for the good of the design.

◀CHRIS KRAVITT: This pouch sheath is entwined with art nouveau vine work.

▲CHRIS KRAVITT: A classic Mexican-loop-style sheath exhibits western floral carving and calfskin lacing on the edge.

▲RICK BRUNER: Any buckskinner would be proud to wear the brown-leather neck sheath with lizard skin insert and colored trade beads.

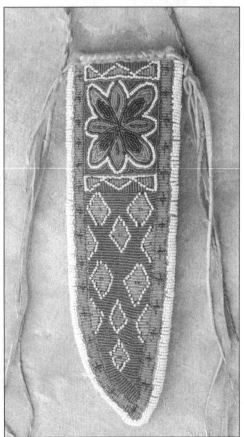

▲PEGGY PATRICK: I've always said, "It's amazing what you can do with antique seed beads and brain tan buckskin."

STATE OF THE ART

JOE KEESLAR: That's some shoulder blade.

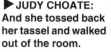

JAY MAINES: It took the hides of a water buffalo and a python to make this sheath, so the lesson is to always save your hides.

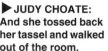

JUDY CHOATE: And she tossed back her tassel and walked out of the room.

SCOTT HENDRYX: When Scott builds sheaths, he considers things like concealment, comfort and safety

ROBERT NIX: Nine knives are dressed to the nines.

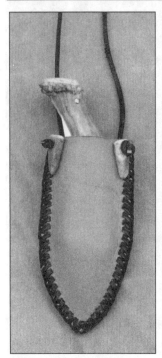

DAVE COLE: He used a couple parts of the deer for the laced neck sheath—the skin for the pouch and antler tips as decoration.

ROBERT ROSSDEUTSCHER: When the knife is in the sheath, the damascus blade pattern becomes the turtle's shell.

Word and Picture Smiths

THERE IS A biohazard seeping into one blade, bats flying across another, the U.S. flag in the bolsters of a folding knife and Mardi Gras-type masks popping up all over the blade of a fourth knife. Anything from creepy spiders to the knifemakers' names can seemingly, willfully be forged into blade and bolster steel.

It's not that easy, but masters always make the extremely difficult look effortless, don't they?

If you've ever watched Michael Jordan play basketball, Pete Sampras hit a tennis ball or Barry Sanders run with a football, you realize that certain individuals are born with so much talent, they exude style and grace while performing the impossible.

Bladesmith Josh Smith's name in the blade and bolster of a folding knife didn't just appear there because he etched it, engraved it or blackened it through heat or with a blade coating. Many bladesmiths today practice "canned" or "canister" steel forging. They make metal pre-forms and insert them into cans or canisters, they select two, three or more types of powdered metal, pour a certain type of metal into one pre-form or another and the others into the containers around the forms. They forge the metal right in the cans, cut the containers, press the metal, pound it, cut it, form it, heat it, pound it and heat it again until shapes emerge, usually the ones they intended to appear, within the steel.

Other word-and-picture smiths forge mosaic damascus, skipping the cans and canisters, but cutting metal into shapes and forging those shapes together with other metals that etch differently, until the desired words and pictures form on the surface of blade steel.

I'd love to record the faces of novice bladesmiths who successfully forge mosaic damascus or powdered, canister steel for the first time. It would be priceless to have a camera running when the stars-and-stripes damascus pattern a rookie bladesmith hoped for, planned for and sweated over actually resulted in stars and stripes. The reaction would be similar to the startled faces of folks reading a book and coming across a section of word-and-picture blades, staring in awe at the steely wonders within the book chapter. That must be a funny sight.

Joe Kertzman

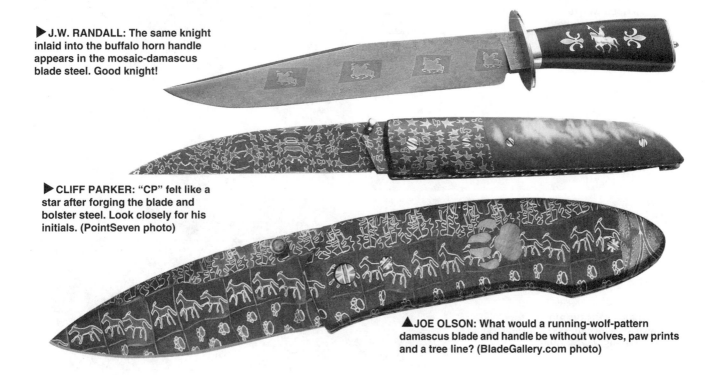

▶J.W. RANDALL: The same knight inlaid into the buffalo horn handle appears in the mosaic-damascus blade steel. Good knight!

▶CLIFF PARKER: "CP" felt like a star after forging the blade and bolster steel. Look closely for his initials. (PointSeven photo)

▲JOE OLSON: What would a running-wolf-pattern damascus blade and handle be without wolves, paw prints and a tree line? (BladeGallery.com photo)

BARRY GALLAGHER: Just in time for Harley Davidson's 100th anniversary celebration is a folder with a blued "Live To Ride" damascus blade forged by Ed Schempp. (BladeGallery.com photo)

GARY HOUSE: A selection of Gary House blade billets illustrates some of the patterning possible using a handful of steels. (PointSeven photo)

RON NEWTON: Ron likes the angel-wing folders (with handles carved to resemble wings) so well that he forged an angels-and-halos blade to complete the heavenly theme. (KnifeShop.tv photo)

KIRK REXROAT: Just to keep the ride-'em-cowboy steel fenced in, Kirk filed a barbed-wire ferrule. (PointSeven photo)

JOSH SMITH: That's his name forged right into the blade and bolster. No joshing! (PointSeven photo)

HANK KNICKMEYER: Why use a tang stamp when you can forge your initials into a blade? (PointSeven photo)

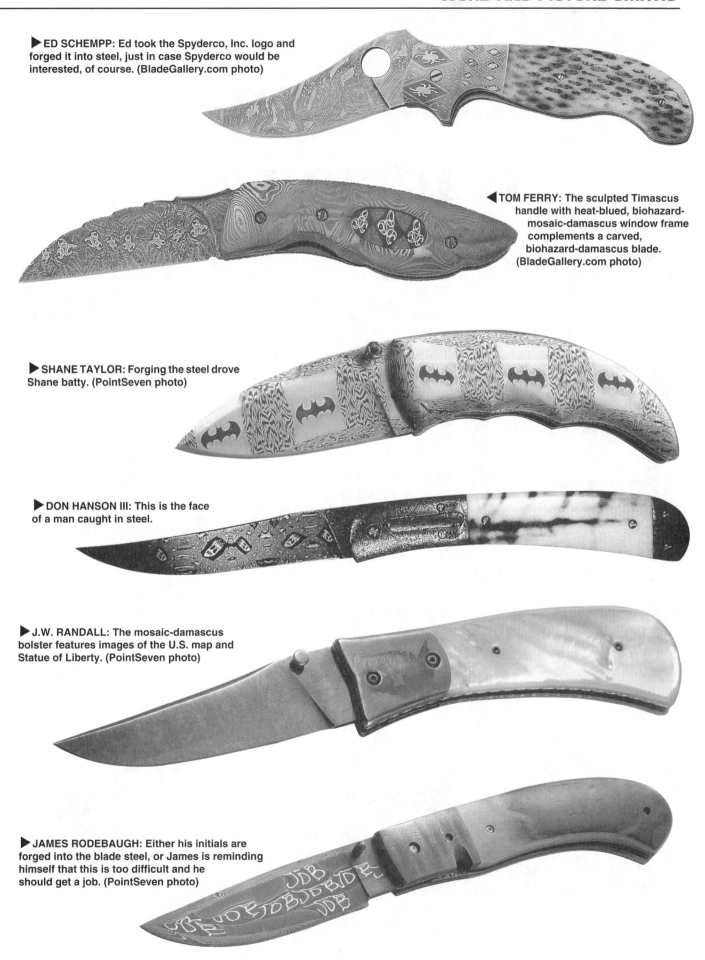

►**ED SCHEMPP:** Ed took the Spyderco, Inc. logo and forged it into steel, just in case Spyderco would be interested, of course. (BladeGallery.com photo)

◄**TOM FERRY:** The sculpted Timascus handle with heat-blued, biohazard-mosaic-damascus window frame complements a carved, biohazard-damascus blade. (BladeGallery.com photo)

►**SHANE TAYLOR:** Forging the steel drove Shane batty. (PointSeven photo)

►**DON HANSON III:** This is the face of a man caught in steel.

►**J.W. RANDALL:** The mosaic-damascus bolster features images of the U.S. map and Statue of Liberty. (PointSeven photo)

►**JAMES RODEBAUGH:** Either his initials are forged into the blade steel, or James is reminding himself that this is too difficult and he should get a job. (PointSeven photo)

Engaging Engraving

MANY COME FROM the gun field. They start by engraving some of the most intricate and sought-after guns man has ever laid his greedy little hands on and held close, admiring the workmanship. Eventually, competition becomes steep, so

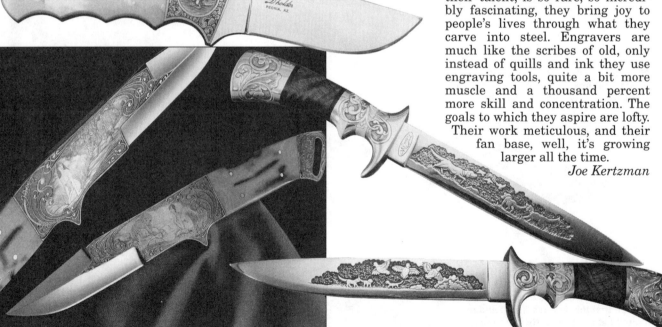

BRUCE SHAW: Nothing less than an 18k-gold eagle disk and scroll engraving would do for a D'Alton Holder knife.

steep, the gun engravers, unless they are the best of the best in their field, start to feel the pressure.

What seems like endless hours peering through magnifying glasses with engravers in their hands, attempting to scratch out a living, literally, turns into years of detailed steel manipulation. Oh, their fan base is large. Many admirers inspect their work, but it is a thankless job, really. No Pulitzer Prizes are granted, no Oscars are accepted, no visits to presidential palaces or the White House. No, it's introspective critiquing and feedback from vocal

customers. Perfecting the art are those who believe in their craft. They give of themselves freely until there is nothing left to give.

Some convert to knives where the competition is a little less steep and the hours, if luck finds them, somewhat less grueling. Some enter the knife world by choice because they realize knives as works of art and prefer the smaller canvasses and different traditional boundaries. In reality, the engravers, themselves, draw the only boundaries.

In the gun and knife fields, but especially in the knife industry, engravers truly are appreciated, whether they realize it or not. They are the ice cream men of the neighborhood, the mailmen and ladies of the community, the volunteer firemen of the township. Their art, their talent, is so rare, so incredibly fascinating, they bring joy to people's lives through what they carve into steel. Engravers are much like the scribes of old, only instead of quills and ink they use engraving tools, quite a bit more muscle and a thousand percent more skill and concentration. The goals to which they aspire are lofty. Their work meticulous, and their fan base, well, it's growing larger all the time.

Joe Kertzman

FRANS VAN ELDIK: The engraver just goes by "Gironi," and the knifemaker goes by "Sir," considering the knives he makes. It's a lady fighter, but the lady doesn't look to be in a fighting mood. (Van Tienhoven photo)

▲MICHAEL PARSONS: This one was literally a Parsons project, doing it the old-fashioned way—with walnut handle, brass bolsters and quail-and-setters engraving.

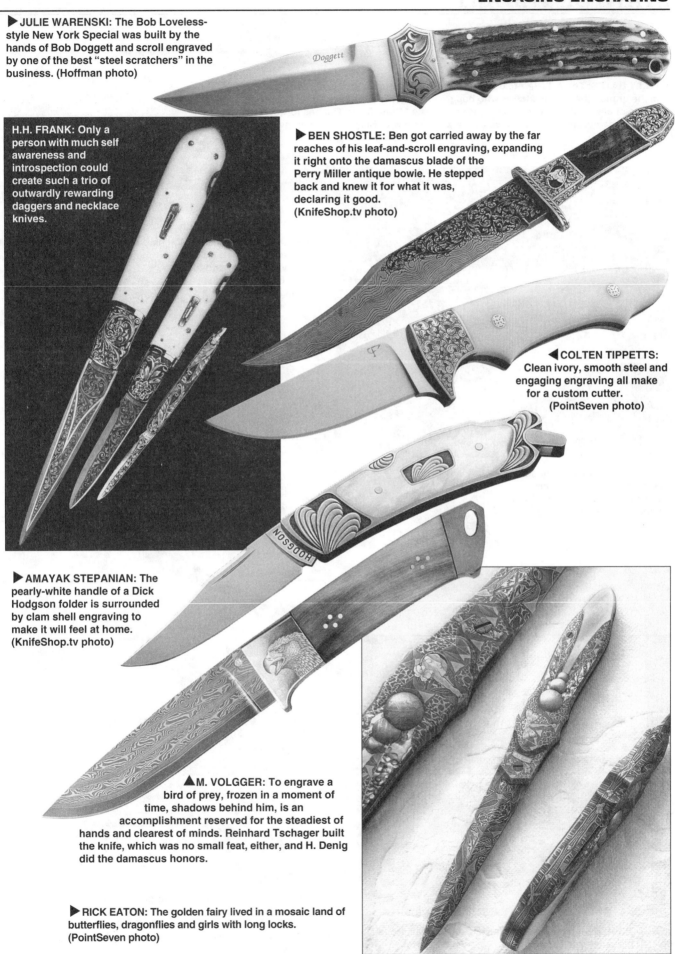

▶ JULIE WARENSKI: The Bob Loveless-style New York Special was built by the hands of Bob Doggett and scroll engraved by one of the best "steel scratchers" in the business. (Hoffman photo)

H.H. FRANK: Only a person with much self awareness and introspection could create such a trio of outwardly rewarding daggers and necklace knives.

▶ BEN SHOSTLE: Ben got carried away by the far reaches of his leaf-and-scroll engraving, expanding it right onto the damascus blade of the Perry Miller antique bowie. He stepped back and knew it for what it was, declaring it good. (KnifeShop.tv photo)

◀ COLTEN TIPPETTS: Clean ivory, smooth steel and engaging engraving all make for a custom cutter. (PointSeven photo)

▶ AMAYAK STEPANIAN: The pearly-white handle of a Dick Hodgson folder is surrounded by clam shell engraving to make it will feel at home. (KnifeShop.tv photo)

▲ M. VOLGGER: To engrave a bird of prey, frozen in a moment of time, shadows behind him, is an accomplishment reserved for the steadiest of hands and clearest of minds. Reinhard Tschager built the knife, which was no small feat, either, and H. Denig did the damascus honors.

▶ RICK EATON: The golden fairy lived in a mosaic land of butterflies, dragonflies and girls with long locks. (PointSeven photo)

▶ **BILLY BATES:** The A.T. Barr folder didn't happen overnight. The handle ivory came from the grandfather of a customer who bought the knife, and it seems Gramps brought the piece of elephant tusk back from Africa in the late 1800s. Devin Thomas forged the Spirograph damascus and A.T. chose to complement it with Billy's scroll engraving. (Hoffman photo)

▼ **BRUCE SHAW:** Michael Vagnino was inspired by Bruce's bolster engraving, so he hand-filed the liners of his damascus locking-liner folder. (Thurber photo)

STEVE DUNN: As a dog flushes wild game, so too does a knifemaker occasionally scare up a rare bird. (PointSeven photo)

◀ **NORVELL FOSTER:** Some guys, like Ernie Self, just want to make a classic damascus hunting knife with jigged-bone handle and engraved bolsters. Done.

GIL RUDOLPH: Hunting rabbits has never been so glamorous as depicted here on a Jim Martin folder. (PointSeven photo)

BARRY LEE HANDS: From the hands of master engraver Barry Lee Hands is a lifelike charging elephant, and though it might be the focal point, the rest of the Charles Sauer knife with elephant-skin-damascus blade and ivory handle is nothing to snub your trunk at. (PointSeven photo)

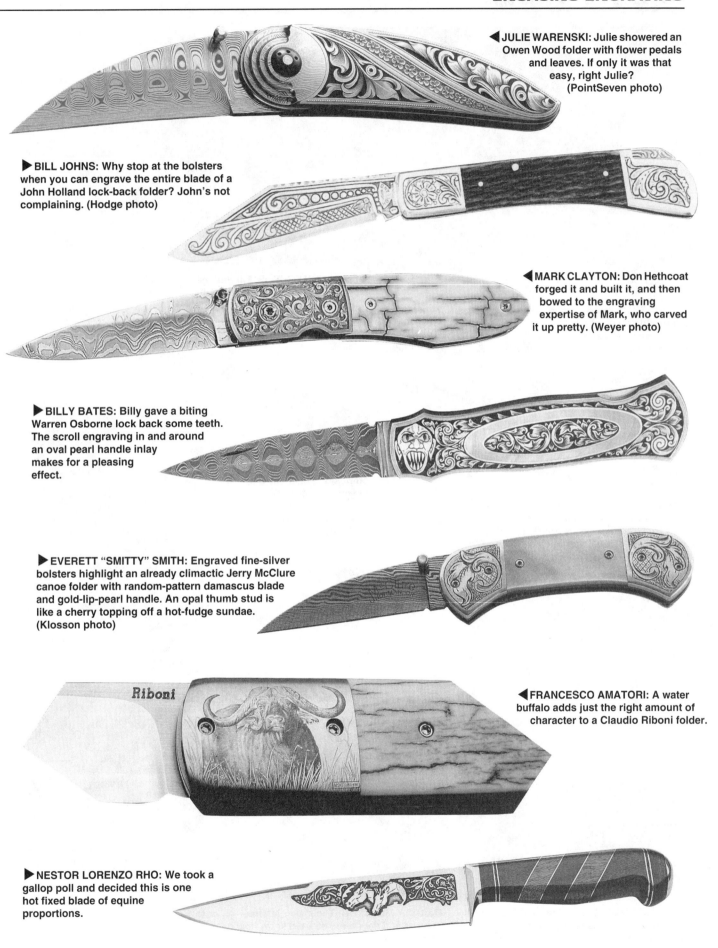

◄ JULIE WARENSKI: Julie showered an Owen Wood folder with flower pedals and leaves. If only it was that easy, right Julie? (PointSeven photo)

► BILL JOHNS: Why stop at the bolsters when you can engrave the entire blade of a John Holland lock-back folder? John's not complaining. (Hodge photo)

◄ MARK CLAYTON: Don Hethcoat forged it and built it, and then bowed to the engraving expertise of Mark, who carved it up pretty. (Weyer photo)

► BILLY BATES: Billy gave a biting Warren Osborne lock back some teeth. The scroll engraving in and around an oval pearl handle inlay makes for a pleasing effect.

► EVERETT "SMITTY" SMITH: Engraved fine-silver bolsters highlight an already climactic Jerry McClure canoe folder with random-pattern damascus blade and gold-lip-pearl handle. An opal thumb stud is like a cherry topping off a hot-fudge sundae. (Klosson photo)

◄ FRANCESCO AMATORI: A water buffalo adds just the right amount of character to a Claudio Riboni folder.

► NESTOR LORENZO RHO: We took a gallop poll and decided this is one hot fixed blade of equine proportions.

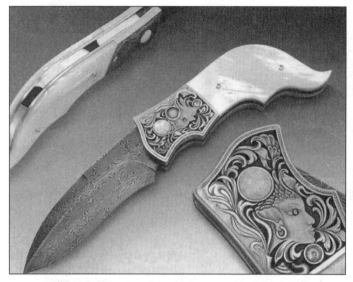

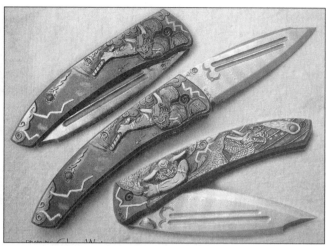

JOT SINGH KHALSA: A magical genie emerges from of a 24k-gold lamp, and you don't even have to rub the pearl knife handle, though you should feel free if you wish. The blade is Robert Eggerling's composite damascus, and the knife is all Khalsa. (Coop photo)

GLENN WATERS: Three-dimensional inlays and engraving depict Rai Jin, the god of thunder, beating on his drums, and Fu Jin, the god of wind, holding his windbag.

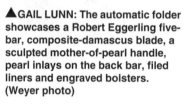

▲**JONNY WALKER NILSSON:** The reindeer-horn handle is three-dimensionally inlaid and engraved by Jonny with traditional bark coloring. Mattias Styrefors forged a dynamite damascus blade for the Sami-style Half Horn. (BladeGallery.com photo)

▲**GAIL LUNN:** The automatic folder showcases a Robert Eggerling five-bar, composite-damascus blade, a sculpted mother-of-pearl handle, pearl inlays on the back bar, filed liners and engraved bolsters. (Weyer photo)

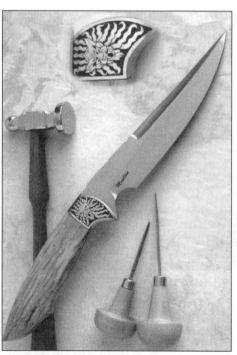

▲**GEORGE DAILEY:** This lovely little lopper is carved, carved some more, inlaid, filed, fit and finished. That's a lot of leg. (PointSeven photo)

▲**DUSTY MOULTON:** The maker left his hammer and engravers so we'd know how he accomplished it.

▲**CHRIS MEYER:** Thanks to Chris's gracious engraving, the Jack Levin folder stands as proud as a peacock. Skilled is the work of a knifemaker who can carve solid knife frames, including guards, from solid pieces of metal. The Peacock knife is decorated with more than 65 precious stones

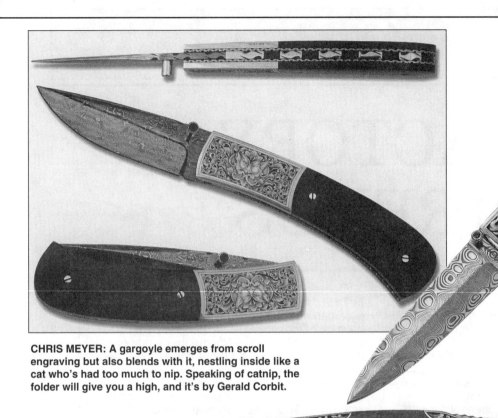

JULIE WARENSKI: Engraving kick starts a Howard Hitchmough folder, and Odin's Eye damascus keeps 'er running. Come to think of it, the pearl handle resembles a bike throttle, doesn't it? (PointSeven photo)

CHRIS MEYER: A gargoyle emerges from scroll engraving but also blends with it, nestling inside like a cat who's had too much to nip. Speaking of catnip, the folder will give you a high, and it's by Gerald Corbit.

HARRY LIMINGS: A good-old wood-handle lockback by Matthew Lerch is engraved as it should be.

JERE DAVIDSON: Entwining and entertaining are branches engraved on the guard and butt of an Edmund Davidson integral knife. Edmund credits Bob Loveless for the original design. (PointSeven photo)

JOYCE MINNICK: It's no fair. Jim Minnick's engraver lives so close by, he just builds the drop-dead-gorgeous knives and hands them off to Joyce like a steel baton. Then she turns them into magical wands. Thank Robert Eggerling for the damascus and Jim for carving it to match the rest of the knife. (PointSeven photo)

TIM HERMAN: Tim's the one who does one-of-a-kind colored rose engraving, one in the same who fashions the sleek Sliver knives. (PointSeven photo)

FACTORY TRENDS

It is a whole new world, a different ballgame when you are the marketing manager, public relations specialist, shop foreman or chief executive officer of a knife company. Production schedules, skids of steel, bins of knife parts, laser-cut blades, computer-numerically-controlled, automated machines with built-in cooling and ventilating systems all need your undivided attention, and all right now.

Inventories take place simultaneously with shipments, bill paying with profit and loss reports, employee payrolls with investment strategy meetings. And among the ruckus, someone needs to stay on top of the game, to keep score, to figure out a way to win!

Pick up the phone, dial the number of any knife production company and ask to speak to someone in charge. Apologize for bothering them and pose one, simple question. Ask, "Is it important to keep coming out with new knife models, patterns and styles, or can you rely on one proven design?" The answer will always be the same. Product development is the lifeblood of the knife industry. Without it, bankruptcy will likely follow.

Come on, how many new designs can there be? How many ways of cutting or improving the slice can a group of innovative individuals develop? Does there really need to be a better blade than what is already out there, and is there even a market for more knives? Yes, yes, yes and a resounding "Yes!" The vitality of the knife industry can be felt in every corner of every forgotten coat closet in all knife factories worldwide. The knife craft is alive and well.

The once-cottage knife industry is a full-blown multi-million-dollar business with devoted customers, informed consumers and discerning enthusiasts anxiously anticipating each new sharp model. They want them to cut, yes, but also to be convenient, comfortable, duty specific, loaded with gadgets, technologically advanced, simple but complex, and stately but exciting, all rolled into one bladed beast of a knife. So, factory heads, get to work. Earn your keep. Lunch break is over, and it's time to show your wares to the other cutting minds in the industry.

Joe Kertzman

Mid-Tech Knives Top the Trendsetters Heap

By Dexter Ewing

To SAY A knife is "handmade" means many things to many knife-makers, but in the author's opinion, it is an edged tool fashioned by one person who controls the processes leading up its completion. To refer to an edged tool as a "production knife" implies that is a commercially made, mass-produced piece. What defines a "mid-tech" knife? By combining handmade and production methods of building a knife or, in other words, by making some parts by hand and others by machine, a knifemaker arrives at a mid-tech knife, one that is a semi-custom or semi-production product.

A mid-tech knife is a bridge that spans the gap between custom and production methods of edged-tool manufacture. Knifemakers have been outputting mid-tech knives for a long time, but Ken Onion, to the author's knowledge, was the first to name them such and, like many catch phrases used by one person, it became popular with other knifemakers. Onion used the term to describe, and differentiate, his semi-custom knives that he assembled and tweaked but did not make in total, from those that took shape by his hands and his hands only. Could a simple term like "mid-tech" fuel customer desire for such pieces? From what the makers of mid-tech knives say, it has done just that.

Branton Knife Co.'s offerings spotlight custom knifemaker Walter Brend's timeless tactical designs. The top knife is the Model 2 fighter, followed by the Merrill's Marauder and the Boot Knife. Custom knifemaker Bobby Branton is a major force behind Branton Knife Co. (Hoffman photo)

Some will always remain true to the handcrafted knife, and others will respect the craft, but speed up production of the edged tools

Combat Elite's complete lineup of available frame-lock folders differs in the various handle treatments, from basic to "decked out," as illustrated here. The two gentlemen behind Combat Elite are certainly no newcomers to the knife industry. Darrel Ralph and Ryan Wilson are accomplished knifemakers in their own right, and through Combat Elite, they are building some of the best in mid-tech tactical folders available today. (Hoffman photo)

Nemesis Knives

Thumbing through knife magazines, readers might have stumbled across ads placed by Nemesis Knives. Who exactly is behind Nemesis Knives? Knifemaker Jeff Hall, who hails from Los Alamitos, California, is the driving force behind the young company's designs. The first Nemesis offering is the Imp, a small gentleman's locking-liner folder available in a variety of hardwood handles. A new Nemesis knife, the Arch Ally fixed blade is a compact tool delivered with a Mini Tek-Lock belt fastener, a neck chain and, thus, multiple carry options.

Worn slung from its bead chain and dangling down from around the neck, the Arch Ally doesn't print from underneath a shirt and is light enough to carry on a daily basis. The 2-1/2-inch modified-clip-point blade is hollow ground to take a keen edge. Steel of choice is CPM S30V, and the G-10 grip features a "worm-groove" milling pattern that enhances hand purchase and adds to the aesthetic quality of the knife. The Arch Ally is a small fixed blade that serves as an excellent utility knife for those who want an edge that's easy to carry.

The Nemesis Hellion fits the definition of a diminutive but tough knife, incorporating a 1-5/8-inch S30V blade. It is of integral construction with holes drilled through the handle to lighten the load. The Hellion comes with a molded-Kydex® sheath and works well in situations that call for a small fixed blade that's easy to access.

What's on the drawing board for upcoming Nemesis Knives projects? Jeff Hall spilled the beans on a mid-tech version of his popular custom tactical folder, the Bounty Hunter. The Nemesis version will have a 4-1/4-inch S30V blade, G-10 bolsters and "complementary handle materials." Overall length will be 9-5/8 inches with .08-inch-thick liners. The Nemesis version of the Bounty Hunter will definitely be a heavy-duty folder!

Muteki

American Bladesmith Society master smith Murray Carter has a piping-hot selection of mid-tech knives in his Muteki line. Each San Mai damascus blade parades a layer of Hitachi white steel sandwiched between two layers of 410 stainless steel. The Hitachi white steel registers 63-64 Rc on the Rockwell Hardness scale, and holds an edge well.

Carter's Muteki line runs the gamut from kitchen knives to hunt/camp knives, utility knives and neck knives. Carter assembles the handles and grinds the blades, so each Muteki piece leaves the shop having been subjected to his own special touch. Handle material choices include Macassar ebony, cocobolo, rosewood and Dymondwood.

One of Carter's most useful Muteki neck knives is the 3-1/4-inch wharncliffe model sporting an ironwood handle and a sizable finger choil for precise cutting control. This model, as with all other Muteki neck knives, comes with a molded-Kydex neck sheath so it can be worn comfortably and discreetly.

For those camp-knife fans out there, why not check out the Matagi? This beast has an 8-1/2-inch San Mai damascus blade, and a cocobolo, rosewood, Macassar ebony or Dymondwood handle. It has the heft to be a great chopping tool but exhibits great balance for tackling some tricky cutting tasks. A beautiful, hand-sewn and tooled-leather sheath completes the package, and the Matagi is one impressive piece of cutlery! Murray Carter's asking prices for the ironwood wharncliffe and the Matagi are $150 and $260, respectively.

American Bladesmith Society master smith Murray Carter's Muteki line of mid-tech knives features San Mai damascus blades and an impressive array of handle materials, from synthetics to bone, wood and mastodon ivory. The Muteki Matagi Camp Knife is an impressive piece with its 8-1/2-inch blade and wood handle. (Hoffman photo)

Simonich Knives, LLC's latest offerings include, from left to right, the Urban Raven, Bitterroot and Kootenai. All three are based on the hard-working designs of custom knifemaker Rob Simonich. (Hoffman photo)

Simonich Knives, LLC

Rob Simonich of Clancy, Mont. became known in knife circles for his stellar, custom Talonite® fixed blades, a reputation that presented him the opportunity to delve into mid-tech knives under the Simonich Knives, LLC umbrella. In 2002, Simonich Knives released its initial mid-tech offering, the Raven combat knife, shortly followed by the highly utilitarian Crowfoot multi-carry neck knife. Now, Simonich Knives has taken the wraps off its newest fixed blade designs, which are sure to prove as successful as the first two offerings.

The Urban Raven is essentially a scaled-down Raven, making it an ideal daily-carry belt knife. A wear-resistant, 4-inch, clip-point D-2 blade showcases double integral guards like its bigger brother, and Simonich's exclusive contoured and styled G-10 Gunner Grip promotes enhanced hand traction in any climate. The Urban Raven comes with a multi-carry Concealex® sheath, giving leeway to tote the knife horizontally or vertically on the belt.

The Kootenai is a medium-size drop-point hunter meant to fill the needs of serious hunters. It features a D-2 blade, and a contoured and rounded, black G-10 handle. Wrapping fingers around the Kootenai handle is like being one with the knife. Rob Simonich knows how to shape a grip. The 1/8-inch-thick, flat-ground D-2 blade proves useful for field dressing and camp chores. The Kootenai carries in a sturdy Concealex belt sheath that employs a Mini Tek-Lok fastener.

For folks who fancy small fixed blades, the Simonich Knives Bitterroot isn't hard to swallow. Its diminutive drop-point blade is 1-5/8 inches long, and the overall length is only 4 inches. A hard-working, tough-wearing S30V blade excels in durability, and as an added touch of class, an arrowhead profile is laser cut out of the handle. The lightweight Bitterroot's molded Concealex sheath permits it to be worn as a neck knife or attached to a key chain.

Branton Knife Co.

Knifemaker Bobby Branton has also jumped into the mid-tech knife arena with both feet. He has formed a close friendship over the years with noted combat knife designer/maker Walter Brend, and Brend lends his expertise in design and execution to three Branton Knife Co. designs.

The Merrill's Marauder fixed blade, with 7-1/2 inches of 1/4-inch-thick D-2 tool steel, is a formidable chopper. An ergonomic canvas-Micarta® handle sports an integral double hand guard to prevent it from sliding around in the palm during use. An Eagle Industries Cordura® sheath of top-notch construction incorporates a Kydex liner for durability, and an exterior accessory pocket is suitable for tot-

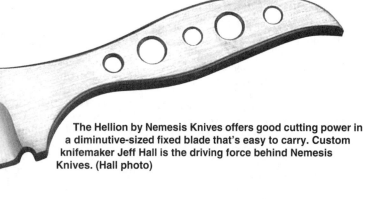

The Hellion by Nemesis Knives offers good cutting power in a diminutive-sized fixed blade that's easy to carry. Custom knifemaker Jeff Hall is the driving force behind Nemesis Knives. (Hall photo)

The Branton Knife Co.'s reproduction of Walter Brend's Model 2 fighter is as close to the original as you can get. (Hoffman photo)

ing a folding knife, multi-tool or sharpening stone.

Through his Branton Knife Co. offerings, Bobby hopes to satisfy a demand from those who long to own one of Brend's ultimate fixed-blade fighters and survival knives. Brend's designs have long been revered as some of the best, if not the best, tactical fixed blades in the custom knife arena. How much will it set you back to own one of the Branton Brends? The Model 2 fighter goes for $299, the Merrill's Marauder for $325, and the Boot Knife is set at $249.

Carson, Obenauf & Carson

The most successful knife design by Kit Carson over the years, the Model 4 folder, has become his signature knife. To further satisfy the demand for the built-like-a-tank tactical folder, Carson has decided to produce a mid-tech version of it with the assistance of his son, Jody, and son-in-law, fellow knifemaker Mike Obenauf. The three have previously collaborated on Carson's F4

neck knife, and Columbia River Knife & Tool is manufacturing a version of that handy little knife.

The mid-tech Model 4 will be the same size as Carson's medium Model 4, with a 3-1/2-inch blade and an overall length of 8 inches. A titanium integral-lock design, it sports machined grooves on the handle surface to enhance purchase. Customers have a choice of four blade styles, including a drop point, modified drop point, double-ground spear point and clip point. Blade steel will be S30V, and Carson hints at the possibility of using other materials. The blades and handle parts are laser cut, and all machining and grinding is done in-house, by hand. Carson says he is planning an initial run of about 100 mid-tech Model 4's, and he holds open the possibility of doing another run with some variations. As of press time, Carson set the price at $400 each. He might offer some or all of the folders with tungsten DLC coating to enhance looks and to bolster the corrosion resistance of the S30V steel.

Combat Elite

Combat Elite is a new name in the mid-tech fray, but the two gentlemen behind it are certainly no newcomers. Darrel Ralph and Ryan Wilson are accomplished knifemakers in their own right, and through Combat Elite, they are building some of the best in mid-tech tactical folders available today.

Their first at-bat resulted in the Tactical Elite frame-lock folder, a tough knife that features a 4-inch spear-point blade, flat ground from 1/8-inch 440C stock. Each blade is subjected to Wilson Combat Armor-Tuff® coating for added corrosion resistance and a subdued appearance.

The Tactical Elite is available in four configurations and price ranges. Level 1 ($275) is the most basic folder, with a ceramic-bead-blasted titanium frame-lock handle, and on the opposite end of the spectrum is the Level 4 ($400), featuring a tricked-out, hand-rubbed, satin-finished titanium frame-lock handle that is anodized and has

The Bitterroot by Simonich Knives LLC is a diminutive fixed blade, designed for carry as either a neck knife or attached to a key chain. (Hoffman photo)

A modern interpretation of the classic stiletto switchblade by Combat Elite features a 440C Teflon®-coated blade and a durable T6-6061 aluminum handle. Handle colors are available in black or green Armor-Tuff® coating. (Hoffman photo)

carbon fiber inlays. In between, are Levels 2 ($325), 3 ($350) and 3G ($375). These showcase handles with green-Armor-Tuff coating, raised G-10 inlays, and green coating with raised G-10 inlays, respectively. No matter the grade, the Tactical Elite is a well-designed and well-built folder.

Combat Elite has also released the Tactical Auto Stiletto, a knife that sports a 4-inch, dagger-style D-2 blade and a T6-6061 aluminum handle with a double integral hand guard. The blade of this one is subjected to a Teflon-based black coating, and customers are given a choice of a black-anodized or green-Armor-Tuff-coated handle. Wilson and Ralph have more knife models planned for release under the Combat Elite banner, possibly to include some fixed blades to complement their established line of folders.

Mid-tech knives excel in quality, blending the best of handmade and production knives and quenching the public's thirst for edged tools designed and built by some of today's most famous knifemakers. Expect to see many more mid-tech knives from these and other makers in the future, as this appears to be a trend that is catching on fast with both the makers and the knife buying public. ●

SUV's: Sport Utility kniVes

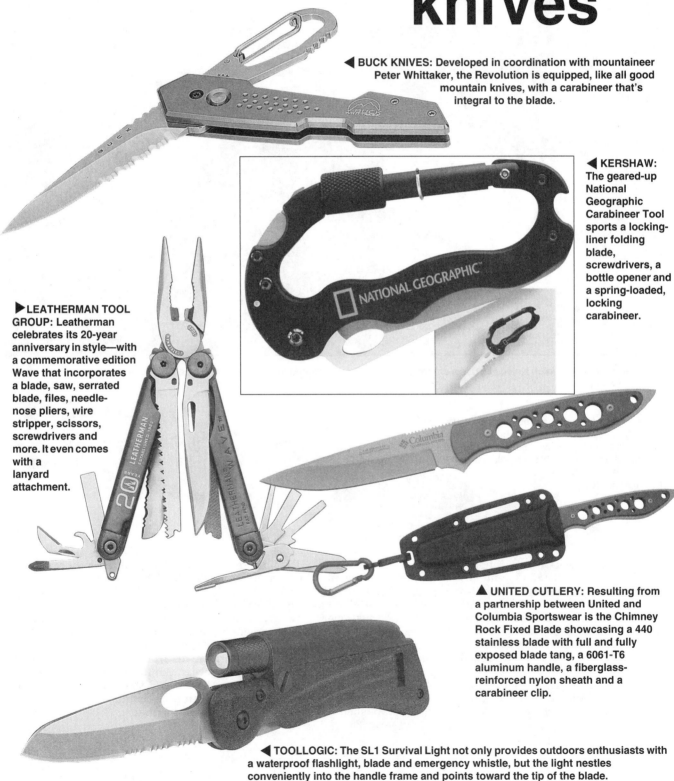

◀ BUCK KNIVES: Developed in coordination with mountaineer Peter Whittaker, the Revolution is equipped, like all good mountain knives, with a carabineer that's integral to the blade.

◀ KERSHAW: The geared-up National Geographic Carabineer Tool sports a locking-liner folding blade, screwdrivers, a bottle opener and a spring-loaded, locking carabineer.

▶ LEATHERMAN TOOL GROUP: Leatherman celebrates its 20-year anniversary in style—with a commemorative edition Wave that incorporates a blade, saw, serrated blade, files, needle-nose pliers, wire stripper, scissors, screwdrivers and more. It even comes with a lanyard attachment.

▲ UNITED CUTLERY: Resulting from a partnership between United and Columbia Sportswear is the Chimney Rock Fixed Blade showcasing a 440 stainless blade with full and fully exposed blade tang, a 6061-T6 aluminum handle, a fiberglass-reinforced nylon sheath and a carabineer clip.

◀ TOOLLOGIC: The SL1 Survival Light not only provides outdoors enthusiasts with a waterproof flashlight, blade and emergency whistle, but the light nestles conveniently into the handle frame and points toward the tip of the blade.

▲ BEAR MGC CUTLERY: In the "Hobo Set," Bear offers you a mess kit that will fit in your pocket.

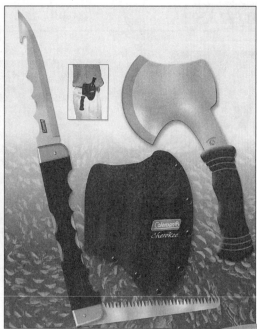

◄ TAYLOR CUTLERY: One canvas belt sheath holds a two-blade Coleman folding knife, including gut hook and saw, and an all-purpose Coleman hatchet.

▼ STANLEY: From the Stanley toolmakers comes the SportUtility Outdoorsman Knife, a combination folding/utility razor-blade knife. The locking-liner folder involves a 3-1/2-inch, semi-serrated "sport" blade, but by pressing a "quick-change" button, the regular knife blade can be replaced with a retractable utility blade.

Freedom Fighters

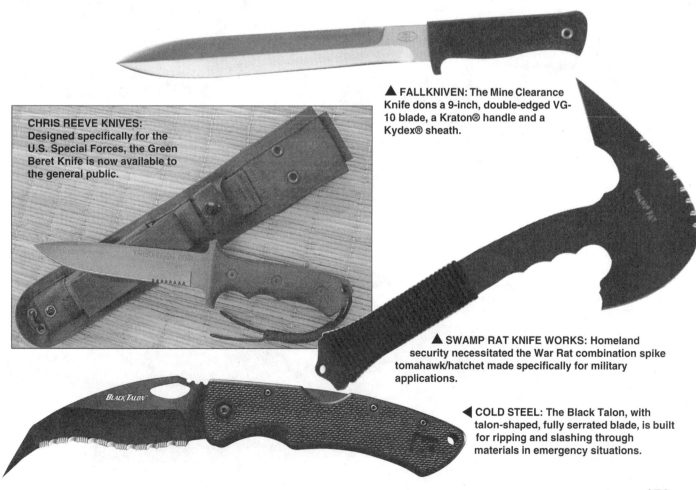

CHRIS REEVE KNIVES: Designed specifically for the U.S. Special Forces, the Green Beret Knife is now available to the general public.

▲ FALLKNIVEN: The Mine Clearance Knife dons a 9-inch, double-edged VG-10 blade, a Kraton® handle and a Kydex® sheath.

▲ SWAMP RAT KNIFE WORKS: Homeland security necessitated the War Rat combination spike tomahawk/hatchet made specifically for military applications.

◄ COLD STEEL: The Black Talon, with talon-shaped, fully serrated blade, is built for ripping and slashing through materials in emergency situations.

FACTORY TRENDS

KUTMASTER: Two X-Treme Military Knives feature stainless blades, Kraton handles and nylon belt sheaths.

SPYDERCO: An all-metal folder manifests itself in the form of the A.T.R. (At the Ready), complete with hollow-ground, folding dagger blade, an integral Compression Lock, titanium handle and Cobra Hood positioned above the one-hand-opening hole in the blade, meant to guide the user's thumb to the hole.

SUREFIRE: A surefire winner is the Millennium M2 flashlight and Strider Knives Model SF tactical fixed blade, together in one package.

EXTREMA RATIO: Watch the bite of the Dobermann II's stainless cobalt steel blade.

BOKER USA: Mikhail Kalashnikov lent his name to the AK-47 and AK-47Ltd locking-liner folders, each with 440C blades, 6061-T6 aluminum handles and G-10 or snake-wood inlays.

BENCHMADE: All black is the Model 9053SBT auto-opening folder with ATS-34 blade, a 6061-T6-aluminum handle, integrated safety for added lockup security and a stainless steel pocket clip.

ONTARIO: In its Freedom Fighter series, Ontario includes several 1095 carbon steel fixed blades married with oval Kraton handles.

Sharp But Stubby Blades

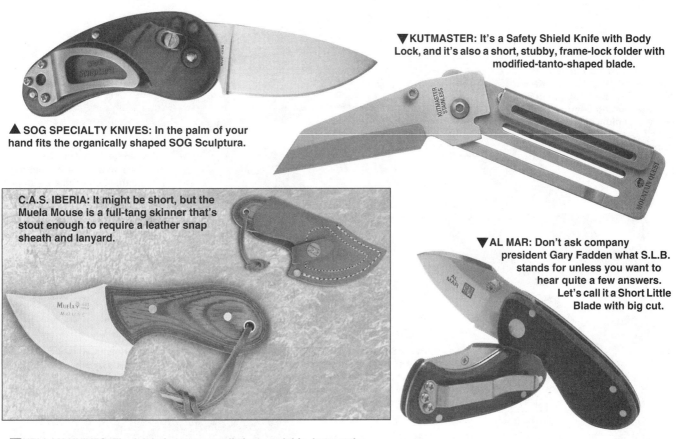

▼**KUTMASTER:** It's a Safety Shield Knife with Body Lock, and it's also a short, stubby, frame-lock folder with modified-tanto-shaped blade.

▲ **SOG SPECIALTY KNIVES:** In the palm of your hand fits the organically shaped SOG Sculptura.

C.A.S. IBERIA: It might be short, but the Muela Mouse is a full-tang skinner that's stout enough to require a leather snap sheath and lanyard.

▼**AL MAR:** Don't ask company president Gary Fadden what S.L.B. stands for unless you want to hear quite a few answers. Let's call it a Short Little Blade with big cut.

▼**KELLAM KNIVES:** Finnish knives are usually long and thin, but not the FinnFolders from Kellam. They're sharp, short and stubby.

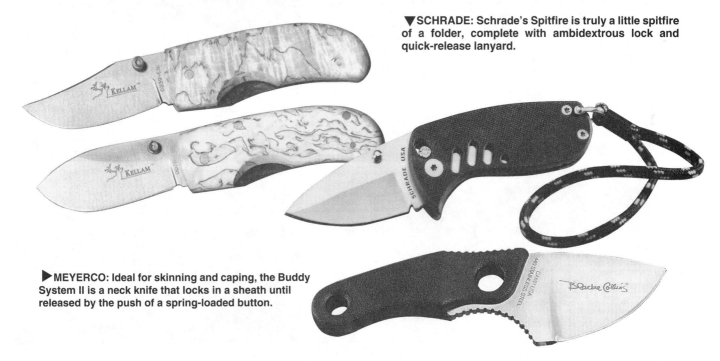

▼**SCHRADE:** Schrade's Spitfire is truly a little spitfire of a folder, complete with ambidextrous lock and quick-release lanyard.

▶**MEYERCO:** Ideal for skinning and caping, the Buddy System II is a neck knife that locks in a sheath until released by the push of a spring-loaded button.

Palpable and Deployable Folders

▼**KA-BAR:** Through its North American distributorship, Ka-Bar offers Italian-made Tecnocut Side Lock folders sporting Sandvik steel blades, titanium bolsters and a choice of red-maple-burl, brown-maple-burl or colored-titanium handles.

◄**BENCHMADE:** The Model 5000 Auto Axis features an unusual aluminum handle that is machined with grooves that face in two directions for a secure grip. Positive blade release is achieved with either hand by drawing the AXIS thumb button back toward the butt of the handle.

▲ **MASTERS OF DEFENSE:** The Allen Elishewitz-designed Phoenix utilizes a Bear-Trac system of shortening and lengthening the 154CM fixed blade by sliding it further into or out of the handle. In the "closed" position, the blade extends outward from the handle 2 inches with no serrations. Sliding it outward results in a full 3-1/2-inch, semi-serrated blade.

►**BOKER:** The folding lock blade of the QuickFlip is released by applying pressure with the forefinger against the blade tang, and a simple snap of the wrist swings the blade open and locks it in place.

►**KA-BAR:** Designed by custom knifemaker Bob Dozier, the Dozier Thorns are sleek, compact and light one-hand-opening side-lock folding knives.

SPYDERCO: A large, palpable, blue G-10 handle and a downward-curving, beak-like blade define the Dodo, but its ambidextrous, one-hand-opening capability and Ball Bearing Lock separate it from other folders.

EMERSON KNIVES, INC.: The Combat Karambit is a folding knife that can be gripped in several positions, including upside down, forward, backward and swinging from the pinkie or index finger. The hook-shaped, one-hand-opening blade incorporates the WAVE feature for ease of extracting the blade while the Karambit is being pulled from within a pants pocket.

TAYLOR CUTLERY: The handle halves of the Smith & Wesson Power Glide pivot and spread apart to slide the tanto- or dagger-shaped blade in or out of the handle frame.

SOG SPECIALTY KNIVES: A twitch of the finger or thumb against either the integral blade guard or the thumb peg will snap the folding blade of the Twitch open, locking it in the extended position.

EMERSON KNIVES, INC.: Allen Elishewitz designs an upscale tactical-utility folding knife with a textured and layered G-10 handle and a sleek 154CM blade.

UNITED CUTLERY: Meet the Harley Davidson Wolf Pup, a locking-liner folder that incorporates an anodized, machined-aluminum handle and a 3-5/16-inch blade.

A Pocketful of Pocketknives

▶BLUE GRASS CUTLERY CORP.: This Winchester Trademark Knife dons a cast, bronze-colored handle engraved with a hunting scene on one side and a Winchester Model 101 on the other.

▶W.R. CASE & SONS CUTLERY CO.: Paying homage to the first Case knives, the company reintroduces the Case Brothers Cutlery brand of pocketknives with never-seen-before tang stamps.

▲ ▶BLUE GRASS CUTLERY CORP.: The first pocketknives released in the Winchester 22 Hornet Shield Cartridge Series are two-blade trappers that come in carbon-steel blades, nickel-silver bolsters and burl-wood-celluloid, glitter-stripe-celluloid or abalone-celluloid handles.

▶VICTORINOX: A clock, timer and alarm are the digital features of the Voyager knife, which also incorporates two knife blades, a can/bottle opener, scissors, corkscrew and screwdriver, among other features.

▲ SANTA FE STONEWORKS: The Santa Fe Kaleidoscope Designs are the handiwork of master inlay artist Steve Rosenblum who inlaid treated hardwoods into the handles of several Camillus pocketknives.

The Game Stalkers

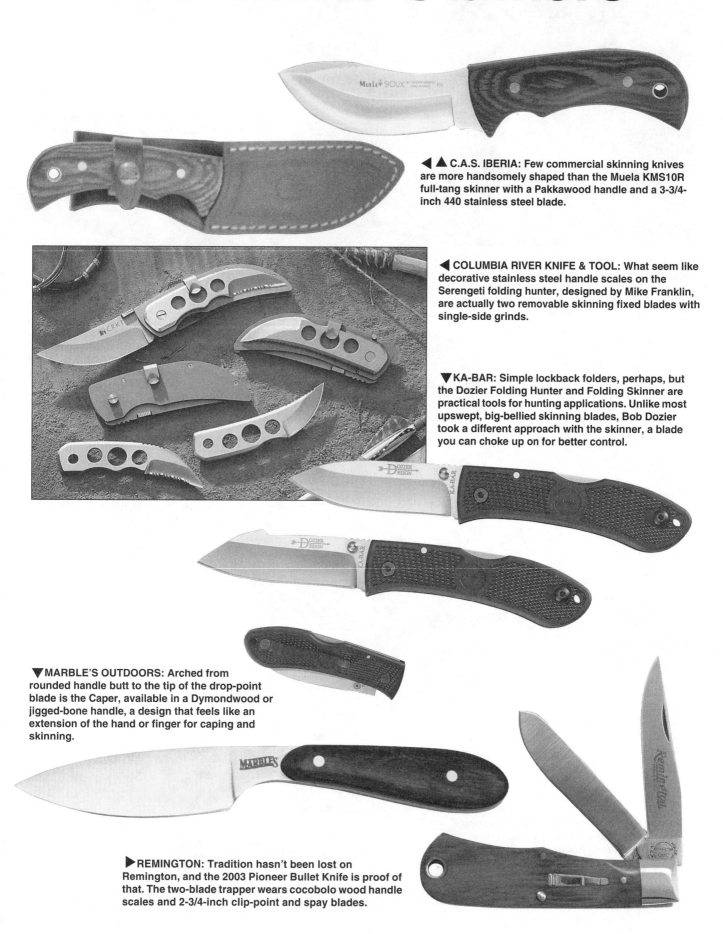

◄▲ **C.A.S. IBERIA:** Few commercial skinning knives are more handsomely shaped than the Muela KMS10R full-tang skinner with a Pakkawood handle and a 3-3/4-inch 440 stainless steel blade.

◄ **COLUMBIA RIVER KNIFE & TOOL:** What seem like decorative stainless steel handle scales on the Serengeti folding hunter, designed by Mike Franklin, are actually two removable skinning fixed blades with single-side grinds.

▼ **KA-BAR:** Simple lockback folders, perhaps, but the Dozier Folding Hunter and Folding Skinner are practical tools for hunting applications. Unlike most upswept, big-bellied skinning blades, Bob Dozier took a different approach with the skinner, a blade you can choke up on for better control.

▼ **MARBLE'S OUTDOORS:** Arched from rounded handle butt to the tip of the drop-point blade is the Caper, available in a Dymondwood or jigged-bone handle, a design that feels like an extension of the hand or finger for caping and skinning.

▶ **REMINGTON:** Tradition hasn't been lost on Remington, and the 2003 Pioneer Bullet Knife is proof of that. The two-blade trapper wears cocobolo wood handle scales and 2-3/4-inch clip-point and spay blades.

▼ MEYERCO: A big, beefy, rubber handle and a full-4-inch 420 blade—what else could a hunter want in the field?

▲ BEAR CUTLERY: There's something about hunting with a damascus folder with genuine India stag bone handle that trips the proverbial trigger, and that's what one gets with the Side Liner Lock.

◄ UNITED CUTLERY: Here's a Deluxe Game Zipper ready to zip game open using the 420 J2 stainless blade and integral gut hook. Two holes in the handle are for grip and even more zip.

▲ FALLKNIVEN: The NL5 Idun Hunter's Knife combines an old-school stacked-leather handle with a new-school 5.1-inch, convex-ground VG-10 blade.

▲ KERSHAW: The Kaper/Gut Hook Combo in leather seems like a hunting knife set made to order.

► KATZ KNIVES: Katz Knives makes working tools, and the Kagemusha fixed blades with cherry wood or Kraton handles are designed to work well in the field. Finger notches along blade spines, deep, upswept blades, grooved and rounded handles, they all say, "use me."

The Edge of Elegance

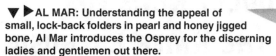

▼ ▶ **AL MAR:** Understanding the appeal of small, lock-back folders in pearl and honey jigged bone, Al Mar introduces the Osprey for the discerning ladies and gentlemen out there.

▼ **TIGERSHARP:** Replaceable-blade knives have always been TigerSharp's claim to fame, and now the company outfits gentlemen's locking-liner folders with such blade wizardry.

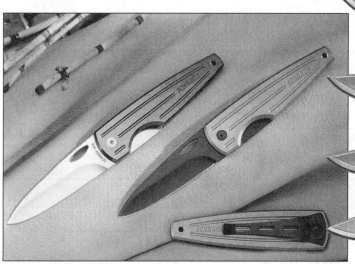

▲ **SCHRADE:** Rugged and lightweight are the Viper locking-liner folders with aircraft-aluminum handles, but what makes them elegant are the taper-point blades and equally sleek grips.

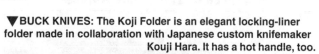

▼ **BUCK KNIVES:** The Koji Folder is an elegant locking-liner folder made in collaboration with Japanese custom knifemaker Kouji Hara. It has a hot handle, too.

▲ **COLUMBIA RIVER KNIFE & Tool:** The company started with the custom Rolox concept (like the Rolex of folding knives, a knife with a blade that slides out the front of the handle) and let custom knifemaker Allen Elishewitz work his magic.

▶ **PRO TECH:** Call them "Custom Titanium Stingers"—Pro Tech does—but the small, titanium-handle automatic folders are more than that. With damascus blades and grip choices including pearl inserts and engraving, they're elegant pocketknives.

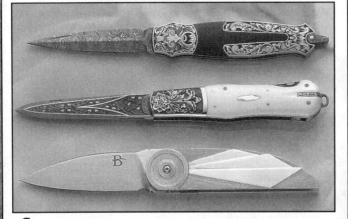
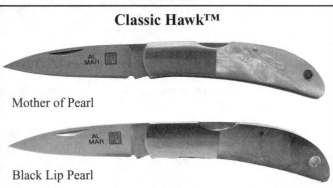

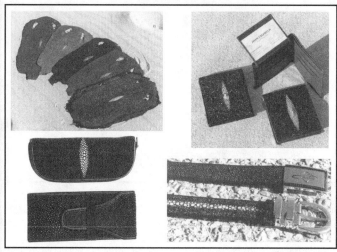

KNIVES MARKETPLACE

SAFARI KIT

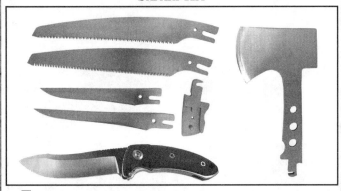

The basic kit includes the handle, a four-inch Kagemusha-style stainless steel hunting blade, and an ax head attachment, all packed in a belt-mounted leather sheath.

Katz offers an optional accessory kit consisting of an 8.5-inch bone/meat saw, an 8.5-inch wood saw, a 6-inch boning blade and a 7.5-inch fillet blade packed in their own belt-mounted leather sheath.

To remove an attachment, simply grasp the locking lever and pull out to release it from the handle. The installed attachment can then be pivoted rearward (like closing a folding knife) until it is released from the pivot pin, then pulled forward and off the handle. The whole process is very smooth.

P.O. Box 730, Chandler, AZ 85244
Phone: 480-786-9334
Fax: 480-786-9338
E-mail: katzkn@aol.com
Web: www.katzknives.com

WWW.KNIFEMAKING.COM

They have it! Pre-shaped hardened and tempered blades, blade stock, brass, nickel silver, guards, pommels, rivets, handle materials, finishing supplies and equipment for sharpening, finishing, drilling, sanding, measuring, and much more. They stock what they sell and ship daily. Their customer service department is rated #1. They offer only the best quality merchandise available and sell to you with confidence.

Don't have access to the web yet? No problem. They offer a complete catalog of their supplies and have a showroom located right off I-35 in Davis, OK, for your convenience.

Shop the web for all your knifemaking supplies, tools, and equipment.

Visit their showroom located at 309 West Main, Davis, OK.
Call 1-800-351-8900 to order yours today. Dealers inquire.

JANTZ SUPPLY
P.O. Box 584
Davis, OK 73030-0584
Phone: 580-369-2316 • Fax: 580-369-3082
Web: www.knifemaking.com

DRAPER KNIVES
Mike & Audra Draper
10 Creek Dr., Riverton, WY 82501
Phone: 307-856-6807 • Cell: 307-851-0426
Web: www.DraperKnives.us

THE GREEN BERET KNIFE

Chris Reeve Knives and Bill Harsey collaborated to produce the "Yarborough" - the first knife ever to be presented to graduates of U.S. Army Special Forces Qualification Course. Identical except for the markings, the knife that is available to all other military and the civilian market is "The Green Beret Knife". With a 7-inch blade of CPM S30V coated with KG Gun-Kote™ and gray canvas micarta handles, this knife is a no-nonsense, hard working tool, that echoes the characteristics of the men for whom it was designed – tough, efficient, exceptional. Also available is a 5.5 inch version – identical handles but with a shorter blade.

CHRIS REEVE KNIVES
11624 W. President Dr., #B, Boise, ID 83713
Phone: 208-375-0367
Web: http://www.chrisreeve.com

KNIVES MARKETPLACE

PREMIER PURVEYOR

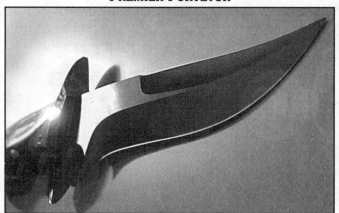

Established in 1992, Arizona Custom Knives (AZCK) has become a market leader in bringing you the finest handmade knives. From one-of-a-kind, investment-grade knives to your everyday carry knife, Arizona Custom Knives tries to "custom fit" the customer with the right knife at the right price. The company brings to you the best of the top makers, along with the latest from the up-and-comers. Years of established relationships with hundreds of custom knifemakers assures you of obtaining those rare gems you seek.

Your collection is their first priority!

ARIZONA CUSTOM KNIVES, INC.

Julie Hyman

9211 Abbott Loop Road, Anchorage, AK 99507

Phone: 907-677-6014 • Fax: 907-677-6610

14 years open to the public. NICA member. Huge selection of custom and production knives and swords. Production lines: Buck, Bench Made, Columbia River Knife & Tool, Boker, Kershaw, Kabar, Spyderco, S&W, Colt, Rigid, United Cutlery, Out Door Edge, Remington, Micro Tech, Timberline, Gerber, Leatherman.

Sharpening: Gatco, Spyderco, DMT.

Specializing in Chris Reeve Knives. Also selling Busse knives and Randall knives.

Sharpening service:

Kitchen knives, hunting, utility knives, scissors, clipper blades, ice skates.

They can also repair clippers.

WORLD OF KNIVES

811 Main Street., Hopkins, MN 55343

Phone: 800-677-6543

GATCO 5-STONE SHARPENING SYSTEM

The GATCO 5-Stone Sharpening System is the only fixed-angle sharpening kit needed to restore a factory perfect edge on even the most well-used knives.

Instructions are permanently mounted inside the storage case to make the job easy.

Just secure the blade in the polymer vise, select the proper angle guide, insert one of the five hone-stone angle guide bars into the guide slot, then put a few drops of mineral oil on the stone and start sharpening.

The GATCO 5-Stone Sharpening System includes extra coarse, coarse, medium and fine honing stones that are made from high-density aluminum oxide for long wear. The fifth, triangular-shaped hone is used for serrated blades.

All stones are mounted in color-coded grips.

To locate a GATCO dealer, call 1-800-LIV-SHARP.

GATCO SHARPENERS

P.O. Box 600, Getzville, NY 14068-0600

Phone: 716-877-2200 • Fax: 716-877-2591

E-mail: gatco@buffnet.net • www.gatcosharpeners.com

SHARPEN YOUR KNIFE THE PROFESSIONAL WAY

You've seen them demonstrated at knife, gun and craft shows, State Fairs, sharpening booths in your local gun and pawn shops, major sporting retailers and by friends in their workshops. These knife wheels have been designed to help professional knifemakers to put a perfect edge on any knife, old or new. Perfected by Jantz Supply, these wheels are now the perfect size and grit to bring you the ultimate sharpening system available. In just seconds you can restore an old rusty knife to an unbelievably sharp useful tool. The two wheel set includes everything needed to start sharpening with your buffer or grinder. Each wheel is 8 x 3/4" and can be used on a 1/2" or 5/8" shaft. Complete sharpening outfits are available which include a Baldor buffer or Delta grinder along with the wheels and compounds necessary to set up a professional sharpening center in your shop.

Visit their showroom located at 309 West Main, Davis, OK.

Call 1-800-351-8900 to order yours today. Dealers inquire.

JANTZ SUPPLY

P.O. Box 584

Davis, OK 73030-0584

Phone: 580-369-2316 • Fax: 580-369-3082

Web: www.knifemaking.com

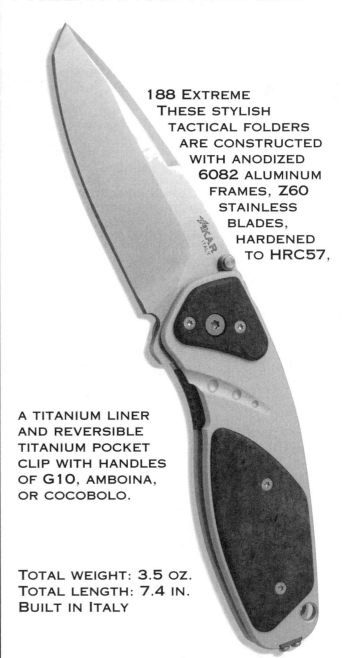

DIRECTORY

Browsing through this book, it's almost certain you will find a couple—or a couple dozen, more likely—creations that you would like to see in your pocket, under your Christmas tree or otherwise tucked in your knife collection.

Now comes the time to find the artisan, call or write that person, and make the deal.

Or perhaps you are a knifemaker yourself, searching for a chunk of mammoth ivory, or stag, or mother-of-pearl or other materials for your project.

Maybe you just want to call a commercial cutlery company for a catalog. Or write to *Blade* magazine or some other knife publication for a subscription.

Whatever your interest in the world of knives, we'll to help you make the connection with this directory. We don't play favorites when it comes to these lists. Most of the listings here were developed following a massive annual mailing that goes to custom knifemakers, companies and other organizations. Each knifemaking organization typically supplies the names of its members to us.

If you weren't listed, or if the listing has erroneous information, please write to Knives Annual at Krause Publications, 700 E. State St., Iola, WI 54990-0001, and we will list you or correct the mistake next year.

If you are a custom knifemaker, feel free to submit complete information about your specialties (using the listings in the book as a guide), along with sample photos of a few of your best works.

Thanks for helping us to make this the best source book—the only complete handbook—of the world's most dazzling, creative cutlery for 24 straight years.

a

A. G., RUSSELL, 1920 North 26th St, Lowell, AR 72745-8489, Phone: 800-255-9037 479-631-0130, Fax: 479-631-8493
Specialties: A. G. Russell Shopmade™ (handmade, custom) knives made in our own shop using the best tool steels: 154CM, A-2, D-2, 52100, Damascus and Stellite. Morseth™ knives made with Norwegian laminated steels. Hunters, camp knives. Working to our own designs in the finest materials.

ABBOTT, WILLIAM M., Box 102A, RR #2, Chandlerville, IL 62627, Phone: 217-458-2325
Specialties: High-grade edged weapons. **Patterns:** Locking folders, Bowies, working straight knives, kitchen cutlery, minis. **Technical:** Grinds D2, ATS-34, 440C and commercial Damascus. Heat-treats; Rockwell tests. Prefers natural handle materials. **Prices:** $100 to $1000. **Remarks:** Part-time maker; first knife sold in 1984. **Mark:** Name.

ABEGG, ARNIE, 5992 Kenwick CR, Huntington Beach, CA 92648, Phone: 714-848-5697

ABERNATHY, PAUL J., 3033 Park St, Eureka, CA 95501, Phone: 707-442-3593
Specialties: Period pieces and traditional straight knives of his design and in standard patterns. **Patterns:** Miniature daggers, fighters and swords. **Technical:** Forges and files SS, brass and sterling silver. **Prices:** $100 to $250; some to $500. **Remarks:** Part-time maker. Doing business as Abernathy's Miniatures. **Mark:** Stylized initials.

ACKERSON, ROBIN E., 119 W Smith St, Buchanan, MI 49107, Phone: 616-695-2911

ADAMS, LES, 6413 NW 200 St, Hialeah, FL 33015, Phone: 305-625-1699
Specialties: Working straight knives of his design. **Patterns:** Fighters, tactical folders, waw enforcing autos. **Technical:** Grinds ATS-34, 440C and D2. **Prices:** $100-$500. **Remarks:** Part-time maker; first knife sold in 1989. **Mark:** First initial, last name, Custom Knives.

ADAMS, WILLIAM D., PO Box 439, Burton, TX 77835, Phone: 713-855-5643, Fax: 713-855-5638
Specialties: Hunter scalpels and utility knives of his design. **Patterns:** Hunters and utility/camp knives. **Technical:** Grinds 1095, 440C and 440V. Uses stabilized wood and other stabilized materials. **Prices:** $100 to $200. **Remarks:** Part-time maker; first knife sold in 1994. **Mark:** Last name in script.

ADDISON, KYLE A., 809 N 20th St, Murray, KY 42071, Phone: 270-759-1564
Specialties: Hand forged blades including Bowies, fighters and hunters. **Patterns:** Custom leather sheaths. **Technical:** Forges 5160, 1084, and my own Damascus. **Prices:** $175 to $1500. **Remarks:** Part-time maker, first knife sold in 1996. **Mark:** First and middle initial, last name under "Trident" with knife and hammer. **Other:** ABS member.

ADKINS, RICHARD L., 138 California Ct, Mission Viejo, CA 92692-4079

AIDA, YOSHIHITO, 26-7 Narimasu 2-Chome, Itabashi-ku, Tokyo 175-0094, JAPAN, Phone: 81-3-3939-0052, Fax: 81-3-3939-0058
Specialties: High-tech working straight knives and folders of his design. **Patterns:** Bowies, lock-backs, hunters, fighters, fishing knives, boots. **Technical:** Grinds CV-134, ATS-34; buys Damascus; works in traditional Japanese fashion for some handles and sheaths. **Prices:** $400 to $900; some higher. **Remarks:** Full-time maker; first knife sold in 1978. **Mark:** Initial logo and Riverside West.

AKAHORI, YOICHIRO, Fuzieda 1-5-4, Shizuoka-ken, 426-0006, JAPAN, Phone: 81 54 641-4830, Fax: 81 54 641 4830
Specialties: Classic & traditional straight knives of his design. **Patterns:** Bowies, hunters & utility/camp knives. **Technical:** Forges Japanese carbon steels; his own Damascus. Prices: $250 to $750; some to $1500. **Remarks:** Full-time maker; first knife sold in 1990. **Mark:** SAEMON in Japanese Kanji.

ALBERICCI, EMILIO, 19 via Masone, 24100, Bergamo, ITALY, Phone: 01139-35-215120
Specialties: Folders and Bowies. **Patterns:** Collector knives. **Technical:** Uses stock removal with extreme lavoration accuracy; offers exotic and high-tech materials. **Prices:** Not currently selling. **Remarks:** Part-time maker. **Mark:** None.

ALDERMAN, ROBERT, 2655 Jewel Lake Rd, Sagle, ID 83860, Phone: 208-263-5996
Specialties: Classic and traditional working straight knives in standard patterns or to customer specs and his design; period pieces. **Patterns:** Bowies, fighters, hunters and utility/camp knives. **Technical:** Casts, forges and grinds 1084; forges and grinds L6 and O1. Prefers an old appearance. **Prices:** $100 to $350; some to $700. **Remarks:** Full-time maker; first knife sold in 1975. Doing business as Trackers Forge. **Mark:** Deer track. **Other:** Knifemaking school. Two-week course for beginners; will cover forging, stock removal, hardening, tempering, case making. All materials supplies - $1250.

ALDRETE, BOB, PO Box 1471, Lomita, CA 90717, Phone: 310-326-3041

ALEXANDER, DARREL, Box 381, Ten Sleep, WY 82442, Phone: 307-366-2699
Specialties: Traditional working straight knives. **Patterns:** Hunters, boots and fishing knives. **Technical:** Grinds D2, 440C, ATS-34 and 154CM. **Prices:** $75 to $120; some to $250. **Remarks:** Full-time maker; first knife sold in 1983. **Mark:** Name, city, state.

ALEXANDER, EUGENE, Box 540, Ganado, TX 77962-0540, Phone: 512-771-3727

ALEXANDER, JERED, 213 Hogg Hill Rd, Dierks, AR 71833, Phone: 870-286-2981

ALLEN, MIKE "WHISKERS", 12745 Fontenot Acres Rd, Malakoff, TX 75148, Phone: 903-489-1026
Specialties: Working and collector-quality lock-backs, liner-locks and automatic folders to customer specs. **Patterns:** Hunters, tantos, Bowies, swords and miniatures. **Technical:** Grinds Damascus, 440C & ATS-34, engraves. **Prices:** $200 and up. **Remarks:** Full-time maker; first knife sold in 1984. **Mark:** Whiskers and date.

ALLRED, BRUCE F., 1764 N Alder, Layton, UT 84041, Phone: 801-825-4612
Specialties: Custom hunting and utility knives. **Patterns:** Custom designs that include a unique grind line, thumb and mosaic pins. **Technical:** ATS-34, 154CM and 440C. **Remarks:** The handle material include but not limited to micarta (in various colors), natural woods and reconstituted stone.

ALVERSON, TIM (R. V.), 4874 Bobbits Bench Rd, Peck, ID 83545, Phone: 208-476-3999
Specialties: Fancy working knives to customer specs; other types on request. **Patterns:** Bowies, daggers, folders and miniatures. **Technical:** Grinds 440C, ATS-34; buys some Damascus. **Prices:** Start at $175. **Remarks:** Full-time maker; first knife sold in 1981. **Mark:** R. V. A. around rosebud.

AMERI, MAURO, Via Riaello No. 20, Trensasco St. Olcese, 16010 Genova, ITALY, Phone: 010-8357077
Specialties: Working and using knives of his design. **Patterns:** Hunters, Bowies and utility/camp knives. **Technical:** Grinds 440C, ATS-34 and 154CM. Handles in wood or Micarta; offers sheaths. **Prices:** $200 to $1200. **Remarks:** Spare-time maker; first knife sold in 1982. **Mark:** Last name, city.

AMES, MICKEY L., 1521 N Central Ave, Monett, MO 65708-1104, Phone: 417-235-5941
Specialties: Traditional working and using straight knives of his design and to customer specs. **Patterns:** Bowies, hunters and utility/camp knives. **Technical:** Forges 5160, 1084, 1095 and makes own Damascus. Filework; silver wire inlay. **Prices:** Start at $100. **Remarks:** Part-time maker; first knife sold in 1990. Doing business as Ames Forge. **Mark:** Last name.

AMMONS, DAVID C., 6225 N Tucson Mtn. Dr, Tucson, AZ 85743, Phone: 520-307-3585
Specialties: Will build to suit. **Patterns:** Yours or mine. **Prices:** $250-$2000. **Mark:** AMMONS.

AMOR JR., MIGUEL, 485-H Judie Lane, Lancaster, PA 17603, Phone: 717-468-5736
Specialties: Working and fancy straight knives in standard patterns; some to customer specs. **Patterns:** Bowies, hunters, fighters and tantos. **Technical:** Grinds 440C, ATS-34, carbon steel and commercial Damascus; forges some in high carbon steels. **Prices:** $125 to $500; some to $1500 and higher. **Remarks:** Part-time maker; first knife sold in 1983. **Mark:** Last name. On collectors' pieces: last name, city, state.

AMOUREUX, A. W., PO Box 776, Northport, WA 99157, Phone: 509-732-6292
Specialties: Heavy-duty working straight knives. **Patterns:** Bowies, fighters, camp knives and hunters for world-wide use. **Technical:** Grinds 440C, ATS-34 and 154CM. **Prices:** $80 to $2000. **Remarks:** Full-time maker; first knife sold in 1974. **Mark:** ALSTAR.

ANDERS, JEROME, 137 Sun Set Ln, Center Ridge, AR 72027, Phone: 501-893-9981
Specialties: Case handles and pin work. **Patterns:** Layered and mosaic steel. **Prices:** $275 and up. **Remarks:** All my knives are truly one-of-a-kind. **Mark:** J. Anders in half moon.

custom knifemakers

ANDERS, DAVID, 157 Barnes Dr, Center Ridge, AR 72027, Phone: 501-893-2294
Specialties: Working straight knives of his design. **Patterns:** Bowies, fighters and hunters. **Technical:** Forges 5160, 1080 and Damascus. **Prices:** $225 to $3200. **Remarks:** Part-time maker; first knife sold in 1988. Doing business as Anders Knives. **Mark:** Last name/MS.

ANDERSEN, HENRIK LEFOLII, Jagtvej 8, Groenholt, 3480, Fredensborg, DENMARK, Phone: 0011-45-48483026
Specialties: Hunters and matched pairs for the serious hunter. **Technical:** Grinds A2; uses materials native to Scandinavia. **Prices:** Start at $250. **Remarks:** Part-time maker; first knife sold in 1985. **Mark:** Initials with arrow.

ANDERSON, TOM, 955 Canal Road Extd., Manchester, PA 17345, Phone: 717-266-6475
Specialties: High-tech one-hand folders. **Patterns:** Fighters, utility, and dress knives. **Technical:** Grinds BG-42, 530V and Damascus. Uses titanium, carbon fiber and select natural handle materials. **Prices:** Start at $400. **Remarks:** First knife sold in 1996. **Mark:** Stylized A over T logo with maker's name.

ANDERSON, MEL, 1718 Lee Lane, Cedaredge, CO 81413, Phone: 970-856-6465, Fax: 970-856-6463
Specialties: Full-size, miniature and one-of-a-kind straight knives and folders of his design. **Patterns:** Bowies, daggers, fighters, hunters and pressure folders. **Technical:** Grinds 440C, 5160, D2, 1095 and Damascus; offers antler, ivory and wood carved handles. **Prices:** Start at $145. **Remarks:** Full-time maker; first knife sold in 1987. **Mark:** Scratchy Hand.

ANDERSON, GARY D., 2816 Reservoir Rd, Spring Grove, PA 17362-9802, Phone: 717-229-2665
Specialties: From working knives to collectors quality blades, some folders. **Patterns:** Traditional and classic designs; customer patterns welcome. **Technical:** Forges Damascus carbon & stainless steels. Offers silver inlay, mokume, filework, checkering. **Prices:** $250 and up. **Remarks:** Part-time maker; first knife sold in 1985. **Mark:** GAND, MS. **Other:** Some engraving, scrimshaw and stone work.

ANDRESS, RONNIE, 415 Audubon Dr. N., Satsuma, AL 36572, Phone: 251-675-7604
Specialties: Working straight knives in standard patterns. **Patterns:** Boots, Bowies, hunters, friction folders and camp knives. **Technical:** Forges 1095, 5160, O1 and his own Damascus. Offers filework and inlays. **Prices:** $125 to $500. **Remarks:** Part-time maker; first knife sold in 1983. Doing business as Andress Knives. **Mark:** Last name, J. S. **Other:** Jeweler, goldsmith, gold work, stone setter. Not currently making knives.

ANDREWS, DON, N. 5155 Ezy St, Coeur D'Alene, ID 83814, Phone: 208-765-8844
Specialties: Plain and fancy folders and straight knives. **Technical:** Grinds D2, 440C, ATS-34; does lost wax casting for guards and pommels. **Prices:** Moderate to upscale. **Remarks:** Full-time maker; first knife sold in 1983. Not currently making knives. **Mark:** Name.

ANDREWS, ERIC, 132 Halbert Street, Grand Ledge, MI 48837, Phone: 517-627-7304
Specialties: Traditional working and using straight knives of his design. **Patterns:** Full-tang hunters, skinners and utility knives. **Technical:** Forges carbon steel; heat-treats. All knives come with sheath; most handles are of wood. **Prices:** $80 to $160. **Remarks:** Part-time maker; first knife sold in 1990. Doing business as The Tinkers Bench.

ANDREWS II, E. R. (RUSS), 131 S Sterling Av, Sugar Creek, MO 64054, Phone: 816-252-3344

ANGELL, JON, 22516 East C R 1474, Hawthorne, FL 32640, Phone: 352-475-5380

ANKROM, W. E., 14 Marquette Dr, Cody, WY 82414, Phone: 307-587-3017, Fax: 307-587-3017
Specialties: Best quality folding knives of his design. **Patterns:** Lockbacks, liner-locks, single 2 blade. **Technical:** ATS-34 commercial Damascus. **Prices:** $500 and up. **Remarks:** Full-time maker; first knife sold in 1975. **Mark:** Name or name, city, state.

ANSO, JENS, GL. Skanderborgveo, 116, 8472 Sporvp, DENMARK, Phone: 45 86968826
Specialties: Working knives of my own design. **Patterns:** Hunters and tacticals. Folders and straight blades. Tantos, drop point, Sheepfoot. **Technical:** Grinds RWL-34 Damasteel ATS-34, B6-42. I use hand rubbed finish on all blades. **Price:** $100 to $400; some up to $1000. **Remarks:** Part-time maker. First knife sold 1997. Doing business as ANSOKNIVES. **Mark:** ANSO. **Other:** Full-time maker since January 2002

ANTONIO JR., WILLIAM J., 6 Michigan State Dr, Newark, DE 19713-1161, Phone: 302-368-8211
Specialties: Fancy working straight knives of his design. **Patterns:** Hunting, survival and fishing knives. **Technical:** Grinds D2, 440C and 154CM;

offers stainless Damascus. **Prices:** $125 to $395; some to $900. **Remarks:** Part-time maker; first knife sold in 1978. **Mark:** Last name, city, state.

AOUN, CHARLES, 69 Nahant St, Wakefield, MA 01880, Phone: 781-224-3353
Specialties: Classic and fancy straight knives of his design. **Patterns:** Fighters, hunters and personal knives. **Technical:** Grinds W2, 1095, ATS-34 and Damascus. Uses natural handle materials; embellishes with silver and semi-precious stones. **Prices:** Start at $290. **Remarks:** Part-time maker; first knife sold in 1995. Doing business as Galeb Knives. **Mark:** G stamped on ricasso or choil.

APPLEBY, ROBERT, 43 N Canal St, Shickshinny, PA 18655, Phone: 570-542-4335
Specialties: Working using straight knives and folders of my own and popular and historical designs. **Patterns:** Variety of straight knives and folders. **Technical:** Hand forged or grinds O-1, 1095, 1084, 5160, 440C, ATS-34, makes own sheaths. **Prices:** Starting at $75. **Remarks:** Part-time maker, first knife sold in 1995. **Mark:** APPLEBY over SHICKSHINNY, PA.

APPLETON, RAY, 244 S Fetzer St, Byers, CO 80103-9748
Specialties: One-of-a-kind folding knives. **Patterns:** Unique folding multilocks and high-tech patterns. **Technical:** All parts machined; D2, S7, 440C, and 6a14v. **Prices:** Start at $8500. **Remarks:** Spare-time maker; first knife sold in 1986. **Mark:** Initials within arrowhead, signed & dated.

ARBUCKLE, JAMES M., 114 Jonathan Jct, Yorktown, VA 23693, Phone: 757-867-9578
Specialties: One-of-a-kind of his design; working knives. **Patterns:** Mostly chefs knives & hunters. **Technical:** Forged & stock removal blades using exotic hardwoods, natural materials, Micarta and stabilized woods. Forge 5160, 1084 & 01; stock remove D2, ATS-34, 440C. Make own pattern welded steel. Prices; $150 to $700. **Remarks:** Forge, grind, heat-treat, finish and embellish all knives myself. Do own leatherwork and wood work. Part-time maker. **Mark:** J. Arbuckle or Arbuckle with maker below it. **Other:** ABS member; ASM member.

ARCHER, RAY & TERRI, PO Box 129, Medicine Bow, WY 82329, Phone: 307-379-2567
Specialties: High finish working straight knives and small one-of-a-kind. **Patterns:** Hunters/skinners, camping. **Technical:** Flat grinds ATS-34, 440C, D2; buys Damascus. **Price:** $100 to $500. **Remarks:** Make own sheaths; first knife sold 1994. **Mark:** Last name over city and state. **Other:** Member of PKA.

ARDWIN, COREY, 4700 North Cedar, North Little Rock, AR 72116, Phone: 501-791-0301, Fax: 501-791-2974

ARNOLD, JOE, 47 Patience Cres., London, Ont., CANADA N6E 2K7, Phone: 519-686-2623
Specialties: Traditional working and using straight knives of his design and to customer specs. **Patterns:** Fighters, hunters and Bowies. **Technical:** Grinds 440C, ATS-34 and 5160. **Prices:** $75 to $500; some to $2500. **Remarks:** Part-time maker; first knife sold in 1988. **Mark:** Last name, country.

ARROWOOD, DALE, 556 Lassetter Rd, Sharpsburg, GA 30277, Phone: 404-253-9672
Specialties: Fancy and traditional straight knives of his design and to customer specs. **Patterns:** Bowies, fighters and hunters. **Technical:** Grinds ATS-34 and 440C; forges high-carbon steel. Engraves and scrimshaws. **Prices:** $125 to $200; some to $245. **Remarks:** Part-time maker; first knife sold in 1989. **Mark:** Anvil with an arrow through it; Old English "Arrowood Knives".

ASHBY, DOUGLAS, 10123 Deermont, Dallas, TX 75243, Phone: 214-238-7531
Specialties: Traditional and fancy straight knives of his design or to customer specs. **Patterns:** Hunters, fighters and utility/camp knives. **Technical:** Grinds 440C, ATS-34 and commercial Damascus. **Prices:** $75 to $200; some to $500. **Remarks:** Part-time maker; first knife sold in 1990. **Mark:** Name, city.

ASHWORTH, BOYD, 3135 Barrett Ct, Powder Springs, GA 30127, Phone: 770-943-4963
Specialties: Fancy Damascus locking folders. **Patterns:** Fighters, hunters and gents. **Technical:** Forges own Damascus; offers filework; uses exotic handle materials. **Prices:** $500 to $2500. **Remarks:** Part-time maker; first knife sold in 1993. **Mark:** Last name.

ATKINSON, DICK, General Delivery, Wausau, FL 32463, Phone: 850-638-8524
Specialties: Working straight knives and folders of his design; some fancy. **Patterns:** Hunters, fighters, boots; locking folders in interframes. **Technical:** Grinds A2, 440C and 154CM. Likes filework. **Prices:** $85 to $300; some exceptional knives. **Remarks:** Full-time maker; first knife sold in 1977. **Mark:** Name, city, state.

AYARRAGARAY, CRISTIAN L., Buenos Aires 250, (3100) Parana-Entre Rios, ARGENTINA, Phone: 043-231753
Specialties: Traditional working straight knives of his design. **Patterns:** Fishing and hunting knives. **Technical:** Grinds and forges carbon steel. Uses native Argentine woods and deer antler. **Prices:** $150 to $250; some to $400. **Remarks:** Full-time maker; first knife sold in 1980. **Mark:** Last name, signature.

b

BABCOCK, RAYMOND G., Rt. 1 Box 328A, Vincent, OH 45784, Phone: 614-678-2688
Specialties: Plain and fancy working straight knives. I will make knives to my design and to custom specifications. I also make folding knives of my design. **Patterns:** Hunting knives, Bowies and folders. **Technical:** Hollow grinds L6. **Prices:** $95 to $500. **Remarks:** Part-time maker; first knife sold in 1973. **Mark:** First initial & last name; R. Babcock.

BACHE-WIIG, TOM, N-5966, Eivindvik, NORWAY, Phone: 4757784290, Fax: 4757784122
Specialties: High-art and working knives of his design. **Patterns:** Hunters, utility knives, hatchets, axes and art knives. **Technical:** Grinds Uddeholm Elmax, powder metallurgy tool stainless steel. Handles made of rear burls of Nordic woods stabilized with vacuum/high-pressure technique. **Prices:** $430 to $900; some to $2300. **Remarks:** Part-time maker; first knife sold 1988. **Mark:** Etched name and eagle head.

BACON, DAVID R., 906 136th St E, Bradenton, FL 34202-9694, Phone: 813-996-4289

BAGLEY, R KEITH, Old Pine Forge, 4415 Hope Acres Dr, White Plains, MD 20695, Phone: 301-932-0990
Specialties: High carbon Damascus with semi-precious stones set in exotic wood handle; tactical and skinner knives. **Technical:** Use ATS-34, 5160, 01, 1085, 1095. **Patterns:** Various patterns; prefer all Tool-Steel and Nickel Damascus. **Price:** Damascus from $250 to $500; stainless from $100 to $225. **Remarks:** Furrier for 25 years, blacksmith for 25 years, knife maker for 10 years.

BAILEY, JOSEPH D., 3213 Jonesboro Dr, Nashville, TN 37214, Phone: 615-889-3172
Specialties: Working and using straight knives; collector pieces. **Patterns:** Bowies, hunters, tactical, folders. **Technical:** 440C, ATS-34, Damascus and wire Damascus. Offers scrimshaw. **Prices:** $85 to $1200. **Remarks:** Part-time maker; first knife sold in 1988. **Mark:** Joseph D Bailey Nashville Tennessee.

BAILEY, KIRBY C., 2055 F. M. 2790 W., Lytle, TX 78052, Phone: 830-772-3376
Specialties: All kinds of knives folders, fixed blade, fighters. **Patterns:** Hunters, folders, fighters, Bowies, miniatures. **Technical:** I do all my own work; heat treating, file work etc. **Prices:** $200 to $1000. **Remarks:** I build any kind of hand cutlery. Have made knives for 45 years; sold knives for 28 years. **Mark:** K. C. B. & serial #. **Other:** Have sold knives in Asia & all states in US.

BAILEY, RYAN, 4185 S St Rt 605, Galena, OH 43021, Phone: 614-577-1040
Specialties: Fancy, high-art, high-tech, collectible straight knives and folders of his design and to customer specs; unique mechanisms, some disassemble. **Patterns:** Daggers, fighters and swords. **Technical:** Does own Damascus & forging from high carbon. Embellishes with file work & gold work. **Prices:** $200 to $2500. **Remarks:** Full-time maker; first knife sold in 1999. Doing business as Briar Knives. **Mark:** RLB.

BAKER, VANCE, 574 Co. Rd. 675, Riceville, TN 37370, Phone: 423-745-9157
Specialties: Traditional working straight knives of his design and to customer specs. Prefers drop-point hunters and small Bowies. **Patterns:** Hunters, utility and kitchen knives. **Technical:** Forges Damascus, cable, L6 and 5160. **Prices:** $100 to $250; some to $500. **Remarks:** Part-time maker; first knife sold in 1985. **Mark:** Initials connected.

BAKER, WILD BILL, Box 361, Boiceville, NY 12412, Phone: 914-657-8646
Specialties: Primitive knives, buckskinners. **Patterns:** Skinners, camp knives and Bowies. **Technical:** Works with L6, files and rasps. **Prices:** $100 to $350. **Remarks:** Part-time maker; first knife sold in 1989. **Mark:** Wild Bill Baker, Oak Leaf Forge, or both.

BAKER, RAY, PO Box 303, Sapulpa, OK 74067, Phone: 918-224-8013
Specialties: High-tech working straight knives. **Patterns:** Hunters, fighters, Bowies, skinners and boots of his design and to customer specs. **Technical:** Grinds 440C, 1095 spring steel or customer request; heat-

treats. Custom-made scabbards for any knife. **Prices:** $125 to $500; some to $1000. **Remarks:** Full-time maker; first knife sold in 1981. **Mark:** First initial, last name.

BAKER, HERB, 14104 NC 87 N, Eden, NC 27288, Phone: 336-627-0338

BALBACH, MARKUS, Heinrich - Worner - Str. 3, 35789 Weilmunster-Laubuseschbach/Ts., GERMANY 06475-8911, Fax: 912986
Specialties: High-art knives and working/using straight knives and folders of his design and to customer specs. **Patterns:** Hunters and daggers. **Technical:** Stainless steel, one of Germany's greatest Smithies. Supplier for the forges of Solingen. **Remarks:** Full-time maker; first knife sold in 1984. Doing business as Schmiedewerkstatte M. Balbach. **Mark:** Initials stamped inside the handle.

BALDWIN, PHILLIP, PO Box 563, Snohomish, WA 98290, Phone: 425-334-5569
Specialties: One-of-a-kind elegant table cutlery; exotics. **Patterns:** Elegant or exotic knives. Likes the challenge of axes, spears and specialty tools. **Technical:** Forges W2, W1 and his own pattern welded steel and mokume-gane. **Prices:** Start at $1000. **Remarks:** Full-time maker; first knife sold in 1973. **Mark:** Last initial marked with chisel.

BALL, KEN, 127 Sundown Manor, Mooresville, IN 46158, Phone: 317-834-4803
Specialties: Classic working/using straight knives of his design and to customer specs. **Patterns:** Hunters and utility/camp knives. **Technical:** Flatgrinds ATS-34. Offers filework. **Prices:** $150 to $400. **Remarks:** Part-time maker; first knife sold in 1994. Doing business as Ball Custom Knives. **Mark:** Last name.

BALLESTRA, SANTINO, via D. Tempesta 11/17, 18039 Ventimiglia (IM), ITALY 0184-215228
Specialties: Using and collecting straight knives. **Patterns:** Hunting, fighting, skinners, Bowies, medieval daggers and knives. **Technical:** Forges ATS-34, D2, O2, 1060 and his own Damascus. Uses ivory and silver. **Prices:** $500 to $2000; some higher. **Remarks:** Full-time maker; first knife sold in 1979. **Mark:** First initial, last name.

BALLEW, DALE, PO Box 1277, Bowling Green, VA 22427, Phone: 804-633-5701
Specialties: Miniatures only to customer specs. **Patterns:** Bowies, daggers and fighters. **Technical:** Files 440C stainless; uses ivory, abalone, exotic woods and some precious stones. **Prices:** $100 to $800. **Remarks:** Part-time maker; first knife sold in 1988. **Mark:** Initials and last name.

BANKS, DAVID L., 99 Blackfoot Ave, Riverton, WY 82501, Phone: 307-856-3154/Cell: 307-851-5599
Specialties: Heavy-duty working straight knives. **Patterns:** Hunters, Bowies and camp knives. **Technical:** Forges Damascus 1084-15N20, L-6-W1 pure nickel, 5160, 52100 and his own Damascus; differential heat treat and tempers. Handles made of horn, antlers and exotic wood. Hand-stitched harness leather sheaths. **Prices:** $300 to $2000. **Remarks:** Part-time maker. **Mark:** Banks Blackfoot forged Dave Banks & initials connected.

BARBER, ROBERT E., 1828 Franklin Dr, Charlottesville, VA 22911-8513, Phone: 804-295-4036
Specialties: Working straight knives and trapper pocket knives, some fancy with filework. **Patterns:** Hunters, skinners, combat knives/fighters and Bowies. **Technical:** Grinds ATS-34, 440C, D2, A2 and CPM 420V. **Prices:** $45 to $1000. **Remarks:** Part-time maker; member North Carolina Custom Knife Makers Guild; first knife sold in 1984. **Mark:** Initials within rebel hat logo.

BARDSLEY, NORMAN P., 197 Cottage St, Pawtucket, RI 02860, Phone: 401-725-9132
Specialties: Working and fantasy knives. **Patterns:** Fighters, boots, fantasy, renaissance & native American in upscale and presentation fashion. **Technical:** Grinds all steels and Damascus. Uses exotic hides for sheaths. **Prices:** $100 to $15,000. **Remarks:** Full-time maker. **Mark:** Last name in script with arrow.

BAREFOOT, JOE W., 117 Oakbrook Dr, Liberty, SC 29657
Specialties: Working straight knives of his design. **Patterns:** Hunters, fighters and boots; tantos and survival knives. **Technical:** Grinds D2, 440C and ATS-34. Mirror finishes. Uses ivory and stag on customer request only. **Prices:** $50 to $160; some to $500. **Remarks:** Part-time maker; first knife sold in 1980. **Mark:** Bare footprint.

BARKER, REGGIE, 603 S Park Dr, Springhill, LA 71075, Phone: 318-539-2958
Specialties: Camp knives & hatchets. **Patterns:** Bowie, skinning, hunting, camping, fighters, kitchen or customer design. **Technical:** Forges carbon steel and own pattern welded steels. Prices $150 to $2000. **Remarks:** Part-time maker. Winner of 1999 & 2000 Spring Hammering Cutting contest. Winner of Best Value of Show 2001; Arkansas Knife Show and journeyman smith. **Mark:** Barker JS. **Other:** Border Guard Forge.

custom knifemakers

BARKER, ROBERT G., 2311 Branch Rd, Bishop, GA 30621, Phone: 706-769-7827
Specialties: Traditional working/using straight knives of his design. **Patterns:** Bowies, hunters and utility knives, ABS Journeyman Smith. **Technical:** Hand forged carbon & Damascus. Forges to shape high-carbon 5160, cable and chain. Differentially heat-treats. **Prices:** $200 to $500; some to $1000. **Remarks:** Spare-time maker; first knife sold in 1987. **Mark:** BARKER/J. S.

BARLOW, JANA POIRIER, 3820 Borland Cir, Anchorage, AK 99517, Phone: 907-243-4581

BARNES, JACK, PO Box 1315, Whitefish, MT 59937-1315, Phone: 406-862-6078

BARNES, AUBREY G., 11341 Rock Hill Road, Hagerstown, MD 21740, Phone: 301-223-4587
Specialties: Classic working and using knives of his design, to customer specs and in standard patterns. **Patterns:** Bowies, hunters, fighters, daggers and utility/camping knives. **Technical:** Forges 5160, 1085, L6 and Damascus, Silver wire inlays. **Prices:** $300 to $2500. **Remarks:** Full-time maker; first knife sold in 1992. Doing business as Falling Waters Forge. **Mark:** First and middle initials, last name, M. S.

BARNES, WENDELL, 2160 Oriole Dr, Missoula, MT 59808, Phone: 406-721-0908
Specialties: Working straight knives. **Patterns:** Hunters, folders, neck knives. **Technical:** Grinds 440C, ATS-34, D2 and Damascus. **Prices:** Start at $75. **Remarks:** Spare-time maker; first knife sold in 1996. **Mark:** First initial and last name around broken heart.

BARNES, MARLEN R., 904 Crestview Dr S, Atlanta, TX 75551-1854, Phone: 903-796-3668
Specialties: Hammer forges random & mosaic Damascus. **Patterns:** Hatchets, straight & folding knives. **Technical:** Hammer forges carbon steel using 5160, 1084 & 52100 with 15N20 & 203E nickel. **Prices:** $150 and up. **Remarks:** Part-time maker; first knife sold 1999. **Mark:** Script M. R. B., other side J. S.

BARNES, WILLIAM, 591 Barnes Rd, Wallingford, CT 06492-1805, Phone: 860-349-0443

BARNES, GREGORY, 266 W. Calaveras St, Altadena, CA 91001, Phone: 626-398-0053

BARNES, GARY L., Box 138, New Windsor, MD 21776-0138, Phone: 410-635-6243, Fax: 410-635-6243
Specialties: Ornate button lock Damascus folders. **Patterns:** Barnes original. **Technical:** Forges own Damascus. **Prices:** Average $2500. **Remarks:** ABS Master Smith since 1983. **Mark:** Hand engraved logo of letter B pierced by dagger.

BARNES, ERIC, H C 74 Box 41, Mountain View, AR 72560, Phone: 501-269-3358

BARNES JR., CECIL C., 141 Barnes Dr, Center Ridge, AR 72027, Phone: 501-893-2267

BARNETT, VAN, Barnett Int'l Inc, 1135 Terminal Way Ste #209, Reno, NV 89502, Phone: 866 ARTKNIFE or 304-727-5512, Fax: 775-201-0038
Specialties: Collector grade one-of-a-kind / embellished high art daggers and art folders. **Patterns:** Art daggers and folders. **Technical:** Forges and grinds own Damascus. **Prices:** Upscale. **Remarks:** Designs and makes one-of-a-kind highly embellished art knives using high karat gold, diamonds and other gemstones, pearls, stone and fossil ivories, carved steel guards and blades, all knives are carved and or engraved, does own engraving, carving and other embellishments, sole authorship; full-time maker since 1981. **Mark:** V. H. Barnett or Van Barnett in script. **Other:** Does one high art collaboration a year with Dellana. Voting Member of Knifemakers Guild. Member of ABS.

BARNGROVER, JERRY, RR #4, Box 1230, Afton, OK 74331, Phone: 918-257-5076

BARR, JUDSON C., 1905 Pickwick Circle, Irving, TX 75060, Phone: 972-790-7195
Specialties: Bowies. **Patterns:** Sheffield & Early American. **Technical:** Forged carbon steel and Damascus. Also stock removal. **Remarks:** Associate member of ABS. **Mark:** Barr.

BARR, A. T., 153 Madonna Dr, Nicholasville, KY 40356, Phone: 859-887-5400
Specialties: Working and collector grade liner-lock folders. **Patterns:** Liner-lock folders. **Technical:** Flat grinds S30V, ATS-34, D-2 and commercial Damascus; hand rubbed satin finish. **Prices:** Start at $300. **Remarks:** Full-time maker, first knives sold in 1979. **Mark:** Full name.

BARRETT, RICK L. (TOSHI HISA), 18943 CR 18, GOSHEN, IN 46528, Phone: 574-533-4297
Specialties: Japanese-style blades from sushi knives to katana and fantasy pieces. **Patterns:** Swords, axes, spears/lances, hunter and utility knives. **Technical:** Forges and grinds Damascus and carbon steels, occasionally uses stainless. **Prices:** $250-$4000+. **Remarks:** Full-time bladesmith, jeweler. **Mark:** Japanese mei on Japanese pieces and stylized initials.

BARRETT, CECIL TERRY, 2514 Linda Lane, Colorado Springs, CO 80909, Phone: 719-473-8325
Specialties: Working and using straight knives and folders of his design, to customer specs and in standard patterns. **Patterns:** Bowies, hunters, kitchen knives, locking folders and slip-joint folders. **Technical:** Grinds 440C, D2 and ATS-34. Wood and leather sheaths. **Prices:** $65 to $500; some to $750. **Remarks:** Full-time maker. **Mark:** Stamped middle name.

BARRON, BRIAN, 123 12th Ave, San Mateo, CA 94402, Phone: 650-341-2683
Specialties: Traditional straight knives. **Patterns:** Daggers, hunters and swords. **Technical:** Grinds 440C, ATS-34 and 1095. Sculpts bolsters using an S-curve. **Prices:** $130 to $270; some to $1500. **Remarks:** Part-time maker; first knife sold in 1993. **Mark:** Diamond Drag "Barron".

BARRY III, JAMES J., 115 Flagler Promenade No, West Palm Beach, FL 33405, Phone: 561-832-4197
Specialties: High-art working straight knives of his design also high art tomahawks. **Patterns:** Hunters, daggers and fishing knives. **Technical:** Grinds 440C only. Prefers exotic materials for handles. Most knives embellished with filework, carving and scrimshaw. Many pieces designed to stand unassisted. **Prices:** $500 to $5000. **Remarks:** Part-time maker; first knife sold in 1975. **Mark:** Branded initials as a J & B together.

BARTH, J. D., 101 4th St, PO Box 186, Alberton, MT 59820, Phone: 406-722-4557
Specialties: Working and fancy straight knives of his design. **Technical:** Grinds ATS-34, 440-C, stainless and carbon Damascus. Uses variety of natural handle materials and Micarta. Likes dovetailed bolsters. Filework on most knives, full and tapered tangs. Makes custom fit sheaths for each knife. **Mark:** Name over maker, city & state.

BARTLOW, JOHN, 5078 Coffeen Ave, Sheridan, WY 82801, Phone: 307 673-4941
Specialties: New liner-locks, working hunters, skinners, bird and trouts. **Patterns:** Working hunters, skinners, capers, bird and trout knives. **Technical:** Working on 6 new liner-lock designs. **Prices:** $200 to $2000. **Remarks:** Full-time maker; first knife sold in 1979. Field-tests knives. **Mark:** Bartlow Sheridan, wyo.

BARTRUG, HUGH E., 2701 34th St. N., #142, St. Petersburg, FL 33713, Phone: 813-323-1136
Specialties: Inlaid straight knives and exotic folders; high-art knives and period pieces. **Patterns:** Hunters, Bowies and daggers; traditional patterns. **Technical:** Diffuses mokume. Forges 100 percent nickel, wrought iron, mosaic Damascus, shokeedo and O1 tool steel; grinds. **Prices:** $210 to $2500; some to $5000. **Remarks:** Retired maker; first knife sold in 1980. **Mark:** Ashley Forge or name.

BASKETT, LEE GENE, 427 Sutzer Ck. Rd, Eastview, KY 42732, Phone: 270-862-5019
Specialties: Fancy working knives and fantasy pieces, often set up in desk stands. **Patterns:** Fighters, Bowies and survival knives; locking folders and traditional styles. **Technical:** Liner-locks. Grinds O1, 440C; buys Damascus. Filework provided on most knives. **Prices:** Start at $135. **Remarks:** Part-time maker; first knife sold in 1980. **Mark:** Last name.

BATLEY, MARK S., PO Box 217, Wake, VA 23176, Phone: 804-776-7794

BATSON, JAMES, 176 Brentwood Lane, Madison, AL 35758, Phone: 540-937-2318
Specialties: Forged Damascus blades and fittings in collectible period pieces. **Patterns:** Integral art knives, Bowies, folders, American-styled blades and miniatures. **Technical:** Forges 52100, 5160 and his Damascus. **Prices:** $150 to $1800; some to $4500. **Remarks:** Full-time maker; first knife sold in 1978. **Mark:** Name, bladesmith with horse's head.

BATSON, RICHARD G., 6591 Waterford Rd, Rixeyville, VA 22737, Phone: 540-937-5932
Specialties: Military, utility and fighting knives in working and presentation grade. **Patterns:** Daggers, combat and utility knives. **Technical:** Grinds O1, 1095 and 440C. Etches and scrimshaws; offers polished, Parkerized finishes. **Prices:** $200 to $450. **Remarks:** Semi-retired, limit production. First knife sold in 1958. **Mark:** Bat in circle, hand-signed and serial numbered.

BATTS, KEITH, 450 Manning Rd, Hooks, TX 75561, Phone: 903-832-1140
Specialties: Working straight knives of his design or to customer specs. **Patterns:** Bowies, hunters, skinners, camp knives and others. **Technical:** Forges 5160 and his Damascus; offers filework. **Prices:** $245 to $895. **Remarks:** Part-time maker; first knife sold in 1988. **Mark:** Last name.

BAUCHOP, ROBERT, PO Box 330, Munster, Kwazulu-Natal 4278, SOUTH AFRICA, Phone: +27 39 3192449
Specialties: Fantasy knives; working and using knives of his design and to customer specs. **Patterns:** Hunters, swords, utility/camp knives, diver's knives and large swords. **Technical:** Grinds Sandvick 12C27, D2, 440C. Uses South African hardwoods red ivory, wild olive, African blackwood, etc.—on handles. **Prices:** $200 to $800; some to $2000. **Remarks:** Full-time maker; first knife sold in 1986. Doing business as Bauchop Custom Knives and swords. **Mark:** Viking helmet with Bauchop (bow and chopper) crest.

BAUCHOP, PETER, c/o Beck's Cutlery Specialties, 107 Edinburgh S #109, Cary, NC 27511, Phone: 919-460-0203, Fax: 919-460-7772
Specialties: Working straight knives and period pieces. **Patterns:** Fighters, swords and survival knives. **Technical:** Grinds O1, D2, G3, 440C and AST-34. Scrimshaws. **Prices:** $100 to $350; some to $1500. **Remarks:** Full-time maker; first knife sold in 1980. **Mark:** Bow and axe (BOW-CHOP).

BAUM, RICK, 435 North Center St, Lehi, UT 84043, Phone: 801-431-7290

BAUMGARDNER, ED, 128 E Main St, Glendale, KY 42740, Phone: 502-435-2675
Specialties: Working fixed blades, some folders. **Patterns:** Drop point & clip point hunters, fighters, small Bowies, traditional slip joint folders and pockbacks. **Technical:** Grinds O-1, 154CM, ARS-34, and Damascus likes using natural handle materials. **Prices:** $100-$700. **Remarks:** Part-time maker, first knife sold in 2001. **Mark:** Last name.

BEAM, JOHN R., 1310 Foothills Rd, Kalispell, MT 59901, Phone: 406-755-2593
Specialties: Classic, high-art and working straight knives of his design. **Patterns:** Bowies and hunters. **Technical:** Grinds 440C, Damascus and scrap. **Prices:** $175 to $600; some to $3000. **Remarks:** Part-time maker; first knife sold in 1950. Doing business as Beam's Knives. **Mark:** Beam's Knives.

BEASLEY, GENEO, PO Box 339, Wadsworth, NV 89442, Phone: 775-575-2584

BEATTY, GORDON H., 121 Petty Rd, Seneca, SC 29672, Phone: 864-882-6278
Specialties: Working straight knives, some fancy. **Patterns:** Traditional patterns, mini-skinners and letter openers. **Technical:** Grinds 440C, D2 and ATS-34; makes knives one at a time. **Prices:** $75 to $450; some to $450. **Remarks:** Part-time maker; first knife sold in 1982. **Mark:** Name.

BEATY, ROBERT B., Cutler, 1995 Big Flat Rd, Missoula, MT 59804, Phone: 406-549-1818
Specialties: Plain & fancy working knives & collector pieces; will accept custom orders. **Patterns:** Hunters, Bowies, utility, kitchen & camp knives; locking folders. **Technical:** Grinds D-2, ATS-34, Dendritie D-2, makes all tool steel Damascus, forges 1095, 5160, 52100. **Prices:** $100 to $450; some to $1100. **Remarks:** Full-time maker; first knife sold 1995. **Mark:** Stainless: First name, middle initial, last name, city & state. Carbon: Last name stamped on Ricasso.

BEAUCHAMP, GAETAN, 125, de la Rivire, Stoneham, PQ, CANADA G0A 4P0, Phone: 418-848-1914, Fax: 418-848-6859
Specialties: Working knives and folders of his design and to customer specs. **Patterns:** Hunters, fighters, fantasy knives. **Technical:** Grinds ATS-34, 440C, Damascus. Scrimshaws on ivory; specializes in buffalo horn and black backgrounds. Offers a variety of handle materials. **Prices:** Start at $125. **Remarks:** Full-time maker; first knife sold in 1992. **Mark:** Signature etched on blade.

BECKER, FRANZ, Am Kreuzberg 2, 84533 Marktl/Inn, GERMANY

BECKER, STEVE, 201 1st Ave NW, Conrad, MT 59425, Phone: 406-278-7753

BECKER, FRANZ, AM Kreuzberg 2, 84533, Marktl/Inn, GERMANY 08678-8020
Specialties: Stainless steel knives in working sizes. **Patterns:** Semi- and full-integral knives; interframe folders. **Technical:** Grinds stainless steels; likes natural handle materials. **Prices:** $200 to $2000. **Mark:** Name, country.

BECKETT, NORMAN L., 1501 N. Chaco Ave, Farmington, NM 87401, Phone: 505-325-4468, Fax: 505-325-4468
Specialties: Fancy, traditional and working folders & straight knives of his design. **Patterns:** Bowies, fighters, folders & hunters. **Technical:** Grinds ATS-34, 440C, CPM 440V and Damascus. File works blades; hollow and flat grinds. Prefers mirror finish; satin finish on working knives. Uses exotic handle material, stabilized woods & Micarta. Hand-tooled or inlaid sheaths. **Prices:** $125 to $900; some to $2500 and up. **Remarks:** Full-time maker; first knife sold in 1993. Doing business as Norm Beckett Knives. **Mark:** First and last name, maker, city and state.

BEERS, RAY, 8 Manorbrook Rd, Monkton, MD 21111, Phone: Summer 410-472-2229, Fax: 410-472-9136

BEERS, RAY, 2501 Lakefront Dr, Lake Wales, FL 33898, Phone: Winter 863-696-3036, Fax: 863-696-9421

BEETS, MARTY, 390 N 5TH Ave, Williams Lake, BC, CANADA V2G 2G4, Phone: 250-392-7199
Specialties: Working and collectable straight knives of my own design. **Patterns:** Hunter, skinners, Bowies and utility knives. **Technical:** Grinds 440C-I do all of my own work including heat treating Uses a variety of handle material specializing in exotic hardwoods, antler and horn. **Price:** $125-$400. **Remarks:** Wife, Sandy does handmade/hand stitched sheaths. First knife sold in 1988. Business name Beets Handmade Knives.

BEGG, TODD M., 420 169 ST. S, Spanaway, WA 98387, Phone: 253-531-2113
Specialties: Hand rubbed satin finished 440c stainless steel. Mirror polished 426 stainless steel. Stabilized mardrone wood.

BEHNKE, WILLIAM, 931 W Sanborn Rd, Lake City, MI 49651-7600, Phone: 231-839-3342
Specialties: Hunters, belt knives and folders. **Patterns:** Traditional styling in moderate-sized straight and folding knives. **Technical:** Forges his own Damascus, cable, saw chain and 5160; likes brass and natural materials. **Prices:** $150 to $2000. **Remarks:** Part-time maker. **Mark:** Bill Behnke Knives.

BELL, MICHAEL, 88321 N Bank Lane, Coquille, OR 97423, Phone: 541-396-3605
Specialties: Full line of traditional Japanese swords. **Patterns:** Complete Japanese line; Tanto, Katana etc. **Technical:** All forged, cable & hand-made steel. **Prices:** Swords from $4000 to $20,000. **Remarks:** Full-time maker; first knife sold in 1972. Served apprenticeship with Japanese sword maker. Doing business as Dragonfly Forge. **Mark:** Dragonfly in shield or tombo Kuni Mitsu.

BELL, DONALD, 2 Division St, Bedford, Nova Scotia, CANADA B4A 1Y8, Phone: 902-835-2623
Specialties: Fancy knives; working/using straight knives and folders of his design. **Patterns:** Hunters, locking folders, jewelry knives. **Technical:** Grinds Damascus and ATS-34; forges and grinds O1; pierces and carves blades. **Prices:** $150 to $650; some to $1200. **Remarks:** Spare-time maker; first knife sold in 1993. **Mark:** Bell symbol with first initial inside.

BENDIK, JOHN, 7076 Fitch Rd, Olmsted Falls, OH 44138

BENFIELD JR., ROBERT O., 532 Bowie, Forney, TX 75126

BENJAMIN JR., GEORGE, 3001 Foxy Lane, Kissimmee, FL 34746, Phone: 407-846-7259
Specialties: Fighters in various styles to include Persian, Moro and military. **Patterns:** Daggers, skinners and one-of-a-kind grinds. **Technical:** Forges O1, D2, A2, 5160 and Damascus. Favors Pakkawood, Micarta, and mirror or Parkerized finishes. Makes unique para-military leather sheaths. **Prices:** $150 to $600; some to $1200. **Remarks:** Doing business as The Leather Box. **Mark:** Southern Pride Knives.

BENNETT, GLEN C., 5821 S Stewart Blvd, Tucson, AZ 85706

BENNETT, PETER, PO Box 143, Engadine N. S. W. 2233, AUSTRALIA, Phone: 02-520-4975 (home), Fax: O2-528-8219 (work)
Specialties: Fancy and embellished working and using straight knives to customer specs and in standard patterns. **Patterns:** Fighters, hunters, bird/trout and fillet knives. **Technical:** Grinds 440C, ATS-34 and Damascus. Uses rare Australian desert timbers for handles. **Prices:** $90 to $500; some to $1500. **Remarks:** Full-time maker; first knife sold in 1985. **Mark:** First and middle initials, last name; country.

BENNETT, BRETT C., 1922 Morrie Ave, Cheyenne, WY 82001, Phone: 307-432-0985

BENNICA, CHARLES, Chemin du Salet, 34190 Moules et Baucels, FRANCE, Phone: +33 4 67 73 42 40
Specialties: Fixed blades and folding knives; the latter with slick closing mechanisms with push buttons to unlock blades. Unique handle shapes, signature to the maker. **Technical:** 416 stainless steel frames for folders and ATS-34 blades. Also specializes in Damascus.

BENSON, DON, 2505 Jackson St, #112, Escalon, CA 95320, Phone: 209-838-7921
Specialties: Working straight knives of his design. **Patterns:** Axes, Bowies, tantos and hunters. **Technical:** Grinds 440C. **Prices:** $100 to $150;

custom knifemakers

some to $400. **Remarks:** Spare-time maker; first knife sold in 1980. **Mark:** Name.

BENTLEY, C. L., 2405 Hilltop Dr, Albany, GA 31707, Phone: 912-432-6656

BER, DAVE, 656 Miller Rd, San Juan Island, WA 98250, Phone: 206-378-7230
Specialties: Working straight and folding knives for the sportsman; welcomes customer designs. **Patterns:** Hunters, skinners, Bowies, kitchen and fishing knives. **Technical:** Forges and grinds saw blade steel, wire Damascus, O1, L6, 5160 and 440C. **Prices:** $100 to $300; some to $500. **Remarks:** Full-time maker; first knife sold in 1985. **Mark:** Last Name.

BERG, LOTHAR, 37 Hillcrest Ln, Kitchener ON, CANADA NZK 1S9, Phone: 519-745-3260
519-745-3260

BERGER, MAX A., 5716 John Richard Ct, Carmichael, CA 95608, Phone: 916-972-9229
Specialties: Fantasy and working/using straight knives of his design. **Patterns:** Fighters, hunters and utility/camp knives. **Technical:** Grinds ATS-34 and 440C. Offers fileworks and combinations of mirror polish and satin finish blades. **Prices:** $200 to $600; some to $2500. **Remarks:** Part-time maker; first knife sold in 1992. **Mark:** Last name.

BERGH, ROGER, PL1137, 83070 NRA, SWEDEN, Phone: +46 613 12046, Fax: +46 613 12046

BERGLIN, BRUCE D., 17441 Lake Terrace Place, Mount Vernon, WA 98274, Phone: 360-422-8603
Specialties: Working and using straight knives of his own design. **Patterns:** Hunters, boots, Bowies, utility/camp knives and period pieces, some made to look old. **Technical:** Forges carbon steel, grinds carbon and stainless steel. Prefers natural handle material and micarta. **Prices:** Start at $200. **Remarks:** Part-time maker since 1998. **Mark:** First initial, middle initial and last name, sometimes surrounded with an oval.

BERTHOLUS, BERNARD, Atelier Du Brute, De Forge 21, rue Fersen 06600, Antibes, FRANCE, Phone: 04 93 34 95 90
Specialties: Traditional working and using straight knives of his design. **Patterns:** Bowies, daggers and hunters. **Technical:** Forges ATS-34, 440, D2 and carbon steels. **Prices:** $720 to $7500. **Remarks:** Full-time maker; first knife sold in 1990. **Mark:** City and last name.

BERTOLAMI, JUAN CARLOS, Av San Juan 575, Neuquen, ARGENTINA 8300
Specialties: Hunting and country labor knives. All of them unique high quality pieces and I supply collectors too. **Technical:** Austrian stainless steel and elephant, hippopotamus and orca ivory, as well as ebony and other fine woods for the handles.

BERTUZZI, ETTORE, Via Partigiani 3, 24068 Seriate (Bergamo), ITALY, Phone: 035-294262, Fax: 035-294262
Specialties: Classic straight knives and folders of his design, to customer specs and in standard patterns. **Patterns:** Bowies, hunters and locking folders. **Technical:** Grinds ATS-34, D3, D2 and various Damascus. **Prices:** $300 to $500. **Remarks:** Part-time maker; first knife sold in 1993. **Mark:** Name etched on ricasso.

BESEDICK, FRANK E., RR 2, Box 802, Ruffsdale, PA 15679, Phone: 724-696-3312
Specialties: Traditional working and using straight knives of his design. **Patterns:** Hunters, utility/camp knives and miniatures; buckskinner blades and tomahawks. **Technical:** Forges and grinds 5160, O1 and Damascus. Offers filework and scrimshaw. **Prices:** $75 to $300; some to $750. **Remarks:** Part-time maker; first knife sold in 1990. **Mark:** Name or initials.

BETHKE, LORA SUE, 13420 Lincoln St, Grand Haven, MI 49417, Phone: 616-842-8268, Fax: 616-844-2696
Specialties: Classic and traditional straight knives of her design. **Patterns:** Boots, Bowies and hunters. **Technical:** Forges 1084 and Damascus. **Prices:** Start at $400. **Remarks:** Part-time maker; first knife sold in 1997. **Mark:** Full name - JS on reverse side. **Other:** Journeyman bladesmith, American Bladesmith Society.

BEUKES, TINUS, 83 Henry St, Risiville, Vereeniging 1939, SOUTH AFRICA, Phone: 27 16 423 2053
Specialties: Working straight knives. **Patterns:** Hunters, skinners and kitchen knives. **Technical:** Grinds D2, 440C and chain, cable and stainless Damascus. **Prices:** $80 to $180. **Remarks:** Part-time maker; first knife sold in 1993. **Mark:** Full name, city, logo.

BEVERLY II, LARRY H., PO Box 741, Spotsylvania, VA 22553, Phone: 540-898-3951
Specialties: Working straight knives, slip-joints and liner-locks. Welcomes customer designs. **Patterns:** Bowies, hunters, guardless fighters and miniatures. **Technical:** Grinds 440C, A2 and O1. **Prices:** $125 to $1000.

Remarks: Part-time maker; first knife sold in 1986. **Mark:** Initials or last name in script.

BEZUIDENHOUT, BUZZ, 30 Surlingham Ave, Malvern, Queensburgh, Natal 4093, SOUTH AFRICA, Phone: 031-4632827, Fax: 031-3631259
Specialties: Traditional working and using straight knives of his design and to customer specs. **Patterns:** Boots, hunters, kitchen knives and utility/camp knives. **Technical:** Grinds 12C27, 440C and ATS-34. Uses local hardwoods, horn - kudu, impala, buffalo - giraffe bone and ivory for handles. **Prices:** $150 to $200; some to $1500. **Remarks:** Spare-time maker; first knife sold in 1988. **Mark:** First name with a bee emblem.

BIGGERS, GARY, Ventura Knives, 1278 Colina Vista, Ventura, CA 93003, Phone: 805-658-6610, Fax: 805-658-6610
Specialties: Fixed blade knives of his design. **Patterns:** Hunters, boots/fighters, Bowies and utility knives. **Technical:** Grinds ATS-34, 01 and commercial Damascus. **Prices:** $150 to $550. **Remarks:** Part-time maker: first knife sold in 1996. Doing business as Ventura Knives. **Mark:** First and last name, city and state.

BILLGREN, PER, Stallgatan 9, S815 76 SODERFORS, SWEDEN, Phone: +46 293 17480, Fax: +46 293 30124
Specialties: Damasteel, stainless Damascus steels. **Patterns:** Bluetounge, Heimskringla, Muhammed's ladder, Rose twist, Odin's eye, Vinland, Hakkapelliitta. **Technical:** Modern Damascus steel made by patented powder metallurgy method. **Prices:** $80 to $180. **Remarks:** Damasteel is available through distributors around the globe.

BIRDWELL, IRA LEE, PO Box 1135, Bagdad, AZ 86321, Phone: 520-633-2516
Specialties: Special orders. **Mark:** engraved signature.

BIRNBAUM, EDWIN, 9715 Hammocks Blvd I 206, Miami, FL 33196

BISH, HAL, 9347 Sweetbriar Trace, Jonesboro, GA 30236, Phone: 770-477-2422

BIZZELL, ROBERT, 145 Missoula Av, Butte, MT 59701, Phone: 406-782-4403
Specialties: Damascus. **Patterns:** Composite, mosaic & traditional. **Technical:** Only fixed blades at this time. **Prices:** Start at $150. **Mark:** Hand signed.

BLACK, EARL, 3466 South, 700 East, Salt Lake City, UT 84106, Phone: 801-466-8395
Specialties: High-art straight knives and folders; period pieces. **Patterns:** Boots, Bowies and daggers; lockers and gents. **Technical:** Grinds 440C and 154CM. Buys some Damascus. Scrimshaws and engraves. **Prices:** $200 to $1800; some to $2500 and higher. **Remarks:** Full-time maker; first knife sold in 1980. **Mark:** Name, city, state.

BLACK, SCOTT, 27100 Leetown Rd, Picayune, MS 39466, Phone: 601-799-5939
Specialties: Friction folders; fighters. **Patterns:** Bowies, fighters, hunters, smoke hawks, friction folders, daggers. **Technical:** All forged, all work done by me, own hand-stitched leather work; own heat-treating. **Prices:** $100 to $2200. **Remarks:** ABS Journeyman Smith. **Mark:** Hot Mark - Copperhead Snake. **Other:** Cabel / Damascus/ High Carbone.

BLACK, SCOTT, 570 Malcom Rd, Covington, GA 30209
Specialties: Working/using folders of his design. **Patterns:** Daggers, hunters, utility/camp knives and friction folders. **Technical:** Forges pattern welded, cable, 1095, O1 and 5160. **Prices:** $100 to $500. **Remarks:** Part-time maker; first knife sold in 1992. Doing business as Copperhead Forge. **Mark:** Hot mark on blade, copperhead snake.

BLACK, TOM, 921 Grecian NW, Albuquerque, NM 87107, Phone: 505-344-2549
Specialties: Working knives to fancy straight knives of his design. **Patterns:** Drop-point skinners, folders, using knives, Bowies and daggers. **Technical:** Grinds 440C, 154CM, ATS-34, A2, D2 and Damascus. Offers engraving and scrimshaw. **Prices:** $185 to $1250; some over $8500. **Remarks:** Full-time maker; first knife sold in 1970. **Mark:** Name, city.

BLACKTON, ANDREW E., 12521 Fifth Isle, Bayonet Point, FL 34667, Phone: 727-869-1406
Specialties: Straight and folding knives, some fancy. **Patterns:** Hunters, Bowies and daggers. **Technical:** Grinds D2, 440C and 154CM. Offers some embellishment. **Prices:** $125 to $450; some to $2000. **Remarks:** Full-time maker. **Mark:** Last name in script.

BLANCHARD, G. R. (GARY), 5917 Negril Ave, Las Vegas, NV 89130, Phone: 702-645-9774
Specialties: Fancy folders and high-art straight knives of his design. **Patterns:** Boots, daggers and locking folders. **Technical:** Grinds 440C and ATS-34 and Damascus. Engraves knives. **Prices:** $1500 to $18,000 or more. **Remarks:** Full-time maker; first knife sold in 1989. **Mark:** First and middle initials, last name.

BLASINGAME, ROBERT, 281 Swanson, Kilgore, TX 75662, Phone: 903-984-8144
Specialties: Classic working and using straight knives and folders of his design and to customer specs. **Patterns:** Bowies, daggers, fighters and hunters; one-of-a-kind historic reproductions. **Technical:** Hand-forges P. W. Damascus, cable Damascus and chain Damascus. **Prices:** $150 to $1000; some to $2000. **Remarks:** Full-time maker; first knife sold in 1968. **Mark:** 'B' inside anvil.

BLAUM, ROY, 319 N. Columbia St, Covington, LA 70433, Phone: 985-893-1060
Specialties: Working straight knives and folders of his design; lightweight easy-open folders. **Patterns:** Hunters, boots, fishing and woodcarving/whittling knives. **Technical:** Grinds A2, D2, O1, 154CM and ATS-34. Offers leatherwork. **Prices:** $40 to $800; some higher. **Remarks:** Full-time maker; first knife sold in 1976. **Mark:** Engraved signature or etched logo.

BLOOMER, ALAN T., 116 E 6th St, Maquon, IL 61458, Phone: 309-875-3583
Specialties: All Damascus folders, making own Damascus. **Patterns:** Bowies, Folders, chef etc. **Technical:** Does own heat treating. **Prices:** $400 to $1000. **Remarks:** Part-time maker; Guild member. **Mark:** Stamp Bloomer. **Other:** No orders.

BLOOMQUIST, R. GORDON, 6206 Tiger Tail Dr, Olympia, WA 98512, Phone: 360-352-7162

BLUM, CHUCK, 743 S. Brea Blvd., #10, Brea, CA 92621, Phone: 714-529-0484
Specialties: Art and investment daggers and Bowies. **Technical:** Flat-grinds; hollow-grinds 440C, ATS-34 on working knives. **Prices:** $125 to $8500. **Remarks:** Part-time maker; first knife sold in 1985. **Mark:** First and middle initials and last name with sailboat logo.

BLUM, KENNETH, 1729 Burleson, Brenham, TX 77833, Phone: 979-836-9577
Specialties: Traditional working straight knives of his design. **Patterns:** Camp knives, Hunters and Bowies. **Technical:** Forges 5160; grinds 440C and D2. Uses exotic woods and Micarta for handles. **Prices:** $150 to $300. **Remarks:** Part-time maker; first knife sold in 1978. **Mark:** Last name on ricasso.

BOARDMAN, GUY, 39 Mountain Ridge R., New Germany 3619, SOUTH AFRICA, Phone: 031-726-921
Specialties: American and South African-styles. **Patterns:** Bowies, American and South African hunters, plus more. **Technical:** Grinds Bohler steels, some ATS-34. **Prices:** $100 to $600. **Remarks:** Part-time maker; first knife sold in 1986. **Mark:** Name, city, country.

BOATRIGHT, BASEL, 11 Timber Point, New Braunfels, TX 78132, Phone: 210-609-0807
Specialties: Working and using knives of his design. **Patterns:** Hunters, skinners and utility/camp knives. **Technical:** Grinds and hand-tempers 5160. **Prices:** $75 to $300. **Remarks:** Part-time maker. **Mark:** Stamped BBB.

BOCHMAN, BRUCE, 183 Howard Place, Grants Pass, OR 97526, Phone: 503-471-1985
Specialties: Working straight knives in standard patterns. **Patterns:** Bowies, hunters, fishing and bird knives. **Technical:** 440C; mirror or satin finish. **Prices:** $140 to $250; some to $750. **Remarks:** Part-time maker; first knife sold in 1977. **Mark:** Custom blades by B. Bochman.

BODEN, HARRY, Via Gellia Mill, Bonsall Matlock, Derbyshire DE4 2AJ, ENGLAND, Phone: 0629-825176
Specialties: Traditional working straight knives and folders of his design. **Patterns:** Hunters, locking folders and utility/camp knives. **Technical:** Grinds Sandvik 12C27, D2 and O1. **Prices:** £70 to £150; some to £300. **Remarks:** Full-time maker; first knife sold in 1986. **Mark:** Full name.

BODNER, GERALD "JERRY", 4102 Spyglass Ct, Louisville, KY 40229, Phone: 502-968-5946
Specialties: Fantasy straight knives in standard patterns. **Patterns:** Bowies, fighters, hunters and micro-miniature knives. **Technical:** Grinds Damascus, 440C and D2. Offers filework. **Prices:** $35 to $180. **Remarks:** Part-time maker; first knife sold in 1993. **Mark:** Last name in script and JAB in oval above knives.

BODOLAY, ANTAL, Rua Wilson Soares Fernandes #31, Planalto, Belo Horizonte MG-31730-700, BRAZIL, Phone: 031-494-1885
Specialties: Working folders and fixed blades of his design or to customer specs; some art daggers and period pieces. **Patterns:** Daggers, hunters, locking folders, utility knives and Khukris. **Technical:** Grinds D6, high carbon steels and 420 stainless. Forges files on request. **Prices:** $30 to $350. **Remarks:** Full-time maker; first knife sold in 1965. **Mark:** Last name in script.

BOEHLKE, GUENTER, Parkstrasse 2, 56412 Grossholbach, GERMANY 2602-5440
Specialties: Classic working/using straight knives of his design. **Patterns:** Hunters, utility/camp knives and ancient remakes. **Technical:** Grinds Damascus, CPM-T-440V and 440C. Inlays gemstones and ivory. **Prices:** $220 to $700; some to $2000. **Remarks:** Spare-time maker; first knife sold in 1985. **Mark:** Name, address and bow and arrow.

BOGUSZEWSKI, PHIL, PO Box 99329, Lakewood, WA 98499, Phone: 253-581-7096
Specialties: Working folders—some fancy—mostly of his design. **Patterns:** Folders, slip-joints and lockers; also makes anodized titanium frame folders. **Technical:** Grinds BG42 & Damascus; offers filework. **Prices:** $450 to $2500. **Remarks:** Full-time maker; first knife sold in 1979. **Mark:** Name, city and state.

BOJTOS, ARPA D., Dobsinskeho 10, 98403 Lucenec, Slovakia, Phone: 00421-47 4333512
Specialties: Fantasy and high-art knives. **Patterns:** Daggers, fighters and hunters. **Technical:** Grinds ATS-34. Carves on steel, handle materials and sheaths. **Prices:** $2000 to $5000; some to $8000. **Remarks:** Full-time maker; first knife sold in 1990. **Mark:** Stylized initials.

BOLD, STU, 63 D'Andrea Tr., Sarnia, Ont., CANADA N7S 6H3, Phone: 519-383-7610
Specialties: Traditional working/using straight knives in standard patterns and to customer specs. **Patterns:** Boots, Bowies and hunters. **Technical:** Grinds ATS-34, 440C and Damascus; mosaic pins. Offers scrimshaw and hand-tooled leather sheaths. **Prices:** $140 to $500; some to $2000. **Remarks:** Part-time maker; first knife sold in 1983. **Mark:** Name, city, province.

BOLEWARE, DAVID, PO Box 96, Carson, MS 39427, Phone: 601-943-5372
Specialties: Traditional and working/using straight knives of his design, to customer specs and in standard patterns. **Patterns:** Bowies, hunters and utility/camp knives. **Technical:** Grinds ATS-34, 440C and Damascus. **Prices:** $85 to $350; some to $600. **Remarks:** Part-time maker; first knife sold in 1989. **Mark:** First and last name, city, state.

BOLTON, CHARLES B., PO Box 6, Jonesburg, MO 63351, Phone: 636-488-5785
Specialties: Working straight knives in standard patterns. **Patterns:** Hunters, skinners, boots and fighters. **Technical:** Grinds 440C and ATS-34. **Prices:** $100 to $300; some to $600. **Remarks:** Full-time maker; first knife sold in 1973. **Mark:** Last name.

BONASSI, FRANCO, Via Superiore 14, Pordenone 33170, ITALY, Phone: 434-550821
Specialties: Fancy and working one-of-a-kind straight knives of his design. **Patterns:** Hunters, skinners, utility and liner-locks. **Technical:** Grinds CPM, ATS-34, 154CM and commercial Damascus. Uses only titanium foreguards and pommels. **Prices:** Start at $250. **Remarks:** Spare-time maker; first knife sold in 1988. Has made cutlery for several celebrities; Gen. Schwarzkopf, Fuzzy Zoeller, etc. **Mark:** FRANK.

BOOCO, GORDON, 175 Ash St, PO Box 174, Hayden, CO 81639, Phone: 970-276-3195
Specialties: Fancy working straight knives of his design and to customer specs. **Patterns:** Hunters and Bowies. **Technical:** Grinds 440C, D2 and A2. Heat-treats. **Prices:** $150 to $350; some $600 and higher. **Remarks:** Part-time maker; first knife sold in 1984. **Mark:** Last name with push dagger artwork.

BOOS, RALPH, 5107 40 Ave, Edmonton, Alberta, CANADA T6L 1B3, Phone: 780-463-7094
Specialties: Classic, fancy and fantasy miniature knives and swords of his design or to customer specs. **Patterns:** Bowies, daggers and swords. **Technical:** Hand files O1, stainless and Damascus. Engraves and carves. Does heat bluing and acid etching. **Prices:** $125 to $350; some to $1000. **Remarks:** Part-time maker; first knife sold in 1982. **Mark:** First initials back to back.

BOOTH, PHILIP W., 301 S. Jeffery Ave, Ithaca, MI 48847, Phone: 989-875-2844
Specialties: Folding knives, various mechanisms, maker of the "minnow" series small folding knife. **Patterns:** Auto lock-backs, liner-locks, classic pattern multi-blades. **Technical:** Grinds ATS-34, 440C, 1095 and commercial Damascus. Prefers natural materials, offers file work and scrimshaw. **Prices:** $200 and up. **Remarks:** Full-time maker; first knife sold in 1991. **Mark:** Last name or name with city and map logo.

BORGER, WOLF, Benzstrasse 8, 76676 Graben-Neudorf, GERMANY, Phone: 07255-72303, Fax: 07255-72304
Specialties: High-tech working and using straight knives and folders, many with corkscrews or other tools, of his design. **Patterns:** Hunters, Bowies and folders with various locking systems. **Technical:** Grinds 440C, ATS-34 and CPM. Uses stainless Damascus. **Prices:** $250 to $900; some

custom knifemakers

to $1500. **Remarks:** Full-time maker; first knife sold in 1975. **Mark:** Howling wolf and name; first name on Damascus blades.

BOSE, REESE, PO Box 61, Shelburn, IN 47879, Phone: 812-397-5114
Specialties: Traditional working and using knives in standard patterns and multi-blade knives. **Patterns:** Multi-blade slip-joints. **Technical:** ATS-34, D2 and CPM 440V. **Prices:** $275 to $1500. **Remarks:** Full-time maker; first knife sold in 1992. Photos by Jack Busfield. **Mark:** R. Bose.

BOSE, TONY, 7252 N. County Rd, 300 E., Shelburn, IN 47879-9778, Phone: 812-397-5114
Specialties: Traditional working and using knives in standard patterns; multi-blade folders. **Patterns:** Multi-blade slip-joints. **Technical:** Grinds commercial Damascus, ATS-34 and D2. **Prices:** $400 to $1200. **Remarks:** Full-time maker; first knife sold in 1972. **Mark:** First initial, last name, city, state.

BOSSAERTS, CARL, Rua Albert Einstein 906, 14051-110, Ribeirao Preto, S. P. BRAZIL, Phone: 016 633 7063
Specialties: Working and using straight knives, to customer specs and in standard patterns. **Patterns:** Hunters, fighters and utility/camp knives. **Technical:** Grinds ATS-34, 440V and 440C; does filework. **Prices:** 60 to $400. **Remarks:** Part-time maker; first knife sold in 1992. **Mark:** Initials joined together.

BOST, ROGER E., 30511 Cartier Dr, Palos Verdes, CA 90275-5629, Phone: 310-541-6833
Specialties: Hunters, fighters, boot, utility. **Patterns:** Loveless-style. **Technical:** ATS-34, 60-61RC, stock removal & forge. **Prices:** $200 & up. **Remarks:** First knife sold in 1990. **Mark:** Diamond with initials inside and Palos Verdes California around outside. **Other:** Cal. Knifemakers Assn, ABS.

BOSTWICK, CHRIS T., 341 Robins Run, Burlington, WI 53105
Specialties: Slipjoints ATS-34. **Patterns:** English jack, gunstock jack, doctors, stockman. **Prices:** $300 and up. **Remarks:** Enjoy traditional patterns/history multiblade slipjoints. **Mark:** CTB.

BOSWORTH, DEAN, 329 Mahogany Dr, Key Largo, FL 33037, Phone: 305-451-1564
Specialties: Free hand hollow ground working knives with hand rubbed satin finish, filework and inlays. **Patterns:** Bird & Trout, hunters, skinners, filet, Bowies, miniatures. **Technical:** Using 440C, ATS-34, D2, Meier Damascus, custom wet formed sheaths. **Prices:** $250 & up. **Remarks:** Part-time maker; first knife made in 1985. **Mark:** BOZ stamped in block letters. **Other:** Member: Florida Knifemakers Assoc.

BOURBEAU, JEAN YVES, 15 Rue Remillard, Notre Dame, Ile Perrot, Quebec, CANADA J7V 8M9, Phone: 514-453-1069
Specialties: Fancy/embellished and fantasy folders of his design. **Patterns:** Bowies, fighters and locking folders. **Technical:** Grinds 440C, ATS-34 and Damascus. Carves precious wood for handles. **Prices:** $150 to $1000. **Remarks:** Part-time maker; first knife sold in 1994. **Mark:** Interlaced initials.

BOUSE, D. MICHAEL, 1010 Victoria Pl., Waldorf, MD 20602, Phone: 301-843-0449
Specialties: Traditional and working/using straight knives of his design. **Patterns:** Daggers, fighters and hunters. **Technical:** Forges 5160 and Damascus; grinds D2; differential hardened blades; decorative handle pins. **Prices:** $125 to $350. **Remarks:** Spare-time maker; first knife sold in 1992. Doing business as Michael's Handmade Knives. **Mark:** Etched last name.

BOWEN, TILTON, Rt. 1, Box 225A, Baker, WV 26801, Phone: 304-897-6159
Specialties: Straight, stout working knives. **Patterns:** Hunters, fighters and boots; also offers buckskinner and throwing knives. All my D2-blades since 1st of year, 1997 are Deep Cryogenic processed. **Technical:** Grinds D2 and 4140. **Prices:** $60 to $275. **Remarks:** Full-time maker; first knife sold in 1982-1983. Sells wholesale to dealers. **Mark:** Initials and BOWEN BLADES, WV.

BOWLES, CHRIS, PO Box 985, Reform, AL 35481, Phone: 205-375-6162
Specialties: Working/using straight knives, and period pieces. **Patterns:** Utility, tactical, hunting, neck knives, machetes, and swords. **Grinds:** 0-1, 154CM, BG-42, 440V. **Prices:** $50-$400; some higher. **Remarks:** Full-time maker. **Mark:** Bowles stamped or Bowles etched in script.

BOXER, BO, Legend Forge, 6477 Hwy 93 S #134, Whitefish, MT 59937, Phone: 505-799-0173
Specialties: Handmade hunting knives, Damascus hunters. Most are antler handled. Also, hand forged Damascus steel. **Patterns:** Hunters and Bowies. **Prices:** $125 to $2500 on some very exceptional Damascus knives. **Mark:** The name "Legend Forge" hand engraved on every blade. **Additional:** Makes his own custom leather sheath stamped with maker

stamp. His knives are used by the outdoorsman of the Smoky Mountains, North Carolina, and the Rockies of Montana and New Mexico. **Other:** Spends one-half of the year in Montana and the other part of the year in Taos New Mexico.

BOYD, FRANCIS, 1811 Prince St, Berkeley, CA 94703, Phone: 510-841-7210
Specialties: Folders and kitchen knives; Japanese swords. **Patterns:** Push-button sturdy locking folders; San Francisco-style chef's knives. **Technical:** Forges and grinds; mostly uses high-carbon steels. **Prices:** Moderate to heavy. **Remarks:** Designer. **Mark:** Name.

BOYE, DAVID, PO Box 1238, Dolan Springs, AZ 86441, Phone: 800-853-1617
Specialties: Folders, hunting and kitchen knives. Forerunner in the use of dendritic steel and dendritic cobalt for blades. **Patterns:** Boye Basics sheath knives, lock-back folders, kitchen knives and hunting knives. **Technical:** Casts blades in stainless 440Cand cobalt. **Prices:** From $79 to $500. **Remarks:** Full-time maker; author of Step-by-Step Knife Making; **Mark:** Name.

BOYER, MARK, 10515 Woodinville Dr, #17, Bothell, WA 98011, Phone: 206-487-9370
Specialties: High-tech and working/using straight knives of his design. **Patterns:** Fighters and utility/camp knives. **Technical:** Grinds 1095 and D2. Offers Kydex sheaths; heat-treats. **Prices:** $45 to $120. **Remarks:** Part-time maker; first knife sold in 1994. Doing business as Boyer Blades. **Mark:** Eagle holding two swords with name.

BOYSEN, RAYMOND A., 125 E St Patrick, Rapid City, SD 57701, Phone: 605-341-7752
Specialties: Hunters and Bowies. **Technical:** High performance blades forged from 52100 & 5160. **Prices:** $200 and up. **Remarks:** American Bladesmith Society journeyman smith. **Mark:** BOYSEN. **Other:** Part-time bladesmith.

BRACK, DOUGLAS D., 119 Camino Ruiz, #71, Camirillo, CA 93012, Phone: 805-987-0490
Specialties: Working straight knives of his design. **Patterns:** Heavy-duty skinners, fighters and boots. **Technical:** Grinds 440C, ATS-34 and 5160; forges cable. **Prices:** $90 to $180; some to $300. **Remarks:** Part-time maker; first knife sold in 1984. **Mark:** tat.

BRADBURN, GARY, 1714 Park Pl., Wichita, KS 67203, Phone: 316-269-4273
Specialties: Straight knives of his design and to customer specs. **Patterns:** Bowies, fighters, hunters and miniatures. **Technical:** Forges 5160 and his own Damascus; grinds D2. **Prices:** $50 to $350; some to $800. **Remarks:** Full-time maker; first knife sold 1991. **Mark:** Last name or last initial inside a shamrock.

BRADFORD, GARRICK, 582 Guelph St, Kitchener ON, CANADA N2H-5Y4, Phone: 519-576-9863

BRADLEY, JOHN, PO Box 37, Pomona Park, FL 32181, Phone: 904-649-4739
Specialties: Fixed-blade using knives. **Patterns:** Skinners, Bowies, camp knives and Sgian Dubhs. **Technical:** Hand forged from 52100, 1095 and own Damascus. **Prices:** $125 to $500; some higher. **Remarks:** Part-time maker; first knife sold in 1988. **Mark:** Last name.

BRADLEY, DENNIS, 2410 Bradley Acres Rd, Blairsville, GA 30512, Phone: 706-745-4364
Specialties: Working straight knives and folders, some high-art. **Patterns:** Hunters, boots and daggers; slip-joints and two-blades. **Technical:** Grinds ATS-34, D2, 440C and commercial Damascus. **Prices:** $100 to $500; some to $2000. **Remarks:** Part-time maker; first knife sold in 1973. **Mark:** BRADLEY KNIVES in double heart logo.

BRADSHAW, BAILEY, 17800 Dickerson St, Ste 112, Dallas, TX 75252, Phone: 972-381-0558, Fax: 972-381-1255
Specialties: Traditional folders and contemporary front lock folders. **Patterns:** Single or multi-blade folders, Bowies. **Technical:** Grind CPM 3V, CPM 440V, CPM 420V, Forge Damascus, 52100. **Prices:** $250 to $3000. **Remarks:** I engrave, carve and do sterling silver sheaths. **Mark:** Tori arch over initials back to back.

BRANDON, MATTHEW, 4435 Meade St, Denver, CO 80211, Phone: 303-458-0786
Specialties: Hunters, skinners, full-tang Bowies. **Prices:** $100-$250. **Remarks:** Satisfaction or full refund. **Mark:** MTB.

BRANDSEY, EDWARD P., 335 Forest Lake Dr, Milton, WI 53563, Phone: 608-868-9010
Specialties: Large Bowies. **Patterns:** Hunters, fighters, Bowies and daggers, some buckskinner-styles. Native American influence on some. **Technical:** ATS-34, 440-C, 0-1, and some Damascus. **Prices:** $200 to $400; some to $3000. **Remarks:** Full-time maker. First knife sold in 1973. **Mark:** Initials connected - registered Wisc. Trademark since March 1983.

BRANDT, MARTIN W, 833 Kelly Blvd, Springfield, OR 97477, Phone: 541-747-5422

BRANTON, ROBERT, 4976 Seewee Rd, Awendaw, SC 29429, Phone: 843-928-3624
Specialties: Working straight knives of his design or to customer specs; throwing knives. **Patterns:** Hunters, fighters and some miniatures. **Technical:** Grinds ATS-34, A2 and 1050; forges 5160, O1. Offers hollow- or convex-grinds. **Prices:** $25 to $400. **Remarks:** Part-time maker; first knife sold in 1985. Doing business as Pro-Flyte, Inc. **Mark:** Last name; or first and last name, city, state.

BRATCHER, BRETT, 11816 County Rd 302, Plantersville, TX 77363, Phone: 936-894-3788, Fax: 936-894-3790
Specialties: Hunting and skinning knives. **Patterns:** Clip & Drop Point. Hand forged. **Technical:** Material 5160, D2, 1095 & Damascus. **Price:** $200 to $500. **Mark:** Bratcher.

BRAY JR., W. LOWELL, 6931 Manor Beach Rd, New Port Richey, FL 34652, Phone: 727-846-0830
Specialties: Traditional working and using straight knives and folders of his design. **Patterns:** Hunters, kitchen knives and utility knives. **Technical:** Grinds 440C & ATS-34; forges high carbon. **Prices:** $70 to $300. **Remarks:** Spare-time maker; first knife sold in 1992. **Mark:** Lowell Bray Knives in shield.

BREED, KIM, 733 Jace Dr, Clarksville, TN 37040, Phone: 931-645-9171
Specialties: High end through working folders and straight knives. **Patterns:** Hunters, fighters, daggers, Bowies. His design or customers. Likes one-of-a-kind designs. **Technical:** Makes own Mosiac and regular Damascus, but will use stainless steels offers filework and sculpted material. **Prices:** $150-$1200. **Remarks:** Part-time maker. First knife sold in 1990. **Mark:** Last name.

BREND, WALTER, 56 Benton Farm Rd, Walterboro, SC 29488, Phone: 843-538-8256

BRENNAN, JUDSON, PO Box 1165, Delta Junction, AK 99737, Phone: 907-895-5153, Fax: 907-895-5404
Specialties: Period pieces. **Patterns:** All kinds of Bowies, rifle knives, daggers. **Technical:** Forges miscellaneous steels. **Prices:** Upscale, good value. **Remarks:** Muzzle-loading gunsmith; first knife sold in 1978. **Mark:** Name.

BRESHEARS, CLINT, 1261 Keats, Manhattan Beach, CA 90266, Phone: 310-372-0739, Fax: 310-372-0739
Specialties: Working straight knives and folders. **Patterns:** Hunters, Bowies and survival knives. Folders are mostly hunters. **Technical:** Grinds 440C, 154CM and ATS-34; prefers mirror finishes. **Prices:** $125 to $750; some to $1800. **Remarks:** Part-time maker; first knife sold in 1978. **Mark:** First name.

BREUER, LONNIE, PO Box 877384, Wasilla, AK 99687-7384
Specialties: Fancy working straight knives. **Patterns:** Hunters, camp knives and axes, folders and Bowies. **Technical:** Grinds 440C, AEB-L and D2; likes wire inlay, scrimshaw, decorative filing. **Prices:** $60 to $150; some to $300. **Remarks:** Part-time maker; first knife sold in 1977. **Mark:** Signature.

BRIDWELL, RICHARD A., Rt. 2, Milford Ch. Rd, Taylors, SC 29687, Phone: 803-895-1715
Specialties: Working straight knives and folders. **Patterns:** Boot and fishing knives, fighters and hunters. **Technical:** Grinds stainless steels and D2. **Prices:** $85 to $165; some to $600. **Remarks:** Part-time maker; first knife sold in 1974. **Mark:** Last name logo.

BRIGHTWELL, MARK, 21104 Creekside Dr, Leander, TX 78641, Phone: 512-267-4110
Specialties: Fancy and plain folders of his design. **Patterns:** Fighters, hunters and gents, some traditional. **Technical:** Hollow- or flat- grinds ATS-34, D2, custom Damascus; elaborate filework; heat-treats. Extensive choice of natural handle materials; no synthetics. **Prices:** $300 to $1500. **Remarks:** Full-time maker. **Mark:** Last name.

BRITTON, TIM, 5645 Murray Rd, Winston-Salem, NC 27106, Phone: 336-922-9582, Fax: 336-923-2062
Specialties: Small and simple working knives, sgian dubhs and special tactical designs. **Technical:** Forges and grinds stainless steel. **Prices:** $110 to $600. **Remarks:** Veteran knife maker. **Mark:** Etched signature.

BROADWELL, DAVID, PO Box 4314, Wichita Falls, TX 76308, Phone: 940-692-1727, Fax: 940-692-4003
Specialties: Sculpted high-art straight and folding knives. **Patterns:** Daggers, sub-hilted fighters, folders, sculpted art knives and some Bowies. **Technical:** Grinds mostly Damascus; carves; prefers natural handle materials, including stone. Some embellishment. **Prices:** $350 to $3000; some higher. **Remarks:** Full-time maker; first knife sold in 1982. **Mark:** Stylized emblem bisecting "B"/with last name below.

BROCK, KENNETH L., PO Box 375, 207 N. Skinner Rd, Allenspark, CO 80510, Phone: 303-747-2547
Specialties: Custom designs, Full-tang working knives and button lock folders of his design. **Patterns:** Hunters, miniatures and minis. **Technical:** Flat-grinds D2 and 440C; makes own sheaths; heat-treats. **Prices:** $50 to $500. **Remarks:** Part-time maker; first knife sold in 1978. **Mark:** Last name, city, state and serial number.

BROMLEY, PETER, Bromley Knives, 1408 S Bettman, Spokane, WA 99212, Phone: 509-534-4235
Specialties: Period Bowies, folder, hunting knives - all sizes and shapes. **Patterns:** Bowies, boot knives, hunters, utility, folder, working knives. **Technical;** High carbon steel (1084, 1095 & 5160). Stock removal & forge. **Prices:** $85 to $750. **Remarks:** Almost full-time, first knife sold in 1987. **Mark:** Bromley, Spokane, WA.

BROOKER, DENNIS, Rt. 1, Box 12A, Derby, IA 50068, Phone: 515-533-2103
Specialties: Fancy straight knives and folders of his design. **Patterns:** Hunters, folders and boots. **Technical:** Forges and grinds. Full-time engraver and designer; instruction available. **Prices:** Moderate to upscale. **Remarks:** Part-time maker. Takes no orders; sells only completed work. **Mark:** Name.

BROOKS, BUZZ, 2345 Yosemite Dr, Los Angles, CA 90041, Phone: 323-256-2892

BROOKS, MICHAEL, 4645 52nd St Apt F4, Lubbock, TX 79414-3802
Specialties: Working straight knives of his design or to customer specs. **Patterns:** Tantos, swords, Bowies, hunters, skinners and boots. **Technical:** Grinds 440C, D2 and ATS-34; offers wide variety of handle materials. **Prices:** $40 to $800. **Remarks:** Part-time maker; first knife sold in 1985. **Mark:** Initials.

BROOKS, STEVE R., 1610 Dunn Ave, Walkerville, MT 59701, Phone: 406-782-5114
Specialties: Working straight knives and folders; period pieces. **Patterns:** Hunters, Bowies and camp knives; folding lockers; axes, tomahawks and buckskinner knives; swords and stilettos. **Technical:** Forges O1, Damascus and mosaic Damascus. Some knives come embellished. **Prices:** $150 to $2000. **Remarks:** Full-time maker; first knife sold in 1982. **Mark:** Lazy initials.

BROOME, THOMAS A., 1212 E. Aliak Ave, Kenai, AK 99611-8205, Phone: 907-283-9128
Specialties: Working hunters & folders **Patterns:** Traditional & custom orders. **Technical:** Grinds ATS-34, BG-42, CPM-S30V. **Prices:** $175 to $350. **Remarks:** Full-time maker; first knife sold in 1979. Doing business as Thom's Custom Knives. **Mark:** Full name, city, state. **Other:** Doing business as: Alaskan Man O; Steel Knives.

BROTHERS, ROBERT L., 989 Philpott Rd, Colville, WA 99114, Phone: 509-684-8922
Specialties: Traditional working and using straight knives and folders of his design and to customer specs. **Patterns:** Bowies, fighters and hunters. **Technical:** Grinds D2; forges Damascus. Makes own Damascus from saw steel wire rope and chain; part-time goldsmith and stone-setter. **Prices:** $100 to $400; some higher. **Remarks:** Part-time maker; first knife sold in 1986. **Mark:** Initials and year made.

BROWER, MAX, 2016 Story St, Boone, IA 50036, Phone: 515-432-2938
Specialties: Working/using straight knives. **Patterns:** Bowies, hunters and boots. **Technical:** Grinds 440C & ATS-34. **Prices:** Start at $150. **Remarks:** Spare-time maker; first knife sold in 1981. **Mark:** Last name.

BROWN, DENNIS G., 1633 North 197th Place, Shoreline, WA 98133, Phone: 206-542-3997

BROWN, HAROLD E., 3654 NW Hwy. 72, Arcadia, FL 34266, Phone: 863-494-7514
Specialties: Fancy and exotic working knives. **Patterns:** Folders, slip-lock, locking several kinds. **Technical:** Grinds D2, 440C and ATS-34. Embellishment available. **Prices:** $175 to $1000. **Remarks:** Part-time maker; first knife sold in 1976. **Mark:** Name and city with logo.

BROWN, JIM, 1097 Fernleigh Cove, Little Rock, AR 72210

BROWN, ROB E., PO Box 15107, Emerald Hill 6011, Port Elizabeth, SOUTH AFRICA, Phone: 27-41-3661086, Fax: 27-41-4511731
Specialties: Contemporary-designed straight knives and period pieces. **Patterns:** Utility knives, hunters, boots, fighters and daggers. **Technical:** Grinds 440C, D2, ATS-34 and commercial Damascus. Knives mostly mirror finished; African handle materials. **Prices:** $100 to $1500. **Remarks:** Full-time maker; first knife sold in 1985. **Mark:** Name and country.

BROWN, TROY L., 22945 W867 Rd, Park Hill, OK 74451, Phone: 918-457-4128
Specialties: Working and using knives and folders. **Patterns:** Bowies, hunters, folders & scagel-style. **Technical:** Forges 5160, 52100, 1084;

custom knifemakers

makes his own Damascus. Prefers stag, wood and Micarta for handles. Offers engraved bolsters and guards. **Prices:** $150 to $750. **Remarks:** Full-time maker; first knife sold in 1994. Knives. **Mark:** Troy Brown. **Other:** Doing business as Elk Creek Forge.

BROWNE, RICK, 980 West 13th St, Upland, CA 91786, Phone: 909-985-1728
Specialties: Sheffield pattern pocket knives. **Patterns:** Hunters, fighters and daggers. No heavy-duty knives. **Technical:** Grinds ATS-34. **Prices:** Start at $450. **Remarks:** Part-time maker; first knife sold in 1975. **Mark:** R. E. Nrowne, Upland, CA

BROWNING, STEVEN W., 3400 Harrison Rd, Benton, AR 72015, Phone: 501-316-2450

BROYLES-SEBENICK, LISA, PO Box 21070, Chattanooga, TN 37424, Phone: 423-892-5007, Fax: 423-899-9456

BRUNCKHORST, LYLE, Country Village, 23706 7th Ave SE, Ste B, Bothell, WA 98021, Phone: 425-402-3484
Specialties: Traditional working and using straight knives and folders of his design. **Patterns:** Bowies, hunters and locking folders. **Technical:** Grinds ATS-34; forges 5160 and his own Damascus. Iridescent RR spike knives. Offers scrimshaw, inlays and animal carvings in horn handles. **Prices:** $225 to $750; some to $3750. **Remarks:** Full-time maker; first knife sold in 1976. Doing business as Bronk's Knife works. **Mark:** Bucking horse.

BRUNER, RICK, 7756 Aster Lane, Jenison, MI 49428, Phone: 616-457-0403
Specialties: Sheath making

BRUNER JR., FRED, BRUNER BLADES, E10910W Hilldale Dr, Fall Creek, WI 54742, Phone: 715-877-2496

BRUNETTA, DAVID, PO Box 4972, Laguna Beach, CA 92652, Phone: 714-497-9611
Specialties: Straights, folders and art knives. **Patterns:** Bowies, camp/hunting, folders, fighters. **Technical:** Grinds ATS-34, D2, BG42. forges O1, 52100, 5160, 1095, makes own Damascus. **Prices:** $300 to $9000. **Mark:** Circle DB logo with last name straight or curved.

BRYAN, TOM, 14822 S Gilbert Rd, Gilbert, AZ 85296, Phone: 480-812-8529
Specialties: Straight & folding knives. **Patterns:** Drop-point hunter fighters. **Technical:** ATS-34, 154CM, 440C & A2. **Prices:** $150 to $800. **Remarks:** Part-time maker; sold first knife in 1994. **Mark:** T. Bryan. **Other:** DBA as T. Bryan Knives.

BUCHMAN, BILL, 63312 South Rd, Bend, OR 97701, Phone: 503-382-8851
Specialties: Working straight knives. **Patterns:** Hunters, Bowies, fighters and boots. Makes full line of leather craft & saddle maker knives. **Technical:** Forges 440C and Sandvik 15N20. Prefers 440C for saltwater. **Prices:** $95 to $400. **Remarks:** Full-time maker; first knife sold in 1982. **Mark:** Initials or last name.

BUCHNER, BILL, PO Box 73, Idleyld Park, OR 97447, Phone: 541-498-2247
Specialties: Working straight knives, kitchen knives and high-art knives of his design. **Technical:** Uses W1, L6 and his own Damascus. Invented "spectrum metal" for letter openers, folder handles and jewelry. Likes sculpturing and carving in Damascus. **Prices:** $40 to $3000; some higher. **Remarks:** Full-time maker; first knife sold in 1978. **Mark:** Signature.

BUCHOLZ, MARK A., PO Box 82, Holualoa, HI 93725, Phone: 808-322-4045
Specialties: Liner-lock folders. **Patterns:** Hunters and fighters. **Technical:** Grinds ATS-34. **Prices:** Upscale. **Remarks:** Full-time maker; first knife sold in 1976. **Mark:** Name, city and state in buffalo skull logo or signature.

BUCKBEE, DONALD M., 243 South Jackson Trail, Grayling, MI 49738, Phone: 517-348-1386
Specialties: Working straight knives, some fancy, in standard patterns; concentrating on kitchen knives. **Patterns:** Kitchen knives, hunters, Bowies. **Technical:** Grinds D2, 440C, ATS-34. Makes ultra-lights in hunter patterns. **Prices:** $100 to $250; some to $350. **Remarks:** Part-time maker; first knife sold in 1984. **Mark:** Antlered bee—a buck bee.

BUCKNER, JIMMIE H., PO Box 162, Putney, GA 31782, Phone: 912-436-4182
Specialties: Camp knives, Bowies (one-of-a-kind), liner-lock folders, tomahawks, camp axes, neck knives for law enforcement and hide-out knives for body guards and professional people. **Patterns:** Hunters, camp knives, Bowies. **Technical:** Forges 1084, 5160 and Damascus (own). own heat treats. **Prices:** $195 to $795 and up. **Remarks:** Full-time maker; first knife sold in 1980, ABS Mastersmith. **Mark:** Name over spade.

BUEBENDORF, ROBERT E., 108 Lazybrooke Rd, Monroe, CT 06468, Phone: 203-452-1769
Specialties: Traditional and fancy straight knives of his design. **Patterns:** Hand-makes and embellishes belt buckle knives. **Technical:** Forges and grinds 440C, O1, W2, 1095, his own Damascus and 154CM. **Prices:** $200 to $500. **Remarks:** Full-time maker; first knife sold in 1978. **Mark:** First and middle initials, last name and MAKER.

BULLARD, RANDALL, 7 Mesa Dr, Canyon, TX 79015, Phone: 806-655-0590
Specialties: Working/using straight knives and folders of his design or to customer specs. **Patterns:** Hunters, locking folders and slip-joint folders. **Technical:** Grinds O1, ATS-34 and 440C. Does file work. **Prices:** $125 to $300; some to $500. **Remarks:** Part-time maker; first knife sold in 1993. Doing business as Bullard Custom Knives. **Mark:** First and middle initials, last name, maker, city and state.

BULLARD, TOM, 117 MC 8068, Flippin, AR 72634, Phone: 870-453-3421
Specialties: Armadillo handle material on hunter and folders. **Patterns:** Bowies, hunters, lock-back folders. **Technical:** Grinds 440-C, ATS-34, commercial Damascus. **Prices:** $150 to $500. **Remarks:** Offers filework and engraving. I do not make screw-together knives. **Mark:** Tbullard.

BULLARD, BILL, Rt. 5, Box 35, Andalusia, AL 36420, Phone: 334-222-9003
Specialties: Traditional working and using straight knives and folders of his design. **Patterns:** Hunters, slip-joint folders and utility/camp knives and folders to customer specs. **Technical:** Forges Damascus, cable. Offers filework. **Prices:** $100 to $500; some to $1500. **Remarks:** Part-time maker; first knife sold in 1974. Doing business as Five Runs Forge. **Mark:** Last name stamped on ricasso.

BUMP, BRUCE D., 1103 Rex Lane, Walla Walla, WA 99362, Phone: 509-522-2219
Specialties: Traditional and Mosaic Damascus. **Patterns:** Black powder pistol/knife combinations 2003 wooden sword award. **Technical:** Sole authorship except for collaborations. **Prices:** $350 to $5500. **Remarks:** American Bladesmith Society journeyman smith ms test in 2003. **Mark:** Bruce D. Bump Walla Walla WA or Bruce D. Bump Custom Walla Walla WA.

BURAK, CHET, Knife Services Photographer, PO Box 14383, E Providence, RI 02914, Phone: 401-431-0625, Fax: 401-434-9821

BURDEN, JAMES, 405 Kelly St, Burkburnett, TX 76354

BURGER, PON, 12 Glenwood Ave, Woodlands, Bulawayo, Zimbabwe 75514
Specialties: Collector's items. **Patterns:** Fighters, locking folders of traditional styles, buckles. **Technical:** Scrimshaws 440C blade. Uses polished buffalo horn with brass fittings. Cased in buffalo hide book. **Prices:** $450 to $1100. **Remarks:** Full-time maker; first knife sold in 1973. Doing business as Burger Products. **Mark:** Spirit of Africa.

BURGER, FRED, Box 436, Munster 4278, Kwa-Zulu Natal, SOUTH AFRICA, Phone: 27 393216
Specialties: Sword canes and tactical walking sticks. **Patterns:** 440C & carbon steel blades. **Technical:** Double hollow ground and Poniard-style blades. **Prices:** $190 to $600. **Remarks:** Full-time maker with son, Barry, since 1987. **Mark:** Last name in oval pierced by a dagger. **Other:** Member South African Guild.

BURKE, BILL, 315 Courthouse Dr, Salmon, ID 83467, Phone: 208-756-3797
Specialties: Hand-forged working knives. **Patterns:** Fowler pronghorn, clip point & drop point hunters. **Technical:** Forges 52100 & 5160. Makes own Damascus from 15N20 and 1084. **Prices:** $250 to $2000. **Remarks:** I am dedicated to fixed-blade high-performance knives. **Mark:** Initials connected. **Other:** Also make "Ed Fowler" miniatures.

BURKE, DAN, 22001 Ole Barn Rd, Edmond, OK 73034, Phone: 405-341-3406, Fax: 405-340-3333
Specialties: Slip joint folders. **Patterns:** Traditional folders. **Technical:** Grinds D2 and BG-42. Prefers natural handle materials; heat-treats. **Prices:** $440 to $1900. **Remarks:** Full-time maker; first knife sold in 1976. **Mark:** First initial and last name.

BURNETT, MAX, 537 Old Dug Mtn. Rd, Paris, AR 72855, Phone: 501-963-2767
Specialties: Forging with coal/charcoal; some stock removal. **Patterns:** Hunters, Bowies, camp, tactical, neck knives & kydex sheaths. **Technical:** Steels used: 1084, 1095, 52100, 5160, L6, 01 & others available. **Prices:** $50 & up for neck knives/Bowies $250 & up. **Remarks:** Full-time since March 2000. **Mark:** M. OGG & omega symbol.

BURROWS, STEPHEN R., 3532 Michigan, Kansas City, MO 64109, Phone: 816-921-1573
Specialties: Fantasy straight knives of his design, to customer specs and in standard patterns; period pieces. **Patterns:** Fantasy, bird and trout knives, daggers, fighters and hunters. **Technical:** Forges 5160 and 1095 high-carbon steel, O1 and his Damascus. Offers lost wax casting in bronze or silver of cross guards and pommels. **Prices:** $65 to $600; some to $2000. **Remarks:** Full-time maker; first knife sold in 1983. Doing business as Gypsy Silk. **Mark:** Etched name.

BUSFIELD, JOHN, 153 Devonshire Circle, Roanoke Rapids, NC 27870, Phone: 252-537-3949, Fax: 252-537-8704
Specialties: Investor-grade folders; high-grade working straight knives. **Patterns:** Original price-style and trailing-point interframe and sculpted-frame folders, drop-point hunters and semi-skinners. **Technical:** Grinds 154CM and ATS-34. Offers interframes, gold frames and inlays; uses jade, agate and lapis. **Prices:** $275 to $2000. **Remarks:** Full-time maker; first knife sold in 1979. **Mark:** Last name and address.

BUSSE, JERRY, 11651 Co. Rd. 12, Wauseon, OH 43567, Phone: 419-923-6471
Specialties: Working straight knives. **Patterns:** Heavy combat knives and camp knives. **Technical:** Grinds D2, A2, INFI. **Prices:** $1100 to $3500. **Remarks:** Full-time maker; first knife sold in 1983. **Mark:** Last name in logo.

BUTLER, JOHN, 777 Tyre Rd, Havana, FL 32333, Phone: 850-539-5742
Specialties: Hunters, Bowies, period. **Technical:** Damascus, 52100, 5160, L6 steels. **Prices:** $80 and up. **Remarks:** Making knives since 1986. **Mark:** JB. **Other:** Journeyman (ABS).

BUTLER, BART, 822 Seventh St, Ramona, CA 92065, Phone: 760-789-6431

BUTLER, JOHN R., 20162 6th Av Ne, Shoreline, WA 98155, Phone: 206-362-3847

BYBEE, BARRY J., 795 Lock Rd. E., Cadiz, KY 42211-8615
Specialties: Working straight knives of his design. **Patterns:** Hunters, fighters, boot knives, tantos and Bowies. **Technical:** Grinds ATS-34, 440C. Likes stag and Micarta for handle materials. **Prices:** $125 to $200; some to $1000. **Remarks:** Part-time maker; first knife sold in 1968. **Mark:** Arrowhead logo with name, city and state.

BYRD, WESLEY L., 189 Countryside Dr, Evensville, TN 37332, Phone: 423-775-3826
Specialties: Hunters, fighters, Bowies, dirks, sign dubh, utility, and camp knives. **Patterns:** Wire rope, random patterns. **Technical:** I use 52100, 1084, 5160, L6, and 15n20. **Prices:** Starting at $180. **Remarks:** I prefer to work with customer for their design preferences. **Mark:** BYRD, WBX. **Other:** ABS journeyman smith.

C

CABE, JERRY (BUDDY), 62 McClaren Lane, Hattieville, AR 72063, Phone: 501-354-3581

CABRERA, SERGIO B., 25711 Frampton Av Apt 113, Harbor City, CA 90710

CAFFREY, EDWARD J., 2608 Central Ave. West, Great Falls, MT 59404, Phone: 406-727-9102
Specialties: Working/using knives and collector pieces; will accept some customer designs. **Patterns:** Hunters, fighters, camp/utility, folders, hawks and hatchets. **Technical:** Forges 5160, 52100, his Damascus, cable and chain Damascus. **Prices:** Start at $125. **Remarks:** ABS mastersmith, Part-time maker; first knife sold in 1989. **Mark:** Last name or engraved initials.

CAIRNES JR., CARROLL B., RT 1 Box 324, Palacios, TX 77465, Phone: 369-588-6815

CALDWELL, BILL, 255 Rebecca, West Monroe, LA 71292, Phone: 318-323-3025
Specialties: Straight knives and folders with machined bolsters and liners. **Patterns:** Fighters, Bowies, survival knives, tomahawks, razors and push knives. **Technical:** Owns and operates a very large, well-equipped blacksmith and bladesmith shop extant with six large forges and eight power hammers. **Prices:** $400 to $3500; some to $10,000. **Remarks:** Full-time maker and self-styled blacksmith; first knife sold in 1962. **Mark:** Wild Bill & Sons.

CALLAHAN, ERRETT, 2 Fredonia, Lynchburg, VA 24503
Specialties: Obsidian knives. **Patterns:** Modern styles and Stone Age replicas. **Technical:** Flakes and knaps to order. **Prices:** $100 to $3400. **Remarks:** Part-time maker; first flint blades sold in 1974. **Mark:** Blade—engraved name, year and arrow; handle—signed edition, year and unit number.

CALLAHAN, F. TERRY, PO Box 880, Boerne, TX 78006, Phone: 830-981-8274, Fax: 830-981-8279
Specialties: Custom hand-forged edged knives, collectible and functional. **Patterns:** Bowies, folders, daggers, hunters, camp knives and swords. **Technical:** Forges 5160, 1095 and his own Damascus. Offers filework and handmade sheaths. **Prices:** $125 to $2000. **Remarks:** First knife sold in 1990. **Mark:** Initials inside a keystone symbol. **Other:** ABS/Journeyman Bladesmith.

CALVERT JR., ROBERT W. (BOB), 911 Julia, PO Box 858, Rayville, LA 71269, Phone: 318-728-4113, Fax: 318-728-0000
Specialties: Using & hunting knives; your design or mine. Since 1990. **Patterns:** Forges own Damascus; all patterns. **Technical:** 5160, D2, 52100, 1084. Prefers natural handle material. **Prices:** $150 & up. **Remarks:** TOMB Member ABS, Journeyman Smith. **Mark:** Calvert (Block) J S.

CAMERON, RON G., PO Box 183, Logandale, NV 89021, Phone: 702-398-3356
Specialties: Fancy and embellished working/using straight knives and folders of his design. **Patterns:** Bowies, hunters and utility/camp knives. **Technical:** Grinds ATS-34, 440C and Devin Thomas Damascus or my own Damascus. Does filework, fancy pins, mokume fittings. Uses exotic hardwoods, stag and Micarta for handles. **Prices:** $150-$500; some to $1000. **Remarks:** Part-time maker; first knife sold in 1994. Doing business as Cameron Handmade Knives. **Mark:** Last name, town, state or last name.

CAMPBELL, DICK, 20000 Silver Ranch Rd, Conifer, CO 80433, Phone: 303-697-0150
Specialties: Working straight knives, period pieces. **Patterns:** Hunters, fighters, boots: 19th century Bowies. **Technical:** Grinds 440C, 154CM. **Prices:** $200 to $2500. **Remarks:** Full-time maker. First knife sold in 1975. **Mark:** Name.

CAMPBELL, COURTNAY M., PO Box 23009, Columbia, SC 29224, Phone: 803-787-0151

CAMPOS, IVAN, R. XI de Agosto, 107, Tatui, SP, BRAZIL 18270-000, Phone: 00-55-15-2518092, Fax: 00-55-15-2594368
Specialties: Brazilian handmade and antique knives.

CANDRELLA, JOE, 1219 Barness Dr, Warminster, PA 18974, Phone: 215-675-0143
Specialties: Working straight knives, some fancy. **Patterns:** Daggers, boots, Bowies. **Technical:** Grinds 440C and 154CM. **Prices:** $100 to $200; some to $1000. **Remarks:** Part-time maker; first knife sold in 1985. Does business as Franjo. **Mark:** FRANJO with knife as J.

CANNADY, DANIEL L., Box 301, Allendale, SC 29810, Phone: 803-584-2813
Specialties: Working straight knives and folders in standard patterns. **Patterns:** Drop-point hunters, Bowies, skinners, fishing knives with concave grind, steak knives and kitchen cutlery. **Technical:** Grinds D2, 440C and ATS-34. **Prices:** $65 to $325; some to $500. **Remarks:** Full-time maker; first knife sold in 1980. **Mark:** Last name above Allendale, S. C.

CANNON, DAN, 9500 Leon, Dallas, TX 75217, Phone: 972-557-0268
Specialties: Damascus, hand forged. **Patterns:** Bowies, hunters, folders. **Prices:** $300. **Remarks:** Full-time maker. **Mark:** CANNON D

CANNON, RAYMOND W., PO Box 1412, Homer, AK 99603, Phone: 907-235-7779
Specialties: Fancy working knives, folders and swords of his design or to customer specs; many one-of-a-kind pieces. **Patterns:** Bowies, daggers and skinners. **Technical:** Forges and grinds O1, A6, 52100, 5160, his combinations for his own Damascus. **Remarks:** First knife sold in 1984. **Mark:** Cannon Alaska or "Hand forged by Wes Cannon".

CANOY, ANDREW B., 3420 Fruchey Ranch Rd, Hubbard Lake, MI 49747, Phone: 810-266-6039

CANTER, RONALD E., 96 Bon Air Circle, Jackson, TN 38305, Phone: 731-668-1780
Specialties: Traditional working knives to customer specs. **Patterns:** Beavertail skinners, Bowies, hand axes and folding lockers. **Technical:** Grinds A1, 440C and 154CM. **Prices:** $65 to $250; some $500 and higher. **Remarks:** Spare-time maker; first knife sold in 1973. **Mark:** Three last initials intertwined.

CANTRELL, KITTY D., 19720 Hiway 78, Ramona, CA 92076, Phone: 760-788-8304

CAPDEPON, RANDY, 553 Joli Rd, Carencro, LA 70520, Phone: 318-896-4113, Fax: 318-896-8753
Specialties: Straight knives and folders of his design. **Patterns:** Hunters and locking folders. **Technical:** Grinds ATS-34, 440C and D2. **Prices:**

custom knifemakers

$200 to $600. **Remarks:** Part-time maker; first knife made in 1992. Doing business as Capdepon Knives. **Mark:** Last name.

CAPDEPON, ROBERT, 829 Vatican Rd, Carencro, LA 70520, Phone: 337-896-8753, Fax: 318-896-8753
Specialties: Traditional straight knives and folders of his design. **Patterns:** Boots, hunters and locking folders. **Technical:** Grinds ATS-34, 440C and D2. Hand-rubbed finish on blades. Likes natural horn materials for handles, including ivory. Offers engraving. **Prices:** $250 to $750. **Remarks:** Full-time maker; first knife made in 1992. **Mark:** Last name.

CAREY JR., CHARLES W., 1003 Minter Rd, Griffin, GA 30223, Phone: 770-228-8994
Specialties: Working and using knives of his design and to customer specs; period pieces. **Patterns:** Fighters, hunters, utility/camp knives and forged-to-shape miniatures. **Technical:** Forges 5160, old files and cable. Offers filework; ages some of his knives. **Prices:** $35 to $400. **Remarks:** Part-time maker; first knife sold in 1991. **Mark:** Knife logo.

CARLISLE, FRANK, 5930 Hereford, Detroit, MI 48224, Phone: 313-882-8349
Specialties: Fancy/embellished and fantasy folders of his design. **Patterns:** Hunters, locking folders and swords. **Technical:** Grinds Damascus and stainless. **Prices:** $80 to $300. **Remarks:** Full-time maker; first knife sold in 1993. Doing business as Carlisle Cutlery. **Mark:** Last name.

CARLISLE, JEFF, PO Box 282 12753 Hwy 200, Simms, MT 59477, Phone: 406-264-5693

CARLSSON, MARC BJORN, Pileatraede 42, 1112 Copenhagen K, DENMARK, Phone: +45 33 91 15 99, Fax: +45 33 91 17 99
Specialties: High-tech knives and folders. **Patterns:** Skinners, tantos, swords, folders and art knives. **Technical:** Grinds ATS-34, Elmax and D2. **Prices:** Start at $250. **Remarks:** Doing business as "Mememto Mori", Professional jeweler and knife maker. Doing business as Metal Point. **Mark:** First name in runic letters within Viking ship.

CARNAHAN, CHARLES A., 27 George Arnold Lane, Green Spring, WV 26722, Phone: 304-492-5891
Specialties: Hand forged fixed blade knives. **Patterns:** Bowies and hunters. **Technical:** Steels used; 5160, 1095, 1085, L6 and A023-E. **Prices:** $300 - $2000. **Remarks:** Part-time maker. First knife sold in 1991. Knives all made by hand forging, no stock removal. **Mark:** Last name.

CAROLINA CUSTOM KNIVES, SEE TOMMY MCNABB,

CARPENTER, RONALD W., RT 4 Box 323, Jasper, TX 75951, Phone: 409-384-4087

CARR, TIM, 3660 Pillon Rd, Muskegon, MI 49445, Phone: 231-766-3582
Specialties: Hunters, camp knives. **Patterns:** Mine or yours. **Technical:** Hand forged 52100 and Damascus. **Prices:** $125 to $700. **Remarks:** Part-time maker. **Mark:** The letter combined from my initials TRC.

CARROLL, CHAD, 12182 McClelland, Grant, MI 49327, Phone: 616-834-9183

CARSON, HAROLD J. "KIT", 1076 Brizendine Lane, Vine Grove, KY 40175, Phone: 270 877-6300, Fax: 270 877 6338
Specialties: Military fixed blades and folders; art pieces. **Patterns:** Fighters, D handles, daggers, combat folders and Crosslock-styles, tactical folders, tactical fixed blades. **Technical:** Grinds Stellite 6K, Talonite, CPM steels, Damascus. **Prices:** $400 to $750; some to $5000. **Remarks:** Full-time maker; first knife sold in 1973. **Mark:** Name stamped or engraved.

CARTER, MURRAY M., 2506 Toyo Oka, Ueki Kamoto, Kumamoto, JAPAN 861-0163, Phone: 81-96-272-6759
Specialties: Traditional Japanese cutlery, utilizing San soh ko (3 layer) or Kata-ha (two layer) blade construction. Laminated neck knives, traditional Japanese etc. **Patterns:** Works from over 200 standard Japanese and North American designs. **Technical:** Forges or grinds Hitachi white steel #1, Hitachi blue super steel or Hitachi ZDP247 stainless steel exclusively. Forges own Damascus. **Prices:** $30 to $3000. **Remarks:** Full-time maker. First knife sold in 1989. Owner & designer of "Muteki" brand knives. **Mark:** Name with Japanese character on forged pieces. "Muteki" with Japanese characters on stock-removal blades.

CARTER, FRED, 5219 Deer Creek Rd, Wichita Falls, TX 76302, Phone: 904-723-4020
Specialties: High-art investor-class straight knives; some working hunters and fighters. **Patterns:** Classic daggers, Bowies; interframe, stainless and blued steel folders with gold inlay. **Technical:** Grinds a variety of steels. Uses no glue or solder. Engraves and inlays. **Prices:** Generally upscale. **Remarks:** Full-time maker. **Mark:** Signature in oval logo.

CASH, TERRY, 113 Sequoyah Circle, Canton, GA 30115, Phone: 770-345-2031
Specialties: Railroad spike knives, traditional straight knives, working/using knives. **Patterns:** Bowies, hunters, utility, camp knives; standard,

own design or to customer spec. **Technical:** Forges 5160, 1095, 52100, heat treatment, makes leather sheaths, presentation boxes & makes own Damascus. **Prices:** $125 to $800. **Remarks:** Full-time maker; first knife sold 1995. **Mark:** First initial and last name. **Other:** Doing business as Cherokee Forge.

CASHEN, KEVIN R., 5615 Tyler St, Hubbardston, MI 48845, Phone: 989-981-6780
Specialties: Working straight knives, high art pattern welded swords, traditional renaissance and ethnic pieces. **Patterns:** Hunters, Bowies, utility knives, swords, daggers. **Technical:** Forges 1095, 1084 and his own O1/L6 Damascus. **Prices:** $100 to $4000+. **Remarks:** Full-time maker; first knife sold in 1985. Doing business as Matherton Forge. **Mark:** Black letter Old English initials and master smith stamp.

CASTEEL, DIANNA, PO Box 63, Monteagle, TN 37356, Phone: 931-723-0851, Fax: 931-723-1856
Specialties: Small, delicate daggers and miniatures; most knives one-of-a-kind. **Patterns:** Daggers, boot knives, fighters and miniatures. **Technical:** Grinds 440C; makes her own Damascus. **Prices:** Start at $350; miniatures start at $250. **Remarks:** Full-time maker. **Mark:** Di in script.

CASTEEL, DOUGLAS, PO Box 63, Monteagle, TN 37356, Phone: 931-723-0851, Fax: 931-723-1856
Specialties: One-of-a-kind collector-class period pieces. **Patterns:** Daggers, Bowies, swords and folders. **Technical:** Grinds 440C; makes his own Damascus. Offers gold and silver castings. **Prices:** Upscale. **Remarks:** Full-time maker; first knife sold in 1982. **Mark:** Last name.

CATOE, DAVID R., 4024 Heutte Dr, Norfolk, VA 23518, Phone: 757-480-3191
Technical: Does own forging, Damascus and heat treatments. **Price:** $200 to $500; some higher. **Remarks:** Part-time maker; trained by Dan Maragni 1985-1988; first knife sold 1989. **Mark:** Leaf of a camillia.

CAUDELL, RICHARD M., PO Box 602, Lawrenceville, IL 62439, Phone: 618-943-5278
Specialties: Classic working/using straight knives in standard patterns. **Patterns:** Boots, fighters, combat fighters and utility/camp knives. **Technical:** Hollow-grinds 440C, ATS-34 and A2. **Prices:** $115 to $600; some to $1200. **Remarks:** First knife sold in 1994. Doing business as Caudell's Custom Knives. **Mark:** Last name.

CAWTHORNE, CHRISTOPHER A., PO Box 604, Wrangell, AK 99929

CENTOFANTE, FRANK, PO Box 928, Madisonville, TN 37354-0928, Phone: 423-442-5767
Specialties: Fancy working folders. **Patterns:** Lockers and liner-locks. **Technical:** Grinds ATS-34; hand-rubbed satin finish on blades. **Prices:** $500 to $1200. **Remarks:** Full-time maker; first knife sold in 1968. **Mark:** Name, city, state.

CHAFFEE, JEFF L., 14314 N Washington St, PO Box 1, Morris, IN 47033, Phone: 812-934-6350
Specialties: Fancy working and utility folders and straight knives. **Patterns:** Fighters, dagger, hunter and locking folders. **Technical:** Grinds commercial Damascus, 440C, ATS-34, D2 and O1. Prefers natural handle materials. **Prices:** $350 to $2000. **Remarks:** Part-time maker; first knife sold in 1988. **Mark:** Last name.

CHAMBERLAIN, JON A., 15 S. Lombard, E. Wenatchee, WA 98802, Phone: 509-884-6591
Specialties: Working and kitchen knives to customer specs; exotics on special order. **Patterns:** Over 100 patterns in stock. **Technical:** Prefers ATS-34, D2, L6 and Damascus. **Prices:** Start at $50. **Remarks:** First knife sold in 1986. Doing business as Johnny Custom Knifemakers. **Mark:** Name in oval with city and state enclosing.

CHAMBERLAIN, JOHN B., 1621 Angela St, Wenatchee, WA 98801, Phone: 509-663-6720
Specialties: Fancy working and using straight knives mainly to customer specs, though starting to make some standard patterns. **Patterns:** Hunters, Bowies and daggers. **Technical:** Grinds D2, ATS-34, M2, M4 and L6. **Prices:** $60 to $190; some to $2500. **Remarks:** Full-time maker; first knife sold in 1943. **Mark:** Name, city, state.

CHAMBERLAIN, CHARLES R., PO Box 156, Barren Springs, VA 24313-0156, Phone: 703-381-5137

CHAMBERLIN, JOHN A., 11535 Our Rd, Anchorage, AK 99516, Phone: 907-346-1524, Fax: 907-562-4583
Specialties: Art and working knives. **Patterns:** Daggers and hunters; some folders. **Technical:** Grinds ATS-34, 440C, A2, D2 and Damascus. Uses Alaskan handle materials such as oosic, jade, whale jawbone, fossil ivory. **Prices:** Start at $150. **Remarks:** Does own heat treating and cryogenic deep freeze. Full-time maker; first knife sold in 1984. **Mark:** Name over English shield and dagger.

CHAMBLIN, JOEL, 296 New Hebron Church Rd, Concord, GA 30206, Phone: 770-884-9055
Specialties: Fancy & working folders. **Patterns:** Fancy locking folders, traditional, multi-blades and utility. **Technical:** Grinds ATS-34, 440V, BG-42 and commercial Damascus. Offers filework. **Prices:** Start at $300. **Remarks:** Full-time maker; first knife sold in 1989. **Mark:** Last name.

CHAMPAGNE, PAUL, 48 Brightman Rd, Mechanicville, NY 12118, Phone: 518-664-4179
Specialties: Rugged, ornate straight knives in the Japanese tradition. **Patterns:** Katanas, wakizashis, tantos and some European daggers. **Technical:** Forges and hand-finishes carbon steels and his own Damascus. Makes Tamahagane for use in traditional blades; uses traditional heat-treating techniques. **Prices:** Start at $750. **Remarks:** Has passed all traditional Japanese cutting tests. Doing business as Twilight Forge. **Mark:** Three diamonds over a stylized crown.

CHAMPION, ROBERT, 1806 Plateau Ln, Amarillo, TX 79106, Phone: 806-359-0446
Specialties: Traditional working straight knives. **Patterns:** Hunters, skinners, camp knives, Bowies, daggers. **Technical:** Grinds 440C & D2. **Prices:** $100 to $600. **Remarks:** Part-time maker; first knife sold in 1979. **Mark:** Last name with dagger logo, city and state. **Other:** Stream-line hunters.

CHAPO, WILLIAM G., 45 Wildridge Rd, Wilton, CT 06897, Phone: 203-544-9424
Specialties: Classic straight knives and folders of his design and to customer specs; period pieces. **Patterns:** Boots, Bowies and locking folders. **Technical:** Forges stainless Damascus. Offers filework. **Prices:** $750 and up. **Remarks:** Full-time maker; first knife sold in 1989. **Mark:** First and middle initials, last name, city, state.

CHARD, GORDON R., 104 S. Holiday Lane, Iola, KS 66749, Phone: 620-365-2311
Specialties: High tech folding knives in one-of-a-kind. **Patterns:** Liner-locking folders of own design. Some fixed blades. **Technical:** Clean work with attention to fit and finish. **Prices:** $150-$2000. **Remarks:** First knife sold in 1983. **Other:** Uses 154CM, ATAS34, and different types of Damascus.

CHASE, JOHN E., 217 Walnut, Aledo, TX 76008, Phone: 817-441-8331
Specialties: Straight high-tech working knives in standard patterns or to customer specs. **Patterns:** Hunters, fighters, daggers and Bowies. **Technical:** Grinds D2, 01, 440C; offers mostly satin finishes. **Prices:** Start at $235. **Remarks:** Part-time maker; first knife sold in 1974. **Mark:** Last name in logo.

CHASE, ALEX, 208 E Pennsylvania Ave, DeLand, FL 32724, Phone: 904-734-9918
Specialties: Historical steels, classic and traditional straight knives of his design and to customer specs. **Patterns:** Art, fighters and hunters. **Technical:** Forges O1-L6 Damascus, meteoric Damascus, 52100, 5160; uses fossil walrus & mastodon ivory etc. **Prices:** $150 to $1000; some to $3500. **Remarks:** Part-time maker; first knife sold in 1990. Doing business as Confederate Forge. **Mark:** Stylized initials-A. C.

CHASTAIN, WADE, Rt. 2, Box 137-A, Horse Shoe, NC 28742, Phone: 704-891-4803
Specialties: Fancy fantasy and high-art straight knives of his design; period pieces. Known for unique mounts. **Patterns:** Bowies, daggers and fighters. **Technical:** Grinds 440C, ATS-34 and O1. Engraves; offers jewelling. **Prices:** $400 to $1200; some to $2000. **Remarks:** Full-time maker; first knife sold in 1984. Doing business as The Iron Master. **Mark:** Engraved last name.

CHAUVIN, JOHN, 200 Anna St, Scott, LA 70583, Phone: 318-237-6138, Fax: 318-237-8079
Specialties: Traditional working and using straight knives of his design, to customer specs and in standard patterns. **Patterns:** Bowies, fighters, and hunters. **Technical:** Grinds ATS-34, 440C and O1 high carbon. Paul Bos heat treating. Uses ivory, stag, oosic and stabilized Louisiana swamp maple for handle materials. Makes sheaths using alligator and ostrich. **Prices:** $125 to $200; Bowies start at $500. **Remarks:** Part-time maker; first knife sold in 1995. **Mark:** Full name, city, state.

CHAUZY, ALAIN, 1 Rue de Paris, 21140 Seur-en-Auxios, FRANCE, Phone: 03-80-97-03-30, Fax: 03-80-97-34-14
Specialties: Fixed blades, folders, hunters, Bowies—scagel-style. **Technical:** Forged blades only. Steels used XC65, 07C, and own Damascus. **Prices:** Contact maker for quote. **Remarks:** Part-time maker. **Mark:** Number 2 crossed by an arrow and name.

CHAVAR, EDWARD V., 1830 Richmond Ave, Bethlehem, PA 18018, Phone: 610-865-1806
Specialties: Working straight knives to his or customer design specifications, folders, high art pieces and some forged pieces. **Patterns:** Fighters,

hunters, tactical, straight and folding knives and high art straight and folding knives for collectors. **Technical:** Grinds ATS-34, 440C, L6, Damascus from various makers and uses Damascus Steel and Mokume of his own creation. **Prices:** Standard models range from $95 to $1500, custom and specialty up to $3000. **Remarks:** Full-time maker; first knife sold in 1990. **Mark:** Name, city, state or signature.

CHEATHAM, BILL, PO Box 636, Laveen, AZ 85339, Phone: 602-237-2786
Specialties: Working straight knives and folders. **Patterns:** Hunters, fighters, boots and axes; locking folders. **Technical:** Grinds 440C. **Prices:** $150 to $350; exceptional knives to $600. **Remarks:** Full-time maker; first knife sold in 1976. **Mark:** Name, city, state.

CHELQUIST, CLIFF, PO Box 91, Arroyo Grande, CA 93421, Phone: 805-489-8095
Specialties: Highly polished sportsman's knives. **Patterns:** Bird knives to Bowies. **Technical:** Grinds D2 and ATS-34. **Prices:** $75 to $150; some to $400. **Remarks:** Spare-time maker; first knife sold in 1983. **Mark:** Last initial.

CHERRY, FRANK J., 3412 Tiley Ne, Albuquerque, NM 87110, Phone: 505-883-8643

CHOATE, MILTON, 1665 W County 17-1/2, Somerton, AZ 85350, Phone: 928-627-7251
Specialties: Classic working and using straight knives of his design, to customer specs and in standard patterns. **Patterns:** Bowies, hunters and utility/camp knives. **Technical:** Grinds 440C; grinds and forges 1095 and 5160. Does filework on top and guards on request. **Prices:** $150 to $600. **Remarks:** Part-time maker; first knife made in 1990. All knives come with handmade sheaths by Judy Choate. **Mark:** Knives marked "Choate".

CHRISTENSEN, JON P., 7814 Spear Dr, Shepherd, MT 59079, Phone: 406-373-0253
Specialties: Patch knives, hunter/utility knives, Bowies, tomahawks. **Technical:** All blades forged, do all my own work including sheaths. **Prices:** $80 on up. **Remarks:** First knife sold in 1999. **Mark:** First and middle initial surrounded by last initial.

CHURCHMAN, T. W., 7402 Tall Cedar, San Antonio, TX 78249, Phone: 210-690-8641
Specialties: Fancy and traditional straight knives and single blade liner-locking folders. Bird/trout knives of his design and to customer specs. **Patterns:** Bird/trout knives, fillet, Bowies, daggers, fighters, boot knives, some miniatures. **Technical:** Grinds 440C and D2. Offers stainless fittings, fancy filework, exotic and stabilized woods and hand sewed lined sheaths. **Prices:** $80 to $650; some to $1500. **Remarks:** Part-time maker; first knife made in 1981 after reading "KNIVES '81". Doing business as "Custom Knives Churchman Made". **Mark:** Last name, dagger.

CLAIBORNE, JEFF, 1470 Roberts Rd, Franklin, IN 46131, Phone: 317-736-7443
Specialties: All one-of-a-kind by hand—no jigs or fixtures—swords, straight knives, period pieces, multi-blade folders. Handle—uses ivory, stag, pearl, oosic, bone or exotic wood. **Technical:** Forges cable Damascus, grinds O1, D2, 1095, 5160, 52100. **Prices:** $100 and up. **Remarks:** Part-time maker; first knife sold in 1989. **Mark:** Stylized initials in an oval.

CLAIBORNE, RON, 2918 Ellistown Rd, Knox, TN 37924, Phone: 615-524-2054
Specialties: Multi blade slip joints, swords, straight knives. **Patterns:** Hunters, daggers, folders. **Technical:** Forges Damascus: mosaic, powder mosaic. Prefers bone and natural handle materials; some exotic woods. **Prices:** $125 to $2500. **Remarks:** Part-time maker; first knife sold in 1979. Doing business as Thunder Mountain Forge Claiborne Knives. **Mark:** Claiborne.

CLARK, D. E. (LUCKY), 126 Woodland St, Mineral Point, PA 15942, Phone: 814-322-4725
Specialties: Working straight knives and folders to customer specs. **Patterns:** Customer designs. **Technical:** Grinds D2, 440C, 154CM. **Prices:** $100 to $200; some higher. **Remarks:** Part-time maker; first knife sold in 1975. **Mark:** Name on one side; "Lucky" on other.

CLARK, DAVE, 82 Valley View Manor Dr, Andrews, NC 28901, Phone: 828-321-8067
Specialties: Folders to customer specs. **Patterns:** Locking folders. **Technical:** Grinds 440C, D2 and stainless Damascus. **Prices:** $400 to $1500. **Remarks:** Full-time maker; first knife sold in 1988. **Mark:** Name.

CLARK, HOWARD F., 115 35th Pl., Runnells, IA 50237, Phone: 515-966-2126
Specialties: Currently Japanese-style swords. **Patterns:** Katana. **Technical:** Forges 1086, L6, 52100 and his own all tool steel Damascus; bar stock; forged blanks. **Prices:** $500 to $3000. **Remarks:** Full-time maker; first knife sold in 1979. Doing business as Morgan Valley Forge. **Prior**

custom knifemakers

Mark: Block letters and serial number on folders; anvil/initials logo on straight knives. Current Mark: Two character kanji "Big Ear".

CLARK, NATE, 484 Baird Dr, Yoncalla, OR 97499, Phone: 541-680-6077

Specialties: Automatics (Push button & hidden release) ATS-34 mirror polish or satin finish, most Damascus, Pearl, Ivory, Abalone, Woods, Bone, Micarta, G-10, filework and carving. **Prices:** $500-$2500. **Remarks:** Full-time knife maker since 1996. **Mark:** Nate Clark.

CLARK, PETER, 1624 Juneau Dr, Anchorage, AK 99501

CLARK, R. W., R. W. Clark Custom Knives, 1069 Golden Meadow, Corona, CA 92882, Phone: 909-279-3494, Fax: 909-279-4394

Specialties: Military field knives and Asian hybrids. Hand carved leather sheaths. **Patterns:** Fixed blade hunters, field utility and military. Also presentation and collector grade knives. **Technical:** First maker to use liquid metals LM1 material in knives. Other materials include S30V, O1, stainless and carbon Damascus. **Prices:** $75 to $2000. Average price $300. **Remarks:** Started knife making in 1990 full-time in 2000. **Mark:** R. W. Clark, Custom, Corona, CA in standard football shape. I also use three Japanese characters, spelling Clark, on my Asian Hybrids.

CLARK, ROGER, Rt. 1, Box 538, Rockdale, TX 76567, Phone: 512-446-3388

Specialties: Traditional working and using straight knives of his design or to customer specs. **Patterns:** Hunters, Bowies and camp knives; primitive styles for black powder hunters. **Technical:** Forges 1084, O1 and Damascus. Sheaths are extra. **Prices:** Primitive styles start at $100; shiny blades start at $150; Damascus start at $250. **Remarks:** Full-time maker; first knife sold in 1989. **Mark:** First initial, last name.

CLASSIC CUTLERY, 230 S Main St Apt 1, Franklin, NH 03235-1565, Phone: 603-226-0885, Fax: same as phone #

Specialties: Custom knives, gemstones, high quality factory knives.

CLAY, J. D., 5050 Hall Rd, Greenup, KY 41144, Phone: 606-473-6769

Specialties: Long known for cleanly finished, collector quality knives of functional design. **Patterns:** Practical hunters and locking folders. **Technical:** Grinds 440C - high mirror finishes. **Prices:** Start at $95. **Remarks:** Full-time maker; first knife sold in 1972. **Mark:** Name stamp in script on blade.

CLAY, WAYNE, Box 125B, Pelham, TN 37366, Phone: 931-467-3472, Fax: 931-467-3076

Specialties: Working straight knives and folders in standard patterns. **Patterns:** Hunters and kitchen knives; gents and hunter patterns. **Technical:** Grinds ATS-34. **Prices:** $125 to $500; some to $1000. **Remarks:** Full-time maker; first knife sold in 1978. **Mark:** Name.

CLICK, JOE, 305 Dodge St #3, Swanton, OH 48558, Phone: 419-825-1220

Specialties: Fancy/embellished and traditional working/using straight knives of his design, to customer specs and in standard patterns. **Patterns:** Bowies, hunters and utility/camp knives. **Technical:** Grinds and forges A2, D2, 5160 and Damascus. Does fancy filework; triple temper. Uses ivory for handle material. **Prices:** $75 to $300; some to $700. **Remarks:** Doing business as Click Custom Knives. **Mark:** Full name.

COCKERHAM, LLOYD, 1717 Carolyn Ave, Denham Springs, IA 70726, Phone: 225-665-1565

COFER, RON, 188 Ozora Road, Loganville, GA 30052

Specialties: Fancy working and using straight knives of his design. **Patterns:** Hunters, Bowies and fighters. **Technical:** Grinds 440C and ATS-34. Heat-treats. Some knives have carved stag handles or scrimshaw. Makes leather sheath for each knife and walnut and deer antler display stands for art knives. **Prices:** $125 to $250; some to $600. **Remarks:** Spare-time maker; first knife sold in 1991. **Mark:** Name, serial number.

COFFMAN, DANNY, 541 Angel Dr S, Jacksonville, AL 36265-5787, Phone: 256-435-1619

Specialties: Straight knives and folders of his design. Now making liner-locks for $650 to $1200 with natural handles and contrasting Damascus blades and bolsters. **Patterns:** Hunters, locking and slip-joint folders. **Technical:** Grinds Damascus, 440C and D2. Offers filework and engraving. **Prices:** $100 to $400; some to $800. **Remarks:** Spare-time maker; first knife sold in 1992. Doing business as Customs by Coffman. **Mark:** Last name stamped or engraved.

COHEN, N. J. (NORM), 2408 Sugarcone Rd, Baltimore, MD 21209, Phone: 410-484-3841

Specialties: Working class knives. **Patterns:** Hunters, skinners, bird knives, push daggers, boots, kitchen and practical customer designs. **Technical:** Stock removal 440C, ATS-34. Uses Micarta, Corian. Some woods in handles. **Prices:** $50 to $250. **Remarks:** Part-time maker; first knife sold in 1982. **Mark:** Etched initials or NJC MAKER.

COHEN, TERRY A., PO Box 406, Laytonville, CA 95454

Specialties: Working straight knives and folders. **Patterns:** Bowies to boot knives and locking folders; mini-boot knives. **Technical:** Grinds stainless; hand rubs; tries for good balance. **Prices:** $85 to $150; some to $325. **Remarks:** Part-time maker; first knife sold in 1983. **Mark:** TERRY KNIVES, city and state.

COIL, JIMMIE J., 2936 Asbury Pl., Owensboro, KY 42303, Phone: 270-684-7827

Specialties: Traditional working and straight knives of his design. **Patterns:** Hunters, Bowies and fighters. **Technical:** Grinds 440C, ATS-34 and D2. Blades are flat-ground with brush finish; most have tapered tang. Offers filework. **Prices:** $65 to $250; some to $750. **Remarks:** Spare-time maker; first knife sold in 1974. **Mark:** Name.

COLE, WELBORN I., 3284 Inman Dr. NE, Atlanta, GA 30319, Phone: 404-261-3977

Specialties: Traditional straight knives of his design. **Patterns:** Hunters. **Technical:** Grinds 440C, ATS-34 and D2. Good wood scales. **Remarks:** Full-time maker; first knife sold in 1983. **Mark:** Script initials.

COLE, DAVE, 620 Poinsetta Dr, Satellite Beach, FL 32937, Phone: 321-773-1687

Specialties: Working straight knives of his design or customer specs. **Patterns:** Utility, hunters. **Technical:** Grinds 01, ATS-34, Damascus; prefers natural handle materials, handmade sheaths. **Prices:** $100 and up. **Remarks:** Part-time maker, member of FKA; first knife sold in 1991. **Mark:** None, DC, or Cole.

COLE, JAMES M., 505 Stonewood Blvd, Bartonville, TX 76226, Phone: 817-430-0302

COLEMAN, KEITH E., 5001 Starfire Pl NW, Albuquerque, NM 87120-2010, Phone: 505-899-3783

Specialties: Affordable collector-grade straight knives and folders; some fancy. **Patterns:** Fighters, tantos, combat folders, gents folders and boots. **Technical:** Grinds ATS-34 and Damascus. Prefers specialty woods; offers filework. **Prices:** $150 to $700; some to $1500. **Remarks:** Full-time maker; first knife sold in 1980. **Mark:** Name, city and state.

COLLINS, LYNN M., 138 Berkley Dr, Elyria, OH 44035, Phone: 440-366-7101

Specialties: Working straight knives. **Patterns:** Field knives, boots and fighters. **Technical:** Grinds D2, 154CM and 440C. **Prices:** Start at $150. **Remarks:** Spare-time maker; first knife sold in 1980. **Mark:** Initials, asterisks.

COLLINS, HAROLD, 503 First St, West Union, OH 45693, Phone: 513-544-2982

Specialties: Traditional using straight knives and folders of his design or to customer specs. **Patterns:** Hunters, Bowies and locking folders. **Technical:** Forges and grinds 440C, ATS-34, D2, O1 and 5160. Flat-grinds standard; filework available. **Prices:** $75 to $300. **Remarks:** Full-time maker; first knife sold in 1989. **Mark:** First initial, last name .

COLTER, WADE, PO Box 2340, Colstrip, MT 59323, Phone: 406-748-4573

Specialties: Fancy and embellished straight knives, folders and swords of his design; historical and period pieces. **Patterns:** Bowies, swords and folders. **Technical:** Hand forges 52100 ball bearing steel and L6, 1090, cable and chain Damascus from 5N20 & 1084. Carves and makes sheaths. **Prices:** $250 to $3500. **Remarks:** Part-time maker; first knife sold in 1990. Doing business as "Colter's Hell" Forge. **Mark:** Initials on left side ricasso.

COLTRAIN, LARRY D., PO Box 1331, Buxton, NC 27920

COMAR, ROGER N., Rt 1 Box 485, Marion, NC 28752, Phone: 828-652-2448

COMPTON, WILLIAM E., 106 N. Sequoia Ct, Sterling, VA 20164, Phone: 703-430-2129

Specialties: Working straight knives of his design or to customer specs; some fancy knives. **Patterns:** Hunters, camp knives, Bowies and some kitchen knives. **Technical:** Also forges 5160, 1095 and make my own Damascus. **Prices:** $150 to $750; some to $1500. **Remarks:** Part-time maker, ABS journeyman smith. first knife sold in 1994. Doing business as Comptons Custom Knives. **Mark:** Stock removal—first and middle initials, last name, city & state. Forged—first & middle initials, last name, city & state, anvil in middle.

COMUS, STEVE, PO Box 68040, Anaheim, CA 92817-9800

CONKEY, TOM, 9122 Keyser Rd, Nokesville, VA 22123, Phone: 703-791-3867

Specialties: Classic straight knives and folders of his design and to customer specs. **Patterns:** Boots, hunters and locking folders. **Technical:** Grinds ATS-34, O1 and commercial Damascus. Lock-backs have jeweled scales and locking bars with dovetailed bolsters. Folders utilize unique 2-piece bushing of his design and manufacture. Sheaths are handmade. Presentation boxes made upon request. **Prices:** $100 to $500. **Remarks:** Part-time maker; first knife sold in 1991. Collaborates with Dan Thomas. **Mark:** Last name with "handcrafted" underneath.

CONKLIN, GEORGE L., Box 902, Ft. Benton, MT 59442, Phone: 406-622-3268, Fax: 406-622-3410
Specialties: Designer and manufacturer of the "Brisket Breaker." **Patterns:** Hunters, utility/camp knives and hatchets. **Technical:** Grinds 440C, ATS-34, D2, 1095, 154CM and 5160. Offers some forging and heat-treats for others. Offers some jewelling. **Prices:** $65 to $200; some to $1000. **Remarks:** Full-time maker. Doing business as Rocky Mountain Knives. **Mark:** Last name in script.

CONLEY, BOB, 1013 Creasy Rd, Jonesboro, TN 37659, Phone: 423-753-3302
Specialties: Working straight knives and folders. **Patterns:** Lockers, two-blades, gents, hunters, traditional styles, straight hunters. **Technical:** Grinds 440C, 154CM and ATS-34. Engraves. **Prices:** $250 to $450; some to $600. **Remarks:** Full-time maker; first knife sold in 1979. **Mark:** Full name, city, state.

CONN JR., C. T., 206 Highland Ave, Attalla, AL 35954, Phone: 205-538-7688
Specialties: Working folders, some fancy. **Patterns:** Full range of folding knives. **Technical:** Grinds O2, 440C and 154CM. **Prices:** $125 to $300; some to $600. **Remarks:** Part-time maker; first knife sold in 1982. **Mark:** Name.

CONNELL, STEVE, 217 Valley St, Adamsville, AL 35005-1852, Phone: 205-674-0440

CONNELLEY, LARRY, 10020 West Markham St, Little Rock, AR 72205, Phone: 501-221-1616

CONNER, ALLEN L., 6399 County Rd 305, Fulton, MO 65251, Phone: 573-642-9200

CONNOLLY, JAMES, 2486 Oro-Quincy Hwy., Oroville, CA 95966, Phone: 916-534-5363
Specialties: Classic working and using knives of his design. **Patterns:** Boots, Bowies and daggers. **Technical:** Grinds ATS-34; forges 5160; forges and grinds O1. **Prices:** $100 to $500; some to $1500. **Remarks:** Full-time maker; first knife sold in 1980. Doing business as Gold Rush Designs. **Mark:** First initial, last name, Handmade.

CONNOR, MICHAEL, Box 502, Winters, TX 79567, Phone: 915-754-5602
Specialties: Straight knives, period pieces, some folders. **Patterns:** Hunters to camp knives to traditional locking folders to Bowies. **Technical:** Forges 5160, O1, 1084 steels and his own Damascus. **Prices:** Moderate to upscale. **Remarks:** Spare-time maker; first knife sold in 1974. **Mark:** Last name, M. S. **Other:** ABS Master Smith 1983.

CONNOR, JOHN W., PO Box 12981, Odessa, TX 79768-2981, Phone: 915-362-6901

CONTI, JEFFREY D., 4640 Feigley Rd. W., Port Orchard, WA 98367, Phone: 360-405-0075
Specialties: Working straight knives. **Patterns:** Fighters and survival knives; hunters, camp knives and fishing knives. **Technical:** Grinds D2, 154CM and O1. Engraves. **Prices:** Start at $80. **Remarks:** Part-time maker; first knife sold in 1980. **Mark:** Initials, year, steel type, name and number of knife.

COOGAN, ROBERT, 1560 Craft Center Dr, Smithville, TN 37166, Phone: 615-597-6801
Specialties: One-of-a-kind knives. **Patterns:** Unique items like ooloo-style Appalachian herb knives. **Technical:** Forges; his Damascus is made from nickel steel and W1. **Prices:** Start at $100. **Remarks:** Part-time maker; first knife sold in 1979. **Mark:** Initials or last name in script.

COOK, LOUISE, 475 Robinson Ln., Ozark, IL 62972, Phone: 618-777-2932
Specialties: Working and using straight knives of her design and to customer specs; period pieces. **Patterns:** Bowies, hunters and utility/camp knives. **Technical:** Forges 5160. Filework; pin work; silver wire inlay. **Prices:** Start at $50/inch. **Remarks:** Part-time maker; first knife sold in 1990. Doing business as Panther Creek Forge. **Mark:** First name and journeyman stamp on one side; panther head on the other.

COOK, MIKE, 475 Robinson Ln, Ozark, IL 62972, Phone: 618-777-2932
Specialties: Traditional working and using straight knives of his design and to customer specs. **Patterns:** Bowies, hunters and utility/camp knives. **Technical:** Forges 5160. Filework; pin work. **Prices:** Start at $50/inch. **Remarks:** Spare-time maker; first knife sold in 1991. **Mark:** First initial, last name and journeyman stamp on one side; panther head on the other.

COOK, JAMES R., 3611 Hwy. 26 W., Nashville, AR 71852, Phone: 870 845 5173
Specialties: Working straight knives and folders of his design or to customer specs. **Patterns:** Bowies, hunters and camp knives. **Technical:** Forges 1084 and high carbon Damascus. **Prices:** $195 to $5500. **Remarks:** Part-time maker; first knife sold in 1986. **Mark:** First and middle initials, last name.

COOK, MIKE A., 10927 Shilton Rd, Portland, MI 48875, Phone: 517-647-2518
Specialties: Fancy/embellished and period pieces of his design. **Patterns:** Daggers, fighters and hunters. **Technical:** Stone bladed knives in agate, obsidian and jasper. Scrimshaws; opal inlays. **Prices:** $60 to $300; some to $800. **Remarks:** Part-time maker; first knife sold in 1988. Doing business as Art of Ishi. **Mark:** Initials and year.

COOMBS JR., LAMONT, 546 State Rt 46, Bucksport, ME 04416, Phone: 207-469-3057, Fax: 207-469-3057
Specialties: Classic fancy and embellished straight knives; traditional working and using straight knives. Knives of his design and to customer specs. **Patterns:** Hunters, folders and utility/camp knives. **Technical:** Hollow- and flat-grinds ATS-34, 440C, A2, D2 and O1; grinds Damascus from other makers. **Prices:** $100 to $500; some to $3500. **Remarks:** Full-time maker; first knife sold in 1988. **Mark:** Last name on banner, handmade underneath.

COON, RAYMOND C., 21135 SE Tillstrom Rd, Gresham, OR 97080, Phone: 503-658-2252
Specialties: Working straight knives in standard patterns. **Patterns:** Hunters, Bowies, daggers, boots and axes. **Technical:** Forges high carbon steel and Damascus. **Prices:** Start at $135. **Remarks:** Full-time maker; does own leatherwork, makes own Damascus, daggers; first knife sold in 1995. **Mark:** First initial, last name.

COOPER, TODD A., 8208 N Pine Haven Pt, Crystal River, FL 34428, Phone: 352-795-6219

COPELAND, THOM, 171 County Line Rd South, Nashville, AR 71852
Specialties: Hand forged fixed blades; hunters, Bowies & camp knives. **Mark:** Copeland. **Other:** Member of ABS and AKA (Arkansas Knifemakers Association)

COPELAND, GEORGE STEVE, 220 Pat Carr Lane, Alpine, TN 38543, Phone: 931-823-5214
Specialties: Traditional and fancy working straight knives and folders. **Patterns:** Friction folders, Congress two- and four-blade folders, button locks and one- and two-blade automatics. **Technical:** Stock removal of 440C, ATS-34 and A2; heat-treats. **Prices:** $180 to $950; some higher. **Remarks:** Full-time maker; first knife sold in 1979. Doing business as Alpine Mountain Knives. **Mark:** G. S. Copeland (HANDMADE); some with four-leaf clover stamp.

COPPINS, DANIEL, 7303 Sherrard Rd, Cambridge, OH 43725, Phone: 740-439-4199
Specialties: Grinds 440 C and etching toll steels, antler, bone handles. **Patterns:** Hunters patch, neck knives, primitive, tomahawk. **Prices:** $20 and up, some to $600. **Remarks:** Sold first knife in 2002. **Mark:** DC. **Other:** Made tomahawk + knives + walking stick for country music band Confederate Railroad.

CORBY, HAROLD, 218 Brandonwood Dr, Johnson City, TN 37604, Phone: 615-926-9781
Specialties: Large fighters and Bowies; self-protection knives; art knives. Along with art knives and combat knives, Corby now has all new automatic MO. PB1, also side lock MO LL-1 with titanium liners G-10 handles. **Patterns:** Sub-hilt fighters and hunters. **Technical:** Grinds 154CM, ATS-34 and 440C. **Prices:** $200 to $6000. **Remarks:** Full-time maker; first knife sold in 1969. Doing business as Knives by Corby. **Mark:** Last name.

CORDOVA, JOSEPH G., PO Box 977, Peralta, NM 87042, Phone: 505-869-3912
Specialties: One-of-a-kind designs, some to customer specs. **Patterns:** Fighter called the "Gladiator", hunters, boots and cutlery. **Technical:** Forges 1095, 5160; grinds ATS-34, 440C and 154CM. **Prices:** Moderate to upscale. **Remarks:** Full-time maker; first knife sold in 1953. **Mark:** Cordova made.

CORKUM, STEVE, 34 Basehoar School Rd, Littlestown, PA 17340, Phone: 717-359-9563

CORRADO, JIM, 255 Rock View Lane, Glide, OR 97443, Phone: 503-496-3951, Fax: 503-496-3595
Specialties: Two-blade pen knife with tip bolsters and inlay. Cast silver knives with engraving. **Patterns:** Slip joint folders, multi-blade folders, lockbacks. **Technical:** Small, accurate, home-made screws & photo etching. **Prices:** $300 to $4000. **Remark:** Close attention to detail & contouring. **Mark:** Etched "CORRADO". **Other:** Rare art knife called "The Wing".

custom knifemakers

CORRIGAN, DAVID P., HCR 65 Box 67, Bingham, ME 04920, Phone: 207-672-4879

COSGROVE, CHARLES G., 2314 W Arbook Blvd, Arlington, TX 76015, Phone: 817-472-6505
Specialties: Traditional fixed or locking blade working knives. **Patterns:** Hunters, Bowies and locking folders. **Technical:** Stock removal using 440C, ATS-34 and D2; heat-treats. Makes heavy, hand-stitched sheaths. **Prices:** $250 to $2500. **Remarks:** Full-time maker; first knife sold in 1968. No longer accepting customer designs. **Mark:** First initial, last name, or full name over city and state.

COSTA, SCOTT, 409 Coventry Rd, Spicewood, TX 78669, Phone: 830-693-3431
Specialties: Working straight knives. **Patterns:** Hunters, skinners, axes, trophy sets, custom boxed steak sets, carving sets and bar sets. **Technical:** Grinds D2, ATS-34, 440 and Damascus. Heat-treats. **Prices:** $225 to $2000. **Remarks:** Full-time maker; first knife sold in 1985. **Mark:** Initials connected.

COSTELLO, DR. TIMOTHY L., 30883 Crest Forest, Farmington Hills, MI 48331, Phone: 248-592-9746

COTTRILL, JAMES I., 1776 Ransburg Ave, Columbus, OH 43223, Phone: 614-274-0020
Specialties: Working straight knives of his design. **Patterns:** Caters to the boating and hunting crowd; cutlery. **Technical:** Grinds O1, D2 and 440C. Likes filework. **Prices:** $95 to $250; some to $500. **Remarks:** Full-time maker; first knife sold in 1977. **Mark:** Name, city, state, in oval logo.

COUGHLIN, MICHAEL M., 414 Northridge Lane, Winder, GA 30680, Phone: 770-307-9509
Specialties: One-of-a-kind large folders and daily carry knives. **Remarks:** Likes customer input and involvement.

COURTNEY, ELDON, 2718 Bullinger, Wichita, KS 67204, Phone: 316-838-4053
Specialties: Working straight knives of his design. **Patterns:** Hunters, fighters and one-of-a-kinds. **Technical:** Grinds and tempers L6, 440C and spring steel. **Prices:** $100 to $500; some to $1500. **Remarks:** Full-time maker; first knife sold in 1977. **Mark:** Full name, city and state.

COURTOIS, BRYAN, 3 Lawn Avenue, Saco, ME 04072, Phone: 207-282-3977
Specialties: Working straight knives; prefers customer designs, no standard patterns. **Patterns:** Functional hunters; everyday knives. **Technical:** Grinds 440C or customer request. Hollow-grinds with a variety of finishes. Specializes in granite handles and custom skeleton knives. **Prices:** Start at $75. **Remarks:** Part-time maker; first knife sold in 1988. Doing business as Castle Knives. **Mark:** A rook chess piece machined into blade using electrical discharge process.

COUSINO, GEORGE, 7818 Norfolk, Onsted, MI 49265, Phone: 517-467-4911, Fax: 517-467-4911
Specialties: Hunters, Bowies using knives. **Patterns:** Hunters, Bowies, buckskinners, folders and daggers. **Technical:** Grinds 440C. **Prices:** $95 to $300. **Remarks:** Part-time maker; first knife sold in 1981. **Mark:** Last name.

COVER, RAYMOND A., Rt. 1, Box 194, Mineral Point, MO 63660, Phone: 314-749-3783
Specialties: High-tech working straight knives and folders in standard patterns. **Patterns:** Bowies and boots; two-bladed folders. **Technical:** Grinds D2, 440C and 154CM. **Prices:** $135 to $250; some to $400. **Remarks:** Part-time maker; first knife sold in 1974. **Mark:** Name.

COWLES, DON, 1026 Lawndale Dr, Royal Oak, MI 48067, Phone: 248-541-4619
Specialties: Straight, non-folding pocket knives of his design. **Patterns:** Gentlemen's pocket knives. **Technical:** Grinds ATS-34, CPM440V, CPM 420V, Talonite. Scrimshaws; pearl inlays in some handles. **Prices:** $300 to $1200. **Remarks:** Part-time maker; first knife sold in 1994. **Mark:** Full name with oak leaf.

COX, COLIN J., 107 N. Oxford Dr, Raymore, MO 64083, Phone: 816-322-1977
Specialties: Working straight knives and folders of his design; period pieces. **Patterns:** Hunters, fighters and survival knives. Folders, two-blades, gents and hunters. **Technical:** Grinds D2, 440C, 154CM and ATS-34. **Prices:** $125 to $750; some to $4000. **Remarks:** Full-time maker; first knife sold in 1981. **Mark:** Full name, city and state.

COX, SAM, 1756 Love Springs Rd, Gaffney, SC 29341, Phone: 864-489-1892, Fax: 864-489-0403
Specialties: Classic high-art working straight knives of his design. Duck knives copyrighted. **Patterns:** Diverse. **Technical:** Grinds 154CM. **Prices:** $300 to $1400. **Remarks:** Full-time maker; first knife sold in 1983. **Mark:** Cox Call, Sam, Sam Cox, unique 2000 logo

CRAIG, ROGER L., 2815 Fairlawn Rd, Topeka, KS 66614, Phone: 785-233-9499
Specialties: Working and camp knives, some fantasy; all his design. **Patterns:** Fighters, hunter. **Technical:** Grinds 1095 and 5160. Most knives have file work. **Prices:** $50 to $250. **Remarks:** Part-time maker; first knife sold in 1991. Doing business as Craig Knives. **Mark:** Last name-Craig.

CRAIN, JACK W., PO Box 212, Granbury, TX 76048, Phone: 817-599-6414
Specialties: Fantasy and period knives; combat and survival knives. **Patterns:** One-of-a-kind art or fantasy daggers, swords and Bowies; survival knives. **Technical:** Forges Damascus; grinds stainless steel. Carves. **Prices:** $350 to $2500; some to $20,000. **Remarks:** Full-time maker; first knife sold in 1969. Designer and maker of the knives seen in the films *Dracula 2000, Executive Decision, Demolition Man, Predator I and II, Commando, Die Hard I and II, Road House, Ford Fairlane* and *Action Jackson,* and television shows *War of the Worlds, Air Wolf, Kung Fu: The Legend Cont.* and *Tales of the Crypt.* **Mark:** Stylized crane.

CRAIN, FRANK, 1127 W. Dalke, Spokane, WA 99205, Phone: 509-325-1596

CRAWFORD, PAT & WES, 205 N Center, West Memphis, AR 72301, Phone: 870-732-2452
Specialties: Stainless steel Damascus. High-tech working self-defense and combat types and folders. **Patterns:** Folding patent locks & interframes. **Technical:** Grinds ATS-34, D2 and 154CM. **Prices:** $125 to $2000. **Remarks:** Full-time maker; first knife sold in 1973. **Mark:** Last name.

CRAWLEY, BRUCE R., 16 Binbrook Dr, Croydon 3136 Victoria, AUSTRALIA
Specialties: Folders. **Patterns:** Hunters, lock-back folders and Bowies. **Technical:** Grinds 440C, ATS-34 and commercial Damascus. Offers filework and mirror polish. **Prices:** $160 to $3500. **Remarks:** Part-time maker; first knife sold in 1990. **Mark:** Initials.

CRENSHAW, AL, Rt. 1, Box 717, Eufaula, OK 74432, Phone: 918-452-2128
Specialties: Folders of his design and in standard patterns. **Patterns:** Hunters, locking folders, slip-joint folders, multi blade folders. **Technical:** Grinds 440C, D2 and ATS-34. Does filework on back springs and blades; offers scrimshaw on some handles. **Prices:** $150 to $300; some higher. **Remarks:** Full-time maker; first knife sold in 1981. Doing business as A. Crenshaw Knives. **Mark:** First initial, last name, Lake Eufaula, state stamped; first initial last name in rainbow; Lake Eufaula across bottom with Okla. in middle.

CROCKFORD, JACK, 1859 Harts Mill Rd, Chamblee, GA 30341, Phone: 770-457-4680
Specialties: Lock-back folders. **Patterns:** Hunters, fishing and camp knives, traditional folders. **Technical:** Grinds A2, D2, ATS-34 and 440C. Engraves and scrimshaws. **Prices:** Start at $175. **Remarks:** Part-time maker; first knife sold in 1975. **Mark:** Name.

CROSS, ROBERT, RMB 200B, Manilla Rd, Tamworth 2340, NSW AUSTRALIA, Phone: 067-618385

CROSSMAN, DANIEL C., BOX 5236, Blakely Island, WA 98222, Phone: 360-375-6542

CROWDER, ROBERT, Box 1374, Thompson Falls, MT 59873, Phone: 406-827-4754
Specialties: Traditional working knives to customer specs. **Patterns:** Hunters, Bowies, fighters and fillets. **Technical:** Grinds ATS-34, 154CM, 440C, Vascowear and commercial Damascus. **Prices:** $160 to $250; some to $2500. **Remarks:** Part-time maker; first knife sold in 1985. **Mark:** First initial, last name.

CROWELL, JAMES L., 7181 Happy Hollow Rd, Mtn. View, AR 72560, Phone: 870-269-4215
Specialties: Bowie knives; fancy period pieces and working knives to customer specs. **Patterns:** Hunters to daggers, war hammers to tantos; locking folders and slip-joints. **Technical:** Forges 1084-5160-01 and his own Damascus. **Prices:** $325 to $3500; some to $7500. **Remarks:** Part-time maker; first knife sold in 1980. Earned ABS Master Smith in 1986. **Mark:** A shooting star.

CROWTHERS, MARK F., PO Box 4641, Rolling Bay, WA 98061-0641, Phone: 206-842-7501

CULPEPPER, JOHN, 2102 Spencer Ave, Monroe, LA 71201, Phone: 318-323-3636
Specialties: Working straight knives. **Patterns:** Hunters, Bowies and camp knives in heavy-duty patterns. **Technical:** Grinds O1, D2 and 440C; hollow-grinds. **Prices:** $75 to $200; some to $300. **Remarks:** Part-time maker; first knife sold in 1970. Doing business as Pepper Knives. **Mark:** Pepper.

CULVER, STEVE, 5682 94th st, Meriden, KS 66512, Phone: 785-484-0146
Specialties: Edged tools and weapons, collectible and functional. **Patterns:** Bowies, daggers, swords, hunters, folders and edged tools. **Technical:** Forges carbon steels and his own pattern welded steels. **Prices:** $200 to $500; some to $4000. **Remarks:** Part-time maker; first knife sold in 1989. **Mark:** Last name, J. S.

CUMMING, R. J., CUMMING KNIVES, 35 Manana Dr, Cedar Crest, NM 87008, Phone: 505-286-0509
Specialties: Custom made Bowie knives, Plains Indians-style knife sheaths. D2, ATS-34 and 1095 Damascus, exotic handles. Custom leather work, Scrimshaw and engraving. **Prices:** $225 to $750; some higher. **Remarks:** Full-time maker; first knife sold in 1978 in Denmark; mentored by late Jim Nolen. Retired US Foreign Service Officer. Member PKA, NCCKG. **Mark:** Stylized CUMMING.

CUTCHIN, ROY D., 960 Hwy. 169 S., Seale, AL 36875, Phone: 334-855-3080
Specialties: Fancy and working folders of his design. **Patterns:** Locking folders. **Technical:** Grinds ATS-34 and commercial Damascus; uses anodized titanium. **Prices:** Start at $250. **Remarks:** Part-time maker. **Mark:** First initial, last name, city and state, number.

CUTE, THOMAS, State Rt. 90-7071, Cortland, NY 13045, Phone: 607-749-4055
Specialties: Working straight knives. **Patterns:** Hunters, Bowies and fighters. **Technical:** Grinds O1, 440C and ATS-34. **Prices:** $100 to $1000. **Remarks:** Full-time maker; first knife sold in 1974. **Mark:** Full name.

d

DACONCEICAO, JOHN M., 138 Perryville Rd, Rehoboth, MA 02769, Phone: 508-252-9686
Specialties: One-of-a-kind straight knives of his design and to customer specs. **Patterns:** Boots, fighters and folders. **Technical:** Grinds O1, 1095 and commercial Damascus. All knives come with leather sheath; cross-draw and shoulder harnesses available. **Prices:** $90 to $200; some to $500. **Remarks:** Part-time maker; first knife sold in 1993. **Mark:** JMD Blades.

DAILEY, G. E., 577 Lincoln St, Seekonk, MA 02771, Phone: 508-336-5088
Specialties: One-of-a-kind exotic designed edged weapons. **Patterns:** Folders, daggers and swords. **Technical:** Reforges and grinds Damascus; prefers hollow-grinding. Engraves, carves, offers filework and sets stones and uses exotic gems and gold. **Prices:** Start at $1100. **Remarks:** Full-time maker. First knife sold in 1982. **Mark:** Last name or stylized initialed logo.

DAKE, MARY H., RT 5 Box 287A, New Orleans, LA 70129, Phone: 504-254-0357

DAKE, C. M., 19759 Chef Menteur Hwy., New Orleans, LA 70129-9602, Phone: 504-254-0357, Fax: 504-254-9501
Specialties: Fancy working folders. **Patterns:** Front-lock lock-backs, button-lock folders. **Technical:** Grinds ATS-34 and Damascus. **Prices:** $500 to $2500; some higher. **Remarks:** Full-time maker; first knife sold in 1988. Doing business as Bayou Custom Cutlery. **Mark:** Last name.

DALAND, B. MACGREGOR, Rt 5 Box 196, Harbeson, DE 19951, Phone: 302-945-2609

DALLYN, KELLY, 14695 Deerridge Dr S E, Calgary AB, CANADA T2J 6A8, Phone: 403-278-3056

DAMLOVAC, SAVA, 10292 Bradbury Dr, Indianapolis, IN 46231, Phone: 317-839-4952
Specialties: Period pieces, Fantasy, Viking, Moran type all Damascus daggers. **Patterns:** Bowies, fighters, daggers, Persian-style knives. **Technical:** Uses own Damascus, some stainless, mostly hand forges. **Prices:** $150 to $2500; some higher. **Remarks:** Full-time maker; first knife sold in 1993. **Mark:** "Sava" stamped in Damascus or etched in stainless. **Other:** Specialty, Bill Moran all Damascus dagger sets, in Moran-style wood case.

D'ANDREA, JOHN, 501 Penn Estates, East Stroudsberg, PA 18301, Phone: 570-420-6050
Specialties: Fancy working straight knives and folders with filework and distinctive leatherwork. **Patterns:** Hunters, fighters, daggers, folders and an occasional sword. **Technical:** Grinds ATS-34, 154CM, 440C and D2. **Prices:** $180 to $600; some to $1000. **Remarks:** Part-time maker; first knife sold in 1986. **Mark:** First name, last initial imposed on samurai sword.

D'ANGELO, LAURENCE, 14703 NE 17th Ave, Vancouver, WA 98686, Phone: 360-573-0546
Specialties: Straight knives of his design. **Patterns:** Bowies, hunters and locking folders. **Technical:** Grinds D2, ATS-34 and 440C. Hand makes all sheaths. **Prices:** $100 to $200. **Remarks:** Full-time maker; first knife sold in 1987. **Mark:** Football logo—first and middle initials, last name, city, state, Maker.

DANIEL, TRAVIS E., 1655 Carrow Rd, Chocowinity, NC 27817, Phone: 252-940-0807
Specialties: Traditional working straight knives of his design or to customer specs. **Patterns:** Hunters, fighters and utility/camp knives. **Technical:** Forges and grinds ATS-34 and his own Damascus. **Prices:** $90 to $1250; some to $2000. **Remarks:** Full-time maker; first knife sold in 1976. **Mark:** Carolina Custom Knives or "TED".

DANIELS, ALEX, 1416 County Rd. 415, Town Creek, AL 35672, Phone: 256-685-0943
Specialties: Working and using straight knives and folders; period pieces, reproduction Bowies. **Patterns:** Mostly reproduction Bowies but offer full line of knives. **Technical:** Now also using BG-42 along with 440C and ATS-34. **Prices:** $200 to $2500. **Remarks:** Full-time maker; first knife sold in 1963. **Mark:** First and middle initials, last name, city and state.

DARBY, DAVID T., 30652 S 533 Rd, Cookson, OK 74427, Phone: 918-457-4868

DARBY, RICK, 71 Nestingrock Lane, Levittown, PA 19054
Specialties: Working straight knives. **Patterns:** Boots, fighters and hunters with mirror finish. **Technical:** Grinds 440C and CPM440V. **Prices:** $125 to $300. **Remarks:** Part-time maker; first knife sold in 1974. **Mark:** First and middle initials, last name.

DARBY, JED, 7878 E. Co. Rd. 50 N., Greensburg, IN 47240, Phone: 812-663-2696
Specialties: Traditional working/using straight knives of his design and to customer specs. **Patterns:** Bowies, hunters and utility/camp knives. **Technical:** Grinds 440C, ATS-34 and Damascus. **Prices:** $70 to $550; some to $1000. **Remarks:** Full-time maker; first knife sold in 1992. Doing business as Darby Knives. **Mark:** Last name and year.

DARCEY, CHESTER L., 1608 Dominik Dr, College Station, TX 77840, Phone: 979-696-1656
Specialties: Lock-back, liner-lock and scale release folders. **Patterns:** Bowies, hunters and utilities. **Technical:** Stock removal on carbon and stainless steels, forge own Damascus. **Prices:** $200 to $1000. **Remarks:** Part-time maker, first knife sold in 1999. **Mark:** Last name in script.

DARPINIAN, DAVE, 15219 W 125th, Olathe, KS 66062, Phone: 913-397-8914
Specialties: Working knives and fancy pieces to customer specs. **Patterns:** Full range of straight knives including art daggers and short swords. **Technical:** Art grinds ATS-34, 440C, 154CM, 5160, 1095. **Prices:** $200 to $1000. **Remarks:** First knife sold in 1996, part-time maker. **Mark:** Last name.

DAVENPORT, JACK, 36842 W. Center Ave, Dade City, FL 33525, Phone: 352-521-4088
Specialties: Titanium liner-lock, button-lock and release. **Patterns:** Boots and double-ground fighters. **Technical:** Grinds ATS-34, 12C27 SS and Damascus; liquid nitrogen quench; heat-treats. **Prices:** $250 to $5000. **Remarks:** Full-time maker; first knife sold in 1986. **Mark:** Last name.

DAVIDSON, EDMUND, 3345 Virginia Ave, Goshen, VA 24439, Phone: 540-997-5651
Specialties: Working straight knives; many integral patterns and upgraded models. **Patterns:** Heavy-duty skinners and camp knives. **Technical:** Grinds A2, ATS-34, BG-42, S7, 440C. **Prices:** $75 to $1500. **Remarks:** Full-time maker; first knife sold in 1986. **Mark:** Name in deer head or custom logos.

DAVIS, BARRY L., 4262 U. S. 20, Castleton, NY 12033, Phone: 518-477-5036
Specialties: Collector-quality and Damascus interframe folders. **Patterns:** Traditional gentlemen's folders. **Technical:** Makes Damascus; uses only natural handle materials. **Prices:** $1000 to $2500; some to $6000. **Remarks:** Part-time maker; first knife sold in 1980. **Mark:** Initials.

DAVIS, JOHN, 235 Lampe Road, Selah, WA 98942, Phone: 509-697-3845, Fax: 509-697-8087
Specialties: Working and using straight knives of his own design, to customer specs and in standard patterns. **Patterns:** Boots, hunters, kitchen and utility/camp knives. **Technical:** Grinds ATS-34, 440C and commercial Damascus; makes own Damascus and mosaic Damascus. Embellishes with stabilized wood, mokume and nickel-silver. **Prices:** Start at $150. **Remarks:** Part-time maker; first knife sold in 1996. **Mark:** Name city and state on Damascus stamp initials.

custom knifemakers

DAVIS, TERRY, Box 111, Sumpter, OR 97877, Phone: 541-894-2307
Specialties: Traditional and contemporary folders. **Patterns:** Multi-blade folders, whittlers and interframe multiblades; sunfish patterns. **Technical:** Flat-grinds ATS-34. **Prices:** $400 to $1000; some higher. **Remarks:** Full-time maker; first knife sold in 1985. **Mark:** Name in logo.

DAVIS, VERNON M., 2020 Behrens Circle, Waco, TX 76705, Phone: 254-799-7671
Specialties: Presentation-grade straight knives. **Patterns:** Bowies, daggers, boots, fighters, hunters and utility knives. **Technical:** Hollow-grinds 440C, ATS-34 and D2. Grinds an aesthetic grind line near choil. **Prices:** $125 to $550; some to $5000. **Remarks:** Part-time maker; first knife sold in 1980. **Mark:** Last name and city inside outline of state.

DAVIS, JESSE W., 7398A Hwy. 3, Sarah, MS 38665, Phone: 662-382-7332
Specialties: Working straight knives and folders in standard patterns and to customer specs. **Patterns:** Boot knives, daggers. **Technical:** Grinds O1, A2, D2, 440C and commercial Damascus. **Prices:** $100 to $650. **Remarks:** Full-time maker; first knife sold in 1977. Former member Knife Makers Guild (in good standing). **Mark:** Name or initials.

DAVIS, STEVE, 3370 Chatsworth Way, Powder Springs, GA 30127, Phone: 770-427-5740
Specialties: Traditional Gents and Ladies folders of his design and to customer specs. **Patterns:** Slip-joint folders, locking-liner folders, lock-back folders. **Technical:** Grinds ATS-34, 440C and Damascus. Offers filework; prefers hand-rubbed finishes and natural handle materials. Uses pearl, ivory, stag and exotic woods. **Prices:** $250 to $600; some to $1500. **Remarks:** Part-time maker; first knife sold in 1988. Doing business as Custom Knives by Steve Davis. **Mark:** Name engraved on blade.

DAVIS, CHARLIE, ANZA Knives, PO Box 710806, Santee, CA 92072, Phone: 619-561-9445, Fax: 619-390-6283
Specialties: Fancy and embellished working straight knives of his design. **Patterns:** Hunters, camp and utility knives. **Technical:** Grinds high-carbon files. **Prices:** $20 to $185 - custom depends. **Remarks:** Full-time maker; first knife sold in 1980. **Mark:** ANZA U. S. A. **Other:** we now offer custom.

DAVIS, W. C., 19300 S. School Rd, Raymore, MO 64083, Phone: 816-331-4491
Specialties: Fancy working straight knives and folders. **Patterns:** Folding lockers and slip-joints; straight hunters, fighters and Bowies. **Technical:** Grinds A2, ATS-34, 154, CPM T490V and CPM 530V. **Prices:** $100 to $300; some to $1000. **Remarks:** Full-time maker; first knife sold in 1972. **Mark:** Name.

DAVIS, DON, 8415 Coyote Run, Loveland, CO 80537-9665, Phone: 970-669-9016, Fax: 970-669-8072
Specialties: Working straight knives in standard patterns or to customer specs. **Patterns:** Hunters, utility knives, skinners and survival knives. **Technical:** Grinds 440C, ATS-34. **Prices:** $75 to $250. **Remarks:** Full-time maker; first knife sold in 1985. **Mark:** Signature, city and state.

DAVISSON, COLE, 25939 Casa Loma Ct, Hemet, CA 92544, Phone: 909-652-8588

DAWKINS, DUDLEY L., 221 NW Broadmoor Ave, Topeka, KS 66606-1254
Specialties: Stylized old or "Dawkins Forged" with anvil in center. New Tang Stamps. **Patterns:** Straight knives. **Technical:** Mostly carbon steel; some Damascus-all knives forged. **Prices:** $125 and up. **Remarks:** All knives supplied with wood-lined sheaths. **Other:** ABS Member - sole authorship.

DAWSON, LYNN, 10A Town Plaza #303, Durango, CO 81301, Fax: 928-772-1729
Specialties: Swords, hunters, utility, and art pieces. **Patterns:** Over 25 patterns to choose from. **Technical:** Grinds 440C, ATS-34, own heat treating. **Prices:** $80 to $1000. **Remarks:** Custom work and my own designs. **Mark:** The name "Lynn" in print or script.

DAWSON, BARRY, 10A Town Plaza, Suite 303, Durango, CO 81301
Specialties: Samurai swords, combat knives, collector daggers, tactical, folding and hunting knives. **Patterns:** Offers over 60 different models. **Technical:** Grinds 440C, ATS-34, own heat-treatment. **Prices:** $75 to $1500; some to $5000. **Remarks:** Full-time maker; first knife sold in 1975. **Mark:** Last name, USA in print or last name in script.

DE CASTRO, MARCO A. M., Rua Bandeira Paulista, 600, Conj. 113, Sao Paulo SP, BRAZIL 04532-001, Phone: 5511 3842-6911, Fax: 5511) 3842-6029

DE MARIA JR., ANGELO, 12 Boronda Rd, Carmel Valley, CA 93924, Phone: 831-659-3381, Fax: 831 659-1315

DE VILLIERS, ANDRE & KIRSTEN, Postnet suite 263, Private bag X6, Cascades 3202, SOUTH AFRICA, Phone: 27 31 785 1278, Fax: 27031078501278

DEAN, HARVEY J., 3266 CR 232, Rockdale, TX 76567, Phone: 512-446-3111, Fax: 512-446-5060
Specialties: Collectible, functional knives. **Patterns:** Bowies, hunters, folders, daggers, swords, battle axes, camp and combat knives. **Technical:** Forges 1095, O1 and his Damascus. **Prices:** $350 to $10,000. **Remarks:** Full-time maker; first knife sold in 1981. **Mark:** Last name and MS.

DEBRAGA, JOSE C., 76 Rue de La Pointe, Aux Lievres Quebec, CANADA G1K 5Y3, Phone: 418-948-0105, Fax: 418-948-0105
Specialties: Art knives, fantasy pieces and working knives of his design or to customer specs. **Patterns:** Knives with sculptured or carved handles, from miniatures to full-size working knives. **Technical:** Grinds and hand-files 440C and ATS-34. A variety of steels and handle materials available. Offers lost wax casting. **Prices:** Start at $300. **Remarks:** Full-time maker; wax modeler, sculptor and knife maker; first knife sold in 1984. **Mark:** Initials in stylized script and serial number.

DEFEO, ROBERT A., 403 Lost Trail Dr, Henderson, NV 89014, Phone: 702-434-3717
Specialties: Working straight knives and period pieces. **Patterns:** Hunters, fighters, daggers and Bowies. **Technical:** Grinds ATS-34 & Damascus. **Prices:** $250 to $500; some higher. **Remarks:** Part-time maker; first knife sold in 1982. **Mark:** Last name.

DEFREEST, WILLIAM G., PO Box 573, Barnwell, SC 29812, Phone: 803-259-7883
Specialties: Working straight knives and folders. **Patterns:** Fighters, hunters and boots; locking folders and slip-joints. **Technical:** Grinds 440C, 154CM and ATS-34; clean lines and mirror finishes. **Prices:** $100 to $700. **Remarks:** Full-time maker; first knife sold in 1974. **Mark:** GORDON.

DEL RASO, PETER, 28 Mayfield Dr, Mt. Waverly, Victoria, 3149, AUSTRALIA, Phone: 613-9807 6771
Specialties: Fixed Blades, some folders, art knives. **Patterns:** Daggers, Bowies, tactical, boot, personal and working knives. **Technical:** Grinds ATS-34, commercial Damascus and any other type of steel on request. **Prices:** $100 to $1500. **Remarks:** Part-time maker, first show in 1993. **Mark:** Makers surname stamped.

DELAROSA, JIM, 202 Macarthur Dr, Mukwonago, WI 53149, Phone: 262-363-9605
Specialties: Working straight knives and folders of my design or customer specs. **Patterns:** Hunters, skinners, fillets, utility and locking folders. **Technical:** Grinds ATS-34, 440-C, D2, 01 and commercial Damascus. **Prices:** $75 to $450; some higher. **Remarks:** Part-time maker. **Mark:** First and last name, city and state.

DELL, WOLFGANG, Am Alten Berg 9, D-73277 Owen-Teck, GERMANY, Phone: 49-7021-81802
Specialties: Fancy high-art straight of his design and to customer specs. **Patterns:** Fighters, hunters, Bowies and utility/camp knives. **Technical:** Grinds ATS-34, RWL-34, Elmax, Damascus (Fritz Schneider). Offers high gloss finish and engraving. **Prices:** $500 to $1000; some to $1600. **Remarks:** Full-time maker; first knife sold in 1992. **Mark:** Hopi hand of peace. **Other:** Member of German Knife maker Guild since 1993. Member of the Italian Knife maker Guild since 2000.

DELLANA, Dellana Inc., 1135 Terminal Way Ste #209, Reno, NV 89502, Phone: 866 Dellana or 304-727-5512, Fax: 775-201-0038
Specialties: Collector grade fancy/embellished high art folders and art daggers. **Patterns:** Locking folders and art daggers. **Technical:** Forges her own Damascus and W-2. Engraves, does stone setting, filework, carving and gold/platinum fabrication. Prefers exotic, high karat gold, platinum, silver, gemstone and mother of pearl handle materials. **Price:** Upscale. **Remarks:** Sole authorship, full-time maker, first knife sold in 1994. **Mark:** First name. **Other:** Does one high art collaboration a year with Van Barnett. **Member:** Art Knife Invitational and ABS; voting member: Knifemakers Guild.

DELONG, DICK, 17561 E. Ohio Circle, Aurora, CO 80017, Phone: 303-745-2652
Specialties: Fancy working knives and fantasy pieces. **Patterns:** Hunters and small skinners. **Technical:** Grinds and files O1, D2, 440C and Damascus. Offers cocobolo and Osage orange for handles. **Prices:** Start at $50. **Remarks:** Part-time maker. **Mark:** Last name; some unmarked.

Other: Member of Art Knife Invitational. Voting member of Knifemakers Guild. Member of ABS.

DEMENT, LARRY, PO Box 1807, Prince Fredrick, MD 20678, Phone: 410-586-9011
Specialties: Fixed blades. **Technical:** Forged & stock removal. **Prices:** $75-$200. **Remarks:** Affordable, good feeling, quality knives. **Other:** Part-time maker.

DEMPSEY, GORDON S., PO Box 7497, N. Kenai, AK 99635, Phone: 907-776-8425
Specialties: Working straight knives. **Patterns:** Pattern welded Damascus and carbon steel blades. **Technical:** Pattern welded Damascus and carbon steel. **Prices:** $80 to $250. **Remarks:** Part-time maker; first knife sold in 1974. **Mark:** Name.

DEMPSEY, DAVID, 103 Chadwick Dr, Macon, GA 31210, Phone: 478-474-4948
Specialties: Tactical, Utility, Working, Classic straight knives. **Patterns:** Fighters, Tantos, Hunters, Neck, Utility or Customer design. **Technical:** Grinds carbon steel and stainless including S30V. (differential heat treatment), Stainless Steels. **Prices:** Start at $150 for Neck Knives. **Remarks:** Full-time maker. First knife sold 1998. **Mark:** First and last name over knives.

DENNEHY, DAN, PO Box 2F, Del Norte, CO 81132, Phone: 719-657-2545
Specialties: Working knives, fighting and military knives, throwing knives. **Patterns:** Full range of straight knives, tomahawks, buckle knives. **Technical:** Forges and grinds A2, O1 and D2. **Prices:** $200 to $500. **Remarks:** Full-time maker; first knife sold in 1942. **Mark:** First name and last initial, city, state and shamrock.

DENNING, GENO, Caveman Engineering, 135 Allenvalley Rd, Gaston, SC 29053, Phone: 803-794-6067
Specialties: Mirror finish. **Patterns:** Hunters, fighters, folders. **Technical:** ATS-34, 440V, S-30-V D-2. **Prices:** $100 and up. **Remarks:** Full-time maker since 1996. Sole income since 1999. **Mark:** Denning with year below. **Other:** A director of SCAK. South Carolina Association of Knifemakers.

DENT, DOUGLAS M., 1208 Chestnut St, S. Charleston, WV 25309, Phone: 304-768-3308
Specialties: Straight and folding sportsman's knives. **Patterns:** Hunters, boots and Bowies, interframe folders. **Technical:** Forges and grinds D2, 440C, 154CM and plain tool steels. **Prices:** $70 to $300; exceptional knives to $800. **Remarks:** Part-time maker; first knife sold in 1969. **Mark:** Last name.

DERINGER, CHRISTOPH, 1559 St. Louis #4, Sherbrooke, Quebec, CANADA J1H 4P7, Phone: 819-345-4260
Specialties: Traditional working/using straight knives and folders of his design and to customer specs. **Patterns:** Boots, hunters, folders, art knives, kitchen knives and utility/camp knives. **Technical:** Forges 5160, O1 and Damascus. Offers a variety of filework. **Prices:** Start at $250. **Remarks:** Full-time maker; first knife sold in 1989. **Mark:** Last name stamped/engraved.

DERR, HERBERT, 413 Woodland Dr, St Albans, WV 25177, Phone: 304-727-3866
Specialties: Damascus one-of-a-kind knives, carbon steels also. **Patterns:** Birdseye, Ladder back, Mosaics. **Technical:** All styles functional as well as artistically pleasing. **Prices:** $90 to $175 carbon, $175 to $600 Damascus. **Remarks:** All Damascus made by maker. **Mark:** H. K. Derr.

DETMER, PHILLIP, 14140 Bluff Rd, Breese, IL 62230, Phone: 618-526-4834
Specialties: Working knives. **Patterns:** Bowies, daggers and hunters. **Technical:** Grinds ATS-34 and D2. **Prices:** $60 to $400. **Remarks:** Part-time maker; first knife sold in 1977. **Mark:** Last name with dagger.

DI MARZO, RICHARD, 2357 Center Pl., Birmingham, AL 35205, Phone: 205-252-3331

DICKERSON, GORDON S., 152 Laurel Ln, Hohenwald, TN 38462, Phone: 931-796-1187
Specialties: Traditional working straight knives; Civil War era period pieces. **Patterns:** Bowies, hunters, tactical, camp/utility knives; some folders. **Technical:** Forges carbon steel; pattern welded and cable Damascus. **Prices:** $150 to $500; some to $3000. **Mark:** Last name. **Other:** ABS member.

DICKERSON, GAVIN, PO Box 7672, Petit 1512, SOUTH AFRICA, Phone: +27 011-965-0988, Fax: +27 011-965-0988
Specialties: Straight knives of his design or to customer specs. **Patterns:** Hunters, skinners, fighters and Bowies. **Technical:** Hollow-grinds D2, 440C, ATS-34, 12C27 and Damascus upon request. Prefers natural han-

dle materials; offers synthetic handle materials. **Prices:** $190 to $2500. **Remarks:** Part-time maker; first knife sold in 1982. **Mark:** Name in full.

DICKISON, SCOTT S., Fisher Circle
Fisher Circle, Portsmouth, RI 02871, Phone: 401-419-4175
Specialties: Working and using straight knives and locking folders of his design and automatics. **Patterns:** Trout knives, fishing and hunting knives. **Technical:** Forges and grinds commercial Damascus and D2, O1. Uses natural handle materials. **Prices:** $400 to $750; some higher. **Remarks:** Part-time maker; first knife sold in 1989. **Mark:** Stylized initials.

DICRISTOFANO, ANTHONY P., PO Box 2369, Northlake, IL 60164, Phone: 847-845-9598
Specialties: Japanese-style swords. **Patterns:** Katana, Wakizashi, Otanto, Kozuka. **Technical:** Tradition and some modern steels. All clay tempered and traditionally hand polished using Japanese wet stones. **Remarks:** Part-time maker. **Prices:** Varied, available on request. **Mark:** Blade tang sighned in "Masatoni" Japanese

DIEBEL, CHUCK, PO Box 13, Broussard, LA 70516-0013

DIETZ, HOWARD, 421 Range Rd, New Braunfels, TX 78132, Phone: 830-885-4662
Specialties: Lock-back folders, working straight knives. **Patterns:** Folding hunters, high grade pocket knives. ATS-34, 440C, CPM 440V, D2 and stainless Damascus. **Prices:** $300 to $1000. **Remarks:** Full-time gun & knife maker; first knife sold in 1995. **Mark:** Name, city, and state.

DIETZEL, BILL, PO Box 1613, Middleburg, FL 32068, Phone: 904-282-1091
Specialties: Forged straight knives and folders. **Patterns:** His interpretations. **Technical:** Forges his Damascus and other steels. **Prices:** Middle ranges. **Remarks:** Likes natural materials; uses titanium in folder liners. **Mark:** Name. **Other:** Master Smith (1997).

DIGANGI, JOSEPH M., Box 950, Santa Cruz, NM 87567, Phone: 505-753-6414, Fax: 505-753-8144
Specialties: Kitchen and table cutlery. **Patterns:** French chef's knives, carving sets, steak knife sets, some camp knives and hunters. Holds patents and trademarks for "System II" kitchen cutlery set. **Technical:** Grinds ATS-34. **Prices:** $150 to $595; some to $1200. **Remarks:** Full-time maker; first knife sold in 1983. **Mark:** DiGangi Designs.

DILL, ROBERT, 1812 Van Buren, Loveland, CO 80538, Phone: 970-667-5144, Fax: 970-667-5144
Specialties: Fancy and working knives of his design. **Patterns:** Hunters, Bowies and fighters. **Technical:** Grinds 440C and D2. **Prices:** $100 to $800. **Remarks:** Full-time maker; first knife sold in 1984. **Mark:** Logo stamped into blade.

DILL, DAVE, 7404 NW 30th St, Bethany, OK 73008, Phone: 405-789-0750
Specialties: Folders of his design. **Patterns:** Various patterns. **Technical:** Hand-grinds 440C, ATS-34. Offers engraving and filework on all folders. **Prices:** Starting at $450. **Remarks:** Full-time maker; first knife sold in 1987. **Mark:** First initial, last name.

DILLUVIO, FRANK J., 13611 Joyce Dr, Warren, MI 48093, Phone: 810-775-1216
Specialties: Traditional working straight knives, some high-tech. **Patterns:** Hunters, Bowies, fishing knives, sub-hilts, liner-lock folders and miniatures. **Technical:** Grinds D2, 440C, CPM; works for precision fits—no solder. **Prices:** $95 to $450; some to $800. **Remarks:** Full-time maker; first knife sold in 1984. **Mark:** Name and state.

DION, GREG, 3032 S. Jackson St, Oxnard, CA 93033, Phone: 805-483-1781
Specialties: Working straight knives, some fancy. Welcomes special orders. **Patterns:** Hunters, fighters, camp knives, Bowies and tantos. **Technical:** Grinds ATS-34, 154CM and 440C. **Prices:** $85 to $300; some to $600. **Remarks:** Part-time maker; first knife sold in 1985. **Mark:** Name.

DIOTTE, JEFF, Diotte Knives, 159 Laurier Dr, LaSalle Ontario, CANADA N9J 1L4, Phone: 519-978-2764

DIPPOLD, AL, 90 Damascus Ln., Perryville, MO 63775, Phone: 573-547-1119
Specialties: Fancy one-of-a-kind locking folders. **Patterns:** Locking folders. **Technical:** Forges and grinds mosaic and pattern welded Damascus. Offers filework on all folders. **Prices:** $500 to $3500; some higher. **Remarks:** Full-time maker; first knife sold in 1980. **Mark:** Last name in logo inside of liner.

DISKIN, MATT, PO Box 653, Freeland, WA 98249, Phone: 360-730-0451
Specialties: Damascus autos. **Patterns:** Dirks & daggers. **Technical:** Forges mosaic Damascus using 15N20, 1084, 02, 06, L6; pure nickel. **Prices:** Start at $500. **Remarks:** Full-time maker. **Mark:** Last name.

DIXON JR., IRA E., PO Box 2581, Ventura, CA 93002-2581, Phone: 805-659-5867
Specialties: Utilitarian straight knives of his design. **Patterns:** Camp, hunters, boot, fighters. **Technical:** Grinds ATS-34, 440C, D2, 5160. **Prices:** $150 to $400. **Remarks:** Part-time maker; first knife sold in 1993. **Mark:** First name, Handmade.

DODD, ROBERT F., 4340 E Canyon Dr, Camp Verde, AZ 86322, Phone: 928-567-3333
Specialties: Useable fixed blade hunter/skinners, some Bowies and collectables. **Patterns:** Drop point. **Technical:** ATS-34 stainless and Damascus. **Prices:** $300 and up. **Remarks:** Worked closely with D. Holder on patterns. **Mark:** R. F. Dodd, Camp Verde AZ.

DOGGETT, BOB, 1310 Vinetree Dr, Brandon, FL 33510, Phone: 813-786-9057
Specialties: Clean, functional working knives. **Patterns:** Classic styled hunter, fighter and utility fixed blades; liner-locking folders. **Technical:** Uses stainless steel and commercial Damascus, 416 stainless for bolsters and hardware, hand-rubbed satin finish, top quality handle materials and titanium liners on folders Uses a variety of modern stainless steels and commercial Damascus. **Prices:** Start at $175. **Remarks:** Part-time maker; specializes in web design for knife makers. **Mark:** Last name

DOIRON, DONALD, 6 Chemin Petit Lac Des Ced, Messines PQ, CANADA JOX-2JO, Phone: 819-465-2489

DOLAN, ROBERT L., 220B Naalae Road, Kula, HI 96790, Phone: 808-878-6406
Specialties: Working straight knives in standard patterns, his designs or to customer specs. **Patterns:** Fixed blades and potter's tools, ceramic saws. **Technical:** Grinds O1, D2, 440C and ATS-34. Heat-treats and engraves. **Prices:** Start at $75. **Remarks:** Full-time tool and knife maker; first knife sold in 1985. **Mark:** Last name, USA.

DOMINY, CHUCK, PO Box 593, Colleyville, TX 76034, Phone: 817-498-4527
Specialties: Titanium liner-lock folders. **Patterns:** Hunters, utility/camp knives and liner-lock folders. **Technical:** Grinds 440C and ATS-34. **Prices:** $250 to $3000. **Remarks:** Full-time maker; first knife sold in 1976. **Mark:** Last name.

DOOLITTLE, MIKE, 13 Denise Ct, Novato, CA 94947, Phone: 415-897-3246
Specialties: Working straight knives in standard patterns. **Patterns:** Hunters and fishing knives. **Technical:** Grinds 440C, 154CM and ATS-34. **Prices:** $125 to $200; some to $750. **Remarks:** Part-time maker; first knife sold in 1981. **Mark:** Name, city and state.

DORNELES, LUCIANO OLIVEIRIRA, Rua 15 De Novembro 2222, Nova Petropolis, RS, BRAZIL 95150-000, Phone: 011-55-54-303-303-90
Specialties: Traditional "true" Brazilian-style working knives and to customer specs. **Patterns:** Brazilian hunters, utility and camp knives, Bowies, Dirk. A master at the making of the true "Faca Campeira Gaucha," the true camp knife of the famous Brazilian Gauchos. A Dorneles knife is 100% hand-forged with sledge hammers only. Can makes spectacular Damascus hunters/daggers. **Technical:** Forges only 52100 and his own Damascus, can put silver wire inlay on customer design handles on special orders; uses only natural handle materials. **Prices:** $250 to $1000. **Mark:** Symbol with L. Dorneles.

DOTSON, TRACY, 1280 Hwy. C-4A, Baker, FL 32531, Phone: 850-537-2407
Specialties: Folding fighters and small folders. **Patterns:** Liner-lock and lock-back folders. **Technical:** Hollow-grinds ATS-34 and commercial Damascus. **Prices:** Start at $250. **Remarks:** Part-time maker; first knife sold in 1995. **Mark:** Last name.

DOUGLAS, JOHN J., 506 Powell Rd, Lynch Station, VA 24571, Phone: 804-369-7196
Specialties: Fancy and traditional straight knives and folders of his design and to customer specs. **Patterns:** Locking folders, swords and sgian dubhs. **Technical:** Grinds 440C stainless, ATS-34 stainless and customer's choice. Offers newly designed non-pivot uni-lock folders. Prefers highly polished finish. **Prices:** $160 to $1400. **Remarks:** Full-time maker; first knife sold in 1975. Doing business as Douglas Keltic. **Mark:** Stylized initial. Folders are numbered; customs are dated.

DOURSIN, GERARD, Chemin des Croutoules, F 84210, Pernes les Fontaines, FRANCE
Specialties: Period pieces. **Patterns:** Liner-locks and daggers. **Technical:** Forges mosaic Damascus. **Prices:** $600 to $4000. **Remarks:** First knife sold in 1983. **Mark:** First initial, last name and I stop the lion.

DOUSSOT, LAURENT, 6262 De La Roche, Montreal, Quebec, CANADA H2H 1W9, Phone: 516-270-6992, Fax: 516-722-1641
Specialties: Fancy and embellished folders and fantasy knives. **Patterns:** Fighters and locking folders. **Technical:** Grinds ATS-34 and commercial Damascus. Scale carvings on all knives; most bolsters are carved titanium. **Prices:** $350 to $3000. **Remarks:** Part-time maker; first knife was sold in 1992. **Mark:** Stylized initials inside circle.

DOWELL, T. M., 139 NW St. Helen's Pl., Bend, OR 97701, Phone: 541-382-8924
Specialties: Integral construction in hunting knives. **Patterns:** Limited to featherweights, lightweights, integral hilt and caps. **Technical:** Grinds D-2, BG-42 & Vasco wear. **Prices:** $185 and up. **Remarks:** Full-time maker; first knife sold in 1967. **Mark:** Initials logo.

DOWNIE, JAMES T., 10076 Estate Dr, Port Franks, Ont., CANADA NOM 2LO, Phone: 519-243-1488, Fax: 519-243-1487
Specialties: Serviceable straight knives and folders; period pieces. **Patterns:** Hunters, Bowies, camp knives and miniatures. **Technical:** Grinds D2, 440C and ATS-34, Damasteel, stainless steel Damascus. **Prices:** $100 to $500; some higher. **Remarks:** Full-time maker, first knife sold in 1978. **Mark:** Signature of first and middle initials, last name.

DOWNING, TOM, 2675 12th St, Cuyahoga Falls, OH 44223, Phone: 330-923-7464
Specialties: Working straight knives; period pieces. **Patterns:** Hunters, fighters and tantos. **Technical:** Grinds 440C, ATs-34 and CPM-T-440V. Prefers natural handle materials. **Prices:** $150 to $900; some to $1500. **Remarks:** Part-time maker; first knife sold in 1979. **Mark:** First and middle initials, last name.

DOWNING, LARRY, 12268 Hwy. 181N, Bremen, KY 42325, Phone: 270-525-3523, Fax: 270-525-3372
Specialties: Working straight knives and folders. **Patterns:** From mini-knives to daggers, folding lockers to interframes. **Technical:** Forges and grinds 154CM, ATS-34 and his own Damascus. **Prices:** $150 to $750; some higher. **Remarks:** Part-time maker; first knife sold in 1979. **Mark:** Name in arrowhead.

DOWNS, JAMES F., 35 Sunset Rd, Londonderry, OH 45647, Phone: 740-887-2099
Specialties: Working straight knives of his design or to customer specs. **Patterns:** Folders, Bowies, boot, hunters, utility. **Technical:** Grinds 440C and other steels. Prefers mastodon ivory, all pearls, stabilized wood and elephant ivory. **Prices:** $75 to $1200. **Remarks:** Full-time maker; first knife sold in 1980. Brochures $2.00. **Mark:** Last name.

DOX, JAN, Zwanebloemlaan 27, B 2900 Schoten, BELGIUM, Phone: 32 3 658 77 43
Specialties: Working/using knives to swords, from kitchen to battlefield. **Patterns:** Own designs, some based on traditional ethnic patterns (Scots, Celtic, Scandinavian and Japanese) or to customer specs. **Technical:** Grinds 4034, 1. 2379(D2) and others on request. Most convex edges. **Handles:** Wrapped in modern or traditional patterns, resin impregnated if desired. Natural or synthetic materials, some carved. Sends out for heat-treating by professionals. **Prices:** Start at 25 to 50 Euro (USD) and up. **Remarks:** Spare-time maker, first knife sold 2001. **Mark:** Name.

DOZIER, BOB, PO Box 1941, Springdale, AR 72765, Phone: 888-823-0023/479-756-0023, Fax: 479-756-9139
Specialties: Using knives (fixed blades and folders). **Patterns:** Some fine collector-grade knives. **Technical:** Uses D2. Prefers Micarta handle material. **Prices:** Using knives $145 to $595. **Remarks:** Full-time maker; first knife sold in 1965. **Mark:** State, made, last name in a circle (for fixed blades); Last name with arrow through 'D' and year over name (for folders). **Other:** Also sells a semi-handmade line of fixed blade with mark; state, knives, last name in circle.

DRAPER, MIKE, #10 Creek Dr, Riverton, WY 82501, Phone: 307-856-6807
Specialties: Hand-forged working straight knives. **Patterns:** Hunters, Bowies and camp knives. **Technical:** Forges 52100 and Damascus. **Prices:** Starting at $150. **Remarks:** Part-time maker; first knife sold in 1996. **Mark:** Initials M. J. D. or Name, city and state.

DRAPER, AUDRA, #10 Creek Dr, Riverton, WY 82501, Phone: 307-856-6807
Specialties: One-of-a-kind straight and folders. **Patterns:** Design custom knives, using, Bowies, and mini's. **Technical:** Forge 52100 and Damascus; I heat-treat all my knives. **Prices:** Start at $60 for key chain knives; up to $3000 for art knives. **Remarks:** Full-time maker; journeyman in the ABS. Member of the PKA; first knife sold in 1995. **Mark:** Audra

DREW, GERALD, 2 Glenn Cable, Asheville, NC 28805, Phone: 828-299-7821
Specialties: Blade ATS-34 5-1/2". Handle spalted Maple. 10" OAL. Straight knives. **Patterns:** Hunters, camp knives, some Bowies & tactical. **Technical:** ATS-34 preferred. **Price:** $110 to $200. **Mark:** GL DREW.

DRISCOLL, MARK, 4115 Avoyer Pl., La Mesa, CA 91941, Phone: 619-670-0695
Specialties: High-art, period pieces and working/using knives of his design or to customer specs; some fancy. **Patterns:** Swords, Bowies, Fighters, daggers, hunters and primitive (mountain man styles). **Technical:** Forges 52100, 5160, O1, L6, 1095, and maker his own Damascus and mokume; also does multiple quench heat treating. Uses exotic hardwoods, ivory and horn, offers fancy file work, carving, scrimshaws. **Prices:** $150 to $550; some to $1500. **Remarks:** Part-time maker; first knife sold in 1986. Doing business as Mountain Man Knives. **Mark:** Double "M".

DRISKILL, BERYL, PO Box 187, Braggadocio, MO 63826, Phone: 573-757-6262
Specialties: Fancy working knives. **Patterns:** Hunting knives, fighters, Bowies, boots, daggers and lock-back folders. **Technical:** Grinds ATS-34. **Prices:** Start at $200. **Remarks:** Part-time maker; first knife sold in 1984. **Mark:** Name.

DROST, JASON D., Rt. 2 Box 49, French Creek, WV 26218, Phone: 304-472-7901
Specialties: Working/using straight knives of his design. **Patterns:** Hunters and utility/camp knives. **Technical:** Grinds 154CM and D2. **Prices:** $125 to $5000. **Remarks:** Spare-time maker; first knife sold in 1995. **Mark:** First and middle initials, last name, maker, city and state.

DROST, MICHAEL B., Rt. 2, Box 49, French Creek, WV 26218, Phone: 304-472-7901
Specialties: Working/using straight knives and folders of all designs. **Patterns:** Hunters, locking folders and utility/camp knives. **Technical:** Grinds ATS-34, D2 and CPM-T-440V. Offers dove-tailed bolsters and spacers, filework and scrimshaw. **Prices:** $125 to $400; some to $740. **Remarks:** Full-time maker; first knife sold in 1990. Doing business as Drost Custom Knives. **Mark:** Name, city and state.

DUBLIN, DENNIS, 728 Stanley St, Box 986, Enderby, BC, CANADA V0E 1V0, Phone: 604-838-6753
Specialties: Working straight knives and folders, plain or fancy. **Patterns:** Hunters and Bowies, locking knives, combination knives/axes. **Technical:** Forges and grinds high carbon steels. **Prices:** $100 to $400; some higher. **Remarks:** Full-time maker; first knife sold in 1970. **Mark:** Name.

DUFF, BILL, 14380 Ghost Rider Dr, Reno, NV 89511, Phone: 775-851-9331
Specialties: Straight knives and folders, some fancy. **Patterns:** Hunters, folders & miniatures. **Technical:** Grinds 440-C and commercial Damascus. **Prices:** $200-$1000; some higher. **Remarks:** First knife some in 1976. **Mark:** Bill Duff, city and state.

DUFOUR, ARTHUR J., 8120 De Armoun Rd, Anchorage, AK 99516, Phone: 907-345-1701
Specialties: Working straight knives from standard patterns. **Patterns:** Hunters, Bowies, camp and fishing knives—grinded thin and pointed. **Technical:** Grinds 440C, ATS-34, AEB-L. Tempers 57-58R; hollow-grinds. **Prices:** $135; some to $250. **Remarks:** Part-time maker; first knife sold in 1970. **Mark:** Prospector logo.

DUGAN, BRAD M., 422 A Cribbage Ln, San Marcos, CA 92069, Phone: 760-752-4417

DUGGER, DAVE, 2504 West 51, Westwood, KS 66205, Phone: 913-831-2382
Specialties: Working straight knives; fantasy pieces. **Patterns:** Hunters, boots and daggers in one-of-a-kind styles. **Technical:** Grinds D2, 440C and 154CM. **Prices:** $75 to $350; some to $1200. **Remarks:** Part-time maker; first knife sold in 1979. Not currently accepting orders. Doing business as Dog Knives. **Mark:** DOG.

DUNKERLEY, RICK, Box 111, Lincoln, MT 59639, Phone: 406-362-3097
Specialties: Mosaic Damascus folders and carbon steel utility knives. **Patterns:** One-of-a-kind folders, standard hunters and utility designs. **Technical:** Forges 52100, Damascus and mosaic Damascus. Prefers natural handle materials. **Prices:** $200 and up. **Remarks:** Full-time maker; first knife sold in 1984, ABS Mastersmith. Doing business as Dunkerley Custom Knives. **Mark:** Dunkerley, MS.

DUNN, STEVE, 376 Biggerstaff Rd, Smiths Grove, KY 42171, Phone: 270-563-9830
Specialties: Working and using straight knives of his design; period pieces. **Patterns:** Hunters, skinners, Bowies, fighters, camp knives, folders, swords and battle axes. **Technical:** Forges his Damascus, O1, 5160, L6 and 1095. **Prices:** Moderate to upscale. **Remarks:** Full-time maker; first knife sold in 1990. **Mark:** Last name and MS.

DUNN, CHARLES K., 17740 GA Hwy. 116, Shiloh, GA 31826, Phone: 706-846-2666
Specialties: Fancy and working straight knives and folders of his design and to customer specs. **Patterns:** Bowies, hunters and locking folders.

Technical: Grinds 440C and ATS-34. Engraves; filework offered. **Prices:** $75 to $300. **Remarks:** Part-time maker; first knife sold in 1988. **Mark:** First initial, last name, city, state.

DURAN, JERRY T., PO Box 80692, Albuquerque, NM 87198-0692, Phone: 505-873-4676
Specialties: Tactical folders, Bowies, fighters, liner-locks and hunters. **Patterns:** Folders, Bowies, hunters & tactical knives. **Technical:** Forges own Damascus and forges carbon steel. **Prices:** Moderate to upscale. **Remarks:** Full-time maker; first knife sold in 1978. **Mark:** Initials in elk rack logo.

DURHAM, KENNETH, Buzzard Roost Forge, 10495 White Pike, Cherokee, AL 35616, Phone: 256-359-4287
Specialties: Bowies, dirks, hunters. **Patterns:** Traditional patterns. **Technical:** Forges 1095, 5160, 52100 and makes own Damascus. **Prices:** $85 to $1250. **Remarks:** Began making knives about 1995. Received journeyman stamp 1999. **Mark:** Bulls head with Ken Durham above and Cherokee AL below.

DURIO, FRED, 144 Gulino St, Opelousas, LA 70570, Phone: 337-948-4831
Specialties: Folders. **Patterns:** Liner-locks; plain & fancy. **Technical:** Makes own Damascus. **Prices:** Moderate to upscale. **Remarks:** Full-time maker. **Mark:** Last name-Durio.

DUVALL, FRED, 10715 Hwy. 190, Benton, AR 72015, Phone: 501-778-9360
Specialties: Working straight knives and folders. **Patterns:** Locking folders, slip joints, hunters, fighters and Bowies. **Technical:** Grinds D2 and CPM440V; forges 5160. **Prices:** $100 to $400; some to $800. **Remarks:** Part-time maker; first knife sold in 1973. **Mark:** Last name.

DUVALL, LARRY E., Rt. 3, Gallatin, MO 64640, Phone: 816-663-2742
Specialties: Fancy working straight knives and folders. **Patterns:** Hunters to swords, minis to Bowies; locking folders. **Technical:** Grinds D2, 440C and 154CM. **Prices:** $150 to $350; some to $2000. **Remarks:** Part-time maker; first knife sold in 1980. **Mark:** Name and address in logo.

DYER, DAVID, 4531 Hunters Glen, Granbury, TX 76048, Phone: 817-573-1198
Specialties: Working skinners & early period knives. **Patterns:** Customer designs, my own patterns. **Technical:** Coal forged blades; 5160 & 52100 steels. **Prices:** $150 for neck-knives & small (3" to 3-1/2"). To $600 for large blades & specialty blades. **Mark:** Last name DYER electro etched. **Other:** Grinds D-2, 1095, L-6.

DYESS, EDDIE, 1005 Hamilton, Roswell, NM 88201, Phone: 505-623-5599
Specialties: Working and using straight knives in standard patterns. **Patterns:** Hunters and fighters. **Technical:** Grinds 440C, 154CM and D2 on request. **Prices:** $85 to $135; some to $250. **Remarks:** Spare-time maker; first knife sold in 1980. **Mark:** Last name.

DYRNOE, PER, Sydskraenten 10, Tulstrup, DK 3400 Hilleroed, DENMARK, Phone: +45 42287041
Specialties: Hand-crafted knives with zirconia ceramic blades. **Patterns:** Hunters, skinners, Norwegian-style tolle knives, most in animal-like ergonomic shapes. **Technical:** Handles of exotic hardwood, horn, fossil ivory, etc. Norwegian-style sheaths. **Prices:** Start at $500. **Remarks:** Part-time maker in cooperation with Hans J. Henriksen; first knife sold in 1993. **Mark:** Initial logo.

e

EAKER, ALLEN L., 416 Clinton Ave, Dept KI, Paris, IL 61944, Phone: 217-466-5160
Specialties: Traditional straight knives and folders of his design. **Patterns:** Hunters, locking folders and slip-joint folders. **Technical:** Grinds 440C; inlays. **Prices:** $125 to $325; some to $500. **Remarks:** Spare-time maker; first knife sold in 1994. **Mark:** Initials in tankard logo stamped on tang, serial number on back side.

EALY, DELBERT, PO Box 121, Indian River, MI 49749, Phone: 231-238-4705

EASLER JR., RUSSELL O., PO Box 301, Woodruff, SC 29388, Phone: 864-476-7830
Specialties: Working straight knives and folders. **Patterns:** Hunters, tantos and boots; locking folders and interframes. **Technical:** Grinds 440C, 154CM and ATS-34. **Prices:** $100 to $350; some to $800. **Remarks:** Part-time maker; first knife sold in 1973. **Mark:** Name or name with bear logo.

EATON, AL, PO Box 43, Clayton, CA 94517, Phone: 925-672-5351
Specialties: One-of-a-kind high-art knives and fantasy knives of his design, full size and miniature. **Patterns:** Hunters, fighters, daggers. **Tech-**

custom knifemakers

nical: Grinds 440C, 154CM and ATS-34; ivory and metal carving. **Prices:** $125 to $3000; some to $5000. **Remarks:** Full-time maker; first knife sold in 1977. **Mark:** Full name, city and state.

EATON, RICK, 9944 McCranie St, Shepherd, MT 59079 3126
Specialties: Interframe folders and one-hand-opening side locks. **Patterns:** Bowies, daggers, fighters and folders. **Technical:** Grinds 154CM, ATS-34, 440C and other maker's Damascus. Offers high-quality hand engraving, Bulino and gold inlay. **Prices:** Upscale. **Remarks:** Full-time maker; first knife sold in 1982. **Mark:** Full name or full name and address.

EBISU, HIDESAKU, 3-39-7 Koi Osako Nishi Ku, Hiroshima City, JAPAN 733 0816

ECHOLS, ROGER, 46 Channing Rd, Nashville, AR 71852-8588, Phone: 870-451-9089
Specialties: Liner-locks, auto-scale release, lock-backs. **Patterns:** My own or yours. **Technical:** Autos. **Prices:** $500 to $1700. **Remarks:** I like to use pearl, ivory & Damascus the most. **Mark:** My name. **Other:** Made first knife in 1984. **Remarks:** Part-time maker; tool & die maker by trade.

EDDY, HUGH E., 211 E Oak St, Caldwell, ID 83605, Phone: 208-459-0536

EDEN, THOMAS, PO Box 57, Cranbury, NJ 08512, Phone: 609-371-0774
Patterns: Fixed blade, working patterns, hand forged. **Technical:** Damascus. **Mark:** Eden (script). **Remarks:** ABS Smith.

EDGE, TOMMY, PO Box 156, Cash, AR 72421, Phone: 501-477-5210
Specialties: Fancy/embellished working knives of his design. **Patterns:** Bowies, hunters and utility/camping knives. **Technical:** Grinds 440C, ATS-34 and D2. Makes own cable Damascus; offers filework. **Prices:** $70 to $250; some to $1500. **Remarks:** Part-time maker; first knife sold in 1993. **Mark:** Stamped first initial, last name and stenciled name, city and state in oval shape.

EDWARDS, LYNN, 778 CR B91, W. Columbia, TX 77486, Phone: 979-345-4080, Fax: 979-345-3472
Specialties: Traditional working and using straight knives of his design and to customer specs. **Patterns:** Bowies, hunters and utility/camp knives. **Technical:** Forges 5168 and O1; forges and grinds D2. Triple-hardens on request; offers silver wire inlay, stone inlays and spacers, filework. **Prices:** $100 to $395; some to $800. **Remarks:** Part-time maker; first knife sold in 1988. Doing business as E&E Emporium. **Mark:** Last name in script.

EDWARDS, MITCH, 303 New Salem Rd, Glasgow, KY 42141, Phone: 270-651-9257
Specialties: Period pieces. **Patterns:** Neck knives, camp, rifleman and Bowie knives. **Technical:** All hand forged, forges own Damascus 01, 1084, 1095, L-6, 15N20. **Prices:** $200 to $1000. **Remarks:** Journeyman smith. **Mark:** Broken heart.

EDWARDS, FAIN E., PO Box 280, Topton, NC 28781, Phone: 828-321-3127

EHRENBERGER, DANIEL ROBERT, 6192 Hiway 168, Shelbyville, MO 63469, Phone: 573-633-2010
Specialties: Affordable working/using straight knives of his design and to custom specs. Patterns: 10" western bowie, fighters, hunting and skinning knives. **Technical:** Forges 1085, 1095, his own Damascus and cable Damascus. **Prices:** $80 to $500. **Remarks:** Full-time maker, first knife sold 1994. **Mark:** Ehrenberger JS.

EKLUND, MAIHKEL, Föne 1111, S-820 41 Farila, SWEDEN
Specialties: Collector-grade working straight knives. **Patterns:** Hunters, Bowies and fighters. **Technical:** Grinds ATS-34, Uddeholm and Dama steel. Engraves and scrimshaws. **Prices:** $150 to $700. **Remarks:** Full-time maker; first knife sold in 1983. **Mark:** Initials or name.

ELDER JR., PERRY B., 1321 Garrettsburg Rd, Clarksville, TN 37042-2516, Phone: 931-647-9416
Specialties: Hunters, combat Bowies, bird and trout. **Technical:** High-carbon steel and Damascus blades. **Prices:** $250 and up depending on blade desired. **Mark:** ELDER.

ELDRIDGE, ALLAN, 7731 Four Winds Dr, Ft Worth, TX 76133, Phone: 817-370-7778
Specialties: Fancy classic straight knives in standard patterns. **Patterns:** Hunters, Bowies, fighters, folders and miniatures. **Technical:** Grinds O1 and Damascus. Engraves silver-wire inlays, pearl inlays, scrimshaws and offers filework. **Prices:** $50 to $500; some to $1200. **Remarks:** Spare-time maker; first knife sold in 1965. **Mark:** Initials.

ELISHEWITZ, ALLEN, 3960 Lariat Ridge, New Braunfels, TX 78132, Phone: 830-227-5325, Fax: 830-899-4595
Specialties: Collectible high-tech working straight knives and folders of his design. **Patterns:** Working, utility and tactical knives. **Technical:** Grinds 154CM and stainless steel Damascus. All designs drafted and field-tested.

Prices: $400 to $600. **Remarks:** Full-time maker; first knife sold in 1989. **Mark:** Last name with a Japanese crane.

ELKINS, R. VAN, PO Box 156, Bonita, LA 71223, Phone: 318-823-2124, Fax: 318-283-6802
Specialties: High-art Bowies, fighters, folders and period daggers; all one-of-a-kind pieces. **Patterns:** Welcomes customer designs. **Technical:** Forges his own Damascus in several patterns, O1 and 5160. **Prices:** $250 to $2800. **Remarks:** First knife sold in 1984. **Mark:** Last name.

ELLEFSON, JOEL, PO Box 1016, 310 S. 1st St, Manhattan, MT 59741, Phone: 406-284-3111
Specialties: Working straight knives, fancy daggers and one-of-a-kinds. **Patterns:** Hunters, daggers and some folders. **Technical:** Grinds A2, 440C and ATS-34. Makes own mokume in bronze, brass, silver and shibuishi; makes brass/steel blades. **Prices:** $75 to $500; some to $2000. **Remarks:** Part-time maker; first knife sold in 1978. **Mark:** Stylized last initial.

ELLERBE, W. B., 3871 Osceola Rd, Geneva, FL 32732, Phone: 407-349-5818
Specialties: Period and primitive knives and sheaths. **Patterns:** Bowies to patch knives, some tomahawks. **Technical:** Grinds Sheffield O1 and files. **Prices:** Start at $35. **Remarks:** Full-time maker; first knife sold in 1971. Doing business as Cypress Bend Custom Knives. **Mark:** Last name or initials.

ELLIOTT, MARCUS, Pen Dinas, Wyddfydd Rd, Great Orme, Llandudno Gwynedd, GREAT BRITAIN LL30 2QL, Phone: 01492-872747
Specialties: Fancy working knives. **Patterns:** Boots and small hunters. **Technical:** Grinds O1, 440C and ATS-34. **Prices:** $160 to $250. **Remarks:** Spare-time maker; first knife sold in 1981. Makes only a few knives each year. **Mark:** First name, middle initial, last name, knife maker, city, state.

ELLIOTT, JERRY, 4507 Kanawha Ave, Charleston, WV 25304, Phone: 304-925-5045
Specialties: Classic and traditional straight knives and folders of his design and to customer specs. **Patterns:** Hunters, locking folders and Bowies. **Technical:** Grinds ATS-34, 154CM, O1, D2 and T-440-V. All guards silver-soldered; bolsters are pinned on straight knives, spot-welded on folders. **Prices:** $80 to $265; some to $1000. **Remarks:** Full-time maker; first knife sold in 1972. **Mark:** First and middle initials, last name, knife maker, city, state.

ELLIS, DAVE/ABS MASTERSMITH, 380 South Melrose Dr #407, Vista, CA 92083, Phone: 760-643-4032 Eves: (760-945-7177
Specialties: Bowies, utility & combat knives. **Patterns:** Using knives to art quality pieces. **Technical:** Forges 5160, L-6, 52100, cable and my own Damascus steels. **Prices:** $300 to $4000. **Remarks:** Part-time maker. California's first ABS Master Smith. **Mark:** Dagger-Rose with name & M. S. mark.

ELLIS, WILLIAM DEAN, 8875 N. Barton, Fresno, CA 93720, Phone: 209-299-0303
Specialties: Classic and fancy knives of his design. **Patterns:** Boots, fighters and utility knives. **Technical:** Grinds ATS-34, D2 and Damascus. Offers tapered tangs and six patterns of filework; tooled multi-colored sheaths. **Prices:** $180 to $350; some to $1300. **Remarks:** Part-time maker; first knife sold in 1991. Doing business as Billy's Blades. **Mark:** "B" in a five-point star next to "Billy," city and state within a rounded-corner rectangle.

ELLIS, WILLY B., Willy B Custom Sticks & Picks, 10 Cutler Rd, Litchfield, NH 03052, Phone: 603-880-9722, Fax: Same
Specialties: One-of-a-kind high art and fantasy knives of my design. Occasional customs full size & miniatures. **Patterns:** Bowies, fighters, hunters and others. **Technical:** Grinds 440C, ATS-34, 1095, carbon Damascus, ivory bone, stone and metal carving. **Prices:** $175-$15,000. **Remarks:** Full-time maker, first knife made in 1973. Probationary member Knifemakers Guild. **Mark:** Willy B. or WB'S C etched or carved. **Other:** Jewel setting inlays.

ELROD, ROGER R., 58 Dale Ave, Enterprise, AL 36330, Phone: 334-347-1863

EMBRETSEN, KAJ, Faluvagen 67, S-82821 Edsbyn, SWEDEN, Phone: 46-271-21057, Fax: 46-271-22961
Specialties: High quality folders. **Patterns:** Scandinavian-style knives. **Technical:** Forges Damascus. Uses only his blades; natural materials. **Prices:** Upscale. **Remarks:** Full-time maker. **Mark:** Name.

EMERSON, ERNEST R., PO Box 4180, Torrance, CA 90510-4180
Specialties: High-tech folders and combat fighters. **Patterns:** Fighters, liner-lock combat folders and SPECWAR combat knives. **Technical:** Grinds 154CM and Damascus. Makes folders with titanium fittings, liners and locks. Chisel grind specialist. **Prices:** $550 to $850; some to $10,000.

Remarks: Full-time maker; first knife sold in 1983. **Mark:** Last name and Specwar knives.

ENCE, JIM, 145 S 200 East, Richfield, UT 84701, Phone: 435-896-6206
Specialties: High-art period pieces (spec in California knives) art knives. **Patterns:** Art, boot knives, fighters, Bowies and occasional folders. **Technical:** Grinds 440C for polish & beauty boys'; makes own Damascus. **Prices:** Upscale. **Remarks:** Full-time maker; first knife sold in 1977. Does own engraving, gold work & stone work. **Mark:** Ence, usually engraved. **Other:** Guild member since 1977. Founding member of the AKI.

ENGLAND, VIRGIL, 1340 Birchwood St, Anchorage, AK 99508, Phone: 907-274-9494
Specialties: Edged weapons and equipage, one-of-a-kind only. **Patterns:** Axes, swords, lances and body armor. **Technical:** Forges and grinds as pieces dictate. Offers stainless and Damascus. **Prices:** Upscale. **Remarks:** A veteran knife maker. No commissions. **Mark:** Stylized initials.

ENGLE, WILLIAM, 16608 Oak Ridge Rd, Boonville, MO 65233, Phone: 816-882-6277
Specialties: Traditional working and using straight knives of his design. **Patterns:** Hunters, Bowies and fighters. **Technical:** Grinds 440C, ATS-34 and 154CM. **Prices:** $250 to $500; some higher. **Remarks:** Part-time maker; first knife sold in 1982. All knives come with certificate of authenticity. **Mark:** Last name in block lettering.

ENGLEBRETSON, GEORGE, 1209 NW 49th St, Oklahoma City, OK 73118, Phone: 405-840-4784
Specialties: Working straight knives. **Patterns:** Hunters and Bowies. **Technical:** Grinds A2, D2, 440C and ATS-34. **Prices:** Start at $150. **Remarks:** Full-time maker; first knife sold in 1967. **Mark:** "By George," name and city.

ENGLISH, JIM, 14586 Olive Vista Dr, Jamul, CA 91935, Phone: 619-669-0833
Specialties: Traditional working straight knives to customer specs. **Patterns:** Hunters, Bowies, fighters, tantos, daggers, boot and utility/camp knives. **Technical:** Grinds 440C, ATS-34, commercial Damascus and customer choice. **Prices:** $130 to $350. **Remarks:** Part-time maker; first knife sold in 1985. In addition to custom line, also does business as Mountain Home Knives. **Mark:** Double "A," Double "J" logo.

ENNIS, RAY, 1220S 775E, Ogden, UT 84404, Phone: 800-410-7603, Fax: 501-621-2683

ENOS III, THOMAS M., 12302 State Rd 535, Orlando, FL 32836, Phone: 407-239-6205
Specialties: Heavy-duty working straight knives; unusual designs. **Patterns:** Swords, machetes, daggers, skinners, filleting, period pieces. **Technical:** Grinds 440C, D2, 154CM. **Prices:** $75 to $1500. **Remarks:** Full-time maker; first knife sold in 1972. **Mark:** Name in knife logo and year, type of steel and serial number. **Other:** No longer accepting custom requests. Will be making my own designs. Send SASE for listing of items for sale.

ENTIN, ROBERT, 127 Pembroke Street 1, Boston, MA 02118

EPTING, RICHARD, 4021 Cody Dr, College Station, TX 77845, Phone: 979-690-6496
Specialties: Folders and working straight knives. **Patterns:** Hunters, Bowies, and locking folders. **Technical:** Forges high-carbon steel and his own Damascus. **Prices:** $200 to $800; some to $1800. **Remarks:** Part-time maker, first knife sold 1996. **Mark:** Name in arch logo.

ERICKSON, WALTER E., 22280 Shelton Tr, Atlanta, MI 49709, Phone: 989-785-5262
Specialties: Unusual survival knives and high-tech working knives. **Patterns:** Butterflies, hunters, tantos. **Technical:** Grinds ATS-34 or customer choice. **Prices:** $150 to $500; some to $1500. **Remarks:** Full-time maker; first knife sold in 1981. **Mark:** Last name in depressed area on blade.

ERICKSON, L. M., PO Box 132, Liberty, UT 84310, Phone: 801-745-2026
Specialties: Straight knives; period pieces. **Patterns:** Bowies, fighters, boots and hunters. **Technical:** Grinds 440C, 154CM and commercial Damascus. **Prices:** $200 to $900; some to $5000. **Remarks:** Part-time maker; first knife sold in 1981. **Mark:** Name, city, state.

ERIKSEN, JAMES THORLIEF, dba Viking Knives, 3830 Dividend Dr, Garland, TX 75042, Phone: 972-494-3667, Fax: 972-235-4932
Specialties: Heavy-duty working and using straight knives and folders utilizing traditional, Viking original and customer specification patterns. Some high-tech and fancy/embellished knives available. **Patterns:** Bowies, hunters, skinners, boot and belt knives, utility/camp knives, fighters, daggers, locking folders, slip-joint folders and kitchen knives. **Technical:** Hollow-grinds 440C, D2, ASP-23, ATS-34, 154CM, Vascowear. **Prices:** $150 to $300; some to $600. **Remarks:** Full-time maker; first knife sold in 1985. Doing business as Viking Knives. For a color catalog showing 50 different models, mail $5 to above address. **Mark:** VIKING or VIKING USA for export.

ESSEGIAN, RICHARD, 7387 E. Tulare St, Fresno, CA 93727, Phone: 309-255-5950
Specialties: Fancy working knives of his design; art knives. **Patterns:** Bowies and some small hunters. **Technical:** Grinds A2, D2, 440C and 154CM. Engraves and inlays. **Prices:** Start at $600. **Remarks:** Part-time maker; first knife sold in 1986. **Mark:** Last name, city and state.

ESSMAN, JUSTUS P., 201 Rialto Way NE, St Petersburg, FL 33704, Phone: 727-894-5327

ETZLER, JOHN, 11200 N. Island, Grafton, OH 44044, Phone: 440-748-2460
Specialties: High-art and fantasy straight knives and folders of his design and to customer specs. **Patterns:** Folders, daggers, fighters, utility knives. **Technical:** Forges and grinds nickel Damascus and tool steel; grinds stainless steels. Prefers exotic, natural materials. **Prices:** $250 to $1200; some to $6500. **Remarks:** Full-time maker; first knife sold in 1992. **Mark:** Name or initials.

EVANS, BRUCE A., 409 CR 1371, Booneville, MS 38829, Phone: 662-720-0193
Specialties: Forges blades. **Patterns:** Hunters, Bowies, or will work with customer. **Technical:** 5160, cable Damascus, pattern welded Damascus. **Prices:** $100 and up. **Mark:** Bruce A. Evans.

EVANS, RONALD B., 209 Hoffer St, Middleton, PA 17057-2723, Phone: 717-944-5464

EVANS, CARLTON, PO Box 815, Aledo, TX 76008, Phone: 817-441-1363
Specialties: Fancy and working liner-locks, full and narrow tang knives, slip-joint folders and locking folders. **Patterns:** Hunters, fighters, tactical and working straight knives. **Technical:** Use the stock removal method. Fancy file work on some knives. The materials I use are of the highest quality like O1, D2, ATS-34, 154CM and Damascus steel. Paul Bos heat treats my blades. **Prices:** Start at $200. **Remarks:** I made my first knife in 1967 (Slip-joint folder). Sold my first knife in 1970. I am a part-time knifemaker.

EVANS, VINCENT K. & GRACE, 6301 Apache Trail, Show Low, AZ 85901, Phone: 928-537-9123
Specialties: Working straight knives; period pieces; swords. **Patterns:** Scottish and central Asian patterns; Bowies, hunters. **Technical:** Forges 5160 and his own Damascus. **Prices:** $100 to $1000; some to $5000. **Remarks:** Full-time maker; first knife sold in 1983. **Mark:** Last initial with fish logo.

EWING, WYMAN, 55 Robertson Rd, Pueblo, CO 81001, Phone: 719-544-9275

EWING, JOHN H., 3276 Dutch Valley Rd, Clinton, TN 37716, Phone: 615-457-5757
Specialties: Working straight knives, hunters, camp knives. **Patterns:** Hunters. **Technical:** Grinds 440, Forges 5160 52100; prefers forging. **Prices:** $150 to $2000. **Remarks:** Part-time maker; first knife sold in 1985. **Mark:** First initial, last name, some embellishing done on knives.

EXTREME RATIO S. A. S, Mauro Chiostri / Maurizio Castrati, Viale Montegrappa 298, 59100 Prato, ITALY, Phone: 0039 0574 58 46 39, Fax: 0039 0574 58 13 12
Specialties: Tactical/military knives and sheaths, blades and sheaths to customer's specs. **Patterns** Tactical fixed blade knives and folders. **Technical:** Grinds stainless cobalt steel. Coatings: Glass-beated, black polymorphic, striped. Handles in CFP, with scales made of high seizure pads. Tactical sheaths with double retention system and multiple anchorage points. **Prices:** $140 to $350. **Remarks:** Full-time maker; first knife sold in 1998. **Mark:** Name of company, steel and knife.

f

FAGAN, JAMES A., 109 S 17 Ave, Lake Worth, FL 33460, Phone: 561-585-9349

FANT JR., GEORGE, 1983 CR 3214, Atlanta, TX 75551-6515, Phone: 903-846-2938

FARID R., MEHR, 8 Sidney Close, Tunbridge Wells, Kent, ENGLAND TN2 5QQ, Phone: 011-44-1892 520345
Specialties: High-tech fixed blades and titanium folders. **Patterns:** Chisel ground liner-lock and integral mechanism folders. **Technical:** Grinds 440C, CPM-T-440V, CPM-420V, CPM-15V, CPMS125V, and T-1 high speed steel and Vasco-max alloy and tool steel. **Prices:** $550 to $15,000. **Remarks:** Full-time maker; first knife sold in 1991. **Mark:** First name and country.

custom knifemakers

FARR, DAN, 285 Glen Ellyn Way, Rochester, NY 14618, Phone: 585-721-1388
Specialties: Hunting, camping, fighting and utility. **Patterns:** Fixed blades. **Technical:** Forged or stock removal. **Prices:** $150-$750.

FASSIO, MELVIN G., 420 Tyler Way, Lolo, MT 59847, Phone: 406-273-9143
Specialties: Working folders to customer specs. **Patterns:** Locking folders, hunters and traditional-style knives. **Technical:** Grinds 440C. **Prices:** $125 to $350. **Remarks:** Part-time maker; first knife sold in 1975. **Mark:** Name and city, dove logo.

FAUCHEAUX, HOWARD J., PO Box 206, Loreauville, LA 70552, Phone: 318-229-6467
Specialties: Working straight knives and folders; period pieces. Also a hatchet with capping knife in the handle. **Patterns:** Traditional locking folders, hunters, fighters and Bowies. **Technical:** Forges W2, 1095 and his own Damascus; stock removal D2. **Prices:** Start at $200. **Remarks:** Full-time maker; first knife sold in 1969. **Mark:** Last name.

FAUST, DICK, 624 Kings Hwy N, Rochester, NY 14617, Phone: 585-544-1948
Specialties: High-performance working straight knives. **Patterns:** Hunters and utility/camp knives. **Technical:** Hollow grinds ATS-34 and 154CM full tang. Exotic woods, stag and Micarta handles. Provides a custom leather sheath with each knife. **Prices:** From $100 to $500; some higher. **Remarks:** Full-time maker. **Mark:** Signature.

FAUST, JOACHIM, Kirchgasse 10, 95497 Goldkronach, GERMANY

FECAS, STEPHEN J., 1312 Shadow Lane, Anderson, SC 29625, Phone: 864-287-4834, Fax: 864-287-4834
Specialties: Front release lock-backs, liner-locks. Folders only. **Patterns:** Gents folders. **Technical:** Grinds ATS-34, Damascus-Ivories and pearl handles. **Prices:** $650 to $1200. **Remarks:** Full-time maker since 1980. First knife sold in 1977. **Mark:** Last name signature. **Other:** All knives hand finished to 1500 grit.

FEIGIN, B, Liir Corp, 3037 Holly Mill Run, Marietta, GA 30062, Phone: 770-579-1631, Fax: 770-579-1199

FELIX, ALEXANDER, PO Box 4036, Torrance, CA 90510, Phone: 310-891-0825
Specialties: Straight working knives, fancy ethnic designs. **Patterns:** Hunters, Bowies, daggers, period pieces. **Technical:** Forges carbon steel and Damascus; forged stainless and titanium jewelry, gold and silver casting. **Prices:** $110 & up. **Remarks:** Jeweler, part-time maker. **Mark:** Signature.

FELLOWS, MIKE, PO Box 166, Velddrie 7365, SOUTH AFRICA, Phone: 27 82 960 3868
Specialties: Miniatures, art knives, subhilt fighters and folders. **Patterns:** Original designs and client's designs. **Technical:** I use my own Damascus (L6 and nickel). **Other:** All my knives carry strong, reliable thru-tang handles screwed & bonded together. I use only indigenous materials for handles, i. e., various hard woods, selected horns, ivory, warthog tusk, hippo tooth, etc. Love to carve animal heads; my favorite-Roses. **Mark:** "Shin" letter from Hebrew alphabet in front of Hebrew word "Karat". **Prices:** R800 - R5500 ($100 to $700 approximately).

FERDINAND, DON, PO Box 1564, Shady Cove, OR 97539-1564, Phone: 503-560-3355
Specialties: One-of-a-kind working knives and period pieces; all tool steel Damascus. **Patterns:** Bowies, push knives and fishing knives. **Technical:** Forges high-carbon alloy steels L6, D2; makes his own Damascus. Exotic handle materials offered. **Prices:** $100 to $500. **Remarks:** Full-time maker since 1980. Does business as Wyvern. **Mark:** Initials connected.

FERGUSON, LEE, 1993 Madison 7580, Hindsville, AR 72738, Phone: 479-443-0084
Specialties: Straight working knives and folders, some fancy. **Patterns:** Hunters, daggers, swords, locking folders and slip-joints. **Technical:** Grinds D2, 440C and ATS-34; heat-treats. **Prices:** $50 to $600; some to $4000. **Remarks:** Part-time maker; first knife sold in 1977. **Mark:** Last name.

FERGUSON, JIM, PO Box 764, San Angelo, TX 76902, Phone: 915-651-6656
Specialties: Straight working knives and folders. **Patterns:** Working belt knives, hunters, Bowies and some folders. **Technical:** Grinds ATS-34, D2 and Vascowear. Flat-grinds hunting knives. **Prices:** $200 to $600; some to $1000. **Remarks:** Full-time maker; first knife sold in 1987. **Mark:** First and middle initials, last name.

FERGUSON, JIM, 32131 Via Bande, Temecula, CA 92592, Phone: 909-719-1552
Specialties: Nickel Damascus - Bowies - Daggers - Push Blades. **Patterns:** All styles. **Technical:** Forges Damascus & sells in US and Canada.

Prices: $120 to $5000. **Remarks:** 1200 Sq. Ft. commercial shop - 75 ton press. **Mark:** Jim Ferguson over push blade. Also make swords, battle axes & utilities.

FERRARA, THOMAS, 122 Madison Dr, Naples, FL 33942, Phone: 813-597-3363, Fax: 813-597-3363
Specialties: High-art, traditional and working straight knives and folders of all designs. **Patterns:** Boots, Bowies, daggers, fighters and hunters. **Technical:** Grinds 440C, D2 and ATS-34; heat-treats. **Prices:** $100 to $700; some to $1300. **Remarks:** Part-time maker; first knife sold in 1983. **Mark:** Last name.

FERRIER, GREGORY K., 3119 Simpson Dr, Rapid City, SD 57702, Phone: 605-342-9280

FERRIS, BILL, 186 Thornton Dr, Palm Beach Garden, FL 33418

FERRY, TOM, 16005 SE 322nd St, Auburn, WA 98092, Phone: 253-939-4468
Specialties: Damascus, fixed blades and folders. **Patterns:** Folders Damascus, and fixed blades. **Technical:** Specialize in Damascus and timascus TM (Titanium Damascus). **Prices:** $400 to $2000. **Remarks:** Name Tom Ferry. **DBA:** Soos Creek Ironworks. **Mark:** Combined T & F in a circle and/or last name on folders. **Other:** Co-developer of Timascus TM (Titanium Damascus).

FIKES, JIMMY L., PO Box 3457, Jasper, AL 35502, Phone: 205-387-9302, Fax: 205-221-1980
Specialties: High-art working knives; artifact knives; using knives with cord-wrapped handles; swords and combat weapons. **Patterns:** Axes to buckskinners, camp knives to miniatures, tantos to tomahawks; spring less folders. **Technical:** Forges W2, O1 and his own Damascus. **Prices:** $135 to $3000; exceptional knives to $7000. **Remarks:** Full-time maker. **Mark:** Stylized initials.

FILIPPOU, IOANNIS-MINAS, 7 Krinis Str Nea Smyrni, Athens 17122, GREECE, Phone: 1 935-2093

FINCH, RICKY D., 2446 HWY 191, West Liberty, KY 41472, Phone: 606-743-7151
Specialties: Traditional working/using straight knives of his design or to customer spec. **Patterns:** Hunters, skinners & utility/camp knives. **Technical:** Grinds 440C & ATS-34, hand rubbed stain finish, use Micarta, stag, stabilized wood - natural & exotic. **Prices:** $55 to $175; some $250. **Remarks:** Part-time maker, first knife made 1994. Doing business as Finch Knives. **Mark:** Last name inside outline of state of Kentucky.

FIORINI, BILL, 390 North St, PO Box 237, Dakota, MN 55925-0237, Phone: 507-643-7946
Specialties: Fancy working knives and lock-backs. **Patterns:** Hunters, boots, Japanese-style knives and kitchen/utility knives. **Technical:** Forges own Damascus. **Prices:** Full range. **Remarks:** Full-time metal smith researching pattern materials. **Mark:** Orchid crest with name KOKA in Japanese.

FISHER, THEO (TED), 8115 Modoc Lane, Montague, CA 96064, Phone: 916-459-3804
Specialties: Moderately priced working knives in carbon steel. **Patterns:** Hunters, fighters, kitchen and buckskinner knives, Damascus miniatures. **Technical:** Grinds ATS-34, L6 and 440C. **Prices:** $65 to $165; exceptional knives to $300. **Remarks:** First knife sold in 1981. **Mark:** Name in banner logo.

FISHER, JAY, 1504 Edwards, PO Box 267, Clouis, NM 88101, Phone: 505-763-2268, Fax: 505-463-2346
Specialties: High-art, ancient and exact working and using straight knives of his design and client's designs. Military working and commemoratives. **Patterns:** Hunters, daggers, folding knives, museum pieces and high-art sculptures. **Technical:** Grinds 440C, ATS-34, 01and D2. Prolific maker of stone-handled knives and swords. **Prices:** $250 to $50,000; some higher. **Remarks:** Full-time maker; first knife sold in 1980. **Mark:** Very fine-JaFisher—Quality Custom Knives. **Other:** High resolution etching, computer and manual engraving.

FISK, JERRY, 145 N Park Ave, Lockesburg, AR 71846, Phone: 870-289-3240
Specialties: Edged weapons, collectible and functional. **Patterns:** Bowies, daggers, swords, hunters, camp knives and others. **Technical:** Forges carbon steels and his own pattern welded steels. **Prices:** $250 to $15,000. **Remarks:** National living treasure. **Mark:** Name, MS.

FISTER, JIM, 5067 Fisherville Rd, Simpsonville, KY 40067, Phone: 502-834-7841
Specialties: One-of-a-kind collectibles and period pieces. **Patterns:** Bowies, camp knives, hunters, buckskinners, and daggers. **Technical:** Forges, 1085, 5160, 52100, his own Damascus, pattern and turkish. **Prices:** $150 to $2500. **Remarks:** Part-time maker; first knife sold in 1982. **Mark:** Name & MS.

FITCH, JOHN S., 45 Halbrook Rd, Clinton, AR 72031-8910, Phone: 501-893-2020

FITZGERALD, DENNIS M., 4219 Alverado Dr, Fort Wayne, IN 46816-2847, Phone: 219-447-1081 **Specialties:** One-of-a-kind collectibles and period pieces. **Patterns:** Skinners, fighters, camp and utility knives; period pieces. **Technical:** Forges 1085, 1095, L6, 5160, 52100, his own pattern and Turkish Damascus. **Prices:** $100 to $500. **Remarks:** Part-time maker; first knife sold in 1985. Doing business as The Ringing Circle. **Mark:** Name and circle logo.

FLETCHER, MICHAEL J., 7415 E 77th St, Tulsa, OK 74133-3536, Phone: 918-252-7816

FLINT, ROBERT, 2902 Aspen Dr, Anchorage, AK 99517, Phone: 907-243-6706 **Specialties:** Working straight knives and folders. **Patterns:** Utility, hunters, fighters and gents. **Technical:** Grinds ATS-34, BG-42, D2 and Damascus. **Prices:** $150 and up. **Remarks:** Part-time maker, first knife sold in 1998. **Mark:** Last name; stylized initials.

FLORES, HENRY, 1000 Kiely Blvd #115, Santa Clara, CA 95051-4819, Phone: 408-246-0491

FLOURNOY, JOE, 5750 Lisbon Rd, El Dorado, AR 71730, Phone: 870-863-7208 **Specialties:** Working straight knives and folders. **Patterns:** Hunters, Bowies, camp knives, folders and daggers. **Technical:** Forges only high-carbon steel, steel cable and his own Damascus. **Prices:** $350 Plus. **Remarks:** First knife sold in 1977. **Mark:** Last name and MS in script.

FOGARIZZU, BOITEDDU, via Crispi, 6, 07016 Pattada, ITALY **Specialties:** Traditional Italian straight knives and folders. **Patterns:** Collectible folders. **Technical:** forges and grinds 12C27, ATS-34 and his Damascus. **Prices:** $200 to $3000. **Remarks:** Full-time maker; first knife sold in 1958. **Mark:** Full name and registered logo.

FOGG, DON, 40 Alma Road, Jasper, AL 35501-8813, Phone: 205-483-0822 **Specialties:** Swords, daggers, Bowies and hunting knives. **Patterns:** Collectible folders. **Technical:** Hand-forged high-carbon and Damascus steel. **Prices:** $200 to $5000. **Remarks:** Full-time maker; first knife sold in 1976. **Mark:** 24K gold cherry blossom.

FONTENOT, GERALD J., 901 Maple Av, Mamou, LA 70554, Phone: 318-468-3180

FORREST, BRIAN, Forrest Knives, PO BOX 203, Descanso, CA 91916, Phone: 619-445-6343 **Specialties:** Working straight knives, some fancy made to customer order. **Patterns:** Traditional patterns, Bowies, hunters, skinners and daggers. **Technical:** Grinds 440C, files & rasps. **Prices:** $125 & up. **Remarks:** Member of California Knifemakers Association. Full-time maker. First knife sold in 1971. **Mark:** Forrest USA.

FORSTALL, AL, 38379 Aunt Massey Rd, Pearl River, LA 70452, Phone: 504-863-2930 **Specialties:** Traditional working and using straight knives of his design or to customer specs. **Patterns:** Fighters, hunters and utility/camp knives. **Technical:** Grinds ATS-34, 440C, commercial Damascus and others upon request. **Prices:** $75 to $250. **Remarks:** Spare-time maker; first knife sold in 1991. **Mark:** Fleur Di Lis with name.

FORTHOFER, PETE, 5535 Hwy. 93S, Whitefish, MT 59937, Phone: 406-862-2674 **Specialties:** Interframes with checkered wood inlays; working straight knives. **Patterns:** Interframe folders and traditional-style knives; hunters, fighters and Bowies. **Technical:** Grinds D2, 440C, 154CM and ATS-34. **Prices:** $350 to $2500; some to $1500. **Remarks:** Part-time maker; full-time gunsmith. First knife sold in 1979. **Mark:** Name and logo.

FORTUNE PRODUCTS, INC., 205 Hickory Creek Rd, Marble Falls, TX 78654, Phone: 830-693-6111, Fax: 830-693-6394 **Specialties:** Knife sharpeners.

FOSTER, NORVELL C., 619 Holmgreen Rd, San Antonio, TX 78220, Phone: 210-333-1675 **Specialties:** Engraving; ivory handle carving. **Patterns:** American-large and small scroll-oak leaf and acorns. **Prices:** $25 to $400. **Mark:** N. C. Foster - S. A., TX & current year.

FOSTER, RONNIE E., 95 Riverview Rd, Morrilton, AR 72110, Phone: 501-354-5389

FOSTER, TIMOTHY L., 723 Sweet Gum Acres Rd, El Dorado, AR 71730, Phone: 870-863-6188

FOSTER, AL, 118 Woodway Dr, Magnolia, TX 77355, Phone: 936-372-9297 **Specialties:** Straight knives and folders. **Patterns:** Hunting, fishing, folders & Bowies. **Technical:** Grinds 440-C, ATS-34 & D2. **Prices:** $100 to

$1000. **Remarks:** Full-time maker; first knife sold in 1981. **Mark:** Scorpion logo & name.

FOSTER, R. L. (BOB), 745 Glendale Blvd., Mansfield, OH 44907

FOSTER, BURT, 21275 Dickinson rd, Moreno Valley, CA 92557, Phone: 909-328-1213, Fax: 909-328-0008 **Specialties:** Working straight knives, Laminated blades, and some art knives of his design. **Patterns:** Bowies, hunters, daggers and Japanese-style knives and swords. **Technical:** Forges 52100, high carbon laminates, and makes own Damascus. Does own heat treating. **Prices:** $150 to $2000 and up. **Remarks:** ABS journeyman smith. Full-time maker, believes in sole authorship. **Mark:** Signed "BF" initials.

FOWLER, CHARLES R., 226 National Forest Rd 48, Ft McCoy, FL 32134-9624, Phone: 904-467-3215

FOWLER, ED A., Willow Bow Ranch, PO Box 1519, Riverton, WY 82501, Phone: 307-856-9815 **Specialties:** High performance working and using straight knives. **Patterns:** Hunter, camp, bird, and trout knives and Bowies. New model, the gentleman's Pronghorn. **Technical:** Low temperature forged 52100 from virgin 5 1/2 round bars, multiple quench heat treating, engraves all knives, all handles domestic sheep horn processed and aged at least 5 years. Makes heavy duty hand-stitched waxed harness leather pouch type sheaths. **Prices:** $800-$7000. **Remarks:** Full-time maker. First knife sold in 1962. **Mark:** Initials connected.

FOWLER, JERRY, 610 FM 1660 N., Hutto, TX 78634, Phone: 512-846-2860 **Specialties:** Using straight knives of his design. **Patterns:** A variety of hunting and camp knives, combat knives. Custom designs considered. **Technical:** Forges 5160, his own Damascus and cable Damascus. Makes sheaths. Prefers natural handle materials. **Prices:** Start at $150. **Remarks:** Part-time maker; first knife sold in 1986. Doing business as Fowler Forge Knife works. **Mark:** First initial, last name, date and J. S.

FOWLER, RICKY & SUSAN, Fowler Custom Knives, PO Box 339, 22080 9th St, Silverhill, AL 36576, Phone: 334-945-3289, Fax: 334-945-3290 **Specialties:** Traditional working/using straight knives of his design or to customer specifications. **Patterns:** Skinners, fighters, tantos, Bowies and utility/camp knives. **Technical:** Grinds O1, ATS-34, 440C, D2, A2 & commercial Damascus. Forges 5160, Damascus, & other steels. **Prices:** Start at $150. **Remarks:** Full-time maker; first knife sold in 1994. Doing business as Fowler Custom Knives. **Mark:** Last name tang stamped & serial numbered.

FOX, WENDELL, 1480 S 39th St, Springfield, OR 97478, Phone: 541-747-2126 **Specialties:** Large camping knives and friction folders of his design and to customer specs. **Patterns:** Hunters, locking folders, slip-joint folders and utility/camp knives. **Technical:** Forges and grinds high carbon steel only. **Prices:** $200 and up. **Remarks:** Full-time maker; first knife sold in 1952. **Mark:** Stamped name or logo. **Other:** All one-of-a-kind pieces. Specializing in early American.

FOX, JACK L., 7085 Canelo Hills Dr, Citrus Heights, CA 95610, Phone: 916-723-8647 **Specialties:** Traditional working/using straight knives of all designs. **Patterns:** Hunters, utility/camp knives and bird/fish knives. **Technical:** Grinds ATS-34, 440C and D2. **Prices:** $125 to $225; some to $350. **Remarks:** Spare-time maker; first knife sold in 1985. Doing business as Fox Knives. **Mark:** Stylized fox head.

FOX, PAUL, 4721 Rock Barn Road, Claremont, NC 28610, Phone: 828-459-2000, Fax: 828-459-9200 **Specialties:** Hi-Tech. **Patterns:** Naibsek, Otnat, & Zorro (tactical) knives. **Technical:** Grinds ATS-34, 440C and D2. **Prices:** $500. **Remarks:** Spare-time maker; first knife sold in 1985. Doing business as Fox Knives. **Mark:** Laser engraved.

FRALEY, D. B., 1355 Fairbanks Ct, Dixon, CA 95620, Phone: 707-678-0393 **Specialties:** Traditional working/using straight knives and folders of his design and in standard patterns. **Patterns:** Fighters, hunters, utility/camp knives. **Technical:** Grinds ATS-34. Offers hand-stitched sheaths. **Prices:** Start at $100. **Remarks:** Part-time maker; first knife sold in 1990. **Mark:** First and middle initials, last name over buffalo.

FRAMSKI, WALTER P., 24 Rek Lane, Prospect, CT 06712, Phone: 203-758-5634

FRANCE, DAN, Box 218, Cawood, KY 40815, Phone: 606-573-6104 **Specialties:** Traditional working and using straight knives of his design. **Patterns:** Hunters, Bowies and utility/camp knives. **Technical:** Forges and grinds O1, 5160 and L6. **Prices:** $35 to $125; some to $350. **Remarks:** Spare-time maker; first knife sold in 1985. **Mark:** First name.

FRANCIS, VANCE, 2612 Alpine Blvd., Alpine, CA 91901, Phone: 619-445-0979
Specialties: Working straight knives. **Patterns:** Bowies and utility knives. **Technical:** Uses ATS-34, A2, D2 and Damascus; differentially tempers large blades. **Prices:** $175 to $600. **Remarks:** Part-time maker. **Mark:** First name, last name, city and state under feather in oval.

FRANCIS, JOHN D., Francis Knives, 18 Miami St, Ft. Loramie, OH 45845, Phone: 937-295-3941
Specialties: Utility and hunting-style fixed bladed knives of ATS-34 steel; micarta, exotic woods, and other types of handle materials.

FRANK, HEINRICH H., 13868 NW Keleka Pl., Seal Rock, OR 97376, Phone: 541-563-3041, Fax: 541-563-3041
Specialties: High-art investor-class folders, handmade and engraved. **Patterns:** Folding daggers, hunter-size folders and gents. **Technical:** Grinds 07 and O1. **Prices:** $4800 to $16,000. **Remarks:** Full-time maker; first knife sold in 1965. Doing business as H. H. Frank Knives. **Mark:** Name, address and date.

FRANKL, JOHN M., 12 Holden St, CAMBRIDGE, MA 02138, Phone: 617-547-0359
Specialties: Hand forged tool steel and Damascus. **Patterns:** Camp knives, Bowies, hunters and fighters. **Technical:** Forge own Damascus, 5160 and V 1084. **Prices:** $150-$1000. **Mark:** Last name "Frankl" on ricasso.

FRANKLIN, MIKE, 9878 Big Run Rd, Aberdeen, OH 45101, Phone: 937-549-2598
Specialties: High-tech tactical folders. **Patterns:** Tactical folders. **Technical:** Grinds CPM-T-440V, 440-C, ATS-34; titanium liners and bolsters; carbon fiber scales. Uses radical grinds and severe serrations. **Prices:** $275 to $600. **Remarks:** Full-time maker; first knife sold in 1969. **Mark:** Stylized boar with HAWG.

FRAPS, JOHN, 3810 Wyandotte Trail, Indianapolis, IN 46240-3422, Phone: 317-849-9419, Fax: 317-842-2224
Specialties: Working and Collector Grade liner-lock and slip joint folders. **Patterns:** Liner-lock foldersand slip joint folders. **Technical:** Flat and hollow grinds ATS-34, Damascus, Talonite, CPM S30V, 154Cm, Stellite 6K; hand rubbed or mirror finish. **Prices:** Start at $175. **Remarks:** Full-time maker; first knife sold in 1997. **Mark:** Cougar Creek Knives and/or name.

FRAZIER, RON, 2107 Urbine Rd, Powhatan, VA 23139, Phone: 804-794-8561
Specialties: Classy working knives of his design; some high-art straight knives. **Patterns:** Wide assortment of straight knives, including miniatures and push knives. **Technical:** Grinds 440C; offers satin, mirror or sand finishes. **Prices:** $85 to $700; some to $3000. **Remarks:** Full-time maker; first knife sold in 1976. **Mark:** Name in arch logo.

FRED, REED WYLE, 3149 X Street, Sacramento, CA 95817, Phone: 916-739-0237
Specialties: Working using straight knives of his design. **Patterns:** Hunting and camp knives. **Technical:** Forges any 10 series, old files and carbon steels. Offers initialing upon request; prefers natural handle materials. **Prices:** $30 to $300; some to $300. **Remarks:** Part-time maker; first knife sold in 1994. Doing business as R. W. Fred Knife maker. **Mark:** Engraved first and last initials.

FREDERICK, AARON, 1213 Liberty Rd, West Liberty, KY 41472, Phone: 606-743-3399

FREEMAN, JOHN, 160 Concession St, Cambridge, Ont., CANADA N1R 2H7, Phone: 519-740-2767, Fax: 519-740-2785
Specialties: Kitchen knives, outdoor knives, sharpeners and folders. **Patterns:** Hunters, skinners, utilities, backpackers. **Technical:** Flat ground 440C. **Prices:** Start at $135 & up. **Remarks:** Full-time maker; first knife sold in 1985. **Mark:** Last name, country.

FREER, RALPH, 114 12th St, Seal Beach, CA 90740, Phone: 562-493-4925, Fax: same
Specialties: Exotic folders, liner-locks, folding daggers, fixed blades. **Patterns:** All original. **Technical:** Lots of Damascus, ivory, pearl, jeweled, thumb studs, carving ATS-34, 420V, 530V. **Prices:** $400-$2500 and up. **Mark:** Freer in German-style text, also freer shield.

FREILING, ALBERT J., 3700 Niner Rd, Finksburg, MD 21048, Phone: 301-795-2880
Specialties: Working straight knives and folders; some period pieces. **Patterns:** Boots, Bowies, survival knives and tomahawks in 4130 and 440C; some locking folders and interframes; ball-bearing folders. **Technical:** Grinds O1, 440C and 154CM. **Prices:** $100 to $300; some to $500. **Remarks:** Part-time maker; first knife sold in 1966. **Mark:** Initials connected.

FREY, STEVE, 19103 131st Drive SE, Snohomish, WA 98296, Phone: 360-668-7351

FREY JR., W. FREDERICK, 305 Walnut St, Milton, PA 17847, Phone: 570-742-9576
Specialties: Working straight knives and folders, some fancy. **Patterns:** Wide range—boot knives to tomahawks. **Technical:** Grinds A2, O1 and D2; hand finishes only. **Prices:** $55 to $170; some to $600. **Remarks:** Spare-time maker; first knife sold in 1983. **Mark:** Last name in script.

FRIEDLY, DENNIS E., 12 Cottontail Ln. - E, Cody, WY 82414, Phone: 307-527-6811
Specialties: Fancy working straight knives and daggers, lock-back folders and liner-locks. **Patterns:** Hunters, fighters, short swords, minis and miniatures; new line of full-tang hunters/boots. **Technical:** Grinds 440C, commercial Damascus, mosaic Damascus and ATS-34 blades; prefers hidden tangs. **Prices:** $135 to $900; some to $2500. **Remarks:** Full-time maker; first knife sold in 1972. **Mark:** Name, city, state.

FRIGAULT, RICK, 3584 Rapidsview Dr, Niagara Falls ON, CANADA L2G 6C4, Phone: 905-295-6695
Specialties: Fixed blades. **Patterns:** Hunting, tactical & large Bowies. **Technical:** Grinds ATS-34, 440-C, D-2, 530V, 560V, carbon fiber & Damascus. Use G-10, Micarta, ivory, antler, ironwood & other stabilized woods for handle material. Makes leather sheaths by hand. Tactical blades include a Concealex sheath made by "On Scene Tactical". **Remarks:** Sold first knife in 1997. Member of Canadian Knifemakers Guild. **Mark:** RFRIGAULT.

FRITZ, JESSE, 900 S. 13th St, Slaton, TX 79364, Phone: 806-828-5083, Fax: 915-530-0508
Specialties: Working and using straight knives in standard patterns. **Patterns:** Hunters, utility/camp knives and skinners with gut hook. **Technical:** Grinds 440C, O1 and 1095. Fline-napped steel design, blued blades, filework and machine jewelling. Inlays handles with turquoise, coral and mother-of-pearl. Makes sheaths. **Prices:** $85 to $275; some to $500. **Mark:** Crossed half ovals: handmade on top, last name in middle, city and state on bottom.

FRIZZELL, TED, 14056 Low Gap Rd, West Fork, AR 72774, Phone: 501-839-2516
Specialties: Swords, axes and self-defense weapons. **Patterns:** Small skeleton knives to large swords. **Technical:** Grinds 5160 almost exclusively—1/4" to 1/2"—bars some O1 and A2 on request. All knives come with Kydex sheaths. **Prices:** $45 to $1200. **Remarks:** Full-time maker; first knife sold in 1984. Doing business as Mineral Mountain Hatchet Works. Wholesale orders welcome. **Mark:** A circle with line in the middle; MM and HW within the circle.

FRONEFIELD, DANIEL, 137 Catherine Dr, Hampton Cove, AL 35763-9732, Phone: 256-536-7827
Specialties: Fixed and folding knives featuring meteorites and other exotic materials. **Patterns:** San-mai Damascus, custom Damascus. **Prices:** $500 to $3000.

FROST, DEWAYNE, 1016 Van Buren Rd, Barnesville, GA 30204, Phone: 770-358-1426

FRUHMANN, LUDWIG, Stegerwaldstr 8, 84489 Burghausen, GERMANY
Specialties: High-tech and working straight knives of his design. **Patterns:** Hunters, fighters and boots. **Technical:** Grinds ATS-34, CPM-T-440V and Schneider Damascus. Prefers natural handle materials. **Prices:** $200 to $1500. **Remarks:** Spare-time maker; first knife sold in 1990. **Mark:** First initial and last name.

FUEGEN, LARRY, 617 N. Coulter Circle, Prescott, AZ 86303, Phone: 928-776-8777
Specialties: High-art folders and classic and working straight knives. **Patterns:** Forged scroll folders, lock-back folders and classic straight knives. **Technical:** Forges 5160, 1095 and his own Damascus. Works in exotic leather; offers elaborate filework and carving; likes natural handle materials, now offers my own engraving. **Prices:** $400 to $7000. **Remarks:** Full-time maker; first knife sold in 1975. **Mark:** Initials connected. **Other:** Sole authorship on all knives.

FUJIKAWA, SHUN, Sawa 1157 Kaizuka, Osaka 597 0062, JAPAN, Phone: 81-724-23-4032, Fax: 81-726-23-9229
Specialties: Folders of his design and to customer specs. **Patterns:** Locking folders. **Technical:** Grinds his own steel. **Prices:** $450 to $2500; some to $3000. **Remarks:** Part-time maker.

FUJISAKA, STANLEY, 45-004 Holowai St, Kaneohe, HI 96744, Phone: 808-247-0017
Specialties: Fancy working straight knives and folders. **Patterns:** Hunters, boots, personal knives, daggers, collectible art knives. **Technical:** Grinds 440C, 154CM and ATS-34; clean lines, inlays. **Prices:** $150 to $1200;

some to $3000. **Remarks:** Full-time maker; first knife sold in 1984. **Mark:** Name, city, state.

FUKUTA, TAK, 38-Umeagae-cho, Seki-City, Gifu-Pref, JAPAN, Phone: 0575-22-0264
Specialties: Bench-made fancy straight knives and folders. **Patterns:** Sheffield-type folders, Bowies and fighters. **Technical:** Grinds commercial Damascus. **Prices:** Start at $300. **Remarks:** Full-time maker. **Mark:** Name in knife logo.

FULLER, JACK A., 7103 Stretch Ct, New Market, MD 21774, Phone: 301-798-0119
Specialties: Straight working knives of his design and to customer specs. **Patterns:** Fighters, camp knives, hunters, tomahawks and art knives. **Technical:** Forges 5160, O1, W2 and his own Damascus. Does silver wire inlay and own leather work, wood lined sheaths for big camp knives. **Prices:** $300 to $850. **Remarks:** Part-time maker. Master Smith in ABS; first knife sold in 1979. **Mark:** Fuller's Forge, MS.

FULLER, BRUCE A., 1305 Airhart Dr, Baytown, TX 77520, Phone: 713-427-1848
Specialties: One-of-a-kind working/using straight knives and folders of his designs. **Patterns:** Bowies, hunters, folders, and utility/camp knives. **Technical:** Forges high-carbon steel and his own Damascus. prefers El Solo Mesquite and natural materials. Offers filework. **Prices:** $200 to $500; some to $1800. **Remarks:** Spare-time maker; first knife sold in 1991. Doing business as Fullco Forge. **Mark:** Fullco, M. S.

FULTON, MICKEY, 406 S Shasta St, Willows, CA 95988, Phone: 530-934-5780
Specialties: Working straight knives and folders of his design. **Patterns:** Hunters, Bowies, lock-back folders and steak knife sets. **Technical:** Hand-filed, sanded, buffed ATS-34, 440C and A2. **Prices:** $65 to $600; some to $1200. **Remarks:** Full-time maker; first knife sold in 1979. **Mark:** Signature.

g

GADBERRY, EMMET, 82 Purple Plum Dr, Hattieville, AR 72063, Phone: 501-354-4842

GADDY, GARY LEE, 205 Ridgewood Lane, Washington, NC 27889, Phone: 252-946-4359
Specialties: Working/using straight knives of his design; period pieces. **Patterns:** Bowies, hunters, utility/camp knives. **Technical:** Grinds ATS-34, O1; forges 1095 **Prices:** $100 to $225; some to $400. **Remarks:** Spare-time maker; first knife sold in 1991. **Mark:** Quarter moon logo.

GAETA, ANGELO, R. Saldanha Marinho, 1295 Centro Jau, SP-17201-310, BRAZIL, Phone: 0146-224543, Fax: 0146-224543
Specialties: Straight using knives to customer specs. **Patterns:** Hunters, fighting, daggers, belt push dagger. **Technical:** Grinds D6, ATS-34 and 440C stainless. titanium nitride golden finish upon request. **Prices:** $60 to $300. **Remarks:** Full-time maker; first knife sold in 1992. **Mark:** First initial, last name.

GAETA, ROBERTO, Rua Shikazu Myai 80, 05351 Sao Paulo, S. P., BRAZIL, Phone: 11-37684626
Specialties: Wide range of using knives. **Patterns:** Brazilian and North American hunting and fighting knives. **Technical:** Grinds stainless steel; likes natural handle materials. **Prices:** $100 to $250; some to $500. **Remarks:** Full-time maker; first knife sold in 1979. **Mark:** BOB'G.

GAGSTAETTER, PETER, Nibelungenschmiede, Bergstrasse 2, 9306 Freidorf TG, SWITZERLAND

GAINES, BUDDY, Gaines Knives, 155 Red Hill Rd, Commerce, GA 30530
Specialties: Collectible and working folders and straight knives. **Patterns:** Folders, hunters, Bowies, tactical knives. **Technical:** Forges own Damascus, grinds ATS-34, D2, commercial Damascus. Prefers Mother of Pearl and Stag. **Prices:** Start at $200. **Remarks:** Part-time maker, sold first knife in 1985. **Mark:** Last name.

GAINEY, HAL, 904 Bucklevel Rd, Greenwood, SC 29649, Phone: 864-223-0225
Specialties: Traditional working and using straight knives and folders. **Patterns:** Hunters, slip-joint folders and utility/camp knives. **Technical:** Hollow-grinds ATS-34 and D2; makes sheaths. **Prices:** $95 to $145; some to $500. **Remarks:** Full-time maker; first knife sold in 1975. **Mark:** Eagle head and last name.

GALLAGHER, SEAN, 24828 114th PL SE, Monroe, WA 98272-7685

GALLAGHER, BARRY, 135 Park St, Lewistown, MT 59457, Phone: 406-538-7056
Specialties: One-of-a-kind Damascus folders. **Patterns:** Folders - utility to high art, some straight knives - hunter, Bowies, and art pieces. **Technical:** Forges own mosaic Damascus and carbon steel, some stainless. **Prices:** $400 to $5000+. **Remarks:** Full-time maker; first knife sold in 1993. Doing business as Gallagher Custom Knives. **Mark:** Last name.

GAMBLE, ROGER, 2801 65 Way N., St. Petersburg, FL 33710, Phone: 727-384-1470
Specialties: Traditional working/using straight knives and folders of his design. **Patterns:** Liner-locks & hunters. **Technical:** Grinds ATS-34 and Damascus. **Prices:** $100 to $1000. **Remarks:** Part-time maker; first knife sold in 1982. Doing business as Gamble Knives. **Mark:** First name in a fan of cards over last name.

GAMBLE, FRANK, 3872 Dunbar Pl., Fremont, CA 94536, Phone: 510-797-7970
Specialties: Fantasy and high-art straight knives and folders of his design. **Patterns:** Daggers, fighters, hunters and special locking folders. **Technical:** Grinds 440C and ATS-34; forges Damascus. Inlays; offers jeweling. Prices $150 to $10,000. **Remarks:** Full-time maker; first knife sold in 1976. **Mark:** First initial, last name.

GANSTER, JEAN-PIERRE, 18, Rue du Vieil Hopital, F-67000 Strasbourg, FRANCE, Phone: 0033 388 32 65 61, Fax: 0033 388 32 52 79
Specialties: Fancy and high-art miniatures of his design and to customer specs. **Patterns:** Bowies, daggers, fighters, hunters, locking folders and miniatures. **Technical:** Forges and grinds stainless Damascus, ATS-34, gold and silver. **Prices:** $100 to $380; some to $2500. **Remarks:** Part-time maker; first knife sold in 1972. **Mark:** Stylized first initials.

GARCIA, MARIO EIRAS, R. Edmundo Scanapieco, 300 Caxingui, Sao Paulo SP-05516-070, BRAZIL, Fax: 011-37214528
Specialties: Fantasy knives of his design; one-of-a-kind only. **Patterns:** Fighters, daggers, boots and two-bladed knives. **Technical:** Forges car leaf springs. Uses only natural handle material. **Prices:** $100 to $200. **Remarks:** Part-time maker; first knife sold in 1976. **Mark:** Two B's, one opposite the other.

GARDNER, ROB, 387 Mustang Blvd., Port Aransas, TX 78373, Phone: 361-749-3597, Fax: 361-749-3597
Specialties: High-art working and using knives of his design and to customer specs. **Patterns:** Daggers, hunters and ethnic-patterned knives. **Technical:** Forges Damascus, L6 and 10-series steels. Engraves and inlays. Handles and fittings may be carved. **Prices:** $175 to $500; some to $2500. **Remarks:** Spare-time maker; first knife sold in 1987. Knives made by custom order only. **Mark:** Engraved or stamped initials.

GARNER, LARRY W., 13069 FM 14, Tyler, TX 75706, Phone: 903-597-6045
Specialties: Fixed blade hunters & Bowies. **Patterns:** My designs or yours. **Technical:** Hand forges 5160. **Prices:** $200 to $500. **Remarks:** Apprentice Bladesmith. **Mark:** Last name.

GARNER JR., WILLIAM O., 2803 East DeSoto St, Pensacola, FL 32503, Phone: 850-438-2009
Specialties: Working straight and art knives. **Patterns:** Hunters and folders. **Technical:** Grinds 440C and ATS-34 steels. **Prices:** $235 to $600. **Remarks:** Full-time maker; first knife sold in 1985. **Mark:** First and last name in oval logo or last name.

GARRITY., TIMOTHY P., 217 S Grandview Blvd, Waukesha, WI 53188, Phone: 414-785-1803

GARVOCK, MARK W., RR 1, Balderson, Ontario, CANADA K1G 1A0, Phone: 613-833-2545, Fax: 613-833-2208
Specialties: Hunters, Bowies, Japanese, daggers & swords. **Patterns:** Cable Damascus, random pattern welded or to suit. **Technical:** Forged blades; hi-carbon. **Prices:** $250 to $900. **Remarks:** Also CKG member & ABS member. **Mark:** Big G with M in middle. **Other:** Shipping & taxes extra.

GASTON, RON, 330 Gaston Dr, Woodruff, SC 29388, Phone: 803-433-0807, Fax: 803-433-9958
Specialties: Working period pieces. **Patterns:** Hunters, fighters, tantos, boots and a variety of other straight knives; single-blade slip-joint folders. **Technical:** Grinds ATS-34. Hand-rubbed satin finish is standard. **Prices:** $200 to $600; some to $1000. **Remarks:** Full-time maker; first knife sold in 1980. **Mark:** Ron Gaston, Woodruff SC.

GAUDETTE, LINDEN L., 5 Hitchcock Rd, Wilbraham, MA 01095, Phone: 413-596-4896
Specialties: Traditional working knives in standard patterns. **Patterns:** Broad-bladed hunters, Bowies and camp knives; wood carver knives; locking folders. **Technical:** Grinds ATS-34, 440C and 154CM. **Prices:** $150 to

custom knifemakers

$400; some higher. **Remarks:** Full-time maker; first knife sold in 1975. **Mark:** Last name in Gothic logo; used to be initials in circle.

GAULT, CLAY, #1225 PR 7022, Lexington, TX 78947, Phone: 979-773-3305
Specialties: Classic straight and folding hunting knives and multi-blade folders of his design. **Patterns:** Folders and hunting knives. **Technical:** Grinds BX-NSM 174 steel, custom rolled from billets to his specifications. Uses exotic leathers for sheaths, and fine natural materials for all knives. **Prices:** $325 to $600; some higher. **Remarks:** Full-time maker; first knife sold in 1970. **Mark:** Name or name with cattle brand.

GEISLER, GARY R., PO Box 294, Clarksville, OH 45113, Phone: 937-383-4055
Specialties: Period Bowies and such; flat ground. **Patterns:** Working knives usually modeled close after an existing antique. **Technical:** Flat grinds 440C, A2 & ATS-34. **Prices:** $300 and up. **Remarks:** Part-time maker; first knife sold in 1982. **Mark:** G. R. Geisler Maker; usually in script on reverse side because I'm left handed.

GENSKE, JAY, 283 Doty St, Fond Du Lac, WI 54935, Phone: 920-921-8019/Cell Phone 920-579-0144
Specialties: Working/using knives and period pieces of his design and to customer specs. **Patterns:** Bowies, fighters, hunters. **Technical:** Grinds ATS-34 and 440C, 01 and 1095 forges and grinds Damascus and 1095. Offers custom-tooled sheaths, scabbards and hand carved handles. **Prices:** $95 to $500; some to $1000. **Remarks:** Full-time maker; first knife sold in 1985. Doing business as Genske Knives. **Mark:** Stamped or engraved last name.

GEORGE, TOM, 550 Aldbury Dr, Henderson, NV 89014
Specialties: Working straight knives, display knives and folders of his design. **Patterns:** Hunters, Bowies, daggers and buckskinners and folders. **Technical:** Uses D2, 440C, ATS-34 and 154CM. **Prices:** $175 to $4500. **Remarks:** First knife sold in 1981. Custom orders accepted. **Mark:** Name.

GEORGE, HARRY, 3137 Old Camp Long Rd, Aiken, SC 29805, Phone: 803-649-1963
Specialties: Working straight knives of his design or to customer specs. **Patterns:** Hunters, skinners and utility knives. **Technical:** Grinds ATS-34. Prefers natural handle materials, hollow-grinds and mirror finishes. **Prices:** Start at $70. **Remarks:** Part-time maker; first knife sold in 1985. Trained under George Herron. Member SCAK. Member Knifemakers Guild. **Mark:** Name, city, state.

GEORGE, LES, 1703 Payne, Wichita, KS 67203, Phone: 316-267-0736
Specialties: Classic, traditional and working/using straight knives of his design and to customer specs. **Patterns:** Fighters, hunters, swords and miniatures. **Technical:** Grinds D2; forges 5160 and Damascus. Uses mosaic handle pins and his own mokume-gane. **Prices:** $35 to $200; some to $800. **Remarks:** No orders taken at this time due to enlistment in the US Marine Corps.; first knife sold in 1992. Doing business as George Custom Knives. **Mark:** Last name or initials stacked.

GEPNER, DON, 2615 E. Tecumseh, Norman, OK 73071, Phone: 405-364-2750
Specialties: Traditional working and using straight knives of his design. **Patterns:** Bowies and daggers. **Technical:** Forges his Damascus, 1095 and 5160. **Prices:** $100 to $400; some to $1000. **Remarks:** Spare-time maker; first knife sold in 1991. Has been forging since 1954; first edged weapon made at 9 years old. **Mark:** Last initial.

GERNER, THOMAS, PO Box 1363, Christchurch, NEW ZEALAND 06398
Specialties: Forged working knives; plain steel and pattern welded. **Patterns:** I try most patterns I hear or read about. **Technical:** 5160, L6, 01, 52100 steels; Australian hardwood handles. **Prices:** $160 & up. **Remarks:** Achieved ABS master smith rating in 2001. **Mark:** Like a standing arrow and a leaning cross, T. G. in the Runic (Viking) alphabet.

GERUS, GERRY, PO Box 2295, G. PO Cairns, Qld. 4870, AUSTRALIA 070-341451, Phone: 019 617935
Specialties: Fancy working and using straight knives of his design. **Patterns:** Hunters, Bowies and fighters. **Technical:** Uses 440C, ATS-34 and commercial Damascus. **Prices:** $275 to $600; some to $1200. **Remarks:** Part-time maker; first knife sold in 1988. **Mark:** Last name; or last name, Hand Made, city, country.

GEVEDON, HANNERS (HANK), 1410 John Cash Rd, Crab Orchard, KY 40419-9770
Specialties: Traditional working and using straight knives. **Patterns:** Hunters, swords, utility and camp knives. **Technical:** Forges and grinds his own Damascus, 5160 and L6. Cast aluminum handles. **Prices:** $50 to $250; some to $400. **Remarks:** Part-time maker; first knife sold in 1983. **Mark:** Initials and LBF tang stamp.

GIAGU, SALVATORE AND DEROMA MARIA ROSARIA, Via V. Emanuele 64, 07016 Pattada (SS), ITALY, Phone: 079-755918, Fax: 079-755918
Specialties: Using and collecting traditional and new folders from Sardegna. **Patterns:** Folding, hunting, utility, skinners and kitchen knives. **Technical:** Forges ATS-34, 440, D2 and Damascus. **Prices:** $200 to $2000; some higher. **Mark:** First initial, last name and name of town and muflon's head.

GIBO, GEORGE, PO Box 4304, Hilo, HI 96720, Phone: 808-987-7002
Specialties: Straight knives and folders. **Patterns:** Hunters, bird and trout, utility, gentlemen and tactical folders. **Technical:** Grinds ATS-34, BG-42, Talonite, Stainless Steel Damascus. **Prices:** $250 to $1000. **Remarks:** Spare-time maker first knife sold in 1995. **Mark:** Name, city and state around Hawaiian "Shaka" sign.

GIBSON SR, JAMES HOOT, 90 Park Place Ave, Bunnell, FL 32110, Phone: 904-437-4383
Specialties: Bowies, folders, daggers, & hunters. **Patterns:** Most all. **Technical:** ATS-440C hand cut & grind. **Prices:** $1250 to $3000. **Remarks:** 100% handmade. **Mark:** Hoot.

GILBERT, CHANTAL, 291 Rue Christophe-Colomb est. #105, Quebec City Quebec, CANADA G1K 3T1, Phone: 418-525-6961, Fax: 418-525-4666
Specialties: Straight art knives that may resemble creatures, often with wings, shells and antennae, always with a beak of some sort, fixed blades in a feminine style. **Technical:** ATS-34 and Damascus. Handle materials usually silver that she forms to shape via special molds and a press; ebony and fossil ivory. **Prices:** Range from $500-$4000. **Other:** Often embellishes her art knives with rubies, meteorite, 18k gold and similar elements.

GILBREATH, RANDALL, 55 Crauswell Rd, Dora, AL 35062, Phone: 205-648-3902
Specialties: Damascus folders and fighters. **Patterns:** Folders and fixed blades. **Technical:** Forges Damascus and high carbon; stock removal stainless steel. **Prices:** $300 to $1500. **Remarks:** Full-time maker; first knife sold in 1979. **Mark:** Name in ribbon.

GILJEVIC, BRANKO, 35 Hayley Crescent, Queanbeyan 2620, N. S. W., AUSTRALIA 0262977613
Specialties: Classic working straight knives and folders of his design. **Patterns:** Hunters, Bowies, skinners and locking folders. **Technical:** Grinds 440C. Offers acid etching, scrimshaw and leather carving. **Prices:** $150 to $1500. **Remarks:** Part-time maker; first knife sold in 1987. Doing business as Sambar Custom Knives. **Mark:** Company name in logo.

GITTINGER, RAYMOND, 6940 S Rt 100, Tiffin, OH 44883, Phone: 419-397-2517

GLASSCOCK, JOHN, 18510 Lippizaner, Cypress, TX 77433, Phone: 713-859-4060

GLOVER, RON, 7702 Misty Springs Ct, Mason, OH 45040, Phone: 513-398-7857
Specialties: High-tech working straight knives and folders. **Patterns:** Hunters to Bowies; some interchangeable blade models; unique locking mechanisms. **Technical:** Grinds 440C, 154CM; buys Damascus. **Prices:** $70 to $500; some to $800. **Remarks:** Part-time maker; first knife sold in 1981. **Mark:** Name in script.

GLOVER, WARREN D., d/b/a Bubba Knives, PO Box 475, Cleveland, GA 30528, Phone: 706-865-3998, Fax: 706-348-7176
Specialties: Traditional and custom working and using straight knives of his design and to customer request. **Patterns:** Hunters, skinners, bird & fish, utility and kitchen knives. **Technical:** Grinds 440, ATS-34 and stainless steel Damascus. **Prices:** $75 to $400 and up. **Remarks:** Part-time maker; sold first knife in 1995. **Mark:** Bubba, year, name, state.

GODDARD, WAYNE, 473 Durham Ave, Eugene, OR 97404, Phone: 541-689-8098
Specialties: Working/using straight knives and folders. **Patterns:** Hunters and folders. **Technical:** Works exclusively with wire Damascus and his own-pattern welded material. **Prices:** $250 to $4000. **Remarks:** Full-time maker; first knife sold in 1963. Three-year backlog on orders. **Mark:** Blocked initials on forged blades; regular capital initials on stock removal.

GOERS, BRUCE, 3423 Royal Ct. S., Lakeland, FL 33813, Phone: 941-646-0984
Specialties: Fancy working and using straight knives of his design and to customer specs. **Patterns:** Hunters, fighters, Bowies and fantasy knives. **Technical:** Grinds ATS-34, some Damascus. **Prices:** $195 to $600; some to $1300. **Remarks:** Part-time maker; first knife sold in 1990. Doing business as Vulture Cutlery. **Mark:** Buzzard with initials.

GOERTZ, PAUL S., 201 Union Ave. SE, #207, Renton, WA 98059, Phone: 425-228-9501
Specialties: Working straight knives of his design and to customer specs. **Patterns:** Hunters, skinners, camp, bird and fish knives, camp axes, some

Bowies, fighters and boots. **Technical:** Grinds ATS-34, BG42, & CPM420V. **Prices:** $75 to $500. **Remarks:** Full-time maker; first knife sold in 1985. **Mark:** Signature.

GOFOURTH, JIM, 3776 Aliso Cyn. Rd, Santa Paula, CA 93060, Phone: 805-659-3814

Specialties: Period pieces and working knives. **Patterns:** Bowies, locking folders, patent lockers and others. **Technical:** Grinds A2 and 154CM. **Prices:** Moderate. **Remarks:** Spare-time maker. **Mark:** Initials interconnected.

GOGUEN, SCOTT, 166 Goguen Rd, Newport, NC 28570, Phone: 919-393-6013

Specialties: Classic and traditional working knives. **Patterns:** Kitchen, camp, hunters, Bowies & swords. **Technical:** Forges high carbon steel and own Damascus. Offers clay tempering and cord wrapped handles. **Prices:** $85 to $1500. **Remarks:** Spare-time maker; first knife sold in1988. **Mark:** Last name or name in Japanese characters.

GOLDBERG, DAVID, 1120 Blyth Ct, Blue Bell, PA 19422, Phone: 215-654-7117

Specialties: Japanese-style designs, will work with special themes in Japanese Genre. **Patterns:** Kozuka, Tanto, Wakazashi, Katana, Tachi, Sword canes, Yari & Naginata. **Technical:** Forges his own Damascus and makes his own handmade steel from straw ash, iron, carbon and clay. Uses traditional materials, carves fittings handles & cases. Hardens all blades in traditional Japanese clay differential technique. **Remarks:** Full-time maker; first knife sold in 1987. **Mark:** Name (kinzan) in Japanese Kanji on Tang under handle. **Other:** Japanese swordsmanship teacher (jaido) and Japanese self defense teach (aikido).

GOLDBERG, METALSMITH, DAVID, 1120 Blyth Ct, Blue Bell, PA 19422, Phone: 215-654-7117

Specialties: Japanese-style swords and fittings. **Patterns:** Kozuka to Dai-Sho, Naginata, Yari and sword canes. **Technical:** Forges and heat treats his own Damascus, cable Damascus, meteorite, and handmade steel from carbonized iron, straw ash and clay. Uses traditional materials, carves fittings, handles and cases. Now making "Tamahagane" (iron sand steel). Sole author. **Prices:** Upon request. **Remarks:** Full-time maker; first knife sold in 1987. **Mark:** Last name in Japanese Kanji-"Kinzan". **Other:** Damascus metalsmithing teacher: C Robbin Hudson. Japanese swordsmithing teacher: Michael Bell; fittings etc self taught.

GOLDING, ROBIN, PO Box 267, Lathrop, CA 95330, Phone: 209-982-0839

Specialties: Working straight knives of his design. **Patterns:** Survival knives, Bowie extractions, camp knives, dive knives and skinners. **Technical:** Grinds 440C, 154CM and ATS-34. **Prices:** $95 to $250; some to $500. **Remarks:** Full-time maker; first knife sold in 1985. Up to 1-1/2 year waiting period on orders. **Mark:** Signature of last name.

GOLTZ, WARREN L., 802 4th Ave. E., Ada, MN 56510, Phone: 218-784-7721

Specialties: Fancy working knives in standard patterns. **Patterns:** Hunters, Bowies and camp knives. **Technical:** Grinds 440C and ATS-34. **Prices:** $120 to $595; some to $950. **Remarks:** Part-time maker; first knife sold in 1984. **Mark:** Last name.

GONZALEZ, LEONARDO WILLIAMS, Ituzaingo 473, Maldonado, CP 20000, URUGUAY, Phone: 598 4222 1617, Fax: 598 4222 1617

Specialties: Classic high-art and fantasy straight knives; traditional working and using knives of his design, in standard patterns or to customer specs. **Patterns:** Hunters, Bowies, daggers, fighters, boots, swords and utility/camp knives. **Technical:** Forges and grinds high carbon and stainless Bohler steels. **Prices:** $100 to $2500. **Remarks:** Full-time maker; first knife sold in 1985. **Mark:** Willy, whale, R. O. U.

GOO, TAI, 5920 W Windy Lou Ln, Tucson, AZ 85742, Phone: 520-744-9777

Specialties: High art, nto-tribal, working knives and fantasy knives. **Technical:** hand forges, does own heat treating, makes own Damascus. **Prices:** $150-$500; some to $10,000. **Remarks:** Full-time maker; first knife sold in 1978. **Mark:** Chiseled signature.

GOODE, BEAR, PO Box 6474, Navajo Dam, NM 87419, Phone: 505-632-8184

Specialties: Working/using straight knives of his design and in standard patterns. **Patterns:** Bowies, hunters and utility/camp knives. **Technical:** Grinds 440C, ATS-34, 154-CM; forges and grinds 1095, 5160 and other steels on request; uses Damascus. **Prices:** $60 to $225; some to $500 and up. **Remarks:** Part-time maker; first knife sold in 1993. Doing business as Bear Knives. **Mark:** First and last name with a three-toed paw print.

GOODLING, RODNEY W., 6640 Old Harrisburg Rd, York Springs, PA 17372

GORDON, LARRY B., 23555 Newell Cir W, Farmington Hills, MI 48336, Phone: 248-477-5483

GORENFLO, JAMES T. (JT), 9145 Sullivan Rd, Baton Rouge, LA 70818, Phone: 225-261-5868

Specialties: Traditional working and using straight knives of his design. **Patterns:** Bowies, hunters and utility/camp knives. **Technical:** Forges 5160, 1095, 52100 and his own Damascus. **Prices:** Start at $200. **Remarks:** Part-time maker; first knife sold in 1992. **Mark:** Last name or initials, J. S. on reverse.

GORENFLO, GABE, 9145 Sullivan Rd, Baton Rouge, LA 70818, Phone: 504-261-5868

GOTTAGE, JUDY, 43227 Brooks Dr, Clinton Twp., MI 48038-5323, Phone: 810-286-7275

Specialties: Custom folders of her design or to customer specs. **Patterns:** Interframes or integral. **Technical:** Stock removal. **Prices:** $300 to $3000. **Remarks:** Full-time maker; first knife sold in 1980. **Mark:** Full name, maker in script.

GOTTAGE, DANTE, 43227 Brooks Dr, Clinton Twp., MI 48038-5323, Phone: 810-286-7275

Specialties: Working knives of his design or to customer specs. **Patterns:** Large and small skinners, fighters, Bowies and fillet knives. **Technical:** Grinds O1, 440C and 154CM and ATS-34. **Prices:** $150 to $600. **Remarks:** Part-time maker; first knife sold in 1975. **Mark:** Full name in script letters.

GOTTSCHALK, GREGORY J., 12 First St. (Ft. Pitt), Carnegie, PA 15106, Phone: 412-279-6692

Specialties: Fancy working straight knives and folders to customer specs. **Patterns:** Hunters to tantos, locking folders to minis. **Technical:** Grinds 440C, 154CM, ATS-34. Now making own Damascus. Most knives have mirror finishes. **Prices:** Start at $150. **Remarks:** Part-time maker; first knife sold in 1977. **Mark:** Full name in crescent.

GOUKER, GARY B., PO Box 955, Sitka, AK 99835, Phone: 907-747-3476

Specialties: Hunting knives for hard use. **Patterns:** Skinners, semi-skinners, and such. **Technical:** Likes natural materials, inlays, stainless steel. **Prices:** Moderate. **Remarks:** New Alaskan maker. **Mark:** Name.

GOYTIA, ENRIQUE, 2120 E PAISANO STE 276, EL PASO, TX 79905

GRAFFEO, ANTHONY I., 100 Riess Place, Chalmette, LA 70043, Phone: 504-277-1428

Specialties: Traditional working and using straight knives of his design, to customer specs and in standard patterns. **Patterns:** Hunters, utility/camp knives and fishing knives. **Technical:** Hollow- and flat-grinds ATS-34, 440C and 154CM. Handle materials include Pakkawood, Micarta and sambar stag. **Prices:** $65 to $100; some to $250. **Remarks:** Part-time maker; first knife sold in 1991. Doing business as Knives by: Graf. **Mark:** First and middle initials, last name city, state, Maker.

GRAHAM, GORDON, RT 3 Box 207, New Boston, TX 75570, Phone: 903-628-6337

GRAVELINE, PASCAL AND ISABELLE, 38, rue de Kerbrezillic, 29350 Moelan-sur-Mer, FRANCE, Phone: 33 2 98 39 73 33, Fax: 33 2 98 39 73 33

Specialties: French replicas from the 17th, 18th and 19th centuries. **Patterns:** Traditional folders and multi-blade pocket knives; traveling knives, fruit knives and fork sets; puzzle knives and friend's knives; rivet less knives. **Technical:** Grind 12C27, ATS-34, Damascus and carbon steel. **Prices:** $500 to $5000; some to $2000. **Remarks:** Full-time makers; first knife sold in 1992. **Mark:** Last name over head of ram.

GRAY, BOB, 8206 N. Lucia Court, Spokane, WA 99208, Phone: 509-468-3924

Specialties: Straight working knives of his own design or to customer specs. **Patterns:** Hunter, fillet and carving knives. **Technical:** Forges 5160, L6 and some 52100; grinds 440C. **Prices:** $100 to $600. **Remarks:** Part-time knife maker; first knife sold in 1991. Doing business as Hi-Land Knives. **Mark:** HI-L.

GRAY, DANIEL, Gray Knives, 686 Main Rd, Brownville, ME 04414, Phone: 207-965-2191

Specialties: Straight knives, Fantasy, folders, automatics and traditional of my own design. **Patterns:** Automatics, fighters, hunters. **Technical:** Grind 01, 154CM & D2. **Prices:** From $155 to $750. **Remarks:** Full-time maker; first knife sold in 1974. **Mark:** Gray Knives.

custom knifemakers

GREBE, GORDON S., PO Box 296, Anchor Point, AK 99556-0296, Phone: 907-235-8242
Specialties: Working straight knives and folders, some fancy. **Patterns:** Tantos, Bowies, boot fighter sets, locking folders. **Technical:** Grinds stainless steels; likes 1/4"-inch stock and glass-bead finishes. **Prices:** $75 to $250; some to $2000. **Remarks:** Full-time maker; first knife sold in 1968. **Mark:** Initials in lightning logo.

GRECO, JOHN, 100 Mattie Jones Road, Greensburg, KY 42743, Phone: 270-932-3335, Fax: 270-932-2225
Specialties: Limited edition knives & swords. **Patterns:** Tactical, fighters, camp knives, short swords. **Technical:** Stock removal carbon steel. **Prices:** Affordable. **Remarks:** Full-time maker since1986. First knife sold in 1979. **Mark:** Greco and steroc w/mo mark. **Other:** Do custom limited edition knives for other designers complete with their logo.

GREEN, BILL, 706 Bradfield, Garland, TX 75042, Phone: 972-272-4748
Specialties: High-art and working straight knives and folders of his design and to customer specs. **Patterns:** Bowies, hunters, kitchen knives and locking folders. **Technical:** Grinds ATS-34, D2 and 440V. Hand-tooled custom sheaths. **Prices:** $70 to $350; some to $750. **Remarks:** Part-time maker; first knife sold in 1990. **Mark:** Last name.

GREEN, WILLIAM (BILL), 46 Warren Rd, View Bank Vic., AUSTRALIA 3084, Fax: 03-9459-1529
Specialties: Traditional high-tech straight knives and folders. **Patterns:** Japanese-influenced designs, hunters, Bowies, folders and miniatures. **Technical:** Forges O1, D2 and his own Damascus. Offers lost wax castings for bolsters and pommels. Likes natural handle materials, gems, silver and gold. **Prices:** $400 to $750; some to $1200. **Remarks:** Full-time maker. **Mark:** Initials.

GREEN, MARK, 1523 S Main St PO Box 20, Graysville, AL 35073, Phone: 205-647-9353

GREEN, RUSS, 6013 Briercrest Ave, Lakewood, CA 90713, Phone: 562-867-2305
Specialties: Sheaths & using knives. **Technical:** Knives 440C, ATS-34, 5160, 01, cable Damascus. **Prices:** Knives-$135 to $850; sheaths- $30 to $200. **Mark:** Russ Green & year.

GREENAWAY, DON, 3325 Dinsmore Trail, Fayetteville, AR 72704, Phone: 501-521-0323

GREENE, STEVE, Dunn Knives Inc, PO Box 204, Rossville, KS 66533, Phone: 785-584-6856, Fax: 785-584-6856

GREENE, DAVID, 570 Malcom Rd, Covington, GA 30209, Phone: 770-784-0657
Specialties: Straight working using knives. **Patterns:** Hunters. **Technical:** Forges mosaic and twist Damascus. Prefers stag and desert ironwood for handle material.

GREENE, CHRIS, 707 Cherry Lane, Shelby, NC 28150, Phone: 704-434-5620

GREENFIELD, G. O., 2605 15th St. #522, Everett, WA 98201, Phone: 425-258-1551
Specialties: High-tech and working straight knives and folders of his design. **Patterns:** Boots, daggers, hunters and one-of-a-kinds. **Technical:** Grinds ATS-34, D2, 440C and T-440V. Makes sheaths for each knife. **Prices:** $100 to $800; some to $10,000. **Remarks:** Part-time maker; first knife sold in 1978. **Mark:** Springfield®, serial number.

GREGORY, MICHAEL, 211 Calhoun Rd, Belton, SC 29627, Phone: 864-338-8898
Specialties: Working straight knives and folders. **Patterns:** Hunters, tantos, locking folders and slip-joints, boots and fighters. **Technical:** Grinds 440C, 154CM and ATS-34; mirror finishes. **Prices:** $95 to $200; some to $1000. **Remarks:** Part-time maker; first knife sold in 1980. **Mark:** Name, city in logo.

GREINER, RICHARD, 1073 E. County Rd. 32, Green Springs, OH 44836

GREISS, JOCKL, Obere Muhlstr. 5, 73252, Gutenberg, GERMANY, Phone: +49 0 7026 3224
Specialties: Classic and working using straight knives of his design. **Patterns:** Bowies, daggers and hunters. **Technical:** Uses only Jerry Rados Damascus. All knives are one-of-a-kind made by hand; no machines are used. **Prices:** $700 to $2000; some to $3000. **Remarks:** Full-time maker; first knife sold in 1984. **Mark:** An "X" with a long vertical line through it.

GRENIER, ROGER, 540 Chemin De La Dague, Saint Jovite, Que., CANADA J0T 2H0, Phone: 819-425-8893
Specialties: Working straight knives. **Patterns:** Heavy-duty Bowies, fighters, hunters, swords and miniatures. **Technical:** Grinds O1, D2 and 440C. **Prices:** $70 to $225; some to $800. **Remarks:** Full-time maker; first knife sold in 1981. **Mark:** Last name on blade.

GREY, PIET, PO Box 363, Naboomspruit 0560, SOUTH AFRICA, Phone: 014-743-3613
Specialties: Fancy working and using straight knives of his design. **Patterns:** Fighters, hunters and utility/camp knives. **Technical:** Grinds ATS-34 and AEB-L; forges and grinds Damascus. Solder less fitting of guards. Engraves and scrimshaws. **Prices:** $125 to $750; some to $1500. **Remarks:** Part-time maker; first knife sold in 1970. **Mark:** Last name.

GRIFFIN, THOMAS J., 591 Quevli Ave, Windom, MN 56101, Phone: 507-831-1089
Specialties: Period pieces and fantasy straight knives of his design. **Patterns:** Daggers and swords. **Technical:** Forges 1095, 52100 and L6. Most blades are his own Damascus; turned fittings and wire-wrapped grips. **Prices:** $250 to $800; some to $2000. **Remarks:** Full-time maker; first knife sold in 1991. Doing business as Griffin Knives. **Mark:** Last name etched.

GRIFFIN, RENDON AND MARK, 9706 Cedardale, Houston, TX 77055, Phone: 713-468-0436
Specialties: Working folders and automatics of their designs. **Patterns:** Standard lockers and slip-joints. **Technical:** Most blade steels; stock removal. **Prices:** Start at $350. **Remarks:** Rendon's first knife sold in 1966; Mark's in 1974. **Mark:** Last name logo.

GRIFFIN JR., HOWARD A., 14299 SW 31st Ct, Davie, FL 33330, Phone: 305-474-5406
Specialties: Working straight knives and folders. **Patterns:** Hunters, Bowies, locking folders with his own push-button lock design. **Technical:** Grinds 440C. **Prices:** $100 to $200; some to $500. **Remarks:** Part-time maker; first knife sold in 1983. **Mark:** Initials.

GRIFFITH, LYNN, PO Box 876, Glenpool, OK 74033, Phone: 918-366-8303
Specialties: Flat ground, full tang tactical knives. **Patterns:** Neck & multi-carry knives, drop and clip points, tantos and Wharncliffes. **Technical:** Grinds ATS-34 and Talonite. **Prices:** $125 to $400; some to $700. **Remarks:** Full-time knife maker; first knife sold in 1987. **Mark:** Last name over year made.

GROSPITCH, ERNIE, 18440 Amityville Dr, Orlando, FL 32820, Phone: 407-568-5438
Specialties: Bowies, hunting, fishing, kitchen, lock-back folders. **Patterns:** My design or customer. **Technical:** Stock removal using most available steels. **Prices:** $140 and up. **Remarks:** Part-time maker, sold first knife in 1990. Mark: Etched name/maker city and state.

GROSS, W. W., 109 Dylan Scott Dr, Archdale, NC 27263-3858
Specialties: Working knives. **Patterns:** Hunters, boots, fighters. **Technical:** Grinds. **Prices:** Moderate. **Remarks:** Full-time maker. **Mark:** Name.

GROSSMAN, STEWART, 24 Water St, #419, Clinton, MA 01510, Phone: 508-365-2291; 800-mysword
Specialties: Miniatures and full-size knives and swords. **Patterns:** One-of-a-kind miniatures—jewelry, replicas—and wire-wrapped figures. Full-size art, fantasy and combat knives, daggers and modular systems. **Technical:** Forges and grinds most metals and Damascus. Uses gems, crystals, electronics and motorized mechanisms. **Prices:** $20 to $300; some to $4500 and higher. **Remarks:** Full-time maker; first knife sold in 1985. **Mark:** G1.

GRUSSENMEYER, PAUL G., 310 Kresson Rd, Cherry Hill, NJ 08034, Phone: 856-428-1088, Fax: 856-428-8997
Specialties: Assembling fancy and fantasy straight knives with his own carved handles. **Patterns:** Bowies, daggers, folders, swords, hunters and miniatures. **Technical:** Uses forged steel and Damascus, stock removal and knapped obsidian blades. **Prices:** $250 to $4000. **Remarks:** Spare-time maker; first knife sold in 1991. **Mark:** First and last initial hooked together on handle.

GUARNERA, ANTHONY R, 42034 Quail Creek Dr, Quartzhill, CA 93536, Phone: 661-722-4032
Patterns: Hunters, camp, Bowies, kitchen, fighter knives. **Technical:** Forged and stock removal. **Prices:** $100 and up.

GUESS, RAYMOND L., 7214 Salineville Rd. NE, Mechanicstown, OH 44651, Phone: 330-738-2793
Specialties: Working straight knives and folders of his design or to customer specs. **Patterns:** Hunters, Bowies, fillet knives, steak and paring knife sets. **Technical:** Grinds 440C. Offers silver inlay work and mirror finishes. Custom-made leather sheath for each knife. **Prices:** $65 to $850; some to $700. **Remarks:** Spare-time maker; first knife sold in 1985. **Mark:** First initial, last name.

GUIDRY, BRUCE, 24550 Adams Av, Murrieta, CA 92562, Phone: 909-677-2384

GUIGNARD, GIB, Box 3413, Quartzsite, AZ 85359, Phone: 928-927-4831
Specialties: Rustic finish on primitive Bowies with stag or ironwood handles & turquoise inlay. **Patterns:** Very large in 5160 & ATS-34 - Small &

med. size hunting knives in ATS-34. **Technical:** Forges 5160 and grind ATS-34. **Prices:** $100 to $1000. **Remarks:** Full-time maker; first knife sold in 1989. Doing business as Cactus Forge. **Mark:** Last name or G+ on period pieces and primitive.

GUILD, DON, Guild Knives, 320 Paani Place 1A, Paia, HI 96779, Phone: 808-877-3109

GUNDERSEN, D. F. "DOC", 5811 S Siesta Lane, Tempe, AZ 85283
Specialties: Small and medium belt knives, sword canes/staffs, kitchen cutlery, slip joint folders, throwers. **Patterns:** Utility, hunters, fighters and sailors' knives. **Technical:** Both forged and stock removal knives available in a variety of steels. Unique carvings available on many items. **Prices:** $65 to $250. **Remarks:** Full-time maker; first knife sold in 1988. Doing business as L & H Knife Works. **Mark:** L&H Knife Works.

GUNN, NELSON L., 77 Blake Road, Epping, NH 03042, Phone: 603-679-5119
Specialties: Classic and working/using straight knives of his design. **Patterns:** Bowies, fighters and hunters. **Technical:** Grinds O1 and 440C. Carved stag handles with turquoise inlays. **Prices:** $125 to $300; some to $700. **Remarks:** Part-time maker; first knife sold in 1996. Doing business as Nelson's Custom Knives. **Mark:** First and last initial.

GUNTER, BRAD, 13 Imnaha Road, Tijeras, NM 87059, Phone: 505-281-8080

GURGANUS, CAROL, 2553 N. C. 45 South, Colerain, NC 27924, Phone: 252-356-4831, Fax: 252-356-4650
Specialties: Working and using straight knives. **Patterns:** Fighters, hunters and kitchen knives. **Technical:** Grinds D2, ATS-34 and Damascus steel. Uses stag, and exotic wood handles. **Prices:** $100 to $300. **Remarks:** Part-time maker; first knife sold in 1992. **Mark:** Female symbol, last name, city, state.

GURGANUS, MELVIN H., 2553 N. C. 45 South, Colerain, NC 27924, Phone: 252-356-4831, Fax: 252-356-4650
Specialties: High-tech working folders. **Patterns:** Leaf-lock and back-lock designs, bolstered and interframe. **Technical:** D2 and 440C; Heat-treats, carves and offers lost wax casting. **Prices:** $300 to $3000. **Remarks:** Part-time maker; first knife sold in 1983. **Mark:** First initial, last name and maker.

GUTHRIE, GEORGE B., 1912 Puett Chapel Rd, Bassemer City, NC 28016, Phone: 704-629-3031
Specialties: Working knives of his design or to customer specs. **Patterns:** Hunters, boots, fighters, locking folders and slip-joints in traditional styles. **Technical:** Grinds D2, 440C and 154CM. **Prices:** $105 to $300; some to $450. **Remarks:** Part-time maker; first knife sold in 1978. **Mark:** Name in state.

h

HAGEN, PHILIP L., PO Box 58, Pelican Rapids, MN 56572, Phone: 218-863-8503
Specialties: High-tech working straight knives and folders. **Patterns:** Defense-related straight knives; wide variety of folders. **Technical:** Automatics; 4 styles. **Prices:** $100 to $800; some to $3000. **Remarks:** Part-time maker; first knife sold in 1975. **Mark:** DOC HAGEN in shield, knife, banner logo; or DOC.

HAGGERTY, GEORGE S., PO Box 88, Jacksonville, VT 05342, Phone: 802-368-7437
Specialties: Working straight knives and folders. **Patterns:** Hunters, claws, camp and fishing knives, locking folders and backpackers. **Technical:** Forges and grinds W2, 440C and 154CM. **Prices:** $85 to $300. **Remarks:** Part-time maker; first knife sold in 1981. **Mark:** Initials or last name.

HAGUE, GEOFF, The Malt House, Hollow Ln., Wilton Marlborough, Wiltshire, ENGLAND SN8 3SR, Phone: +44 01672-870212, Fax: +44 01672 870212
Specialties: Fixed blade and folding knives. **Patterns:** Locking and friction folders, hunters & small knives. **Technical:** Grinds ATS-34, RWL34 and Damascus; others by agreement. **Prices:** Start at $200. **Remarks:** Full-time maker. **Mark:** Last name. **Other:** British voting member of the Knife Makers Guild.

HAINES, JEFF, HAINES CUSTOM KNIVES, 302 N. Mill St, Wauzeka, WI 53826, Phone: 608-875-5002
Patterns: Hunters, skinners, camp knives, customer designs welcome. **Technical:** Forges 1095, 5160, & Damascus, grinds A2. **Prices:** $40 and up. **Remarks:** Part-time maker since 1995. **Mark:** Last name.

HALL, JEFF, PO Box 435, Los Alamitos, CA 90720, Phone: 562-594-4740
Specialties: Collectible and working folders of his design. **Technical:** Grinds ATS-34, 154CM, 440V and various makers' Damascus. **Patterns:** Fighters, gentleman's, hunters and utility knives. **Prices:** $300 to $500; some to $1000. **Remarks:** Full-time maker. First knife sold 1998. **Mark:** Last name.

HALLIGAN, ED, 14 Meadow Way, Sharpsburg, GA 30277, Phone: 770-251-7720, Fax: 770-251-7720
Specialties: Working straight knives and folders, some fancy. **Patterns:** Liner-locks, hunters, skinners, boots, fighters and swords. **Technical:** Grinds ATS-34; forges 5160; makes cable and pattern Damascus. **Prices:** $160 to $2500. **Remarks:** Full-time maker; first knife sold in 1985. Doing business as Halligan Knives. **Mark:** Last name, city, state and USA.

HAMLET JR., JOHNNY, 300 Billington, Clute, TX 77531, Phone: 409-265-6929
Specialties: Working straight knives and folders. **Patterns:** Hunters, fighters, fillet and kitchen knives, locking folders. Likes upswept knives and trailing-points. **Technical:** Grinds 440C, D2, ATS-34. Makes sheaths. **Prices:** $55 to $225; some to $500. **Remarks:** Part-time maker; first knife sold in 1988. **Mark:** Hamlet's Handmade in script.

HAMMOND, JIM, PO Box 486, Arab, AL 35016, Phone: 256-586-4151, Fax: 256-586-0170
Specialties: High-tech fighters and folders. **Patterns:** Proven-design fighters. **Technical:** Grinds 440C, 440V, ATS-34 and other specialty steels. **Prices:** $385 to $1200; some to $8500. **Remarks:** Full-time maker; first knife sold in 1977. Designer for Columbia River Knife & Tool. **Mark:** Full name, city, state in shield logo.

HANCOCK, TIM, 10805 N. 83rd St, Scottsdale, AZ 85260, Phone: 480-998-8849
Specialties: High-art and working straight knives and folders of his design and to customer preferences. **Patterns:** Bowies, fighters, daggers, tantos, swords, folders. **Technical:** Forges Damascus and 52100; grinds ATS-34. Makes Damascus. Silver-wire inlays; offers carved fittings and file work. **Prices:** $500 to $10,000. **Remarks:** Full-time maker; first knife sold in 1988. **Mark:** Last name or heart. **Other:** Mastersmith ABS

HAND, BILL, PO Box 773, 1103 W. 7th St, Spearman, TX 79081, Phone: 806-659-2967, Fax: 806-659-5117
Specialties: Traditional working and using straight knives and folders of his design or to customer specs. **Patterns:** Hunters, Bowies, folders and fighters. **Technical:** Forges 5160, 52100 and Damascus. **Prices:** Start at $150. **Remarks:** Part-time maker; Journeyman Smith. Current delivery time twelve to sixteen months. **Mark:** Stylized initials.

HANKINS, R., 9920 S Rural Rd #10859, Tempe, AZ 85284, Phone: 480-940-0559
Specialties: Completely hand-made tactical, practical and custom Bowie knives. **Technical:** Use Damascus, ATS-34 and 440C stainless steel for blades. Stock removal method of grinding. Handle material varies from ivory, stag to Micarta, depending on application and appearance. **Remarks:** Part-time maker.

HANSEN, ROBERT W., 35701 University Ave. N. E., Cambridge, MN 55008, Phone: 612-689-3242
Specialties: Working straight knives, folders and integrals. **Patterns:** From hunters to minis, camp knives to miniatures; folding lockers and slip-joints in original styles. **Technical:** Grinds O1, 440C and 154CM; likes filework. **Prices:** $75 to $175; some to $550. **Remarks:** Part-time maker; first knife sold in 1983. **Mark:** Fish with last initial inside.

HANSEN, LONNIE, PO Box 4956, Spanaway, WA 98387, Phone: 253-847-4632
Specialties: Working straight knives of his design. **Patterns:** Tomahawks, tantos, hunters, filet. **Technical:** Forges 1086, 52100, grinds 440V, BG-42. **Prices:** Starting at $300. **Remarks:** Part-time maker since 1989. **Mark:** First initial and last name. Also first and last initial

HANSON III, DON L., PO Box 13, Success, MO 65570-0013, Phone: 573-674-3045
Specialties: One-of-a-kind Damascus folders. **Patterns:** Small, fancy pocket knives, large folding fighters. **Technical:** I forge my own pattern welded Damascus, file work & carving. **Prices:** $800 & up. **Remarks:** Full-time maker, first knife sold in 1984. **Mark:** Sunfish. **Other:** Member of ABS, ABANA, BAM.

HARA, KOUJI, 292-2 Ohsugi, Seki-City, Gifu-Pref. 501-32, JAPAN, Phone: 0575-24-7569, Fax: 0575-24-7569
Specialties: High-tech and working straight knives of his design; some folders. **Patterns:** Hunters, locking folders and utility/camp knives. **Technical:** Grinds Cowry X, Cowry Y and ATS-34. Prefers high mirror polish; pearl handle inlay. **Prices:** $80 to $500; some to $1000. **Remarks:** Full-time maker; first knife sold in 1980. Doing business as Knife House "Hara". **Mark:** First initial, last name in fish.

HARDY, SCOTT, 639 Myrtle Ave, Placerville, CA 95667, Phone: 530-622-5780
Specialties: Traditional working and using straight knives of his design. **Patterns:** Most anything with an edge. **Technical:** Forges carbon steels. Japanese stone polish. Offers mirror finish; differentially tempers. **Prices:** $100 to $1000. **Remarks:** Part-time maker; first knife sold in 1982. **Mark:** First initial, last name and Handmade with bird logo.

HARDY, DOUGLAS E., 114 Cypress Rd, Franklin, GA 30217, Phone: 706-675-6305

HARILDSTAD, MATT, 18627 68 Ave, Edmonton, AB, T5T 2M8, CANADA, Phone: 780-481-3165
Specialties: Working knives, fancy fighting knives, kitchen cutlery, letter openers. **Patterns:** Full range of straight knives in classic patterns. **Technical:** Grinds ATS-34, 440C, commercial Damascus and some high carbon. **Prices:** $120 to $500 (US). **Remarks:** Part-time maker, first knife sold in 1997. **Mark:** Name, city province.

HARKINS, J. A., PO Box 218, Conner, MT 59827, Phone: 406-821-1060
Specialties: Investment grade folders. **Patterns:** flush buttons, lockers. **Technical:** Grinds ATS-34 . Engraves; offers gem work. **Prices:** Start at $550. **Remarks:** Full-time maker and engraver; first knife sold in 1988. **Mark:** First and middle initials, last name.

HARLEY, LARRY W., 348 Deerfield Dr, Bristol, TN 37620, Phone: 423-878-5368 (shop)/Cell 423-571-0638, Fax: 276-466-6771
Specialties: One-of-a-kind Persian in one-of-a-kind Damascus. Working knives, period pieces. **Technical:** Forges and grinds ATS-34, 440c, L6, 15, 20, 1084, and 52100. **Patterns:** Full range of straight knives, tomahawks, razors, buck skinners and hog spears. **Prices:** $200 and up. **Mark:** Pine tree.

HARM, PAUL W., 818 Young Rd, Attica, MI 48412, Phone: 810-724-5582
Specialties: Early American working knives. **Patterns:** Hunters, skinners, patch knives, fighters, folders. **Technical:** Forges and grinds 1084, 01, 52100 and own Damascus. **Prices:** $75 to $1000. **Remarks:** First knife sold in 1990. **Mark:** Connected initials.

HARMON, JAY, 462 Victoria Rd, Woodstock, GA 30189, Phone: 770-928-2734
Specialties: Working straight knives and folders of his design or to customer specs; collector-grade pieces. **Patterns:** Bowies, daggers, fighters, boots, hunters and folders. **Technical:** Grinds 440C, 440V, ATS-34, D2 1095 and Damascus; heat-treats; makes own mokume. **Prices:** Start at $185. **Remarks:** Part-time maker; first knife sold in 1984. **Mark:** Last name.

HARRINGTON, ROGER, 3 Beech Farm Cottages, Bugsell Lane, East Sussex, ENGLAND TN 32 5 EN, Phone: 44 0 1580 882194
Specialties: Working straight knives to his or customer's designs, flat saber Norwegian-style grinds on full tang knives. **Technical:** Grinds 01, D2. Prices: $100-$500. **Remarks:** First knife made by hand in 1997 whilst traveling around the world. **Mark:** Bison with bison written under.

HARRIS, RALPH DEWEY, 2607 Bell Shoals Rd, Brandon, FL 33511, Fax: 813-654-8175
Specialties: Collector quality interframe folders. **Patterns:** High tech locking folders of his own design with various mechanisms. **Technical:** Grinds 440C, ATS-34 and commercial Damascus. Offers various frame materials including 416ss, and titanium; file worked frames and his own engraving. **Prices:** $400 to $3000. **Remarks:** Full-time maker; first knife sold in 1978. **Mark:** Last name, or name and city.

HARRIS, CASS, 19855 Frasier Hill Lane, Bluemont, VA 20135, Phone: 540-554-8774
Prices: $160 to $500.

HARRIS, JAY, 991 Johnson St, Redwood City, CA 94061, Phone: 415-366-6077
Specialties: Traditional high-tech straight knives and folders of his design. **Patterns:** Daggers, fighters and locking folders. **Technical:** Uses 440C, ATS-34 and CPM. **Prices:** $250 to $850. **Remarks:** Spare-time maker; first knife sold in 1980.

HARRIS, JEFFERY A., 705 Olive St Ste 325, St. Louis, MO 63101, Phone: 314-241-2442
Remarks: Purveyor and collector of handmade knives.

HARRISON, JIM (SEAMUS), 721 Fairington View Dr, St. Louis, MO 63129, Phone: 314-894-2525
Specialties: Gent's locking liner folders. Compact straight blades for hunting, backpacking and canoeing. **Patterns:** Preference for modified Wharncliffes. Most patterns developed in BWCAW and Quetico. **Technical:** Grinds 440C, 154CM, talonite, S-30V and pattern welded. Heat treats. **Prices:** Straight blades $150-$400; folders $225-$400. **Remarks:** Likes knives to be carry friendly. **Mark:** Seamus.

HARRISON, JAMES, 721 Fairington View Dr, St Louis, MO 63129, Phone: 314-894-2525
Specialties: Liner-lock folder. **Technical:** 440C

HARSEY, WILLIAM H., 82710 N. Howe Ln., Creswell, OR 97426, Phone: 519-895-4941
Specialties: High-tech kitchen and outdoor knives. **Patterns:** Folding hunters, trout and bird folders; straight hunters, camp knives and axes. **Technical:** Grinds; etches. **Prices:** $125 to $300; some to $1500. Folders start at $350. **Remarks:** Full-time maker; first knife sold in 1979. **Mark:** Full name, state, U. S. A.

HART, BILL, 647 Cedar Dr, Pasadena, MD 21122, Phone: 410-255-4981
Specialties: Fur-trade era working straight knives and folders. **Patterns:** Springbuck folders, skinners, Bowies and patch knives. **Technical:** Forges and stock removes 1095 and 5160 wire Damascus. **Prices:** $100 to $600. **Remarks:** Part-time maker; first knife sold in 1986. **Mark:** Name.

HARTGROVE, WM. ANTHONY, PO Box 771482, Eagle River, AR 99577, Phone: 901-696-0156

HARTMAN, ARLAN (LANNY), 340 Ruddiman, N. Muskegon, MI 49445, Phone: 616-744-3635
Specialties: Working straight knives and folders. **Patterns:** Drop-point hunters, coil spring lockers, slip-joints. **Technical:** Flat-grinds D2, 440C and ATS-34. **Prices:** $200 to $2000. **Remarks:** Part-time maker; first knife sold in 1982. **Mark:** Last name.

HARTSFIELD, PHILL, PO Box 1637, Newport Beach, CA 92659-0637, Phone: 949-722-9792 & 714-636-7633
Specialties: Heavy-duty working and using straight knives. **Patterns:** Fighters, swords and survival knives, most in Japanese profile. **Technical:** Grinds A2. **Prices:** $350 to $20,000. **Remarks:** Full-time maker; first knife sold about 1966. Doing business as A Cut Above. **Mark:** Initials, chiseled character plus register mark. **Other:** Color catalog $10.

HARVEY, MAX, 14 Bass Rd, Bull Creek, Perth 6155, WESTERN AUSTRALIA, Phone: 09-332-7585
Specialties: Daggers, Bowies, fighters and fantasy knives. **Patterns:** Hunters, Bowies, tantos and skinners. **Technical:** Hollow-and flat-grinds 440C, ATS-34, 154CM and Damascus. Offers gem work. **Prices:** $250 to $4000. **Remarks:** Part-time maker; first knife sold in 1981. **Mark:** First and middle initials, last name.

HARVEY, HEATHER, Heavin Forge, PO Box 768, Belfast 1100, SOUTH AFRICA, Phone: 27-13-253-0914
Specialties: Integral hand forged knives, traditional African weapons, primitive folders and by-gone forged styles. **Patterns:** All forged knives, war axes, spears, arrows, forks, spoons, and swords. **Technical:** Own carbon Damascus and mokume. Also forges stainless, brass, copper and titanium. Traditional forging and heat-treatment methods used. **Prices:** $300-$5000, average $1000. **Remarks:** Full-time maker and knifemaking instructor. First Damascus sold in 1995, first knife sold in 1998. Often collaborate with my husband, Kevin (A. B. S. J. S) using the logo "Heavin". **Mark:** First name in calligraphy.

HARVEY, KEVIN, Heavin Forge, PO Box 768, Belfast 1100, SOUTH AFRICA, Phone: 27-13-253-0914
Specialties: Large knives of presentation quality and creative art knives. **Patterns:** Fixed blades of bowie, dagger and fighter-styles, occasionally folders. **Technical:** Stock removal of stainless and forging of carbon steel and own Damascus. Indigenous African handle materials preferred. Stacked file worked handles. Ostrich, bull frog, fish, crocodile and snake leathers used on unique sheaths. Surface texturing and heat coloring of materials. Often collaborate with my wife, Heather (A. B. S. J. S) under the logo "Heavin". **Prices:** $500-$5000 average $1500. **Remarks:** Full-time maker and knifemaking instructor. First knife sold in 1984. **Mark:** First name in calligraphy.

HASLINGER, THOMAS, 164 Fairview Dr SE, Calgary AB, CANADA T2H 1B3, Phone: 403-253-9628
Specialties: One-of-a-kind using, working & art knives HCK signature sweeping grind liners . **Patterns:** No fixed patterns, likes to work with customers on design. **Technical:** Grinds Various specialty alloys, including Damascus, High end satin finish. Prefers natural handle materials e. g. Ancient Ivory Stag, Pearl, Abalone, Stone and exotic woods. I do inlay work with stone, some sterling silver, niobium and gold wire work. Custom sheaths using matching woods or hand stitched with unique leather like sturgeon, Nile perch or carp. Offers engraving. **Prices:** Starting at $150. **Remarks:** Full-time maker; first knife sold in 1994. Doing business as Haslinger Custom Knives. **Mark:** Two marks used, high end work uses stylized initials, other uses elk antler with Thomas Haslinger, Canada, Handcrafted above

HATCH, KEN, PO Box 244, La-Point, UT 84039
Specialties: Indian and early trade knives. **Patterns:** Buckskinners and period Bowies. **Technical:** Forges and grinds 1095, O1, W2, ATS-34. Pre-

fers natural handle materials. **Prices:** $85 to $400. **Remarks:** Part-time maker, custom leather & bead work; first knife sold in 1977. **Mark:** Last name or dragonfly stamp.

HAWES, CHUCK, Hawes Forge, PO Box 176, Weldon, IL 61882, Phone: 217-736-2479
Specialties: 95% of all work in own Damascus. **Patterns:** Slip-joints, liner-locks, hunters, Bowie's, swords, anything in between. **Technical:** Forges everything use all high carbon steels, no stainless. **Prices:** $150-$4000. **Remarks:** Like to do custom orders, my style or yours. Sells Damascus. **Mark:** Small football shape. Chuck Hawes maker Weldon,IL. **Other:** Full-time maker sine 1995.

HAWK, GRANT AND GAVIN, Box 401, Idaho City, ID 83631, Phone: 208-392-4911
Specialties: Large folders with unique locking systems D. O. G. lock, toad lock. **Technical:** Grinds ATS-34, titanium folder parts. **Prices:** $450 and up. **Remarks:** Full-time maker. **Mark:** First initials and last names.

HAWK, JACK L., Rt. 1, Box 771, Ceres, VA 24318, Phone: 703-624-3878
Specialties: Fancy and embellished working and using straight knives of his design or to customer specs. **Patterns:** Hunters, Bowies and daggers. **Technical:** Hollow-grinds 440C, ATS-34 and D2; likes bone and ivory handles. **Prices:** $75 to $1200. **Remarks:** Full-time maker; first knife sold in 1982. **Mark:** Full name and initials.

HAWK, JOEY K., Rt. 1, Box 196, Ceres, VA 24318, Phone: 703-624-3282
Specialties: Working straight knives, some fancy. Welcomes customer designs. **Patterns:** Hunters, fighters, daggers, Bowies and miniatures. **Technical:** Grinds 440C or customer preference. Offers some knives with jewelling. **Prices:** $100 to $250; some to $500. **Remarks:** Part-time maker; first knife sold in 1983. **Mark:** First and middle initials, last name stamped.

HAWKINS, BUDDY, PO Box 5969, Texarkana, TX 75505-5969, Phone: 903-838-7917

HAWKINS, RADE, 110 Buckeye Rd, Fayetteville, GA 30214, Phone: 770-964-1177, Fax: 770-306-2877
Specialties: Exotic steels, custom designs, one-of-a-kind knives. **Patterns:** All styles. **Technical:** Grinds CPM10V, CPM440V, Vascomax C-350, and Damascus. **Prices:** Start at $190. **Remarks:** Full-time maker; first knife sold in 1972. **Mark:** Rade Hawkins Custom Knives.

HAYES, DOLORES, PO Box 41405, Los Angeles, CA 90041, Phone: 213-258-9923
Specialties: High-art working and using straight knives of her design. **Patterns:** Art knives and miniatures. **Technical:** Grinds 440C, stainless AEB, commercial Damascus and ATS-34. **Prices:** $50 to $500; some to $2000. **Remarks:** Spare-time maker; first knife sold in 1978. **Mark:** Last name.

HAYES, WALLY, 1026 Old Montreal Rd, Orleans, Ont., CANADA K4A-3N2, Phone: 613-824-9520
Specialties: Classic and fancy straight knives and folders. **Patterns:** Daggers, Bowies, fighters, tantos. **Technical:** Forges own Damascus and O1; engraves. **Prices:** $150 to $14,000. **Mark:** Last name, M. S. and serial number.

HAYES, SCOTTY, Texarkana College, 2500 N ROBINSON RD, TEXARKANA, TX 75501, Phone: 903-838-4541, x3236, Fax: 903-832-5030
Specialties: ABS School of Bladesmithing.

HAYNES, JERRY, 6902 Teton Ridge, San Antonio, TX 78233, Phone: 210-599-2928
Specialties: Working straight knives and folders of his design, also historical blades. **Patterns:** Hunters, skinners, carving knives, fighters, renaissance daggers, locking folders and kitchen knives. **Technical:** Grinds ATS-34, CPM, Stellite 6K, and acquired Damascus. Prefers exotic handle materials. Has B. A. in design. Studied with R. Buckminster Fuller. **Prices:** $200 to $1200. **Remarks:** Part-time maker - will go full-time after retirement in 2007. First knife sold in 1953. **Mark:** Arrowhead and last name.

HAYNIE, CHARLES, 125 Cherry Lane, Toccoa, GA 30577, Phone: 706-886-8665

HAYS, MARK, Hays Handmade Knives, 1008 Kavanagh Dr, Austin, TX 78748, Phone: 512-292-4410
Specialties: Working straight knives and folders. Patterns inspired by Randall & Stone. **Patterns:** Bowies, hunters and slip-joint folders. **Technical:** 440C stock removal. Repairs and restores Stone knives. **Prices:** Start at $200. **Remarks:** Part-time maker, brochure available, with Stone knives 1974-1983, 1990-1991. **Mark:** First initial, last name, state and serial number.

HAZEN, MARK, 9600 Surrey Rd, Charlotte, NC 28227, Phone: 704-573-0904, Fax: 704-573-0052
Specialties: Working/using straight knives of his design and to customer specs. **Patterns:** Hunters/skinners, fillet, utility/camp, fighters, short swords. **Technical:** Grinds 154CM, ATS-34, 440C. **Prices:** $75 to $450; some to $1500. **Remarks:** Part-time maker. First knife sold 1982. **Mark:** Name with cross in it, stamped in blade.

HEADRICK, GARY, 122 Blvd Wilson, Juan Les Pins, FRANCE 06160, Phone: 04 93 61 25 15
Specialties: Hi-tech folders with natural furnishings. **Patterns:** Damascus & Mokumes. **Prices:** $500 to $2000. **Remarks:** Full-time maker for last 5 years. **Mark:** G/P in a circle. **Other:** 8 years active.

HEARN, TERRY L., Rt 14 Box 7676, Lufkin, TX 75904, Phone: 936-632-5045

HEASMAN, H. G., 28 St. Mary's Rd, Llandudno, N. Wales U. K. LL302UB, Phone: UK)0492-876351
Specialties: Miniatures only. **Patterns:** Bowies, daggers and swords. **Technical:** Files from stock high-carbon and stainless steel. **Prices:** $400 to $600. **Remarks:** Part-time maker; first knife sold in 1975. Doing business as Reduced Reality. **Mark:** NA.

HEDRICK, DON, 131 Beechwood Hills, Newport News, VA 23608, Phone: 757-877-8100
Specialties: Working straight knives; period pieces and fantasy knives. **Patterns:** Hunters, boots, Bowies and miniatures. **Technical:** Grinds 440C and commercial Damascus. Also makes micro-mini Randall replicas. **Prices:** $150 to $550; some to $1200. **Remarks:** Part-time maker; first knife sold in 1982. **Mark:** First initial, last name in oval logo.

HEFLIN, CHRISTOPHER M., 6013 Jocelyn Hollow Rd, Nashville, TN 37205, Phone: 615-352-3909

HEGWALD, J. L., 1106 Charles, Humboldt, KS 66748, Phone: 316-473-3523
Specialties: Working straight knives, some fancy. **Patterns:** Makes Bowies, miniatures. **Technical:** Forges or grinds O1, L6, 440C; mixes materials in handles. **Prices:** $35 to $200; some higher. **Remarks:** Part-time maker; first knife sold in 1983. **Mark:** First and middle initials.

HEHN, RICHARD KARL, Lehnmuehler Str. 1, 55444 Dorrebach, GERMANY, Phone: 06724 3152
Specialties: High-tech, full integral working knives. **Patterns:** Hunters, fighters & daggers. **Technical:** Grinds CPM T-440V, CPM T-420V, forges his own stainless Damascus. **Prices:** $1000 to $10,000. **Remarks:** Full-time maker; first knife sold in 1963. **Mark:** Runic last initial in logo.

HEINZ, JOHN, 611 Cafferty Rd, Upper Black Eddy, PA 18972, Phone: 610-847-8535

HEITLER, HENRY, PO Box 15025, Tampa, FL 33684-5025, Phone: 813-933-1645
Specialties: Traditional working and using straight knives of his design and to customer specs. **Patterns:** Fighters, hunters, utility/camp knives and fillet knives. **Technical:** Flat-grinds ATS-34; offers tapered tangs. **Prices:** $135 to $450; some to $600. **Remarks:** Part-time maker; first knife sold in 1990. **Mark:** First initial, last name, city, state circling double H's.

HELSCHER, JOHN W., 2645 Highway 1, Washington, IA 52353, Phone: 319-653-7310

HELTON, ROY, Helton Knives, 2941 Comstock St, San Diego, CA 92111, Phone: 858-277-5024

HEMBROOK KNIVES, Ron Hembrook, PO Box 201, Neosho, WI 53059, Phone: 920-625-3607
Specialties: Hunters, working knives. **Technical:** Grinds ATS-34, 440C, 01 & Damascus. **Prices:** $125 to $750; some to $1000. **Remarks:** First knife sold in 1980. **Mark:** Hembrook plus a serial number. Part-time maker, makes hunters, daggers, Bowies, folders and miniatures.

HEMPERLEY, GLEN, 21106 Roydencrest, Spring, TX 77388, Phone: 281-350-0283
Specialties: Specializes in hunting knives, does fixed and folding knives.

HENDRICKS, SAMUEL J., 2162 Van Buren Rd, Maurertown, VA 22644, Phone: 703-436-3305
Specialties: Integral hunters and skinners of thin design. **Patterns:** Boots, hunters and locking folders. **Technical:** Grinds ATS-34, 440C and D2. Integral liners and bolsters of N-S and 7075 T6 aircraft aluminum. Does leatherwork. **Prices:** $50 to $250; some to $500. **Remarks:** Full-time maker; first knife sold in 1992. **Mark:** First and middle initials, last name, city and state in football-style logo.

HENDRICKSON, SHAWN, 2327 Kaetzel Rd, Knoxville, MD 21758, Phone: 301-432-4306
Specialties: Hunting knives. **Patterns:** Clip points, drop points and trailing point hunters. **Technical:** Forges 5160, 1084 and L6. **Prices:** $175 to $400.

custom knifemakers

HENDRICKSON, E. JAY, 4204 Ballenger Creek Pike, Frederick, MD 21703, Phone: 301-663-6923
Specialties: Classic collectors and working straight knives of his design. **Patterns:** Bowies, Kukri's, camp, hunters, and fighters. **Technical:** Forges 06, 1084, 5160, 52100, D2, L6 and W2; makes Damascus; offers silver wire inlay. Moran-styles on order. **Prices:** $400 to $5000. **Remarks:** Full-time maker; first knife sold in 1975. **Mark:** Last name, M. S.

HENDRIX, WAYNE, 9636 Burton's Ferry Hwy, Allendale, SC 29810, Phone: 803-584-3825, Fax: 803-584-3825
Specialties: Working/using knives of his design. **Patterns:** Hunters and fillet knives. **Technical:** Grinds ATS-34, D2 and 440C. **Prices:** $55 to $300. **Remarks:** Full-time maker; first knife sold in 1985. **Mark:** Last name.

HENDRIX, JERRY, Hendrix Custom Knives, 175 Skyland Dr. Ext., Clinton, SC 29325, Phone: 864-833-2659
Specialties: Traditional working straight knives of all designs. **Patterns:** Hunters, utility, boot, bird and fishing. **Technical:** grinds ATS-34 and 440C. **Prices:** $85-$275. **Remarks:** Full-time maker. **Mark:** Full name in shape of knife. **Other:** Hand stitched, waxed leather sheaths.

HENNON, ROBERT, 940 Vincent Lane, Ft. Walton Beach, FL 32547, Phone: 904-862-9734

HENRIKSEN, HANS J., Birkegaardsvej 24, DK 3200 Helsinge, DEN-MARK, Fax: 45 4879 4899
Specialties: Zirconia ceramic blades. **Patterns:** Customer designs. **Technical:** Slip-cast zirconia-water mix in plaster mould; offers hidden or full tang. **Prices:** White blades start at $10cm; colored +50 percent. **Remarks:** Part-time maker; first ceramic blade sold in 1989. **Mark:** Initial logo.

HENRY & SON, PETER, 332 Nine Mile Ride, Wokingham, Berkshire, ENGLAND RG40 3NJ, Phone: 0118-9734475
Specialties: Period pieces. **Patterns:** Period pieces only—Scottish dirks, sgian dubhs and Bowies, modern hunters. **Technical:** Grinds O1. **Prices:** £50 to £250 or $80 to $400; Bowies £110 to £120. **Remarks:** Full-time maker; first knife sold in 1974. **Mark:** P. Henry & Son.

HENSLEY, WAYNE, PO Box 904, Conyers, GA 30012, Phone: 770-483-8938
Specialties: Period pieces and fancy working knives. **Patterns:** Boots to Bowies, locking folders to miniatures. Large variety of straight knives. **Technical:** Grinds ATS-34, 440C, D2 and commercial Damascus. **Prices:** $85 and up. **Remarks:** Full-time maker; first knife sold in 1974. **Mark:** Last name.

HERBST, PETER, Komotauer Strasse 26, 91207 Lauf a. d. Pegn., GERMANY, Phone: 09123-13315, Fax: 09123-13379
Specialties: Working/using knives and folders of his design. **Patterns:** Hunters, fighters and daggers; interframe and integral. **Technical:** Grinds CPM-T-440V, UHB-Elmax, ATS-34 and stainless Damascus. **Prices:** $300 to $3000; some to $8000. **Remarks:** Full-time maker; first knife sold in 1981. **Mark:** First initial, last name.

HERGERT, BOB, 12 Geer Circle, Port Orford, OR 97465, Phone: 541-332-3010

HERMAN, TIM, 7721 Foster, Overland Park, KS 66204, Phone: 913-649-3860, Fax: 913-649-0603
Specialties: Investment-grade folders of his design; interframes and bolster frames. **Patterns:** Interframes and new designs in carved stainless. **Technical:** Grinds ATS-34 and damasteel Damascus. Engraves and gold inlays with pearl, jade, lapis and Australian opal. **Prices:** $1000 to $15,000. **Remarks:** Full-time maker; first knife sold in 1978. **Mark:** Etched signature.

HERMES, DANA E., 39594 Kona Ct, Fremont, CA 94538, Phone: 415-490-0393
Specialties: Fancy and embellished classic straight knives of his design. **Patterns:** Hunters and Bowies. **Technical:** Grinds 440C and D2. **Prices:** $200 to $600; some to $1000. **Remarks:** Spare-time maker; first knife sold in 1985. **Mark:** Last name.

HERNDON, WM. R. "BILL", 32520 Michigan St, Acton, CA 93510, Phone: 661-269-5860, Fax: 661-269-4568
Specialties: Straight knives, plain and fancy. **Technical:** Carbon steel (white and blued), Damascus, stainless steels. **Prices:** Start at $120. **Remarks:** Full-time maker; first knife sold in 1976. **Mark:** Signature and/or helm logo.

HERRING, MORRIS, Box 85 721 W Line St, Dyer, AR 72935, Phone: 501-997-8861

HERRON, GEORGE, 474 Antonio Way, Springfield, SC 29146, Phone: 803-258-3914
Specialties: High-tech working and using straight knives; some folders. **Patterns:** Hunters, fighters, boots in personal styles. **Technical:** Grinds 154CM, ATS-34. **Prices:** $150 to $1000; some to $2000. **Remarks:** Full-time maker; first knife sold in 1963. About 12 year back log. Not excepting orders. No catalog. **Mark:** Last name in script.

HESSER, DAVID, PO Box 1079, Dripping Springs, TX 78620, Phone: 512-894-0100
Specialties: High-art daggers and fantasy knives of his design; court weapons of the Renaissance. **Patterns:** Daggers, swords, axes, miniatures and sheath knives. **Technical:** Forges 1065, 1095, O1, D2 and recycled tool steel. Offers custom lapidary work and stone-setting, stone handles and custom hardwood scabbards. **Prices:** $95 to $500; some to $6000. **Remarks:** Full-time maker; first knife sold in 1989. Doing business as Exotic Blades. **Mark:** Last name, year.

HETHCOAT, DON, Box 1764, Clovis, NM 88101, Phone: 505-762-5721
Specialties: Liner-lock and multi-blade folders. **Patterns:** Hunters, Bowies. **Technical:** Grinds stainless; forges Damascus. **Prices:** Moderate to upscale. **Remarks:** Full-time maker; first knife sold in 1969. **Mark:** Last name on all.

HIBBEN, WESTLEY G., 14101 Sunview Dr, Anchorage, AK 99515
Specialties: Working straight knives of his design or to customer specs. **Patterns:** Hunters, fighters, daggers, combat knives and some fantasy pieces. **Technical:** Grinds 440C mostly. Filework available. **Prices:** $200 to $400; some to $3000. **Remarks:** Part-time maker; first knife sold in 1988. **Mark:** Signature.

HIBBEN, JOLEEN, PO Box 172, LaGrange, KY 40031, Phone: 502-222-0983
Specialties: Miniature straight knives of her design; period pieces. **Patterns:** Hunters, axes and fantasy knives. **Technical:** Grinds Damascus, 1095 tool steel and stainless 440C or ATS-34. Uses wood, ivory, bone, feathers and claws on/for handles. **Prices:** $60 to $200. **Remarks:** Spare-time maker; first knife sold in 1991. **Mark:** Initials or first name.

HIBBEN, DARYL, PO Box 172, LaGrange, KY 40031-0172, Phone: 502-222-0983
Specialties: Working straight knives, some fancy to customer specs. **Patterns:** Hunters, fighters, Bowies, short sword, art and fantasy. **Technical:** Grinds 440C, ATS-34, 154CM, Damascus; prefers hollow-grinds. **Prices:** $175 to $3000. **Remarks:** Full-time maker; first knife sold in 1979. **Mark:** Etched full name in script.

HIBBEN, GIL, PO Box 13, LaGrange, KY 40031, Phone: 502-222-1397, Fax: 502-222-2676
Specialties: Working knives and fantasy pieces to customer specs. **Patterns:** Full range of straight knives, including swords, axes and miniatures; some locking folders. **Technical:** Grinds ATS-34, 440C and 154CM. **Prices:** $300 to $2000; some to $10,000. **Remarks:** Full-time maker; first knife sold in 1957. Maker and designer of *Rambo III* knife; made swords for movie *Marked for Death* and throwing knife for movie *Under Seige*; made belt buckle knife and knives for movie *Perfect Weapon*; made knives featured in movie *Star Trek the Next Generation,* Star Trek Nemesis 1990 inductee cutlery hall of fame; designer for United Cutlery. Official klingon armourer for Star Trek, over 34 movies and TV productions. **Mark:** Hibben Knives. City and state, or signature.

HIGGINS, J. P. DR., Art Knives By, 120 N Pheasant Run, Coupeville, WA 98239, Phone: 360-678-9269, Fax: 360-678-9269
Specialties: Since 2003 Dr. J. P. Higgins and Tom Sterling have created a unique collaboration of one-of-a-kind, ultra-quality art knives with percussion or pressured flaked stone blades and creatively sculpted handles. Their knives are often highly influenced by the traditions of Japanese netsuke and unique fusions of cultures, reflecting stylistically integrated choices of exotic hardwoods, fossil ivories and semi-precious materials, contrasting inlays and polychromed and pyrographed details. **Prices:** $300-$900. Limited output ensures highest quality artwork and exceptional levels of craftsmanship. Signatures Sterling and Higgins.

HIGH, TOM, 5474 S. 112. 8 Rd, Alamosa, CO 81101, Phone: 719-589-2108
Specialties: Hunters, some fancy. **Patterns:** Drop-points in several shapes; some semi-skinners. Knives designed by and for top outfitters and guides. **Technical:** Grinds ATS-34; likes hollow-grinds, mirror finishes; prefers scrim able handles. **Prices:** $175 to $8000. **Remarks:** Full-time maker; first knife sold in 1965. Limited edition wildlife series knives. **Mark:** Initials connected; arrow through last name on fancy knives.

HILKER, THOMAS N., PO Box 409, Williams, OR 97544, Phone: 541-846-6461
Specialties: Traditional working straight knives and folders. **Patterns:** Folding skinner in two sizes, Bowies, fork and knife sets, camp knives and interchangeable. **Technical:** Grinds D2, 440C and ATS-34. Heat-treats. **Prices:** $50 to $350; some to $400. Doing business as Thunderbolt Artisans. Only limited production models available; not currently taking orders. **Remarks:** Full-time maker; first knife sold in 1983. **Mark:** Last name.

HILL, HOWARD E., 111 Mission Lane, Polson, MT 59860, Phone: 406-883-3405, Fax: 406-883-3486
Specialties: Autos, complete new design, legal in Montana (with permit). **Patterns:** Bowies, daggers, skinners and lock-back folders. **Technical:** Grinds 440C; uses micro and satin finish. **Prices:** $150 to $1000. **Remarks:** Full-time maker; first knife sold in 1981. **Mark:** Persuader.

HILL, STEVE E., 40 Rand Pond Rd, Goshen, NH 03752, Phone: 603-863-4762, Fax: 603-863-4762
Specialties: Fancy manual and automatic liner-lock folders, some working grade. **Patterns:** Classic to cool folding and fixed blade designs. **Technical:** Grinds Damascus and occasional 440C, D2. Prefers natural handle materials; offers elaborate filework, carving, and inlays. **Prices:** $375 to $5000; some higher. **Remarks:** Full-time maker; first knife sold in 1978. **Mark:** First initial, last name and handmade. **Other:** Knife maker to Rock 'n' Roll stars.

HILL, RICK, 20 Nassau, Maryville, IL 62062-5618, Phone: 618-288-4370
Specialties: Working knives and period pieces to customer specs. **Patterns:** Hunters, locking folders, fighters and daggers. **Technical:** Grinds D2, 440C and 154CM; forges his own Damascus. **Prices:** $75 to $500; some to $3000. **Remarks:** Part-time maker; first knife sold in 1983. **Mark:** Full name in hill shape logo.

HILLMAN, CHARLES, 225 Waldoboro Rd, Friendship, ME 04547, Phone: 207-832-4634
Specialties: Working knives of my own or custom design. Heavy Scagel influence. **Patterns:** Hunters, fishing, camp and general utility. Occasional folders. **Technical:** Grinds D2 and 440C. File work, blade and handle carving, engraving. Natural handle materials-antler, bone, leather, wood, horn. Sheaths made to order. **Prices:** $60 to $500. **Remarks:** Part-time maker; first knife sold 1986. **Mark:** Last name in oak leaf.

HINDERER, RICK, 5423 Kister Rd, Wooster, OH 44691, Phone: 216-263-0962
Specialties: Working knives to one-of-a-kind Damascus straight knives and folders. **Patterns:** All. **Technical:** Grinds ATS-34 and D2; forges O1, W2 and his own nickel Damascus steel. **Prices:** $50 to $3200. **Remarks:** Part-time maker; first knife sold in 1988. Doing business as Mustang Forge. **Mark:** Initials or first initial, last name.

HINK III, LES, 1599 Aptos Lane, Stockton, CA 95206, Phone: 209-547-1292
Specialties: Working straight knives and traditional folders in standard patterns or to customer specs. **Patterns:** Hunting and utility/camp knives; others on request. **Technical:** Grinds carbon and stainless steels. **Prices:** $80 to $200; some higher. **Remarks:** Part-time maker; first knife sold in 1980. **Mark:** Last name, or last name 3.

HINMAN, TED, 183 Highland Ave, Watertown, MA 02472

HINSON AND SON, R., 2419 Edgewood Rd, Columbus, GA 31906, Phone: 706-327-6801
Specialties: Working straight knives and folders. **Patterns:** Locking folders, liner-locks, combat knives and swords. **Technical:** Grinds 440C and commercial Damascus. **Prices:** $100 to $350; some to $1500. **Remarks:** Part-time maker; first knife sold in 1983. Son Bob is co-worker. **Mark:** HINSON, city and state.

HINTZ, GERALD M., 5402 Sahara Ct, Helena, MT 59602, Phone: 406-458-5412
Specialties: Fancy, high-art, working/using knives of his design. **Patterns:** Bowies, hunters, daggers, fish fillet and utility/camp knives. **Technical:** Forges ATS-34, 440C and D2. Animal art in horn handles or in the blade. **Prices:** $75 to $400; some to $1000. **Remarks:** Part-time maker; first knife sold in 1980. Doing business as Big Joe's Custom Knives. Will take custom orders. **Mark:** F. S. or W. S. with first and middle initials and last name.

HIRAYAMA, HARUMI, 4-5-13 Kitamachi, Warabi City, Saitama Pref. 335-0001, JAPAN, Phone: 048-443-2248, Fax: 048-443-2248
Specialties: High-tech working knives of her design. **Patterns:** Locking folders, interframes, straight gents and slip-joints. **Technical:** Grinds 440C or equivalent; uses natural handle materials and gold. **Prices:** Start at $700. **Remarks:** Part-time maker; first knife sold in 1985. **Mark:** First initial, last name.

HIROTO, FUJIHARA, 2-34-7 Koioosako Nishi-ku Hiroshima-city, Hiroshima, JAPAN, Phone: 082-271-8389

HITCHMOUGH, HOWARD, 95 Old Street Road, Peterborough, NH 03458-1637, Phone: 603-924-9646, Fax: 603-924-9595
Specialties: High class folding knives. **Patterns:** Lock-back folders, liner-locks, pocket knives. **Technical:** Uses ATS-34, stainless Damascus, titanium, gold and gemstones. Prefers hand-rubbed finishes and natural handle materials. **Prices:** $850 to $3500; some to $4500. **Remarks:** Full-time maker; first knife sold in 1967. **Mark:** Last name.

HOBART, GENE, 100 Shedd Rd, Windsor, NY 13865, Phone: 607-655-1345

HOCKENBARY, WARREN E., 1806 Vallecito Dr, San Pedro, CA 90732

HOCKENSMITH, DAN, 21390 Cty Line Rd 1, Berthoud, CO 80513, Phone: 970-669-5404
Specialties: Traditional working and using straight knives of his design. **Patterns:** Hunters, Bowies, folders and utility/camp knives. **Technical:** Uses his Damascus, 5160, carbon steel. Hand forged. **Prices:** $150 to $600; some to $1000. **Remarks:** full-time maker; first knife sold in 1987. **Mark:** Name, town & state, anvil

HODGE, J. B., 1100 Woodmont Ave. SE, Huntsville, AL 35801, Phone: 205-536-8388
Specialties: Fancy working folders. **Patterns:** Slip-joints. **Technical:** Grinds 154CM and ATS-34. **Prices:** Start at $175. **Remarks:** Part-time maker; first knife sold in 1978. Not currently taking orders. **Mark:** Name, city and state.

HODGE III, JOHN, 422 S. 15th St, Palatka, FL 32177, Phone: 904-328-3897
Specialties: Fancy straight knives and folders. **Patterns:** Various. **Technical:** Pattern-welded Damascus—"Southern-style." **Prices:** To $1000. **Remarks:** Part-time maker; first knife sold in 1981. **Mark:** JH3 logo.

HODGSON, RICHARD J., 9081 Tahoe Lane, Boulder, CO 80301, Phone: 303-665-9460
Specialties: Straight knives and folders in standard patterns. **Patterns:** High-tech knives in various patterns. **Technical:** Grinds 440C, AEB-L and CPM. **Prices:** $850 to $2200. **Remarks:** Part-time maker. **Mark:** None.

HOEL, STEVE, PO Box 283, Pine, AZ 85544, Phone: 602-476-4278
Specialties: Investor-class folders, straight knives and period pieces of his design. **Patterns:** Folding interframes lockers and slip-joints; straight Bowies, boots and daggers. **Technical:** Grinds 154CM, ATS-34 and commercial Damascus. **Prices:** $600 to $1200; some to $7500. **Remarks:** Full-time maker. **Mark:** Initial logo with name and address.

HOFER, LOUIS, Gen Del, Rose Prairie BC, CANADA V0C 2H0, Phone: 250-630-2513

HOFFMAN, KEVIN L., 14672 Kristenright Lane, Orlando, FL 32826-5305, Phone: 407 207-2643, Fax: 407 207-2643
Specialties: High-tech working knives, distinctive folders. **Patterns:** Frame lock folders. **Technical:** Grinds ATS-34, Damascus; titanium folders. Makes Kydex sheaths. **Prices:** $400 to $2000. **Remarks:** Full-time maker since 1981. **Mark:** KLH.

HOFFMANN, UWE H., PO Box 60114, Vancouver, BC, CANADA V5W 4B5, Phone: 604-572-7320 (after 5 p. m.)
Specialties: High-tech working knives, folders and fantasy knives of his design or to customer specs. **Patterns:** Hunters, fishing knives, combat and survival knives, folders and diver's knives. **Technical:** Grinds 440C, ATS-34, D2 and commercial Damascus. **Prices:** $95 to $900; some to $2000 and higher. **Remarks:** Full-time maker; first knife sold in 1985. **Mark:** Hoffmann Handmade Knives.

HOGAN, THOMAS R., 2802 S. Heritage Av, Boise, ID 83709, Phone: 208-362-7848

HOGSTROM, ANDERS T., 2130 Valerga Dr, Apt 8, Belmont, CA 94002
Specialties: Short Dirks of own design. For select pieces makes wooden display boxes. **Patterns:** Dirks, Daggers, Fighters and an occasional sword. **Technical:** Grinds 1050 high carbon, ATS-34, 440C, occasional Damascus and ancient ivories. Does clay tempering and uses exotic hardwoods. **Prices:** Start at $225. **Marks:** Last name in various typefaces.

HOKE, THOMAS M., 3103 Smith Ln, LaGrange, KY 40031, Phone: 502-222-0350
Specialties: Working/using knives, straight knives. Own designs and customer specs. **Patterns:** Daggers, Bowies, hunters, fighters, short swords. **Technical:** Grind 440C, Damascus and ATS-34. Filework on all knives. Tooling on sheaths (custom fit on all knives). Any handle material, mostly exotic. **Prices:** $100 to $700; some to $1500. **Remarks:** Full-time maker, first knife sold in 1986. **Mark:** Dragon on banner which says T. M. Hoke.

HOLBROOK, H. L., Rt. #3, Box 585, Olive Hill, KY 41164, Phone: 606-738-6542/606-738-6842 Shop
Specialties: Traditional working using straight knives and folders of his design, to customer specs and in standard patterns. **Patterns:** Hunters, folders. **Technical:** Grinds 440C, ATS-34 and D2. Blades have hand-rubbed satin finish. Uses exotic woods, stag and Micarta. Hand-sewn sheath with each straight knife. **Prices:** $90 to $270; some to $400. **Remarks:** Part-time maker; first knife sold in 1983. Doing business as Holbrook knives. **Mark:** Name, city, state.

custom knifemakers

HOLDEN, LARRY, PO Box 2017, Ridgecrest, CA 93555, Phone: 760-375-7955
Specialties: Sculptured high art, fantasy, and classical fixed blade knives of his design. **Patterns:** Sculptured art knives, fantasy, Bowies, bustier, traditional or non traditional. Will work with customer on designs. **Technical:** Hand grinds modern steels, Boye dendritic blanks, Damascus. Sculpts integrated blade, handle, and sheath designs. Mastodon ivory, natural, and exotic materials. Casts in precious metals. **Prices:** $300 and up. **Remarks:** Full-time maker, first complete knife sold 1995. **Mark:** Dragon logo followed by makers name and city.

HOLDER, D'ALTON, 7148 W. Country Gables Dr, Peoria, AZ 85381, Phone: 623-878-3064, Fax: 623-878-3964
Specialties: Deluxe working knives and high-art hunters. **Patterns:** Drop-point hunters, fighters, Bowies, miniatures and locking folders. **Technical:** Grinds 440C and 154CM; uses amber and other materials in combination on stick tangs. **Prices:** $300 to $1000; some to $2000. **Remarks:** Full-time maker; first knife sold in 1966. **Mark:** D'HOLDER, city and state.

HOLLAND, JOHN H., 1580 Nassau St, Titusville, FL 32780, Phone: 321-267-4378
Specialties: Traditional and fancy working/using straight knives and folders of his design, to customer specs and in standard patterns. **Patterns:** Hunters, and slip-joint folders. **Technical:** Grinds 440V and 440C. Offers engraving. **Prices:** $200 to $500; some to $1000. **Remarks:** Part-time maker; first knife sold in 1988. doing business as Holland Knives. **Mark:** First and last name, city, state.

HOLLAR, BOB, 701 2nd Ave SW, Great Falls, MT 59404, Phone: 406-268-8252
Specialties: Working/using straight knives and folders of his design and to customer specs; period pieces. **Patterns:** Fighters, hunters, liners & back lock folders. **Technical:** Forges 52100, 5160, 15N20 & 1084 (Damascus)*. **Prices:** $225 to $650; some to $1500. **Remarks:** Full-time maker. Doing business as Goshawk Knives. **Mark:** Goshawk stamped. **Other:** *Burled woods, stag, ivory; all stabilized material for handles.

HOLLOWAY, PAUL, 714 Burksdale Rd, Norfolk, VA 23518, Phone: 804-588-7071
Specialties: Working straight knives and folders to customer specs. **Patterns:** Lockers and slip-joints; fighters and boots; fishing and push knives, from swords to miniatures. **Technical:** Grinds A2, D2, 154CM, 440C and ATS-34. **Prices:** $125 to $400; some to $1200. **Remarks:** Part-time maker; first knife sold in 1981. **Mark:** Last name, or last name and city in logo.

HOLMES, ROBERT, 1431 S Eugene St, Baton Rouge, LA 70808-1043, Phone: 504-291-4864
Specialties: Using straight knives and folders of his design or to customer specs. **Patterns:** Bowies, utility hunters, camp knives, skinners, slip-joint and lock-back folders. **Technical:** Forges 1065, 1095 and L6. Makes his own Damascus and cable Damascus. Offers clay tempering. **Prices:** $150 to $1500. **Remarks:** Part-time maker; first knife sold in 1988. **Mark:** DOC HOLMES, or anvil logo with last initial inside.

HOLUM, MORTEN, Bolerskrenten 28, 0691, Oslo, NORWAY, Phone: 011-47-22-27-69-96
Specialties: Working straight knives. **Patterns:** Traditional Norwegian knives, hunters, fighters, axes. **Technical:** Forges Damascus. Uses his own blades. **Prices:** $200 to $800; some to $1500. **Remarks:** Part-time maker; first knife sold in 1986. **Mark:** Last name.

HORN, JESS, 2526 Lansdown Rd, Eugene, OR 97404, Phone: 541-463-1510
Specialties: Investor-class working folders; period pieces; collectibles. **Patterns:** High-tech design and finish in folders; liner-locks, traditional slip-joints and featherweight models. **Technical:** Grinds ATS-34, 154CM. **Prices:** Start at $1000. **Remarks:** Full-time maker; first knife sold in 1968. **Mark:** Full name or last name.

HORN, DES, 5 Wenlock Rd, Newlands, 7700 Cape Town, SOUTH AFRICA, Phone: 27 21 671 5795, Fax: 27 21 671 5795
Specialties: Folding knives. **Patterns:** Ball release side lock mechanism and interframe automatics. **Technical:** Prefers working in totally stainless materials. **Prices:** $400 to $2000. **Remarks:** Enjoys working in gold, titanium, meteorite, pearl & mammoth. **Mark:** Des Horn.

HORNE, GRACE, 182 Crimicar Ln, Sheffield Britian, UNITED KINGDOM s10 4EJ
Specialties: Knives of own design including kitchen and utility knives for people with reduced hand use. **Technical:** Working at Sheffield Hallam University researching innovative, contemporary Damascus steels using non-traditional methods of manufacture. **Remarks:** Spare-time maker/full-time researcher. **Mark:** 'gH' & 'Sheffield'.

HORTON, SCOT, PO Box 451, Buhl, ID 83316, Phone: 208-543-4222
Specialties: Traditional working stiff knives and folders. **Patterns:** Hunters, skinners, utility and show knives. **Technical:** Grinds ATS-34. Uses stag, abalone and exotic woods. **Prices:** $200 to $2500. **Remarks:** First knife sold in 1990. **Mark:** Full name in arch underlined with arrow, city, state.

HOSSOM, JERRY, 3585 Schilling ridge, Duluth, GA 30096, Phone: 770-449-7809
Specialties: Working straight knives of his own design. **Patterns:** Fighters, combat knives, modern Bowies and daggers, modern swords, concealment knives for military and LE uses. **Technical:** Grinds 154CM, S30V, CPM-3V and stainless Damascus. Uses natural and synthetic handle materials. **Prices:** $250-1500; some higher. **Remarks:** Full-time maker since 1997. First knife sold in 1983. **Mark:** First initial and last name, includes city and state since 2002.

HOUSE, LAWRENCE, 932 Eastview Dr, Canyon Lake, TX 78133, Phone: 830-899-6932

HOUSE, GARY, 2851 Pierce Rd, Ephrata, WA 98823, Phone: 509-754-3272
Specialties: Mosaic Damascus bar stock. **Patterns:** Unlimited, SW Indian designs, geometric patterns, using 1084, 15N20 & some nickel. **Prices:** $50 per inch and up. **Remarks:** Some of the finest and most unique patterns available.

HOWARD, DURVYN M., 4220 McLain St. S., Hokes Bluff, AL 35903, Phone: 256-492-5720
Specialties: Collectible upscale folders; one of kinds, gentlemen's folders. Multiple patents. **Patterns:** Conceptual designs; each unique and different. **Technical:** Uses natural and exotic materials and precious metals. **Prices:** $5000 to $25,000. **Remarks:** Full-time maker; by commission or available work. **Mark:** Howard: new for 2000; Howard in Garamond Narrow "etched". **Other:** Work displayed at select shows, K. G. Show etc.

HOWE, TORI, 13000 E Stampede Rd, Athol, ID 83801

HOWELL, TED, 1294 Wilson Rd, Wetumpka, AL 36092, Phone: 205-569-2281, Fax: 205-569-1764
Specialties: Working/using straight knives and folders of his design; period pieces. **Patterns:** Bowies, fighters, hunters. **Technical:** Forges 5160, 1085 and cable. Offers light engraving and scrimshaw; filework. **Prices:** $75 to $250; some to $450. **Remarks:** Part-time maker; first knife sold in 1991. Doing business as Howell Co. **Mark:** Last name, Slapout AL.

HOWELL, ROBERT L., Box 1617, Kilgore, TX 75663, Phone: 903-986-4364
Specialties: Straight knives and folders of his design. **Patterns:** Hunters and locking folders. **Technical:** Grinds D2 and ATS-34; forges and grinds Damascus. **Prices:** $75 to $200; some to $2500. **Remarks:** Part-time maker; first knife sold in 1978. Doing business as Howell Knives. **Mark:** Last name.

HOWELL, JASON G., 213 Buffalo Trl, Lake Jackson, TX 77566, Phone: 979-297-9454
Specialties: Fixed blades and liner-lock folders. Makes own Damascus. **Patterns:** Clip & drop point. **Prices:** $150 to $750. **Remarks:** I like making Mosaic Damascus out of the ordinary stuff. Member of TX Knifemakers & Collectors Association; apprentice in ABS; working towards Journeyman Stamp. **Mark:** Name, city, state.

HOWELL, LEN, 550 Lee Rd. 169, Opelika, AL 36804, Phone: 334-749-1942
Specialties: Traditional and working knives of his design and to customer specs. **Patterns:** Buckskinner, hunters and utility/camp knives. **Technical:** Forges cable Damascus, 1085 and 5160; makes own Damascus. **Mark:** Engraved last name.

HOWSER, JOHN C., 54 Bell Ln., Frankfort, KY 40601, Phone: 502-875-3678
Specialties: Slip joint folders (old patterns-multi blades). **Patterns:** traditional slip joint folders, lock-backs, hunters & fillet knives. **Technical:** ATS-34 standard steel, will use D-2, 440V-hand rubbed satin finish natural materials. **Prices:** $100-$400; some to $500. **Remarks:** Full-time maker; first knife sold in 1974. **Mark:** Signature or stamp.

HOY, KEN, 54744 Pinchot Dr, North Fork, CA 93643, Phone: 209-877-7805

HRISOULAS, JIM, 330 S. Decatur Ave, Suite 109, Las Vegas, NV 89107, Phone: 702-566-8551
Specialties: Working straight knives; period pieces. **Patterns:** Swords, daggers and sgian dubhs. **Technical:** Double-edged differential heat treating. **Prices:** $85 to $175; some to $600 and higher. **Remarks:** Full-time maker; first knife sold in 1973. Author of *The Complete Bladesmith, The Pattern Welded Blade* and *The Master Bladesmith*. Doing business as Salamander Armory. **Mark:** 8R logo and sword and salamander.

HUCKABEE, DALE, 254 Hwy 260, Maylene, AL 35114
Specialties: Fixed blade hunter & Bowies of my design. **Technical:** Steel used: 5160, 1095, 1084 & some Damascus. **Prices:** Starting at $95 & up,

depending on materials used. **Remarks:** Hand forged & stock removal. **Mark:** Stamped HUCKABEE. **Other:** Part-time maker.

HUDSON, C. ROBBIN, 22280 Frazier Rd, Rock Hall, MD 21661, Phone: 410-639-7273
Specialties: High-art working knives. **Patterns:** Hunters, Bowies, fighters and kitchen knives. **Technical:** Forges W2, nickel steel, pure nickel steel, composite and mosaic Damascus; makes knives one at a time. **Prices:** 500 to $1200; some to $5000. **Remarks:** Full-time maker; first knife sold in 1970. **Mark:** Last name and MS.

HUDSON, ROB, 340 Roush Rd, Northumberland, PA 17857, Phone: 570-473-9588
Specialties: Custom hunters, Bowies, daggers, tantos, custom orders. **Technical:** Grinds ATS-34, stainless, Damascus, hollow grinds or flat. Filework, finger grooves. Engraving and scrimshaw available. **Prices:** $200 to $700. **Remarks:** Full-time maker. Business: Rob's Custom Knives. **Mark:** Capital R, Capital H in script.

HUDSON, ANTHONY B., 279 Valley St, Midland, OH 45148, Phone: 937-783-5822

HUDSON, ROBERT, 3802 Black Cricket Ct, Humble, TX 77396, Phone: 713-454-7207
Specialties: Working straight knives of his design. **Patterns:** Bowies, hunters, skinners, fighters and utility knives. **Technical:** Grinds D2, 440C, 154CM and commercial Damascus. **Prices:** $85 to $350; some to $1500. **Remarks:** Part-time maker; first knife sold in 1980. **Mark:** Full name, handmade, city and state.

HUEY, STEVE, 5060 W Port St, Eugene, OR 97402, Phone: 541-484-7344
Specialties: Working straight knives, some one-of-a-kind. **Patterns:** Folders, fixed hunting, fighters, kitchen knives, some one-of-a-kind. **Technical:** D2 and ATS-34 carbon on request. **Prices:** $75 to $600. **Remarks:** Part-time maker; first knife sold in 1981. **Mark:** Last name in rectangle.

HUGHES, ED, 280 1/2 Holly Lane, Grand Junction, CO 81503, Phone: 970-243-8547
Specialties: Working and art folders. **Patterns:** Buys Damascus. **Technical:** Grinds stainless steels. Engraves. **Prices:** $300 and up. **Remarks:** Full-time maker; first knife sold in 1978. **Mark:** Name or initials.

HUGHES, LAWRENCE, 207 W. Crestway, Plainview, TX 79072, Phone: 806-293-5406
Specialties: Working and display knives. **Patterns:** Bowies, daggers, hunters, buckskinners. **Technical:** Grinds D2, 440C and 154CM. **Prices:** $125 to $300; some to $2000. **Remarks:** Full-time maker; first knife sold in 1979. **Mark:** Name with buffalo skull in center.

HUGHES, DAN, 13743 Persimmon Blvd., West Palm Beach, FL 33411
Specialties: Working straight knives to customer specs. **Patterns:** Hunters, fighters, fillet knives. **Technical:** Grinds 440C and ATS-34. **Prices:** $55 to $175; some to $300. **Remarks:** Part-time maker; first knife sold in 1984. **Mark:** Initials.

HUGHES, BILL, 110 Royale Dr, Texarkana, TX 75503, Phone: 903-838-0134

HUGHES, DARYLE, 10979 Leonard, Nunica, MI 49448, Phone: 616-837-6623
Specialties: Working knives. **Patterns:** Buckskinners, hunters, camp knives, kitchen and fishing knives. **Technical:** Forges and grinds W2, O1 and D2. **Prices:** $40 to $100; some to $400. **Remarks:** Part-time maker; first knife sold in 1979. **Mark:** Name and city in logo.

HULETT, STEVE, 115 Yellowstone Ave, West Yellowstone, MT 59758, Phone: 406-646-4116
Specialties: Classic, working/using knives, straight knives, folders. Your design, custom specs. **Patterns:** Utility/camp knives, hunters, and linerlock folders. **Technical:** Grinds 440C stainless steel, O1 Carbon, 1095. Shop is retail and knife shop—people watch their knives being made. We do everything in house—"all but smelt the ore, or tan the hide." **Prices:** $125 to $7000. **Remarks:** Full-time maker; first knife sold in 1994. **Mark:** Seldom seen knives/West Yellowstone Montana

HULL, MICHAEL J., 1330 Hermits Circle, Cottonwood, AZ 86326, Phone: 928-634-2871
Specialties: Period pieces and working knives. **Patterns:** Hunters, fighters, Bowies, camp and Mediterranean knives, etc. **Technical:** Grinds 440C, ATS-34 and BG42 and S30V. **Prices:** $125 to $750; some to $1000. **Remarks:** Full-time maker; first knife sold in 1983. **Mark:** Name, city, state.

HULSEY, HOYT, 379 Shiloh, Attalla, AL 35954, Phone: 256-538-6765
Specialties: Traditional working straight knives and folders of his design. **Patterns:** Hunters and utility/camp knives. **Technical:** Grinds 440C, ATS-34, O1 and A2. **Prices:** $75 to $250. **Remarks:** Part-time maker; first knife sold in 1989. **Mark:** Hoyt Hulsey Attalla AL.

HUMENICK, ROY, PO Box 55, Rescue, CA 95672
Specialties: Multiblade folders. **Patterns:** Original folder & fixed blade designs, also traditional patterns. **Technical:** Grinds premium steels and Damascus. **Prices:** $350 and up; some to $1500. **Remarks:** First knife sold in 1984. **Mark:** Last name in ARC.

HUMPHREYS, JOEL, 3260 Palmer Rd, Bowling Green, FL 33834-9801, Phone: 863-773-0439
Specialties: Traditional working/using straight knives and folders of his design and in standard patterns. **Patterns:** Hunters, folders and utility/camp knives. **Technical:** Grinds ATS-34, D2, 440C. All knives have tapered tangs, mitered bolster/handle joints, handles of horn or bone fitted sheaths. **Prices:** $135 to $225; some to $350. **Remarks:** Part-time maker; first knife sold in 1990. Doing business as Sovereign Knives. **Mark:** First name or "H" pierced by arrow.

HUNT, MAURICE, 2492 N 800 E, Winter: 2925 Argyle Rd Venice FL 34293, AVON, IN 46123, Phone: 317 272-2669/Winter: 941-493-4027, Fax: 317 272-2159
Patterns: Bowies, hunters, fighters. **Prices:** $200 to $800. **Remarks:** Spare-time maker prior to 1995; Part-time maker after 1995. **Other:** Journeyman smith.

HUNTER, RICHARD D., 7230 NW 200th Terrace, Alachua, FL 32615, Phone: 904-462-3150
Specialties: Traditional working/using knives of his design or customer suggestions; filework. **Patterns:** Folders of various types, Bowies, hunters, daggers. **Technical:** Traditional blacksmith; hand forges high carbon steel (5160, 1084, 52100) and makes own Damascus; grinds 440C and ATS-34. **Prices:** $200 & up. **Remarks:** Part-time maker; first knife sold in 1992. **Mark:** Last name in capital letters.

HUNTER, HYRUM, 285 N. 300 W., PO Box 179, Aurora, UT 84620, Phone: 435-529-7244
Specialties: Working straight knives of my design or to customer specs. **Patterns:** Drop and clip, fighters dagger, some folders. **Technical:** Forged from two piece Damascus. **Prices:** Prices are adjusted according to size, complexity and material used. **Remarks:** I will consider any design you have. Part-time maker; first knife sold in 1990. **Mark:** Initials encircled with first initial and last name and city, then state. Some patterns are numbered.

HURST, GERARD T., PO Box 8742, Albuquerque, NM 87198, Phone: 505-401-1900
Mark: Hurst inside logo. **Prices:** Start at $225 and up to $5000. Upscale folders, utility knives, and art pieces. Grinds BG42, Damasteel, Mike Norris Damascus.

HURST, JEFF, PO Box 247, Rutledge, TN 37861, Phone: 865-828-5729
Specialties: Working straight knives and folders of his design. **Patterns:** Tomahawks, hunters, boots, folders and fighters. **Technical:** Forges W2, O1 and his own Damascus. Makes mokume. **Prices:** $175 to $350; some to $500. **Remarks:** Full-time maker; first knife sold in 1984. Doing business as Buzzard's Knob Forge. **Mark:** Last name; partnered knives are marked with Newman L. Smith, handle artisan, and SH in script.

HURST, COLE, 1583 Tedford, E. Wenatchee, WA 98802, Phone: 509-884-9206
Specialties: Fantasy, high-art and traditional straight knives. **Patterns:** Bowies, daggers and hunters. **Technical:** Blades are made of stone; handles are made of stone, wood or ivory and embellished with fancy woods, ivory or antlers. **Prices:** $100 to $300; some to $2000. **Remarks:** Spare-time maker; first knife sold in 1985. **Mark:** Name and year.

HURT, WILLIAM R., 9222 Oak Tree Cir., Frederick, MD 21701, Phone: 301-898-7143
Specialties: Traditional and working/using straight knives. **Patterns:** Bowies, hunters, fighters and utility knives. **Technical:** Forges 5160, O1 and O6; makes own Damascus. Offers silver wire inlay. **Prices:** $200 to $600; some higher. **Remarks:** Full-time maker; first knife sold in 1989. **Mark:** First and middle initials, last name.

HUSIAK, MYRON, PO Box 238, Altona 3018, Victoria, AUSTRALIA, Phone: 03-315-6752
Specialties: Straight knives and folders of his design or to customer specs. **Patterns:** Hunters, fighters, lock-back folders, skinners and boots. **Technical:** forges and grinds his own Damascus, 440C and ATS-34. **Prices:** $200 to $900. **Remarks:** Part-time maker; first knife sold in 1974. **Mark:** First initial, last name in logo and serial number.

HYDE, JIMMY, 5094 Stagecoach Rd, Ellenwood, GA 30049, Phone: 404-968-1951, Fax: 404-209-1741
Specialties: Working straight knives of any design; period pieces. **Patterns:** Bowies, hunters and utility knives. **Technical:** Grinds 440C; forges 5160, 1095 & O1. Makes his own Damascus and cable Damascus. **Prices:** $150 to $600. **Remarks:** Part-time maker; first knife sold in 1978. **Mark:** First initial, last name.

custom knifemakers

HYTOVICK, JOE "HY", 14872 SW 111th St, Dunnellon, FL 34432, Phone: 800-749-5339
Specialties: Straight, Folder & Miniature. **Technical:** Blades from Wootz, Damascus and Alloy steel. **Prices:** To $5000. **Mark:** HY.

i

IKOMA, FLAVIO YUJI, R. MANOEL R. TEIXEIRA, 108, Centro Presidente Prudente, SP-19031-220, BRAZIL, Phone: 0182-22-0115
Specialties: Straight knives and folders of all designs. **Patterns:** Fighters, hunters, Bowies, swords, folders, skinners, utility and defense knives. **Technical:** Grinds and forges D6, 440C, high-carbon steels and Damascus. **Prices:** $60 to $350; some to $3300. **Remarks:** Full-time maker; first knife sold in 1991. All stainless steel blades are ultra sub-zero quenched. **Mark:** Ikoma Knives beside eagle.

IMBODEN II, HOWARD L., 620 Deauville Dr, Dayton, OH 45429, Phone: 513-439-1536
Specialties: One-of-a-kind hunting, flint, steel and art knives. **Technical:** Forges and grinds stainless, high-carbon and Damascus. Uses obsidian, cast sterling silver, 14K and 18K gold guards. Carves ivory animals and more. **Prices:** $65 to $25,000. **Remarks:** Full-time maker; first knife sold in 1986. Doing business as Hill Originals. **Mark:** First and last initials, II.

IMEL, BILLY MACE, 1616 Bundy Ave, New Castle, IN 47362, Phone: 765-529-1651
Specialties: High-art working knives, period pieces and personal cutlery. **Patterns:** Daggers, fighters, hunters; locking folders and slip-joints with interframes. **Technical:** Grinds D2, 440C and 154CM. **Prices:** $300 to $2000; some to $6000. **Remarks:** Part-time maker; first knife sold in 1973. **Mark:** Name in monogram.

INMAN III, PAUL R., 3120 B Blake Ave #224, Glenwood Springs, CO 81601, Phone: 970-963-5951
Specialties: Bowies in the Moran-style. **Prices:** $300-$1000.

IRIE, MICHAEL L., Mike Irie Handcraft, 1606 Auburn Dr, Colorado Springs, CO 80909, Phone: 719-572-5330
Specialties: Working fixed blade knives and handcrafted blades for the do-it-yourselfer. **Patterns:** Twenty standard designs along with custom. **Technical:** Blades are ATS-34, BG-43, 440C with some outside Damascus. **Prices:** Fixed blades $95 & up, blade work $45 and up. **Remarks:** Formerly dba Wood, Irie & Co. with Barry Wood. Full-time maker since 1991. **Mark:** Name.

IRON WOLF FORGE, SEE NELSON, KEN

ISAO, OHBUCHI, 702-1 Nouso Yame-City, Fukuoka, JAPAN, Phone: 0943-23-4439

ISGRO, JEFFERY, 1516 First St, West Babylon, NY 11704, Phone: 631-587-7516
Specialties: File work, glass beading, kydex, leather. **Patterns:** Tactical use knives, skinners, capers, Bowies, camp, hunters. **Technical:** ATS-34, 440C & D2. **Price:** $120 to $600. **Remarks:** Part-time maker. **Mark:** First name, last name, Long Island, NY.

ISHIHARA, HANK, 86-18 Motomachi, Sakura City, Chiba Pref., JAPAN, Phone: 043-485-3208, Fax: 043-485-3208
Specialties: Fantasy working straight knives and folders of his design. **Patterns:** Boots, Bowies, daggers, fighters, hunters, fishing, locking folders and utility camp knives. **Technical:** Grinds ATS-34, 440C, D2, 440V, CV-134, COS25 and Damascus. Engraves. **Prices:** $250 to $1000; some to $10,000. **Remarks:** Full-time maker; first knife sold in 1987. **Mark:** HANK.

j

JACKS, JIM, 344 S. Hollenbeck Ave, Covina, CA 91723-2513, Phone: 626-331-5665
Specialties: Working straight knives in standard patterns. **Patterns:** Bowies, hunters, fighters, fishing and camp knives, miniatures. **Technical:** Grinds Stellite 6K, 440C and ATS-34. **Prices:** Start at $100. **Remarks:** Spare-time maker; first knife sold in 1980. **Mark:** Initials in diamond logo.

JACKSON, DAVID, 214 Oleander Av, Lemoore, CA 93245, Phone: 559-925-8547
Specialties: Forged steel. **Patterns:** Hunters, camp knives, Bowies. **Prices:** $150 and up. **Mark:** G. D. Jackson - Maker - Lemoore CA.

JACKSON, JIM, 7 Donnington Close, Chapel Row Bucklebury RG7 6PU, ENGLAND, Phone: 011-89-712743, Fax: 011-89-710495
Specialties: Large Bowies, concentrating on form and balance; collector quality Damascus daggers. **Patterns:** With fancy filework & engraving

available. **Technical:** Forges O1, 5160 and CS70 and 15N20 Damascus. **Prices:** From $1000. **Remarks:** Part-time maker. **Mark:** Jackson England with in a circle M. S. **Other:** All knives come with a custom tooled leather swivel sheath or exotic materials.

JACKSON, CHARLTON R., 6811 Leyland Dr, San Antonio, TX 78239, Phone: 210-601-5112

JAKSIK JR., MICHAEL, 427 Marschall Creek Rd, Fredericksburg, TX 78624, Phone: 830-997-1119
Mark: MJ or M. Jaksik

JAMES, PETER, 2549 W. Golf Rd, #290, Hoffman Estates, IL 60194, Phone: 708-310-9113, Fax: 708-885-1716
Specialties: Working/using straight knives of his design and in standard patterns. **Patterns:** Bowies, daggers and urban companion knives. **Technical:** Grinds 440C and soligen tool. Makes a variety of sheaths for urban companion series. **Prices:** $48 to $250. **Remarks:** Part-time maker; first knife sold in 1986. Doing business as Peter James & Sons. **Mark:** Initials overlapped.

JANIGA, MATTHEW A., 15950 Xenia St. NW, Andover, MN 55304-2346, Phone: 612-427-2510
Specialties: Period pieces, swords, daggers. **Patterns:** Daggers, fighters and swords. **Technical:** Forges 5160, Damascus and 52100. Does own heat treating. Forges own pattern-welded steel. **Prices:** $100 - $1000; some to $5000. **Remarks:** Spare-time maker; first knife sold in 1991. **Mark:** Interwoven initials.

JARVIS, PAUL M., 30 Chalk St, Cambridge, MA 02139, Phone: 617-547-4355 or 617-666-9090
Specialties: High-art knives and period pieces of his design. **Patterns:** Japanese and Mid-Eastern knives. **Technical:** Grinds Myer Damascus, ATS-34, D2 and O1. Specializes in height-relief Japanese-style carving. Works with silver, gold and gems. **Prices:** $200 to $17,000. **Remarks:** Part-time maker; first knife sold in 1978.

JEAN, GERRY, 25B Cliffside Dr, Manchester, CT 06040, Phone: 860-649-6449
Specialties: Historic replicas. **Patterns:** Survival and camp knives. **Technical:** Grinds A2, 440C and 154CM. Handle slabs applied in unique tongue-and-groove method. **Prices:** $125 to $250; some to $1000. **Remarks:** Spare-time maker; first knife sold in 1973. **Mark:** Initials and serial number.

JEFFRIES, ROBERT W., Route 2, Box 227, Red House, WV 25168, Phone: 304-586-9780
Specialties: Straight knives and folders. **Patterns:** Hunters, skinners and folders. **Technical:** Uses 440C, ATS-34; makes his own Damascus. **Prices:** Moderate. **Remarks:** Part-time maker; first knife sold in 1988. **Mark:** NA.

JENSEN, JOHN LEWIS, dba Magnus Design Studio, PO Box 60547, Pasadena, CA 91116, Phone: 626-449-1148, Fax: 626-449-1148
Specialties: Designer & fabricator of modern, unique, elegant, innovative, original, one-of-a-kind, hand crafted, custom ornamental edged weaponry. Combines skill, precision, distinction & the finest materials, geared toward the discriminating art collector. **Patterns:** Folding knives & fixed blades, daggers, fighters & swords. **Technical:** High embellishment, BFA 96 Rhode Island School of Design: Jewelry & metalsmithing. Grinds 440C, ATS-34, Damascus. Works with custom made Damascus to his specs. Uses gold, silver, gemstones, pearl, titanium, fossil mastodon and walrus ivories. Carving, file work, soldering, deep etches Damascus, engraving, layers, bevels, blood grooves Also forges his own Damascus. **Prices:** Start at $3500. **Remarks:** Available on a first come basis & via commission based on his designs Knifemakers guild voting member and ABS apprenticesmith and member of the Society of North American Goldsmiths. **Mark:** Maltese cross/butterfly shield.

JENSEN JR., CARL A., 8957 Country Road P-35, Blair, NE 68008, Phone: 402-426-3353
Specialties: Working knives of his design; some customer designs. **Patterns:** Hunters, fighters, boots and Bowies. **Technical:** Grinds A2, D2, O1, 440C, 5160 and ATS-34; recycles old files, leaf springs; heat-treats. **Prices:** $35 to $350. **Remarks:** Part-time maker; first knife sold in 1980. **Mark:** Stamp "BEAR'S CUTLERY" or etch of letters "BEAR" forming silhouette of a Bear.

JERNIGAN, STEVE, 3082 Tunnel Rd, Milton, FL 32571, Phone: 850-994-0802, Fax: 850-994-0802
Specialties: Investor-class folders and various theme pieces. **Patterns:** Array of models and sizes in side plate locking interframes and conventional liner construction. **Technical:** Grinds ATS-34, CPM-T-440V and Damascus. Inlays mokume (and minerals) in blades and sculpts marble cases. **Prices:** $650 to $1800; some to $6000. **Remarks:** Full-time maker; first knife sold in 1982. Takes orders for folders only. **Mark:** Last name.

JOBIN, JACQUES, 46 St. Dominique, Levis Quebec, CANADA G6V 2M7, Phone: 418-833-0283, Fax: 418-833-8378
Specialties: Fancy and working straight knives and folders; miniatures. **Patterns:** Minis, fantasy knives, fighters and some hunters. **Technical:** ATS-34, some Damascus and titanium. Likes native snake wood. Heat-treats. **Prices:** Start at $250. **Remarks:** Full-time maker; first knife sold in 1986. **Mark:** Signature on blade.

JOEHNK, BERND, Posadowskystrasse 22, 24148 Kiel, GERMANY, Phone: 0431-7297705, Fax: 0431-7297705
Specialties: One-of-a-kind fancy/embellished and traditional straight knives of his design and to customer specs. **Patterns:** Daggers, fighters, hunters and letter openers. **Technical:** Grinds 440C, ATS-34, commercial Damascus and various stainless and corrosion-resistant steels. Likes filework. Leather sheaths. Offers engraving. **Prices:** Upscale. **Remarks:** Part-time maker; first knife sold in1990. **Mark:** Full name and city.

JOHANNING CUSTOM KNIVES, TOM, 1735 Apex Rd, Sarasota, FL 34240 9386, Phone: 941-371-2104, Fax: 941-378-9427

JOHANSSON, ANDERS, Konstvartarevagen 9, S-772 40 Grangesberg, SWEDEN, Phone: 46 240 23204, Fax: +46 21 358778
Specialties: Scandinavian traditional and modern straight knives. **Patterns:** Hunters, fighters and fantasy knives. **Technical:** Grinds stainless steel and makes own Damascus. Prefers water buffalo and mammoth for handle material. **Prices:** Start at $100. **Remarks:** Spare-time maker; first knife sold in 1994. Works together with scrimshander Viveca Sahlin. **Mark:** Stylized initials.

JOHNS, ROB, 1423 S. Second, Enid, OK 73701, Phone: 405-242-2707
Specialties: Classic and fantasy straight knives of his design or to customer specs; fighters for use at Medieval fairs. **Patterns:** Bowies, daggers and swords. **Technical:** Forges and grinds 440C, D2 and 5160. Handles of nylon, walnut or wire-wrap. **Prices:** $150 to $350; some to $2500. **Remarks:** Full-time maker; first knife sold in 1980. **Mark:** Medieval Customs, initials.

JOHNSON, STEVEN R., 202 E. 200 N., PO Box 5, Manti, UT 84642, Phone: 435-835-7941
Specialties: Investor-class working knives. **Patterns:** Hunters, fighters, boots & folders of locking liner variety. **Technical:** Grinds ATS-34, 440-C, RWL-34. **Prices:** $500 to $5000. **Remarks:** Full-time maker; first knife sold in 1972. **Mark:** Name, city, state and optional signature mark.

JOHNSON, C. E. GENE, 5648 Redwood Ave, Portage, IN 46368, Phone: 219-762-5461
Specialties: Lock-back folders and sprinters of his design or to customer specs. **Patterns:** Hunters, Bowies, survival lock-back folders. **Technical:** Grinds D2, 440C, A18, O1, Damascus; likes filework. **Prices:** $100 to $2000. **Remarks:** Full-time maker; first knife sold in 1975. **Mark:** "Gene" city, state and serial number.

JOHNSON, DURRELL CARMON, PO Box 594, Sparr, FL 32192, Phone: 352-622-5498
Specialties: Old-fashioned working straight knives and folders of his design or to customer specs. **Patterns:** Bowies, hunters, fighters, daggers, camp knives and Damascus miniatures. **Technical:** Forges 5160, his own Damascus, W2, wrought iron, nickel and horseshoe rasps. Offers filework. **Prices:** $100 to $2000. **Remarks:** Full-time maker and blacksmith; first knife sold in 1957. **Mark:** Middle name.

JOHNSON, GORDEN W., 5426 Sweetbriar, Houston, TX 77017, Phone: 713-645-8990
Specialties: Working knives and period pieces. **Patterns:** Hunters, boots and Bowies. **Technical:** Flat-grinds 440C; most knives have narrow tang. **Prices:** $90 to $450. **Remarks:** Full-time maker; first knife sold in 1974. **Mark:** Name, city, state.

JOHNSON, HAROLD "HARRY" C., 98 Penn St, Trion, GA 30753-1520
Specialties: Working straight knives. **Patterns:** Mostly hunters and large Bowies. **Technical:** Grinds popular steels. Offers leatherwork, sheaths and cases. **Prices:** $125 to $2000; some higher. **Remarks:** Part-time maker; first knife sold in 1973. **Mark:** First initial, last name, city, state. **Other:** Also makes wood and leather cases for knives and guns.

JOHNSON, RANDY, 2575 E. Canal Dr, Turlock, CA 95380, Phone: 209-632-5401
Specialties: Folders. **Patterns:** Locking folders. **Technical:** Grinds Damascus. **Prices:** $200 to $400. **Remarks:** Spare-time maker; first knife sold in 1989. Doing business as Puedo Knifeworks. **Mark:** PUEDO

JOHNSON, R. B., Box 11, Clearwater, MN 55320, Phone: 320-558-6128
Specialties: Liner-locks with Titanium, mosaic damascus. **Patterns:** Liner-lock folders, skeleton hunters, frontier Bowies. **Technical:** Damascus,

Mosaic Damascus, A-2, O-1, 1095. **Prices:** $200 and up. **Remarks:** Full-time maker since 1973. Not accepting orders. **Mark:** R B Johnson (signature).

JOHNSON, RUFFIN, 215 LaFonda Dr, Houston, TX 77060, Phone: 281-448-4407
Specialties: Working straight knives and folders. **Patterns:** Hunters, fighters and locking folders. **Technical:** Grinds 440C and 154CM; hidden tangs and fancy handles. **Prices:** $200 to $400; some to $1095. **Remarks:** Full-time maker; first knife sold in 1972. **Mark:** Wolf head logo and signature.

JOHNSON, RYAN M., 7320 Foster Hixson Cemetery Rd, Hixson, TN 37343, Phone: 615-842-9323
Specialties: Working and using straight knives of his design and to customer specs. **Patterns:** Bowies, hunters and utility/camp knives. **Technical:** Forges 5160, Damascus and files. **Prices:** $70 to $400; some to $800. **Remarks:** Full-time maker; first knife sold in 1986. **Mark:** Sledge-hammer with halo.

JOHNSON, RICHARD, W165 N10196 Wagon Trail, Germantown, WI 53022, Phone: 262-251-5772
Specialties: Custom knives and knife repair.

JOHNSON, DAVID A., 1791 Defeated Creek Rd, Pleasant Shade, TN 37145, Phone: 615-774-3596

JOHNSON, JOHN R., 5535 Bob Smith Ave, Plant City, FL 33565, Phone: 813-986-4478

JOHNSTON, DR. ROBT, PO Box 9887 1 Lomb Mem Dr, Rochester, NY 14623

JOKERST, CHARLES, 9312 Spaulding, Omaha, NE 68134, Phone: 402-571-2536
Specialties: Working knives in standard patterns. **Patterns:** Hunters, fighters and pocketknives. **Technical:** Grinds 440C, ATS-34. **Prices:** $90 to $170. **Remarks:** Spare-time maker; first knife sold in 1984. **Mark:** Early work marked RCJ; current work marked with last name and city.

JONES, ENOCH, 7278 Moss Ln., Warrenton, VA 20187, Phone: 540-341-0292
Specialties: Fancy working straight knives. **Patterns:** Hunters, fighters, boots and Bowies. **Technical:** Forges and grinds O1, W2, 440C and Damascus. **Prices:** $100 to $350; some to $1000. **Remarks:** Part-time maker; first knife sold in 1982. **Mark:** First name.

JONES, BOB, 6219 Aztec NE, Albuquerque, NM 87110, Phone: 505-881-4472
Specialties: Fancy working knives of his design. **Patterns:** Mountain man/buckskinner-type knives; multi-blade folders, locking folders, and slip-joints. **Technical:** Grinds A2, O1, 1095 and commercial Damascus; uses no stainless steel. Engraves. **Prices:** $100 to $500; some to $1500. **Remarks:** Full-time maker; first knife sold in 1960. **Mark:** Initials on fixed blades; initials encircled on folders.

JONES, FRANKLIN (FRANK) W., 6030 Old Dominion Rd, Columbus, GA 31909, Phone: 706-563-6051
Specialties: Traditional/working/tactical/period straight knives of his or your design. **Patterns:** Liner-lock folders. Hunters, skinners, utility/camp, Bowies, fighters, kitchen, carving sets. **Technical:** Forges all straight knives using 5160, 01, 52100, 1085 and 1095. **Prices:** $150 to $1000. **Remarks:** Full-time, American Bladesmith Society Journeyman Smith. **Mark:** F. W. Jones, Columbus, GA.

JONES, JOHN, 12 Schooner Circuit, Manly West, QLD 4179, AUSTRALIA, Phone: 07-339-33390
Specialties: Straight knives and folders. **Patterns:** Working hunters, folding lock-backs, fancy daggers and miniatures. **Technical:** Grinds 440C, O1 and L6. **Prices:** $180 to $1200; some to $2000. **Remarks:** Part-time maker; first knife sold in 1986. **Mark:** Jones

JONES, CURTIS J., 39909 176th St. E., Palmdale, CA 93591, Phone: 805-264-2753
Specialties: Big Bowies, daggers, his own style of hunters. **Patterns:** Bowies, daggers, hunters, swords, boots and miniatures. **Technical:** Grinds 440C, ATS-34 and D2. Fitted guards only; does not solder. Heat-treats. Custom sheaths-hand-tooled and stitched. **Prices:** $125 to $1500; some to $3000. **Remarks:** Full-time maker; first knife sold in 1975. Mail orders accepted. **Mark:** Stylized initials on either side of three triangles interconnected.

JONES, CHARLES ANTHONY, 36 Broadgate Close, Bellaire Barnstaple, No. Devon E31 4AL, ENGLAND, Phone: 0271-75328
Specialties: Working straight knives. **Patterns:** Simple hunters, fighters and utility knives. **Technical:** Grinds 440C, O1 and D2; filework offered. Engraves. **Prices:** $100 to $500; engraving higher. **Remarks:** Spare-time maker; first knife sold in 1987. **Mark:** Tony engraved.

custom knifemakers

JONES, BARRY M. AND PHILLIP G., 221 North Ave, Danville, VA 24540, Phone: 804-793-5282
Specialties: Working and using straight knives and folders of their design and to customer specs; combat and self-defense knives. **Patterns:** Bowies, fighters, daggers, swords, hunters and liner-lock folders. **Technical:** Grinds 440C, ATS-34 and D2; flat-grinds only. All blades hand polished. **Prices:** $100 to $1000; some higher. **Remarks:** Part-time makers; first knife sold in 1989. **Mark:** Jones Knives, city, state.

JONES, JOHN A., 779 SW 131 Hwy, Holden, MO 64040, Phone: 816-850-4318
Specialties: Working, using knives. Hunters, skinners & fighters. **Technical:** Grinds D2, 01, 440C, 1095. Prefers forging; creates own Damascus. File working on most blades. **Prices:** $50 to $500. **Remarks:** Part-time maker; first knife sold in 1996. Doing business as Old John Knives. **Mark:** OLD JOHN & serial number.

JONES, ROGER MUDBONE, PO Box 367, Waverly, OH 45601, Phone: 740-947-5684
Specialties: Working in cutlery to suit working woodsman and fine collector. **Patterns:** Bowies, hunters, folders, hatchets in both period and modern style, scale miniatures a specialty. **Technical:** All cutlery hand forged to shape with traditional methods; multiple quench and draws, limited Damascus production hand carves wildlife and historic themes in stag/antler/ivory, full line of functional and high art leather. All work sole authorship. **Prices:** $50-$5000 **Remarks:** Full-time maker/first knife sold in 1979. **Mark:** Stamped R. Jones hand made or hand engraved sig. W/bowie knife mark.

JORGENSEN, GERD, Jernbanegata 8, N-3262 Larvik, NORWAY, Phone: +47 33 18 66 06, Fax: +47 33 18 66 06
Specialties: Scandinavian-styles hunters, working/using straight knives of my design, flint knives. **Patterns:** Mild modifications of traditional Scandinavian patterns, hunters, camp knives and fighters/tactical. **Technical:** Grinds Sandvik 12C27, forges own blades collaborates with other Scandinavian blacksmiths. Buys Damascus blades. **Prices:** $100 to $400. **Remarks:** Part-time maker; first knife sold in 1990. **Mark:** First name or initials.

JURGENS, JOHN, 3650 Emerald St Apt Y-1, Torrence, CA 90503, Phone: 310-542-3985

JUSTICE, SHANE, 425 South Brooks St, Sheridan, WY 82801, Phone: 307-673-4432
Specialties: Fixed blade working knives. **Patterns:** Hunters, skinners and camp knives. Other designs produced on a limited basis. **Technical:** Hand forged 5160 and 52100. **Remarks:** Part-time maker. Sole author. **Mark:** Cross over a Crescent.

k

K B S, KNIVES, RSD 181, North Castlemaine, Vic 3450, AUSTRALIA, Phone: 0011 61 3 54 705864, Fax: 0011 61 3 54 706233
Specialties: Bowies, daggers and miniatures. **Patterns:** Art daggers, traditional Bowies, fancy folders and miniatures. **Technical:** Hollow or flat grind, most steels. **Prices:** $200 to $600+. **Remarks:** Full-time maker; first knife sold in 1983. **Mark:** Initials and address in Southern Cross motif.

KACZOR, TOM, 375 Wharncliffe Rd. N., Upper London, Ont., CANADA N6G 1E4, Phone: 519-645-7640

KADASAH, AHMED BIN, PO Box 1969, Jeddah 21441, SAUDI ARABIA, Phone: 26 913-0082

KAGAWA, KOICHI, 1556 Horiyamashita, Hatano-Shi, Kanagawa, JAPAN
Specialties: Fancy high-tech straight knives and folders to customer specs. **Patterns:** Hunters, locking folders and slip-joints. **Technical:** Uses 440C and ATS-34. **Prices:** $500 to $2000; some to $20,000. **Remarks:** Part-time maker; first knife sold ln 1986. **Mark:** First initial, last name-YOKOHAMA.

KAIN, CHARLES, Kain Designs, 5412 N College Ave, Indianapolis, IN 46220
Specialties: Damascus Art Pieces. **Patterns:** Any. **Remarks:** Specialize in unique art pieces. **Mark:** Kain and signed stamp for unique pieces.

KAJIN, AL, PO Box 1047, Forsyth, MT 59327, Phone: 406-356-2442
Specialties: Damascus, utility knives, working knives; make my own Damascus. **Patterns:** All types. **Technical:** Maker since 1989; ABS member. **Prices:** $175 & up. **Remarks:** Like to work with customer on design. **Mark:**

AK on forged blades. Stylized Kajin in outline of Montana for stock removal knives.

KALFAYAN, EDWARD N., 410 Channing, Ferndale, MI 48220, Phone: 248-548-4882
Specialties: Working straight knives and lock-back folders; some art and fantasy pieces. **Patterns:** Bowies, toothpicks, fighters, daggers, swords and hunters. **Technical:** Grinds ATS-34, 440C, O1, 5160 and Damascus. **Prices:** $150 to $5000. **Remarks:** Full-time maker; first knife sold in 1973. **Mark:** Last name.

KALUZA, WERNER, Lochnerstr. 32, 90441 Nurnberg, GERMANY, Phone: 0911 666047
Specialties: Fancy high-art straight knives of his design. **Patterns:** Boots and ladies knives. **Technical:** Grinds ATS-34, CPM-T-440V and Schneider Damascus. Engraving available. **Prices:** NA. **Remarks:** Part-time maker. **Mark:** First initial and last name.

KANDA, MICHIO, 7-32-5 Shinzutumi-cho, Shinnanyo-shi, Yamaguchi 746 0033, JAPAN, Phone: 0834-62-1910, Fax: 011-81-83462-1910
Specialties: Fantasy knives of his design. **Patterns:** Animal knives. **Technical:** Grinds ATS-34. **Prices:** $300 to $3000. **Remarks:** Full-time maker; first knife sold in 1985. Doing business as Shusui Kanda. **Mark:** Last name inside "M".

KANKI, IWAO, 14-25 3-Chome Fukui Miki, Hyougo, JAPAN 673-0433, Phone: 07948-3-2555
Specialties: Plane, knife. **Prices:** Not determined yet. **Mark:** Chiyozuru Sadahide. **Other:** Masters of traditional crafts designated by the Minister of International Trade & Industry (Japan).

KANSEI, MATSUNO, 109-8 Uenomachi Nishikaiden, Gitu-city, JAPAN 501-1168, Phone: 81-58-234-8643
Specialties: Folders of original design. **Patterns:** Liner-lock folder. **Technical:** Grinds VG-10, Damascus. **Prices:** $350-$2000. **Remarks:** Full-time maker. First knife sold in 1993. **Mark:** Name.

KANTER, MICHAEL, Adam Michael Knives, 14550 West Honey Ln, New Berlin, WI 53151, Phone: 262-860-1136
Specialties: Fixed blades and liner-lock folders. **Patterns:** Drop point hunters, and Bowies. **Technical:** My own Damascus, BG42, ATS-34 and CPMS60V. **Prices:** $200-$1000. **Mark:** Adam Michael over wavy line. **Other:** Ivory, Mamoth Ivory, stabilized woods, and pearl handles.

KARP, BOB, PO Box 47304, Phoenix, AZ 85068, Phone: 602 870-1234, Fax: 602 331-0283

KATO, SHINICHI, 3233-27-5-410 Kikko Taikogane, Moriyama-ku Nagoya, JAPAN 463-0004, Phone: 81-52-736-6032
Specialties: Flat grind and hand finish. **Patterns:** Bowie, fighter. Hunting knife. **Technical:** Flat grind ATS-34. **Prices:** $100-$1500. **Remarks:** Part-time maker. First knife sold in 1995. **Mark:** Name.

KATO, KIYOSHI, 4-6-4 Himonya Meguro-ku, Tokyo 152, JAPAN
Specialties: Swords, Damascus knives, working knives and paper knives. **Patterns:** Traditional swords, hunters, Bowies and daggers. **Technical:** Forges his own Damascus and carbon steel. Grinds ATS-34. **Prices:** $260 to $700; some to $4000. **Remarks:** Full-time maker. **Mark:** First initial, last name.

KATSUMARO, SHISHIDO, 2-6-11 Kamiseno Aki-ku, Hiroshima, JAPAN, Phone: 090-3634-9054, Fax: 082-227-4438

KAUFFMAN, DAVE, 120 Clark Creek Loop, Montana City, MT 59634, Phone: 406-442-9328
Specialties: Field grade & exhibition grade hunting knives & ultra light folders. **Patterns:** Fighters, Bowies and drop-point hunters. **Technical:** ATS-34 and Damascus. **Prices:** $60 to $1200. **Remarks:** Full-time maker; first knife sold in 1989. On the cover of Knives '94. **Mark:** First and last name, city and state.

KAUFMAN, SCOTT, 302 Green Meadows Cr., Anderson, SC 29624, Phone: 864-231-9201
Specialties: Classic and working/using straight knives in standard patterns. **Patterns:** Fighters, hunters and utility/camp knives. Technical Grinds ATS-34, 440C, O1. **Prices:** $100 to $500. **Remarks:** Part-time maker; first knife sold in 1987. **Mark:** Kaufman Knives with Bible in middle.

KAWASAKI, AKIHISA, 11-8-9 Chome Minamiamachi, Suzurandai Kita-Ku, Kobe, JAPAN, Phone: 078-593-0418, Fax: 078-593-0418
Specialties: Working/using knives of his design. **Patterns:** Hunters, kit camp knives. **Technical:** Forges and grinds Molybdenum Panadium. Grinds ATS-34 and stainless steel. Uses Chinese Quince wood, desert ironwood and cow leather. **Prices:** $300 to $800; some to $1000. **Remarks:** Full-time maker. **Mark:** A. K.

KAY, J. WALLACE, 332 Slab Bridge Rd, Liberty, SC 29657

KAZSUK, DAVID, PO Box 39, Perris, CA 92572-0039, Phone: 909-780-2288

KEARNEY, JAROD, 7200 Townsend Forest Ct, Brown Summit, NC 27214, Phone: 336-656-4617

KEELER, ROBERT, 623 N Willett St, Memphis, TN 38107, Phone: 901-278-6538

KEESLAR, STEVEN C., 115 Lane 216, Hamilton, IN 46742, Phone: 219-488-3161, Fax: 219-488-3149
Specialties: Traditional working/using straight knives of his design and to customer specs. **Patterns:** Bowies, hunters, utility/camp knives. **Technical:** Forges 5160, files 52100. **Prices:** $100 to $600; some to $1500. **Remarks:** Part-time maker; first knife sold in 1976. **Mark:** First initial, last name.

KEESLAR, JOSEPH F., 391 Radio Rd, Almo, KY 42020, Phone: 270-753-7919, Fax: 270-753-7919
Specialties: Classic and contemporary Bowies, combat, hunters, daggers & folders. **Patterns:** Decorative filework, engraving and custom leather sheaths available. **Technical:** Forges 5160, 52100 and his own Damascus steel. **Prices:** $300 to $3000. **Remarks:** Full-time maker; first knife sold in 1976. **Mark:** First and middle initials, last name in hammer, knife and anvil logo, M. S. **Other:** ABS Master Smith.

KEETON, WILLIAM L., 6095 Rehobeth Rd. SE, Laconia, IN 47135-9550, Phone: 812-969-2836
Specialties: Plain and fancy working knives. **Patterns:** Hunters and fighters; locking folders and slip-joints. Names patterns after Kentucky Derby winners. **Technical:** Grinds D2, ATS-34, 440C, 440V and 154CM; mirror and satin finishes. **Prices:** $95 to $2000. **Remarks:** Full-time maker; first knife sold in 1971. **Mark:** Logo of key.

KEHIAYAN, ALFREDO, Cuzco 1455, Ing. Maschwitz, CP B1623GXU Buenos Aires, ARGENTINA, Phone: 03488-4-42212
Specialties: Functional straight knives. **Patterns:** Utility knives, skinners, hunters and boots. **Technical:** Forges and grinds SAE 52. 100, SAE 6180, SAE 9260, SAE 5160, 440C and ATS-34, titanium with nitride. All blades mirror-polished; makes leather sheath and wood cases. **Prices:** $70 to $800; some to $6000. **Remarks:** Full-time maker; first knife sold in 1983. **Mark:** Name. **Other:** Some knives are satin finish (utility knives).

KEIDEL, GENE W. AND SCOTT J., 4661 105th Ave. SW, Dickinson, ND 58601
Specialties: Fancy/embellished and working/using straight knives of his design. **Patterns:** Bowies, hunters and miniatures. **Technical:** Grind 440C and O1 tool steel. Offer scrimshaw and filework. **Prices:** $95 to $500. **Remarks:** Full-time makers; first knife sold in1990. Doing business as Keidel Knives. **Mark:** Last name.

KEISUKE, GOTOH, 105 Cosumo-City Otozu 202 Ohita-city, Ohita, JAPAN, Phone: 097-523-0750

KELLEY, THOMAS P., 4711 E Ashler Hills Dr, Cave Creek, AZ 85331, Phone: 480-488-3101

KELLEY, GARY, 17485 SW Pheasant Lane, Aloha, OR 97006, Phone: 503-649-7867
Specialties: Primitive knives and blades. **Patterns:** Fur trade era rifleman's knives, patch and throwing knives. **Technical:** Hand-forges and precision investment casts. **Prices:** $25 to $55. **Remarks:** Part-time maker. Staff photographer/writer for *Tactical Knives* magazine; does illustrative knife photography. Doing business as Reproduction Blades. **Mark:** Full name or initials.

KELLOGG, BRIAN R., 19048 Smith Creek Rd, New Market, VA 22844, Phone: 540-740-4292
Specialties: Fancy and working straight knives of his design and to customer specs. **Patterns:** Fighters, hunters and utility/camp knives. **Technical:** Grinds 440C, D2 and A2. Offers filework and fancy pin and cable pin work. Prefers natural handle materials. **Prices:** $75 to $225; some to $350. **Remarks:** Part-time maker; first knife sold in 1983. **Mark:** Last name.

KELLY, LANCE, 1723 Willow Oak Dr, Edgewater, FL 32132, Phone: 904-423-4933
Specialties: Investor-class straight knives and folders. **Patterns:** Kelly-style in contemporary outlines. **Technical:** Grinds O1, D2 and 440C; engraves; inlays gold and silver. **Prices:** $600 to $3500. **Remarks:** Full-time engraver and knife maker; first knife sold in 1975. **Mark:** Last name.

KELSO, JIM, 577 Collar Hill Rd, Worcester, VT 05682, Phone: 802-229-4254, Fax: 802-229-0595
Specialties: Fancy high-art straight knives and folders that mix Eastern and Western influences. Only uses own designs, but accepts suggestions for themes. **Patterns:** Daggers, swords and locking folders. **Technical:** Grinds only custom Damascus. Works with top Damascus blade smiths.

Prices: $3000 to $8000; some to $15,000. **Remarks:** Full-time maker; first knife sold in 1980. **Mark:** Stylized initials.

KENNEDY JR., BILL, PO Box 850431, Yukon, OK 73085, Phone: 405-354-9150
Specialties: Working straight knives. **Patterns:** Hunters, fighters, minis and fishing knives. **Technical:** Grinds D2, 440C and Damascus. **Prices:** $80 & higher. **Remarks:** Part-time maker; first knife sold in 1980. **Mark:** Last name and year made.

KERBY, MARLIN W., RT1 Box 114D, Brashear, TX 75420, Phone: 903-485-6201

KERN, R W, 20824 Texas Trail W, San Antonio, TX 78257-1602, Phone: 210-698-2549
Specialties: Damascus, straight and folders. **Patterns:** Hunters, Bowies & folders. **Technical:** Grinds ATS-34, 440C & BG42. Forge own Damascus. **Prices:** $200 & up. **Remarks:** First knives 1980; retired; work as time permits. **Mark:** Outline of Alamo with kern over outline. **Other:** Member ABS, Texas Knife maker & Collectors Association.

KESSLER, RALPH A., PO Box 61, Fountain Inn, SC 29644-0061
Specialties: Traditional-style knives. **Patterns:** Folders, hunters, fighters, Bowies and kitchen knives. **Technical:** Grinds D2, O1, A2 and ATS-34. Forges 1090 and 1095. **Prices:** $100 to $500. **Remarks:** Part-time maker; first knife sold in 1982. **Mark:** Last name or initials with last name.

KEYES, DAN, 6688 King St, Chino, CA 91710, Phone: 909-628-8329

KHALSA, JOT SINGH, 368 Village St, Millis, MA 02054, Phone: 508-376-8162, Fax: 508-376-8081
Specialties: Liner-locks, one-of-a-kind daggers, swords, and kirpans (Sikh daggers) all original designs. **Technical:** Forges own Damascus, uses others high quality Damascus including stainless, and grinds stainless steels. Uses natural handle materials frequently unusual minerals. Pieces are frequently engraved and more recently carved. **Prices:** Start at $700.

KHARLAMOV, YURI, Oboronnay 46, 2, Tula, 300007, RUSSIA
Specialties: Classic, fancy and traditional knives of his design. **Patterns:** Daggers and hunters. **Technical:** Forges only Damascus with nickel. Uses natural handle materials; engraves on metal, carves on nut-tree; silver and pearl inlays. **Prices:** $600 to $2380; some to $4000. **Remarks:** Full-time maker; first knife sold in 1988. **Mark:** Initials.

KI, SHIVA, 5222 Ritterman Ave, Baton Rouge, LA 70805, Phone: 225-356-7274
Specialties: Fancy working straight knives and folders to customer specs. **Patterns:** Emphasis on personal defense knives, martial arts weapons. **Technical:** Forges and grinds; makes own Damascus; prefers natural handle materials. **Prices:** $135 to $850; some to $1800. **Remarks:** Full-time maker; first knife sold in 1981. **Mark:** Name with logo.

KIEFER, TONY, 112 Chateaugay Dr, Pataskala, OH 43062, Phone: 740-927-6910
Specialties: Traditional working and using straight knives in standard patterns. **Patterns:** Bowies, fighters and hunters. **Technical:** Grinds 440C and D2; forges D2. Flat-grinds Bowies; hollow-grinds drop-point and trailing-point hunters. **Prices:** $95 to $140; some to $200. **Remarks:** Spare-time maker; first knife sold in 1988. **Mark:** Last name.

KILBY, KEITH, 1902 29th St, Cody, WY 82414, Phone: 307-587-2732
Specialties: Works with all designs. **Patterns:** Mostly Bowies, camp knives and hunters of his design. **Technical:** Forges 52100, 5160, 1095, Damascus and mosaic Damascus. **Prices:** $250 to $3500. **Remarks:** Part-time maker; first knife sold in 1974. Doing business as Foxwood Forge. **Mark:** Name

KIMBERLEY, RICHARD L., 86-B Arroyd Hondo Rd, Santa Fe, NM 87508, Phone: 505-820-2727
Specialties: Fixed-blade and period knives. **Technical:** O1, 52100, 9260 steels. **Remarks:** Member ABS. **Mark:** "By D. KIMBERLEY SANTA FE NM". **Other:** Marketed under "Kimberleys of Santa Fe".

KIMSEY, KEVIN, 198 Cass White Rd. N. W., Cartersville, GA 30121, Phone: 770-387-0779 & 770-655-8879
Specialties: Tactical fixed blades & folders. **Patterns:** Fighters, folders, hunters and utility knives. **Technical:** Grinds 440C, ATS-34 and D2 carbon. **Prices:** $100 to $400; some to $600. **Remarks:** Three-time "Blade" award winner, knifemaker since 1983. **Mark:** Rafter and stylized KK.

KING, JASON M., Box 151, Eskridge, KS 66423, Phone: 785-449-2638
Specialties: Working and using straight knives of his design and sometimes to customer specs. Some slip joint & lock-back folders. **Patterns:** Hunters, Bowies, tacticals, fighters; some miniatures. **Technical:** Grinds D2, 440C and other Damascus. **Prices:** $75 to $200; some up to $500. **Remarks:** Full-time maker since 2000. First knife sold in 1998. **Mark:** JMK. **Other:** Likes to use height quality stabilized wood.

custom knifemakers

KING, HERMAN, PO Box 122, Millington, TN 38083, Phone: 901-876-3062

KING, BILL, 14830 Shaw Road, Tampa, FL 33625, Phone: 813-961-3455
Specialties: Folders, lock-backs, liner-locks and stud openers. **Patterns:** Wide varieties; folders. **Technical:** ATS-34 and some Damascus; single and double grinds. Offers filework and jewel embellishment; nickel-silver Damascus and mokume bolsters. **Prices:** $150 to $475; some to $850. **Remarks:** Full-time maker; first knife sold in 1976. All titanium fitting on liner-locks; screw or rivet construction on lock-backs. **Mark:** Last name in crown.

KING, FRED, 430 Grassdale Rd, Cartersville, GA 30120, Phone: 770-382-8478
Specialties: Fancy and embellished working straight knives and folders. **Patterns:** Hunters, Bowies and fighters. **Technical:** Grinds ATS-34 and D2; forges 5160 and Damascus. Offers filework. **Prices:** $100 to $3500. **Remarks:** Spare-time maker; first knife sold in 1984. **Mark:** Kings Edge.

KING JR., HARVEY G., Box 184, Eskridge, KS 66423-0184, Phone: 785-449-2487
Specialties: Traditional working and using straight knives of his design and to customer specs. **Patterns:** Hunters, Bowies and fillet knives. **Technical:** Grinds O1, A2 and D2. Prefers natural handle materials; offers leatherwork. **Prices:** Start at $70. **Remarks:** 3/4-time maker; first knife sold in 1988. **Mark:** Name and serial number based on steel used, year made and number of knives made that year.

KINKADE, JACOB, 197 Rd. 154, Carpenter, WY 82054, Phone: 307-649-2446
Specialties: Working/using knives of his design or to customer specs; some miniature swords, daggers and battle axes. **Patterns:** Hunters, daggers, boots; some miniatures. **Technical:** Grinds carbon and stainless and commercial Damascus. Prefers natural handle material. **Prices:** Start at $30. **Remarks:** Part-time maker; first knife sold in 1990. **Mark:** Connected initials or none.

KINKER, MIKE, 8755 E County Rd 50 N, Greensburg, IN 47240, Phone: 812-663-5277, Fax: 812-662-8131
Specialties: Working/using knives, straight knives. Starting to make folders. Your design. **Patterns:** Boots, daggers, hunters, skinners, hatchets. **Technical:** Grind 440C & ATS-34, others if required. Damascus, dovetail bolsters, jeweled blade. **Prices:** $125 to 375; some to $1000. **Remarks:** Part-time maker; first knife sold in 1991. Doing business as Kinker Knives. **Mark:** Kinker and Kinker plus year.

KINNIKIN, TODD, Eureka Forge, 8356 John McKeever Rd, House Springs, MO 63051, Phone: 314-938-6248
Specialties: Mosaic Damascus. **Patterns:** Hunters, fighters, folders and automatics. **Technical:** Forges own mosaic Damascus with tool steel Damascus edge. Prefers natural, fossil and artifact handle materials. **Prices:** $400 to $2400. **Remarks:** Full-time maker; first knife sold in 1994. **Mark:** Initials connected.

KIOUS, JOE, 1015 Ridge Pointe Rd, Kerrville, TX 78028, Phone: 830-367-2277, Fax: 830-367-2286
Specialties: Investment-quality interframe & bolstered folders. **Patterns:** Folder specialist - all types. **Technical:** Both stainless and non stainless Damascus. **Prices:** $450 to $3000; some to $10,000. **Remarks:** Full-time maker; first knife sold in 1969. **Mark:** Last name, city and state or last name only.

KIRK, RAY, PO Box 1445, Tahlequah, OK 74465, Phone: 918-456-1519
Specialties: Using knives with natural handles. **Patterns:** Neck knives & small hunters & skinners. **Technical:** Uses 52100 and 15N20 for Damascus. Some stock removal. **Prices:** $65 to $800. **Remarks:** Started forging in 1989; makes some Damascus. Has some 52100 and Damascus in custom flat bar 512E3 for sale **Mark:** Stamped "Raker" on blade.

KITSMILLER, JERRY, 67277 Las Vegas Dr, Montrose, CO 81401, Phone: 970-249-4290
Specialties: Working straight knives in standard patterns. **Patterns:** Hunters, boots. **Technical:** Grinds ATS-34 and 440C only. **Prices:** $75 to $200; some to $300. **Remarks:** Spare-time maker; first knife sold in 1984. **Mark:** J&S Knives.

KLINGBEIL, RUSSELL K., 1120 Shaffer Trail, Oviedo, FL 32765, Phone: 407-366-3223, Fax: 407-977-0329
Specialties: Frontier and Sheffield Bowies, gentlemen's fancy folders. **Patterns:** Bowies, daggers & fighters. **Technical:** Forges Damascus & Mosaic as well as straight carbon. **Prices:** $250 to $1200. **Remarks:** Part-time maker, ABS Journeyman; sold first knife 199 2. **Mark:** R. Klingbeil maker Oviedo, FL dated. **Other:** Steels used: 52100, 5160, 1095, 203E, 0-1.

KNICKMEYER, HANK, 6300 Crosscreek, Cedar Hill, MO 63016, Phone: 314-285-3210
Specialties: Complex mosaic Damascus constructions. **Patterns:** Fixed blades, swords, folders and automatics. **Technical:** Mosaic Damascus with all tool steel Damascus edges. **Prices:** $500 to $2000; some $3000 and higher. **Remarks:** Part-time maker; first knife sold in 1989. Doing business as Dutch Creek Forge & Foundry. **Mark:** Initials connected.

KNICKMEYER, KURT, 6344 Crosscreek, Cedar Hill, MO 63016, Phone: 314-274-0481

KNIGHT, JASON, Jason Knight & Family, 110 Paradie Pond Ln, Harleyville, SC 29448, Phone: 843-452-1163
Specialties: Bowies. **Patterns:** Bowies and anything from history or my own design. **Technical:** 1084, 5160, 01, 52102, Damascus/forged blades. **Prices:** $200 and up. **Remarks:** Bladesmith. **Mark:** KNIGHT.

KNIPSCHIELD, TERRY, 808 12th Ave. NE, Rochester, MN 55906, Phone: 507-288-7829
Specialties: Working straight and some folding knives in standard patterns. **Patterns:** Lock-back and slip-joint knives. **Technical:** Grinds ATS-34. **Prices:** $55 to $350; some to $600. **Remarks:** Part-time maker; first knife sold in 1986. Doing business as Knip Custom Knives. **Mark:** KNIP in Old English with shield logo.

KNIPSTEIN, R. C. (JOE), 731 N. Fielder, Arlington, TX 76012, Phone: 817-265-0573;817-265-2021, Fax: 817-265-3410
Specialties: Traditional pattern folders along with custom designs. **Patterns:** Hunters, Bowies, folders, fighters, utility knives. **Technical:** Grinds 440C, D2, 154CM and ATS-34. Natural handle materials and full tangs are standard. **Prices:** Start at $300. **Remarks:** Part-time maker; first knife sold in 1989. **Mark:** Last name.

KNUTH, JOSEPH E., 3307 Lookout Dr, Rockford, IL 61109, Phone: 815-874-9597
Specialties: High-art working straight knives of his design or to customer specs. **Patterns:** Daggers, fighters and swords. **Technical:** Grinds 440C, ATS-34 and D2. **Prices:** $150 to $1500; some to $15,000. **Remarks:** Full-time maker; first knife sold in 1989. **Mark:** Initials on bolster face.

KOHLS, JERRY, N4725 Oak Rd, Princeton, WI 54968, Phone: 920-295-3648
Specialties: Working knives & period pieces. **Patterns:** Hunters-boots & Bowies - your designs or mine. **Technical:** Grinds, ATS-34 440c 154CM & 1095 & commercial Damascus. **Remarks:** Part-time maker. **Mark:** Last Name.

KOJETIN, W., 20 Bapaume Rd, Delville, Germiston 1401, SOUTH AFRICA, Phone: 27118733305/mobile 21836256208
Specialties: High-art and working straight knives of all designs. **Patterns:** Daggers, hunters and his own Man hunter Bowie. **Technical:** Grinds D2 and ATS-34; forges and grinds 440B/C. Offers "wrap-around" pava and abalone handles, scrolled wood or ivory, stacked filework and setting of faceted semi-precious stones. **Prices:** $185 to $600; some to $11,000. **Remarks:** Spare-time maker; first knife sold in 1962. **Mark:** Billy K.

KOLITZ, ROBERT, W9342 Canary Rd, Beaver Dam, WI 53916, Phone: 920-887-1287
Specialties: Working straight knives to customer specs. **Patterns:** Bowies, hunters, bird and trout knives, boots. **Technical:** Grinds O1, 440C; commercial Damascus. **Prices:** $50 to $100; some to $500. **Remarks:** Spare-time maker; first knife sold in 1979. **Mark:** Last initial.

KOMMER, RUSS, 9211 Abbott Loop Rd, Anchorage, AK 99507, Phone: 907-346-3339
Specialties: Working straight knives with the outdoorsman in mind. **Patterns:** Hunters, semi-skinners, fighters, folders and utility knives, art knives. **Technical:** Hollow-grinds ATS-34, 440C and 440V. **Prices:** $125 to $850; some to $3000. **Remarks:** Full-time maker; first knife sold in 1995. **Mark:** Bear paw—full name, city and state or full name and state.

KOPP, TODD M., PO Box 3474, Apache Jct., AZ 85217, Phone: 602-983-6143
Specialties: Classic and traditional straight knives. **Patterns:** Bowies, boots, daggers, fighters and hunters. **Technical:** Grinds M1, ATS-34 and 4160. Some engraving and filework. **Prices:** $125 to $400; some to $800. **Remarks:** Part-time maker; first knife sold in 1989. **Mark:** Name, city and state.

KOSTER, STEVEN C, 16261 Gentry Ln, Hunting Beach, CA 92647, Phone: 714-840-8621
Specialties: Bowies, daggers, skinners, camp knives. **Technical:** Use 5160, 52100, 1084, 1095 steels. **Prices:** $200 to $1000. **Remarks:** Wood & leather sheaths with silver furniture. **Mark:** Koster squeezed between lines. **Other:** ABS apprentice, member California Knives Assoc.

KOVAL, MICHAEL T., 5819 Zarley St, New Albany, OH 43054, Phone: 614-855-0777
Specialties: Working straight knives of his design; period pieces. **Patterns:** Bowies, boots and daggers. **Technical:** Grinds D2, 440C and ATS-34. **Prices:** $95 to $195; some to $495. **Remarks:** Full-time knife maker supply house; spare-time knife maker. **Mark:** Last name.

KOVAR, EUGENE, 2626 W. 98th St, Evergreen Park, IL 60642, Phone: 708-636-3724
Specialties: One-of-a-kind miniature knives only. **Patterns:** Fancy to fantasy miniature knives; knife pendants and tie tacks. **Technical:** Files and grinds nails, nickel-silver and sterling silver. **Prices:** $5 to $35; some to $100. **Mark:** GK.

KOYAMA, CAPTAIN BUNSHICHI, 3-23 Shirako-cho, Nakamura-ku, Nagoya City 453-0817, JAPAN, Phone: 052-461-7070
Specialties: Innovative folding knife. **Patterns:** General purpose one hand. **Technical:** Grinds ATS-34 and Damascus. **Prices:** $400 to $900; some to $1500. **Remarks:** Part-time maker; first knife sold in 1994. **Mark:** Captain B. Koyama and the shoulder straps of CAPTAIN.

KOZAI, SHINGO, 934 Toyo Oka, Ueki, Kamoto Kumamoto, JAPAN 8611063, Phone: 8196 272-2988

KRAFT, STEVE, 315 S. E. 6th, Abilene, KS 67410, Phone: 785-263-1411
Specialties: Folders, lock-backs, scale release auto, push button auto. **Patterns:** Hunters, boot knives and fighters. **Technical:** Grinds ATS-34, Damascus; uses titanium, pearl, ivory etc. **Prices:** $500 to $2500. **Remarks:** Part-time maker; first knife sold in 1984. **Mark:** Kraft.

KRAFT, ELMER, 1358 Meadowlark Lane, Big Arm, MT 59910, Phone: 406-849-5086, Fax: 406-883-3056
Specialties: Traditional working/using straight knives of all designs. **Patterns:** Fighters, hunters, utility/camp knives. **Technical:** Grinds 440C, D2. Custom makes sheaths. **Prices:** $125 to $350; some to $500. **Remarks:** Part-time maker; first knife sold in 1984. **Mark:** Last name.

KRANNING, TERRY L., 548 W Wyeth St, Pocatello, ID 83204, Phone: 208-234-1812
Specialties: Miniature and full-size fantasy and working knives of his design. **Patterns:** Miniatures and some mini straight knives including razors, tomahawks, hunters, Bowies and fighters. **Technical:** Grinds 1095, 440C, commercial Damascus and nickel-silver. Uses exotic materials like meteorite. **Prices:** $40 to $150. **Remarks:** Part-time maker; first knife sold in 1978. **Mark:** Last initial or full initials in eagle head logo.

KRAPP, DENNY, 1826 Windsor Oak Dr, Apopka, FL 32703, Phone: 407-880-7115
Specialties: Fantasy and working straight knives of his design. **Patterns:** Hunters, fighters and utility/camp knives. **Technical:** Grinds ATS-34 and 440C. **Prices:** $85 to $300; some to $800. **Remarks:** Spare-time maker; first knife sold in 1988. **Mark:** Last name.

KRAUSE, ROY W., 22412 Corteville, St. Clair Shores, MI 48081, Phone: 810-296-3995, Fax: 810-296-2663
Specialties: Military and law enforcement/Japanese-style knives and swords. **Patterns:** Combat and back-up, Bowies, fighters, boot knives, daggers, tantos, wakazashis and katanas. **Technical:** Grinds ATS-34, A2, D2, 1045, O1 and commercial Damascus; differentially hardened Japanese-style blades. **Prices:** Moderate to upscale. **Remarks:** Full-time maker. **Mark:** Last name on traditional knives; initials in Japanese characters on Japanese-style knives.

KRAVITT, CHRIS, Treestump Leather, HC 31, Box 6484, Ellsworth, ME 04605-9320, Phone: 207-584-3000, Fax: 207-584-3000

KREH, LEFTY, 210 Wichersham Way, Cockeysville, MD 21030

KREIBICH, DONALD L., 6082 Boyd Ct, San Jose, CA 95123, Phone: 408-225-8354
Specialties: Working straight knives in standard patterns. **Patterns:** Bowies, boots and daggers; camp and fishing knives. **Technical:** Grinds 440C, 154CM and ATS-34; likes integrals. **Prices:** $100 to $200; some to $500. **Remarks:** Part-time maker; first knife sold in 1980. **Mark:** First and middle initials, last name.

KRESSLER, D. F., Schloss Odetzhausen, Schlossberg 1-85235, Odetzhausen, GERMANY, Phone: 08134-998 7290, Fax: 08134-998 7290
Specialties: High-tech Integral and Interframe knives. **Patterns:** Hunters, fighters, daggers. **Technical:** Grinds new state-of-the-art steels; prefers natural handle materials. **Prices:** Upscale. **Mark:** Name in logo.

KRETSINGER JR., PHILIP W., 17536 Bakersville Rd, Boonsboro, MD 21713, Phone: 301-432-6771
Specialties: Fancy and traditional period pieces. **Patterns:** Hunters, Bowies, camp knives, daggers, carvers, fighters. **Technical:** Forges W2, 5160

and his own Damascus. **Prices:** Start at $200. **Remarks:** Full-time knife maker. **Mark:** Name.

KUBAIKO, HANK, 10765 Northvale, Beach City, OH 44608, Phone: 330-359-2418
Specialties: Reproduce antique Bowies. Distal tapering and clay zone tempering. **Patterns:** Bowies, fighters, fishing knives, kitchen cutlery, lockers, slip-joints, camp knives, axes and miniatures. Also makes American, European and traditional samurai swords and daggers. **Technical:** Grinds 440C, ATS-34 and D2; will use CPM-T-440V at extra cost. **Prices:** Moderate. **Remarks:** Full-time maker. Allow three months for sword order fulfillment. **Mark:** Alaskan Maid and name. **Other:** This is my 25th year as a knife maker. I will be making 25 serial numbered knives-folder (liner-locks).

KUBASEK, JOHN A., 74 Northhampton St, Easthampton, MA 01027, Phone: 413-532-3288
Specialties: Left- and right-handed liner-lock folders of his design or to customer specs Also new knives made with Ripcord patent. **Patterns:** Fighters, tantos, drop points, survival knives, neck knives and belt buckle knives. **Technical:** Grinds ATS-34 and Damascus. **Prices:** $395 to $1500. **Remarks:** Part-time maker; first knife sold in 1985. **Mark:** Name and address etched.

I

LA GRANGE, FANIE, 22 Sturke Rd, Selborne, Bellville 7530, SOUTH AFRICA, Phone: 27-021-9134199, Fax: 27-021-9134199
Specialties: Fancy high-tech straight knives and folders of his design and to customer specs. **Patterns:** Daggers, hunters and locking folders. **Technical:** Grinds Sandvik 12C27 and ATS-34; forges and grinds Damascus. Engraves, enamels and anodizes bolsters. Uses rare and natural handle materials. **Prices:** $250 to $500; some higher. **Remarks:** Full-time maker; first knife sold in 1987. **Mark:** Name, town, country under Table Mountain.

LADD, JIMMIE LEE, 1120 Helen, Deer Park, TX 77536, Phone: 713-479-7186
Specialties: Working straight knives. **Patterns:** Hunters, skinners and utility knives. **Technical:** Grinds 440C and D2. **Prices:** $75 to $225. **Remarks:** First knife sold in 1979. **Mark:** First and middle initials, last name.

LADD, JIM S., 1120 Helen, Deer Park, TX 77536, Phone: 713-479-7286
Specialties: Working knives and period pieces. **Patterns:** Hunters, boots and Bowies plus other straight knives. **Technical:** Grinds D2, 440C and 154CM. **Prices:** $125 to $225; some to $550. **Remarks:** Part-time maker; first knife sold in 1965. Doing business as The Tinker. **Mark:** First and middle initials, last name.

LAGRANGE, FANIE, 12 Canary Crescent, Table View 7441, South Africa, Phone: 27 21 55 76 805
Specialties: African influenced styles in folders & fixed blades. **Patterns:** All original patterns with many one-of-a-kinds. **Technical:** Mostly stock removal in 12c27, ATS-34, stainless Damascus. **Prices:** $350-$3000. **Remarks:** Professional maker. S A Guild Member. **Mark:** Name over spear.

LAINSON, TONY, 114 Park Ave, Council Bluffs, IA 51503, Phone: 712-322-5222
Specialties: Working straight knives, liner-locking folders. **Technical:** Grinds 154CM, ATS-34, 440C buys Damascus. Handle materials include Micarta, carbon fiber G-10 ivory pearl and bone. **Prices:** $95 to $600. **Remarks:** Part-time maker; first knife sold in 1987. **Mark:** Name and state.

LAIRSON SR., JERRY, H C 68 Box 970, Ringold, OK 74754, Phone: 580-876-3426
Specialties: Fighters and hunters. **Patterns:** Damascus, random, raindrop, ladder, twist & others. **Technical:** All knives hammer forged. **Prices:** Carbon steel $150 to $400; Damascus $600 to $900. **Remarks:** I make any style knife but prefer fighters and hunters.

LAKE, RON, 3360 Bendix Ave, Eugene, OR 97401, Phone: 541-484-2683
Specialties: High-tech working knives; inventor of the modern interframe folder. **Patterns:** Hunters, boots, etc.; locking folders. **Technical:** Grinds 154CM and ATS-34. Patented interframe with special lock release tab. **Prices:** $2200 to $3000; some higher. **Remarks:** Full-time maker; first knife sold in 1966. **Mark:** Last name.

LALA, PAULO RICARDO P. AND LALA, ROBERTO P., R. Daniel Martins, 636, Centro, Presidente Prudente, SP-19031-260, BRAZIL, Phone: 0182-210125
Specialties: Straight knives and folders of all designs to customer specs. **Patterns:** Bowies, daggers fighters, hunters and utility knives. **Technical:** Grinds and forges D6, 440C, high-carbon steels and Damascus. **Prices:**

custom knifemakers

$60 to $400; some higher. **Remarks:** Full-time makers; first knife sold in 1991. All stainless steel blades are ultra sub-zero quenched. **Mark:** Sword carved on top of anvil under KORTH.

LAMB, CURTIS J., 3336 Louisiana Terrace, Ottawa, KS 66067-8996, Phone: 785-242-6657

LAMBERT, RONALD S., 24 Vermont St, Johnston, RI 02919, Phone: 401-831-5427
Specialties: Traditional working and using straight knives of his design. **Patterns:** Boots, Bowies and hunters. **Technical:** Grinds O1 and 440C; forges 1070. Offers exotic wood handles; sheaths have exotic skin overlay. **Prices:** $100 to $500; some to $850. **Remarks:** Part-time maker; first knife sold in 1991. Doing business as RL Custom Knives. **Mark:** Initials; each knife is numbered.

LAMBERT, JARRELL D., 2321 FM 2982, Granado, TX 77962, Phone: 512-771-3744
Specialties: Traditional working and using straight knives of his design and to customer specs. **Patterns:** Bowies, hunters, tantos and utility/camp knives. **Technical:** Grinds ATS-34; forges W2 and his own Damascus. Makes own sheaths. **Prices:** $80 to $600; some to $1000. **Remarks:** Part-time maker; first knife sold in 1982. **Mark:** Etched first and middle initials, last name; or stamped last name.

LAMEY, ROBERT M., 15800 Lamey Dr, Biloxi, MS 39532, Phone: 228-396-9066, Fax: 228-396-9022
Specialties: Bowies, fighters, hard use knives. **Patterns:** Bowies, fighters, hunters & camp knives. **Technical:** Forged and stock removal. **Prices:** $125 to $350. **Remarks:** Lifetime reconditioning; will build to customer designs, specializing in hard use, affordable knives. **Mark:** LAMEY.

LAMPREY, MIKE, 32 Pathfield, Great Torrington, Devon EX38 7BX, ENGLAND, Phone: 01805 601331
Specialties: High-tech locking folders of his design. **Patterns:** Side lock folders. **Technical:** Grinds ATS-34, Dendritic 440C, PM stainless Damascus. Linerless handle shells in titanium. Belt clips in ATS-34. **Prices:** $300 to $750; some to $1000. **Remarks:** Part-time maker; first knife sold in 1982. **Mark:** Signature or Celtic knot.

LAMPSON, FRANK G., 3215 Saddle Bag Circle, Rimrock, AZ 86335, Phone: 928-567-7395
Specialties: Working folders; one-of-a-kinds. **Patterns:** Folders, hunters, utility knives, fillet knives and Bowies. **Technical:** Grinds ATS-34, 440C and 154CM. **Prices:** $100 to $750; some to $3500. **Remarks:** Full-time maker; first knife sold in 1971. **Mark:** Name in fish logo.

LANCASTER, C. G., No 2 Schoonwinkel St, Parys, Free State, SOUTH AFRICA, Phone: 0568112090
Specialties: High-tech working and using knives of his design and to customer specs. **Patterns:** Hunters, locking folders and utility/camp knives. **Technical:** Grinds Sandvik 12C27, 440C and D2. Offers anodized titanium bolsters. **Prices:** $450 to $750; some to $1500. **Remarks:** Part-time maker; first knife sold in 1990. **Mark:** Etched logo.

LANCE, BILL, PO Box 4427, Eagle River, AK 99577, Phone: 907-694-1487
Specialties: Ooloos and working straight knives; limited issue sets. **Patterns:** Several ooloo patterns, drop-point skinners. **Technical:** Uses ATS-34, Vascomax 350; ivory, horn and high-class wood handles. **Prices:** $85 to $300; art sets to $3000. **Remarks:** First knife sold in 1981. **Mark:** Last name over a lance.

LANDERS, JOHN, 758 Welcome Rd, Newnan, GA 30263, Phone: 404-253-5719
Specialties: High-art working straight knives and folders of his design. **Patterns:** hunters, fighters and slip-joint folders. **Technical:** Grinds 440C, ATS-34, 154CM and commercial Damascus. **Prices:** $85 to $250; some to $500. **Remarks:** Part-time maker; first knife sold in 1989. **Mark:** Last name.

LANE, BEN, 4802 Massie St, North Little Rock, AR 72218, Phone: 501-753-8238
Specialties: Fancy straight knives of his design and to customer specs; period pieces. **Patterns:** Bowies, hunters, utility/camp knives. **Technical:** Grinds D2 and 154CM; forges and grinds 1095. Offers intricate handle work including inlays and spacers. **Prices:** $120 to $450; some to $5000. **Remarks:** Part-time maker; first knife sold in 1989. **Mark:** Full name, city, state.

LANG, KURT, 4908 S. Wildwood Dr, McHenry, IL 60050, Phone: 708-516-4649
Specialties: High-art working knives. **Patterns:** Bowies, utilitarian-type knives with rough finishes. **Technical:** Forges welded steel in European- and Japanese-styles. **Prices:** Moderate to upscale. **Remarks:** Part-time maker. **Mark:** "Crazy Eye" logo.

LANG, BUD, 265 S Anita Dr Ste 120, Orange, CA 92868-3310, Phone: 714-939-9991

LANGLEY, GENE H., 1022 N. Price Rd, Florence, SC 29506, Phone: 843-669-3150
Specialties: Working knives in standard patterns. **Patterns:** Hunters, boots, fighters, locking folders and slip-joints. **Technical:** Grinds 440C, 154CM and ATS-34. **Prices:** $125 to $450; some to $1000. **Remarks:** Part-time maker; first knife sold in 1979. **Mark:** Name.

LANKTON, SCOTT, 8065 Jackson Rd. R-11, Ann Arbor, MI 48103, Phone: 313-426-3735
Specialties: Pattern welded swords, krisses and Viking period pieces. **Patterns:** One-of-a-kind. **Technical:** Forges W2, L6 nickel and other steels. **Prices:** $600 to $12,000. **Remarks:** Part-time bladesmith, full-time smith; first knife sold in 1976. **Mark:** Last name logo.

LAPEN, CHARLES, Box 529, W. Brookfield, MA 01585
Specialties: Chefs knives for the culinary artist. **Patterns:** camp knives, Japanese-style swords and wood working tools, hunters. **Technical:** Forges 1075, car spring and his own Damascus. Favors narrow and Japanese tangs. **Prices:** $200 to $400; some to $2000. **Remarks:** Part-time maker; first knife sold in 1972. **Mark:** Last name.

LAPLANTE, BRETT, 4545 CR412, McKinney, TX 75071, Phone: 972-838-9191
Specialties: Working straight knives and folders to customer specs. **Patterns:** Survival knives, Bowies, skinners, hunters. **Technical:** Grinds D2 and 440C. Heat-treats. **Prices:** $175 to $600. **Remarks:** Part-time maker; first knife sold in 1987. **Mark:** Last name in Canadian maple leaf logo.

LARAMIE, MARK, 181 Woodland St, Fitchburg, MA 01420, Phone: 978-353-6979
Specialties: Fancy and working folders and straight knives. **Patterns:** Locking folders, hunters. **Technical:** Grinds 440c, ATS-34, and commercial Damascus. **Prices:** $100 to $1500. **Remarks:** part-time maker, first knife sold in 2000. **Mark:** name, city, state or initials.

LARGIN, Kelgin Knives, PO Box 151, Metamora, IN 47030, Phone: 765-969-5012
Remarks: Teach classes across U. S. in mobile knife shop.

LARSON, RICHARD, 549 E. Hawkeye Ave, Turlock, CA 95380, Phone: 209-668-1615
Specialties: Traditional working/using straight knives in standard patterns. **Patterns:** Bowies, hunters and utility/camp knives. **Technical:** Grinds ATS-34, 440C, and 154CM. Engraves and scrimshaws holsters and handles. Hand-sews sheaths with tooling. **Prices:** $150 to $300; some to $1000. **Remarks:** Part-time maker; first knife sold in 1986. Doing business as Larson Knives. **Mark:** Knife logo spelling last name.

LARY, ED, 651 Rangeline Rd, Mosinee, WI 54455, Phone: 715-693-3940
Specialties: Upscale hunters and art knives. **Patterns:** Hunters, fighters, period pieces. **Technical:** Grinds all steels, heat treats, fancy file work. **Prices:** Upscale. **Remarks:** Since 1974. **Mark:** Lary.

LAUGHLIN, DON, 190 Laughlin Dr, Vidor, TX 77662, Phone: 409-769-3390
Specialties: Straight knives and folders of his design. **Patterns:** Hunters, spring-back folders, drop points and trailing points. **Technical:** Grinds D2, 440C and 154CM; stock removal; makes his own Damascus. **Prices:** $175 to $250 for stock removal blades; $250 to $800 for Damascus blades. **Remarks:** Full-time maker; first knife sold in 1973. **Mark:** DEER or full name.

LAURENT, KERMIT, 1812 Acadia Dr, LaPlace, LA 70068, Phone: 504-652-5629
Specialties: Traditional and working straight knives and folders of his design. **Patterns:** Bowies, hunters, utilities and folders. **Technical:** Forges own Damascus, plus uses most tool steels & stainless. Specializes in altering cable patterns. Uses stabilized handle materials, especially select exotic woods. **Prices:** $100 to $2500; some to $50,000. **Remarks:** Full-time maker; first knife sold in 1982. Doing business as Kermit's Knife Works. Favorite material is meteorite Damascus **Mark:** First name.

LAWLER, TIM, Sabersmith, 11073 S Hartel, Grand Ledge, ME 48837, Phone: 517-281-8327

LAWRENCE, ALTON, 201 W Stillwell, De Queen, AR 71832, Phone: 870-642-7643, Fax: 870-642-4023
Specialties: Classic straight knives and folders to customer specs. **Patterns:** Bowies, hunters, folders and utility/camp knives. **Technical:** Forges 5160, 1095, 1084, Damascus and railroad spikes. **Prices:** Start at $100. **Remarks:** Part-time maker; first knife sold in 1988. **Mark:** Last name inside fish symbol.

LAY, R. J. (BOB), Box 122, Falkland BC, CANADA V0E 1W0, Phone: 250-379-2265, Fax: Same
Specialties: Traditional styled, fancy straight knifes of his design. Specializing in hunters. **Patterns:** Bowies, fighters and hunters. **Technical:** Grinds 440C, forges and grinds tool steels. Uses exotic handle and spacer material. File cut, prefers narrow tang. Sheaths available. **Price:** $200 to $500; some to $1500. **Remarks:** Full-time maker, first knife sold in 1976. Doing business as Lay's Custom Knives. **Mark:** Signature acid etched.

LAY, L. J., 602 Mimosa Dr, Burkburnett, TX 76354, Phone: 817-569-1329
Specialties: Working straight knives in standard patterns; some period pieces. **Patterns:** Drop-point hunters, Bowies and fighters. **Technical:** Grinds ATS-34 to mirror finish; likes Micarta handles. **Prices:** Moderate. **Remarks:** Full-time maker; first knife sold in 1985. **Mark:** Name or name with ram head and city or stamp L J Lay.

LEACH, MIKE J., 5377 W. Grand Blanc Rd, Swartz Creek, MI 48473, Phone: 810-655-4850
Specialties: Fancy working knives. **Patterns:** Hunters, fighters, Bowies and heavy-duty knives; slip-joint folders and integral straight patterns. **Technical:** Grinds D2, 440C and 154CM; buys Damascus. **Prices:** Start at $150. **Remarks:** Full-time maker; first knife sold in 1952. **Mark:** First initial, last name.

LEAVITT JR., EARL F., Pleasant Cove Rd, Box 306, E. Boothbay, ME 04544, Phone: 207-633-3210
Specialties: 1500-1870 working straight knives and fighters; pole arms. **Patterns:** Historically significant knives, classic/modern custom designs. **Technical:** Flat-grinds O1; heat-treats. Filework available. **Prices:** $90 to $350; some to $1000. **Remarks:** Full-time maker; first knife sold in 1981. Doing business as Old Colony Manufactory. **Mark:** Initials in oval.

LEBATARD, PAUL M., 14700 Old River Rd, Vancleave, MS 39565, Phone: 228-826-4137, Fax: 228-826-2933
Specialties: Sound working knives; lightweight folders. **Patterns:** Hunters, fillets, camp and kitchen knives, combat/survival utility knives, Bowies, toothpicks and one- and two-blade folders. **Technical:** Grinds ATS-34, A-2, D-2, 440-C; forges 52100 & 5160. Machines folder frames from aircraft aluminum. **Prices:** $50 to $550. **Remarks:** Part-time maker; first knife sold in 1974. Offers knife repair, restoration and sharpening. **Mark:** Last name. **Other:** Knives are serial numbered.

LEBER, HEINZ, Box 446, Hudson's Hope, BC, CANADA V0C 1V0, Phone: 250-783-5304
Specialties: Working straight knives of his design. **Patterns:** 20 models, form capers to Bowies. **Technical:** Hollow-grinds D2 and M2 steel; mirror-finishes and full tang only. Likes moose, elk, stone sheep for handles. **Prices:** $175 to $1000. **Remarks:** Full-time maker; first knife sold in 1975. **Mark:** Initials connected.

LEBLANC, JOHN, Rt. 2, Box 22950, Winnsboro, TX 75494, Phone: 903-629-7745

LECK, DAL, Box 1054, Hayden, CO 81639, Phone: 970-276-3663
Specialties: Classic, traditional and working knives of his design and in standard patterns; period pieces. **Patterns:** Boots, daggers, fighters, hunters and push daggers. **Technical:** Forges O1 and 5160; makes his own Damascus. **Prices:** $175 to $700; some to $1500. **Remarks:** Part-time maker; first knife sold in 1990. Doing business as The Moonlight Smithy. **Mark:** Stamped: hammer & anvil with initials.

LEE, RANDY, PO Box 1873, St. Johns, AZ 85936, Phone: 928-337-2594, Fax: 928-337-5002
Specialties: Traditional working and using straight knives of his design. **Patterns:** Bowies, fighters, hunters, daggers and professional throwing knives. **Technical:** Grinds ATS-34, 440C and D2. Offers sheaths. **Prices:** $235 to $1500; some to $800. **Remarks:** Part-time maker; first knife sold in 1979. **Mark:** Full name, city, state.

LEET, LARRY W., 14417 2nd Ave. S. W., Burien, WA 98166-1505
Specialties: Heavy-duty working knives. **Patterns:** Hunters, tantos, camp knives and Bowies. **Technical:** Grinds stainless steels; likes filework. **Remarks:** Full-time maker; first knife sold in 1970. **Mark:** Stylized initials.

LELAND, STEVE, 2300 Sir Francis Drake Blvd., Fairfax, CA 94930-1118, Phone: 415-457-0318, Fax: 415-457-0995
Specialties: Traditional and working straight knives and folders of his design and to customer specs. Makes straight & locking folder sets. **Patterns:** Boots, hunters, fighters, Bowies. **Technical:** Grinds O1, ATS-34 and 440C. Does own heat treat. Makes nickel silver sheaths. **Prices:** $150 to $550; some to $1500. **Remarks:** Part-time maker; first knife sold in 1987. Doing business as Leland Handmade Knives. **Mark:** Last name.

LEMCKE, JIM L., 10649 Haddington, Ste 180, Houston, TX 77043, Phone: 888-461-8632, Fax: 713-461-8221
Specialties: Large supply of custom ground and factory finished blades; knife kits; leather sheaths; in-house heat treating and cryogenic tempering; exotic handle material (wood, ivory, oosik, horn, stabilized woods); machines & supplies for knife making; polishing and finishing supplies; heat treat ovens; etching equipment; bar, sheet and rod material (brass, stainless steel, nickel silver); titanium sheet material. Catalog. $4.

LEONARD, RANDY JOE, 188 Newton Rd, Sarepta, LA 71071, Phone: 318-994-2712

LEONE, NICK, 9 Georgetown, Pontoon Beach, IL 62040, Phone: 618-797-1179
Specialties: Working straight knives and art daggers. **Patterns:** Bowies, skinners, hunters, camp/utility, fighters, daggers and primitive knives. **Technical:** Forges 5160, W2, O1, 1098, 52100 and his own Damascus. **Prices:** t$100 to $1000; some to $3500. **Remarks:** Full-time maker; first knife sold in 1987. Doing business as Anvil Head Forge. **Mark:** Last name, NL, AHF.

LEPORE, MICHAEL J., 66 Woodcutters Dr, Bethany, CT 06524, Phone: 203-393-3823
Specialties: One-of-a-kind designs to customer specs; mostly handmade. **Patterns:** Fancy working straight knives and folders. **Technical:** Forges and grinds W2, W1 and O1; prefers natural handle materials. **Prices:** Start at $350. **Remarks:** Spare-time maker; first knife sold in 1984. **Mark:** Last name.

LERCH, MATTHEW, N88 W23462 North Lisbon Road, Sussex, WI 53089, Phone: 262-246-6362
Specialties: Gentlemen's folders. **Patterns:** Interframe and integral folders; lock-backs, slip-joints, side locks, button locks and liner-locks. **Technical:** Grinds ATS-34, 1095, 440 and Damascus. Offers filework and embellished bolsters. **Prices:** $400 to $3000. **Remarks:** Part-time maker; first knife sold in 1995. **Mark:** Last name.

LEVENGOOD, BILL, 15011 Otto Rd, Tampa, FL 33624, Phone: 813-961-5688
Specialties: Working straight knives and folders. **Patterns:** Hunters, Bowies, folders and collector pieces. **Technical:** Grinds ATS-34, BG-42 and Damascus. **Prices:** $175 to $1500. **Remarks:** Part-time maker; first knife sold in 1983. **Mark:** Last name, city, state.

LEVERETT, KEN, PO Box 696, Lithia, FL 33547, Phone: 813-689-8578
Specialties: High-tech and working straight knives and folders of his design and to customer specs. **Patterns:** Bowies, hunters and locking folders. **Technical:** Grinds ATS-34, Damascus. **Prices:** $100 to $350; some to $1500. **Remarks:** Part-time maker; first knife sold in 1991. **Mark:** Name, city, state.

LEVIN, JACK, 7216 Bay Pkwy, Brooklyn, NY 11204, Phone: 718-232-8574

LEVINE, BOB, 101 Westwood Dr, Tullahoma, TN 37388, Phone: 931-454-9943
Specialties: Working left- and right-handed Liner-lock folders. **Patterns:** Hunters and folders. **Technical:** Grinds ATS-34, 440C, D2, O1 and some Damascus; hollow and some flat grinds. Uses sheep horn, fossil ivory, Micarta and exotic woods. Provides custom leather sheath with each fixed knife. **Prices:** $125 to $500; some higher. **Remarks:** Full-time maker; first knife sold in 1984. Voting member Knife Makers Guild. **Mark:** Name and logo.

LEWIS, TOM R., 1613 Standpipe Rd, Carlsbad, NM 88220, Phone: 505-885-3616
Specialties: Traditional working straight knives and pocketknives. **Patterns:** Outdoor knives, hunting knives and Bowies and pocketknives. **Technical:** Grinds ATS-34 forges 5168 & 01. Makes wire, pattern welded and chainsaw Damascus. **Prices:** $100 to $900. **Remarks:** Part-time maker; first knife sold in 1980. Doing business as TR Lewis Handmade Knives. **Mark:** Lewis family crest.

LEWIS, MIKE, 21 Pleasant Hill Dr, DeBary, FL 32713, Phone: 386-753-0936
Specialties: Traditional straight knives. **Patterns:** Swords and daggers. **Technical:** Grinds 440C, ATS-34 and 5160. Frequently uses cast bronze and cast nickel guards and pommels. **Prices:** $100 to $750. **Remarks:** Part-time maker; first knife sold in 1988. **Mark:** Dragon Steel and serial number.

LEWIS, K. J., 374 Cook Rd, Lugoff, SC 29078, Phone: 803-438-4343

LEWIS, STEVE, Knife Dealer, PO Box 9056, Woodland Park, CO 80866, Phone: 719-686-1120 or 888-685-2322
Specialties: Buy, sell, trade and consign W. F. Moran and other fine custom-made knives. Mail order and major shows.

LICATA, STEVEN, Licata Custom Knives, 89 Fenner Ave, Clifton, NJ 07013, Phone: 973-523-6964
Prices: $200-$25,000

custom knifemakers

LIEBENBERG, ANDRE, 8 Hilma Rd, Bordeauxrandburg 2196, SOUTH AFRICA, Phone: 011-787-2303
Specialties: High-art straight knives of his design. **Patterns:** Daggers, fighters and swords. **Technical:** Grinds 440C and 12C27. **Prices:** $250 to $500; some $4000 and higher. Giraffe bone handles with semi-precious stones. **Remarks:** Spare-time maker; first knife sold in 1990. **Mark:** Initials.

LIEGEY, KENNETH R., 132 Carney Dr, Millwood, WV 25262, Phone: 304-273-9545
Specialties: Traditional working/using straight knives of his design and to customer specs. **Patterns:** Hunters, utility/camp knives, miniatures. **Technical:** Grinds 440C. **Prices:** $75 to $150; some to $300. **Remarks:** Spare-time maker; first knife sold in 1977. **Mark:** First and middle initials, last name.

LIGHTFOOT, GREG, RR #2, Kitscoty AB, CANADA T0B 2P0, Phone: 780-846-2812
Specialties: Stainless steel and Damascus. **Patterns:** Boots, fighters and locking folders. **Technical:** Grinds BG-42, 440C, D2, CPM steels, Stellite 6K. Offers engraving. **Prices:** $250 to $500; some to $850. **Remarks:** Full-time maker; first knife sold in 1988. Doing business as Lightfoot Knives. **Mark:** Shark with Lightfoot Knives below.

LIKARICH, STEVE, 26075 Green Acres Rd, Colfax, CA 95713, Phone: 530-346-8480
Specialties: Fancy working knives; art knives of his design. **Patterns:** Hunters, fighters and art knives of his design. **Technical:** Grinds ATS-34, 154CM and 440C; likes high polishes and filework. **Prices:** $200 to $2000; some higher. **Remarks:** Full-time maker; first knife sold in 1987. **Mark:** Name.

LINDSAY, CHRIS A., 1324 N. E. Locksley Dr, Bend, OR 97701, Phone: 541-389-3875
Specialties: Working knives in standard patterns. **Patterns:** Hunters and camp knives. **Technical:** Hollow- and flat-grinds 440C and ATS-34; offers brushed finishes, tapered tangs. **Prices:** $75 to $160; knife kits $60 to $80. **Remarks:** Part-time maker; first knife sold in 1980. **Mark:** Last name, town and state in oval.

LINKLATER, STEVE, 8 Cossar Dr, Aurora, Ont., CANADA L4G 3N8, Phone: 905-727-8929
Specialties: Traditional working/using straight knives and folders of his design. **Patterns:** Fighters, hunters and locking folders. **Technical:** Grinds ATS-34, 440V and D2. **Prices:** $125 to $350; some to $600. **Remarks:** Part-time maker; first knife sold in 1987. Doing business as Links Knives. **Mark:** LINKS.

LISTER JR., WELDON E., 9140 Sailfish Dr, Boerne, TX 78006, Phone: 210-981-2210
Specialties: One-of-a-kind fancy and embellished folders. **Patterns:** Locking and slip-joint folders. **Technical:** Commercial Damascus and O1. All knives embellished. Engraves, inlays, carves and scrimshaws. **Prices:** Upscale. **Remarks:** Spare-time maker; first knife sold in 1991. **Mark:** Last name.

LITTLE, GARY M., HC84 Box 10301, PO Box 156, Broadbent, OR 97414, Phone: 503-572-2656
Specialties: Fancy working knives. **Patterns:** Hunters, tantos, Bowies, axes and buckskinners; locking folders and interframes. **Technical:** Forges and grinds O1, L6, 1095; makes his own Damascus; bronze fittings. **Prices:** $85 to $300; some to $2500. **Remarks:** Full-time maker; first knife sold in 1979. Doing business as Conklin Meadows Forge. **Mark:** Name, city and state.

LITTLE, JIMMY L., PO Box 871652, Wasilla, AK 99687, Phone: 907-373-7831
Specialties: Working straight knives; fancy period pieces. **Patterns:** Bowies, bush swords and camp knives. **Technical:** Grinds 440C, 154CM and ATS-34. **Prices:** $100 to $1000. **Remarks:** Full-time maker; first knife sold in 1984. **Mark:** First and middle initials, last name.

LITTLE, GUY A., 486 West Lincoln Av, Oakhurst, NJ 07755

LITTLE, LARRY, 1A Cranberry Ln, Spencer, MA 01562, Phone: 508-885-2301
Specialties: Working straight knives of his design or to customer specs. Likes Scagel-style. **Patterns:** Hunters, fighters…can grind other patterns. **Technical:** Grinds L6 and O1, most have file work. Prefers natural handle material especially antler. Uses nickel silver. Makes own heavy duty leather sheath. **Prices:** start at $100. **Remarks:** Part-time maker. First knife sold in 1985. Offers knife repairs. **Mark:** Last name.

LIVELY, TIM AND MARIAN, PO Box 8784 CRB, Tucson, AZ 85738
Specialties: Multi-cultural primitive knives of their design on speculation. **Patterns:** Neo-tribal one-of-a-kinds. **Technical:** Hand forges using ancient techniques; hammer finish. **Prices:** Moderate. **Remarks:** Full-time makers; first knife sold in 1974. **Mark:** Last name.

LIVESAY, NEWT, 3306 S. Dogwood St, Siloam Springs, AR 72761, Phone: 479-549-3356, Fax: 479-549-3357
Specialties: Combat utility knives, hunting knives, titanium knives, swords, axes, KYDWX sheaths for knives and pistols, custom orders.

LIVINGSTON, ROBERT C., PO Box 6, Murphy, NC 28906, Phone: 704-837-4155
Specialties: Art letter openers to working straight knives. **Patterns:** Minis to machetes. **Technical:** Forges and grinds most steels. **Prices:** Start at $20. **Remarks:** Full-time maker; first knife sold in 1988. Doing business as Mystik Knife works. **Mark:** MYSTIK.

LOCKE, KEITH, PMB 141, 7120 Rufe Snow Dr Ste 106, Watauga, TX 76148-1867, Phone: 817-514-7272
Technical: Forges carbon steel and handcrafts sheaths for his knives. **Remarks:** Sold first knife in 1996.

LOCKETT, STERLING, 527 E. Amherst Dr, Burbank, CA 91504, Phone: 818-846-5799
Specialties: Working straight knives and folders to customer specs. **Patterns:** Hunters and fighters. **Technical:** Grinds. **Prices:** Moderate. **Remarks:** Spare-time maker. **Mark:** Name, city with hearts.

LOCKETT, LOWELL C., 66653 Gunderson Rd, North Bend, OR 97459-9210, Phone: 541-756-1614
Specialties: Traditional & working/using knives. **Patterns:** Bowies, hunters, utility/camp knives. **Technical:** Forges 5160, 1095, 1084, 02, L6. Makes own guards & sheaths. **Prices:** Start at $90. **Remarks:** Full-time maker. **Mark:** L C lockett (on side of blade) ABS Journeyman Smith, member OKCA.

LOERCHNER, WOLFGANG, Wolfe Fine Knives, PO Box 255, Bayfield, Ont., CANADA N0M 1G0, Phone: 519-565-2196
Specialties: Traditional straight knives, mostly ornate. **Patterns:** Small swords, daggers and stilettos; locking folders and miniatures. **Technical:** Grinds D2, 440C and 154CM; all knives hand-filed and flat-ground. **Prices:** $300 to $5000; some to $10,000. **Remarks:** Part-time maker; first knife sold in 1983. Doing business as Wolfe Fine Knives. **Mark:** WOLFE.

LONEWOLF, J. AGUIRRE, 481 Hwy 105, Demorest, GA 30535, Phone: 706-754-4660, Fax: 706-754-8470
Specialties: High-art working and using straight knives of his design. **Patterns:** Bowies, hunters, utility/camp knives and fine steel blades. **Technical:** Forges Damascus and high-carbon steel. Most knives have hand-carved moose antler handles. **Prices:** $55 to $500; some to $2000. **Remarks:** Full-time maker; first knife sold in 1980. Doing business as Lonewolf Trading Post. **Mark:** Stamp.

LONG, GLENN A., 10090 SW 186th Ave, Dunnellon, FL 34432, Phone: 352-489-4272
Specialties: Classic working and using straight knives of his design and to customer specs. **Patterns:** Hunters, Bowies, utility. **Technical:** Grinds 440C D2 and 440V. **Prices:** $85 to $300; some to $800. **Remarks:** Part-time maker; first knife sold in 1990. **Mark:** Last name inside diamond.

LONGWORTH, DAVE, 1811 SR 774, Hamersville, OH 45130, Phone: 513-876-3637
Specialties: High-tech working knives. **Patterns:** Locking folders, hunters, fighters and elaborate daggers. **Technical:** Grinds O1, ATS-34, 440C; buys Damascus. **Prices:** $125 to $600; some higher. **Remarks:** Part-time maker; first knife sold in 1980. **Mark:** Last name.

LOOS, HENRY C., 210 Ingraham, New Hyde Park, NY 11040, Phone: 516-354-1943
Specialties: Miniature fancy knives and period pieces of his design. **Patterns:** Bowies, daggers and swords. **Technical:** Grinds O1 and 440C. Uses sterling, 18K, rubies and emeralds. All knives come with handmade hardwood cases. **Prices:** $90 to $195; some to $250. **Remarks:** Spare-time maker; first knife sold in 1990. **Mark:** Script last initial.

LORO, GENE, 2457 State Route 93 NE, Crooksville, OH 43731, Phone: 740-982-4521, Fax: 740-982-1249
Specialties: Hand forged knives. **Patterns:** Damascus, Random, Ladder, Twist, etc. **Technical:** ABS Journeyman Smith. **Prices:** $100 and up. **Remarks:** I do not make folders. **Mark:** Loro. Retired engineer.

LOTT, SHERRY, 1098 Legion Park Rd, Greensburg, KY 42743, Phone: 270-932-2212, Fax: 270-932-6442
Specialties: One-of-a-kind, usually carved handles. **Patterns:** Art. **Technical:** Carbon steel, stock removal. Prices: Moderate. **Mark:** Sherry Lott. **Other:** First knife sold in 1994.

LOVELESS, R. W., PO Box 7836, Riverside, CA 92503, Phone: 909-689-7800
Specialties: Working knives, fighters and hunters of his design. **Patterns:** Contemporary hunters, fighters and boots. **Technical:** Grinds 154CM and ATS-34. **Prices:** $850 to $4950. **Remarks:** Full-time maker since 1969. **Mark:** Name in logo.

LOVESTRAND, SCHUYLER, 1136 19th St SW, Vero Beach, FL 32962, Phone: 561-778-0282, Fax: 561-466-1126
Specialties: Fancy working straight knives of his design and to customer specs; unusual fossil ivories. **Patterns:** Hunters, fighters, Bowies and fishing knives. **Technical:** Grinds stainless steel. **Prices:** $275 and up . **Remarks:** Part-time maker; first knife sold in 1982. **Mark:** Name in logo.

LOZIER, DON, 5394 SE 168th Ave, Ocklawaha, FL 32179, Phone: 352-625-3576
Specialties: Fancy and working straight knives of his design and in standard patterns. **Patterns:** Daggers, fighters, boot knives, and hunters. **Technical:** Grinds ATS-34, 440C & Damascus. Most Pieces are highly embellished by notable artisans. Taking limited number of orders per annum. **Prices:** Start at $250; most are $1250 to $3000; some to $12,000. **Remarks:** Full-time maker. **Mark:** Name.

LUCHAK, BOB, 15705 Woodforest Blvd., Channelview, TX 77530, Phone: 281-452-1779
Specialties: Presentation knives; start of The Survivor series. **Patterns:** Skinners, Bowies, camp axes, steak knife sets and fillet knives. **Technical:** Grinds 440C. Offers electronic etching; filework. **Prices:** $50 to $1500. **Remarks:** Full-time maker; first knife sold in 1983. Doing business as Teddybear Knives. **Mark:** Full name, city and state with Teddybear logo.

LUCHINI, BOB, 1220 Dana Ave, Palo Alto, CA 94301, Phone: 650-321-8095

LUCIE, JAMES R., 4191 E. Fruitport Rd, Fruitport, MI 49415, Phone: 231-865-6390, Fax: 231-865-3170
Specialties: Hand-forges William Scagel-style knives. **Patterns:** Authentic scagel-style knives and miniatures. **Technical:** Forges 5160, 52100 & 1084 and forges his own pattern welded Damascus steel. **Prices:** Start at $750. **Remarks:** Full-time maker; first knife sold in 1975. Believes in sole authorship of his work. ABS Journeyman Smith. **Mark:** Scagel Kris with maker's name and address.

LUCKETT, BILL, 108 Amantes Ln., Weatherford, TX 76088, Phone: 817-613-9412
Specialties: Uniquely patterned robust straight knives. **Patterns:** Fighters, Bowies, hunters. **Technical:** Grinds 440C and commercial Damascus; makes heavy knives with deep grinding. **Prices:** $275 to $1000; some to $2000. **Remarks:** Part-time maker; first knife sold in 1975. **Mark:** Last name over Bowie logo.

LUDWIG, RICHARD O., 57-63 65 St, Maspeth, NY 11378, Phone: 718-497-5969
Specialties: Traditional working/using knives. **Patterns:** Boots, hunters and utility/camp knives. Technical Grinds 440C, ATS-34 and 154CM. File work on guards and handles; silver spacers. Offers scrimshaw. **Prices:** $325 to $400; some to $2000. **Remarks:** Full-time maker. **Mark:** Stamped first initial, last name, state.

LUI, RONALD M., 4042 Harding Ave, Honolulu, HI 96816, Phone: 808-734-7746
Specialties: Working straight knives and folders in standard patterns. **Patterns:** Hunters, boots and liner-locks. **Technical:** Grinds 440C and ATS-34. **Prices:** $100 to $700. **Remarks:** Spare-time maker; first knife sold in 1988. **Mark:** Initials connected.

LUM, ROBERT W., 901 Travis Ave, Eugene, OR 97404, Phone: 541-688-2737
Specialties: High-art working knives of his design. **Patterns:** Hunters, fighters, tantos and folders. **Technical:** Grinds 440C, 154CM and ATS-34; plans to forge soon. **Prices:** $175 to $500; some to $800. **Remarks:** Full-time maker; first knife sold in 1976. **Mark:** Chop with last name underneath.

LUMAN, JAMES R., Clear Creek Trail, Anaconda, MT 59711, Phone: 406-560-1461
Specialties: San Mai and composite end patterns. **Patterns:** Pool and eye Spiro graph southwest composite patterns. **Technical:** All patterns with blued steel; all made by myself. **Prices:** $200 to $800. **Mark:** Stock blade removal. Pattern welded steel. Bottom ricasso JRL.

LUNDSTROM, JAN-AKE, Mastmostigen 8, 66010 Dals-Langed, SWEDEN, Phone: 0531-40270
Specialties: Viking swords, axes and knives in cooperation with handle makers. **Patterns:** All traditional styles, especially swords and inlaid blades. **Technical:** Forges his own Damascus and laminated steel. **Prices:** $200 to $1000. **Remarks:** Full-time maker; first knife sold in 1985; collaborates with museums. **Mark:** Runic.

LUNN, LARRY A., PO Box 48931, St Petersburg, FL 33743, Phone: 727-345-7455
Specialties: Fancy folders & double action autos; some straight blades. **Patterns:** All types; my own designs. **Technical:** Stock removal; commer-

cial Damascus. **Prices:** $125 & up. **Remarks:** File work inlays and exotic materials. **Mark:** Name in script.

LUNN, GAIL, PO Box 48931, St Petersburg, FL 33743, Phone: 727-345-7455
Specialties: Fancy folders & double action autos, some straight blades. **Patterns:** One-of-a-kind - All types. **Technical:** Stock removal - Hand made. **Prices:** $300 and up. **Remarks:** Fancy file work, exotic materials, inlays, stone etc. **Mark:** Name in script.

LUTZ, GREG, 127 Crescent Rd, Greenwood, SC 29646, Phone: 864-229-7340
Specialties: Working and using knives and period pieces of his design and to customer specs. **Patterns:** Fighters, hunters and swords. **Technical:** Forges 1095 and O1; grinds ATS-34. Differentially heat-treats forged blades; uses cryogenic treatment on ATS-34. **Prices:** $50 to $350; some to $1200. **Remarks:** Part-time maker; first knife sold in 1986. Doing business as Scorpion Forge. **Mark:** First initial, last name.

LYLE III, ERNEST L., Lyle Knives, PO Box 1755, Chiefland, FL 32644, Phone: 352-490-6693
Specialties: Fancy period pieces; one-of-a-kind and limited editions. **Patterns:** Arabian/Persian influenced fighters, military knives, Bowies and Roman short swords; several styles of hunters. **Technical:** Grinds 440C, D2 and 154CM. Engraves. **Prices:** Upscale. **Remarks:** Full-time maker; first knife sold in 1972. **Mark:** Last name in capital letters - LYLE over a much smaller Chief land.

LYONS, WILLIAM R., 1109 Hillside Ct, Ft Collins, CO 80524, Phone: 970-493-3009

LYTTLE, BRIAN, Box 5697, High River, AB, CANADA T1V 1M7, Phone: 403-558-3638
Specialties: Fancy working straight knives and folders; art knives. **Patterns:** Bowies, daggers, dirks, Sgian Dubhs, folders, dress knives. **Technical:** Forges Damascus steel; engraving; scrimshaw; heat-treating; classes. **Prices:** $200 to $1000; some to $5000. **Remarks:** Full-time maker; first knife sold in 1983. **Mark:** Last name, country.

m

MACDONALD, JOHN, 9 David Dr, Raymond, NH 03077, Phone: 603-895-0918
Specialties: Working/using straight knives of his design and to customer specs. **Patterns:** Japanese cutlery, Bowies, hunters and working knives. **Technical:** Grinds O1, L6 and ATS-34. Swords have matching handles and scabbards with Japanese flair. **Prices:** $70 to $250; some to $500. **Remarks:** Part-time maker; first knife sold in 1988. Wood/glass-topped custom cases. **Mark:** Initials.

MACDONALD, DAVID, 2824 Hwy 47, Los Lunas, NM 87031, Phone: 505-866-5866

MACKIE, JOHN, 13653 Lanning, Whittier, CA 90605, Phone: 562-945-6104
Specialties: Forged. **Patterns:** Bowie & camp knives. **Technical:** Attended ABS Bladesmith School. **Prices:** $75 to $500. **Mark:** JSM in a triangle.

MACKRILL, STEPHEN, PO Box 1580, Pinegowrie 2123, Johannesburg, SOUTH AFRICA, Phone: 27-11-886-2893, Fax: 27-11-334-6230
Specialties: Art fancy, historical, collectors and corporate gifts cutlery. **Patterns:** Fighters, hunters, camp, custom lock-back and liner-lock folders. **Technical:** N690, 12C27, ATS-34, silver and gold inlay on handles; wooden and silver sheaths. **Prices:** $330 and upwards. **Remarks:** First knife sold in 1978. **Mark:** Oval with first initial, last name, "Maker" country of origin.

MADISON II, BILLY D., 2295 Tyler Rd, Remlap, AL 35133, Phone: 205-680-6722
Specialties: Traditional working and using straight knives and folders of his design or yours. **Patterns:** Hunters, locking folders, utility/camp knives, and fighters. **Technical:** Grinds 440C, ATS-34, D2 & BG-42; forges some high carbons. Prefers natural handle material. Ivory, bone, exotic woods & horns. **Prices:** $100 to $400; some to $1000. **Remarks:** Limited part-time maker (disabled machinist); first knife sold in 1978. **Mark:** Last name and year. Offers sheaths. **Other:** Wife makes sheaths. All knives have unconditional lifetime warranty. Never had a knife returned in 23 years.

MADRULLI, MME. JOELLE, Residence Ste Catherine B1, Salon De Provence, FRANCE 13330

MAE, TAKAO, 1-119, 1-4 Uenohigashi, Toyonaka, Osaka, JAPAN 560-0013, Phone: 81-6-6852-2758, Fax: 81-6-6481-1649
Remarks: Distinction stylish in art-forged blades, with lacquered ergonomic handles.

custom knifemakers

MAESTRI, PETER A., S11251 Fairview Rd, Spring Green, WI 53588, Phone: 608-546-4481
Specialties: Working straight knives in standard patterns. **Patterns:** Camp and fishing knives, utility green-river styled. **Technical:** Grinds 440C, 154CM and 440A. **Prices:** $15 to $45; some to $150. **Remarks:** Full-time maker; first knife sold in 1981. Provides professional cutler service to professional cutters. **Mark:** CARISOLO, MAESTRI BROS., or signature.

MAGEE, JIM, 319 N 12th, Salina, KS 67401, Phone: 785-820-8535
Specialties: Working and fancy folding knives. **Patterns:** Liner-locking folders, favorite is my Persian. **Technical:** Grinds ATS-34, George woth Damascus, titanium. Liners Prefer Mother of Pearl handles. **Prices:** Start at $175 some to $1000. **Remarks:** Part-time maker, first knife sold in 2001. Purveyor since 1982. Currently President of the Professional Knifemakers Assn. **Mark:** Last name.

MAIENKNECHT, STANLEY, 38648 S. R. 800, Sardis, OH 43946

MAINES, JAY, Sunrise River Custom Knives, 5584 266th St, Wyoming, MN 55092, Phone: 651-462-5301
Specialties: Heavy duty working, classic and traditional fixed blades. Some high-tech and fancy embellished knives available. **Patterns:** Hunters, skinners, Bowies, Tantos, fillet, fighters, daggers, boot and cutlery sets. **Technical:** Hollow ground, stock removal blades of 440C, ATS-34 and CPM S-90V. Prefers natural handle materials, exotic hard woods, and stag, rams and buffalo horns. Offers dovetailed bolsters in brass, stainless steel and nickel silver. Custom sheaths from matching wood or hand-stitched from heavy duty water buffalo hide. **Prices:** Moderate to up-scale. **Remarks:** Part-time maker; first knife sold in 1992. Color brochure available upon request. Doing business as Sunrise River Custom Knives. **Mark:** Full name under a Rising Sun logo. **Other:** Offers fixed blade knives repair and handle conversions.

MAISEY, ALAN, PO Box 197, Vincentia 2540, NSW AUSTRALIA, Phone: 2-4443 7829
Specialties: Daggers, especially krisses; period pieces. **Technical:** Offers knives and finished blades in Damascus and nickel Damascus. **Prices:** $75 to $2000; some higher. **Remarks:** Part-time maker; provides complete restoration service for krisses. Trained by a Javanese Kris smith. **Mark:** None, triangle in a box, or three peaks.

MAJER, MIKE, 50 Palmetto Bay Rd, Hilton Head, SC 29928, Phone: 843-681-3483

MAKOTO, KUNITOMO, 3-3-18 Imazu-cho Fukuyama-city, Hiroshima, JAPAN, Phone: 084-933-5874

MALABY, RAYMOND J., 835 Calhoun Ave, Juneau, AK 99801, Phone: 907-586-6981

MALLETT, JOHN, 760 E Francis St #N, Ontario, CA 91761, Phone: 800-532-3336/ 909-923-4116, Fax: 909-923-9932
Specialties: Complete line of 3/M, Norton and Hermes belts for grinding and polishing 24-2000 grit; also hard core, Bader and Burr King grinders. Baldor motors and buffers. ATS-34, 440C, BG42 and 416 stainless steel.

MALLOY, JOE, 1039 Schwabe St, Freeland, PA 18224, Phone: 570-636-2781
Specialties: Working straight knives and lock-back folders-plain and fancy-of his design. **Patterns:** Hunters, utility, Bowie, survival knives, folders. **Technical:** Grinds ATS-34, 440C, D2 and A2 and Damascus. Makes own leather and kyder sheaths. **Prices:** $100 to $1800. **Remarks:** Part-time maker; first knife sold in 1982. **Mark:** First and middle initials, last name, city and state.

MANABE, MICHAEL K., 3659 Tomahawk Lane, San Diego, CA 92117, Phone: 619-483-2416
Specialties: Classic and high-art straight knives of his design or to customer specs. **Patterns:** Bowies, fighters, hunters, utility/camp knives; all knives one-of-a-kind. **Technical:** Forges and grinds 52100, 5160 and 1095. Does multiple quenching for distinctive temper lines. Each blade triple-tempered. **Prices:** Start at $200. **Remarks:** Part-time maker; first knife sold in 1994. **Mark:** First and middle initials, last name and J. S. on other side.

MANEKER, KENNETH, RR 2, Galiano Island, B. C., CANADA V0N 1P0, Phone: 604-539-2084
Specialties: Working straight knives; period pieces. **Patterns:** Camp knives and hunters; French chef knives. **Technical:** Grinds 440C, 154CM and Vascowear. **Prices:** $50 to $200; some to $300. **Remarks:** Part-time maker; first knife sold in 1981. Doing business as Water Mountain Knives. **Mark:** Japanese Kanji of initials, plus glyph.

MANKEL, KENNETH, 7836 Cannonsburg Rd, Cannonsburg, MI 49317, Phone: 616-874-6955

MANLEY, DAVID W., 3270 Six Mile Hwy, Central, SC 29630, Phone: 864-654-1125
Specialties: Working straight knives of his design or to custom specs. **Patterns:** Hunters, boot & fighters. **Technical:** Grinds 440C & ATS-34.

Prices: $60 to $250. **Remarks:** Part-time maker; first knife sold in 1994. **Mark:** First initial, last name, year and serial number.

MANN, TIM, Bladeworks, PO Box 1196, Honokaa, HI 96727, Phone: 808-775-0949, Fax: 808-775-0949
Specialties: Hand-forged knives and swords. **Patterns:** Bowies, Tantos, pesh kabz, daggers. **Technical:** Use 5160, 1050, 1075, 1095 & ATS-34 steels, cable Damascus. **Prices:** $200 to $800. **Remarks:** Just learning to forge Damascus. **Mark:** None yet.

MANN, MICHAEL L., Idaho Knife Works, PO Box 144, Spirit Lake, ID 83869, Phone: 509 994-9394
Specialties: Good working blades-historical reproduction, modern or custom design. **Patterns:** Cowboy Bowies, Mountain Man period blades, old style folders, designer & maker of "The Cliff Knife", hunter and hook knives, hand ax, fish fillet and kitchen knives. **Technical:** High carbon steel blades-hand forged 5160 or grind L6 tool steel. **Prices:** $100 to $630+. **Remarks:** Made first knife in 1965. Full-time making knives as Idaho Knife Works since 1986. Functional as well as collectible. Each knife truly unique! **Mark:** Four mountain peaks are his initials MM.

MARAGNI, DAN, R. D. 1, Box 106, Georgetown, NY 13072, Phone: 315-662-7490
Specialties: Heavy-duty working knives, some investor class. **Patterns:** Hunters, fighters and camp knives, some Scottish types. **Technical:** Forges W2 and his own Damascus; toughness and edge-holding a high priority. **Prices:** $125 to $500; some to $1000. **Remarks:** Full-time maker; first knife sold in 1975. **Mark:** Celtic initials in circle.

MARKLEY, KEN, 7651 Cabin Creek Lane, Sparta, IL 62286, Phone: 618-443-5284
Specialties: Traditional working and using knives of his design and to customer specs. **Patterns:** Fighters, hunters and utility/camp knives. **Technical:** Forges 5160, 1095 and L6; makes his own Damascus; does file work. **Prices:** $150 to $800; some to $2000. **Remarks:** Part-time maker; first knife sold in 1991. Doing business as Cabin Creek Forge. **Mark:** Last name, JS.

MARKS, CHRIS, RT 2 Box 527, Ava, MO 65608, Phone: 417-683-1065
Specialties: Mosaic Damascus. **Patterns:** Too numerous to list - ever changing. **Technical:** W1, W2, 1095, 203E, Nickel 200. **Prices:** $20 and up. **Mark:** Anvil with name in center.

MARLOWE, DONALD, 2554 Oakland Rd, Dover, PA 17315, Phone: 717-764-6055
Specialties: Working straight knives in standard patterns. **Patterns:** Bowies, fighters, boots and utility knives. **Technical:** Grinds D2 and 440C. **Prices:** $120 to $525. **Remarks:** Spare-time maker; first knife sold in 1977. **Mark:** Last name.

MARSHALL, STEPHEN R., 975 Harkreader Rd, Mt. Juliet, TN 37122

MARSHALL, GLENN, PO Box 1099, 1117 Hofmann St, Mason, TX 76856, Phone: 915-347-6207
Specialties: Working knives and period pieces. **Patterns:** Straight and folding hunters, fighters and camp knives. **Technical:** Steel used 440C, D2, CPM & 440V. **Prices:** $90 and up according to options. **Remarks:** Full-time maker; first knife sold in 1932. **Mark:** First initial, last name, city and state with anvil logo.

MARTIN, BRUCE E., Rt. 6, Box 164-B, Prescott, AR 71857, Phone: 501-887-2023
Specialties: Fancy working straight knives of his design. **Patterns:** Bowies, camp knives, skinners and fighters. **Technical:** Forges 5160, 1095 and his own Damascus. Uses natural handle materials; filework available. **Prices:** $75 to $350; some to $500. **Remarks:** Full-time maker; first knife sold in 1979. **Mark:** Name in arch.

MARTIN, TONY, 108 S. Main St, PO Box 324, Arcadia, MO 63621, Phone: 573-546-2254
Specialties: Specializes in historical designs. Puko, etc.

MARTIN, ROBB, 7 Victoria St, Elmira, Ontario, CANADA N3B 1R9

MARTIN, RANDALL J., 1477 Country Club Rd, Middletown, CT 06457, Phone: 860-347-1161
Specialties: High-performance using knives. **Patterns:** Neck knives, tactical liner-locks, survival, utility and Japanese knives. **Technical:** Grinds BG42, CPMM4, D2 and A2; aerospace composite materials; carbon fiber sheaths. **Prices:** Start at $150. **Remarks:** Part-time maker; first knife sold in 1976. Doing business as Martinsite Knives. **Mark:** First and middle initials, last name.

MARTIN, PETER, 28220 N. Lake Dr, Waterford, WI 53185, Phone: 262-895-2815
Specialties: Fancy, fantasy and working straight knives and folders of his design and in standard patterns. **Patterns:** Bowies, fighters, hunters, locking folders and liner-locks. **Technical:** Forges own Mosaic Damascus, powdered steel and his own Damascus. Prefers natural handle material;

offers file work and carved handles. **Prices:** Moderate. **Remarks:** Part-time maker; first knife sold in 1988. Doing business as Martin Custom Products. Uses only natural handle materials. **Mark:** Martin Knives.

MARTIN, MICHAEL W., Box 572, Jefferson St, Beckville, TX 75631, Phone: 903-678-2161
Specialties: Classic working/using straight knives of his design and in standard patterns. **Patterns:** Hunters. **Technical:** Grinds ATS-34, 440C, O1 and A2. Bead blasted, Parkerized, high polish and satin finishes. Sheaths are handmade. Also hand forges cable Damascus. **Prices:** $145 to $230. **Remarks:** Part-time maker; first knife sold in 1995. Doing business as Michael W. Martin Knives. **Mark:** Name and city, state in arch.

MARTIN, GENE, PO Box 396, Williams, OR 97544, Phone: 541-846-6755
Specialties: Straight knives and folders. **Patterns:** Fighters, hunters, skinners, boot knives, spring back and lock-back folders. **Technical:** Grinds ATS-34, 440C, Damascus and 154CM. Forges; makes own Damascus; scrimshaws. **Prices:** $100 TO $1200; some higher. **Remarks:** Full-time maker; first knife sold in 1993. Doing business as Provision Forge. **Mark:** Name and/or crossed staff and sword.

MARTIN, HAL W., 781 Hwy 95, Morrilton, AR 72110, Phone: 501-354-1682

MARTIN, JOHN ALEXANDER, 20100 NE 150th, Luther, OK 73054, Phone: 405-277-3992
Specialties: Inlaid and engraved mother of pearl. **Patterns:** Bowies, fighters, hunters & traditional patterns. **Technical:** Forges 5160 & 1084. **Prices:** Start at $175. **Remarks:** Part-time maker. **Mark:** Initials JAM.

MARTIN, WALTER E., 570 Cedar Flat Rd, Williams, OR 97544, Phone: 541-846-6755

MARTIN, JIM, 1120 S. Cadiz Ct, Oxnard, CA 93035, Phone: 805-985-9849
Specialties: Fancy and working/using folders of his design. **Patterns:** Automatics, locking folders and miniatures. **Technical:** Grinds 440C, AEB-L, 304SS and Damascus. **Prices:** $350 to $700; some to $1500. **Remarks:** Full-time maker; first knife sold in 1992. Doing business as Jim Martin Custom Knives.

MARZITELLI, PETER, 19929 35A Ave, Langley, BC, CANADA V3A 2R1, Phone: 604-532-8899
Specialties: Specializes in unique functional knife shapes & designs using natural and synthetic handle materials. **Patterns:** Mostly folders, some daggers and art knives. **Technical:** Grinds ATS-34, S/S Damascus & others. **Prices:** $220 to $1000 (average $375). **Remarks:** Full-time maker; first knife sold in 1984. **Mark:** Stylized logo reads "Marz."

MASON, BILL, 1114 St. Louis, #33, Excelsior Springs, MO 64024, Phone: 816-637-7335
Specialties: Combat knives; some folders. **Patterns:** Fighters to match knife types in book *Cold Steel.* **Technical:** Grinds O1, 440C and ATS-34. **Prices:** $115 to $250; some to $350. **Remarks:** Spare-time maker; first knife sold in 1979. **Mark:** Initials connected.

MASSEY, RON, 61638 El Reposo St, Joshua Tree, CA 92252, Phone: 760-366-9239 after 5 p. m., Fax: 763-366-4620
Specialties: Classic, traditional, fancy/embellished, high art, period pieces, working/using knives, straight knives, folders, and automatics. Your design, customer specs, about 175 standard patterns. **Patterns:** Automatics, hunters and fighters. All are side-locking folders. Unless requested as lock books slip joint I specialize or custom design. **Technical:** ATS-34, 440C, D-2 upon request. Engraving, filework, scrimshaw, most of the exotic handle materials. All aspects are performed by me - inlay work in pearls or stone, hand made Pem' work. **Prices:** $110 to $2500; some to $6000. **Remarks:** Part-time maker; first knife sold in 1976.

MASSEY, ROGER, 4928 Union Rd, Texarkana, AR 71854, Phone: 870-779-1018
Specialties: Traditional and working straight knives and folders of his design and to customer specs. **Patterns:** Bowies, hunters, daggers and utility knives. **Technical:** Forges 1084 & 52100, makes his own Damascus. Offers filework and silver wire inlay in handles. **Prices:** $200 to $1500; some to $2500. **Remarks:** Part-time maker; first knife sold in 1991. **Mark:** Last name, M. S.

MASSEY, AL, Box 14, Site 15, RR#2, Mount Uniacke, Nova Scotia, CANADA B0N 1Z0, Phone: 902-866-4754
Specialties: Working knives and period pieces. **Patterns:** Swords and daggers of Celtic to medieval design, Bowies. **Technical:** Forges 5160, 1084 and 1095. Makes own Damascus. **Prices:** $100 to $400; some to $900. **Remarks:** Part-time maker, first blade sold in 1988. **Mark:** Initials and JS on Ricasso.

MATA, LEONARD, 3583 Arruza St, San Deigo, CA 92154, Phone: 619-690-6935

MATSUSAKI, TAKESHI, Matsusaki Knives, 151 Ono-Cho Saseboshi, Nagasaki, JAPAN, Phone: 0956-47-2938
Specialties: Working and collector grade front look and slip joint. **Patterns:** Sheffierd type folders. **Technical:** Grinds ATS-34 k-120. **Price:** $250-$1000; some to $8000. **Remarks:** Part-time maker, first knife sold in 1990. **Mark:** Name and initials.

MAXEN, MICK, 2 Huggins Lane Welham Green, Hatfield, Herts, UNITED KINGDOM AL97LR, Phone: 01707 261213
Specialties: Damascus & Mosaic. **Patterns:** Medieval-style daggers & Bowies. **Technical:** Forges CS75 & 15N20 / nickel Damascus. **Mark:** Last name with axe above.

MAXFIELD, LYNN, 382 Colonial Ave, Layton, UT 84041, Phone: 801-544-4176
Specialties: Sporting knives, some fancy. **Patterns:** Hunters, fishing, fillet, special purpose; some locking folders. **Technical:** Grinds 440-C, ATS-34, 154-CM, D2, CPM-S60V, S90V, 530V, CPM-3, Talonite, and Damascus. **Prices:** $125 to $400; some to $900. **Remarks:** Part-time maker; first knife sold in 1979. **Mark:** Name, city and state.

MAXWELL, DON, 3164 N. Marks, Suite 122, Fresno, CA 93722, Phone: 559-497-8441
Specialties: Fancy working and using straight knives of his design. **Patterns:** Hunters, fighters, utility/camp knives, liner-lock folders and fantasy knives. **Technical:** Grinds 440C, ATS-34, D2 and commercial Damascus. **Prices:** $250 to $1000; some to $2500. **Remarks:** Full-time maker; first knife sold in 1987. **Mark:** Last name, city, state or last name only.

MAYNARD, WILLIAM N., 2677 John Smith Rd, Fayetteville, NC 28306, Phone: 910-425-1615
Specialties: Traditional and working straight knives of all designs. **Patterns:** Combat, Bowies, fighters, hunters and utility knives. **Technical:** Grinds 440C, ATS-34 and commercial Damascus. Offers fancy filework; handmade sheaths. **Prices:** $100 to $300; some to $750. **Remarks:** Full-time maker; first knife sold in 1988. **Mark:** Last name.

MAYNARD, LARRY JOE, PO Box 493, Crab Orchard, WV 25827
Specialties: Fancy and fantasy straight knives. **Patterns:** Big knives; a Bowie with a full false edge; fighting knives. **Technical:** Grinds standard steels. **Prices:** $350 to $500; some to $1000. **Remarks:** Full-time maker; first knife sold in 1986. **Mark:** Middle and last initials.

MAYO JR., TOM, 67-420 Alahaka St, Waialua, HI 96791, Phone: 808-637-6560
Specialties: Presentation grade working knives. **Patterns:** Combat knives, hunters, Bowies and folders. **Technical:** Uses BG-42 & 440V (ATS-34 and 440C upon request). **Prices:** Start at $250. **Remarks:** Part-time maker; first knife sold in 1983. **Mark:** Volcano logo with name and state.

MAYVILLE, OSCAR L., 2130 E. County Rd. 910S., Marengo, IN 47162, Phone: 812-338-3103
Specialties: Working straight knives; period pieces. **Patterns:** Kitchen cutlery, Bowies, camp knives and hunters. **Technical:** Grinds A2, O1 and 440C. **Prices:** $50 to $350; some to $500. **Remarks:** Full-time maker; first knife sold in 1984. **Mark:** Initials over knife logo.

MC CORNOCK, CRAIG, McC Mtn Outfitters, 4775 Rte 212, Willow, NY 12495, Phone: 914-679-9758

MCABEE, WILLIAM, 27275 Norton Grade, Colfax, CA 95713, Phone: 530-389-8163
Specialties: Working/using knives. **Patterns:** Fighters, Bowies, Hunters. **Technical:** Grinds ATS-34. **Prices:** $75 to $200; some to $350. **Remarks:** Part-time maker; first knife sold in 1990. **Mark:** Stylized WM stamped.

MCADAMS, DENNIS, 1709 Ichabod Lane, Chattanooga, TN 37405-2250, Phone: 423-267-4743

MCBURNETTE, HARVEY, PO Box 227, Eagle Nest, NM 87718, Phone: 505-377-6254, Fax: 505-377-6218
Specialties: Fancy working folders; some to customer specs. **Patterns:** Front-locking folders. **Technical:** Grinds D2, 440C and 154CM; engraves. **Prices:** $450 to $3000. **Remarks:** Full-time maker; first knife sold in 1972. **Mark:** Last name, city and state.

MCCALLEN JR., HOWARD H., 110 Anchor Dr, So Seaside Park, NJ 08752

MCCARLEY, JOHN, 4165 Harney Rd, Taneytown, MD 21787
Specialties: Working straight knives; period pieces. **Patterns:** Hunters, Bowies, camp knives, miniatures, throwing knives. **Technical:** Forges W2, O1 and his own Damascus. **Prices:** $150 to $300; some to $1000. **Remarks:** Part-time maker; first knife sold in 1977. **Mark:** Initials in script.

custom knifemakers

MCCARTY, HARRY, 1479 Indian Ridge Rd, Blaine, TN 37709 **Specialties:** Period pieces. **Patterns:** Trade knives, Bowies, 18th & 19th century folders & hunting swords. **Technical:** Forges & grinds high carbon steel. **Prices:** $75 to $1300. **Remarks:** Full-time maker; first knife sold in 1977. **Mark:** Stylized initials inside a shamrock. **Other:** Doing business as Indian Ridge Forge.

MCCLURE, MICHAEL, 803 17th Ave, Menlo Park, CA 94025, Phone: 650-323-2596 **Specialties:** Working/using straight knives of his design and to customer specs. **Patterns:** Bowies, hunters, skinners, utility/camp, tantos, fillets and boot knives. **Technical:** Forges high carbon and Damascus; also grinds stainless, all grades. **Prices:** Start at $100. **Remarks:** Part-time maker; first knife sold in 1991. **Mark:** Mike McClure. **Other:** ABS journeyman smith

MCCONNELL, CHARLES R., 158 Genteel Ridge, Wellsburg, WV 26070, Phone: 304-737-2015 **Specialties:** Working straight knives. **Patterns:** Hunters, Bowies, daggers, minis and push knives. **Technical:** Grinds 440C and 154CM; likes full tangs. **Prices:** $65 to $325; some to $800. **Remarks:** Part-time maker; first knife sold in 1977. **Mark:** Name.

MCCONNELL JR., LOYD A., 1710 Rosewood, Odessa, TX 79761, Phone: 915-363-8344 **Specialties:** Working straight knives and folders, some fancy. **Patterns:** Hunters, boots, Bowies, locking folders and slip-joints. **Technical:** Grinds CPM Steels, ATS-34 and BG-42 and commercial Damascus. **Prices:** $175 to $900; some to $10,000. **Remarks:** Full-time maker; first knife sold in 1975. Doing business as Cactus Custom Knives. **Mark:** Name, city and state in cactus logo.

MCCOUN, MARK, 14212 Pine Dr, DeWitt, VA 23840, Phone: 804-469-7631 **Specialties:** Working/using straight knives of his design and in standard patterns; custom miniatures. **Patterns:** Locking liners, integrals. **Technical:** Grinds Damascus, ATS-34 and 440C. **Prices:** $150 to $500. **Remarks:** Part-time maker; first knife sold in 1989. **Mark:** Name, city and state.

MCCRACKIN, KEVIN, 3720 Hess Rd, House Springs, MO 63051, Phone: 636-677-6066

MCCRACKIN AND SON, V. J., 3720 Hess Rd, House Springs, MO 63051, Phone: 636-677-6066 **Specialties:** Working straight knives in standard patterns. **Patterns:** Hunters, Bowies and camp knives. **Technical:** Forges L6, 5160, his own Damascus, cable Damascus. **Prices:** $125 to $700; some to $1500. **Remarks:** Part-time maker; first knife sold in 1983. Son Kevin helps make the knives. **Mark:** Last name, M. S.

MCCULLOUGH, JERRY, 274 West Pettibone Rd, Georgiana, AL 36033, Phone: 334-382-7644 **Specialties:** Standard patterns or custom designs. **Technical:** Forge and grind scrap-tool and Damascus steels. Use natural handle materials & turquoise trim on some. Filework on others. **Prices:** $65 to $250 and up. **Remarks:** Part-time maker. **Mark:** Initials (JM) combined.

MCDERMOTT, MICHAEL, 151 Hwy F, Defiance, MO 63341, Phone: 314-798-2077

MCDONALD, ROBIN J., 6509 E Jeffrey Dr, Fayetteville, NC 28314 **Specialties:** Working knives of my design. **Patterns:** Bowies, hunters, camp knives & fighters. **Technical:** Forges primarily 5160. **Prices:** $100 to $500. **Remarks:** Part-time maker; first knife sold in 1999. **Mark:** initials RJM.

MCDONALD, ROBERT J., 14730 61 Court N., Loxahatchee, FL 33470, Phone: 561-790-1470 **Specialties:** Traditional working straight knives to customer specs. **Patterns:** Fighters, swords and folders. **Technical:** Grinds 440C, ATS-34 and forges own Damascus. **Prices:** $150 to $1000. **Remarks:** Part-time maker; first knife sold in 1988. **Mark:** Electro-etched name.

MCDONALD, W. J. "JERRY", 7173 Wickshire Cove E., Germantown, TN 38138, Phone: 901-756-9924 **Specialties:** Classic and working/using straight knives of his design and in standard patterns. **Patterns:** Bowies, hunters kitchen and traditional spring back pocket knives. **Technical:** Grinds ATS-34, 154CM, D2, 440V, BG42 & 440C. **Prices:** $125 to $1000. **Remarks:** Full-time maker; first knife sold in 1989. **Mark:** First and middle initials, last name, maker, city and state. Some of my knives are stamped McDonald in script.

MCDONALD, RICH, 4590 Kirk Rd, Columbiana, OH 44408, Phone: 330-482-0007, Fax: 330-482-0007 **Specialties:** Traditional working/using and art knives of his design. **Patterns:** Bowies, hunters, folders, primitives and tomahawks. **Technical:** Forges 5160, 1084, 1095, 52100 and his own Damascus. Fancy filework.

Prices: $200 to $1500. **Remarks:** Full-time maker; first knife sold in 1994. **Mark:** First and last initials connected.

MCFALL, KEN, PO Box 458, Lakeside, AZ 85929, Phone: 928-537-2026, Fax: 928-537-8066 **Specialties:** Fancy working straight knives and some folders. **Patterns:** Daggers, boots, tantos, Bowies. Some miniatures. **Technical:** Grinds D2, ATS-34 and 440C. Forges his own Damascus. **Prices:** $200 to $1200. **Remarks:** Part-time maker; first knife sold in 1984. **Mark:** Name, city and state.

MCFARLIN, J. W., 3331 Pocohantas Dr, Lake Havasu City, AZ 86404, Phone: 928-855-8095, Fax: 928-855-8095 **Technical:** Flat grinds, D2, ATS-34, 440C, Thomas & Peterson Damascus. **Remarks:** From working knives to investment. Customer designs always welcome. 100% hand made. **Prices:** $150 to $3000. **Mark:** Hand written in the blade.

MCFARLIN, ERIC E., PO Box 2188, Kodiak, AK 99615, Phone: 907-486-4799 **Specialties:** Working knives of his design. **Patterns:** Bowies, skinners, camp knives and hunters. **Technical:** Flat and convex grinds 440C, A2 and AEB-L. **Prices:** Start at $200. **Remarks:** Part-time maker; first knife sold in 1989. **Mark:** Name and city in rectangular logo.

MCGILL, JOHN, PO Box 302, Blairsville, GA 30512, Phone: 404-745-4686 **Specialties:** Working knives. **Patterns:** Traditional patterns; camp knives. **Technical:** Forges L6 and 9260; makes Damascus. **Prices:** $50 to $250; some to $500. **Remarks:** Full-time maker; first knife sold in 1982. **Mark:** XYLO.

MCGOVERN, JIM, 105 Spinnaker Way, Portsmouth, NH 03801-3331 **Specialties:** Working straight knives and folders. **Patterns:** Hunters and boots. **Technical:** Hollow-grinds 440C, ATS-34; prefers full tapered tangs. Offers filework. **Prices:** Straight knives, $165 to $250; folders start at $325. **Remarks:** Full-time maker; first knife sold in 1985. **Mark:** Name.

MCGOWAN, FRANK E., 12629 Howard Lodge Dr, Sykesville, MD 21784, Phone: 410-489-4323 **Specialties:** Fancy working knives & folders to customer specs. **Patterns:** Survivor knives, fighters, fishing knives, folders and hunters. **Technical:** Grinds and forges O1, 440C, 5160, ATS-34, 52100, or customer choice. **Prices:** $100 to $1000; some more. **Remarks:** Full-time maker; first knife sold in 1986. **Mark:** Last name.

MCGRATH, PATRICK T., 8343 Kenyon Av, Westchester, CA 90045, Phone: 310-338-8764

MCGRODER, PATRICK J., 5725 Chapin Rd, Madison, OH 44057, Phone: 216-298-3405, Fax: 216-298-3405 **Specialties:** Traditional working/using knives of his design. **Patterns:** Bowies, hunters and utility/camp knives. **Technical:** Grinds ATS-34, D2 and customer requests. Does reverse etching; heat-treats; prefers natural handle materials; custom made sheath with each knife. **Prices:** $125 to $250. **Remarks:** Part-time maker. **Mark:** First and middle initials, last name, maker, city and state.

MCGUANE IV, THOMAS F., 410 South 3rd Ave, Bozeman, MT 59715, Phone: 406-586-0248 **Specialties:** Multi metal inlaid knives of handmade steel. **Patterns:** Lockback and liner-lock folders, fancy straight knives. **Technical:** 1084/1SN20 Damascus and Mosaic steels by maker. **Prices:** $1000 and up. **Mark:** Surname or name and city, state.

MCHENRY, WILLIAM JAMES, Box 67, Wyoming, RI 02898, Phone: 401-539-8353 **Specialties:** Fancy high-tech folders of his design. **Patterns:** Locking folders with various mechanisms. **Technical:** One-of-a-kind only, no duplicates. Inventor of the Axis Lock. Most pieces disassemble and feature top-shelf materials including gold, silver and gems. **Prices:** Upscale. **Remarks:** Full-time maker; first knife sold in 1988. Former goldsmith. **Mark:** Last name or first and last initials.

MCINTOSH, DAVID L., PO Box 948, Haines, AK 99827, Phone: 907-766-3673 **Specialties:** Working straight knives and folders of all designs. **Patterns:** All styles, except swords. **Technical:** Grinds ATS-34 and top name maker Damascus. Engraves; offers tooling on sheaths. Uses fossil ivory. **Prices:** $60 to $800; some to $2000. **Remarks:** Full-time maker; first knife sold in 1984. **Mark:** Last name, serial number, steel type, city and state.

MCKENZIE, DAVID BRIAN, 2311 B Ida Rd, Campbell River B., CANADA V9W-4V7

MCKIERNAN, STAN, 205 E. Park St, Vandalia, MO 63382, Phone: 573-594-6135 **Specialties:** Self-sheathed knives and miniatures. **Patterns:** Daggers, ethnic designs and individual styles. **Technical:** Grinds Damascus and

440C. **Prices:** $200-$500; some to $1500. **Mark:** "River's Bend" inside two concentric circles.

MCLENDON, HUBERT W., 125 Thomas Rd, Waco, GA 30182, Phone: 770-574-9796
Specialties: Using knives; my design or customer's. **Patterns:** Bowies & hunters. **Technical:** Hand ground or forged ATS-34, 440C & D2. **Prices:** $100 to $300. **Remarks:** First knife sold in 1978. **Mark:** McLendon or Mc.

MCLUIN, TOM, 36 Fourth St, Dracut, MA 01826, Phone: 978-957-4899
Specialties: Working straight knives and folders of his design. **Patterns:** Boots, hunters and folders. **Technical:** Grinds ATS-34, 440C, O1 and Damascus; makes his own mokume. **Prices:** $100 to $400; some to $700. **Remarks:** Part-time maker; first knife sold in 1991. **Mark:** Last name.

MCLURKIN, ANDREW, 2112 Windy Woods Dr, Raleigh, NC 27607, Phone: 919-834-4693
Specialties: Collector grade folders, working folders, fixed blades, and miniatures. Knives made to order and to his design. **Patterns:** Locking liner and lock-back folders, hunter, working and tactical designs. **Technical:** Using patterned Damascus, Mosaic Damascus, ATS_34, BG-42, and CPM steels. Prefers natural handle materials such as pearl, ancient ivory and stabilized wood. Also using synthetic materials such as carbon fiber, titanium, and G10. **Prices:** $250 and up. **Mark:** Last name. Mark is often on inside of folders.

MCMANUS, DANNY, 413 Fairhaven Dr, Taylors, SC 29687, Phone: 864-268-9849, Fax: 864-268-9699
Specialties: High-tech and traditional working/using straight knives of his design, to customer specs and in standard patterns. **Patterns:** Boots, Bowies, fighters, hunters and utility/camp knives. **Technical:** Forges stainless steel Damascus; grinds ATS-34. Offers engraving and scrimshaw. **Prices:** $300 to $2000; some to $3000. **Remarks:** Full-time maker; first knife sold in 1997. Doing business as Stamascus KnifeWorks Corp. **Mark:** Stamascus.

MCNABB, TOMMY, Carolina Custom Knives, 4015 Brownsboro Rd, Winston-Salem, NC 27106, Phone: 336-759-0640, Fax: 336-759-0641

MCNEIL, JIMMY, 1175 Mt. Moriah Rd, Memphis, TN 38117, Phone: 901-544-0710 or 901-683-8133
Specialties: Fancy high-art straight knives of his design. **Patterns:** Bowies, daggers and swords. **Technical:** Grinds O1 and Damascus. Engraves, carves and inlays. **Prices:** $50 to $300; some to $2000. **Remarks:** Spare-time maker; first knife sold in 1993. Doing business as McNeil's Minerals and Knives. **Mark:** Crossed mining picks and serial number.

MCRAE, J. MICHAEL, 7750 Matthews-Mint Hill Rd, Mint Hill, NC 28227, Phone: 704-545-2929
Specialties: Scottish dirks and sgian dubhs. **Patterns:** Traditional blade styles with traditional and slightly non-traditional handle treatments. **Technical:** Forges 1095, 5160 and his own Damascus. Prefers Stag and exotic hardwoods for handles, many intricately carved. **Prices:** Starting at $125, some to $2000. **Remarks:** Journeyman Smith in ABS, member of North Carolina Custom Knifemakers Guild and ABANA. Full-time maker, first knife sold in 1982. Doing business as Scotia Metalwork. **Mark:** Last name underlined with a claymore.

MEERDINK, KURT, 120 Split Rock Dr, Barryville, NY 12719, Phone: 845-557-0783
Specialties: Working straight knives. **Patterns:** Hunters, Bowies, tactical & neck knives. **Technical:** Grinds ATS-34, 440C, D2, Damascus. **Prices:** $95 to $1100. **Remarks:** Full-time maker; first knife sold in 1994. **Mark:** Meerdink Maker, Rio NY.

MEIER, DARYL, 75 Forge Rd, Carbondale, IL 62901, Phone: 618-549-3234
Specialties: One-of-a-kind knives and swords. **Patterns:** Collaborates on blades. **Technical:** Forges his own Damascus, W1 and A203E, 440C, 431, nickel 200 and clad steel. **Prices:** $250 to $450; some to $6000. **Remarks:** Full-time smith and researcher since 1974; first knife sold in 1974. **Mark:** Name or circle/arrow symbol or SHAWNEE.

MELIN, GORDON C., 11259 Gladhill Road Unit 4, Whittier, CA 90604, Phone: 562-946-5753

MELLARD, J. R., 17006 Highland Canyon Dr, Houston, TX 77095, Phone: 281-550-9464

MELOY, SEAN, 7148 Rosemary Lane, Lemon Grove, CA 91945-2105, Phone: 619-465-7173
Specialties: Traditional working straight knives of his design. **Patterns:** Bowies, fighters and utility/camp knives. **Technical:** Grinds 440C, ATS-34 and D2. **Prices:** $125 to $300. **Remarks:** Part-time maker; first knife sold in 1985. **Mark:** Broz Knives.

MENSCH, LARRY C., RD #3, Box 1444, Milton, PA 17847, Phone: 570-742-9554
Specialties: Custom orders. **Patterns:** Bowies, daggers, hunters, tantos, short swords and miniatures. **Technical:** Grinds ATS-34, carbon and stainless steel Damascus; blade grinds hollow, flat and slack. Filework; bending guards and fluting handles with finger grooves. Offers engraving and scrimshaw. **Prices:** $100 to $300; some to $1000. **Remarks:** Full-time maker; first knife sold in 1993. Doing business as Larry's Knife Shop. **Mark:** Connected capital "L" and small "m" in script.

MERCER, MIKE, 149 N. Waynesville Rd, Lebanon, OH 45036, Phone: 513-932-2837
Specialties: Jeweled gold and ivory daggers; multi-blade folders. **Patterns:** 1-1/4" folders, hunters, axes, replicas. **Technical:** Uses O1 Damascus and mokume. **Prices:** $150 to $1500. **Remarks:** Full-time maker since 1991. **Mark:** Last name in script.

MERCHANT, TED, 7 Old Garrett Ct, White Hall, MD 21161, Phone: 410-343-0380
Specialties: Traditional and classic working knives. **Patterns:** Bowies, hunters, camp knives, fighters, daggers and skinners. **Technical:** Forges W2 and 5160; makes own Damascus. Makes handles with wood, stag, horn, silver and gem stone inlay; fancy filework. **Prices:** $125 to $600; some to $1500. **Remarks:** Full-time maker; first knife sold in 1985. **Mark:** Last name.

MERZ III, ROBERT L., 1447 Winding Canyon, Katy, TX 77493, Phone: 281-391-2897
Specialties: Working straight knives and folders, some fancy, of his design. **Patterns:** Hunters, skinners, fighters and camp knives. **Technical:** Flat-grinds 440C, 154CM, ATS-34, 440V and commercial Damascus. **Prices:** $150 to $450; some to $600. **Remarks:** Part-time maker; first knife sold in 1974. **Mark:** MERZ KNIVES, city and state, or last name in oval.

MESHEJIAN, MARDI, 33 Elm Dr, E. Northport, NY 11731, Phone: 631-757-4541
Specialties: One-of-a-kind fantasy and high-art straight knives of his design. **Patterns:** Swords, daggers, finger knives and other edged weapons. **Technical:** Forged Damascus & Chain Damascus. **Prices:** $150 to $2500; some to $3000. **Remarks:** Full-time maker; first knife sold in 1996. Doing business as Tooth and Nail Metalworks. **Mark:** Stamped Etched stylized "M".

MESSER, DAVID T., 134 S. Torrence St, Dayton, OH 45403-2044, Phone: 513-228-6561
Specialties: Fantasy period pieces, straight and folding, of his design. **Patterns:** Bowies, daggers and swords. **Technical:** Grinds 440C, O1, 06 and commercial Damascus. Likes fancy guards and exotic handle materials. **Prices:** $100 to $225; some to $375. **Remarks:** Spare-time maker; first knife sold in 1994. **Mark:** Name stamp.

METHENY, H. A. "WHITEY", 7750 Waterford Dr, Spotsylvania, VA 22553, Phone: 703-582-3228
Specialties: Working and using straight knives of his design and to customer specs. **Patterns:** Hunters and kitchen knives. **Technical:** Grinds 440C and ATS-34. Offers filework; tooled custom sheaths. **Prices:** $200 to $350. **Remarks:** Spare-time maker; first knife sold in 1990. **Mark:** Initials/full name football logo.

METZ, GREG T., c/o James Ranch HC 83, Cascade, ID 83611, Phone: 208-382-4336
Specialties: Hunting & utility knives. **Prices:** $300 and up. **Remarks:** Natural handle materials; hand forged blades; 1084 & 1095. **Mark:** METZ (last name).

MICHINAKA, TOSHIAKI, I-679 Koyamacho-nishi, Totton-shi, Tottori 680-0947, JAPAN, Phone: 0857-28-5911

MICHO, KANDA, 7-32-5 Shinzutsumi-cho Shinnanyo-city, Yamaguchi, JAPAN, Phone: 0834-62-1910

MILFORD, BRIAN A., RD 2 Box 294, Knox, PA 16232, Phone: 814-797-2595, Fax: 814-226-4351
Specialties: Traditional and working/using straight knives of his design or to customer specs. **Patterns:** Fighters, hunters and utility/camp knives. **Technical:** Forges Damascus and 52100; grinds 440C. **Prices:** $50 to $300; some to $750. **Remarks:** Part-time maker; first knife sold in 1991. Doing business as BAM Forge. **Mark:** Full name or initials.

MILITANO, TOM, Custom Knives, 77 Jason Rd, Jacksonville, AL 36265-6655, Phone: 256-435-7132
Specialties: Fixed blade, one-of-a-kind knives. **Patterns:** Bowies, fighters, hunters and tactical knives. **Technical:** Grinds 440C, ATS-34, A2, and Damascus. Hollow grinds, flat grinds, and decorative filework. **Prices:** $150 plus. **Remarks:** Part-time maker. **Mark:** Name, city and state in oval with maker in the center. Sold first knives in the mid to late 1980s. Memberships: Arkansas Knifemakers Association, Mississippi Noisemakers Association and Flint River Knife Club.

custom knifemakers

MILLARD, FRED G., 5317 N. Wayne, Chicago, IL 60640, Phone: 773-769-5160
Specialties: Working/using straight knives of his design or to customer specs. **Patterns:** Bowies, hunters, utility/camp knives, kitchen/steak knives. **Technical:** Grinds ATS-34, O1, D2 and 440C. Makes sheaths. **Prices:** $80 to $250. **Remarks:** Full-time maker; first knife sold in 1993. Doing business as Millard Knives. **Mark:** Mallard duck in flight with serial number.

MILLER, R. D., 10526 Estate Lane, Dallas, TX 75238, Phone: 214-348-3496
Specialties: One-of-a-kind collector-grade knives. **Patterns:** Boots, hunters, Bowies, camp and utility knives, fishing and bird knives, miniatures. **Technical:** Grinds a variety of steels to include O1, D2, 440C, 154CM and 1095. **Prices:** $65 to $300; some to $900. **Remarks:** Full-time maker; first knife sold in 1984. **Mark:** R. D. Custom Knives with date or bow and arrow logo.

MILLER, RICK, 516 Kanaul Rd, Rockwood, PA 15557, Phone: 814-926-2059
Specialties: Working/using straight knives of his design and in standard patterns. **Patterns:** Bowies, daggers, hunters and friction folders. **Technical:** Grinds L6. Forges 5160, L6 and Damascus. Patterns for Damascus are random, twist, rose or ladder. **Prices:** $75 to $250; some to $400. **Remarks:** Part-time maker; first knife sold in 1982. **Mark:** Script stamp "R. D. M.".

MILLER, MICHAEL E., 1508 Crestwood Dr, Wagoner, OK 74467, Phone: 918-485-6166
Specialties: Traditional working/using knives of his design. **Patterns:** Bowies, hunters and kitchen knives. **Technical:** Grinds ATS-34, CPM 440V; forges Damascus and cable Damascus and 52100. Prefers scrimshaw, fancy pins, basket weave and embellished sheaths. **Prices:** $80 to $300; some to $500. **Remarks:** Part-time maker; first knife sold in 1984. Doing business as Miller Custom Knives. **Mark:** First and middle initials, last name, maker, city and state.

MILLER, JAMES P., 9024 Goeller Rd, RR 2, Box 28, Fairbank, IA 50629, Phone: 319-635-2294
Specialties: All tool steel Damascus; working knives and period pieces. **Patterns:** Hunters, Bowies, camp knives and daggers. **Technical:** Forges and grinds 1095, 52100, 440C and his own Damascus. **Prices:** $100 to $350; some to $1500. **Remarks:** Full-time maker; first knife sold in 1970. **Mark:** First and middle initials, last name with knife logo.

MILLER, HANFORD J., Box 97, Cowdrey, CO 80434, Phone: 970-723-4708
Specialties: Working knives in Moran-style; period pieces. **Patterns:** Bowies, fighters, camp knives and other large straight knives. **Technical:** Forges W2, 1095, 5160 and his own Damascus; differential tempers; offers wire inlay. **Prices:** $300 to $800; some to $3000. **Remarks:** Full-time maker; first knife sold in 1968. **Mark:** Initials or name within Bowie logo.

MILLER, DON, 1604 Harrodsburg Rd, Lexington, KY 40503, Phone: 606-276-3299

MILLER, BOB, 7659 Fine Oaks Pl., Oakville, MO 63129, Phone: 314-846-8934
Specialties: Mosaic Damascus; collector using straight knives and folders. **Patterns:** Hunters, Bowies, utility/camp knives, daggers. **Technical:** Forges own Damascus, mosaic-Damascus and 52100. **Prices:** $125 to $500. **Remarks:** Part-time maker; first knife sold in 1983. **Mark:** First and middle initials and last name, or initials.

MILLER, RONALD T., 12922 127th Ave. N., Largo, FL 34644, Phone: 813-595-0378 (after 5 p. m.)
Specialties: Working straight knives in standard patterns. **Patterns:** Combat knives, camp knives, kitchen cutlery, fillet knives, locking folders and butterflies. **Technical:** Grinds D2, 440C and ATS-34; offers brass inlays and scrimshaw. **Prices:** $45 to $325; some to $750. **Remarks:** Part-time maker; first knife sold in 1984. **Mark:** Name, city and state in palm tree logo.

MILLER, MICHAEL K., 28510 Santiam Hwy., Sweet Home, OR 97386, Phone: 541-367-4927
Specialties: Specializes in kitchen cutlery of his design or made to customer specs. **Patterns:** Hunters, utility/camp knives and kitchen cutlery. **Technical:** Grinds ATS-34, AEBL & 440-C. Wife does scrimshaw as well. Makes custom sheaths and holsters. **Prices:** $200. **Remarks:** Full-time maker; first knife sold in 1989. **Mark:** M&M Kustom Krafts.

MILLER, M. A., 11625 Community Center Dr, Unit 1531, Northglenn, CO 80233, Phone: 303-427-8756
Specialties: Using knives for hunting. 3-1/2"-4" Loveless drop-point. Made to customer specs. **Patterns:** Skinners and camp knives. **Technical:** Grinds 440C, D2, O1 and ATS-34 Damascus miniatures. **Prices:** $225 to $275; miniatures $75. **Remarks:** Part-time maker; first knife sold in 1988.

Mark: Last name stamped in block letters or first and middle initials, last name, maker, city and state with triangles on either side etched.

MILLS, LOUIS G., 9450 Waters Rd, Ann Arbor, MI 48103, Phone: 734-668-1839
Specialties: High-art Japanese-style period pieces. **Patterns:** Traditional tantos, daggers and swords. **Technical:** Makes steel from iron; makes his own Damascus by traditional Japanese techniques. **Prices:** $900 to $2000; some to $8000. **Remarks:** Spare-time maker. **Mark:** Yasutomo in Japanese Kanji.

MINK, DAN, PO Box 861, 196 Sage Circle, Crystal Beach, FL 34681, Phone: 727-786-5408
Specialties: Traditional and working knives of his design. **Patterns:** Bowies, fighters, folders and hunters. **Technical:** Grinds ATS-34, 440C and D2. Blades and tanges embellished with fancy filework. Uses natural and rare handle materials. **Prices:** $125 to $450. **Remarks:** Part-time maker; first knife sold in 1985. **Mark:** Name and star encircled by custom made, city, state.

MINNICK, JIM, 144 North 7th St, Middletown, IN 47356, Phone: 765-354-4108
Specialties: Lever-lock folding art knives, liner-locks. **Patterns:** Stilettos, Persian and one-of-a-kind folders. **Technical:** Grinds and carves Damascus, stainless, and high carbon. **Prices:** $950 to $7000. **Remarks:** Part-time maker; first knife sold in 1976. **Mark:** Minnick and JMJ. **Other:** Husband & wife team.

MIRABILE, DAVID, 1715 Glacier Av., Juneau, AK 99801, Phone: 907-463-3404
Specialties: Elegant edged weapons. **Patterns:** Fighters, Bowies, claws, tklinget daggers, executive desk knives. **Technical:** Forged high carbon steels, his own Damascus; uses ancient walrus ivory and prehistoric bone extensively, very rarely uses wood. **Prices:** $350 to $7000. **Remarks:** Full-time maker. Knives sold through art gallery in Juneau, AK. **Mark:** Last name etched or engraved.

MITCHELL, JAMES A., PO Box 4646, Columbus, GA 31904, Phone: 404-322-8582
Specialties: Fancy working knives. **Patterns:** Hunters, fighters, Bowies and locking folders. **Technical:** Grinds D2, 440C and commercial Damascus. **Prices:** $100 to $400; some to $900. **Remarks:** Part-time maker; first knife sold in 1976. Sells knives in sets. **Mark:** Signature and city.

MITCHELL, MAX, DEAN AND BEN, 3803 V. F. W. Rd, Leesville, LA 71440, Phone: 318-239-6416
Specialties: Hatchet and knife sets with folder & belt & holster all match. **Patterns:** Hunters, 200 L6 steel. **Technical:** L6 steel; soft back, hand edge. **Prices:** $300 to $500. **Remarks:** Part-time makers; first knife sold in 1965. Custom orders only; no stock. **Mark:** First names.

MITCHELL, WM. DEAN, 8438 Cty Rd One, Lamar, CO 81052, Phone: 719-336-8807
Specialties: Classic and period knives. **Patterns:** Bowies, hunters, daggers and swords. **Technical:** Forges carbon steel and Damascus 52100, 1095, 5160; makes pattern, composite and mosaic Damascus; offers filework. Makes wooden display cases. **Prices:** Mid-scale. **Remarks:** Part-time maker since 1986; first knife sold in 1986. Doing business as Pioneer Forge & Woodshop. **Mark:** Full name with anvil, MS.

MITSUYUKI, ROSS, 94-1071 Kepakepa St, C-3, Waipahu, Hawaii 96797, Phone: 808-671-3335, Fax: 808-671-3335
Specialties: Working straight knives and folders. **Patterns:** Hunting, fighters, utility knives and boot knives. **Technical:** BG-42 530V S. S. Damascus. **Prices:** $100-$500. **Remarks:** Spare-time maker, first knife sold in 1998. **Mark:** Name, state, Hawaiian sea turtle.

MIZE, RICHARD, Fox Creek Forge, 2038 Fox Creek Rd, Lawrenceburg, KY 40342, Phone: 502-859-0602
Specialties: Forges spring steel, 5160, 10xx steels, natural handle materials. **Patterns:** Traditional working knives, period flavor Bowies, rifle knives. **Technical:** Does own heat treating, differential temper. **Prices:** $100 to $400. **Remarks:** Strongly advocates sole authorship. **Mark:** Initial M hot stamped.

MOMCILOVIC, GUNNAR, Nordlysv, 16, N-30055 Krokstadelva, NORWAY, Phone: 0111-47-3287-3586

MONCUS, MICHAEL STEVEN, 1803 US 19 North, Smithville, GA 31787, Phone: 912-846-2408

MONK, NATHAN P., 1304 4th Ave. SE, Cullman, AL 35055, Phone: 205-737-0463
Specialties: Traditional working and using straight knives of his design and to customer specs; fancy knives. **Patterns:** Bowies, daggers, fighters, hunters, utility/camp knives, bird knives and one-of-a-kinds. **Technical:** Grinds ATS-34, 440C and A2. **Prices:** $50 to $175. **Remarks:** Spare-time maker; first knife sold in 1990. **Mark:** First and middle initials, last name, city, state.

MONTANO, GUS A., 11217 Westonhill Dr, San Diego, CA 92126-1447, Phone: 619-273-5357
Specialties: Traditional working/using straight knives of his design. **Patterns:** Boots, Bowies and fighters. **Technical:** Grinds 1095 and 5160; grinds and forges cable. Double or triple hardened and triple drawn; hand-rubbed finish. Prefers natural handle materials. **Prices:** $200 to $400; some to $600. **Remarks:** Spare-time maker; first knife sold in 1997. **Mark:** First initial and last name.

MONTEIRO, VICTOR, 31, Rue D'Opprebais, 1360 Maleves Ste Marie, BELGIUM, Phone: 010 88 0441
Specialties: Working and fancy straight knives, folders and integrals of his design. **Patterns:** Bowies, fighters and hunters. **Technical:** Grinds ATS-34, 440C and commercial Damascus, embellishment, filework and domed pins. **Prices:** $300 to $1000; some higher. **Remarks:** Part-time maker; first knife sold in 1989. **Mark:** Logo with initials connected.

MONTJOY, CLAUDE, 706 Indian Creek Rd, Clinton, SC 29325, Phone: 864-697-6160
Specialties: Folders, slip joint, lock, lock liner & inter frame. **Patterns:** Hunters, boots, fighters, some art knives and folders. **Technical:** Grinds ATS-34 and Damascus. Offers inlaid handle scales. **Prices:** $100 to $500. **Remarks:** Full-time maker; first knife sold in 1982. **Mark:** Montjoy. **Other:** Custom orders, no catalog.

MOORE, MARVE, 1216 Paintersville-New Jasper Rd, Xenia, OH 45385, Phone: 937-256-8235

MOORE, MICHAEL ROBERT, 61 Beaulieu St, Lowell, MA 01850, Phone: 978-459-2163, Fax: 978-441-1819

MOORE, JAMES B., 1707 N. Gillis, Ft. Stockton, TX 79735, Phone: 915-336-2113
Specialties: Classic working straight knives and folders of his design. **Patterns:** Hunters, Bowies, daggers, fighters, boots, utility/camp knives, locking folders and slip-joint folders. **Technical:** Grinds 440C, ATS-34, D2, L6, CPM and commercial Damascus. **Prices:** $85 to $700; exceptional knives to $1500. **Remarks:** Full-time maker; first knife sold in 1972. **Mark:** Name, city and state.

MOORE, BILL, 806 Community Ave, Albany, GA 31705, Phone: 912-438-5529
Specialties: Working and using folders of his design and to customer specs. **Patterns:** Bowies, hunters and locking folders. **Technical:** Grinds ATS-34, forges 5168 and cable Damascus. Filework. **Prices:** $100 to $400. **Remarks:** Part-time maker; first knife sold in 1988. **Mark:** Moore Knives.

MOORE, TED, 340 E Willow St, Elizabethtown, PA 17022-1946, Phone: 717-367-3939
Specialties: Damascus folders, cigar cutters. **Patterns:** Locking folders & slip joint. **Technical:** Grinds Damascus, high carbon & stainless; also ATS-34 & D2. **Prices:** $250 to $1500. **Remarks:** Part-time maker; first knife sold 1993. **Mark:** Moore U. S. A.

MORAN JR., WM. F., PO Box 68, Braddock Heights, MD 21714, Phone: 301-371-7543
Specialties: High-art working knives of his design. **Patterns:** Fighters, camp knives, Bowies, daggers, axes, tomahawks, push knives and miniatures. **Technical:** Forges W2, 5160 and his own Damascus; puts silver wire inlay on most handles; uses only natural handle materials. **Prices:** $400 to $7500; some to $9000. **Remarks:** Full-time maker. **Mark:** W. F. Moran Jr. Master Smith MS.

MORETT, DONALD, 116 Woodcrest Dr, Lancaster, PA 17602-1300, Phone: 717-746-4888

MORGAN, JEFF, 9200 Arnaz Way, Santee, CA 92071, Phone: 619-448-8430
Specialties: Fancy working straight knives. **Patterns:** Hunters, fighters, boots, miniatures. **Technical:** Grinds D2, 440C and ATS-34; likes exotic handles. **Prices:** $65 to $140; some to $500. **Remarks:** Full-time maker; first knife sold in 1977. **Mark:** Initials connected.

MORGAN, TOM, 14689 Ellett Rd, Beloit, OH 44609, Phone: 330-537-2023
Specialties: Working straight knives and period pieces. **Patterns:** Hunters, boots and presentation tomahawks. **Technical:** Grinds O1, 440C and 154CM. **Prices:** Knives, $65 to $200; tomahawks, $100 to $325. **Remarks:** Full-time maker; first knife sold in 1977. **Mark:** Last name and type of steel used.

MORRIS, DARRELL PRICE, 92 Union, St. Plymouth, Devon, ENGLAND PL1 3EZ, Phone: 0752 223546
Specialties: Traditional Japanese knives, Bowies and high-art knives. **Technical:** Nickel Damascus and mokamame. **Prices:** $1000 to $4000. **Remarks:** Part-time maker; first knife sold in 1990. **Mark:** Initials and Japanese name—Kuni Shigae.

MORRIS, ERIC, 306 Ewart Ave, Beckley, WV 25801, Phone: 304-255-3951

MORRIS, C. H., 1590 Old Salem Rd, Frisco City, AL 36445, Phone: 334-575-7425
Specialties: Liner-lock folders. **Patterns:** Interframe liner-locks. **Technical:** Grinds 440C and ATS-34. **Prices:** Start at $350. **Remarks:** Full-time maker; first knife sold in 1973. Doing business as Custom Knives. **Mark:** First and middle initials, last name.

MORTENSON, ED, 2742 Hwy. 93 N, Darby, MT 59829, Phone: 406-821-3146, Fax: 406-821-3146
Specialties: Period pieces and working/using straight knives of his design, to customer specs and in standard patterns. **Patterns:** Bowies, hunters and kitchen knives. **Technical:** Grinds ATS-34, 5160 and 1095. Sheath combinations - flashlight/knife, hatchet/knife, etc. **Prices:** $60 to $140; some to $300. **Remarks:** Full-time maker; first knife sold in 1993. Doing business as The Blade Lair. **Mark:** M with attached O.

MOSES, STEVEN, 1610 West Hemlock Way, Santa Ana, CA 92704

MOSIER, RICHARD, 52 Dapplegray Ln, Rolling Hills Est, CA 90274

MOSIER, JOSHUA J., Spring Creek Knife Works, PO Box 442/802 6th St, Edgar, NE 68935
Specialties: Working straight and folding knives of my designs with customer specs. **Patterns:** Hunters, utilities, locking liner folders, kitchen and camp knives. **Technical:** Forges and grinds 5160, W2, L6, simple carbon steels and my own Damascus, uses some antique materials, provides a history of the materials used in each knife. **Prices:** $55 and up. **Remarks:** Part-time maker, sold first knife in 1986. **Mark:** SCKW .

MOSSER, GARY E., 11827 NE 102nd Place, Kirkland, WA 98033-5170, Phone: 425-827-2279
Specialties: Working knives. **Patterns:** Hunters, skinners, camp knives, some art knives. **Technical:** Stock removal method; prefers ATS-34. **Prices:** $100 to $250; special orders and art knives are higher. **Remarks:** Part-time maker; first knife sold in 1976. **Mark:** Name.

MOULTON, DUSTY, 135 Hillview Lane, Loudon, TN 37774, Phone: 865-408-9779
Specialties: Fancy and working straight knives. **Patterns:** Hunters, fighters, fantasy and miniatures. **Technical:** Grinds ATS-34 and Damascus. **Prices:** $300 to $2000. **Remarks:** Full-time maker; first knife sold in 1991. **Mark:** Last name. **Other:** Now doing engraving on own knives as well as other makers.

MOUNT, DON, 4574 Little Finch Ln., Las Vegas, NV 89115, Phone: 702-531-2925
Specialties: High-tech working and using straight knives of his design. **Patterns:** Bowies, fighters and utility/camp knives. **Technical:** Uses 440C and ATS-34. **Prices:** $150 to $300; some to $1000. **Remarks:** Part-time maker; first knife sold in 1985. **Mark:** Name below a woodpecker.

MOUNTAIN HOME KNIVES, PO Box 167, Jamul, CA 91935, Phone: 619-669-0833
Specialties: High-quality working straight knives. **Patterns:** Hunters, fighters, skinners, tantos, utility and fillet knives, Bowies and san-mai Damascus Bowies. **Technical:** Hollow-grind 440C by hand. Feature linen Micarta handles, nickel-silver handle bolts and handmade sheaths. **Prices:** $65 to $270. **Remarks:** Company owned by Jim English. **Mark:** Mountain Home Knives.

MOYER, RUSS, HC 36 Box 57C, Havre, MT 59501, Phone: 406-395-4423
Specialties: Working knives to customer specs. **Patterns:** Hunters, Bowies and survival knives. **Technical:** Forges W2. **Prices:** $150 to $350. **Remarks:** Part-time maker; first knife sold in 1976. **Mark:** Initials in logo.

MULLER, JODY & PAT, PO Box 35, Pittsburg, MO 65724, Phone: 417-852-4306/417-752-3260
Specialties: Hand engraving, carving and inlays. One-of-a-kind personal carry knives with billfold cases, cleavers. **Patterns:** One-of-a-kind fixed blades in all styles. **Technical:** Forges 1095, L6 and Nickel into our own patterned Damascus. **Prices:** $150-$1500. **Remarks:** Son and father team of part-time makers. Jody made first knife at age 12. Now does fine hand-engraving, carving and inlay. **Mark:** Muller Forge in script. **Other:** Cross reference Muller Forge.

MULLIN, STEVE, 500 Snowberry Lane, Sandpoint, ID 83864, Phone: 208-263-7492
Specialties: Damascus period pieces and folders. **Patterns:** Full range of folders, hunters and Bowies. **Technical:** Forges and grinds O1, D2, 154CM and his own Damascus. Engraves. **Prices:** $100 to $2000. **Remarks:** Full-time maker; first knife sold in 1975. Sells line of using knives under Pack River Knife Co. **Mark:** Full name, city and state.

custom knifemakers

MUNROE, DERYK C., PO Box 3454, Bozeman, MT 59772

MURRAY, BILL, 1632 Rio Mayo, Green Valley, AZ 85614

MURSKI, RAY, 12129 Captiva Ct, Reston, VA 22091-1204, Phone: 703-264-1102
Specialties: Fancy working/using folders of his design. **Patterns:** Hunters, slip-joint folders and utility/camp knives. **Technical:** Grinds CPM-3V **Prices:** $125-$500. **Remarks:** Spare-time maker; first knife sold in 1996. **Mark:** Etched name with serial number under name.

MYERS, PAUL, 644 Maurice St, Wood River, IL 62095, Phone: 618-258-1707
Specialties: Fancy working straight knives and folders. **Patterns:** Full range of folders, straight hunters and Bowies; tie tacks; knife and fork sets. **Technical:** Grinds D2, 440C, ATS-34 and 154CM. **Prices:** $100 to $350; some to $3000. **Remarks:** Full-time maker; first knife sold in 1974. **Mark:** Initials with setting sun on front; name and number on back.

n

NATEN, GREG, 1804 Shamrock Way, Bakersfield, CA 93304-3921
Specialties: Fancy and working/using folders of his design. **Patterns:** Fighters, hunters and locking folders. **Technical:** Grinds 440C, ATS-34 and CPM440V. Heat-treats; prefers desert ironwood, stag and mother of pearl. Designs and sews leather sheaths for straight knives. **Prices:** $175 to $600; some to $950. **Remarks:** Spare-time maker; first knife sold in 1992. **Mark:** Last name above battle-ax, handmade.

NAVAGATO, ANGELO, 5 Commercial Apt 2, Camp Hill, PA 17011

NEALEY, IVAN F. (FRANK), Anderson Dam Rd, Box 65, HC #87, Mt. Home, ID 83647, Phone: 208-587-4060
Specialties: Working straight knives in standard patterns. **Patterns:** Hunters, skinners and utility knives. **Technical:** Grinds D2, 440C and 154CM. **Prices:** $90 to $135; some higher. **Remarks:** Part-time maker; first knife sold in 1975. **Mark:** Name.

NEALY, BUD, 1439 Poplar Valley Rd, Stroudsburg, PA 18360, Phone: 570-402-1018, Fax: 570-402-1019
Specialties: Original design concealment knives with designer multi-concealment sheath system. **Patterns:** Concealment knives, boots, combat and collector pieces. **Technical:** Grinds ATS-34; uses Damascus. **Prices:** $200 to $2500. **Remarks:** Full-time maker; first knife sold in 1980. **Mark:** Name, city, state or signature.

NEDVED, DAN, 206 Park Dr, Kalispell, MT 59901, Phone: 406-752-5060
Specialties: Slip joint folders, liner-locks, straight knives. **Patterns:** Mostly traditional or modern blend with traditional lines. **Technical:** Grinds ATS-34, 440C, 1095 and uses other maker's Damascus. **Prices:** $95 and up. Mostly in the $150 to $200 range. **Remarks:** Part-time maker, averages 2 a month. **Mark:** Dan Nedved or Nedved with serial # on opposite side.

NEELY, GREG, 5419 Pine St, Bellaire, TX 77401, Phone: 713-991-2677
Specialties: Traditional patterns and his own patterns for work and/or collecting. **Patterns:** Hunters, Bowies and utility/camp knives. **Technical:** Forges own Damascus, 1084, 5160 and some tool steels. Differentially tempers. **Prices:** $225 to $5000. **Remarks:** Part-time maker; first knife sold in 1987. **Mark:** Last name or interlocked initials, MS.

NEILSON, J., RR 2 Box 16, Wyalusing, PA 18853, Phone: 570-746-4944
Specialties: Working and collectable fixed blade knives. **Patterns:** Hunter/fighters, Bowies, neck knives and historical replicas. **Technical:** Flat grinds, 1095, 1084, 5160, 440C, Damascus (Forging my own). **Prices:** $150-$450. **Remarks:** Full-time maker, first knife sold in 2000. Doing business at Mountain Hollow Blade & Hide Co. **Mark:** Mountain Hollow and full name. **Other:** Each knife comes with a sheath by Tess.

NELSON, KEN, 11059 Hwy 73, Pittsville, WI 54466, Phone: 715-884-6448
Specialties: Working straight knives, period pieces. **Patterns:** Utility, hunters, dirks, daggers, throwers, hawks, axes, swords, and pole arms. **Technical:** Forges 5160, 52100, W2, 10xx, L6, and own Damascus. Multiple and differential heat treating. **Prices:** $50 to $350; some to $3000. **Remarks:** Part-time maker. First knife sold in 1995. Doing business as Iron Wolf Forge. Member of ABS. **Mark:** Stylized wolf paw print.

NELSON, TOM, PO Box 2298, Wilropark 1731, Gauteng, SOUTH AFRICA

NELSON, BOB, 21 Glen Rd, Sparta, NJ 07871

NELSON, DR. CARL, 2500 N Robison Rd, Texarkana, TX 75501

NETO JR., NELSON AND DE CARVALHO, HENRIQUE M., R. Joao Margarido, No. 20-V, Guerra, Braganca Paulista, SP-12900-000, BRAZIL, Phone: 011-7843-6889, Fax: 011-7843-6889
Specialties: Straight knives and folders. **Patterns:** Bowies, katanas, jambyias and others. **Technical:** Forges high carbon steels. **Prices:** $70 to $3000. **Remarks:** Full-time makers; first knife sold in 1990. **Mark:** H&N.

NEUHAEUSLER, ERWIN, Heiligenangerstrasse 15, 86179 Augsburg, GERMANY, Phone: 0821/81 49 97
Specialties: Using straight knives of his design. **Patterns:** Hunters, boots, Bowies. **Technical:** Grinds ATS-34, RWL-34 and Damascus. **Prices:** $200 to $750. **Remarks:** Spare-time maker; first knife sold in 1991. **Mark:** Etched logo, last name and city.

NEVLING, MARK, Burr Oak Knives, PO Box 9, Hume, IL 61932, Phone: 217-887-2522
Specialties: Straight knives and folders of his own design. **Patterns:** Hunters, fighters, Bowies, folders, and small executive knives. **Technical:** Convex grinds, Forges, uses only high carbon and Damascus. **Prices:** $200 - $2000. **Remarks:** Full-time maker, first knife sold 1988.

NEWCOMB, CORBIN, 628 Woodland Ave, Moberly, MO 65270, Phone: 660-263-4639
Specialties: Working straight knives and folders; period pieces. **Patterns:** Hunters, axes, Bowies, folders, buckskinned blades and boots. **Technical:** Hollow-grinds D2, 440C and 154CM; prefers natural handle materials. Makes own Damascus; offers cable Damascus. **Prices:** $100 to $500. **Remarks:** Full-time maker; first knife sold in 1982. Doing business as Corbin Knives. **Mark:** First name and serial number.

NEWHALL, TOM, 3602 E 42nd Stravenue, Tucson, AZ 85713, Phone: 520-721-0562

NEWTON, RON, 223 Ridge Lane, London, AR 72847, Phone: 479-293-3001
Specialties: Mosaic Damascus folders with accelerated actions. **Patterns:** One-of-a-kind. **Technical:** 1084-15N20 steels used in my mosaic Damascus steels. **Prices:** $1000 to $5000. **Remarks:** Also making antique Bowie repros and various fixed blades. **Mark:** All capital letters in NEWTON "Western Invitation" font.

NEWTON, LARRY, 1758 Pronghorn Ct, Jacksonville, FL 32225, Phone: 904-221-2340, Fax: 904-220-4098
Specialties: Traditional and slender high-grade gentlemen's automatic folders, locking liner type tactical, and working straight knives. **Patterns:** Front release locking folders, interframes, hunters, and skinners. **Technical:** Grinds Damascus, ATS-34, 440C and D2. **Prices:** Folders start at $350, straights start at $150. **Remarks:** Spare-time maker; first knife sold in 1989. **Mark:** Last name.

NICHOLSON, R. KENT, PO Box 204, Phoenix, MD 21131, Phone: 410-323-6925
Specialties: Large using knives. **Patterns:** Bowies and camp knives in the Moran-style. **Technical:** Forges W2, 9260, 5160; makes Damascus. **Prices:** $150 to $995. **Remarks:** Part-time maker; first knife sold in 1984. **Mark:** Name.

NIELSON, JEFF V., PO Box 365, Monroe, UT 84754, Phone: 801-527-4242
Specialties: Classic knives of his design and to customer specs. **Patterns:** Fighters, hunters, locking folders; miniatures. **Technical:** Grinds 440C stainless & Damascus. **Prices:** $100 to $1200. **Remarks:** Part-time maker; first knife sold in 1991. **Mark:** Name, location.

NIEMUTH, TROY, 3143 North Ave, Sheboygan, WI 53083, Phone: 414-452-2927
Specialties: Period pieces and working/using straight knives of his design and to customer specs. **Patterns:** Hunters and utility/camp knives. **Technical:** Grinds 440C, 1095 and A2. **Prices:** $85 to $350; some to $500. **Remarks:** Full-time maker; first knife sold in 1995. **Mark:** Etched last name.

NILSSON, JOHNNY WALKER, Tingsstigen 11, SE-133 33 Arvidsjaur, SWEDEN, Phone: 46-960-130-48
Specialties: High-end hand-carved and engraved Sami-style horn knives. **Patterns:** Nordic and Scandinavian-styles. **Technical:** Grinds carbon and Damascus steels himself as of 2003. Uses Damascus forged to specification by Conny Persson, Kaj Embretsen, Matttias Styrefors. **Prices:** $650-$2500. **Remarks:** Nordic (five countries) champion of horn knives for many years. Yearly award in his name in future Nordic Championships. Inspired by the 10,000-year-old Sami culture, he combines traditional designs and techniques with his own innovations. Handles in Arctic burls and reindeer

horn, bark dye, bark and pewter spacers. Engraved horn sheaths with wood and horn inlays, 3D inlays, cutouts and filework. Full-time maker since 1988. **Mark:** JN

NISHIUCHI, MELVIN S., 6121 Forest Park Dr, Las Vegas, NV 89156, Phone: 702-438-2327
Specialties: Collectable quality using/working knives. **Patterns:** Locking liner folders, fighters, hunters and fancy personal knives. **Technical:** Grinds ATS-34 and Devin Thomas Damascus; prefers semi-precious stone and exotic natural handle materials. **Prices:** $375-$2000. **Remarks:** Part-time maker; first knife sold in 1985. **Mark:** Circle with a line above it.

NIX, ROBERT T., 4194 Cadillac, Wayne, MI 48184, Phone: 734-729-6468
Specialties: Hunters, skinners, art, bowie, camp/survival/boot folders. Most are file worked. Custom leather work available also, mainly sheaths/overlays, inlays, tooling, combinations of material/leather, micarta, wood, kydex, nylon. **Technical:** Stock removal, ATS-34, stainless Damascus, 440C, 420V, 440V, BG42, D2, 01, carbon Damascus. Every blade gets Rockwelled. I like the natural handle materials best, but will use anything that's available; ivory, bone, horn, pearl, stabilized woods, micarta. **Prices:** Knives from $125 to $2500. Sheaths from $40 to $400. **Remarks:** Part-time maker, first knife sold in 1993. Make each piece as if it were for me. **Mark:** R. T. Nix in script or Nix in bold face.

NOLEN, R. D. AND STEVE, 1110 Lakeshore Dr, Estes Park, CO 80517-7113, Phone: 970-586-5814, Fax: 970-586-8827
Specialties: Working knives; display pieces. **Patterns:** Wide variety of straight knives, butterflies and buckles. **Technical:** Grind D2, 440C and 154CM. Offer filework; make exotic handles. **Prices:** $150 to $800; some higher. **Remarks:** Full-time makers; first knife sold in 1968. Steve is third generation maker. **Mark:** NK in oval logo.

NORDELL, INGEMAR, Skarpå 2103, 82041 Färila, SWEDEN, Phone: 0651-23347
Specialties: Classic working and using straight knives. **Patterns:** Hunters, Bowies and fighters. **Technical:** Forges and grinds ATS-34, D2 and Sandvik. **Prices:** $120 to $1500. **Remarks:** Part-time maker; first knife sold in 1985. **Mark:** Initials or name.

NOREN, DOUGLAS E., 14676 Boom Rd, Springlake, MI 49456, Phone: 616-842-4247
Specialties: Hand forged blades, custom built & made to order. Hand file work, carving & casting. Stag & stacked handles. Replicas of Scagel & Joseph Rogers. Hand tooled custom made sheaths. **Technical:** 5160, 52100 & 1084 steel. **Prices:** Start at $250. **Remarks:** Sole authorship, works in all mediums, ABS journey man msn., all knives come with a custom hand-tooled sheath. Also makes anvils. **Other:** I enjoy the challenge & meeting people.

NORFLEET, ROSS W., 3947 Tanbark Rd, Richmond, VA 23235, Phone: 804-276-4169
Specialties: Classic, traditional and working/using knives of his design or in standard patterns. **Patterns:** Hunters and folders. **Technical:** Hollow-grinds 440C and ATS-34. **Prices:** $150 to $550. **Remarks:** Part-time maker; first knife sold in 1992. **Mark:** Last name.

NORRIS, DON, 8861 N Shadow Rock Dr, Tucson, AZ 85743, Phone: 520-744-2494
Specialties: Classic and traditional working/using straight knives and folders of his design, or to customer specs etc. **Patterns:** Bowies, daggers, fighters, hunters and utility/camp knives. **Technical:** Grinds and forges Damascus; grinds ATS-34 and 440C. Cast sterling guards and bolsters on Bowies. **Prices:** $350 to $2000; some to $3500. **Remarks:** Full-time maker; first knife sold in 1990. Doing business as Norris Custom Knives. **Mark:** Last name.

NORRIS, MIKE, 2115 W Main St, Albermarle, NC 28001, Phone: 704-982-8445

NORTON, DON, 7517 Mountain Quail Dr, Las Vegas, NV 89146, Phone: 703-642-5036
Specialties: Fancy and plain straight knives. **Patterns:** Hunters, small Bowies, tantos, boot knives, fillets. **Technical:** Prefers 440C, Micarta, exotic woods and other natural handle materials. Hollow-grinds all knives except fillet knives. **Prices:** $165 to $1500; average is $200. **Remarks:** Full-time maker; first knife sold in 1980. **Mark:** Full name, Hsi Shuai, city, state.

NOTT, RON P., PO Box 281, Summerdale, PA 17093, Phone: 717-732-2763
Specialties: High-art folders and some straight knives. **Patterns:** Scale release folders. **Technical:** Grinds ATS-34, 416 and nickel-silver. Engraves, inlays gold. **Prices:** $250 to $3000. **Remarks:** Full-time maker; first knife sold in 1993. Doing business as Knives By Nott, customer engraving. **Mark:** First initial, last name and serial number.

NOWLAND, RICK, 3677 E Bonnie Rd, Waltonville, IL 62894, Phone: 618-279-3170
Specialties: Fancy single blade slip joints & trappers using Damascus & Mokume. **Patterns:** Uses several Remington patterns and also his own designs. **Technical:** Uses ATS-34, 440C; forges his own Damascus; makes Mokume. **Prices:** Start at $200. **Remarks:** Part-time maker; first knife sold in 1986. **Mark:** Last name.

NUNN, GREGORY, HC64 Box 2107, Castle Valley, UT 84532, Phone: 435-259-8607
Specialties: High-art working and using knives of his design; new edition knife with handle made from anatomized dinosaur bone - first ever made. **Patterns:** Flaked stone knives. **Technical:** Uses gem-quality agates, jaspers and obsidians for blades. **Prices:** $250 to $2300. **Remarks:** Full-time maker; first knife sold in 1989. **Mark:** Name, knife and edition numbers, year made.

O

OAKES, WINSTON, 431 Deauville Dr, Dayton, OH 45429, Phone: 937-434-3112
Specialties: Dealer. **Prices:** $200 to $10,000. **Remarks:** Dealer in Jess Horn folders and other high quality hunters.

OBENAUF, MIKE, 355 Sandy Ln, Vine Grove, KY 40175, Phone: 270-828-4138/270-877-6300
Specialties: Tactical and gentleman's type folders, tactical fixed blades. **Technical:** Grinds CPM Steels, Damascus, etc. **Prices:** $275 and up. **Remarks:** Full-time maker since 2000. First knife sold in 2000. **Mark:** OBENAUF engraved or stamped.

OBRIEN, GEORGE, 22511 Tullis Trails Ct, Katy, TX 77494-8265

O'CEILAGHAN, MICHAEL, 1623 YC Rd, Baltimore, MD 21226, Phone: 410-355-1660, Fax: 410-355-1661
Specialties: High-art and traditional straight knives of his design and to customer specs. **Patterns:** Fighters, hunters and utility/camp knives. **Technical:** Forges 5160, O6, 1045 and railroad spikes. Blades are "Hamon" tempered and drawn; handles are either horn or hand-carved wood. **Prices:** $100 to $325; some to $750. **Remarks:** First knife sold in 1992. Doing business as Howling Wolf Forge. **Mark:** Howling Wolf Forge, signed signature, date forged.

OCHS, CHARLES F., 124 Emerald Lane, Largo, FL 33771, Phone: 727-536-3827, Fax: 727-536-3827
Specialties: Working knives; period pieces. **Patterns:** Hunters, fighters, Bowies, buck skinners and folders. **Technical:** Forges 52100, 5160 and his own Damascus. **Prices:** $150 to $1800; some to $2500. **Remarks:** Full-time maker; first knife sold in 1978. **Mark:** OX Forge.

O'DELL, CLYDE, 176 Ouachita 404, Camden, AR 71701, Phone: 870-574-2754
Specialties: Working knives. **Patterns:** Hunters, camp knives, tomahawks. **Technical:** Forges 5160 and 1084. **Prices:** Starting at $50. **Remarks:** Spare-time maker. **Mark:** Last name.

ODGEN, RANDY W., 10822 SAGE ORCHARD, HOUSTON, TX 77089, Phone: 713-481-3601

ODOM, VIC, PO BOX 572, NORTH, SC 29112, Phone: 803-247-5614
Specialties: Forged knives & tomahawks; stock removal knives. **Patterns:** Hunters, Bowies. **Prices:** $50 and up. **Mark:** Steel stamp "ODOM" and etched "Odom Forge North, SC" plus a serial number.

OGDEN, BILL, Ogden Knives, PO Box 52, Avis, PA 17721, Phone: 570-753-5568
Specialties: One-of-a-kind, liner-lock folders, hunters, skinners, minis. **Technical:** Grinds ATS-34, 440-C, D2, 52100, Damascus, natural & unnatural handle materials, hand-stitched custom sheaths. **Prices:** $50 and up. **Remarks:** Part-time maker since 1992. **Mark:** Last name or "OK" stamp (Ogden Knives).

OGLETREE JR., BEN R., 2815 Israel Rd, Livingston, TX 77351, Phone: 409-327-8315
Specialties: Working/using straight knives of his design. **Patterns:** Hunters, kitchen and utility/camp knives. **Technical:** Grinds ATS-34, W1 and 1075; heat-treats. **Prices:** $200 to $400. **Remarks:** Part-time maker; first knife sold in 1955. **Mark:** Last name, city and state in oval with a tree on either side.

OKAYSU, KAZOU, 12-2 1 Chome Higashi Ueno, Taito-Ku, Tokyo, JAPAN 110-0015, Phone: 81-33834-2323, Fax: 81-33831-3012
Mark: Okayasu Steel Co Ltd. **Other:** Steel Co. Ltd. Hitachi ATS - 34, XD0189

custom knifemakers

OLIVE, MICHAEL E., HC 78 Box 442, Leslie, AR 72645, Phone: 870-363-4452

OLIVER, TODD D., RR5 Box 659, Spencer, IN 47460, Phone: 812-829-1762
Specialties: Damascus hunters and daggers. High carbon. **Patterns:** Ladder, twist random. **Technical:** Sole author of all blades. **Prices:** $350 and up. **Remarks:** Learned bladesmithing from Jim Batson at the ABS school & Damascus from Billy Merritt in Indiana. **Mark:** T. D. Oliver Spencer IN. **Other:** Two crossed swords and a battle ax.

OLIVER, ANTHONY CRAIG, 1504 Elaine Pl., Ft. Worth, TX 76106, Phone: 817-625-0825
Specialties: Fancy and embellished traditional straight knives of his design. **Patterns:** Hunters, full-size folders, Bowies, daggers and miniatures in stainless and nickel Damascus with tempered blades. **Technical:** Grinds 440C and ATS-34. **Prices:** $40 to $500. **Remarks:** Part-time maker; first knife sold in 1988. **Mark:** Initials and last name.

OLOFSON, CHRIS, 29 Knives, 1 Kendall SQ Bldg 600, Cambridge, MA 02139, Phone: 617-492-0451

OLSON, WAYNE C., 890 Royal Ridge Dr, Bailey, CO 80421, Phone: 303-816-9486
Specialties: High-tech working knives. **Patterns:** Hunters to folding lockers; some integral designs. **Technical:** Grinds 440C, 154CM and ATS-34; likes hand-finishes; precision-fits stainless steel fittings—no solder, no nickel silver. **Prices:** $275 to $600; some to $3000. **Remarks:** Part-time maker; first knife sold in 1979. **Mark:** Name, maker.

OLSON, DARROLD E., PO Box 1539, Springfield, OR 97477, Phone: 541-726-8300/541-914-7238
Specialties: Straight knives and folders of his design and to customer specs. **Patterns:** Hunters, liner-locks and locking folders. **Technical:** Grinds 440C, ATS-34 and 154CM. Uses anodized titanium; sheaths wet-molded. **Prices:** $150 to $350. **Remarks:** Part-time maker; first knife sold in 1989. **Mark:** Etched logo, year, type of steel & name.

OLSON, ROD, Box 5973, High River, AB, CANADA T1V 1P6, Phone: 403-652-2744, Fax: 403-646-5838
Specialties: Lock-back folders with gold toothpicks. **Patterns:** Locking folders. **Technical:** Grinds ATS-34 blades and spring - filework- 14kt bolsters & liners. **Prices:** Mid range. **Remarks:** Part-time maker; first knife sold in 1979. **Mark:** Last name on blade.

OLSZEWSKI, STEPHEN, 1820 Harkney Hill Rd, Coventry, RI 02816, Phone: 401-397-4774
Specialties: Lock-back, liner-locks, automatics (art knives). **Patterns:** One-of-a-kind art knives specializing in figurals. **Technical:** Damascus steel, titanium file worked liners, fossil ivory & pearl. **Prices:** $1800 to $6500. **Remarks:** Will custom build to your specifications. **Other:** Quality work with guarantee. **Mark:** SCO inside fish symbol.

O'MALLEY, DANIEL, 4338 Evanston Ave N, Seattle, WA 98103, Phone: 206-527-0315
Specialties: Custom chef's knives. **Remarks:** Making knives since 1997.

ONION, KENNETH J., 91-990 Oaniani St, Kapolei, HI 96707, Phone: 808-674-1300, Fax: 808-674-1403
Specialties: Straight knives and folders. **Patterns:** Bowies, daggers, tantos, fighters, boots, hunters, utility knives and art knives. **Technical:** ATS-34, 440C, Damascus, 5160, D2. **Prices:** $135 to $1500. **Remarks:** Part-time maker; first knife sold in 1991. All knives fully guaranteed. Call for availability. **Mark:** Name and state.

ORTEGA, BEN M., 165 Dug Road, Wyoming, PA 18644, Phone: 717-696-3234

ORTON, RICHARD, PO Box 7002, La Verne, CA 91750, Phone: 909-621-5948
Specialties: Collectible folders, using and collectible straight knives. **Patterns:** Wharncliffe, gents, tactical, boot, neck knives, bird & trout, hunters, camp, bowie. **Technical:** Grinds ATS-34, Jim Fergeson Damascus titanium liners, bolsters, anodize, lots of filework, jigged and picked bone, giraffe bone. Scrimshaw on some. **Prices:** Folders $300 to $600; straight $100 to $750. **Remarks:** Full-time maker; first knife sold in 1992. Doing business as Orton Knife Works. Now making folders. **Mark:** Last name, city and state.

OSBORNE, WARREN, 215 Edgefield, Waxahachie, TX 75165, Phone: 972-935-0899, Fax: 972-937-9004
Specialties: Investment grade collectible, interframes, one-of-a-kinds; unique locking mechanisms. **Patterns:** Folders; bolstered and interframes; conventional lockers, front lockers and back lockers; some slip-joints; some high-art pieces; fighters. **Technical:** Grinds ATS-34, 440 and 154; some Damascus and CPM400V. **Prices:** $400 to $2000; some to $4000. Interframes $650 to $1500. **Remarks:** Full-time maker; first knife sold in 1980. **Mark:** Last name in boomerang logo.

OSBORNE, DONALD H., 5840 N McCall, Clovis, CA 93611, Phone: 559-299-9483, Fax: 559-298-1751
Specialties: Traditional working and using straight knives of his design. **Patterns:** Working straight knives, hunters, Bowies and camp knives. **Technical:** Forges 5160, 1084, 1095; grinds 440C & 154CM. **Prices:** $150 to $500. **Remarks:** Part-time maker. **Mark:** Last name.

OSBORNE, MICHAEL, 585 Timber Ridge Dr, New Braunfels, TX 78132, Phone: 210-609-0118
Specialties: Traditional and working/using straight knives of his design. **Patterns:** Bowies, fighters and hunters. **Technical:** Forges 5160, 52100 and 10. Tempers all blades. Some filework. Embellishes with silver wire inlay. **Prices:** $125 to $500; some to $1000. **Remarks:** Part-time maker; first knife sold in 1988. **Mark:** Engraved signature and year.

OSTERMAN, DANIEL E., 1644 W. 10th, Junction City, OR 97448, Phone: 541-998-1503
Specialties: One-third scale copies of period pieces, museum class miniatures. **Patterns:** Antique Bowies. **Technical:** Grinds all cutlery grade steels, engraves, etches, inlays and overlays. **Remarks:** Full-time maker; first miniature knife sold in 1975. **Mark:** Initials.

OTT, FRED, 1257 Rancho Durango Rd, Durango, CO 81303, Phone: 970-375-9669
Patterns: Bowies, camp knives & hunters. **Technical:** Forges 1084 Damascus **Prices:** $150 to $800. **Remarks:** Full-time maker. **Mark:** Last name.

OVEREYNDER, T. R., 1800 S. Davis Dr, Arlington, TX 76013, Phone: 817-277-4812, Fax: 817-277-4812
Specialties: Highly finished collector-grade knives. **Patterns:** Fighters, Bowies, daggers, locking folders, slip-joints and 90 percent collector-grade interframe folders. **Technical:** Grinds D2, BG-42, 5-60V, 5-30V 440V,154CM, vendor supplied Damascus. Has been making titanium-frame folders since 1977. **Prices:** $500 to $1500; some to $7000. **Remarks:** Full-time maker; first knife sold in 1977. Doing business as TRO Knives. **Mark:** T. R. OVEREYNDER KNIVES, city and state.

OWENS, DONALD, 2274 Lucille Ln, Melbourne, FL 32935, Phone: 321-254-9765

OWENS, JOHN, 14500 CR 270, Nathrop, CO 81236, Phone: 719-395-0870
Specialties: Hunters. **Prices:** $175 to $235; some to $650. **Remarks:** Spare-time maker. **Mark:** Last name.

OWNBY, JOHN C., 3316 Springbridge Ln, Plano, TX 75025
Specialties: Hunters, utility/camp knives. **Patterns:** Hunters, locking folders and utility/camp knives. **Technical:** 440C, D2 & ATS-34. All blades are flat ground. Prefers natural materials for handles—exotic woods, horn and antler. **Prices:** $150 to $350; some to $500. **Remarks:** Part-time maker; first knife sold in 1993. **Mark:** Name, city, state. **Other:** Doing business as John C. Ownby Handmade Knives

OYSTER, LOWELL R., 543 Grant Road, Corinth, ME 04427, Phone: 207-884-8663
Specialties: Traditional and original designed multi-blade slip-joint folders. **Patterns:** Hunters, minis, camp and fishing knives. **Technical:** Grinds O1; heat-treats. **Prices:** $55 to $450; some to $750. **Remarks:** Full-time maker; first knife sold in 1981. **Mark:** A scallop shell.

p

PACHI, FRANCESCO, Via Pometta, 1, 17046 Sassello (SV), ITALY, Phone: 019 720086, Fax: 019 720086
Specialties: Folders and straight knives of his design. **Patterns:** Utility, hunters and skinners. **Technical:** Grinds ATS-34, Rul-3l and Damascus. **Prices:** $400 to $2500. **Remarks:** Full-time maker; first knife sold in 1991. **Mark:** Logo with last name.

PACKARD, BOB, PO Box 311, Elverta, CA 95626, Phone: 916-991-5218
Specialties: Traditional working/using straight knives of his design and to customer specs. **Patterns:** Hunters, fishing knives, utility/camp knives. **Technical:** Grinds ATS-34, 440C; Forges 52100, 5168 and cable Damascus. **Prices:** $75 to $225. **Mark:** Engraved name and year.

PADGETT JR., EDWIN L., 340 Vauxhall St, New London, CT 06320-3838, Phone: 860-443-2938
Specialties: Skinners and working knives of any design. **Patterns:** Straight and folding knives. **Technical:** Grinds ATS-34 or any tool steel upon request. **Prices:** $50 to $300. **Mark:** Name.

PADILLA, GARY, PO Box 6928, Auburn, CA 95604, Phone: 530-888-6992
Specialties: Native American influenced working and using straight knives of his design. **Patterns:** Hunters, kitchen knives, utility/camp knives and obsidian ceremonial knives. **Technical:** Grinds 440C, ATS-34, O1 and

Damascus. **Prices:** Generally $100-$200. **Remarks:** Part-time maker; first knife sold in 1977. Doing business as Bighorn Knifeworks. **Mark:** Stylized initials or name over company name.

PAGE, LARRY, 165 Rolling Rock Rd, Aiken, SC 29803, Phone: 803-648-0001
Specialties: Working knives of his design. **Patterns:** Hunters, boots and fighters. **Technical:** Grinds ATS-34. **Prices:** Start at $85. **Remarks:** Part-time maker; first knife sold in 1983. **Mark:** Name, city and state in oval.

PAGE, REGINALD, 6587 Groveland Hill Rd, Groveland, NY 14462, Phone: 716-243-1643
Specialties: High-art straight knives and one-of-a-kind folders of his design. **Patterns:** Hunters, locking folders and slip-joint folders. **Technical:** Forges O1, 5160 and his own Damascus. Prefers natural handle materials but will work with Micarta. **Remarks:** Spare-time maker; first knife sold in 1985. **Mark:** First initial, last name.

PALAZZO, TOM, 207-30 Jordon Dr, Bayside, NY 11360, Phone: 718-352-2170
Specialties: Fixed blades, custom sheaths, neck knives. **Patterns:** No fixed patterns. **Prices:** $150 and up.

PALMER, TAYLOR, Taylor-Made Scenic Knives Inc, Box 97, Blanding, UT 84511, Phone: 435-678-2523
Specialties: Bronze carvings inside of blade area. **Prices:** $250 and up. **Mark:** Taylor Palmer Utah.

PANKIEWICZ, PHILIP R., RFD #1, Waterman Rd, Lebanon, CT 06249
Specialties: Working straight knives. **Patterns:** Hunters, daggers, minis and fishing knives. **Technical:** Grinds D2, 440C and 154CM. **Prices:** $60 to $125; some to $250. **Remarks:** Spare-time maker; first knife sold in 1975. **Mark:** First initial in star.

PARDUE, MELVIN M., Rt. 1, Box 130, Repton, AL 36475, Phone: 334-248-2447
Specialties: Folders, collectable, combat, utility and tactical. **Patterns:** Lock-back, liner-lock, pushbutton; all blade and handle patterns. **Technical:** Grinds 154-CM, 440-C, 12-C-27. Forges Mokume and Damascus. Uses Titanium. **Prices:** $400 to $1600. **Remarks:** Full-time maker; Guild member, ABS member, AFC member. **Mark:** Mel Pardue or Pardue. **Other:** First knife made 1957; first knife sold professionally 1974.

PARK, VALERIE, PO Box 85319, Seattle, WA 98145-1319

PARKER, CLIFF, 6350 Tulip Dr, Zephyrhills, FL 33544, Phone: 813-973-1682
Specialties: Damascus folders & straight knives. **Patterns:** Skinners & locking liners. **Technical:** Mostly use 1095, 1084, 15N20, 203E & powdered steel. **Prices:** $300 to $1500. **Remarks:** Making own Damascus & specializing in mosaics; first knife sold in 1996. **Mark:** CP. **Other:** Full-time beginning in 2000.

PARKER, ROBERT NELSON, 5223 Wilhelm Rd. N. W., Rapid City, MI 49676, Phone: 231-331-6173, Fax: 248-545-8211
Specialties: Traditional working and using straight knives of his design. **Patterns:** Hunters, fighters, utility/camp knives; some Bowies. **Technical:** Grinds ATS-34;GB-42, forges 01-516-L6 hollow and flat grinds, full and hidden tangs. Hand-stitched leather sheaths. **Prices:** $225 to $500; some to $1000. **Remarks:** Part-time maker; first knife sold in 1986. **Mark:** Full name.

PARKER, J. E., 11 Domenica Cir, Clarion, PA 16214, Phone: 814-226-4837
Specialties: Fancy/embellished, traditional and working straight knives of his design and to customer specs. Engraving & scrimshaw by the best in the business. **Patterns:** Bowies, hunters and liner-lock folders. **Technical:** Grinds 440C, 440V, ATS-34 and nickel Damascus. Prefers mastodon, oosik, amber and malachite handle material. **Prices:** $75 to $5200. **Remarks:** Full-time maker; first knife sold in 1991. Doing business as Custom Knife. **Mark:** J E Parker & Clarion PA stamped or etched in blade.

PARKS, BLANE C., 15908 Crest Dr, Woodbridge, VA 22191, Phone: 703-221-4680
Specialties: Knives of his design. **Patterns:** Boots, Bowies, daggers, fighters, hunters, kitchen knives, locking and slip-joint folders, utility/camp knives, letter openers and friction folders. **Technical:** Grinds ATS-34, 440C, D2 and other carbon steels. Offers filework, silver wire inlay and wooden sheaths. **Prices:** Start at $250 & up. **Remarks:** Part-time maker; first knife sold in 1993. Doing business as B. C. Parks Knives. **Mark:** First and middle initials, last name.

PARKS, JOHN, 3539 Galilee Church Rd, Jefferson, GA 30549, Phone: 706-367-4916
Specialties: Traditional working and using straight knives of his design. **Patterns:** Trout knives, hunters and integral bolsters. **Technical:** Forges 1095 and 5168. **Prices:** $175 to $450; some to $650. **Remarks:** Part-time maker; first knife sold in 1989. **Mark:** Initials.

PARLER, THOMAS O., 11 Franklin St, Charleston, SC 29401, Phone: 803-723-9433

PARRISH, ROBERT, 271 Allman Hill Rd, Weaverville, NC 28787, Phone: 828-645-2864
Specialties: Heavy-duty working knives of his design or to customer specs. **Patterns:** Survival and duty knives; hunters and fighters. **Technical:** Grinds 440C, D2, O1 and commercial Damascus. **Prices:** $200 to $300; some to $6000. **Remarks:** Part-time maker; first knife sold in 1970. **Mark:** Initials connected, sometimes with city and state.

PARRISH III, GORDON A., 940 Lakloey Dr, North Pole, AK 99705, Phone: 907-488-0357
Specialties: Classic and high-art straight knives of his design and to customer specs. **Patterns:** Bowies and hunters. **Technical:** Grinds tool steel and ATS-34. Uses mostly Alaskan handle materials. **Prices:** $125 to $750. **Remarks:** Spare-time maker; first knife sold in 1980. **Mark:** Last name, state.

PARSONS, MICHAEL R., McKee Knives, 7042 McFarland Rd, Indianapolis, IN 46227, Phone: 317-784-7943
Specialties: Hand-forged fixed-blade knives, all fancy but all are useable knives. **Patterns:** Engraves, carves, wire inlay, and leather work. All knives one-of-a-kind. **Technical:** Blades forged from files, all work hand done. **Prices:** $350-$2000. **Mark:** McKee.

PASSMORE, JIMMY D., 316 SE Elm, Hoxie, AR 72433, Phone: 870-886-1922

PATE, LLOYD D., 219 Cottontail Ln., Georgetown, TX 78626, Phone: 512-863-7805
Specialties: Traditional working straight knives. **Patterns:** Hunters, fighters and Bowies. **Technical:** Hollow-grinds D2, 440C and ATS-34; likes mirror-finishes. **Prices:** $75 to $350; some to $500. **Remarks:** Part-time maker; first knife sold in 1983. **Mark:** Last name.

PATRICK, PEGGY, PO Box 127, Brasstown, NC 28902, Phone: 828-837-7627
Specialties: Authentic period and Indian sheaths, braintan, rawhide, beads and quill work. **Technical:** Does own braintan, rawhide; uses only natural dyes for quills, old color beads.

PATRICK, BOB, 12642 24A Ave, S. Surrey, B. C., CANADA V4A 8H9, Phone: 604-538-6214, Fax: 604-888-2683
Specialties: Presentation pieces of his design only. **Patterns:** Bowies, push daggers, art pieces. **Technical:** D2, 5160, Damascus. **Prices:** Fair. **Remarks:** Full-time maker; first knife sold in 1987. Doing business as Crescent Knife Works. **Mark:** Logo with name and province or Crescent Knife Works.

PATRICK, CHUCK, PO Box 127, Brasstown, NC 28902, Phone: 828-837-7627
Specialties: Period pieces. **Patterns:** Hunters, daggers, tomahawks, pre-Civil War folders. **Technical:** Forges hardware, his own cable and Damascus, available in fancy pattern and mosaic. **Prices:** $150 to $1000; some higher. **Remarks:** Full-time maker. **Mark:** Hand-engraved name or flying owl.

PATRICK, WILLARD C., PO Box 5716, Helena, MT 59604, Phone: 406-458-6552
Specialties: Working straight knives and one-of-a-kind art knives of his design or to customer specs. **Patterns:** Hunters, Bowies, fish, patch and kitchen knives. **Technical:** Grinds ATS-34, 1095, O1, A2 and Damascus. **Prices:** $85 to $350; some to $600. **Remarks:** Full-time maker; first knife sold in 1989. Doing business as Wil-A-Mar Cutlery. **Mark:** Shield with last name and a dagger.

PATTAY, RUDY, 510 E. Harrison St, Long Beach, NY 11561, Phone: 516-431-0847
Specialties: Fancy and working straight knives of his design. **Patterns:** Bowies, hunters, utility/camp knives. **Technical:** Hollow-grinds ATS-34, 440C, O1. Offers commercial Damascus, stainless steel soldered guards; fabricates guard and butt cap on lathe and milling machine. Heat-treats. Prefers synthetic handle materials. Offers hand-sewn sheaths. **Prices:** $100 to $350; some to $500. **Remarks:** Part-time maker; first knife sold in 1990. **Mark:** First initial, last name in sorcerer logo.

PATTERSON, ALAN W., Rt. 3, Box 131, Hayesville, NC 28904, Phone: 704-389-9103
Specialties: Working straight knives and folders of his design or to customer specs; period pieces. **Patterns:** Forged knives, swords, tomahawks and folders. **Technical:** Damascus, cable and tool steels. Some custom leatherwork; wife offers scrimshaw. **Prices:** $125 to $5000. **Remarks:** Full-time maker; first knife sold in 1990. **Mark:** Patterson Forge.

PATTERSON, PAT, Box 246, Barksdale, TX 78828, Phone: 830-234-3586, Fax: 830-234-3587
Specialties: Traditional fixed blades & liner-lock folders. **Patterns:** Hunters & folders. **Technical:** Grinds 440C, ATS-34, D2, 01 & Damascus.

custom knifemakers

Prices: $250 to $1000. **Remarks:** Full-time maker. First knife sold in 1991. **Mark:** Name & city.

PATTON, DICK & ROB, 206-F W. 38th St, Garden City, ID 83714, Phone: 208-377-5704 or 208-327-7641
Specialties: Custom Damascus, hand forged, fighting knives-Bowie & tactical. **Patterns:** Mini Bowie, Merlin Fighter, Mandrita Fighting Bowie. **Prices:** $100 to $2000.

PAULICHECK, GARTH, PO Box 812, Williston, ND 58802-0812, Phone: 701-774-8803

PAULO, FERNANDES R, Raposo Tavares, no 213, Lencois Paulista, SP, 18680, Sao Paulo, BRAZIL, Phone: 014-263-4281
Specialties: An apprentice of Jose Alberto Paschoarelli, his designs are heavily based on the later designs. **Technical:** Grinds tool steels and stainless steels. Part-time knife maker. **Prices:** Start from $100. **Mark:** P. R. F.

PAWLOWSKI, JOHN R., 804 Iron Gate Ct, Newport News, VA 23602, Phone: 757-890-9098
Specialties: Traditional working and using straight knives and folders. **Patterns:** Hunters, Bowies, Fighters and Camp Knives. **Technical:** Stock removal, grinds 440C, ATS-34, 154CM and buys Damascus. **Prices:** $150 to $500; some higher. **Remarks:** Part-time maker, first knife sold in 1983. **Mark:** Early mark, name over attacking Eagle and Alaska. Current mark, name over attacking Eagle and Virginia.

PEAGLER, RUSS, PO Box 1314, Moncks Corner, SC 29461, Phone: 803-761-1008
Specialties: Traditional working straight knives of his design and to customer specs. **Patterns:** Hunters, fighters, boots. **Technical:** Hollow-grinds 440C, ATS-34 and O1; uses Damascus steel. Prefers bone handles. **Prices:** $85 to $300; some to $500. **Remarks:** Spare-time maker; first knife sold in 1983. **Mark:** Initials.

PEASE, W. D., 657 Cassidy Pike, Ewing, KY 41039, Phone: 606-845-0387
Specialties: Display-quality working folders. **Patterns:** Fighters, tantos and boots; locking folders and interframes. **Technical:** Grinds ATS-34 and commercial Damascus; has own side-release lock system. **Prices:** $500 to $1000; some to $3000. **Remarks:** Full-time maker; first knife sold in 1970. **Mark:** First and middle initials, last name.

PEELE, BRYAN, 219 Ferry St, PO Box 1363, Thompson Falls, MT 59873, Phone: 406-827-4633
Specialties: Fancy working and using knives of his design. **Patterns:** Hunters, Bowies and fighters. **Technical:** Grinds 440C, ATS-34, D2, O1 and commercial Damascus. **Prices:** $110 to $300; some to $900. **Remarks:** Part-time maker; first knife sold in 1985. **Mark:** The Elk Rack, full name, city, state.

PENDLETON, LLOYD, 24581 Shake Ridge Rd, Volcano, CA 95689, Phone: 209-296-3353, Fax: 209-296-3353
Specialties: Contemporary working knives in standard patterns. **Patterns:** Hunters, fighters and boots. **Technical:** Grinds 154CM and ATS-34; mirror finishes. **Prices:** $300 to $700; some to $2000. **Remarks:** Full-time maker; first knife sold in 1973. **Mark:** First initial, last name logo, city and state.

PENDRAY, ALFRED H., 13950 NE 20th St, Williston, FL 32696, Phone: 352-528-6124
Specialties: Working straight knives and folders; period pieces. **Patterns:** Fighters and hunters, axes, camp knives and tomahawks. **Technical:** Forges Wootz steel; makes his own Damascus; makes traditional knives from old files and rasps. **Prices:** $125 to $1000; some to $3500. **Remarks:** Part-time maker; first knife sold in 1954. **Mark:** Last initial in horseshoe logo.

PENFOLD, MICK, Penfold Custom Knives, 131 Mojave Court, Vacaville, CA 95688, Phone: 707-448-0584
Specialties: Hunters, fighters, Bowies. **Technical:** Grinds 440C, ATS-34, & Damascus. **Prices:** $150-$1200. **Remarks:** Full-time maker. First knives sold in 1999. **Mark:** Last names.

PENNINGTON, C. A., 163 Kainga Rd, Kainga Christchurch 8009, NEW ZEALAND, Phone: 03-3237292
Specialties: Classic working and collectors knives. Folders a specialty. **Patterns:** Classical styling for hunters and collectors. **Technical:** Forges his own all tool steel Damascus. Grinds D2 when requested. **Prices:** $240 to $2000. **Remarks:** Full-time maker; first knife sold in 1988. **Mark:** Name, country. **Other:** Color brochure $3.

PEPIOT, STEPHAN, 73 Cornwall Blvd., Winnipeg, Man., CANADA R3J-1E9, Phone: 204-888-1499
Specialties: Working straight knives in standard patterns. **Patterns:** Hunters and camp knives. **Technical:** Grinds 440C and industrial hack-saw blades. **Prices:** $75 to $125. **Remarks:** Spare-time maker; first knife sold in 1982. Not currently taking orders. **Mark:** PEP.

PERRY, JIM, Hope Star PO Box 648, Hope, AR 71801

PERRY, CHRIS, 1654 W. Birch, Fresno, CA 93711, Phone: 209-498-2342
Specialties: Traditional working/using straight knives of his design. **Patterns:** Boots, hunters and utility/camp knives. **Technical:** Grinds ATS-34 and 416 ss fittings. **Prices:** $190 to $225. **Remarks:** Spare-time maker. **Mark:** Name above city and state.

PERRY, JOHNNY, PO Box 4666, Spartanburg, SC 29305-4666, Phone: 803-578-3533

PERRY, JOHN, 9 South Harrell Rd, Mayflower, AR 72106, Phone: 501-470-3043
Specialties: Investment grade and working folders; some straight knives. **Patterns:** Front and rear lock folders, liner-locks and hunters. **Technical:** Grinds CPM440V, D2 and making own Damascus. Offers filework. **Prices:** $375 to $950; some to $2500. **Remarks:** Part-time maker; first knife sold in 1990. Doing business as Perry Custom Knives. **Mark:** Initials or last name in high relief set in a diamond shape.

PERSSON, CONNY, PL 605, 820 50 Loos, SWEDEN, Phone: +46 657 10305, Fax: +46 657 413 435

PETEAN, FRANCISCO AND MAURICIO, R. Dr. Carlos de Carvalho Rosa, 52, Centro, Birigui, SP-16200-000, BRAZIL, Phone: 0186-424786
Specialties: Classic knives to customer specs. **Patterns:** Bowies, boots, fighters, hunters and utility knives. **Technical:** Grinds D6, 440C and high carbon steels. Prefers natural handle material. **Prices:** $70 to $500. **Remarks:** Full-time maker; first knife sold in 1985. **Mark:** Last name, hand made.

PETERSEN, DAN L., 3015 SW Clark Ct, Topeka, KS 66604
Specialties: Period pieces and forged integral hilts on hunters and fighters. **Patterns:** Texas-style Bowies, boots and hunters in high carbon and Damascus steel. **Technical:** Austempers forged high-carbon blades. **Prices:** $200 to $3000. **Remarks:** First knife sold in 1978. **Mark:** Stylized initials, MS.

PETERSON, LLOYD (PETE) C., 64 Halbrook Rd, Clinton, AR 72031, Phone: 501-893-0000
Specialties: Miniatures, and mosaic folders. **Prices:** $250 & up. **Remarks:** Lead time is 6-8 months. **Mark:** Pete.

PETERSON, KAREN, The Pen And The Sword Ltd, PO Box 290741, Brooklyn, NY 11229-0741, Phone: 718-382-4847, Fax: 718-376-5745

PETERSON, CHRIS, Box 143, 2175 W. Rockyford, Salina, UT 84654, Phone: 801-529-7194
Specialties: Working straight knives of his design. **Patterns:** Large fighters, boots, hunters and some display pieces. **Technical:** Forges O1 and meteor. Makes and sells his own Damascus. Engraves, scrimshaws and inlays. **Prices:** $150 to $600; some to $1500. **Remarks:** Full-time maker; first knife sold in 1986. **Mark:** A drop in a circle with a line through it.

PETERSON, ELDON G., 260 Haugen Heights Rd, Whitefish, MT 59937, Phone: 406-862-2204
Specialties: Fancy and working folders, any size. **Patterns:** Lock-back interframes, integral bolster folders, liner-locks, and two-blades. **Technical:** Grinds 440C and ATS-34. Offers gold inlay work, gem stone inlays and engraving. **Prices:** $285 to $5000. **Remarks:** Full-time maker; first knife sold in 1974. **Mark:** Name, city and state.

PFANENSTIEL, DAN, 1824 Lafayette Av, Modesto, CA 95355, Phone: 209-575-5937
Specialties: Japanese tanto, swords. One-of-a-kind knives. **Technical:** Forges simple carbon steels, some Damascus. **Prices:** $200-$1000. **Mark:** Circle with wave inside.

PHILIPPE, D. A., PO Box 306, Cornish, NH 03746, Phone: 603-543-0662
Specialties: Traditional working straight knives. **Patterns:** Hunters, trout & bird, camp knives etc. **Technical:** Grinds ATS-34, 440c, A-2, Damascus, flat and hollow ground. Exotic woods and antler handles. Brass, nickel silver and stainless components. **Prices:** $125 - $800. **Remarks:** Full-time maker, first knife sold in 1984. **Mark:** First initial, last name.

PHILLIPS, DENNIS, 16411 West Bennet Rd, Independence, LA 70443, Phone: 985-878-8275
Specialties: Specializes in fixed blade military combat tacticals.

PHILLIPS, RANDY, 759 E. Francis St, Ontario, CA 91761, Phone: 909-923-4381
Specialties: Hunters, collector-grade liner-locks and high-art daggers. **Technical:** Grinds D2, 440C and 154CM; embellishes. **Prices:** Start at $200. **Remarks:** Part-time maker; first knife sold in 1981. Not currently taking orders. **Mark:** Name, city and state in eagle head.

PHILLIPS, JIM, PO Box 168, Williamstown, NJ 08094, Phone: 609-567-0695

PHILLIPS, SCOTT C., 671 California Rd, Gouverneur, NY 13642, Phone: 315-287-1280
Specialties: Sheaths in leather. Fixed blade hunters, boot knives, Bowies, buck skinners (hand forged & stock removal). **Technical:** 440C, 5160, 1095 & 52100. **Prices:** Start at $125. **Remarks:** Part-time maker; first knife sold in 1993. **Mark:** Before "2000" as above after S Mangus.

PICKENS, SELBERT, Rt. 1, Box 216, Liberty, WV 25124, Phone: 304-586-2190
Specialties: Using knives. **Patterns:** Standard sporting knives. **Technical:** Stainless steels; stock removal method. **Prices:** Moderate. **Remarks:** Part-time maker. **Mark:** Name.

PIENAAR, CONRAD, 19A Milner Rd, Bloemfontein 9300, SOUTH AFRICA, Phone: 051 436 4180, Fax: 051 436 7400
Specialties: Fancy working and using straight knives and folders of his design, to customer specs and in standard patterns. **Patterns:** Hunters, locking folders, cleavers, kitchen and utility/camp knives. **Technical:** Grinds 12C27, D2 and ATS-34. Uses some Damascus. Scrimshaws; inlays gold. Knives come with wooden box and custom-made leather sheath. **Prices:** $300 to $1000. **Remarks:** Part-time maker; first knife sold in 1981. Doing business as C. P. Knife maker. **Mark:** Initials and serial number. **Other:** I make slip joint folders and liner-locking folders.

PIERCE, RANDALL, 903 Wyndham, Arlington, TX 76017, Phone: 817-468-0138

PIERCE, HAROLD L., 106 Lyndon Lane, Louisville, KY 40222, Phone: 502-429-5136
Specialties: Working straight knives, some fancy. **Patterns:** Big fighters and Bowies. **Technical:** Grinds D2, 440C, 154CM; likes sub-hilts. **Prices:** $150 to $450; some to $1200. **Remarks:** Full-time maker; first knife sold in 1982. **Mark:** Last name with knife through the last initial.

PIERGALLINI, DANIEL E., 4011 N. Forbes Rd, Plant City, FL 33565, Phone: 813-754-3908
Specialties: Traditional and fancy straight knives and folders of my design or to customer's specs. **Patterns:** Hunters, fighters, three-fingered skinners, fillet, working and camp knives. **Technical:** Grinds 440C, O1, D2, ATS-34, some Damascus; forges his own mokume. Uses natural handle material. **Prices:** $250-$600; some to $600; some to $1600. **Remarks:** Part-time maker; sold first knife in 1994. **Mark:** Last name, city, state or last name in script.

PIESNER, DEAN, 30 King St, St. Jacobs, Ont., CANADA N0B 2N0, Phone: 519-664-3622, Fax: 519-664-1828
Specialties: Classic and period pieces of his design and to customer specs. **Patterns:** Bowies, skinners, fighters and swords. **Technical:** Forges 5160, 52100, steel Damascus and nickel-steel Damascus. Makes own mokume gane with copper, brass and nickel silver. Silver wire inlays in wood. **Prices:** Start at $150. **Remarks:** Full-time maker; first knife sold in 1990. **Mark:** First initial, last name, JS.

PIOREK, JAMES S., PO Box 335, Rexford, MT 59930, Phone: 406-889-5510
Specialties: True custom and semi-custom production (SCP), specialized concealment blades; advanced sheaths and tailored body harnessing systems. **Patterns:** Tactical/personal defense fighters, swords, utility and custom patterns. **Technical:** Grinds A2 and Talonite®; heat-treats. Sheaths: Kydex or Kydex-lined leather laminated or Kydex-lined with Rigger Coat™. Exotic materials available. **Prices:** $50 to $10,000. **Remarks:** Full-time maker. Doing business as Blade Rigger L. L. C. **Mark:** For true custom: Initials with abstract cutting edge and for SCP: Blade Rigger. **Other:** Martial artist and unique defense industry tools and equipment.

PITMAN, DAVID, PO Drawer 2566, Williston, ND 58802, Phone: 701-572-3325

PITT, DAVID F., 6812 Digger Pine Ln, Anderson, CA 96007, Phone: 530-357-2393
Specialties: Fixed blade, hunters & hatchets. Flat ground mirror finish. **Patterns:** Hatchets with gut hook, small gut hooks, guards, bolsters or guard less. **Technical:** Grinds A2, 440C, 154CM, ATS-34, D2. **Prices:** $150 to $750. **Remarks:** Guild member since 1982. **Mark:** Bear paw with name David F. Pitt.

PLUNKETT, RICHARD, 29 Kirk Rd, West Cornwall, CT 06796, Phone: 860-672-3419; Toll free: 888-KNIVES-8
Specialties: Traditional, fancy folders and straight knives of his design. **Patterns:** Slip-joint folders and small straight knives. **Technical:** Grinds O1 and stainless steel. Offers many different file patterns. **Prices:** $150 to $450. **Remarks:** Full-time maker; first knife sold in 1994. **Mark:** Signature and date under handle scales.

POAG, JAMES, RR 1, Box 212A, Grayville, IL 62844, Phone: 618-375-7106
Specialties: Working straight knives and folders; period pieces; of his design or to customer specs. **Patterns:** Bowies and camp knives, lockers and slip-joints. **Technical:** Forges and grinds stainless steels and others; provides serious leather; offers embellishments; scrimshaws, engraves and does leather work for other makers. **Prices:** $65 to $1200. **Remarks:** Full-time maker; first knife sold in 1967. **Mark:** Name.

POLK, CLIFTON, 4625 Webber Creek Rd, Van Buren, AR 72956, Phone: 479-474-3828
Specialties: Fancy working straight knives and folders. **Patterns:** Locking folders, slip-joints, two-blades, straight knives. **Technical:** Offers 440C, D2 ATS-34 and Damascus. **Prices:** $150 to $3000. **Remarks:** Full-time maker. **Mark:** Last name.

POLKOWSKI, AL, 8 Cathy Ct, Chester, NJ 07930, Phone: 908-879-6030
Specialties: High-tech straight knives and folders for adventurers and professionals. **Patterns:** Fighters, side-lock folders, boots and concealment knives. **Technical:** Grinds D2 and ATS-34; features satin and bead-blast finishes; Kydex sheaths. **Prices:** Start at $100. **Remarks:** Full-time maker; first knife sold in 1985. **Mark:** Full name, Handmade.

POLLOCK, WALLACE J., 806 Russet Vly Dr, Cedar Park, TX 78613
Specialties: Using knives, dressed up or not. **Patterns:** Use my own patterns or yours. **Patterns:** Traditional hunters, daggers, fighters, camp knives. **Technical:** Grinds ATS-34, d-2, bg-42, makes own Damascus, dentritic d-2, 440c handles exotic wood, horn, bone, ivory. **Remarks:** Full-time maker, sold first knife 1973. **Prices:** $250 to $2500. **Mark:** Last name, maker, city/state.

POLZIEN, DON, 1912 Inler Suite-L, Lubbock, TX 79407, Phone: 806-791-0766
Specialties: Traditional Japanese-style blades; restores antique Japanese swords, scabbards and fittings. **Patterns:** Hunters, fighters, one-of-a-kind art knives. **Technical:** 1045-1050 carbon steels, 440C, D2, ATS-34, standard and cable Damascus. **Prices:** $150 to $2500. **Remarks:** Full-time maker. First knife sold in 1990. **Mark:** Oriental characters inside square border.

PONZIO, DOUG, 3212 93rd St, Pleasant Prairie, WI 53158, Phone: 262-694-3188
Specialties: Damascus - Gem stone handles. **Mark:** P. F.

POOLE, MARVIN O., PO Box 552, Commerce, GA 30529, Phone: 803-225-5970
Specialties: Traditional working/using straight knives and folders of his design and in standard patterns. **Patterns:** Bowies, fighters, hunters, locking folders, bird and trout knives. **Technical:** Grinds 440C, D2, ATS-34. **Prices:** $50 to $150; some to $750. **Remarks:** Part-time maker; first knife sold in 1980. **Mark:** First initial, last name, year, serial number.

POOLE, STEVE L., 200 Flintlock Trail, Stockbridge, GA 30281, Phone: 770-474-9154
Specialties: Traditional working and using straight knives and folders of his design, to customer specs and in standard patterns. **Patterns:** Bowies, fighters, hunters, utility and locking folders. **Technical:** Grinds ATS-34 and 440V; buys Damascus. Heat-treats; offers leatherwork. **Prices:** $85 to $350; some to $800. **Remarks:** Spare-time maker; first knife sold in 1991. **Mark:** Stylized first and last initials.

POPP SR., STEVE, 6573 Winthrop Dr, Fayetteville, NC 28311, Phone: 910-822-3151
Specialties: Working straight knives. **Patterns:** Hunters, Bowies and fighters. **Technical:** Forges and grinds his own Damascus, O1, L6 and spring steel. **Prices:** $75 to $600; some to $1000. **Remarks:** Full-time maker; first knife sold in 1984. **Mark:** Initials and last name.

POSKOCIL, HELMUT, Oskar Czeijastrasse 2, A-3340 Waidhofen/Ybbs, AUSTRIA, Phone: 0043-7442-54519, Fax: 0043-7442-54519
Specialties: High-art and classic straight knives and folders of his design. **Patterns:** Bowies, daggers, hunters and locking folders. **Technical:** Grinds ATS-34 and stainless and carbon Damascus. Hardwoods, fossil ivory, horn and amber for handle material; silver wire and gold inlays; silver butt caps. Offers engraving and scrimshaw. **Prices:** $350 to $850; some to $3500. **Remarks:** Part-time maker; first knife sold in 1991. **Mark:** Name.

POSNER, BARRY E., 12501 Chandler Blvd., Suite 104, N. Hollywood, CA 91607, Phone: 818-752-8005, Fax: 818-752-8006
Specialties: Working/using straight knives. **Patterns:** Hunters, kitchen and utility/camp knives. **Technical:** Grinds ATS-34; forges 1095 and nickel. **Prices:** $95 to $400. **Remarks:** Part-time maker; first knife sold in 1987. Doing business as Posner Knives. Supplier of finished mosaic handle pin stock. **Mark:** First and middle initials, last name.

POTIER, TIMOTHY F., PO Box 711, Oberlin, LA 70655, Phone: 337-639-2229
Specialties: Classic working and using straight knives to customer specs; some collectible. **Patterns:** Hunters, Bowies, utility/camp knives and belt axes. **Technical:** Forges carbon steel and his own Damascus; offers file-work. **Prices:** $300 to $1800; some to $4000. **Remarks:** Part-time maker; first knife sold in 1981. **Mark:** Last name, MS.

POTOCKI, ROGER, Route 1, Box 333A, Goreville, IL 62939, Phone: 618-995-9502

POTTER, FRANK, 25 Renfrew Ave, Middletown, RI 02842, Phone: 401-846-5352
Specialties: Autos. **Patterns:** Liner-lock; my own design. **Technical:** Damascus bolters & blades; ivory & pearl. **Prices:** $1000 to $3000. **Remarks:** Full-time maker, first knife sold 1996. **Mark:** Frank Potter

POWELL, ROBERT CLARK, PO Box 321, 93 Gose Rd, Smarr, GA 31086, Phone: 478-994-5418
Specialties: Composite bar Damascus blades. **Patterns:** Art knives, hunters, combat, tomahawks. **Patterns:** Hand forge all blades. **Prices:** $300 & up. **Remarks:** Member ABS. **Mark:** Powell.

POWELL, JAMES, 2500 North Robison Rd, Texarkana, TX 75501

POYTHRESS, JOHN, PO Box 585, 625 Freedom St, Swainsboro, GA 30401, Phone: 478-237-9233 day/478-237-9478 night
Specialties: Traditional working and using straight knives of his design or to customer specs. **Patterns:** Hunters, liner-lock folders, dagger, tanto. **Technical:** Uses 440C, ATS-34 and D2. **Prices:** $150 and up. **Remarks:** Part-time maker; first knife sold in 1983. Member N. C. Customer Knifemaker's Guild. **Mark:** J. W. Poythress Handcrafted.

PRATER, MIKE, Prater and Company, 81 Sanford Ln, Flintstone, GA 30725
Specialties: Variety of horn- and stag-handled belt knives. **Patterns:** Standard patterns in large and small narrow-tang construction. **Technical:** Grind O1, D2 and Damascus. **Prices:** $165 to $10,000. **Remarks:** First knife sold in 1980. **Mark:** Prater Knives.

PRESSBURGER, RAMON, 59 Driftway Rd, Howell, NJ 07731, Phone: 732-363-0816
Specialties: BG-42. I am the only knife maker in USA that has a complete line of affordable hunting knives made from BG-42. **Patterns:** All types hunting styles. **Technical:** Uses all steels; my main steels are D-2 & BG-42. **Prices:** $75 to $500. **Remarks:** Full-time maker; I have been making hunting knives for 30 years. **Mark:** NA. **Other:** I will make knives to your patterning.

PRICE, TIMMY, PO Box 906, Blairsville, GA 30514, Phone: 706-745-5111

PRIMOS, TERRY, 932 Francais Dr, Shreveport, LA 71118, Phone: 318-686-6625
Specialties: Traditional forged straight knives. **Patterns:** Hunters, Bowies, camp knives, and fighters. **Technical:** Forges primarily 1084 and 5160; also forges Damascus. **Prices:** $250 to $600. **Remarks:** Full-time maker; first knife sold in 1993. **Mark:** Last name.

PRITCHARD, RON, 613 Crawford Ave, Dixon, IL 61021, Phone: 815-284-6005
Specialties: Plain and fancy working knives. **Patterns:** Variety of straight knives, locking folders, interframes and miniatures. **Technical:** Grinds 440C, 154CM and commercial Damascus. **Prices:** $100 to $200; some to $1500. **Remarks:** Part-time maker; first knife sold in 1979. **Mark:** Name and city.

PROVENZANO, JOSEPH D., 3024 Ivy Place, Chalmette, LA 70043, Phone: 504-279-3154
Specialties: Working straight knives and folders in standard patterns. **Patterns:** Hunters, Bowies, folders, camp and fishing knives. **Technical:** Grinds ATS-34, 440C, 154CM, CPM 4400V, CPM420V and Damascus. Hollow-grinds hunters. **Prices:** $90 to $300; some to $600. **Remarks:** Part-time maker; first knife sold in 1980. **Mark:** Joe-Pro.

PRYOR, STEPHEN L., HC Rt 1, Box 1445, Boss, MO 65440, Phone: 573-626-4838, Fax: Same
Specialties: Working & fancy straight knives, some to customer specs. **Patterns:** Bowies, hunting/fishing, utility/camp, fantasy/art. **Technical:** Grinds 440C, ATS-34, 1085, some Damascus, and does filework. Stag & exotic hardwood handles. **Prices:** $250 and up. **Remarks:** Full-time maker; first knife sold in 1991. **Mark:** Stylized first initial and last name over city & state.

PUGH, JIM, PO Box 711, Azle, TX 76020, Phone: 817-444-2679, Fax: 817-444-5455
Specialties: Fancy/embellished limited editions by request. **Patterns:** 5- to 7-inch Bowies, wildlife art pieces, hunters, daggers and fighters; some commemoratives. **Technical:** Multi color transplanting in solid 18K gold, fine gems; grinds 440C and ATS-34. Offers engraving, fancy file etching and leather sheaths for wildlife art pieces. Ivory and coco bolo handle material on limited editions. Designs animal head butt caps and paws or bear claw guards; sterling silver heads and guards. **Prices:** $60,000 to $80,000 each in the Big Five 2000 edition. **Remarks:** Full-time maker; first knife sold in 1970. **Mark:** Pugh (old English).

PUGH, VERNON, 701-525 3rd Ave North, Saskatoon SK, CANADA S7K 2J6, Phone: 306-652-9274

PULIS, VLADIMIR, Horna Ves 43/B/25, 96 701 Kremnica, SLOVAKIA, Phone: 421-857-6757-x214
Specialties: Fancy and high-art straight knives of his design. **Patterns:** Daggers and hunters. **Technical:** Forges Damascus steel. All work done by hand. **Prices:** $250 to $3000; some to $10,000. **Remarks:** Full-time maker; first knife sold in 1990. **Mark:** Initials in sixtagon.

PULLIAM, MORRIS C., 560 Jeptha Knob Rd, Shelbyville, KY 40065, Phone: 502-633-2261
Specialties: Working knives; classic Bowies. Cherokee River pattern Damascus. **Patterns:** Bowies, hunters, and 376 tomahawks. **Technical:** Forges L6, W2, 1095, Damascus and nickel-sheet and bar 320 layer Damascus. **Prices:** $165 to $1200. **Remarks:** Full-time maker; first knife sold in 1974. Makes knives for Native American festivals. Doing business as Knob Hill Forge. Member of Piqua Sept Shawnee of Ohio. No nickel sheet. **Mark:** Small and large - Pulliam **Other:** Member of a state tribe, American Indian artist & craftsman by federal law.

PURSLEY, AARON, Box 1037, Big Sandy, MT 59520, Phone: 406-378-3200
Specialties: Fancy working knives. **Patterns:** Locking folders, straight hunters and daggers, personal wedding knives and letter openers. **Technical:** Grinds O1 and 440C; engraves. **Prices:** $300 to $600; some to $1500. **Remarks:** Full-time maker; first knife sold in 1975. **Mark:** Initials connected with year.

PURVIS, BOB & ELLEN, 2416 N Loretta Dr, Tucson, AZ 85716, Phone: 520-795-8290
Specialties: Hunter, skinners, Bowies, using knives, gentlemen's folders and collectible knives. **Technical:** Grinds ATS-34, 440C, Damascus, Dama steel, heat-treats and cryogenically quenches. We do gold-plating, salt bluing, scrimshawing, filework and fashion hand made leather sheaths. Materials used for handles include exotic woods, mammoth ivory, mother of pearl, G-10 and micarta. **Prices:** $165 to $800. **Remarks:** Knifemaker since retirement in 1984. Selling them since 1993. **Mark:** Script or print R. E. Purvis ~ Tucson, AZ or last name only.

PUTNAM, DONALD S., 590 Wolcott Hill Rd, Wethersfield, CT 06109, Phone: 203-563-9718, Fax: 203-563-9718
Specialties: Working knives for the hunter and fisherman. **Patterns:** His design or to customer specs. **Technical:** Uses stock removal method, O1, W2, D2, ATS-34, 154CM, 440C and CPM REX 20; stainless steel Damascus on request. **Prices:** NA. **Remarks:** Full-time maker; first knife sold in 1985. **Mark:** Last name with a knife outline.

q

QUAKENBUSH, THOMAS C., 2426 Butler Rd, Ft. Wayne, IN 46808, Phone: 219-483-0749

QUARTON, BARR, PO Box 4335, McCall, ID 83638, Phone: 208-634-3641
Specialties: Plain and fancy working knives; period pieces. **Patterns:** Hunters, tantos and swords. **Technical:** Forges and grinds 154CM, ATS-34 and his own Damascus. **Prices:** $180 to $450; some to $4500. **Remarks:** Part-time maker; first knife sold in 1978. Doing business as Barr Custom Knives. **Mark:** First name with bear logo.

QUATTLEBAUM, CRAIG, 2 Ridgewood Ln., Searcy, AR 72143
Specialties: Traditional straight knives and one-of-a-kind knives of his design; period pieces. **Patterns:** Bowies and fighters. **Technical:** Forges 5168, 52100 and own Damascus. **Prices:** $100 to $1200. **Remarks:** Part-time maker; first knife sold in 1988. **Mark:** Stylized initials.

QUICK, MIKE, 23 Locust Ave, Kearny, NJ 07032, Phone: 201-991-6580
Specialties: Traditional working/using straight knives. **Patterns:** Bowies. **Technical:** 440C and ATS-34 for blades; Micarta, wood and stag for handles.

r

R. BOYES KNIVES, N81 W16140 Robin Hood Dr, Menomonee Falls, WI 53051, Phone: 262-255-7341
Specialties: Hunters, working knives. **Technical:** Grinds ATS-34, 440C, 01 tool steel & Damascus. **Prices:** $60 to $500. **Remarks:** First knife sold in 1998. Tom Boyes changed to R. Boyes Knives.

RACHLIN, LESLIE S., 1200 W. Church St, Elmira, NY 14905, Phone: 607-733-6889
Specialties: Classic and working/using straight knives and folders of his design. **Patterns:** Hunters, locking folders and utility/camp knives. **Technical:** Grinds 440C and Damascus. **Prices:** $110 to $200; some to $450. **Remarks:** Spare-time maker; first knife sold in 1989. Doing business as Tinkermade Knives. **Mark:** Stamped initials or Tinkermade, city and state.

RADOS, JERRY F., 7523 E 5000 N Rd, Grant Park, IL 60940, Phone: 815-472-3350, Fax: 815-472-3944
Specialties: Deluxe period pieces. **Patterns:** Hunters, fighters, locking folders, daggers and camp knives. **Technical:** Forges and grinds his own Damascus which he sells commercially; makes pattern-welded Turkish Damascus. **Prices:** Start at $900. **Remarks:** Full-time maker; first knife sold in 1981. **Mark:** Last name.

RAGSDALE, JAMES D., 3002 Arabian Woods Dr, Lithonia, GA 30038, Phone: 770-482-6739
Specialties: Fancy and embellished working knives of his design or to customer specs. **Patterns:** Hunters, folders and fighters. **Technical:** Grinds 440C, ATS-34 and A2. **Prices:** $150 and up. **Remarks:** Full-time maker; first knife sold in 1984. **Mark:** Fish symbol with name above, town below.

RAINVILLE, RICHARD, 126 Cockle Hill Rd, Salem, CT 06420, Phone: 860-859-2776
Specialties: Traditional working straight knives. **Patterns:** Outdoor knives, including fishing knives. **Technical:** L6, 400C, ATS-34. **Prices:** $100 to $800. **Remarks:** Full-time maker; first knife sold in 1982. **Mark:** Name, city, state in oval logo.

RALEY, R. WAYNE, 825 Poplar Acres Rd, Collierville, TN 38017, Phone: 901-853-2026

RALPH, DARREL, Briar Knives, 4185 S St Rt 605, Galena, OH 43021, Phone: 740-965-9970
Specialties: Fancy, high-art, high-tech, collectible straight knives and folders of his design and to customer specs; unique mechanisms, some disassemble. **Patterns:** Daggers, fighters and swords. **Technical:** Forges his own Damascus, nickel and high carbon. Uses mokume and Damascus; mosaics and special patterns. Engraves and heat-treats. Prefers pearl, ivory and abalone handle material; uses stones and jewels. **Prices:** $250 to six figures. **Remarks:** Full-time maker; first knife sold in 1987. Doing business as Briar Knives. **Mark:** DDR.

RAMEY, LARRY, 1315 Porter Morris Rd, Chapmansboro, TN 37035-5120, Phone: 615-307-4233
Specialties: Titanium knives. **Technical:** Pictures taken by Hawkinson Photography.

RAMEY, MARSHALL F., PO Box 2589, West Helena, AR 72390, Phone: 501-572-7436, Fax: 501-572-6245
Specialties: Traditional working knives. **Patterns:** Designs military combat knives; makes butterfly folders, camp knives and miniatures. **Technical:** Grinds D2 and 440C. **Prices:** $100 to $500. **Remarks:** Full-time maker; first knife sold in 1978. **Mark:** Name with ram's head.

RAMSEY, RICHARD A., 8525 Trout Farm Rd, Neosho, MO 64850, Phone: 417-451-1493

RANDALL JR., JAMES W., 11606 Keith Hall Rd, Keithville, LA 71047, Phone: 318-925-6480, Fax: 318-925-1709
Specialties: Mosaic Damascus. **Patterns:** Swords. **Technical:** Custom inlay work on handles. **Prices:** $350 and up. **Mark:** J. W. Randall.

RANDALL MADE KNIVES, PO Box 1988, Orlando, FL 32802, Phone: 407-855-8075, Fax: 407-855-9054
Specialties: Working straight knives. **Patterns:** Hunters, fighters and Bowies. **Technical:** Forges and grinds O1 and 440B. **Prices:** $65 to $250; some to $450. **Remarks:** Full-time maker; first knife sold in 1937. **Mark:** Randall, city and state in scimitar logo.

RANDOW, RALPH, 4214 Blalock Rd, Pineville, LA 71360, Phone: 318-640-3369

RANKL, CHRISTIAN, Possenhofenerstr. 33, 81476 Munchen, GERMANY, Phone: 089-75967265, Fax: 0727-3662679
Specialties: Tail-lock knives. **Patterns:** Fighters, hunters and locking folders. **Technical:** Grinds ATS-34, D2, CPM1440V, RWL 34 also stainless

Damascus . **Prices:** $450 to $950; some to $2000. **Remarks:** Full-time maker; first knife sold in 1989. **Mark:** Electrochemical etching on blade.

RAPP, STEVEN J., 7273 South 245 East, Midvale, UT 84047, Phone: 801-567-9553
Specialties: Gold quartz; mosaic handles. **Patterns:** Daggers, Bowies, fighters and San Francisco knives. **Technical:** Hollow- and flat-grinds 440C and Damascus. **Prices:** Start at $500. **Remarks:** Full-time maker; first knife sold in 1981. **Mark:** Name and state.

RAPPAZZO, RICHARD, 142 Dunsbach Ferry Rd, Cohoes, NY 12047, Phone: 518-783-6843
Specialties: Damascus locking folders and straight knives. **Patterns:** Folders, dirks, fighters and tantos in original and traditional designs. **Technical:** Hand-forges all blades; specializes in Damascus; uses only natural handle materials. **Prices:** $400 to $1500. **Remarks:** Part-time maker; first knife sold in 1985. **Mark:** Name, date, serial number.

RARDON, A. D., 1589 S. E. Price Dr, Polo, MO 64671, Phone: 660-354-2330
Specialties: Folders, miniatures. **Patterns:** Hunters, buck skinners, Bowies, miniatures and daggers. **Technical:** Grinds O1, D2, 440C and ATS-34. **Prices:** $150 to $2000; some higher. **Remarks:** Full-time maker; first knife sold in 1954. **Mark:** Fox logo.

RARDON, ARCHIE F., 1589 SE Price Dr, Polo, MO 64671, Phone: 660-354-2330
Specialties: Working knives. **Patterns:** Hunters, Bowies and miniatures. **Technical:** Grinds O1, D2, 440C, ATS-34, cable and Damascus. **Prices:** $50 to $500. **Remarks:** Part-time maker. **Mark:** Boar hog.

RAY, ALAN W., PO Box 479, Lovelady, TX 75851, Phone: 936-636-2350, Fax: 936-636-2931
Specialties: Working straight knives of his design. **Patterns:** Hunters, camp knives, steak knives and carving sets. **Technical:** Forges L6 and 5160 for straight knives; grinds D2 and 440C for folders and kitchen cutlery. **Prices:** $200 to $1000. **Remarks:** Full-time maker; first knife sold in 1979. **Mark:** Stylized initials.

REBELLO, INDIAN GEORGE, 358 Elm St, New Bedford, MA 02740-3837, Phone: 208-999-7090
Specialties: One-of-a-kind fighters and Bowies. **Patterns:** To customers' specs, hunters and utilities. **Technical:** Forges his own Damascus, 5160, 52100, 1084, 1095, cable and O-1. Grinds S30V, ATS-34, 154CM, 440C, D2 and A2. Makes own Mokumme. **Prices:** Starting at $250. **Remarks:** Full-time maker, first knife sold in 1991. Doing business as Indian George's Knives. President and founding father of the New England Custom Knives Association. **Mark:** Indian George's Knives.

RED, VERNON, 2020 Benton Cove, Conway, AR 72032, Phone: 501-450-7284
Specialties: Traditional straight knives and folders of my design and special orders. Most are one-of-a-kind. **Patterns:** Hunters, fighters, Bowies, fillet, skinners & lock-blades. **Technical:** Hollow Grind 90%; use 440C, D-2, ATS-34, Stamascus and Damascus. Uses natural woods, pearl, horn, stag, ivory & bone. **Prices:** $125 and up. **Remarks:** Part-time maker; first knife sold in 1992. Do scrimshaw on ivory & micarta. **Mark:** Last name. **Other:** Member Arkansas Knives Assoc. (aka) Custom Made Knives by Vernon Red.

REDDIEX, BILL, 27 Galway Ave, Palmerston North, NEW ZEALAND, Phone: 06-357-0383, Fax: 06-358-2910
Specialties: Collector-grade working straight knives. **Patterns:** Traditional-style Bowies and drop-point hunters. **Technical:** Grinds 440C, D2 and O1; offers variety of grinds and finishes. **Prices:** $130 to $750. **Remarks:** Full-time maker; first knife sold in 1980. **Mark:** Last name around kiwi bird logo.

REED, DAVE, Box 132, Brimfield, MA 01010, Phone: 413-245-3661
Specialties: Traditional styles. Makes knives from chains, rasps, gears, etc. **Patterns:** Bush swords, hunters, working minis, camp and utility knives. **Technical:** Forges 1075 and his own Damascus. **Prices:** Start at $50. **Remarks:** Part-time maker; first knife sold in 1970. **Mark:** Initials.

REED, JOHN M., 1095 Spalding Cir, Goose Creek, SC 29445, Phone: 843-797-6287
Specialties: Hunter, utility, some survival knives. **Patterns:** Trailing Point, and drop point sheath knives. **Technical:** ATS-34, rockwell 60 exotic wood or natural material handles. **Prices:** $135-$300. Depending on handle material. **Remarks:** I like the stock removal method. "Old Fashioned trailing point blades". **Mark:** "Reed" acid etched on left side of blade. **Other:** Hand made and sewn leather sheaths.

REEVE, CHRIS, 11624 W. President Dr, Ste. B, Boise, ID 83713, Phone: 208-375-0367, Fax: 208-375-0368
Specialties: Originator and designer of the One Piece range of fixed blade utility knives and of the Sebenza Integral Lock folding knives made by Chris Reeve Knives. Currently makes only one or two pieces per year him-

self. **Patterns:** Art folders and fixed blades; one-of-a-kind. **Technical:** Grinds BG-42, Damascus and other materials to his own design. **Prices:** $1000 and upwards. **Remarks:** Full-time in knife business; first knife sold in 1982. **Mark:** Signature and date.

REEVES, WINFRED M., PO Box 300, West Union, SC 29696, Phone: 803-638-6121
Specialties: Working straight knives; some elaborate pieces. **Patterns:** Hunters, tantos and fishing knives. **Technical:** Grinds D2, 440C and ATS-34. Does not solder joints; does not use buffer unless requested. **Prices:** $75 to $150; some to $300. **Remarks:** Part-time maker; first knife sold in 1975. **Mark:** Last name, Walhalla, state.

REGGIO JR., SIDNEY J., PO Box 851, Sun, LA 70463, Phone: 504-886-5886
Specialties: Miniature classic and fancy straight knives of his design or in standard patterns. **Patterns:** Fighters, hunters and utility/camp knives. **Technical:** Grinds 440C, ATS-34 and commercial Damascus. Engraves; scrimshaws; offers filework. Hollow grinds most blades. Prefers natural handle material. Offers handmade sheaths. **Prices:** $85 to $250; some to $500. **Remarks:** Part-time maker; first knife sold in 1988. Doing business as Sterling Workshop. **Mark:** Initials.

REMINGTON, DAVID W., 12928 Morrow Rd, Gentry, AR 72734-9781, Phone: 501-846-3526
Specialties: Fancy and traditional straight knives of his design and to customer specs. **Patterns:** Bowies, daggers and hunters. **Technical:** Grinds ATS-34, A2 and D2. Makes own twist and random-pattern Damascus. Wholesale D2, A2, stag and ossic sheep horn. Rope and thorn pattern filework; tapered tangs; heat treats. **Prices:** $65 to $250; some to $1000. **Remarks:** Part-time maker; first knife sold in 1991. **Mark:** First and last name, Custom.

REPKE, MIKE, 4191 N. Euclid Ave, Bay City, MI 48706, Phone: 517-684-3111
Specialties: Traditional working and using straight knives of their design or to customer specs; classic knives; display knives. **Patterns:** Hunters, Bowies, skinners, fighters boots, axes and swords. **Technical:** Grind 440C. Offer variety of handle materials. **Prices:** $99 to $1500. **Remarks:** Full-time makers. Doing business as Black Forest Blades. **Mark:** Knife logo.

REVERDY, PIERRE, 5 Rue de L'egalite', 26100 Romans, FRANCE, Phone: 334 75 05 10 15, Fax: 334 75 02 28 40
Specialties: Art knives; legend pieces. **Patterns:** Daggers, Bowies, hunters and other large patterns. **Technical:** Forges his Damascus and "poetique Damascus"; works with his own EDM machine to create any kind of pattern inside the steel with his own touch. **Prices:** $2000 and up. **Remarks:** Full-time maker; first knife sold in 1986. Nicole (wife) collaborates with enamels. **Mark:** Initials connected.

REVISHVILI, ZAZA, 2102 Linden Ave, Madison, WI 53704, Phone: 608-243-7927
Specialties: Fancy/embellished and high-art straight knives and folders of his design. **Patterns:** Daggers, swords and locking folders. **Technical:** Uses Damascus; silver filigree, silver inlay in wood; enameling. **Prices:** $1000 to $9000; some to $15,000. **Remarks:** Full-time maker; first knife sold in 1987. **Mark:** Initials, city.

REXROAT, KIRK, 527 Sweetwater Circle, Box 224, Wright, WY 82732, Phone: 307-464-0166
Specialties: Using and collectible straight knives and folders of his design or to customer specs. **Patterns:** Bowies, hunters, folders. **Technical:** Forges Damascus patterns, mosaic and 52100. **Prices:** $400 and up. **Remarks:** Part-time maker, Mastersmith in the ABS; first knife sold in 1984. Doing business as Rexroat Knives. **Mark:** Last name.

REYNOLDS, DAVE, Rt. 2, Box 36, Harrisville, WV 26362, Phone: 304-643-2889
Specialties: Working straight knives of his design. **Patterns:** Bowies, kitchen and utility knives. **Technical:** Grinds and forges L6, 1095 and 440C. Heat-treats. **Prices:** $50 to $85; some to $175. **Remarks:** Full-time maker; first knife sold in 1980. Doing business as Terra-Gladius Knives. **Mark:** Mark on special orders only; serial number on all knives.

REYNOLDS, JOHN C., #2 Andover, HC77, Gillette, WY 82716, Phone: 307-682-6076
Specialties: Working knives, some fancy. **Patterns:** Hunters, Bowies, tomahawks and buck skinners; some folders. **Technical:** Grinds D2, ATS-34, 440C and I forge my own Damascus and Knifes now. Scrimshaws. **Prices:** $200 to $3000. **Remarks:** Spare-time maker; first knife sold in 1969. **Mark:** On ground blades JC Reynolds Gillette, WY; on forged blades, initials make mark-JCR.

RHO, NESTOR LORENZO, Primera Junta 589, (6000) Junin, Buenos Aires, ARGENTINA, Phone: 02362 15670686
Specialties: Classic and fancy straight knives of his design. **Patterns:** Bowies, fighters and hunters. **Technical:** Grinds 420C, 440C and 1050.

Offers semi-precious stones on handles, acid etching on blades and blade engraving. **Prices:** $60 to $300; some to $1200. **Remarks:** Full-time maker; first knife sold in 1975. **Mark:** Name.

RHODES, JAMES D., 205 Woodpoint Ave, Hagerstown, MD 21740, Phone: 301-739-2657
Specialties: Traditional working and using straight knives of his design. **Patterns:** Bowies, fighters, hunters and kitchen knives. **Technical:** Forges 5160, 1085, and 9260; makes own Damascus. Hard edges, soft backs, dead soft tangs. Heat-treats. **Prices:** $150 to $350. **Remarks:** Part-time maker. **Mark:** Last name, JS.

RICARDO ROMANO, BERNARDES, Ruai Coronel Rennò, 1261, Itajuba MG, BRAZIL 37500, Phone: 0055-2135-622-5896
Specialties: Hunters, fighters, Bowies. **Technical:** Grinds blades of stainless and tools steels. **Patterns:** Hunters. **Prices:** $100 to $700. **Mark:** Romano.

RICE, STEPHEN E., 11043 C Oak Spur Ct, St. Louis, MO 63146, Phone: 314-432-2025

RICHARD, RON, 4875 Calaveras Ave, Fremont, CA 94538, Phone: 510-796-9767
Specialties: High-tech working straight knives of his design. **Patterns:** Bowies, swords and locking folders. **Technical:** Forges and grinds ATS-34, 154CM and 440V. All folders have dead-bolt button locks. **Prices:** $650 to $850; some to $1400. **Remarks:** Full-time maker; first knife sold in 1968. **Mark:** Full name.

RICHARDS JR., ALVIN C., 2889 Shields Ln, Fortuna, CA 95540-3241, Phone: 707-725-2526
Specialties: Fixed blade Damascus. One-of-a-kind. **Patterns:** Hunters, fighters. **Prices:** $125 to $500. **Remarks:** Like to work with customers on a truly custom knife. **Mark:** A C Richards or ACR.

RICHARDSON JR., PERCY, PO Box 973, Hemphill, TX 75948, Phone: 409-787-2279
Specialties: Traditional and working straight knives and folders in standard patterns and to customer specs. **Patterns:** Bowies, daggers, hunters, automatics, locking folders, slip-joints and utility/camp knives. **Technical:** Grinds ATS-34, 440C and D2. **Prices:** $125 to $600; some to $1800. **Remarks:** Full-time maker; first knife sold in 1990. Doing business as Lone Star Custom Knives. **Mark:** Lone Star with last name across it.

RICHTER, JOHN C., 932 Bowling Green Trail, Chesapeake, VA 23320
Specialties: Hand-forged knives in original patterns. **Patterns:** Hunters, fighters, utility knives and other belt knives, folders, swords. **Technical:** Hand-forges high carbon and his own Damascus; makes mokume gane. **Prices:** $75 to $1500. **Remarks:** Part-time maker. **Mark:** Richter Forge.

RICHTER, SCOTT, 516 E. 2nd St, S. Boston, MA 02127, Phone: 617-269-4855
Specialties: Traditional working/using folders. **Patterns:** Locking folders, swords and kitchen knives. **Technical:** Grinds ATS-34, 5160 and A2. High-tech materials. **Prices:** $150 to $650; some to $1500. **Remarks:** Full-time maker; first knife sold in 1991. Doing business as Richter Made. **Mark:** Last name, Made.

RICKE, DAVE, 1209 Adams, West Bend, WI 53090, Phone: 262-334-5739
Specialties: Working knives; period pieces. **Patterns:** Hunters, boots, Bowies; locking folders and slip-joints. **Technical:** Grinds ATS-34, A2, 440C and 154CM. **Prices:** $125-$1600. **Remarks:** Full-time maker; first knife sold in 1976. **Mark:** Last name.

RIDER, DAVID M., PO Box 5946, Eugene, OR 97405-0911, Phone: 541-343-8747

RIEPE, RICHARD A., 17604 East 296 Street, Harrisonville, MO 64701

RIETVELD, BERTIE, PO Box 53, Magaliesburg 1791, SOUTH AFRICA, Phone: +2714 577 1294, Fax: 014 577 1294
Specialties: Damascus, Persian, art daggers, button-lock folders. **Patterns:** Mostly one-ofs. **Technical:** Work only in own stainless Damascus and other exotics. **Prices:** $500 to $8000. **Remarks:** First knife made in 1979. Past chairman of SA Knifemakers Guild. Member SA Knifemakers Guild & Knifemakers Guild (USA). Also a member of the Italian Guild. **Mark:** Elephant with last name.

RIGNEY JR., WILLIE, 191 Colson Dr, Bronston, KY 42518, Phone: 606-679-4227
Specialties: High-tech period pieces and fancy working knives. **Patterns:** Fighters, boots, daggers and push knives. **Technical:** Grinds 440C and 154CM; buys Damascus. Most knives are embellished. **Prices:** $150 to $1500; some to $10,000. **Remarks:** Full-time maker; first knife sold in 1978. **Mark:** First initial, last name.

RINALDI, T. H., Rinaldi Custom Blades, PO Box 718, Winchester, CA 92596, Phone: 909-926-5422
Technical: Grinds S30V, 3V, A2 and talonite fixed blades. **Prices:** $175-600. **Remarks:** Tactical and utility for the most part.

RINKES, SIEGFRIED, Am Sportpl 2, D 91459, Markterlbach, GERMANY

RIZZI, RUSSELL J., 37 March Rd, Ashfield, MA 01330, Phone: 413-625-2842
Specialties: Fancy working and using straight knives and folders of his design or to customer specs. **Patterns:** Hunters, locking folders and fighters. **Technical:** Grinds 440C, D2 and commercial Damascus. **Prices:** $150 to $750; some to $2500. **Remarks:** Part-time maker; first knife sold in 1990. **Mark:** Last name, Ashfield, MA.

ROATH, DEAN, 3050 Winnipeg Dr, Baton Rouge, LA 70819, Phone: 225-272-5562
Specialties: Classic working knives; focusing on fillet knives for salt water fishermen. **Patterns:** Hunters, filets, canoe/trail, and boating/sailing knives. **Technical:** Grinds 440C. **Prices:** $85 to $500; some to $1500. **Remarks:** Part-time maker; first knife sold in 1978. **Mark:** Name, city and state.

ROBBINS, HOWARD P., 1407 S. 217th Ave, Elkhorn, NE 68022, Phone: 402-289-4121
Specialties: High-tech working knives with clean designs, some fancy. **Patterns:** Folders, hunters and camp knives. **Technical:** Grinds 440C. Heat-treats; likes mirror finishes. Offers leatherwork. **Prices:** $100 to $500; some to $1000. **Remarks:** Full-time maker; first knife sold in 1982. **Mark:** Name, city and state.

ROBERTS, MICHAEL, 601 Oakwood Dr, Clinton, MS 39056, Phone: 601-924-3154; Pager 601-978-8180
Specialties: Working and using knives in standard patterns and to customer specs. **Patterns:** Hunters, Bowies, tomahawks and fighters. **Technical:** Forges 5160, O1, 1095 and his own Damascus. Uses only natural handle materials. **Prices:** $145 to $500; some to $1100. **Remarks:** Part-time maker; first knife sold in 1988. **Mark:** Last name or first and last name in Celtic script.

ROBERTS, CHUCK, PO Box 7174, Golden, CO 80403, Phone: 303-642-0512
Specialties: Sheffield Bowies; historic styles only. **Patterns:** Bowies and California knives. **Technical:** Grinds 440C, 5160 and ATS-34. Handles made of stag, ivory or mother-of-pearl. **Prices:** Start at $750. **Remarks:** Full-time maker. **Mark:** Last initial or last name.

ROBERTS, MIKE, 601 Oakwood Dr, Clinton, MS 39056-4332, Phone: 601-924-3154

ROBERTS, JACK, 10811 Sagebluff Dr, Houston, TX 77089, Phone: 218-481-1784
Specialties: Hunting knives and folders, offers scrimshaw by wife Barbara. **Patterns:** Drop point hunters and liner-lock folders. **Technical:** Grinds 440-C, offers file work, texturing, natural handle materials and micarta. **Prices:** $200 to $800; some higher. **Remarks:** Part-time maker, sold first knife in 1965. **Mark:** Name, city, state.

ROBERTS, GEORGE A., PO Box 31228, 211 Main St, Whitehorse, YT, CANADA Y1A 5P7, Phone: 867-667-7099, Fax: 867-667-7099
Specialties: Masadon Ivory, fossil walrus ivory handled knives, scrimshawed or carved. **Patterns:** Side lockers, fancy bird & trout knives, hunters, fillet blades. **Technical:** Grinds stainless Damascus, all surgical steels. **Prices:** Up to $3500 U. S. **Remarks:** Full-time maker; first knives sold in 1986. Doing business as Bandit Blades. **Mark:** Bandit Yukon with pick & shovel crossed. **Other:** Most recent works have gold nuggets in fossilized Mastodon ivory. Something new using mosaic pins in mokume bolster and in mosaic Damascus, it creates a new look.

ROBERTS, E. RAY, 191 Nursery Rd, Monticello, FL 32344, Phone: 850-997-4403
Specialties: High-Carbon Damascus knives & tomahawks.

ROBERTSON, LEO D., 3728 Pleasant Lake Dr, Indianapolis, IN 46227, Phone: 317-882-9899
Specialties: Hunting and folders. **Patterns:** Hunting, fillet, bowie, utility, folders and tantos. **Technical:** Uses ATS-34, 440C, 1095, D2 and Damascus steels. **Prices:** Fixed knives $75 to $350, folders $350 to $600. **Remarks:** Handles made with stag, wildwoods, laminates, mother of pearl. **Mark:** Logo with full name in oval around logo. **Other:** Made first knife in 1990. Member of American bladesmith society.

ROBINSON, ROBERT W., 1569 N. Finley Pt., Polson, MT 59860, Phone: 406-887-2259, Fax: 406-887-2259
Specialties: High-art straight knives, folders and automatics of his design. **Patterns:** Hunters and locking folders. **Technical:** Grinds ATS-34, 154CM and 440V. Inlays pearl and gold; engraves sheep horn and ivory. **Prices:** $150 to $500; some to $2000. **Remarks:** Full-time maker; first knife sold in 1983. Doing business as Robbie Knife. **Mark:** Name on left side of blade.

ROBINSON, CHARLES (DICKIE), PO Box 221, Vega, TX 79092, Phone: 806-267-2629
Specialties: Classic and working/using knives. **Patterns:** Bowies, daggers, fighters, hunters and camp knives. **Technical:** Forges O1, 5160, 52100 and his own Damascus. **Prices:** $125 to $850; some to $2500. **Remarks:** Part-time maker; first knife sold in 1988. Doing business as Robinson Knives. **Mark:** Last name, JS.

ROBINSON, CHUCK, Sea Robin Forge, 1423 Third Ave, Picayune, MS 39466, Phone: 601-798-0060
Specialties: Deluxe period pieces and working/using knives of his design and to customer specs. **Patterns:** Bowies, RR spike knives, hunters, folders, utility knives and original designs. **Technical:** Forges own Damascus, 52100, O1, L6, 1070 through 1095, 15N20 and cable. **Prices:** Start at $225. **Remarks:** First knife 1958. Recently transitioned to full-time maker. **Mark:** Dolphin entwined on anchor and initials C. R. **Other:** Makes bladesmithing anvils, hammers & finishing jigs.

ROBINSON III, REX R., 10531 Poe St, Leesburg, FL 34788, Phone: 352-787-4587
Specialties: One-of-a-kind high-art automatics of his design. **Patterns:** Automatics, liner-locks and lock-back folders. **Technical:** Uses tool steel and stainless Damascus and mokume; flat grinds. Hand carves folders. **Prices:** $1800 to $7500. **Remarks:** First knife sold in 1988. **Mark:** First name inside oval.

ROCHFORD, MICHAEL R., PO Box 577, Dresser, WI 54009, Phone: 715-755-3520
Specialties: Working straight knives and folders. Classic Bowies and Moran traditional. **Patterns:** Bowies, fighters, hunters: slip-joint, locking and liner-locking folders. **Technical:** Grinds ATS-34, 440C, 154CM and D-2; forges W2, 5160, and his own Damascus. Offers metal & metal and leather sheaths. Filework and wire inlay. **Prices:** $150 to $1000; some to $2000. **Remarks:** Part-time maker; first knife sold in 1984. **Mark:** Name.

RODEBAUGH, JAMES L., 9374 Joshua Rd, Oak Hills, CA 92345

RODEWALD, GARY, 447 Grouse Court, Hamilton, MT 59840, Phone: 406-363-2192
Specialties: Bowies of my design as inspired from his torical pieces. **Patterns:** Hunters, Bowies & camp/combat. Forges 5160 1084 & my own Damascus of 1084, 15N20, field grade hunters AT-34 - 440C, 440V, and BG42. **Prices:** $200-$1500 **Remarks:** Sole author on knives - sheaths done by saddle maker. **Mark:** Rodewald

RODKEY, DAN, 18336 Ozark Dr, Hudson, FL 34667, Phone: 727-863-8264
Specialties: Traditional straight knives of his design and in standard patterns. **Patterns:** Boots, fighters and hunters. **Technical:** Grinds 440C, D2 and ATS-34. **Prices:** Start at $200. **Remarks:** Full-time maker; first knife sold in 1985. Doing business as Rodkey Knives. **Mark:** Etched logo on blade.

ROE JR., FRED D., 4005 Granada Dr, Huntsville, AL 35802, Phone: 205-881-6847
Specialties: Highly finished working knives of his design; period pieces. **Patterns:** Hunters, fighters and survival knives; locking folders; specialty designs like divers' knives. **Technical:** Grinds 154CM, ATS-34 and Damascus. Field-tests all blades. **Prices:** $125 to $250; some to $2000. **Remarks:** Part-time maker; first knife sold in 1980. **Mark:** Last name.

ROGERS, RICHARD, PO Box 769, Magdalena, NM 87825, Phone: 505-854-2567
Specialties: Sheffield-style folders & multi-blade folders. **Patterns:** Folders: various traditional patterns. One-of-a-kind fixed blades. Fixed blades: Bowies, daggers, hunters, utility knives. **Technical:** Use various steels, like natural handle materials. **Prices:** $400 on up. **Mark:** Last name.

ROGERS, RODNEY, 602 Osceola St, Wildwood, FL 34785, Phone: 352-748-6114
Specialties: Traditional straight knives and folders. **Patterns:** Fighters, hunters, skinners. **Technical:** Flat-grinds ATS-34 and Damascus. Prefers natural materials. **Prices:** $150 to $1400. **Remarks:** Full-time maker; first knife sold in 1986. **Mark:** Last name, Handmade.

ROGERS, CHARLES W., Rt 1 Box 1552, Douglass, TX 75943, Phone: 409-326-4496

ROGERS JR., ROBERT P., 3979 South Main St, Acworth, GA 30101, Phone: 404-974-9982
Specialties: Traditional working knives. **Patterns:** Hunters, 4-inch trailing-points. **Technical:** Grinds D2, 154CM and ATS-34; likes ironwood and ivory Micarta. **Prices:** $125 to $175. **Remarks:** Spare-time maker; first knife sold in 1975. **Mark:** Name.

ROGHMANS, MARK, 607 Virginia Ave, LaGrange, GA 30240, Phone: 706-885-1273
Specialties: Classic and traditional knives of his design. **Patterns:** Bowies, daggers and fighters. **Technical:** Grinds ATS-34, D2 and 440C.

custom knifemakers

Prices: $250 to $500. **Remarks:** Part-time maker; first knife sold in 1984. Doing business as LaGrange Knife. **Mark:** Last name and/or LaGrange Knife.

ROHN, FRED, 7675 W Happy Hill Rd, Coeur d'Alene, ID 83814, Phone: 208-667-0774
Specialties: Hunters, boot knives, custom patterns. **Patterns:** Drop points, double edge etc. **Technical:** Grinds 440 or 154CM. **Prices:** $85 and up. **Remarks:** Part-time maker. **Mark:** Logo on blade; serial numbered.

ROLLERT, STEVE, PO Box 65, Keenesburg, CO 80643-0065, Phone: 303-732-4858
Specialties: Highly finished working knives. **Patterns:** Variety of straight knives; locking folders and slip-joints. **Technical:** Forges and grinds W2, 1095, ATS-34 and his pattern-welded, cable Damascus and nickel Damascus. **Prices:** $300 to $1000; some to $3000. **Remarks:** Full-time maker; first knife sold in 1980. Doing business as Dove Knives. **Mark:** Last name in script.

ROLLICK, WALTER D., 2001 Cochran Rd, Maryville, TN 37803, Phone: 423-681-6105

RONZIO, N. JACK, PO Box 248, Fruita, CO 81521, Phone: 970-858-0921

ROSA, PEDRO GULLHERME TELES, R. das Magnolias, 45 CECAP Presidente Prudente, SP-19065-410, BRAZIL, Phone: 0182-271769
Specialties: Using straight knives and folders to customer specs; some high-art. **Patterns:** Fighters, Bowies and daggers. **Technical:** Grinds and forges D6, 440C, high carbon steels and Damascus. **Prices:** $60 to $400. **Remarks:** Full-time maker; first knife sold in 1991. **Mark:** A hammer over "Hammer."

ROSE, DEREK W., 14 Willow Wood Rd, Gallipolis, OH 45631, Phone: 740-446-4627

ROSENFELD, BOB, 955 Freeman Johnson Road, Hoschton, GA 30548, Phone: 770-867-2647
Specialties: Fancy and embellished working/using straight knives of his design and in standard patterns. **Patterns:** Daggers, hunters and utility/camp knives. **Technical:** Forges 52100, A203E, 1095 and L6 Damascus. Offers engraving. **Prices:** $125 to $650; some to $1000. **Remarks:** Full-time maker; first knife sold in 1984. Also makes folders; ABS journeyman. **Mark:** Last name or full name, Knife maker.

ROSS, D. L., 27 Kinsman St, Dunedin, NEW ZEALAND, Phone: 64 3 464 0239, Fax: 64 3 464 0239
Specialties: Working straight knives of his design. **Patterns:** Hunters, various others. **Technical:** Grinds 440C. **Prices:** $100 to $450; some to $700 NZ dollars. **Remarks:** Part-time maker; first knife sold in 1988. **Mark:** Dave Ross, Maker, city and country.

ROSS, GREGG, 4556 Wenhart Rd, Lake Worth, FL 33463, Phone: 407-439-4681
Specialties: Working/using straight knives. **Patterns:** Bowies, hunters and utility/camp knives. **Technical:** Forges and grinds ATS-34, Damascus and cable Damascus. Uses decorative pins. **Prices:** $125 to $250; some to $400. **Remarks:** Part-time maker; first knife sold in 1992. **Mark:** Name, city and state.

ROSS, STEPHEN, 534 Remington Dr, Evanston, WY 82930, Phone: 307-789-7104
Specialties: One-of-a-kind collector-grade classic and contemporary straight knives and folders of his design and to customer specs; some fantasy pieces. **Patterns:** Combat and survival knives, hunters, boots and folders. **Technical:** Grinds stainless; forges spring and tool steel. Engraves, scrimshaws. Makes leather sheaths. **Prices:** $160 to $3000. **Remarks:** Part-time-time maker; first knife sold in 1971. **Mark:** Last name in modified Roman; sometimes in script.

ROSS, TIM, 3239 Oliver Rd, RR #17, Thunder Bay, ONT, CANADA P7B 6C2, Phone: 807-935-2667
Specialties: Fancy working knives of his design. **Patterns:** Fishing and hunting knives, Bowies, daggers and miniatures. **Technical:** Uses D2, Stellite 6K and 440C; forges 52100 and Damascus. Makes antler handles and sheaths; has supply of whale teeth and moose antlers for trade. Prefers natural materials only. Wife Katherine scrimshaws. **Prices:** $100 to $350; some to $2100. **Remarks:** Part-time maker; first knife sold in 1975. **Mark:** Last name stamped on tang.

ROSSDEUTSCHER, ROBERT N., 133 S Vail Ave, Arlington Hts, IL 60005, Phone: 847-577-0404
Specialties: Frontier-style and historically inspired knives. **Patterns:** Trade knives, Bowies, camp knives & hunting knives. **Technical:** Most knives are hand forged, a few are stock removal. **Prices:** $85 to $600. **Remarks:** Journeyman Smith of the American Bladesmith Society and Neo-Tribal Metalsmiths. **Mark:** Back-to-back "R's", one upside down and backwards, one right side up & forward in an oval. Sometimes with name, town & state; depending on knife style.

ROTELLA, RICHARD, 643 75th St, Niagara Falls, NY 14304
Specialties: Working knives of his design. **Patterns:** Various fishing, hunting and utility knives; folders. **Technical:** Grinds ATS-34. Prefers hand-rubbed finishes. **Prices:** $65 to $450; some to $900. **Remarks:** Spare-time maker; first knife sold in 1977. Not taking orders at this time; only sells locally. **Mark:** Name and city in stylized waterfall logo.

ROULIN, CHARLES, 113 B Rt. de Soral, 1233 Geneva, SWITZERLAND, Phone: 022-757-4479, Fax: 022-757-4479
Specialties: Fancy high-art straight knives and folders of his design. **Patterns:** Bowies, locking folders, slip-joint folders and miniatures. **Technical:** Grinds 440C, ATS-34 and D2. Engraves; carves nature scenes and detailed animals in steel, ivory, on handles and blades. **Prices:** $500 to $3000; some to $10,000. **Remarks:** Full-time maker; first knife sold in 1988. **Mark:** Symbol of fish with name or name engraved.

ROWE, KENNY, 1406 W Ave C, Hope, AR 71801, Phone: 870-777-8216, Fax: 870-777-2974

ROWE, STEWART G., 8-18 Coreen Court, Mt. Crosby, Brisbane 4306, AUSTRALIA, Phone: Ph: 073-201-0906, Fax: Fax: 073-201-2406
Specialties: Designer knives, reproduction of ancient weaponry, traditional Japanese tantos and edged tools. **Patterns:** "Shark"—blade range. **Technical:** Forges W1, W2, D2; creates own Tamahagne steel and composite pattern-welded billets. Gold, silver and ivory fittings available. **Prices:** $300 to $11,000. **Remarks:** Full-time maker; first knife sold in 1981. Doing business as Stewart Rowe Productions Pty Ltd .

ROY, ROBERT F., 16180 Schaeffer St, PO Box 262, Bayview, ID 83803, Phone: 208-683-9396

ROZAS, CLARK D., 1436 W "G" Street, Wilmington, CA 90744, Phone: 310-518-0488
Specialties: Hand forged blades. **Patterns:** Pig stickers, toad stabbers, whackers, choppers. **Technical:** Damascus, 52100, 1095, 1084, 5160. **Prices:** $200 to $600. **Remarks:** A. B. S. member; part-time maker since 1995. **Mark:** Name over dagger.

RUANA KNIFE WORKS, Box 520, Bonner, MT 59823, Phone: 406-258-5368
Specialties: Working knives and period pieces. **Patterns:** Variety of straight knives. **Technical:** Forges 5160 chrome alloy for Bowies and 1095. **Prices:** $105 and up. **Remarks:** Full-time maker; first knife sold in 1938. **Mark:** Name.

RUBLEY, JAMES A., 4609 W Nevada Mills Rd, Angola, IN 46703, Phone: 219-833-1255
Specialties: Working American knives and collectibles for hunters, buckskinners and re-enactment groups from Pre-Revolutionary War through the Civil War. **Patterns:** Anything authentic, barring folders. **Technical:** Iron fittings, natural materials; forges files. **Prices:** $175 to $2500. **Remarks:** Museum consultant and blacksmith for two decades. Offers classes in beginning, intermediate and advanced traditional knife making. **Mark:** Lightning bolt.

RUPERT, BOB, 301 Harshaville Rd, Clinton, PA 15026, Phone: 724-573-4569
Specialties: Wrought period pieces with natural elements. **Patterns:** Elegant straight blades - friction folders. **Technical:** Forges colonial 7; 1095; 5160; diffuse mokume-gane and form Damascus. **Prices:** $150 to $1500; some higher. **Remarks:** Part-time maker; first knife sold in 1980. Evening hours studio since 1980. **Mark:** R etched in Old English. **Other:** Likes simplicity that disassembles.

RUPLE, WILLIAM H., PO Box 370, Charlotte, TX 78011, Phone: 830-277-1371
Specialties: Multi blade folders, slip joints, some lock-backs. **Patterns:** Like to reproduce old patterns. **Technical:** Grinds 440C, ATS-34, D2 and commercial Damascus. Offers filework on back springs and liners. **Prices:** $300 to $500; some to $1000. **Remarks:** Full-time maker; first knife sold in 1988. **Mark:** Ruple.

RUSS, RON, 5351 NE 160th Ave, Williston, FL 32696, Phone: 352-528-2603
Specialties: Damascus and Mokume. **Patterns:** Ladder, rain drop and butterfly. **Technical:** Most knives, including Damascus, are forged from 52100-E. **Prices:** $65 to $2500. **Mark:** Russ.

RUSSELL, MICK, 4 Rossini Rd, Pari Park, Port Elizabeth 6070, SOUTH AFRICA
Specialties: Art knives. **Patterns:** Working and collectible bird, trout and hunting knives, defense knives and folders. **Technical:** Grinds D2, 440C, ATS-34 and Damascus. Offers mirror or satin finishes. **Prices:** Start at $100. **Remarks:** Full-time maker; first knife sold in 1986. **Mark:** Stylized rhino incorporating initials.

RUSSELL, TOM, 6500 New Liberty Rd, Jacksonville, AL 36265, Phone: 205-492-7866
Specialties: Straight working knives of his design or to customer specs. **Patterns:** Hunters, folders, fighters, skinners, Bowies and utility knives. **Technical:** Grinds D2, 440C and ATS-34; offers filework. **Prices:** $75 to $225. **Remarks:** Part-time maker; first knife sold in 1987. Full-time tool and die maker. **Mark:** Last name with tulip stamp.

RUTH, MICHAEL G, 3101 New Boston Rd, Texarkana, TX 75501, Phone: 903-832-7166

RYAN, C. O., 902-A Old Wormley Creek Rd, Yorktown, VA 23692, Phone: 757-898-7797
Specialties: Working/using knives. **Patterns:** Hunters, kitchen knives, locking folders. **Technical:** Grinds 440C and ATS-34. **Prices:** $45 to $130; some to $450. **Remarks:** Part-time maker; first knife sold in 1980. **Mark:** Name-C. O. Ryan.

RYBAR JR., RAYMOND B., 726 W Lynwood St, Phoenix, AZ 85007, Phone: 605-523-0201
Specialties: Fancy/embellished, high-art and traditional working using straight knives and folders of his design and in standard patterns; period pieces. **Patterns:** Daggers, fighters and swords. **Technical:** Forges Damascus. All blades have etched biblical scripture or biblical significance. **Prices:** $120 to $1200; some to $4500. **Remarks:** Full-time maker; first knife sold in 1972. Doing business as Stone Church Forge. **Mark:** Last name or business name.

RYBERG, GOTE, Faltgatan 2, S-562 00 Norrahammar, SWEDEN, Phone: 4636-61678

RYDBOM, JEFF, PO Box 548, Annandale, MI 55302, Phone: 320-274-9639

RYDER, BEN M., PO Box 133, Copperhill, TN 37317, Phone: 615-496-2750
Specialties: Working/using straight knives of his design and to customer specs. **Patterns:** Fighters, hunters, utility/camp knives. **Technical:** Grinds 440C, ATS-34, D2, commercial Damascus. **Prices:** $75 to $400. **Remarks:** Part-time maker; first knife sold in 1992. **Mark:** Full name in double butterfly logo.

RYUICHI, KUKI, 504-7 Tokorozawa-Shinmachi Tokorozawa-City, Saitama, JAPAN, Phone: 042-943-3451

RZEWNICKI, GERALD, 8833 S Massbach Rd, Elizabeth, IL 61028-9714, Phone: 815-598-3239

S

SAINDON, R. BILL, 233 Rand Pond Rd, Goshen, NH 03752, Phone: 603-863-1874
Specialties: Collector-quality folders of his design or to customer specs. **Patterns:** Latch release, liner-lock and lock-back folders. **Technical:** Offers limited amount of own Damascus; also uses Damas makers steel. Prefers natural handle material, gold and gems. **Prices:** $500 to $4000. **Remarks:** Full-time maker; first knife sold in 1981. Doing business as Daynia Forge. **Mark:** Sun logo or engraved surname.

ST. CLAIR, THOMAS K., 12608 Fingerboard Rd, Monrovia, MD 21770, Phone: 301-482-0264

ST. AMOUR, MURRAY, RR 3, 222 Dicks Rd, Pembroke ON, CANADA K8A 6W4, Phone: 613-735-1061
Specialties: Working fixed blades. **Patterns:** Hunters, fish, fighters, Bowies and utility knives. **Technical:** Grinds ATS-34, 154-CM, CPM-440V and Damascus. **Prices:** $75 and up. **Remarks:** Full-time maker; sold first knife in 1992. **Mark:** Last name over Canada.

ST. CYR, H. RED, 1218 N Cary Av., Wilmington, CA 90744, Phone: 310-518-9525

SAKAKIBARA, MASAKI, 20-8 Sakuragaoka, 2-Chome Setagaya-ku, Tokyo 156-0054, JAPAN, Phone: 81-3-3420-0375

SAKMAR, MIKE, 2470 Melvin, Rochester, MI 48307, Phone: 248-852-6775, Fax: 248-852-8544
Specialties: Mokume in various patterns and alloy combinations. **Patterns:** Bowies, fighters, hunters and integrals. **Technical:** Grinds ATS-34, Damascus and high-carbon tool steels. Uses mostly natural handle materials—elephant ivory, walrus ivory, stag, wildwood, oosic, etc. Makes mokume for resale. **Prices:** $250 to $2500; some to $4000. **Remarks:** Part-time maker; first knife sold in 1990. **Mark:** Last name. **Other:** Supplier of Mokume.

SALLEY, JOHN D., 3965 Frederick-Ginghamsburg Rd, Tipp City, OH 45371, Phone: 937-698-4588, Fax: 937-698-4131
Specialties: Fancy working knives and art pieces. **Patterns:** Hunters, fighters, daggers and some swords. **Technical:** Grinds ATS-34, 12C27 and W2; buys Damascus. **Prices:** $85 to $1000; some to $6000. **Remarks:** Part-time maker; first knife sold in 1979. **Mark:** First initial, last name.

SAMPSON, LYNN, 381 Deakins Rd, Jonesborough, TN 37659, Phone: 423-348-8373
Specialties: Highly finished working knives, mostly folders. **Patterns:** Locking folders, slip-joints, interframes and two-blades. **Technical:** Grinds D2, 440C and ATS-34; offers extensive filework. **Prices:** Start at $300. **Remarks:** Full-time maker; first knife sold in 1982. **Mark:** Name and city in logo.

SANDERS, A. A., 3850 72 Ave. NE, Norman, OK 73071, Phone: 405-364-8660
Specialties: Working straight knives and folders. **Patterns:** Hunters, fighters, daggers and Bowies. **Technical:** Forges his own Damascus; offers stock removal with ATS-34, 440C, A2, D2, O1, 5160 and 1095. **Prices:** $85 to $1500. **Remarks:** Full-time maker; first knife sold in 1985. Formerly known as Athern Forge. **Mark:** Name.

SANDERS, MICHAEL M., PO Box 1106, Ponchatoula, LA 70454, Phone: 225-294-3601
Specialties: Working straight knives and folders, some deluxe. **Patterns:** Hunters, fighters, Bowies, daggers, large folders and deluxe Damascus miniatures. **Technical:** Grinds O1, D2, 440C, ATS-34 and Damascus. **Prices:** $75 to $650; some higher. **Remarks:** Full-time maker; first knife sold in 1967. **Mark:** Name and state.

SANDERS, BILL, 335 Bauer Ave, PO Box 957, Mancos, CO 81328, Phone: 970-533-7223
Specialties: Working straight knives, some fancy and some fantasy, of his design. **Patterns:** Hunters, boots, utility knives, using belt knives. **Technical:** Grinds 440C, ATS-34 and commercial Damascus. Provides wide variety of handle materials. **Prices:** $170 to $350; some to $800. **Remarks:** Full-time maker. **Mark:** Name, city and state.

SANDERSON, RAY, 4403 Uplands Way, Yakima, WA 98908, Phone: 509-965-0128
Specialties: One-of-a-kind Buck knives; traditional working straight knives and folders of his design. **Patterns:** Bowies, hunters and fighters. **Technical:** Grinds 440C and ATS-34. **Prices:** $200 to $750. **Remarks:** Part-time maker; first knife sold in 1984. **Mark:** Sanderson Knives in shape of Bowie.

SANDLIN, LARRY, 4580 Sunday Dr, Adamsville, AL 35005, Phone: 205-674-1816
Specialties: High-art straight knives of his design. **Patterns:** Boots, daggers, hunters and fighters. **Technical:** Forges 1095, L6, O1, carbon steel and Damascus. **Prices:** $200 to $1500; some to $5000. **Remarks:** Part-time maker; first knife sold in 1990. **Mark:** Chiseled last name in Japanese.

SARVIS, RANDALL J., 110 West park Ave, Fort Pierre, SD 57532, Phone: 605-223-2772

SAWBY, SCOTT, 480 Snowberry Ln, Sandpoint, ID 83864, Phone: 208-263-4171
Specialties: Folders, working and fancy. **Patterns:** Locking folders, patent locking systems and interframes. **Technical:** Grinds D2, 440C, 154CM, CPM-T-440V and ATS-34. **Prices:** $400 to $1000. **Remarks:** Full-time maker; first knife sold in 1974. **Mark:** Last name, city and state.

SCARROW, WIL, c/o L&W Mail Service, 6012 Pearce, Lakewood, CA 90712, Phone: 626-286-6069
Specialties: Carving knives, also working straight knives in standard patterns or to customer specs. **Patterns:** Carving, fishing, hunting, skinning, utility, swords & Bowies. **Technical:** Forges and grinds: A2, L6, D2, 5160, 1095, 440C, AEB-L, ATS-34 and others on request. Offers some filework. **Prices:** $65 to $850; some higher. Prices include sheath (carver's $40 and up). **Remarks:** Spare-time maker; first knife sold in 1983. Two to eight month construction time on custom orders. Doing business as Scarrow's Custom Stuff and Gold Hill Knife works (in Oregon). **Mark:** SC with arrow and date/year made. **Other:** Carving knives available at the 'Wild Duck' Woodcarvers Supply. Contact at duckstore@aol.com

SCHALLER, ANTHONY BRETT, 5609 Flint Ct. NW, Albuquerque, NM 87120, Phone: 505-899-0155
Specialties: Straight knives and locking-liner folders of his design and in standard patterns. **Patterns:** Boots, fighters, utility knives and folders. **Technical:** Grinds ATS-34, BG42 and stainless Damascus. Offers filework, mirror finishes and full and narrow tangs. Prefers exotic woods or Micarta for handle materials. **Prices:** $60 to $350; some to $500. **Remarks:** Part-time maker; first knife sold in 1990. **Mark:** A. B. Schaller - Albuquerque NM - handmade.

custom knifemakers

SCHEID, MAGGIE, 124 Van Stallen St, Rochester, NY 14621-3557
Specialties: Simple working straight knives. **Patterns:** Kitchen and utility knives; some miniatures. **Technical:** Forges 5160 high-carbon steel. **Prices:** $100 to $200. **Remarks:** Part-time maker; first knife sold in 1986. **Mark:** Full name.

SCHEMPP, ED, PO Box 1181, Ephrata, WA 98823, Phone: 509-754-2963, Fax: 509-754-3212
Specialties: Mosaic Damascus and unique folder designs **Patterns:** Primarily folders. **Technical:** Grinds CPM440V; forges many patterns of mosaic using powdered steel. **Prices:** $100 to $400; some to $2000. **Remarks:** Part-time maker; first knife sold in 1991. Doing business as Ed Schempp Knives. **Mark:** Ed Schempp Knives over five heads of wheat, city and state.

SCHEMPP, MARTIN, PO Box 1181, 5430 Baird Springs Rd. N. W., Ephrata, WA 98823, Phone: 509-754-2963, Fax: 509-754-3212
Specialties: Fantasy and traditional straight knives of his design, to customer specs and in standard patterns; Paleolithic-styles. **Patterns:** Fighters and Paleolithic designs. **Technical:** Uses opal, Mexican rainbow and obsidian. Offers scrimshaw. **Prices:** $15 to $100; some to $250. **Remarks:** Spare-time maker; first knife sold in 1995. **Mark:** Initials and date.

SCHEPERS, GEORGE B., PO Box 395, Shelton, NE 68876-0395
Specialties: Fancy period pieces of his design. **Patterns:** Bowies, swords, tomahawks; locking folders and miniatures. **Technical:** Grinds W1, W2 and his own Damascus; etches. **Prices:** $125 to $600; some higher. **Remarks:** Full-time maker; first knife sold in 1981. **Mark:** Schep.

SCHEURER, ALFREDO E. FAES, Av. Rincon de los Arcos 104, Col. Bosque Res. del Sur, C. P. 16010, MEXICO, Phone: 5676 47 63
Specialties: Fancy and fantasy knives of his design. **Patterns:** Daggers. **Technical:** Grinds stainless steel; casts and grinds silver. Sets stones in silver. **Prices:** $2000 to $3000. **Remarks:** Spare-time maker; first knife sold in 1989. **Mark:** Symbol.

SCHILLING, ELLEN, 95 Line Rd, Hamilton Square, NJ 08690, Phone: 609-448-0483

SCHIPPNICK, JIM, PO Box 326, SANBORN, NY 14132, Phone: 716-731-3715
Specialties: Nordic, early American, rustic. **Mark:** Runic R. **Remarks:** Also import Nordic knives from Norway, Sweden & Finland.

SCHIRMER, MIKE, 28 Biltmore Rd, PO Box 534, Twin Bridges, MT 59754, Phone: 406-684-5868
Specialties: Working straight knives of his design or to customer specs; mostly hunters and personal knives. **Patterns:** Hunters, camp, kitchen, Bowies and fighters. **Technical:** Grinds O1, D2, A2 and Damascus and Talonoite. **Prices:** Start at $150. **Remarks:** Full-time maker; first knife sold in 1992. Doing business as Ruby Mountain Knives. **Mark:** Name or name & location.

SCHLOMER, JAMES E., 2543 Wyatt Pl, Kissimmee, FL 34741, Phone: 407-348-8044
Specialties: Working and show straight knives. **Patterns:** Hunters, Bowies and skinners. **Technical:** Stock removal method, 440C. Scrimshaws; carves sambar stag handles. Works on corean and Micarta. **Prices:** $150 to $750. **Remarks:** Full-time maker. **Mark:** Name and steel number.

SCHLUETER, DAVID, PO Box 463, Syracuse, NY 13209, Phone: 315-485-0829
Specialties: Japanese-style swords, handmade fittings, leather wraps. **Patterns:** Kozuka to Tach, blades with bo-hi and o-kissaki. **Technical:** Sole author, forges and grinds, high carbon steels. Blades are tempered after clay-coated and water-quenched heat treatment. All fittings are handmade. **Prices:** $800 to $5000 plus. **Remarks:** Full-time maker, doing business as Odd Frog Forge. **Mark:** Full name and date.

SCHMIDT, RICK, PO Box 1318, Whitefish, MT 59937, Phone: 406-862-6471, Fax: 406-862-6078
Specialties: Traditional working and using straight knives and folders of his design and to customer specs. **Patterns:** Fighters, hunters, cutlery and utility knives. **Technical:** Flat-grinds D2 and ATS-34. Custom leather sheaths. **Prices:** $120 to $250; some to $1900. **Remarks:** Full-time maker; first knife sold in 1975. **Mark:** Stylized initials.

SCHMITZ, RAYMOND E., PO Box 1787, Valley Center, CA 92082, Phone: 760-749-4318

SCHMOKER, RANDY, Spirit of the Hammer, HC 63 BOX 1085, Slana, AK 99586, Phone: 907-822-3371
Specialties: Hand carved, natural materials, mastodon ivory, moose antler. **Patterns:** Hunter, skinner, bowie, fighter, artistic collectables. **Technical:** Hand forged. **Prices:** $300 to $600. **Remarks:** 01 tool steel, 1095, 5160, 52100. **Mark:** Sheep with an S. **Other:** Custom sheaths, display stands.

SCHNEIDER, KARL A., 209 N. Brownleaf Rd, Newark, DE 19713, Phone: 302-737-0277
Specialties: Traditional working and using straight knives of his design. **Patterns:** Hunters, kitchen and fillet knives. **Technical:** Grinds ATS-34. Shapes handles to fit hands; uses Micarta, Pakkawood and exotic woods. Makes hand-stitched leather cases. **Prices:** $95 to $225. **Remarks:** Part-time maker; first knife sold in 1984-85. **Mark:** Name, address; also name in shape of fish.

SCHNEIDER, CRAIG M., 285 County Rd. 1400 N., Seymour, IL 61875, Phone: 217-687-2651
Specialties: Straight knives of my own design. **Patterns:** Bowies & hunters. **Technical:** Stock removal stainless and forged high carbon steels & Damascus. Uses a wide selection of handle materials and various guard and boster material **Prices:** $75 to $2000. **Remarks:** Part-time maker; first knife sold in 1985. **Mark:** Stylized initials.

SCHOEMAN, CORRIE, Box 28596, Danhof 9310, SOUTH AFRICA, Phone: 027 51 4363528 Cell: 027 82-3750789
Specialties: High-tech folders of his design or to customer's specs. **Patterns:** Linerlock folders and automatics. **Technical:** ATS-34, Damascus or stainless Damascus with titanium frames; prefers exotic materials for handles. **Prices:** $500 to $2000. **Remarks:** Full-time maker; first knife sold in 1984. **Mark:** Logo in knife shape engraved on inside of back bar. **Other:** All folders come with filed liners and back and jewled inserts.

SCHOENFELD, MATTHEW A., RR #1, Galiano Island, B. C., CANADA V0N 1P0, Phone: 250-539-2806
Specialties: Working knives of his design. **Patterns:** Kitchen cutlery, camp knives, hunters. **Technical:** Grinds 440C. **Prices:** $85 to $500. **Remarks:** Part-time maker; first knife sold in 1978. **Mark:** Signature, Galiano Is. B. C., and date.

SCHOENINGH, MIKE, 49850 Miller Rd, North Powder, OR 97867, Phone: 541-856-3239

SCHOLL, TIM, 1389 Langdon Rd, Angier, NC 27501, Phone: 910-897-2051, Fax: 910-897-4742
Specialties: Fancy and working/using straight knives and folders of his design and to customer specs. **Patterns:** tomahawks, swords, tantos, hunters and fantasy knives. **Technical:** Grinds ATS-34 & D2; forges carbon and tool steel and Damascus. Offers filework, engraving and scrimshaw. **Prices:** $85; some to $3000. **Remarks:** Full-time maker; first knife sold in 1990. Doing business as Tim Scholl Custom Knives. **Mark:** Last name or last initial with arrow.

SCHRADER, ROBERT, 55532 Gross De, Bend, OR 97707, Phone: 541-385-3259

SCHRAP, ROBERT G., Custom Leather Knife Sheath Co, 7024 W. Wells St, Wauwatosa, WI 53213-3717, Phone: 414-771-6472, Fax: 414-479-9765
Specialties: Leatherwork. **Prices:** $35 to $100. **Mark:** Schrap in oval.

SCHROEN, KARL, 4042 Bones Rd, Sebastopol, CA 95472, Phone: 707-823-4057, Fax: 707-823-2914
Specialties: Using knives made to fit. **Patterns:** Sgian dubhs, carving sets, wood-carving knives, fishing knives, kitchen knives and new cleaver design. **Technical:** Forges A2, ATS-34,D2 and L-6 cruwear S30V 590V. **Prices:** $150 to $6000. **Remarks:** Full-time maker; first knife sold in 1968. Author of *The Hand Forged Knife.* **Mark:** Last name.

SCHULTZ, ROBERT W., PO Box 70, Cocolalla, ID 83813-0070

SCHWARZER, STEPHEN, PO Box 4, Pomona Park, FL 32181, Phone: 386-649-5026, Fax: 386-649-8585
Specialties: Mosaic Damascus & picture mosaic in folding knives. **Patterns:** Folders, axes and buckskinner knives. **Technical:** Specializes in picture mosaic Damascus and powder metal mosaic work. Sole authorship; all work including carving done in-house. Most knives have file work & carving. **Prices:** $1500 to $5000; some higher; carbon steel & primitive knives much less. **Remarks:** Full-time maker; first knife sold in 1976, considered by many to be one of the top mosaic Damascus specialists in the world. Mosaic Master level work. **Mark:** Schwarzer + anvil.

SCIMIO, BILL, HC 01 Box 24A, Spruce Creek, PA 16683, Phone: 814-632-3751

SCOFIELD, EVERETT, 2873 Glass Mill Rd, Chickamauga, GA 30707, Phone: 706-375-2790
Specialties: Historic and fantasy miniatures. **Patterns:** All patterns. **Technical:** Uses only the finest tool steels and other materials. Uses only natural, precious and semi-precious materials. **Prices:** $100 to $1500. **Remarks:** Full-time maker; first knife sold in 1971. Doing business as Three Crowns Cutlery. **Mark:** Three Crowns logo.

SCORDIA, PAOLO, Via Terralba 143, 00050 Torrimpietra, ROMA, ITALY, Phone: 06-61697231
Specialties: Working and using knives of my own design. **Patterns:** Any pattern. **Technical:** I forge my own Damascus and grind ATS-34, 420C, 440C; use hardwoods & Micarta for handles, brass & nickel-silver for fittings. Makes sheaths. **Prices:** $80 to $500. **Remarks:** Part-time maker; first knife sold in 1988. **Mark:** Initials with sun and moon logo.

SCOTT, AL, 2245 Harper Valley Rd, Harper, TX 78631, Phone: 830-864-4182
Specialties: High-art straight knives of his design. **Patterns:** Daggers, swords, early European, Middle East and Japanese knives. **Technical:** Uses ATS-34, 440C and Damascus. Hand engraves; does file work cuts filigree in the blade; offers ivory carving and precious metal inlay. **Remarks:** Full-time maker; first knife sold in 1994. Doing business as Al Scott Maker of Fine Blade Art. **Mark:** Name engraved in old English, sometime inlaid in 24K gold.

SCRIMSHAW BY LYNN BENADE, 2610 Buckhurst Dr, Beachwood, OH 44122, Phone: 216-464-0777

SCROGGS, JAMES A., 108 Murray Hill Dr, Warrensburg, MO 64093, Phone: 660-747-2568
Specialties: Straight knives, prefers light weight. **Patterns:** Hunters, hide-outs, and fighters. **Technical:** Grinds 5160, 01, and 52-100. Prefers handles of walnut in English, bastonge, American black Also uses myrtle, maple, Osage orange. **Prices:** $200-$1000. **Remarks:** 1st knife sold in 1985. Part-time maker, no orders taken. **Mark:** SCROGGS in block or script.

SCULLEY, PETER E., 340 Sunset Dr, Rising Fawn, GA 30738, Phone: 706-398-0169

SEARS, MICK, 1697 Peach Orchard Rd. #302, Sumter, SC 29154, Phone: 803-499-5074
Specialties: Scots and confederate reproductions; Bowies and fighters. **Patterns:** Bowies, fighters. **Technical:** Grinds 440C and 1095. **Prices:** $50 to $150; some to $300. **Remarks:** Part-time maker; first knife sold in 1975. Doing business as Mick's Custom Knives. **Mark:** First name.

SELENT, CHUCK, PO Box 1207, Bonners Ferry, ID 83805-1207, Phone: 208-267-5807
Specialties: Period, art and fantasy miniatures; exotics; one-of-a-kinds. **Patterns:** Swords, daggers and others. **Technical:** Works in Damascus, meteorite, 440C and tool steel. Offers scrimshaw. Offers his own casting and leatherwork; uses jewelry techniques. Makes display cases for miniatures. **Prices:** $75 to $400. **Remarks:** Part-time maker; first knife sold in 1990. **Mark:** Last name and bear paw print logo scrimshawed on handles or leatherwork.

SELF, ERNIE, 950 O'Neill Ranch Rd, Dripping Springs, TX 78620-9760, Phone: 512-858-7133, Fax: 512-858-9363
Specialties: Traditional and working straight knives and folders of his design and in standard patterns. **Patterns:** Hunters, locking folders and slip-joints. **Technical:** Grinds 440C, D2, 440V, ATS-34 and Damascus. Offers fancy filework. **Prices:** $125 to $500; some to $1500. **Remarks:** Full-time maker; first knife sold in 1982. **Mark:** In oval shape - Ernie Self Maker Dripping Springs TX. **Other:** I also customize Buck 110's and 112's folding knives.

SELLEVOLD, HARALD, S. Kleivesmau: 2, PO Box 4134, N5834 Bergen, NORWAY, Phone: 55-310682
Specialties: Norwegian-styles; collaborates with other Norse craftsmen. **Patterns:** Distinctive ferrules and other mild modifications of traditional patterns; Bowies and friction folders. **Technical:** Buys Damascus blades; blacksmiths his own blades. Semi-gemstones used in handles; gemstone inlay. **Prices:** $350 to $2000. **Remarks:** Full-time maker; first knife sold in 1980. **Mark:** Name and country in logo.

SELVIDIO, RALPH, PO Box 1464, Crystal River, FL 34423, Phone: 352-628-1883
Specialties: Collector grade folders with unique mechanisms. **Patterns:** Locking folders. **Technical:** Grinds Damascus. **Prices:** $1000 to $6000. **Remarks:** Full-time maker; first knife sold in 1986. **Mark:** Rattler. **Other:** Doing business as Rattler brand Knives.

SELZAM, FRANK, Martin Reinhard Str 23, 97631, Bad Koenigshofen, GERMANY, Phone: 09761-5980
Specialties: Hunters, working knives to customers specs, hand tooled & stitched leather sheaths large stock of wood and German stag horn. **Patterns:** Mostly own design. **Technical:** Forged blades, own Damascus, also stock removal stainless. **Prices:** $250 - $1500. **Remark:** First knife sold in 1978. **Mark:** Last name stamped.

SENTZ, MARK C., 4084 Baptist Rd, Taneytown, MD 21787, Phone: 410-756-2018
Specialties: Fancy straight working knives of his design. **Patterns:** Hunters, fighters, folders and utility/camp knives. **Technical:** Forges 1085,

1095, 5160, 5155 and his Damascus. Most knives come with wood-lined leather sheath or wooden presentation sheath. **Prices:** Start at $275. **Remarks:** Full-time maker; first knife sold in 1989. Doing business as M. Charles Sentz Gunsmithing, Inc. **Mark:** Last name.

SERAFEN, STEVEN E., 24 Genesee St, New Berlin, NY 13411, Phone: 607-847-6903
Specialties: Traditional working/using straight knives of his design and to customer specs. **Patterns:** Bowies, fighters, hunters. **Technical:** Grinds ATS-34, 440C, high-carbon steel. **Prices:** $175 to $600; some to $1200. **Remarks:** Part-time maker; first knife sold in 1990. **Mark:** First and middle initial, last name in script.

SERVEN, JIM, PO Box 1, Fostoria, MI 48435, Phone: 517-795-2255
Specialties: Highly finished unique folders. **Patterns:** Fancy working folders, axes, miniatures and razors; some straight knives. **Technical:** Grinds 440C; forges his own Damascus. **Prices:** $150 to $800; some to $1500. **Remarks:** Full-time maker; first knife sold in 1971. **Mark:** Name in map logo.

SEVEY CUSTOM KNIFE, 94595 Chandler Rd, Gold Beach, OR 97450, Phone: 541-247-2649
Specialties: Fixed blade hunters. **Patterns:** Drop point, trailing paint, clip paint, full tang, hidden tang. **Technical:** D-2, & ATS-34 blades, stock removal. Heat treatment by Paul Bos. **Prices:** $225 and up depending on overall length & grip material. **Mark:** Sevey Custom Knife.

SFREDDO, RODRITO MENEZES, Rua 15 De Novembro 2222, Nova Petropolis, RS, BRASIL 95150-000, Phone: 011-55-54-303-303-90
Specialties: Traditional Brazilian-style working and high-art knives of his design. **Patterns:** Fighters, Bowies, utility and camp knives, classic Mediterranean Dirk. Welcome customer design. **Technical:** Forges only with sledge hammers (no power hammer here) 100% to shape in 52100 and his own Damascus. Makes own sheaths in the true traditional Brazilian-style. **Remark:** Full-time maker. **Prices:** $250 to $1100 for his elaborate Mediterranean Dirk. Uses only natural handle materials. Considered by many to be Brazil's best bladesmith.

SHADLEY, EUGENE W., 26315 Norway Dr, Bovey, MN 55709, Phone: 218-245-3820, Fax: 218-245-1639
Specialties: Classic multi-blade folders. **Patterns:** Whittlers, stockman, sowbelly, congress, trapper, etc. **Technical:** Grinds ATS-34, 416 frames. **Prices:** Start at $300. **Remarks:** Full-time maker; first knife sold in 1985. Doing business as Shadley Knives. **Mark:** Last name.

SHADMOT, BOAZ, Moshav Paran D N, Arava, ISRAEL 86835

SHARRIGAN, MUDD, 111 Bradford Rd, Wiscasset, ME 04578-4457, Phone: 207-882-9820, Fax: 207-882-9835
Specialties: Wood carvers knives, custom designs, seaman's knives; repair straight knives, handles and blades on heirloom pieces; custom leather sheaths. **Patterns:** Daggers, fighters, hunters, buckskinner, Indian crooked knives and seamen working knives; traditional Scandinavian-styles. **Technical:** Forges 1095, O1. Laminates 1095 and mild steel. **Prices:** $50 to $325; some to $1200. **Remarks:** Full-time maker; first knife sold in 1982. **Mark:** First name and swallow tail carving.

SHAVER II, JAMES R., 1529 Spider Ridge Rd, Parkersburg, WV 26104, Phone: 304-422-2692
Specialties: Hunting and working straight knives in carbon and Damascus steel. **Patterns:** Bowies and daggers in Damascus and carbon steels. **Technical:** Forges 5160 carbon and Damascus in O101018 mild steel and pvee nickel. **Prices:** $85 to $225 some to $750. **Remarks:** Part-time maker; sold first knife in 1998. Believes in sole authorship. **Mark:** Last name.

SHEEHY, THOMAS J., 4131 NE 24th Ave, Portland, OR 97211-6411, Phone: 503-493-2843
Specialties: Hunting knives and ULUs. **Patterns:** Own or customer designs. **Technical:** 1095/01 and ATS-34 steel. **Prices:** $35 to $200. **Remarks:** Do own heat treating; forged or ground blades. **Mark:** Name.

SHEETS, STEVEN WILLIAM, 6 Stonehouse Rd, Mendham, NJ 07945, Phone: 201-543-5882

SHELTON, PAUL S., 1406 Holloway, Rolla, MO 65401, Phone: 314-364-3151
Specialties: Fancy working straight knives of his design or to customer specs. **Patterns:** All types from camp knives to miniatures, except folders. **Technical:** Grinds ATS-34 and commercial Damascus. Offers filework, texturing, natural handle materials and exotic leather sheaths. **Prices:** Start at $100. **Remarks:** Part-time maker; first knife sold in 1984. **Mark:** Last name and serial number.

SHIKAYAMA, TOSHIAKI, 259-2 Suka Yoshikawa City, Saitama 342-0057, JAPAN, Phone: 04-89-81-6605, Fax: 04-89-81-6605
Specialties: Folders in standard patterns. **Patterns:** Locking and multi-blade folders. **Technical:** Grinds ATS, carbon steel, high speed steel.

custom knifemakers

Prices: $400 to $2500; $4500 with engraving. **Remarks:** Full-time maker; first knife sold in 1952. **Mark:** First initial, last name.

SHINOSKY, ANDY, 3117 Meanderwood Dr, Canfield, OH 44406, Phone: 330-702-0299
Specialties: Collectible fancy folders and interframes. **Patterns:** Drop points, trailing points and daggers. **Technical:** Grinds ATS-34 and Damascus. Prefers natural handle materials. **Prices:** Start at $450. **Remarks:** Part-time maker; first knife sold in 1992. **Mark:** Name or bent folder logo.

SHIPLEY, STEVEN A., 800 E Campbell Rd Ste 137, Richardson, TX 75081, Phone: 972-644-7981, Fax: 972-644-7985
Specialties: Hunters, skinners and traditional straight knives. **Technical:** Hand grinds ATS-34, 440C and Damascus steels. Each knife is custom sheathed by my son, Dan. **Prices:** $175 to $2000. **Remarks:** Part-time maker; like smooth lines and unusual handle materials. **Mark:** S A Shipley.

SHOEBOTHAM, HEATHER, Heather's Blacksmith Shop, POB 768, Belfast 1100, SOUTH AFRICA, Phone: +27 11 496 1600, Fax: +27 11 835 2932
Specialties: All steel hand forged knives of my own design. **Patterns:** Traditional African weapons, friction folders and by-gone forged styles. **Technical:** Own Damascus, specializing in drive chain and steel wire rope, Meteorite, 420 & Mokume. Also using forged brass, copper and titanium fittings. All work hand-forged using a traditional coal fire. Differential heat-treatment used. **Prices:** $150 to $3000. **Remarks:** Full-time practicing blacksmith and furrier and part-time bladesmith. First Damascus sold in 1995. First knife sold in 1998. Member of ABS. **Mark:** Knives: Rearing unicorn in horseshoe surrounded with first name. Damascus: Sold under "Damsel Damascus".

SHOEMAKER, SCOTT, 316 S. Main St, Miamisburg, OH 45342, Phone: 513-859-1935
Specialties: Twisted, wire-wrapped handles on swords, fighters and fantasy blades; new line of seven models with quick-draw, multi-carry Kydex sheaths. **Patterns:** Bowies, boots and one-of-a-kinds in his design or to customer specs. **Technical:** Grinds A6 and ATS-34; buys Damascus. Hand satin finish is standard. **Prices:** $100 to $1500; swords to $8000. **Remarks:** Part-time maker; first knife sold in 1984. **Mark:** Angel wings with last initial, or last name.

SHOEMAKER, CARROLL, 380 Yellowtown Rd, Northup, OH 45658, Phone: 740-446-6695
Specialties: Working/using straight knives of his design. **Patterns:** Hunters, utility/camp and early American backwoodsmen knives. **Technical:** Grinds ATS-34; forges old files, O1 and 1095. Uses some Damascus; offers scrimshaw and engraving. **Prices:** $100 to $175; some to $350. **Remarks:** Spare-time maker; first knife sold in 1977. **Mark:** Name and city or connected initials.

SHOGER, MARK O., 14780 SW Osprey Dr, Suite 345, Beaverton, OR 97007, Phone: 503-579-2495
Specialties: Working and using straight knives and folders of his design; fancy and embellished knives. **Patterns:** Hunters, Bowies, daggers and locking folders. **Technical:** Forges O1, W2 and his own pattern-welded Damascus. **Remarks:** Spare-time maker. **Mark:** Last name or stamped last initial over anvil.

SHORE, JOHN I., Alaska Knifemaker, 2901 Sheldon Jackson St, Anchorage, AK 99508, Phone: 907-272-2253
Specialties: Working straight knives, hatchets, and folders. **Patterns:** Hunters, skinners, Bowies, fighters, working using knives. **Technical:** Prefer using exotic steels, grinds most CPM's, Damasteel, RWL34, BG42, D2 and some ATS-34. Prefers exotic hardwoods, stabilized materials, Micarta, and Pearl. **Prices:** Start at $200. **Remarks:** Full-time maker; first knife sold in 1985. **Mark:** Name in script, Anchorage, AK.

SHOSTLE, BEN, 1121 Burlington, Muncie, IN 47302, Phone: 765-282-9073, Fax: 765-282-5270
Specialties: Fancy high-art straight knives of his design. **Patterns:** Bowies, daggers and fighters. **Technical:** Uses 440C, ATS-34 and commercial Damascus. All knives and engraved. **Prices:** $900 to $3200; some to $4000. **Remarks:** Full-time maker; first knife sold in 1987. Doing business as The Gun Room (T. G. R.). **Mark:** Last name.

SIBRIAN, AARON, 4308 Dean Dr, Ventura, CA 93003, Phone: 805-642-6950
Specialties: Tough working knives of his design and in standard patterns. **Patterns:** Makes a "Viper utility"—a kukri derivative and a variety of straight using knives. **Technical:** Grinds 440C and ATS-34. Offers traditional Japanese blades; soft backs, hard edges, temper lines. **Prices:** $60 to $100; some to $250. **Remarks:** Spare-time maker; first knife sold in 1989. **Mark:** Initials in diagonal line.

SIGMAN, CORBET R., Rt. 1, Box 260, Liberty, WV 25124, Phone: 304-586-9131
Specialties: Collectible working straight knives and folders. **Patterns:** Hunters, fighters, boots, camp knives and exotics such as sgian dubhs—

distinctly Sigman lines; folders. **Technical:** Grinds D2, 154CM, plain carbon tool steel and ATS-34. **Prices:** $60 to $800; some to $4000. **Remarks:** Full-time maker; first knife sold in 1970. **Mark:** Name or initials.

SIGMAN, JAMES P., 10391 Church Rd, North Adams, MI 49262, Phone: 517-523-3028
Specialties: High-tech working knives of his design. **Patterns:** Daggers, hunters, fighters and folders. **Technical:** Forges and grinds L6, O1, W2 and his Damascus. **Prices:** $150 to $750. **Remarks:** Part-time maker; first knife sold in 1982. **Mark:** Sig or Sig Forge.

SIMMONS, H. R., 1100 Bay City Road, Aurora, NC 27806, Phone: 252-322-5969
Specialties: Working/using straight knives of his design. **Patterns:** Fighters, hunters and utility/camp knives. **Technical:** Forges and grinds Damascus and L6; grinds ATS-34. **Prices:** $150 to $250; some to $400. **Remarks:** Part-time maker; first knife sold in 1987. Doing business as HRS Custom Knives, Royal Forge & Trading Company. **Mark:** Initials.

SIMONELLA, GIANLUIGI, 15, via Rosa Brustolo, 33085 Maniago, ITALY, Phone: 01139-427-730350
Specialties: Traditional and classic folding and working/using knives of his design and to customer specs. **Patterns:** Bowies, fighters, hunters, utility/camp knives. **Technical:** Forges ATS-34, D2, 440C. **Prices:** $250 to $400; some to $1000. **Remarks:** Full-time maker; first knife sold in 1988. **Mark:** Wilson.

SIMONICH, ROB, PO Box 278, Clancy, MT 59634, Phone: 406-933-8274
Specialties: Working knives in standard patterns. **Patterns:** Hunters, combat knives, Bowies and small fancy knives. **Technical:** Grinds D2, ATS-34 and 440C; forges own cable Damascus. Offers filework on most knives. **Prices:** $75 to $300; some to $1000. **Remarks:** Spare-time maker; first knife sold in 1984. Not currently taking orders. **Mark:** Last name in buffalo logo.

SIMONS, BILL, 6217 Michael Ln., Lakeland, FL 33811, Phone: 863-646-3783
Specialties: Working folders. **Patterns:** Locking folders, liner-locks, hunters, slip joints most patterns; some straight camp knives. **Technical:** Grinds D2, ATS-34 and O1. **Prices:** Start at $100. **Remarks:** Full-time maker; first knife sold in 1970. **Mark:** Last name.

SIMS, BOB, PO Box 772, Meridian, TX 76665, Phone: 254-435-6240
Specialties: Traditional working straight knives and folders in standard patterns; banana/sheep foot blade combinations in trapper patterns. **Patterns:** Locking folders, slip-joint folders and hunters. **Technical:** Grinds D2, ATS-34 and O1. Offers filework on some knives. **Prices:** $150 to $275; some to $600. **Remarks:** Part-time maker; first knife sold in 1975. **Mark:** The division sign.

SINCLAIR, J. E., 520 Francis Rd, Pittsburgh, PA 15239, Phone: 412-793-5778
Specialties: Fancy hunters & fighters, liner-locking folders. **Patterns:** Fighters, hunters and folders. **Technical:** Flat-grinds & hollow grind, prefers hand rubbed satin finish. Uses natural handle materials. **Prices:** $185 to $800. **Remarks:** Part-time maker; first knife sold in 1995. **Mark:** First and middle initials, last name and maker.

SINYARD, CLESTON S., 27522 Burkhardt Dr, Elberta, AL 36530, Phone: 334-987-1361
Specialties: Working straight knives and folders of his design. **Patterns:** Hunters, buckskinners, Bowies, daggers, fighters and all-Damascus folders. **Technical:** Makes Damascus from 440C, stainless steels, D2 and regular high-carbon steel; forges "forefinger pad" into hunters and skinners. **Prices:** In Damascus $450 to $1500; some $2500. **Remarks:** Full-time maker; first knife sold in 1980. Doing business as Nimo Forge. **Mark:** Last name, U. S. A. in anvil.

SISEMORE, CHARLES RUSSEL, RR 2 Box 329AL, Mena, AR 71953, Phone: 918-383-1360

SISKA, JIM, 6 Highland Ave, Westfield, MA 01085, Phone: 413-568-9787, Fax: 413-568-6341
Specialties: Traditional working straight knives and folders. **Patterns:** Hunters, fighters, Bowies and one-of-a-kinds; folders. **Technical:** Grinds D2 and ATS-34; buys Damascus. Likes exotic woods. **Prices:** $195 to $2500. **Remarks:** Part-time maker; first knife sold in 1983. **Mark:** Last name in Old English.

SJOSTRAND, KEVIN, 1541 S. Cain St, Visalia, CA 93292, Phone: 209-625-5254
Specialties: Traditional and working/using straight knives and folders of his design or to customer specs. **Patterns:** Bowies, hunters, utility/camp knives, lock-back, springbuck and liner-lock folders. **Technical:** Grinds ATS-34, 440C and 1095. Prefers high polished blades and full tang. Natural and stabilized hardwoods, Micarta and stag handle material. **Prices:** $75 to $300. **Remarks:** Part-time maker; first knife sold in 1992. Doing

business as Black Oak Blades. **Mark:** Oak tree, Black Oak Blades, name, or just last name.

SKOW, H. A. "TEX", Tex Custom Knives, 3534 Gravel Springs Rd, Senatobia, MS 38668, Phone: 662-301-1568
Specialties: One-of-a-kind daggers, Bowies, boot knives & hunters. **Patterns:** Different Damascus patterns (By Bob Eggerling). **Technical:** 440C, 58, 60 Rockwell hardness. **Prices:** Negotiable. **Remarks:** 30 hunters, 10 collector knives per year. **Mark:** TEX.

SLEE, FRED, 9 John St, Morganville, NJ 07751, Phone: 908-591-9047
Specialties: Working straight knives, some fancy, to customer specs. **Patterns:** Hunters, fighters, boots, fancy daggers and folders. **Technical:** Grinds D2, 440C and ATS-34. **Prices:** $125 to $550. **Remarks:** Part-time maker; first knife sold in 1980. **Mark:** Last name in old English.

SLOAN, SHANE, 4226 FM 61, Newcastle, TX 76372, Phone: 940-846-3290
Specialties: Collector-grade straight knives and folders. **Patterns:** I use stainless Damascus, ATS-34 and 12-C-27. Bowies, lockers, slip-joints, fancy folders, fighters and period pieces. **Technical:** Grinds D2 and ATS-34. Uses hand-rubbed satin finish. Prefers rare natural handle materials. **Prices:** $250 to $6500. **Remarks:** Full-time maker; first knife sold in 1985. **Mark:** Name and city.

SLOBODIAN, SCOTT, 4101 River Ridge Dr, PO Box 1498, San Andreas, CA 95249, Phone: 209-286-1980, Fax: 209-286-1982
Specialties: Japanese-style knives and swords, period pieces, fantasy pieces and miniatures. **Patterns:** Small kweikens, tantos, wakazashis, katanas, traditional samurai swords. **Technical:** Flat-grinds 1050, commercial Damascus. **Prices:** $800 to $3500; some to $7500. **Remarks:** Full-time maker; first knife sold in 1987. **Mark:** Blade signed in Japanese characters and various scripts.

SMALE, CHARLES J., 509 Grove Ave, Waukegan, IL 60085, Phone: 847-244-8013

SMALL, ED, Rt. 1, Box 178-A, Keyser, WV 26726, Phone: 304-298-4254
Specialties: Working knives of his design; period pieces. **Patterns:** Hunters, daggers, buckskinners and camp knives; likes one-of-a-kinds. **Technical:** Forges and grinds W2, L6 and his own Damascus. **Prices:** $150 to $1500. **Remarks:** Full-time maker; first knife sold in 1978. Doing business as Iron Mountain Forge Works. **Mark:** Script initials connected.

SMALLWOOD, WAYNE, 146 Poplar Dr, Kalispell, MT 59901

SMART, STEVE, 1 Meadowbrook Cir., Melissa, TX 75454, Phone: 214-837-4216, Fax: 214-837-4111
Specialties: Working/using straight knives and folders of his design, to customer specs and in standard patterns. **Patterns:** Bowies, hunters, kitchen knives, locking folders, utility/camp, fishing and bird knives. **Technical:** Grinds ATS-34, D2, 440C and O1. Prefers mirror polish or satin finish; hollow-grinds all blades. All knives come with sheath. Offers some filework. **Prices:** $95 to $225; some to $500. **Remarks:** Spare-time maker; first knife sold in 1983. **Mark:** Name, Custom, city and state in oval.

SMART, STEATEN, 15815 Acorn Circle, Tavares, FL 32778, Phone: 352-343-8423

SMIT, CORN, PO Box 31, Darwendale, Zimbabwe, SOUTH AFRICA, Phone: 110-263-69-3107
Specialties: Working/using knives, custom made collectors knives. Your design and customer specs. **Patterns:** Daggers, Bowies, hunters, and exclusive one off designs. **Technical:** Grind 440C stainless and D-2. We photo etch animals, names, logos, etc. on the blades. We do gold plating of etches and scrimshaw on handles. Guards can be brass or sterling sclens or horn. Handles indigenous wood or horns. **Prices:** $150 to $1000; some to $5000. **Remarks:** Full-time maker; first knife sold in 1984. We give a limited lifetime guarantee. **Mark:** Blacksmith - Zimbabwe with SMIT underneath.

SMIT, GLENN, 627 Cindy Ct, Aberdeen, MD 21001, Phone: 410-272-2959
Specialties: Working and using straight and folding knives of his design or to customer specs. Customizes and repairs all types of cutlery. Exclusive maker of Dave Murphy-style knives. **Patterns:** Hunters, Bowies, daggers, fighters, utility/camp, folders, kitchen knives and miniatures, Murphy combat, C. H. A. I. K., Little 88 and Tiny 90-styles. **Technical:** Grinds 440C, ATS-34, O1, A2 also grinds 6AL4V titanium allox for blades. Reforges commercial Damascus and makes own Damascus, cast aluminum handles. **Prices:** Miniatures start at $20; full-size knives start at $40. **Remarks:** Spare-time maker; first knife sold in 1986. Doing business as Wolf's Knives. **Mark:** G. P. SMIT, with year on reverse side, Wolf's knives-Murphy's way with date.

SMITH, J. D., 516 E. Second St, No. 38, S. Boston, MA 02127, Phone: 617-828-4293
Specialties: Fighters, Bowies, Persian, locking folders & swords. **Patterns:** Bowies, fighters and locking folders. **Technical:** Forges and grinds D2, his Damascus, O1, 52100 etc. and wootz-pattern hammer steel. **Prices:** $500 to $2000; some to $5000. **Remarks:** Full-time maker; first knife sold in 1987. Doing business as Hammersmith. **Mark:** Last initial alone or in cartouche.

SMITH, RICK, Bear Bone Knife Works, 1843 W Evans Creek Rd, Rogue River, OR 97537, Phone: 541-582-4144, Fax: 541-582-4151
Specialties: Classic, historical-style Bowies for re-enactors and custom sheaths. **Patterns:** Historical-style Bowies, varied contemporary knife styles. **Technical:** Mostly made by stock removal method; also forge weld tri-cable Damascus blades. Do own heat treating & tempering using an even heat digital kiln. Preferred steels are ATS-34, 154CM, 5160, D-2, 1095 and 01 tool & various carbon Damascus. **Prices:** $250 to $1000. **Remarks:** Full-time maker since 1997 Now forging random pattern Damascus up to 600 layers. Discontinued using BG42 steel. Serial numbers now appear under log. Damascus knives are not given a serial number. **Mark:** "Bear Bone" over initials "R S" (separated by downward arrow) on blade; initials R S (separated by downward arrow) within a 3/8" circle; 2 shooting stars & a Bowie. Serial numbers appear on ricasso area of blade unless otherwise requested.

SMITH, LENARD C., PO Box D68, Valley Cottage, NY 10989, Phone: 914-268-7359

SMITH, JOHN M., 3450 E Beguelin Rd, Centralia, IL 62801, Phone: 618-249-6444, Fax: 618-249-6444
Specialties: Traditional work knives, art knives. **Patterns:** daggers, Bowies, folders. **Technical:** Forges Damascus & hi-carbon. Also uses stainless. **Prices:** $250 to $2500. **Remarks:** Full-time maker; first knife sold in 1980. **Mark:** Etched signature or logo.

SMITH, JOHN W., 1322 Cow Branch Rd, West Liberty, KY 41472, Phone: 606-743-3599
Specialties: Fancy and working locking folders of his design or to customer specs. **Patterns:** Interframes, traditional and daggers. **Technical:** Grinds 530V and my own Damascus. Offers gold inlay, engraving with gold inlay, hand-fitted mosaic pearl inlay and filework. Prefers hand-rubbed finish. Pearl and ivory available. **Prices:** Utility pieces $375-$650. Art knives $1200 to $10,000 **Remarks:** Full-time maker. **Mark:** Initials engraved inside diamond.

SMITH, W. M., 802 W. Hwy. 90, Bonifay, FL 32425, Phone: 904-547-5935

SMITH, RAYMOND L., 217 Red Chalk Rd, Erin, NY 14838, Phone: 607-795-5257
Specialties: Working/using straight knives and folders to customer specs and in standard patterns; period pieces. **Patterns:** Bowies, hunters, slip-joints. **Technical:** Forges 5160, 52100, 1018 Damascus and wire cable Damascus. Filework. **Prices:** $75 to $750; estimates for custom orders. **Remarks:** Part-time maker; first knife sold in 1991. ABS Master Smith. Doing business as The Anvils Edge. **Mark:** Initials in script.

SMITH, NEWMAN L., 676 Glades Rd, Shop #3, Gatlinburg, TN 37738, Phone: 423-436-3322
Specialties: Collector-grade and working knives. **Patterns:** Hunters, slip-joint and lock-back folders, some miniatures. **Technical:** Grinds O1 and ATS-34; makes fancy sheaths. **Prices:** $110 to $450; some to $1000. **Remarks:** Full-time maker; first knife sold in 1984. Partners part-time to handle Damascus blades by Jeff Hurst; marks these with SH connected. **Mark:** First and middle initials, last name.

SMITH, JOSH, Box 753, Frenchtown, MT 59834, Phone: 406-626-5775
Specialties: Mosaic, Damascus, liner-lock folders, Bowies, fighters,etc. **Patterns:** Bowies, designs and folders. **Technical:** Advanced Mosaic and Damascus. **Prices:** $450-$3000. **Mark:** JOSH. **Other:** A. B. S. Mastersmith.

SMITH, GREGORY H., 8607 Coddington Ct, Louisville, KY 40299, Phone: 502-491-7439
Specialties: Traditional working straight knives and fantasy knives to customer specs. **Patterns:** Fighters and modified Bowies; camp knives and swords. **Technical:** Grinds O1, 440C and commercial Damascus bars. **Prices:** $55 to $300. **Remarks:** Part-time maker; first knife sold in 1985. **Mark:** JAGED, plus signature.

SMITH, D. NOEL, 12018 NE Lonetree Ct, Poulsbo, WA 98370, Phone: 360-697-6992
Specialties: Fantasy art knives of his own design or to standard patterns. **Patterns:** Daggers, hunters and art knives. **Technical:** Grinds O1, D2, 440C stainless and Damascus. Offers natural and synthetic carved handles, engraved and acid etched blades, sculptured guards, butt caps and

custom knifemakers

bases. **Prices:** Start at $250. **Remarks:** Full-time maker; first knife sold in 1990. Doing business as Minds' Eye Metal master. **Mark:** Signature.

SMITH, BOBBIE D., 802 W. Hwy. 90., Bonifay, FL 32425, Phone: 904-547-5935
Specialties: Working straight knives and folders. **Patterns:** Bowies, hunters and slip-joints. **Technical:** Grinds 440C and ATS-34; custom sheaths for each knife. **Prices:** $75 to $250. **Remarks:** Part-time maker. **Mark:** NA.

SMITH, MICHAEL J., 1418 Saddle Gold Ct, Brandon, FL 33511, Phone: 813-431-3790
Specialties: Fancy high art folders of his design. **Patterns:** Locking locks and automatics. **Technical:** Uses ATS-34, non-stainless & stainless Damascus; hand carves folders, prefers ivory & pearl. Hand-rubbed satin finish. Liners are 6AL4V titanium. **Prices:** $500 to $3000. **Remarks:** Full-time maker; first knife sold in 1989. **Mark:** Name, city, state.

SMITH JR., JAMES B. "RED", Rt. 2, Box 1525, Morven, GA 31638, Phone: 912-775-2844
Specialties: Folders. **Patterns:** Rotating rear-lock folders. **Technical:** Grinds ATS-34, D2 and Vascomax 350. **Prices:** Start at $350. **Remarks:** Full-time maker; first knife sold in 1985. **Mark:** GA RED in cowboy hat.

SMOCK, TIMOTHY E., 1105 N Sherwood Dr, Marion, IN 46952, Phone: 765-664-0123

SMOKER, RAY, 113 Church Rd, Searcy, AR 72143, Phone: 501-796-2712
Specialties: Working/using fixed blades of his design only. **Patterns:** Hunters, skinners, utility/camp and flat-ground knives. **Technical:** Forges his own Damascus and 52100; makes sheaths. Uses improved multiple edge quench he developed. **Prices:** $140 to $200; price includes sheath. **Remarks:** Full-time maker; first knife sold in 1992. **Mark:** Last name.

SNARE, MICHAEL, 3352 E. Mescal St, Phoenix, AZ 85028

SNELL, JERRY L., 235 Woodsong Dr, Fayetteville, GA 30214, Phone: 770-461-0586
Specialties: Working straight knives of his design and in standard patterns. **Patterns:** Hunters, boots, fighters, daggers and a few folders. **Technical:** Grinds 440C, ATS-34; buys Damascus. **Prices:** $175 to $1000. **Remarks:** Part-time maker. **Mark:** Last name, or name, city and state.

SNODY, MIKE, 7169 Silk Hope Rd, Liberty, NC 27298, Phone: 888-393-9534
Specialties: High performance straight knives in traditional & Japanese-styles. **Patterns:** Skinners, hunters, tactical, Kwaiken &Tantos. **Technical:** Grinds BG-42, ATS-34, 440C & A-2. Offers full or tapered tangs, upgraded handle materials such as fossil ivory, coral and exotic woods. Traditional diamond wrap over stingray on Japanese-style knives. Sheaths available in leather or Kydex. **Prices:** $100 to $1000. **Remarks:** Part-time maker; first knife sold in 1999. **Mark:** Name over knife maker.

SNOW, BILL, 4824 18th Ave, Columbus, GA 31904, Phone: 706-576-4390
Specialties: Traditional working/using straight knives and folders of his design and to customer specs. Offers engraving and scrimshaw. **Patterns:** Bowies, fighters, hunters and folders. **Technical:** Grinds ATS-34, 440V, 440C, 420V, CPM350, BG42, A2, D2, 5160, 52100 and O1; forges if needed. Cryogenically quenches all steels; inlaid handles; some integrals; leather or Kydex sheaths. **Prices:** $125 to $700; some to $3500. **Remarks:** Full-time maker; first knife sold in 1958. Doing business as Tipi Knife works. **Mark:** Old English scroll "S" inside a tipi.

SNYDER, MICHAEL TOM, PO Box 522, Zionsville, IN 46077-0522, Phone: 317-873-6807

SOLOMON, MARVIN, 23750 Cold Springs Rd, Paron, AR 72122, Phone: 501-821-3170, Fax: 501-821-6541
Specialties: Traditional working and using straight knives of his design and to customer specs also lock-back 7 liner-lock folders. **Patterns:** Single blade folders. **Technical:** Forges 5160, 1095, O1 and random Damascus. **Prices:** $125 to $1000. **Remarks:** Part-time maker; first knife sold in 1990. Doing business as Cold Springs Forge. **Mark:** Last name.

SONNTAG, DOUGLAS W., 906 N 39 St, Nixa, MO 65714, Phone: 417-693-1640, Fax: 417-582-1392
Specialties: Working knives; art knives. **Patterns:** Hunters, boots, straight working knives; Bowies, some folders, camp/axe sets. **Technical:** Grinds D-2, ATS-34, forges own Damascus; does own heat treating. **Prices:** $175 to $500; some higher. **Remarks:** Part-time maker; first knife sold in 1986. **Mark:** Etched name in arch.

SONTHEIMER, G. DOUGLAS, 12604 Bridgeton Dr, Potomac, MD 20854, Phone: 301-948-5227
Specialties: Fixed blade knives. **Patterns:** Whitetail deer, backpackers, camp, claws, filet, fighters. **Technical:** Hollow Grinds. **Price:** $325 and up. **Remarks:** Spare-time maker; first knife sold in 1976. **Mark:** LORD.

SOPPERA, ARTHUR, Morgenstalstr. 37, PO Box 708, CH-8038 Zurich, SWITZERLAND, Phone: 1-482 86 12, Fax: 1-481 62 71
Specialties: High-art, high-tech knives of his design. **Patterns:** Mostly locking folders, some straight knives. **Technical:** Grinds ATS-34 and commercial Damascus. Folders have button lock of his own design; some are fancy folders in jeweler's fashion. Also makes jewelry with integrated small knives. **Prices:** $200 to $1000; some $2000 and higher. **Remarks:** Full-time maker; first knife sold in 1986. **Mark:** Stylized initials, name, country.

SORNBERGER, JIM, 25126 Overland Dr, Volcano, CA 95689, Phone: 209-295-7819
Specialties: Classic San Francisco-style knives. Collectible straight knives. **Patterns:** Forges 1095-1084/15W2. Makes own Damascus and powder metal. Fighters, daggers, Bowies; miniatures; hunters, custom canes, liner-locks folders. **Technical:** Grinds 440C, 154CM and ATS-34; engraves, carves and embellishes. **Prices:** $500 to $14,000 in gold with gold quartz inlays. **Remarks:** Full-time maker; first knife sold in 1970. **Mark:** First initial, last name, city and state.

SOWELL, BILL, 100 Loraine Forest Ct, Macon, GA 31210, Phone: 478- 994-9863
Specialties: Hunters, boot, Bowies, fighters, tactical. **Patterns:** Makes own Damascus, forges L-6, 5160, 1095-1-84/15N2. Makes own Damascus and powder metal. **Technical:** Grinds ATS-34. **Prices:** Start at $150. **Remarks:** Part-time maker; first knife sold 1998. **Mark:** Iron Horse Knives; Iron Horse Forge. **Other:** Does own leather work.

SPARKS, BERNARD, PO Box 73, Dingle, ID 83233, Phone: 208-847-1883
Specialties: Maker engraved, working and art knives. Straight knives and folders of his own design. **Patterns:** Locking inner-frame folders, hunters, fighters, one-of-a-kind art knives. **Technical:** Grinds 530V steel, 440-C, 154CM, ATS-34, D-2 and forges by special order; triple temper, cryogenic soak. Mirror or hand finish. New Liquid metal steel. **Prices:** $300 to $2000. **Remarks:** Full-time maker, first knife sold in 1967. **Mark:** Last name over state with a knife logo on each end of name. Prior 1980, stamp of last name.

SPICKLER, GREGORY NOBLE, 5614 Mose Circle, Sharpsburg, MD 21782, Phone: 301-432-2746

SPINALE, RICHARD, 4021 Canterbury Ct, Lorain, OH 44053, Phone: 440-282-1565
Specialties: High-art working knives of his design. **Patterns:** Hunters, fighters, daggers and locking folders. **Technical:** Grinds 440C, ATS-34 and 07; engraves. Offers gold bolsters and other deluxe treatments. **Prices:** $300 to $1000; some to $3000. **Remarks:** Spare-time maker; first knife sold in 1976. **Mark:** Name, address, year and model number.

SPIVEY, JEFFERSON, 9244 W. Wilshire, Yukon, OK 73099, Phone: 405-721-4442
Specialties: The Saber tooth: a combination hatchet, saw and knife. **Patterns:** Built for the wilderness, all are one-of-a-kind. **Technical:** Grinds chromemoly steel. The saw tooth spine curves with a double row of biangular teeth. **Prices:** Start at $300. **Remarks:** First knife sold in 1977. **Mark:** Name and serial number.

SPRAGG, WAYNE E., PO Box 508, 1314 3675 East Rd, Ashton, ID 83420
Specialties: Working straight knives, some fancy. **Patterns:** Folders. **Technical:** Forges carbon steel and makes Damascus. **Prices:** $110 to $400; some higher. **Remarks:** All stainless heat-treated by Paul Bos. Carbon steel in shop heat treat. **Mark:** Name, city and state with bucking horse logo.

SPROUSE, TERRY, 1633 Newfound Rd, Asheville, NC 28806, Phone: 704-683-3400
Specialties: Traditional and working straight knives of his design. **Patterns:** Bowies and hunters. **Technical:** Grinds ATS-34, 440C and D2. Makes sheaths. **Prices:** $85 to $125; some to $225. **Remarks:** Part-time maker; first knife sold in 1989. **Mark:** NA.

STAFFORD, RICHARD, 104 Marcia Ct, Warner Robins, GA 31088, Phone: 912-923-6372
Specialties: High-tech straight knives and some folders. **Patterns:** Hunters in several patterns, fighters, boots, camp knives, combat knives and period pieces. **Technical:** Grinds ATS-34 and 440C; satin finish is standard. **Prices:** Starting at $75. **Remarks:** Part-time maker; first knife sold in 1983. **Mark:** Last name.

STALCUP, EDDIE, PO Box 2200, Gallup, New Mexico 87305, Phone: 505-863-3107
Specialties: Working and fancy hunters, bird and trout. Special custom orders. **Patterns:** Drop point hunters, locking liner and muti blade folders. **Technical:** ATS-34. **Prices:** $150 to $500. **Mark:** E. F. Stalcup, Gallup, NM. **Other:** Scrimshaw, Exotic handle material, wet formed sheaths. Membership Arizona knife collectors association.

STANCER, CHUCK, 62 Hidden Ranch Rd Nw, Calgary AB, CANADA T3A 5S5, Phone: 403-295-7370

STANLEY, JOHN, 604 Elm Street, Crossett, AR 71635, Phone: 870-304-3005
Specialties: Hand forged fixed blades with engraving and carving. **Patterns:** Scottish dirks, skeans and fantasy blades. **Technical:** Forge high carbon steel, own Damascus. Prices $70 to $500. **Remarks:** All work is sole authorship. **Mark:** Varies. **Other:** Offer engraving and carving services on other knives and handles.

STAPEL, CRAIG, Box 1617, Glendale, CA 91209, Phone: 213-668-2669
Specialties: Working knives. **Patterns:** Hunters, tantos and fishing knives. **Technical:** Grinds 440C and AEB-L. **Prices:** $80 to $150. **Remarks:** Spare-time maker; first knife sold in 1981. **Mark:** First and middle initials, last name.

STAPEL, CHUCK, Box 1617, Glendale, CA 91209, Phone: 213-66-KNIFE, Fax: 213-669-1577
Specialties: Working knives of his design. **Patterns:** Variety of straight knives tantos, hunters, folders and utility knives. **Technical:** Grinds D2, 440C and AEB-L. **Prices:** $185 to $3000. **Remarks:** Full-time maker; first knife sold in 1974. **Mark:** Last name or last name, U. S. A.

STAPLETON, WILLIAM E., 5425 Country Lane, Merritt Island, FL 32953, Phone: 407-452-8946

STECK, VAN R., 260 W. Dogwood Ave, Orange City, FL 32763, Phone: 386-775-7303
Specialties: Hollow and distal tapers. **Patterns:** Neck knives, hunters, fighters, Bowies and Japanese swords. **Technical:** ATS-34, D-2, A-2, titanium, ebony, coco-bolo, ironwood. **Prices:** $75-$450.

STEFFEN, CHUCK, 504 Dogwood Ave NW, St Michael, MN, Phone: 763-497-6315
Specialties: Custom hunting knives, fixed blades folders. Specializing in exotic materials, Damascus excellent fit form & finishes.

STEGALL, KEITH, 2101 W. 32nd, Anchorage, AK 99517, Phone: 907-276-6002
Specialties: Traditional working straight knives. **Patterns:** Most patterns. **Technical:** Grinds 440C and 154CM. **Prices:** $100 to $300. **Remarks:** Spare-time maker; first knife sold in 1987. **Mark:** Name and state with anchor.

STEGNER, WILBUR G., 9242 173rd Ave. SW, Rochester, WA 98579, Phone: 360-273-0937
Specialties: Working/using straight knives and folders of his design. **Patterns:** Hunters and locking folders. **Technical:** Grinds ATS-34 and other tool steels. Quenches, tempers and hardness tests each blade. **Prices:** $80 to $600; some to $3000. **Remarks:** Full-time maker; first knife sold in 1979. **Mark:** First and middle initials, last name in bar over shield logo.

STEIGER, MONTE L., Box 186, Genesee, ID 83832, Phone: 208-285-1769
Specialties: Traditional working/using straight knives of all designs. **Patterns:** Hunters, utility/camp knives, filet and chefs. **Technical:** Grinds 1095, O1, 440C, ATS-34. Handles of stacked leather, natural wood, Micarta or Pakkawood. Each knife comes with right- or left-handed sheath. **Prices:** $70 to $220. **Remarks:** Spare-time maker; first knife sold in 1988. **Mark:** First initial, last name, city and state.

STEIGERWALT, KEN, PO Box 172, Orangeville, PA 17859, Phone: 717-683-5156
Specialties: Fancy classic folders of his design. **Patterns:** Folders, button locks and rear locks. **Technical:** Grinds ATS-34, 440C and commercial Damascus. Experiments with unique filework. **Prices:** $200 to $600; some to $1500. **Remarks:** Full-time maker; first knife sold in 1981. **Mark:** Initials.

STEINAU, JURGEN, Julius-Hart Strasse 44, Berlin 0-1162, GERMANY, Phone: 372-6452512, Fax: 372-645-2512
Specialties: Fantasy and high-art straight knives of his design. **Patterns:** Boots, daggers and switch-blade folders. **Technical:** Grinds 440B, 2379 and X90 Cr. Mo. V. 78. **Prices:** $1500 to $2500; some to $3500. **Remarks:** Full-time maker; first knife sold in 1984. **Mark:** Symbol, plus year, month day and serial number.

STEINBERG, AL, 5244 Duenas, Laguna Woods, CA 92653, Phone: 949-951-2889
Specialties: Fancy working straight knives to customer specs. **Patterns:** Hunters, Bowies, fishing, camp knives, push knives and high end kitchen knives. **Technical:** Grinds O1, 440C and 154CM. **Prices:** $60 to $2500. **Remarks:** Full-time maker; first knife sold in 1972. **Mark:** Signature, city and state.

STEINBRECHER, MARK W., 4725 Locust Ave, Glenview, IL 60025, Phone: 847-298-5721
Specialties: Working & fancy folders. **Patterns:** Daggers, pocket knives, fighters and gents of my own design or to customer specs. **Technical:** Hollow grinds ATS-34, O-1 other makers Damascus. Uses natural handle materials: stag, ivories, mother of pearl. File work and some inlays. **Prices:** $500 to $1200; some to $2500. **Remarks:** Part-time maker, first folder sold in 1989. **Mark:** Name etched or handwritten on ATS-34; stamped on Damascus.

STEKETEE, CRAIG A., 871 N. Hwy. 60, Billings, MO 65610, Phone: 417-744-2770
Specialties: Classic and working straight knives and swords of his design. **Patterns:** Bowies, hunters, and Japanese-style swords. **Technical:** Forges his own Damascus; bronze, silver and Damascus fittings, offers filework. Prefers exotic and natural handle materials. **Prices:** $200 to $4000. **Remarks:** Full-time maker. **Mark:** STEK.

STEPHAN, DANIEL, 2201 S. Miller Rd, Valrico, FL 33594, Phone: 813-684-2781

STERLING, MURRAY, 693 Round Peak Church Rd, Mount Airy, NC 27030, Phone: 336-352-5110, Fax: Fax: 336-352-5105
Specialties: Single & dual blade folders. Interframes & integral dovetail frames. **Technical:** Grinds ATS-34 or Damascus by Mike Norris and/or Devin Thomas. **Prices:** $300 & up. **Remarks:** Full-time maker; first knife sold in 1991. **Mark:** Last name stamped.

STEVENS, BARRY B., 901 Amherst, Cridersville, OH 45806, Phone: 419-221-2446
Specialties: Small fancy folders of his design and to customer specs; mini-hunters and fighters. **Patterns:** Fighters, hunters, liner-locks, lock-back and bolster release folders. **Technical:** Grinds ATS-34, 440C, Damascus and SS Damascus. Prefers hand-rubbed finishes and natural handle materials-horn, ivory, pearls, exotic woods. **Prices:** $300 to $1000; some to $2500. **Remarks:** Part-time maker; first knife sold in 1991. Doing business as Bare Knives. **Mark:** First and middle initials, last name.

STEWART, EDWARD L., 4297 Audrain Rd 335, Mexico, MO 65265, Phone: 573-581-3883
Specialties: Fixed blades, working knives some art. **Patterns:** Hunters, Bowies, Utility/camp knives. **Technical:** Forging 1095-W-2-I-6-52100 makes own Damascus. **Prices:** $85-$500. **Remarks:** Part-time maker first knife sold in 1993. **Mark:** First and last initials-last name.

STIDHAM, RHETT & JANIE, PO Box 570, Roseland, FL 32957, Phone: 772-589-0618
Specialties: Loveless, randaus. Scagels, antique pocket knife. **Other:** Starting our 33rd year full-time.

STIMPS, JASON M., 374 S Shaffer St, Orange, CA 92866, Phone: 714-744-5866

STIPES, DWIGHT, 2651 SW Buena Vista Dr, Palm City, FL 34990, Phone: 772-597-0550
Specialties: Traditional and working straight knives in standard patterns. **Patterns:** Boots, Bowies, daggers, hunters and fighters. **Technical:** Grinds 440C, D2 and D3 tool steel. Handles of natural materials, animal, bone or horn. **Prices:** $75 to $150. **Remarks:** Full-time maker; first knife sold in 1972. **Mark:** Stipes.

STOCKWELL, WALTER, 368 San Carlos Ave, Redwood City, CA 94061, Phone: 650-363-6069
Specialties: Scottish dirks. **Patterns:** All knives one-of-a-kind. **Technical:** Grinds ATS-34, forges 5160, 52100, L6. **Prices:** $125 - $500. **Remarks:** Part-time maker since 1992; graduate of ABS bladesmithing school. **Mark:** Shooting star over "STOCKWELL". Pre-2000, "WKS".

STODDARD'S, INC., COPLEY PLACE, 100 Huntington Ave, Boston, MA 02116, Phone: 617-536-8688, Fax: 617-536-8689
Specialties: Cutlery (kitchen, pocket knives, Randall-made Knives, custom knives, scissors, & manicure tools) binoculars, low vision aids, personal care items (hair brushes, manicure sets, mirrors.)

STODDART, W. B. BILL, 917 Smiley, Forest Park, OH 45240, Phone: 513-851-1543
Specialties: Sportsmen's working knives and multi-blade folders. **Patterns:** Hunters, camp and fish knives; multi-blade reproductions of old standards. **Technical:** Grinds A2, 440C and ATS-34; makes sheaths to match handle materials. **Prices:** $80 to $300; some to $850. **Remarks:** Part-time maker; first knife sold in 1976. **Mark:** Name, Cincinnati, state.

STOKES, ED, 22614 Cardinal Dr, Hockley, TX 77447, Phone: 713-351-1319
Specialties: Working straight knives and folders of all designs. **Patterns:** Boots, Bowies, daggers, fighters, hunters and miniatures. **Technical:** Grinds ATS-34, 440C and D2. Offers decorative butt caps, tapered spacers on handles and finger grooves, nickel-silver inlays, hand-made sheaths. **Prices:** $185 to $290; some to $350. **Remarks:** Full-time maker;

custom knifemakers

first knife sold in 1973. **Mark:** First and last name, Custom Knives with Apache logo.

STONE, JERRY, PO Box 1027, Lytle, TX 78052, Phone: 512-772-4502
Specialties: Traditional working and using folders of his design and to customer specs; fancy knives. **Patterns:** Fighters, hunters, locking folders and slip-joints. **Technical:** Grinds 440C and ATS-34. Offers filework. **Prices:** $125 to $375; some to $700. **Remarks:** Full-time maker; first knife sold in 1973. **Mark:** Initials.

STORCH, ED, R. R. 4 Mannville, Alberta T0B 2W0, CANADA, Phone: 780-763-2214
Specialties: Working knives, fancy fighting knives, kitchen cutlery and art knives. **Patterns:** Working patterns, Bowies and folders. **Technical:** Forges his own Damascus. Grinds ATS-34. Builds friction folders. **Prices:** $45 to $750 (US). **Remarks:** Part-time maker; first knife sold in 1984. **Mark:** Last Name.

STORMER, BOB, 10 Karabair Rd, St Peters, MO 63376, Phone: 636-441-6807
Specialties: Straight knives - Using collector grade. **Patterns:** Bowies, skinners, hunters, camp knives. **Technical:** Forges 5160, 1095. **Prices:** $150-$400. **Remarks:** Part-time maker ABS journeyman smith 2001. **Mark:** Setting Sun/Fall trees/Initials.

STOUT, CHARLES, RT3 178 Stout Rd, Gillham, AR 71841, Phone: 870-386-5521

STOUT, JOHNNY, 1205 Forest Trail, New Braunfels, TX 78132, Phone: 830-606-4067
Specialties: Folders, some fixed blades. Working knives, some fancy. **Patterns:** Hunters, tactical, Bowies, automatics, liner-locks and slip-joints. **Technical:** Grinds stainless and carbon steels; forges own Damascus. **Prices:** $450 to $895; some to $3500. **Remarks:** Full-time maker; first knife sold in 1983. **Mark:** Name and city in logo with serial number. **Other:** Hosts semi-annual Guadalupe forge hammer-in & knifemakers rendezvous.

STOVER, HOWARD, 100 Palmetto Dr Apt 7, Pasadena, CA 91105, Phone: 765-452-3928

STOVER, TERRY "LEE", 1809 N. 300 E., Kokomo, IN 46901, Phone: 765-452-3928
Specialties: Damascus folders with filework; Damascus Bowies of his design or to customer specs. **Patterns:** Lock-back folders and Sheffield-style Bowies. **Technical:** Forges 1095, Damascus using O2, 203E or O2, pure nickel. Makes mokume. Uses only natural handle material. **Prices:** $300 to $1700; some to $2000. **Remarks:** Part-time maker; first knife sold in 1984. **Mark:** First and middle initials, last name in knife logo; Damascus blades marked in Old English.

STOVER, JAMES K., HC 60 Box 1260, Lakeview, OR 97630, Phone: 541-947-4008

STRAIGHT, KENNETH J., 11311 103 Lane N., Largo, FL 33773, Phone: 813-397-9817

STRAIGHT, DON, PO Box 12, Points, WV 25437, Phone: 304-492-5471
Specialties: Traditional working straight knives of his design. **Patterns:** Hunters, Bowies and fighters. **Technical:** Grinds 440C, ATS-34 and D2. **Prices:** $75 to $125; some to $225. **Remarks:** Spare-time maker; first knife sold in 1978. **Mark:** Last name.

STRANDE, POUL, Soster Svenstrup Byvej 16, Dastrup 4130 Viby Sj., DENMARK, Phone: 46 19 43 05, Fax: 46 19 53 19
Specialties: Classic fantasy working knives; Damasceret blade, Nikkel Damasceret blade, Lamineret - Lamineret blade with Nikkel. **Patterns:** Bowies, daggers, fighters, hunters and swords. **Technical:** Uses carbon steel and 15C20 steel. **Prices:** NA. **Remarks:** Full-time maker; first knife sold in 1985. **Mark:** First and last initials.

STRICKLAND, DALE, 1440 E. Thompson View, Monroe, UT 84754, Phone: 435-896-8362
Specialties: Traditional and working straight knives and folders of his design and to customer specs. **Patterns:** Hunters, folders, miniatures and utility knives. **Technical:** Grinds Damascus and 440C. **Prices:** $120 to $350; some to $500. **Remarks:** Part-time maker; first knife sold in 1991. **Mark:** Oval stamp of name, Maker.

STRIDER, MICK, Strider Knives, 234 1/2 S. Coast Hwy, Oceanside, CA 92084, Phone: 760-967-6445

STRONG, SCOTT, 2138 Oxmoor Dr, Beavercreek, OH 45431, Phone: 937-426-9290
Specialties: Working knives, some deluxe. **Patterns:** Hunters, fighters, survival and military-style knives, art knives. **Technical:** Forges and grinds O1, A2, D2, 440C and ATS-34. Uses no solder; most knives disassemble.

Prices: $75 to $450; some to $1500. **Remarks:** Spare-time maker; first knife sold in 1983. **Mark:** Strong Knives.

STROYAN, ERIC, Box 218, Dalton, PA 18414, Phone: 717-563-2603
Specialties: Classic and working/using straight knives and folders of his design. **Patterns:** Hunters, locking folders, slip-joints. **Technical:** Forges Damascus; grinds ATS-34, D2. **Prices:** $200 to $600; some to $2000. **Remarks:** Part-time maker; first knife sold in 1968. **Mark:** Signature or initials stamp.

STUART, STEVE, Box 168, Gores Landing, Ont., CANADA K0K 2E0, Phone: 905-342-5617
Specialties: Straight knives. **Patterns:** Tantos, fighters, skinners, file and rasp knives. **Technical:** Uses 440C, files, Micarta and natural handle materials. **Prices:** $60 to $400. **Remarks:** Part-time maker. **Mark:** Interlocking SS with last name.

SUEDMEIER, HARLAN, RFD 2, Box 299D, Nebraska City, NE 68410, Phone: 402-873-4372
Specialties: Working straight knives. **Patterns:** Hunters, fighters and Bowies. **Technical:** Grinds ATS-34 and 440C; forges 52100. **Prices:** Start at $75. **Remarks:** Part-time maker; first knife sold in 1982. Not currently taking orders. **Mark:** First initial, last name.

SUGIHARA, KEIDOH, 4-16-1 Kamori-Cho, Kishiwada City, Osaka, F596-0042, JAPAN, Fax: 0724-44-2677
Specialties: High-tech working straight knives and folders of his design. **Patterns:** Bowies, hunters, fighters, fishing, boots, some pocket knives and liner-lock folders. **Technical:** Grinds ATS-34, COS-25, buys Damascus and high carbon steels. Prices $60 to $4000. **Remarks:** Full-time maker, first knife sold in 1980. **Mark:** Initial logo with fish design.

SUGIYAMA, EDDY K., 2361 Nagayu Naoirimachi Naoirigun, Ohita, JAPAN, Phone: 0974-75-2050
Specialties: One-of-a-kind, exotic style knives. **Patterns:** Working, utility and miniatures. **Technical:** CT rind, ATS-34 & D2. **Prices:** $400-$1200. **Remarks:** Full-time maker. **Mark:** Name or cedar mark.

SUMMERS, DAN, 2675 NY Rt. 11, Whitney Pt., NY 13862, Phone: 607-692-2391
Specialties: Period knives and tomahawks. **Technical:** All hand forging. **Prices:** Most $100 to $400.

SUMMERS, ARTHUR L., 1310 Hess Rd, Concord, NC 28025, Phone: 704-795-2863
Specialties: Collector-grade knives in drop points, clip points or straight blades. **Patterns:** Fighters, hunters, Bowies and personal knives. **Technical:** Grinds 440C, ATS-34, D2 and Damascus. **Prices:** $150 to $650; some to $2000. **Remarks:** Full-time maker; first knife sold in 1987. **Mark:** Last name and serial number.

SUMMERS, DENNIS K., 827 E. Cecil St, Springfield, OH 45503, Phone: 513-324-0624
Specialties: Working/using knives. **Patterns:** Fighters and personal knives. **Technical:** Grinds 440C, A2 and D2. Makes drop and clip point. **Prices:** $75 to $200. **Remarks:** Part-time maker; first knife sold in 1995. **Mark:** First and middle initials, last name, serial number.

SUNDERLAND, RICHARD, Box 248, Quathiaski Cove, BC, CANADA V0P 1N0, Phone: 250-285-3038
Specialties: Personal and hunting knives with carved handles in oosic and ivory. **Patterns:** Hunters, Bowies, daggers, camp and personal knives. **Technical:** Grinds 440C, ATS-34 and O1. Handle materials of rosewoods, fossil mammoth ivory and oosic. **Prices:** $150 to $1000. **Remarks:** Full-time maker; first knife sold in 1983. Doing business as Sun Knife Co. **Mark:** SUN.

SUTTON, S. RUSSELL, 4900 Cypress Shores Dr, New Bern, NC 28562, Phone: 252-637-3963
Specialties: Straight knives and folders to customer specs and in standard patterns. **Patterns:** Boots, hunters, interframes and locking liners. **Technical:** Grinds ATS-34, 440C and stainless Damascus. **Prices:** $185 to $650; some to $950. **Remarks:** Full-time maker; first knife sold in 1992. **Mark:** Etched last name.

SWEAZA, DENNIS, 4052 Hwy 321 E, Austin, AR 72007, Phone: 501-941-1886

SWEDER, JORAM, Tilaru Metalsmithing, PO Box 4175, Ocala, FL 34470, Phone: 352-546-4438
Specialties: Hand forged one-of-a-kind and custom pieces. **Prices:** $100 and up.

SWEENEY, COLTIN D., 1216 S 3 St W, Missoula, MT 59801, Phone: 406-721-6782

SWYHART, ART, 509 Main St, PO Box 267, Klickitat, WA 98628, Phone: 509-369-3451
Specialties: Traditional working and using knives of his design. **Patterns:** Bowies, hunters and utility/camp knives. **Technical:** Forges 52100, 5160

and Damascus 1084 mixed with either 15N20 or 0186. Blades differentially heat-treated with visible temper line. **Prices:** $75 to $250; some to $350. **Remarks:** Part-time maker; first knife sold in 1983. **Mark:** First name, last initial in script.

SYMONDS, ALBERTO E., Rambla M Gandhi 485, Apt 901, Montevideo 11300, URUGUAY, Phone: 011 598 2 7103201(Phone & Fax), Fax: 011 598 5608207 (Phone & Fax)

SYSLO, CHUCK, 3418 South 116 Ave, Omaha, NE 68144, Phone: 402-333-0647
Specialties: High-tech working straight knives. **Patterns:** Hunters, daggers and survival knives; locking folders. **Technical:** Flat-grinds D2, 440C and 154CM; hand polishes only. **Prices:** $175 to $500; some to $3000. **Remarks:** Part-time maker; first knife sold in 1978. **Mark:** CISCO in logo.

SZAREK, MARK G., 94 Oakwood Av, Revere, MA 02151, Phone: 781-289-7102
Specialties: Classic period working & using straight knives and tools. **Patterns:** Hunting knives, American & Japanese woodworking tools. **Technical:** Forges 5160, 1050, Damascus; differentially hardens blades with fireclay. **Prices:** $50 to $750. **Remarks:** Part-time maker; first knife sold in 1989. **Mark:** Last name. **Other:** Produces Japanese alloys for sword fittings and accessories. Custom builds knife presentation boxes and cabinets.

SZILASKI, JOSEPH, 29 Carroll Dr, Wappingers Falls, NY 12590, Phone: 845-297-5397
Specialties: Straight knives, folders and tomahawks of his design, to customer specs and in standard patterns. Many pieces are one-of-a-kind. **Patterns:** Bowies, daggers, fighters, hunters, art knives and early American styles. **Technical:** Forges A2, D2, O1 and Damascus. **Prices:** $450 to $4000; some to $10,000. **Remarks:** Full-time maker; first knife sold in 1990. **Mark:** Snake logo. **Other:** ABS mastersmith and voting member KMG.

t

TAKAHASHI, KAORU, 2506 TOYO OKA YADO UEKI, KAMOTO, KUMAMOTO, JAPAN 861-01, Phone: 8196 272-6759

TAKAHASHI, MASAO, 39-3 Sekine-machi, Maebashi-shi, Gunma 371 0047, JAPAN, Phone: 81 27 234 2223, Fax: 81 27 234 2223
Specialties: Working straight knives. **Patterns:** Daggers, fighters, hunters, fishing knives, boots. **Technical:** Grinds ATS-34 & Damascus. **Prices:** $350 to $1000 & up. **Remarks:** Full-time maker; first knife sold in 1982. **Mark:** M. Takahashi.

TALLY, GRANT, 26961 James Ave, Flat Rock, MI 48134, Phone: 734-789-8961
Straight knives and folders of his design. **Patterns:** Bowies, daggers, fighters. **Technical:** Grinds ATS-34, 440C and D2. Offers filework. **Prices:** $250 to $1000. **Remarks:** Part-time maker; first knife sold in 1985. Doing business as Tally Knives. **Mark:** Tally (last name).

TAMBOLI, MICHAEL, 12447 N. 49 Ave, Glendale, AZ 85304, Phone: 602-978-4308
Specialties: Miniatures, some full size. **Patterns:** Miniature hunting knives to fantasy art knives. **Technical:** Grinds 440C, 154CM and Damascus. **Prices:** $75 to $500; some to $1000. **Remarks:** Part-time maker; first knife sold in 1978. **Mark:** Initials or last name, city and state.

TASMAN, KERLEY, 9 Avignon Retreat, Pt. Kennedy, 6172, Western Australia, AUSTRALIA, Phone: 61-0407821460
Specialties: Knife/harness/sheath systems for elite military personnel & body guards. **Patterns:** Utility/tactical knives, hunters small game & presentation grade knives. **Technical:** ATS-34 & 440C, Damascus, flat & hollow grids. **Prices:** US $200 to $1800. **Remarks:** Will take presentation grade commissions. **Mark:** Makers Initials. **Other:** Multi award winning maker and custom jeweler.

TAY, LARRY C-G, Siglap PO Box 315, Singapore 9145, SINGAPORE, Phone: 65-2419421, Fax: 65-2434879
Specialties: Push knives, working and using straight knives and folders of his design; Marble's Safety Knife with stained or albino Asian buffalo horn and bone or rosewood handles. **Patterns:** Fighters and utility/camp knives. **Technical:** Forges and grinds D2, truck leaf springs. **Prices:** $200 to $1000. **Remarks:** Spare-time maker; first knife sold in 1957. **Mark:** LDA/ LAKELL, from 1999 initials L. T.

TAYLOR, SCOTT, 18124 B La Salle Av, Gardena, CA 90248, Phone: 310-538-8104

TAYLOR, SHANE, 18 Broken Bow Ln., Miles City, MT 59301, Phone: 406-232-7175
Specialties: One-of-a-kind fancy Damascus straight knives and folders. **Patterns:** Bowies, folders and fighters. **Technical:** Forges own mosaic

and pattern welded Damascus. **Prices:** $450 and up. **Remarks:** ABS mastersmith, full-time maker; first knife sold in 1982. **Mark:** First name.

TAYLOR, BILLY, 10 Temple Rd, Petal, MS 39465, Phone: 601-544-0041
Specialties: Straight knives of his design. **Patterns:** Bowies, skinners, hunters and utility knives. **Technical:** Flat-grinds 440C, ATS-34 and 154CM. **Prices:** $60 to $300. **Remarks:** Part-time maker; first knife sold in 1991. **Mark:** Full name, city and state.

TAYLOR, C. GRAY, 560 Poteat Ln, Fall Branch, TN 37656, Phone: 423-348-8304
Specialties: High-art display knives; period pieces. **Patterns:** Fighters, Bowies, daggers, locking folders and interframes. **Technical:** Grinds 440C, 154CM and ATS-34. **Prices:** $350 and up. **Remarks:** Full-time maker; first knife sold in 1975. **Mark:** Name, city and state.

TERAUCHI, TOSHIYUKI, 7649-13 219-11 Yoshida, Fujita-Cho Gobo-Shi, JAPAN

TERRILL, STEPHEN, 21363 Rd. 196, Lindsay, CA 93247, Phone: 209-562-4395
Specialties: Deluxe working straight knives and folders. **Patterns:** Fighters, tantos, boots, locking folders and axes; traditional oriental patterns. **Technical:** Forges 440C, 1084 and his Damascus. **Prices:** Moderate. **Remarks:** Part-time maker; first knife sold in 1972. **Mark:** Name, city, state in logo.

TERZUOLA, ROBERT, 3933 Agua Fria St, Santa Fe, NM 87501, Phone: 505-473-1002, Fax: 505-438-8018
Specialties: Working folders of his design; period pieces. **Patterns:** High-tech utility, defense and gentleman's folders. **Technical:** Grinds154CM and CPM S30V/odd carbon fiber. Offers titanium, carbon fiber and G10 composite for side-lock folders & tactical folders. **Prices:** $400 to $1200. **Remarks:** Full-time maker; first knife sold in 1980. **Mark:** Mayan dragon head, name.

THAYER, DANNY O., 8908S 100W, Romney, IN 47981, Phone: 765-538-3105
Specialties: Hunters, fighters, Bowies. **Prices:** $250 and up.

THEIS, TERRY, 21452 FM 2093, Harper, TX 78631, Phone: 830-864-4438
Specialties: All European and American engraving styles. **Prices:** $200 to $2000. **Remarks:** Engraver only.

THEUNS PRINSLOO KNIVES, PO Box 2263, Bethlehem, 9700, SOUTH AFRICA, Phone: 27 58 3037111, Fax: same
Specialties: Fancy Folders. **Technical:** Own Damascus and Mokume. **Prices:** $450-$1500.

THEVENOT, JEAN-PAUL, 16 Rue De La Prefecture, Dijon, FRANCE 21000

THIE, BRIAN, 11987 Sperry Rd, Sperry, IA 52650, Phone: 319-985-2276
Specialties: Working using knives from basic to fancy. **Patterns:** Hunters, fighters, camp and folders. **Technical:** Forges blades and own Damascus. **Prices:** $100 and up. **Remarks:** Member of ABS, Part-time maker. Sole author of blades including forging, heat treat, engraving and sheath making. **Mark:** Last name, with last name initial inside, serial number all hand engraved into the blade.

THILL, JIM, 10242 Bear Run, Missoula, MT 59803, Phone: 406-251-5475
Specialties: Traditional and working/using knives of his design. **Patterns:** Fighters, hunters and utility/camp knives. **Technical:** Grinds D2 and ATS-34; forges 10-95-85, 52100, 5160, 10 series, reg. Damascus-mosaic. Offers hand cut sheaths with rawhide lace. **Prices:** $145 to $350; some to $1250. **Remarks:** Full-time maker; first knife sold in 1962. **Mark:** Running bear in triangle.

THOMAS, DEVIN, 90 N. 5th St, Panaca, NV 89042, Phone: 775-728-4363
Specialties: Traditional straight knives and folders in standard patterns. **Patterns:** Bowies, fighters, hunters. **Technical:** Forges stainless Damascus, nickel and 1095. Uses, makes and sells Mokume with brass, copper and nickel-silver. **Prices:** $300 to $1200. **Remarks:** Full-time maker; first knife sold in 1979. **Mark:** First and last name, city and state with anvil, or first name only.

THOMAS, ROCKY, 1716 Waterside Blvd, Moncks Corner, SC 29461, Phone: 843-761-7761
Specialties: Traditional working and using straight knives in standard patterns. **Patterns:** Hunters and utility/camp knives. **Technical:** Grinds 440C, ATS-34 and commercial Damascus. **Prices:** $85 to $150. **Remarks:** Spare-time maker; first knife sold in 1986. **Mark:** First name in script and/or block.

custom knifemakers

THOMAS, KIM, PO Box 531, Seville, OH 44273, Phone: 330-769-9906
Specialties: Fancy and traditional straight knives of his design and to customer specs; period pieces. **Patterns:** Boots, daggers, fighters, swords. **Technical:** Forges own Damascus from 5160, 1010 and nickel. **Prices:** $135 to $1500; some to $3000. **Remarks:** Part-time maker; first knife sold in 1986. Doing business as Thomas Iron Works. **Mark:** KT.

THOMAS, BOB G., RR 1 Box 121, Thebes, IL 62990-9718

THOMAS, DAVID E., 8502 Hwy 91, Lillian, AL 36549, Phone: 334-961-7574
Specialties: Bowies & hunters. **Technical:** Hand forged blades in 5160, 1095 and own Damascus. **Prices:** $400 & up. **Mark:** Stylized DT, maker's last name, serial number.

THOMPSON, KENNETH, 4887 Glenwhite Dr, Duluth, GA 30136, Phone: 770-446-6730
Specialties: Traditional working and using knives of his design. **Patterns:** Hunters, Bowies and utility/camp knives. **Technical:** Forges 5168, O1, 1095 and 52100. **Prices:** $75 to $1500; some to $2500. **Remarks:** Part-time maker; first knife sold in 1990. **Mark:** P/W; or name, P/W, city and state.

THOMPSON, TOMMY, 4015 NE Hassalo, Portland, OR 97232-2607, Phone: 503-235-5762
Specialties: Fancy and working knives; mostly liner-lock folders. **Patterns:** Fighters, hunters and liner-locks. **Technical:** Grinds D2, ATS-34, CPM440V and T15. Handles are either hardwood inlaid with wood banding and stone or shell, or made of agate, jasper, petrified woods, etc. **Prices:** $75 to $500; some to $1000. **Remarks:** Part-time maker; first knife sold in 1987. Doing business as Stone Birds. **Mark:** First and last name, city and state. **Other:** Knife making temporarily stopped due to family obligations.

THOMPSON, LLOYD, PO Box 1664, Pagosa Springs, CO 81147, Phone: 970-264-5837
Specialties: Working and collectible straight knives and folders of his design. **Patterns:** Straight blades, lock-back folders & slip joint folders. **Technical:** Hollow-grinds ATS-34, D2 and O1. Uses sambar stag and exotic woods. **Prices:** $150 to upscale. **Remarks:** Full-time maker; first knife sold in 1985. Doing business as Trapper Creek Knife Co. **Remarks:** Offers 3-day knife-making classes. **Mark:** Name.

THOMPSON, LEON, 45723 S. W. Saddleback Dr, Gaston, OR 97119, Phone: 503-357-2573
Specialties: Working knives. **Patterns:** Locking folders, slip-joints and liner-locks. **Technical:** Grinds ATS-34, D2 and 440C. **Prices:** $200 to $600. **Remarks:** Full-time maker; first knife sold in 1976. **Mark:** First and middle initials, last name, city and state.

THOMSEN, LOYD W., HCR-46, Box 19, Oelrichs, SD 57763, Phone: 605-535-6162
Specialties: High-art and traditional working/using straight knives and presentation pieces of his design and to customer specs; period pieces. Hand carved animals in crown of stag on handles and carved display stands. **Patterns:** Bowies, hunters, daggers and utility/camp knives. **Technical:** Forges and grinds 1095HC, 1084, L6, 15N20, 440C stainless steel, nickel 200; special restoration process on period pieces. Makes sheaths. **Prices:** $350 to $1000. **Remarks:** Full-time maker; first knife sold in 1995. Doing business as Horsehead Creek Knives. **Mark:** Initials and last name over a horse's head.

THOUROT, MICHAEL W., T-814 Co. Road 11, Napoleon, OH 43545, Phone: 419-533-6832, Fax: 419-533-3516
Specialties: Working straight knives to customer specs. Designed two-handled skinning ax and limited edition engraved knife and art print set. **Patterns:** Fishing and fillet knives, Bowies, tantos and hunters. **Technical:** Grinds O1, D2, 440C and Damascus. **Prices:** $200 to $5000. **Remarks:** Part-time maker; first knife sold in 1968. **Mark:** Initials.

THUESEN, KEVIN, 10649 Haddington, Suite 180, Houston, TX 77043, Phone: 713-461-8632
Specialties: Working straight knives. **Patterns:** Hunters, including upswept skinners, and custom walking sticks. **Technical:** Grinds D2, 440C, 154CM and ATS-34. **Prices:** $85 to $125; some to $200. **Remarks:** Part-time maker; first knife sold in 1985. **Mark:** Initials on slant.

THUESEN, ED, 21211 Knolle Rd, Damon, TX 77430, Phone: 979-553-1211, Fax: 979-553-1211
Specialties: Working straight knives. **Patterns:** Hunters, fighters and survival knives. **Technical:** Grinds D2, 440C, ATS-34 and Vascowear. **Prices:** $150 to $275; some to $600. **Remarks:** Part-time maker; first knife sold in 1979. Runs knife maker supply business. **Mark:** Last name in script.

TICHBOURNE, GEORGE, 7035 Maxwell Rd. #5, Mississauga, Ont., CANADA L5S 1R5, Phone: 905-670-0200
Specialties: Traditional working and using knives as well as unique collectibles. **Patterns:** Bowies, hunters, outdoor, kitchen, integrals, art, mili-

tary, Scottish dirks, folders. **Technical:** Stock removal 440C, Stellite 6K, stainless damasteel Damascus, liquid metal. Handle materials include Mammoth, Meteorite, Mother of Pearl, Precious gems, Mosiac, Abalone, Stag, Micarta, Exotic High Resin Woods. Corian scrimshawed by George. Leather sheaths are hand stitched and tooled by George as well as the silver adornments for the Dirk sheaths. **Prices:** $55 US up to $5000 US. **Remarks:** Full-time maker, first knife sold in 1990. **Mark:** Full name over maple lear. **Other:** There will be a "new" mark coming out for George's "Signature" line.

TIENSVOLD, JASON, PO Box 795, Rushville, NE 69360, Phone: 308-327-2046
Specialties: Working & using straight knives of my design; period pieces. **Patterns:** Hunters, skinners, Bowies, fighters, daggers. **Technical:** Forge my own Damascus using 15N20 & 1084, custom file work. **Prices:** $200 & up. **Remarks:** Part-time maker, first knife sold in 1994; doing business under Tiensvold Custom Knives. **Mark:** Tiensvold USA Handmade in a circle.

TIENSVOLD, ALAN L., PO Box 355, Rushville, NE 69360, Phone: 308-327-2046
Specialties: Working knives, tomahawks & period pieces, high end Damascus knives. **Patterns:** Random, ladder, twist and many more. **Technical:** Hand forged blades, we forge our own Damascus. **Prices:** Working knives start at $300. **Remarks:** I received my journeyman rating with the ABS in 2002. **Mark:** Tiensvold hand made U. S. A. on left side, JS on right. **Other:** I also do my own engraving and fine work.

TIGHE, BRIAN, RR 1, Ridgeville, Ont, CANADA L0S 1M0, Phone: 905-892-2734, Fax: 905-892-2734
Specialties: High tech tactical folders. **Patterns:** Boots, daggers, locking and slip-joint folders. **Technical:** CPM 440V & CPM 420V. Prefers natural handle material inlay; hand finishes. **Prices:** $450 to $2000. **Remarks:** Part-time maker; first knife sold in 1989. **Mark:** Etched signature.

TILL, CALVIN E. AND RUTH, 211 Chaping, Chadron, NE 69337
Specialties: Straight knives, hunters, Bowies no folders **Patterns:** Training point, drop point hunters, Bowies. **Technical:** ATS-34 sub zero quench RC-59, 61. **Prices:** $700 to $1200. **Remarks:** I sell only the absolute best knives I can make. **Mark:** RC Till. The R is for my wife Ruth. **Other:** I manufacture every part in my knives.

TILTON, JOHN, 24041 Hwy 383, Iowa, LA 70647, Phone: 337-582-6785
Specialties: Camp knives and skinners. **Technical:** All forged blades. **Prices:** $125 and up. **Mark:** Initials J. E. T. **Other:** ABS Journeyman Smith.

TINDERA, GEORGE, Burning River Forge, 751 Hadcock Rd, Brunswick, OH 44212-2648, Phone: 330-220-6212
Specialties: Straight knives; my designs. **Patterns:** Personal knives; classic Bowies and fighters. **Technical:** Hand-forged high carbon; my own cable and pattern welded Damascus. **Prices:** $100 to $400. **Remarks:** Spare-time maker; sold first knife in 1995. **Other:** Natural handle materials.

TINGLE, DENNIS P., 19390 E Clinton Rd, Jackson, CA 95642, Phone: 209-223-4586

TODD, RICHARD C., RR 1, Chambersburg, IL 62323, Phone: 217-327-4380
Specialties: Multi blade folders & silver sheaths. **Patterns:** Blacksmithing and tool making. **Mark:** RT with letter R crossing the T.

TOICH, NEVIO, Via Pisacane 9, Rettorgole di Caldogna, Vincenza, ITALY 36030, Phone: 0444-985065, Fax: 0444-301254
Specialties: Working/using straight knives of his design or to customer specs. **Patterns:** Bowies, hunters, skinners and utility/camp knives. **Technical:** Grinds 440C, D2 and ATS-34. Hollow-grinds all blades and uses mirror polish. Offers hand-sewn sheaths. Uses wood and horn. **Prices:** $120 to $300; some to $450. **Remarks:** Spare-time maker; first knife sold in 1989. Doing business as Custom Toich. **Mark:** Initials and model number punched.

TOKAR, DANIEL, Box 1776, Shepherdstown, WV 25443
Specialties: Working knives; period pieces. **Patterns:** Hunters, camp knives, buckskinners, axes, swords and battle gear. **Technical:** Forges L6, 1095 and his Damascus; makes mokume, Japanese alloys and bronze daggers; restores old edged weapons. **Prices:** $25 to $800; some to $3000. **Remarks:** Part-time maker; first knife sold in 1979. Doing business as The Willow Forge. **Mark:** Arrow over rune and date.

TOLLEFSON, BARRY A., 177 Blackfoot Trail, Gunnison, CO 81230-9720, Phone: 970-641-0752
Specialties: Working straight knives, some fancy. **Patterns:** Hunters, skinners, fighters and camp knives. **Technical:** Grinds 440C, ATS-34 and D2. Likes mirror-finishes; offers some fancy filework. Handles made from elk, deer and exotic hardwoods. **Prices:** $75 to $300; some higher. **Remarks:** Part-time maker; first knife sold in 1990. **Mark:** Stylized initials.

TOMES, P. J., 594 Highpeak Lane, Shipman, VA 22971, Phone: 434-263-8662, Fax: 804-263-4439
Specialties: Lock blade folders, forged scagels and Bowies. **Technical:** MS forges 52100 only. **Mark:** Tomes MS USA on forged blades.

TOMEY, KATHLEEN, 146 Buford Pl, Macon, GA 31204, Phone: 478-746-8454
Specialties: Working hunters, skinners, daily users in fixed blades, plain and embellished. Tactical neck and tanto. Bowies. **Technical:** Grinds 01, ATS-34, flat or hollow grind, filework, satin and mirror polish finishes. High quality sheaths with tooling. Kydex with tactical. **Prices:** $150 to $500. **Remarks:** Almost full-time maker. **Mark:** Last name in diamond.

TOMPKINS, DAN, PO Box 398, Peotone, IL 60468, Phone: 708-258-3620
Specialties: Working knives, some deluxe, some folders. **Patterns:** Hunters, boots, daggers and push knives. **Technical:** Grinds D2, 440C, ATS-34 and 154CM. **Prices:** $85 to $150; some to $400. **Remarks:** Part-time maker; first knife sold in 1975. **Mark:** Last name, city, state.

TONER, ROGER, 531 Lightfoot Place, Pickering, Ont., CANADA L1V 5Z8, Phone: 905-420-5555
Specialties: Exotic Sword canes. **Patterns:** Bowies, daggers and fighters. **Technical:** Grinds 440C, D2 and Damascus. Scrimshaws and engraves. Silver cast pommels and guards in animal shapes; twisted silver wire inlays. Uses semi-precious stones. **Prices:** $200 to $2000; some to $3000. **Remarks:** Part-time maker; first knife sold in 1982. **Mark:** Last name.

TOPLISS, M. W. "IKE", 1668 Hermosa Ct, Montrose, CO 81401, Phone: 970-249-4703
Specialties: Working/using straight knives of his design and to customer specs. **Patterns:** Boots, hunters, utility/camp knives. **Technical:** Prefers ATS-34. Other steels available on request. Likes stabilized wood, natural hardwoods, antler and Micarta. **Prices:** $175 to $300; some to $800. **Remarks:** Part-time maker; first knife sold in 1984. **Mark:** Name, city, state.

TORGESON, SAMUEL L., 25 Alpine Ln, Sedona, AZ 86336-6809

TOSHIFUMI, KURAMOTO, 3435 Higashioda Asakura-gun, Fukuoka, JAPAN, Phone: 0946-42-4470

TOWELL, DWIGHT L., 2375 Towell Rd, Midvale, ID 83645, Phone: 208-355-2419
Specialties: Solid, elegant working knives; art knives. **Patterns:** Hunters, Bowies, daggers; folders in several weights. **Technical:** Grinds 154CM; some engraving. **Prices:** $250 to $800; some $3500 and higher. **Remarks:** Part-time maker; first knife sold in 1970. **Mark:** Last name.

TOWNSEND, ALLEN MARK, 6 Pine Trail, Texarkana, AR 71854, Phone: 870-772-8945

TRACY, BUD, 495 Flanders Rd, Reno, NV 8951-4784

TREIBER, LEON, PO Box 342, Ingram, TX 78025, Phone: 830-367-2246
Specialties: Folders of his design and to customer specs. **Patterns:** Locking folders. **Technical:** Grinds CPM-T-440V, D2, 440C, Damascus, 420v & ats34. **Prices:** $250 to $1500. **Remarks:** Part-time maker; first knife sold in 1992. Doing business as Treiber Knives. **Mark:** First initial, last name, city, state.

TREML, GLENN, RR #14, Site 11-10, Thunder Bay, Ont., CANADA P7B 5E5, Phone: 807-767-1977
Specialties: Working straight knives of his design and to customer specs. **Patterns:** Hunters, kitchen knives and double-edged survival knives. Technical Grinds 440C, ATS-34 and O1; stock removal method. Uses various woods and Micarta for handle material. **Prices:** $60 to $400; some higher. **Mark:** Stamped last name.

TRINDLE, BARRY, 1660 Ironwood Trail, Earlham, IA 50072-8611, Phone: 515-462-1237
Specialties: Engraved folders. **Patterns:** Mostly small folders, classical styles and pocket knives. **Technical:** 440 only. Engraves. Handles of wood or mineral material. **Prices:** Start at $1000. **Mark:** Name on tang.

TRISLER, KENNETH W., 6256 Federal 80, Rayville, LA 71269, Phone: 318-728-5541

TRITZ, JEAN JOSE, Schopstrasse 23, 20255 Hamburg, GERMANY, Phone: 040-49 78 21
Specialties: Scandinavian knives, Japanese kitchen knives, friction folders, swords. **Patterns:** Puukkos, Tollekniven, Hocho, friction folders, swords. **Technical:** Forges tool steels, carbon steels, 52100 Damascus Mokume, San Maj. **Prices:** $200 to $2000; some higher. **Remarks:** Full-time maker; first knife sold in 1989. **Mark:** Initials in monogram. **Other:** Does own leatherwork, prefers natural materials. Sole authorship. Speaks French, German, English, Norwegian.

TRUDEL, PAUL, 525 Braydon Ave, Ottawa ON, CANADA K1G 0W7
Remarks: Part-time knife maker.

TRUJILLO, ALBERT MB, 2035 Wasmer Circle, Bosque Farms, NM 87068, Phone: 505-869-0428
Specialties: Working/using straight knives of his design or to customer specs. **Patterns:** Hunters, skinners, fighters, working/using knives. File work offered. **Technical:** Grinds ATS-34, D2, 440C. Tapers tangs, all blades cryogenically treated. **Prices:** $75 to $500. **Remarks:** Part-time maker; first knife sold in 1997. **Mark:** First and last name under logo.

TRUJILLO, ADAM, 3001 Tanglewood Dr, Anchorage, AK 99517, Phone: 907-243-6093
Specialties: Working/using straight knives of his design. **Patterns:** Hunters and utility/camp knives. **Technical:** Grinds 440C, ATS-34 and O1; ice tempers blades. Sheaths are dipped in wax and oil base. **Prices:** $200 to $500; some to $1000. **Remarks:** Spare-time maker; first knife sold in 1995. Doing business as Alaska Knife & Service Co. **Mark:** NA.

TRUJILLO, THOMAS A., 3001 Tanglewood Dr, Anchorage, AK 99517, Phone: 907-243-6093
Specialties: High-end art knives. **Patterns:** Hunters, Bowies, daggers and locking folders. **Technical:** Grinds to customer choice, including rock and commercial Damascus. Inlays jewels and carves handles. **Prices:** $150 to $900; some to $6000. **Remarks:** Full-time maker; first knife sold in 1976. Doing business as Alaska Knife & Service Co. **Mark:** Alaska Knife and/or Thomas Anthony.

TRUJILLO, MIRANDA, 3001 Tanglewood Dr, Anchorage, AK 99517, Phone: 907-243-6093
Specialties: Working/using straight knives of her design. **Patterns:** Hunters and utility/camp knives. **Technical:** Grinds ATS-34 and 440C. Sheaths are water resistant. **Prices:** $145 to $400; some to $600. **Remarks:** Spare-time maker; first knife sold in 1989. Doing business as Alaska Knife & Service Co. **Mark:** NA.

TSCHAGER, REINHARD, Piazza Parrocchia 7, I-39100 Bolzano, ITALY, Phone: 0471-970642, Fax: 0471-970642
Specialties: Classic, high-art, collector-grade straight knives of his design. **Patterns:** Hunters. **Technical:** Grinds ATS-34, D2 and Damascus. Oval pins. Gold inlay. Offers engraving. **Prices:** $500 to $1200; some to $4000. **Remarks:** Spare-time maker; first knife sold in 1979. **Mark:** Gold inlay stamped with initials.

TURANSKI, TED, 30 Ladoga Pk, Lansing, NY 14882, Phone: 607-533-3594

TURCOTTE, LARRY, 1707 Evergreen, Pampa, TX 79065, Phone: 806-665-9369, 806-669-0435
Specialties: Fancy and working/using knives of his design and to customer specs. **Patterns:** Hunters, kitchen knives, utility/camp knives. **Technical:** Grinds 440C, D2, ATS-34. Engraves, scrimshaws, silver inlays. **Prices:** $150 to $350; some to $1000. **Remarks:** Part-time maker; first knife sold in 1977. Doing business as Knives by Turcotte. **Mark:** Last name.

TURECEK, JIM, 12 Elliott Rd, Ansonia, CT 06401, Phone: 203-734-8406
Specialties: Exotic folders, art knives and some miniatures. **Patterns:** Trout and bird knives with split bamboo handles and one-of-a-kind folders. **Technical:** Grinds and forges stainless and carbon Damascus. **Prices:** $750 to $1500; some to $3000. **Remarks:** Full-time maker; first knife sold in 1983. **Mark:** Last initial in script, or last name.

TURNBULL, RALPH A., 14464 Linden Dr, Spring Hill, FL 34609, Phone: 352-688-7089
Specialties: Fancy folders. **Patterns:** Primarily gents pocket knives. **Technical:** Wire EDM work on bolsters. **Prices:** $650 and up. **Remarks:** Full-time maker; first knife sold in 1973. **Mark:** Signature or initials.

TURNER, KEVIN, 17 Hunt Ave, Montrose, NY 10548, Phone: 914-739-0535
Specialties: Working straight knives of his design and to customer specs; period pieces. **Patterns:** Daggers, fighters and utility knives. **Technical:** Forges 5160 and 52100. **Prices:** $90 to $500. **Remarks:** Part-time maker; first knife sold in 1991. **Mark:** Acid-etched signed last name and year.

TWO KNIFE GUYS, PO Box 24477, Chattanooga, TN 37422, Phone: 423-894-6640

TYCER, ART, 23820 N Cold Springs Rd, Paron, AR 72122, Phone: 501-821-4487
Specialties: Fancy working/using straight knives of his design, to customer specs and standard patterns. **Patterns:** Boots, Bowies, daggers, fighters, hunters, kitchen and utility knives. **Technical:** Grinds ATS-34, 440C, 52100 & carbon steel. Uses exotic woods with spacer material, stag and water buffalo. Offers filework. **Prices:** $125 & up depending on size & embellishments. **Remarks:** Making and using own Damascus and other Damascus also. **Mark:** Flying "T" over first initial inside an oval. **Other:** Full-time maker.

custom knifemakers

TYSER, ROSS, 1015 Hardee Court, Spartanburg, SC 29303, Phone: 864-585-7616
Specialties: Traditional working and using straight knives and folders of his design and in standard patterns. **Patterns:** Bowies, hunters and slip-joint folders. **Technical:** Grinds 440C and commercial Damascus. Mosaic pins; stone inlay. Does filework and scrimshaw. Offers engraving and cutwork and some inlay on sheaths. **Prices:** $45 to $125; some to $400. **Remarks:** Part-time maker; first knife sold in 1995. Doing business as RT Custom Knives. **Mark:** Stylized initials.

U

UCHIDA, CHIMATA, 977-2 Oaza Naga Shisui Ki, Kumamoto, JAPAN 861-1204
UEKAMA, NOBUYUKI, 3-2-8-302 Ochiai, Tama City, Tokyo, JAPAN

V

VAGNINO, MICHAEL, PO Box 67, Visalia, CA 93279, Phone: 559-528-2800
Specialties: Working & fancy straight knives & folders of his design & to customer specs. **Patterns:** Hunters, Bowies, camp, kitchen & folders: locking liners, slip-joint, lock-back & double-action autos. **Technical:** Forges 52100, A2, 1084 & 15N20 Damascus and grinds stainless. **Prices:** $275 to $2000 plus.

VAIL, DAVE, 554 Sloop Point Rd, Hampstead, NC 28443, Phone: 910-270-4456
Specialties: Working/using straight knives of my own design or to the customer's specs. **Patterns:** Hunters/skinners, camp/utility, fillet, Bowies. **Technical:** Grinds ATS-34, 440c, 154CM and 1095 carbon steel. **Prices:** $90-$450. **Remarks:** Part-time maker. Member of NC Custom Knifemakers Guild. **Mark:** Etched oval with "Dave Vail Hampstead NC" inside.

VALLOTTON, BUTCH AND AREY, 621 Fawn Ridge Dr, Oakland, OR 97462, Phone: 541-459-2216, Fax: 541-459-7473
Specialties: Quick opening knives w/complicated mechanisms. **Patterns:** Tactical, fancy, working, and some art knives. **Technical:** Grinds all steels, uses others' Damascus. Uses Spectrum Metal. **Prices:** From $350 to $4500. **Remarks:** Full-time maker since 1984; first knife sold in 1981. **Mark:** Name w/viper head in the "V". **Other:** Co/designer, Appelgate Fairbarn folding w/Bill Harsey.

VALLOTTON, RAINY D., 1295 Wolf Valley Dr, Umpqua, OR 97486, Phone: 541-459-0465
Specialties: Folders, one-handed openers and art pieces. **Patterns:** All patterns. **Technical:** Stock removal all steels; uses titanium liners and bolsters; uses all finishes. **Prices:** $350 to $3500. **Remarks:** Full-time maker. **Mark:** Name.

VALLOTTON, SHAWN, 621 Fawn Ridge Dr, Oakland, OR 97462, Phone: 503-459-2216
Specialties: Left-hand knives. **Patterns:** All styles. **Technical:** Grinds 440C, ATS-34 and Damascus. Uses titanium. Prefers bead-blasted or anodized finishes. **Prices:** $250 to $1400. **Remarks:** Full-time maker. **Mark:** Name and specialty.

VALLOTTON, THOMAS, 621 Fawn Ridge Dr, Oakland, OR 97462, Phone: 541-459-2216
Specialties: Custom autos. **Patterns:** Tactical, fancy. **Technical:** File work, uses Damascus, uses Spectrum Metal. **Prices:** From $350 to $700. **Remarks:** Full-time maker. **Mark:** T and a V mingled. **Other:** Maker of Protégé 3 canoe.

VALOIS, A. DANIEL, 3552 W. Lizard Ck. Rd, Lehighton, PA 18235, Phone: 717-386-3636
Specialties: Big working knives; various sized lock-back folders with new safety releases. **Patterns:** Fighters in survival packs, sturdy working knives, belt buckle knives, military-style knives, swords. **Technical:** Forges and grinds A2, O1 and 440C; likes full tangs. **Prices:** $65 to $240; some to $600. **Remarks:** Full-time maker; first knife sold in 1969. **Mark:** Anvil logo with last name inside.

VAN CLEVE, STEVE, Box 372, Sutton, AK 99674, Phone: 907-745-3038

VAN DE MANAKKER, THIJS, Koolweg 34, 5759 px Helenaveen, HOLLAND, Phone: 0493539369
Specialties: Classic high-art knives. **Patterns:** Swords, utility/camp knives and period pieces. **Technical:** Forges soft iron, carbon steel and Bloomery Iron. Makes own Damascus, Bloomery Iron and patterns. **Prices:** $20 to $2000; some higher. **Remarks:** Full-time maker; first knife sold in 1969. **Mark:** Stylized "V".

VAN DEN ELSEN, GERT, Purcelldreef 83, 5012 AJ Tilburg, NETHERLANDS, Phone: 013-4563200
Specialties: Fancy, working/using, miniatures and integral straight knives of the maker's design or to customer specs. **Patterns:** Bowies, fighters, hunters and Japanese-style blades. **Technical:** Grinds ATS-34 and 440C; forges Damascus. Offers filework, differentially tempered blades and some mokume-gane fittings. **Prices:** $350 to $1000; some to $4000. **Remarks:** Part-time maker; first knife sold in 1982. Doing business as G-E Knives. **Mark:** Initials GE in lozenge shape.

VAN EIZENGA, JERRY W., 14227 Cleveland, Nunica, MI 49448, Phone: 616-842-2699
Specialties: Hand forged blades, Scagel patterns and other styles. **Patterns:** Camp, hunting, bird, trout, folders, axes, miniatures. **Technical:** 5160, 52100, 1084. **Prices:** Start at $250. **Remarks:** Part-time maker, sole author of knife and sheath. **Mark:** Interconnecting letters spelling VAN, city and state. **Other:** First knife made early 1970s. ABS member who believes in the beauty of simplicity.

VAN ELDIK, FRANS, Ho Flaan 3, 3632BT Loenen, NETHERLANDS, Phone: 0031 294 233 095, Fax: 0031 294 233 095
Specialties: Fancy collector-grade straight knives and folders of his design. **Patterns:** Hunters, fighters, boots and folders. **Technical:** Forges and grinds D2, 154CM, ATS-34 and stainless Damascus. **Prices:** Start at $225. **Remarks:** Spare-time maker; first knife sold in 1979. **Mark:** Lion with name and Amsterdam.

VAN HOY, ED & TANYA, 1826 McCallum Road, Candor, NC 27229, Phone: 910-974-7933, Fax: 928-563-7551
Specialties: Traditional and working/using straight knives of his design, make folders. **Patterns:** Fighters, straight knives, folders, hunters and art knives. **Technical:** Grinds ATS-34 and 440V; forges D2. Offers filework, engraves, acid etching, mosaic pins, decorative bolsters and custom fitted English bridle leather sheaths. **Prices:** $250 to $3000. **Remarks:** Full-time maker; first knife sold in 1977. Wife also engraves. Doing business as Van Hoy Custom Knives. **Mark:** Acid etched last name.

VAN RIJSWIJK, AAD, AvR Knives, Arij Koplaan 16B, 3132 AA Vlaardingen, NETHERLANDS, Phone: +31 10 2343227, Fax: +31 10 2343648
Specialties: High-art interframe folders of his design and in shaving sets. **Patterns:** Hunters and locking folders. **Technical:** Uses semi precious stones, mammoth, ivory, walrus ivory, iron wood. **Prices:** $550 to $3800. **Remarks:** Full-time maker; first knife sold in 1993. **Mark:** NA.

VAN RIPER, JAMES N., PO Box 7045, Citrus Heights, CA 95621-7045, Phone: 916-721-0892

VAN SCHAIK, BASTIAAN, Post Box 75269, 1070 AG, Amsterdam, NETHERLANDS, Phone: 31-20-633-80-25, Fax: same as phone #
Specialties: Working/using straight knives and axes of his design. **Patterns:** Daggers, fighters, push daggers and battle axes. **Technical:** Grinds ATS-34 and 440C; forges high-carbon steel. Uses Damascus and high-tech coatings. **Prices:** $400 to $1500; some to $2000. **Remarks:** Full-time maker; first knife sold in 1993. Doing business as Licorne Edged Creations. **Mark:** Unicorn head.

VANDERFORD, CARL G., Rt. 9, Box 238B, Columbia, TN 38401, Phone: 615-381-1488
Specialties: Traditional working straight knives and folders of his design. **Patterns:** Hunters, Bowies and locking folders. **Technical:** Forges and grinds 440C, O1 and wire Damascus. **Prices:** $60 to $125. **Remarks:** Part-time maker; first knife sold in 1987. **Mark:** Last name.

VANDEVENTER, TERRY L., 3274 Davis Rd, Terry, MS 39170-9750, Phone: 601-371-7414
Specialties: Camp knives, Bowies, friction folders. **Technical:** 1095, 1084, L-6, Damascus & Mokume; natural handles. **Prices:** $250 to $1200. **Remarks:** Sole author; makes everything here. **Mark:** T L Vandeventer (with silhouette of snake), handcrafted knives. **Other:** Part-time since 1994. ABS Journeyman Smith.

VASQUEZ, JOHNNY DAVID, 1552 7th St, Wyandotte, MI 48192, Phone: 734-281-2455

VAUGHAN, IAN, 351 Doe Run Rd, Manheim, PA 17545-9368, Phone: 717-665-6949

VEATCH, RICHARD, 2580 N. 35th Pl., Springfield, OR 97477, Phone: 541-747-3910
Specialties: Traditional working and using straight knives of his design and in standard patterns; period pieces. **Patterns:** Daggers, hunters, swords, utility/camp knives and minis. **Technical:** Forges and grinds his own Damascus; uses L6 and O1. Prefers natural handle materials; offers leatherwork. **Prices:** $50 to $300; some to $500. **Remarks:** Full-time maker; first knife sold in 1991. **Mark:** Stylized initials.

VEIT, MICHAEL, 3289 E. Fifth Rd, LaSalle, IL 61301, Phone: 815-223-3538
Specialties: Damascus folders. **Technical:** Engraver-sole author. **Prices:** $2500 to $6500. **Remarks:** Part-time maker; first knife sold in 1985. **Mark:** Name in script.

VELARDE, RICARDO, 7240 N Greefield Dr, Park City, UT 84098, Phone: 435-940-1378/Cell 801-360-1413/801-361-0204
Specialties: Investment grade integrals and interframs. **Patterns:** Boots, fighters and hunters; hollow grind. **Technical:** BG on Integrals. **Prices:** Start at $650. **Remarks:** First knife sold in 1992. **Mark:** First initial, last name on blade; city, state, U. S. A. at bottom of tang.

VENSILD, HENRIK, Gl Estrup, Randersvei 4, DK-8963 Auning, DENMARK, Phone: +45 86 48 44 48
Specialties: Classic and traditional working and using knives of his design; Scandinavian influence. **Patterns:** hunters and using knives. **Technical:** Forges Damascus. Hand makes handles, sheaths and blades. **Prices:** $350 to $1000. **Remarks:** Part-time maker; first knife sold in 1967. **Mark:** Initials.

VIALLON, HENRI, Les Belins, 63300 Thiers, FRANCE, Phone: 04-73-80-24-03, Fax: 04 73-51-02-02
Specialties: Folders and complex Damascus **Patterns:** My draws. **Technical:** Forge. **Prices:** $1000-$5000. **Mark:** H. Viallon

VIELE, H. J., 88 Lexington Ave, Westwood, NJ 07675, Phone: 201-666-2906
Specialties: Folding knives of distinctive shapes. **Patterns:** High-tech folders. **Technical:** Grinds 440C and ATS-34. **Prices:** Start at $475. **Remarks:** Full-time maker; first knife sold in 1973. **Mark:** Last name with stylized throwing star.

VIKING KNIVES (SEE JAMES THORLIEF ERIKSEN)

VILAR, RICARDO AUGUSTO FERREIRA, Rua Alemada Dos Jasmins, NO 243, Parque Petropolis, Mairipora Sao Paulo, BRASIL 07600-000, Phone: 011-55-11-44-85-43-46
Specialties: Traditional Brazilian-style working knives of the Sao Paulo state. **Patterns:** Fighters, hunters, utility, and camp knives, welcome customer design. Specialize in the "true" Brazilian camp knife "Soracabana." **Technical:** Forges only with sledge hammer to 100% shape in 5160 and 52100 and his own Damascus steels. Makes own sheaths in the "true" traditional "Paulista"-style of the state of Sao Paulo. **Remark:** Full-time maker. **Prices:** $250 to $600. Uses only natural handle materials. **Mark:** Special designed signature styled name R. Vilar.

VILLA, LUIZ, R. Com. Miguel Calfat, 398 Itaim Bibi, Sao Paulo, SP-04537-081, BRAZIL, Phone: 011-8290649
Specialties: One-of-a-kind straight knives and jewel knives of all designs. **Patterns:** Bowies, hunters, utility/camp knives and jewel knives. **Technical:** Grinds D6, Damascus and 440C; forges 5160. Prefers natural handle material. **Prices:** $70 to $200. **Remarks:** Part-time maker; first knife sold in 1990. **Mark:** Last name and serial number.

VILLAR, RICARDO, Al. dos Jasmins, 243, Mairipora, S. P. 07600-000, BRAZIL, Phone: 011-4851649
Specialties: Straight working knives to customer specs. **Patterns:** Bowies, fighters and utility/camp knives. **Technical:** Grinds D6, ATS-34 and 440C stainless. **Prices:** $80 to $200. **Remarks:** Part-time maker; first knife sold in 1993. **Mark:** Percor over sword and circle.

VISTE, JAMES, Edgewize Forge, 13401 Mt Elliot, Detroit, MI 48212, Phone: 313-664-7455
Mark: EWF touch mark.

VISTNES, TOR, N-6930 Svelgen, NORWAY, Phone: 047-57795572
Specialties: Traditional and working knives of his design. **Patterns:** Hunters and utility knives. **Technical:** Grinds Uddeholm Elmax. Handles made of rear burls of different Nordic stabilized woods. **Prices:** $300 to $1100. **Remarks:** Part-time maker; first knife sold in 1988. **Mark:** Etched name and deer head.

VOGT, PATRIK, Kungsvagen 83, S-30270 Halmstad, SWEDEN, Phone: 46-35-30977
Specialties: Working straight knives. **Patterns:** Bowies, hunters & fighters. **Technical:** Forges carbon steel and own Damascus. **Prices:** From $100. **Remarks:** Not currently making knives. **Mark:** Initials or last name.

VOGT, DONALD J., 9007 Hogans Bend, Tampa, FL 33647, Phone: 813 973-3245
Specialties: Art knives, folders, automatics, large fixed blades. **Technical:** Uses Damascus steels for blade and bolsters, filework, hand carving on blade bolsters and handles. Other materials used - jewels, gold, stainless steel, mokume. Prefers to use natural handle materials. **Prices:** $800 to $7000. **Remarks:** Part-time maker; first knife sold in 1997. **Mark:** Last name.

VOORHIES, LES, 14511 Lk Mazaska Tr, Faribault, MN 55021, Phone: 507-332-0736
Specialties: Steels. **Technical:** ATS-34 Damascus. **Prices:** $75-$450.

VOSS, BEN, 362 Clark St, Galesburg, IL 61401, Phone: 309-342-6994
Specialties: Fancy working knives of his design. **Patterns:** Bowies, fighters, hunters, boots and folders. **Technical:** Grinds 440C, ATS-34 and D2. **Prices:** $35 to $1200. **Remarks:** Part-time maker; first knife sold in 1986. **Mark:** Name, city and state.

VOTAW, DAVID P., Box 327, Pioneer, OH 43554, Phone: 419-737-2774
Specialties: Working knives; period pieces. **Patterns:** Hunters, Bowies, camp knives, buckskinners and tomahawks. **Technical:** Grinds O1 and D2. **Prices:** $100 to $200; some to $500. **Remarks:** Part-time maker; took over for the late W. K. Kneubuhler. Doing business as W-K Knives. **Mark:** WK with V inside anvil.

VOWELL, DONALD J., 815 Berry Dr, Mayfield, KY 42066, Phone: 270-247-2157

VUNK, ROBERT, 3166 Breckenridge Dr, Colorado Springs, CO 80906, Phone: 719-576-5505
Specialties: Working knives, some fancy; period pieces. **Patterns:** Variety of tantos, fillet knives, kitchen knives, camp knives and folders. **Technical:** Grinds O1, 440C and ATS-34; provides mountings, cases, stands. **Prices:** $55 to $1300. **Remarks:** Part-time maker; first knife sold in 1985. Doing business as RV Knives. **Mark:** Initials.

W

WADA, YASUTAKA, Fujinokidai 2-6-22, Nara City, Nara prefect 631-0044, JAPAN, Phone: 0742 46-0689
Specialties: Fancy and embellished one-of-a-kind straight knives of his design. **Patterns:** Bowies, daggers and hunters. **Technical:** Grinds ATS-34, Cowry X and Cowry X L-30 laminate. **Prices:** $400 to $2500; some higher. **Remarks:** Part-time maker; first knife sold in 1990. **Mark:** Owl eyes with initial and last name underneath.

WAGAMAN, JOHN K., 903 Arsenal Ave, Fayetteville, NC 28305, Phone: 910-485-7860
Specialties: Fancy working knives. **Patterns:** Bowies, miniatures, hunters, fighters and boots. **Technical:** Grinds D2, 440C, 154CM and commercial Damascus; inlays mother-of-pearl. **Prices:** $110 to $2000. **Remarks:** Part-time maker; first knife sold in 1975. **Mark:** Last name.

WAHLSTER, MARK DAVID, 1404 N. Second St, Silverton, OR 97381, Phone: 503-873-3775
Specialties: Automatics, antique and high-tech folders in standard patterns and to customer specs. **Patterns:** Hunters, fillets and combat knives. **Technical:** Flat grinds 440C, ATS-34, D2 and Damascus. Uses titanium in folders. **Prices:** $100 to $1000. **Remarks:** Full-time maker; first knife sold in 1981. **Mark:** Name, city and state or last name.

WALDROP, MARK, 14562 SE 1st Ave. Rd, Summerfield, FL 34491, Phone: 352-347-9034
Specialties: Period pieces. **Patterns:** Bowies and daggers. **Technical:** Uses stock removal. Engraves. **Prices:** Moderate to upscale. **Remarks:** Part-time maker; first knife sold in 1978. **Mark:** Last name.

WALKER, GEORGE A., PO Box 3272, 483 Aspen Hills, Alpine, WY 83128-0272, Phone: 307-883-2372, Fax: 307-883-2372
Specialties: Deluxe working knives. **Patterns:** Hunters, boots, fighters, Bowies and folders. **Technical:** Forges his own Damascus and cable; engraves, carves, scrimshaws. Makes sheaths. **Prices:** $125 to $750; some to $1000. **Remarks:** Full-time maker; first knife sold in 1979. Partners with wife. **Mark:** Name, city and state.

WALKER, JIM, 22 Walker Lane, Morrilton, AR 72110, Phone: 501-354-3175
Specialties: Period pieces and working/using knives of his design and to customer specs. **Patterns:** Bowies, fighters, hunters, camp knives. **Technical:** Forges 5160, O1, L6, 52100, 1084, 1095. **Prices:** Start at $325. **Remarks:** Full-time maker; first knife sold in 1993. **Mark:** Three arrows with last name/MS.

WALKER, MICHAEL L., PO Box 1924, Rancho de Taos, NM 87571, Phone: 505-737-3086, Fax: 505-751-0284
Specialties: Innovative knife designs and locking systems; Titanium and SS furniture and art. **Patterns:** Folders from utility grade to museum quality art; others upon request. **Technical:** State-of-the-art materials: titanium, stainless Damascus, gold, etc. **Prices:** $3500 and above. **Remarks:** Designer/MetalCrafts; Full-time professional knife maker since 1980; Four U. S. Patents; Invented Liner-lock and was awarded Registered U. S.

custom knifemakers

Trademark No. 1,585,333. **Mark:** Early mark MW, Walker's Lockers by M. L. Walker; current M. L. Walker or Michael Walker.

WALKER, JOHN W., 10620 Moss Branch Rd, Bon Aqua, TN 37025, Phone: 931-670-4754
Specialties: Straight knives, daggers and folders; sterling rings, 14K gold wire wrap; some stone setting. **Patterns:** Hunters, boot knives, others. **Technical:** Grinds 440C, ATS-34, L6, etc. Buys Damascus. **Prices:** $150 to $500; some to $1500. **Remarks:** Part-time maker; first knife sold in 1982. **Mark:** Hohenzollern Eagle with name, or last name.

WALKER, BILL, 431 Walker Rd, Stevensville, MD 21666, Phone: 410-643-5041

WALKER, DON, 3236 Halls Chapel Rd, Burnsville, NC 28714, Phone: 828-675-9716

WALKER III, JOHN WADE, 2595 Hwy 1647, Paintlick, KY 40461, Phone: 606-792-3498

WALLACE, ROGER L., 4902 Collins Lane, Tampa, FL 33603, Phone: 813-239-3261
Specialties: Working straight knives, Bowies and camp knives to customer specs. **Patterns:** Hunters, skinners and utility knives. **Technical:** Forges high-carbon steel. **Prices:** Start at $75. **Remarks:** Part-time maker; first knife sold in 1985. **Mark:** First initial, last name.

WALLINGFORD JR., CHARLES W, 9024 US 42, Union, KY 41091, Phone: 606-384-4141
Specialties: 18th & 19th century styles - Patch knives, Rifleman knives. **Technical:** 1084 & 5160 forged blades. **Prices:** $125 to $300. **Mark:** CW.

WALTERS, A. F., PO Box 523, 275 Crawley Rd, TyTy, GA 31795, Phone: 229-528-6207
Specialties: Working knives, some to customer specs. **Patterns:** Locking folders, straight hunters, fishing and survival knives. **Technical:** Grinds D2, 154CM and 13C26. **Prices:** Start at $200. **Remarks:** Part-time maker. Label: "The jewel knife". **Mark:** "J" in diamond and knife logo.

WARD, J. J., 7501 S. R. 220, Waverly, OH 45690, Phone: 614-947-5328
Specialties: Traditional and working/using straight knives and folders of his design. **Patterns:** Hunters and locking folders. **Technical:** Grinds ATS-34, 440C and Damascus. Offers handmade sheaths. **Prices:** $125 to $250; some to $500. **Remarks:** Spare-time maker; first knife sold in 1980. **Mark:** Etched name.

WARD, KEN, 5122 Lake Shastina Blvd, Weed, CA 96094, Phone: 530-938-9720
Specialties: Working knives, some to customer specs. **Patterns:** Straight and folding hunters, axes, Bowies, buckskinners and miniatures. **Technical:** Grinds ATS-34, Damascus and Stellite 6K. **Prices:** $100 to $700. **Remarks:** Part-time maker; first knife sold in 1977. **Mark:** Name.

WARD, W. C., 817 Glenn St, Clinton, TN 37716, Phone: 615-457-3568
Specialties: Working straight knives; period pieces. **Patterns:** Hunters, Bowies, swords and kitchen cutlery. **Technical:** Grinds O1. **Prices:** $85 to $150; some to $500. **Remarks:** Part-time maker; first knife sold in 1969. He styled the Tennessee Knife Maker. **Mark:** TKM.

WARD, CHUCK, 1010 E. North St, Benton, AR 72015, Phone: 501-778-4329
Specialties: Traditional working and using straight knives and folders of his design. **Technical:** Grinds 440C, D2, A2, ATS-34 and O1; uses natural and composite handle materials. **Prices:** $90 to $400; some higher. **Remarks:** Part-time maker; first knife sold in 1990. **Mark:** First initial, last name.

WARDELL, MICK, 20, Clovelly Rd, Bideford, N Devon EX39 3BU, ENGLAND, Phone: 01237 475312, Fax: 01237 475312
Specialties: Folders of his design. **Patterns:** Locking and slip-joint folder, hunters and Bowies. **Technical:** Grinds ATS-34, D2 and Damascus. Heat-treats. **Prices:** $200 to $800. **Remarks:** Full-time maker; first knife sold in 1986. **Mark:** M. Wardell - England

WARDEN, ROY A., 275 Tanglewood Rd, Union, MO 63084, Phone: 314-583-8813
Specialties: Complex mosaic designs of "EDM wired figures" and "Stack up" patterns and "Lazer Cut" and "Torch cut" and "Sawed" patterns combined. **Patterns:** Mostly "all mosaic" folders, automatics, fixed blades. **Technical:** Mosaic Damascus with all tool steel edges. **Prices:** $500 to $2000 and up. **Remarks:** Part-time maker; first knife sold in 1987. **Mark:** WARDEN stamped or initials connected.

WARE, TOMMY, PO Box 488, Datil, NM 87821, Phone: 505-772-5817
Specialties: Traditional working and using straight knives, folders and automatics of his design and to customer specs. **Patterns:** Hunters, auto-matics and locking folders. **Technical:** Grinds ATS-34, 440C and D2. Offers engraving and scrimshaw. **Prices:** $275 to $575; some to $1000. **Remarks:** Full-time maker; first knife sold in 1990. Doing business as Wano Knives. **Mark:** Last name inside oval, business name above, city and state below, year on side.

WARENSKI, BUSTER, PO Box 214, Richfield, UT 84701, Phone: 435-896-5319
Specialties: Investor-class straight knives. **Patterns:** Daggers, swords. **Technical:** Grinds, engraves and inlays; offers surface treatments. All engraved by Julie Warenski. **Prices:** Upscale. **Remarks:** Full-time maker. **Mark:** Warenski (hand engraved on blade).

WARREN, AL, 1423 Sante Fe Circle, Roseville, CA 95678, Phone: 916-784-3217/Cell Phone 916-257-5904
Specialties: Working straight knives and folders, some fancy. **Patterns:** Hunters, Bowies, daggers, short swords, fillets, folders and kitchen knives. **Technical:** Grinds D2, ATS-34 and 440C, 440V. **Prices:** $110 to $1100; some to $3700. **Remarks:** Part-time maker; first knife sold in 1978. **Mark:** First and middle initials, last name.

WARREN, DANIEL, 571 Lovejoy Rd, Canton, NC 28716, Phone: 828-648-7351
Specialties: Using knives. **Patterns:** Drop point hunters. **Prices:** $200 to $500. **Mark:** Warren-Bethel NC.

WARREN (SEE DELLANA)

WARTHER, DALE, 331 Karl Ave, Dover, OH 44622, Phone: 216-343-7513
Specialties: Working knives; period pieces. **Patterns:** Kitchen cutlery, daggers, hunters and some folders. **Technical:** Forges and grinds O1, D2 and 440C. **Prices:** $250 to $7000. **Remarks:** Full-time maker; first knife sold in 1967. Takes orders only at shows or by personal interviews at his shop. **Mark:** Warther Originals.

WASHBURN, ARTHUR D., ADW Custom Knives, 10 Hinman St/POB 625, Pioche, NV 89043, Phone: 775-962-5463
Specialties: Locking liner folders. **Patterns:** Slip joint folders (single & multiplied), lock-back folders, some fixed blades. Do own heat-treating; Rockwell test each blade. **Technical:** Carbon & stainless Damascus, some 1084, 1095, ATS-34. **Prices:** $200 to $1000 and up. **Remarks:** Sold first knife in 1997. Part-time maker. **Mark:** ADW enclosed in an oval or ADW.

WASHBURN JR., ROBERT LEE, 244 Lovett Scott Rd, Adrian, GA 31002, Phone: 475-275-7926, Fax: 475-272-6849
Specialties: Hand-forged period, Bowies, tactical, boot & hunters. **Patterns:** Bowies, tantos, loot hunters, tactical and folders. **Prices:** $100 to $2500. **Remarks:** All hand forged. 52100 being my favorite steel. **Mark:** Washburn Knives W of Dublin GA.

WATANABE, WAYNE, PO Box 3563, Montebello, CA 90640
Specialties: Straight knives in Japanese-styles. One-of-a-kind designs; welcomes customer designs. **Patterns:** Tantos to katanas, Bowies. **Technical:** Flat grinds A2, O1 and ATS-34. Offers hand-rubbed finishes and wrapped handles. **Prices:** Start at $200. **Remarks:** Part-time maker. **Mark:** Name in characters with flower.

WATERS, HERMAN HAROLD, 2516 Regency, Magnolia, AR 71753, Phone: 870-234-5409

WATERS, GLENN, 11 Shinakawa Machi, Hirosaki City 036-8183, JAPAN, Phone: 172-33-8881
Specialties: One-of-a-kind collector-grade highly embellished art knives. Folders, fixed blades, and automatics. **Patterns:** Locking liner folders, automatics and fixed art knives. **Technical:** Grinds blades from Damasteel, and selected Damascus makers, mostly stainless. Does own engraving, gold inlaying and stone setting, filework, and carving. Gold and Japanese precious metal fabrication. Prefers exotic material, high karat gold, silver, Shyaku Dou, Shibu Ichi Gin, precious gemstones. **Prices:** Upscale. **Remarks:** Designs and makes some-of-a-kind highly embellished art knives often with fully engraved handles and blades. A jeweler by trade for 20 years before starting to make knives. Full-time since 1999, first knife sold in 1994. **Mark:** Glenn Waters maker Japan, G. Waters or Glen in Japanese writing.

WATERS, LU, 2516 Regency, Magnolia, AR 71753, Phone: 870-234-5409

WATSON, BILLY, 440 Forge Rd, Deatsville, AL 36022, Phone: 334-365-1482
Specialties: Working and using straight knives and folders of his design; period pieces. **Patterns:** Hunters, Bowies and utility/camp knives. **Technical:** Forges and grinds his own Damascus, 1095, 5160 and 52100. **Prices:** $25 to $1500. **Remarks:** Full-time maker; first knife sold in 1970. Doing business as Billy's Blacksmith Shop. **Mark:** Last name.

WATSON, TOM, 1103 Brenau Terrace, Panama City, FL 32405, Phone: 850-785-9209
Specialties: Liner-lock folders. **Patterns:** Tactical, utility and art investment pieces. **Technical:** Flat-grinds ATS-34, 440-V, Damascus. **Prices:** Tactical start at $250, investment pieces $500 & up. **Remarks:** In business since 1978. **Mark:** Name and city.

WATSON, DANIEL, 350 Jennifer Ln., Driftwood, TX 78619, Phone: 512-847-9679
Specialties: One-of-a-kind knives and swords. **Patterns:** Hunters, daggers, swords. **Technical:** Hand-purify and carbonize his own high-carbon steel, pattern-welded Damascus, cable and carbon-induced crystalline Damascus. European and Japanese tempering. **Prices:** $125 to $25,000. **Remarks:** Full-time maker; first knife sold in 1979. **Mark:** "Angel Sword" on forged pieces; "Bright Knight" for stock removal.

WATSON, PETER, 66 Kielblock St, La Hoff 2570, SOUTH AFRICA, Phone: 018-84942
Specialties: Traditional working and using straight knives and folders of his design. **Patterns:** Hunters, locking folders and utility/camp knives. **Technical:** Sandvik and 440C. **Prices:** $120 to $250; some to $1500. **Remarks:** Part-time maker; first knife sold in 1989. **Mark:** Buffalo head with name.

WATSON, BERT, PO Box 26, Westminster, CO 80036-0026, Phone: 303-426-7577
Specialties: Working/using straight knives of his design and to customer specs. **Patterns:** Hunters, utility/camp knives. **Technical:** Grinds O1, ATS-34, 440C, D2, A2 and others. **Prices:** $50 to $250. **Remarks:** Part-time maker; first knife sold in 1974. Doing business as Game Trail Knives. **Mark:** GTK stamped or etched, sometimes with first or last name.

WATT III, FREDDIE, PO Box 1372, Big Spring, TX 79721, Phone: 915-263-6629
Specialties: Working straight knives, some fancy. **Patterns:** Hunters, fighters and Bowies. **Technical:** Grinds A2, D2, 440C and ATS-34; prefers mirror finishes. **Prices:** $150 to $350; some to $750. **Remarks:** Full-time maker; first knife sold in 1979. **Mark:** Last name, city and state.

WATTELET, MICHAEL A., PO Box 649, 125 Front, Minocqua, WI 54548, Phone: 715-356-3069
Specialties: Working and using straight knives of his design and to customer specs; fantasy knives. **Patterns:** Daggers, fighters and swords. **Technical:** Grinds 440C and L6; forges and grinds O1. Silversmith. **Prices:** $75 to $1000; some to $5000. **Remarks:** Full-time maker; first knife sold in 1966. Doing business as M & N Arts Ltd. **Mark:** First initial, last name.

WATTS, WALLY, 9560 S. Hwy. 36, Gatesville, TX 76528, Phone: 254-487-2866
Specialties: Unique traditional folders of his design. **Patterns:** One- to five-blade folders and single-blade gents in various blade shapes. **Technical:** Grinds ATS-34; D2 and 440C on request. **Prices:** $150 to $250; some to $500. **Remarks:** Full-time maker; first knife sold in 1986. **Mark:** Last name.

WEDDLE JR., DEL, 2703 Green Valley Rd, St. Joseph, MO 64505, Phone: 816-364-1981
Specialties: Working knives; some period pieces. **Patterns:** Hunters, fighters, locking folders, push knives. **Technical:** Grinds D2 and 440C; can provide precious metals and set gems. Offers his own forged wire-cable Damascus in his finished knives. **Prices:** $80 to $250; some to $2000. **Remarks:** Full-time maker; first knife sold in 1972. **Mark:** Signature with last name and date.

WEHNER, RUDY, 297 William Warren Rd, Collins, MS 39428, Phone: 601-765-4997
Specialties: Reproduction antique Bowies and contemporary Bowies in full and miniature. **Patterns:** Skinners, camp knives, fighters, axes and Bowies. **Technical:** Grinds 440C, ATS-34, 154CM and Damascus. **Prices:** $100 to $500; some to $850. **Remarks:** Full-time maker; first knife sold in 1975. **Mark:** Last name on Bowies and antiques; full name, city and state on skinners.

WEILAND JR., J. REESE, PO Box 2337, Riverview, FL 33568, Phone: 813-671-0661
Specialties: Hawk bills; tactical to fancy folders. **Patterns:** Hunters, tantos, Bowies, fantasy knives, spears and some swords. **Technical:** Grinds ATS-34, 154CM, 440C, D2, 01, A2, Damascus. Titanium hardware on locking liners and button locks. **Prices:** $150 to $4000. **Other:** Full-time maker, first knife sold in 1978. Knifemakers Guild member since 1988.

WEILER, DONALD E., PO Box 1576, Yuma, AZ 85366-9576, Phone: 928-782-1159
Specialties: Working straight knives; period pieces. **Patterns:** Strong springbuck folders, blade & spring ATS-34. **Technical:** Forges O1, W2, 5160, ATS-34 and cable Damascus. Makes his own high-carbon steel

Damascus. **Prices:** $80 to $1000. **Remarks:** Full-time maker; first knife sold in 1952. **Mark:** Last name, city.

WEINAND, GEROME M., 14440 Harpers Bridge Rd, Missoula, MT 59808, Phone: 406-543-0845
Specialties: Working straight knives. **Patterns:** Bowies, fishing and camp knives, large special hunters. **Technical:** Grinds O1, 440C, ATS-34, 1084, L6, also stainless Damascus, Aebl and 304; makes all-tool steel Damascus; Dendritic D2 from powdered steel. Heat-treats. **Prices:** $30 to $100; some to $500. **Remarks:** Full-time maker; first knife sold in 1982. **Mark:** Last name.

WEINSTOCK, ROBERT, PO Box 170028, San Francisco, CA 94117-0028, Phone: 415-731-5968
Specialties: Fancy and high-art straight knives of his design. **Patterns:** Daggers, folders, poignards and miniatures. **Technical:** Grinds A2, O1 and 440C. Chased and hand-carved blades and handles. Also using various Damascus steels from other makers. **Prices:** $3000 to 7,000+. **Remarks:** Full-time maker; first knife sold in 1994. **Mark:** Last name carved.

WEISS, CHARLES L., 18847 N. 13th Ave, Phoenix, AZ 85027, Phone: 623-582-6147
Specialties: High-art straight knives and folders; deluxe period pieces. **Patterns:** Daggers, fighters, boots, push knives and miniatures. **Technical:** Grinds 440C, 154CM and ATS-34. **Prices:** $300 to $1200; some to $2000. **Remarks:** Full-time maker; first knife sold in 1975. **Mark:** Name and city.

WELCH, WILLIAM H., 8232 W. Red Snapper Dr, Kimmell, IN 46760, Phone: 219-856-3577
Specialties: Working knives; deluxe period pieces. **Patterns:** Hunters, tantos, Bowies. **Technical:** Grinds ATS-34, D2 and 440C. **Prices:** $100 to $600. **Remarks:** Part-time maker; first knife sold in 1976. **Mark:** Last name.

WERNER JR., WILLIAM A., 336 Lands Mill, Marietta, GA 30067, Phone: 404-988-0074
Specialties: Fantasy and working/using straight knives. **Patterns:** Bowies, daggers, fighters. **Technical:** Grinds 440C stainless, 10 series carbon and Damascus. **Prices:** $150 to $400; some to $750. **Remarks:** Part-time maker. Doing business as Werner Knives. **Mark:** Last name.

WERTH, GEORGE W., 5223 Woodstock Rd, Poplar Grove, IL 61065, Phone: 815-544-4408
Specialties: Period pieces, some fancy. **Patterns:** Straight fighters, daggers and Bowies. **Technical:** Forges and grinds O1, 1095 and his Damascus, including mosaic patterns. **Prices:** $200 to $650; some higher. **Remarks:** Full-time maker. Doing business as Fox Valley Forge. **Mark:** Name in logo or initials connected.

WESCOTT, CODY, 5330 White Wing Rd, Las Cruces, NM 88012, Phone: 505-382-5008
Specialties: Fancy and presentation-grade working knives. **Patterns:** Hunters, locking folders and Bowies. **Technical:** Hollow-grinds D2 and ATS-34; all knives file worked. Offers some engraving. Makes sheaths. **Prices:** $80 to $300; some to $950. **Remarks:** Full-time maker; first knife sold in 1982. **Mark:** First initial, last name.

WEST, CHARLES A., 1315 S. Pine St, Centralia, IL 62801, Phone: 618-532-2777
Specialties: Classic, fancy, high tech, period pieces, traditional and working/using straight knives and folders. **Patterns:** Bowies, fighters and locking folders. **Technical:** Grinds ATS-34, O1 and Damascus. Prefers hot blued finishes. **Prices:** $100 to $1000; some to $2000. **Remarks:** Full-time maker; first knife sold in 1963. Doing business as West Custom Knives. **Mark:** Name or name, city and state.

WEST, PAT, PO Box 9, Charlotte, TX 78011, Phone: 830-277-1290
Specialties: Classic working and using straight knives and folders. **Patterns:** Hunters, kitchen knives, slip-joint folders. **Technical:** Grinds ATS-34, D2 and Vascowear. Offers filework and decorates liners on folders. **Prices:** $300 to $600. **Remarks:** Spare-time maker; first knife sold in 1984. **Mark:** Name.

WESTBERG, LARRY, 305 S. Western Hills Dr, Algona, IA 50511, Phone: 515-295-9276
Specialties: Traditional and working straight knives of his design and in standard patterns. **Patterns:** Bowies, hunters, utility knives and miniatures. **Technical:** Grinds 440C, D2 and 1095. Heat-treats. Uses natural handle materials. **Prices:** $85 to $600; some to $1000. **Remarks:** Part-time maker; first knife sold in 1987. **Mark:** Last name-town & state.

WHEELER, ROBERT, 289 S Jefferson, Bradley, IL 60915, Phone: 815-932-5854

WHETSELL, ALEX, 1600 Palmetto Tyrone Rd, Sharpsburg, GA 30277, Phone: 770-463-4881
Specialties: Knifekits.com, a source for fold locking liner type and straight knife kits. Our kits are industry standard for folding knife kits. **Technical:**

custom knifemakers

Many selections of colored G10 carbon fiber, and wood handle material for our kits as well as bulk sizes for the custom knife maker, heat treated folding knife pivots, screws, bushings, etc.

WHIPPLE, WESLEY A., PO Box 3771, Kodiak, AK 99615, Phone: 907-486-6737
Specialties: Working straight knives, some fancy. **Patterns:** Hunters, Bowies, camp knives, fighters. **Technical:** Forges high carbon steels, Damascus, offers relief carving & silver wire inlay. **Prices:** $200 to $800; some higher. **Remarks:** Part-time maker; first knife sold in 1989. **Mark:** Last name/JS. **Other:** A. K. A. Wilderness Knife and Forge, Box 3771 Kodiak, AK 99615 907-486-6737

WHITE, ROBERT J., RR 1, 641 Knox Rd. 900 N., Gilson, IL 61436, Phone: 309-289-4487
Specialties: Working knives, some deluxe. **Patterns:** Bird and trout knives, hunters, survival knives and locking folders. **Technical:** Grinds A2, D2 and 440C; commercial Damascus. Heat-treats. **Prices:** $125 to $250; some to $600. **Remarks:** Full-time maker; first knife sold in 1976. **Mark:** Last name in script.

WHITE, BRYCE, 1415 W Col. Glenn Rd, Little Rock, AR 72210, Phone: 501-821-2956
Specialties: Hunters, fighters, makes Damascus, file work, handmade only. **Technical:** L6, 1075, 1095, 01 steels used most. **Patterns:** I will do any pattern or use my own. **Prices:** $200 to $300. Sold first knife in 1995. **Mark:** White.

WHITE, RICHARD T., 359 Carver St, Grosse Pointe Farms, MI 48236, Phone: 313-881-4690

WHITE, LOU, 7385 Red Bud Rd Ne, Ranger, GA 30734, Phone: 706-334-2273

WHITE, DALE, 525 CR 212, Sweetwater, TX 79556, Phone: 325-798-4178
Specialties: Working and using knives. **Patterns:** Hunters, skinners, utilities and Bowies. **Technical:** Grinds 440C, offers file work, fancy pins and scrimshaw by Sherry Sellers. **Prices:** From $45 to $300. **Remarks:** Sold first knife in 1975. **Mark:** Full name, city and state.

WHITE, GENE E., 6620 Briarleigh Way, Alexandria, VA 22315, Phone: 703-924-1268
Specialties: Small utility/gents knives. **Patterns:** Eight standard hunters; most other patterns on commission basis. Currently no swords, axes and fantasy knives. **Technical:** Stock removal 440C and D2; others on request. Mostly hollow grinds; some flat grinds. Prefers natural handle materials. Makes own sheaths. **Prices:** Start at $85. **Remarks:** Part-time maker; first knife sold in 1971. **Mark:** First and middle initials, last name.

WHITE JR., ROBERT J. BUTCH, RR 1, Gilson, IL 61436, Phone: 309-289-4487
Specialties: Folders of all sizes. **Patterns:** Hunters, fighters, boots and folders. **Technical:** Forges Damascus; grinds tool and stainless steels. **Prices:** $500 to $1800. **Remarks:** Spare-time maker; first knife sold in 1980. **Mark:** Last name in block letters.

WHITENECT, JODY, Elderbank, Halifax County, Nova Scotia, CANADA B0N 1K0, Phone: 902-384-2511
Specialties: Fancy and embellished working/using straight knives of his design and to customer specs. **Patterns:** Bowies, fighters and hunters. **Technical:** Forges 1095 and O1; forges and grinds ATS-34. Various filework on blades and bolsters. **Prices:** $200 to $400; some to $800. **Remarks:** Part-time maker; first knife sold in 1996. **Mark:** Longhorn stamp or engraved.

WHITLEY, WELDON G., 1308 N Robin Ave, Odessa, TX 79764, Phone: 915-584-2274
Specialties: Working knives of his design or to customer specs. **Patterns:** Hunters, folders and various double-edged knives. **Technical:** Grinds 440C, 154CM and ATS-34. **Prices:** $150 to $1250. **Mark:** Name, address, road-runner logo.

WHITLEY, L. WAYNE, 1675 Carrow Rd, Chocowinity, NC 27817-9495, Phone: 252-946-5648

WHITMAN, JIM, 21044 Salem St, Chugiak, AK 99567, Phone: 907-688-4575, Fax: 907-688-4278
Specialties: Working straight knives and folders; some art pieces. **Patterns:** Hunters, skinners, Bowies, camp knives, working fighters, swords and hatchets. **Technical:** Grinds AEB-L Swedish, 440C, 154CM, ATS-34, and Damascus in full convex. Prefers exotic hardwoods, natural and native handle materials—whale bone, antler, ivory and horn. **Prices:** Start at $150. **Remarks:** Full-time maker; first knife sold in 1983. **Mark:** Name, city, state.

WHITMIRE, EARL T., 725 Colonial Dr, Rock Hill, SC 29730, Phone: 803-324-8384
Specialties: Working straight knives, some to customer specs; some fantasy pieces. **Patterns:** Hunters, fighters and fishing knives. **Technical:** Grinds D2, 440C and 154CM. **Prices:** $40 to $200; some to $250. **Remarks:** Full-time maker; first knife sold in 1967. **Mark:** Name, city, state in oval logo.

WHITTAKER, WAYNE, 2900 Woodland Ct, Metamore, MI 48455, Phone: 810-797-5315
Specialties: Folders, hunters on request. **Patterns:** Bowies, daggers and hunters. **Technical:** ATS-34 S. S. and Damascus **Prices:** $300 to $500; some to $2000. **Remarks:** Full-time maker; first knife sold in 1985. **Mark:** Etched name on one side.

WHITTAKER, ROBERT E., PO Box 204, Mill Creek, PA 17060
Specialties: Using straight knives. Has a line of knives for buckskinners. **Patterns:** Hunters, skinners and Bowies. **Technical:** Grinds O1, A2 and D2. Offers filework. **Prices:** $35 to $100. **Remarks:** Part-time maker; first knife sold in 1980. **Mark:** Last initial or full initials.

WHITTAKER, RANDY, 6930 Burruss Mill Rd, Cummings, GA 30131, Phone: 770-889-5263

WHITWORTH, KEN J., 41667 Tetley Ave, Sterling Heights, MI 48078, Phone: 313-739-5720
Specialties: Working straight knives and folders. **Patterns:** Locking folders, slip-joints and boot knives. **Technical:** Grinds 440C, 154CM and D2. **Prices:** $100 to $225; some to $450. **Remarks:** Part-time maker; first knife sold in 1976. **Mark:** Last name.

WICKER, DONNIE R., 2544 E. 40th Ct, Panama City, FL 32405, Phone: 904-785-9158
Specialties: Traditional working and using straight knives of his design or to customer specs. **Patterns:** Hunters, fighters and slip-joint folders. **Technical:** Grinds 440C, ATS-34, D2 and 154CM. Heat-treats and does hardness testing. **Prices:** $90 to $200; some to $400. **Remarks:** Part-time maker; first knife sold in 1975. **Mark:** First and middle initials, last name.

WIGGINS, HORACE, 203 Herndon, Box 152, Mansfield, LA 71502, Phone: 318-872-4471
Specialties: Fancy working knives. **Patterns:** Straight and folding hunters. **Technical:** Grinds O1, D2 and 440C. **Prices:** $90 to $275. **Remarks:** Part-time maker; first knife sold in 1970. **Mark:** Name, city and state in diamond logo.

WILCHER, WENDELL L., RR 6 Box 6573, Palestine, TX 75801, Phone: 903-549-2530
Specialties: Fantasy, miniatures and working/using straight knives and folders of his design and to customer specs. **Patterns:** Fighters, hunters, locking folders. **Technical:** Hand works (hand file and hand sand knives), not grind. **Prices:** $75 to $250; some to $600. **Remarks:** Part-time maker; first knife sold in 1987. **Mark:** Initials, year, serial number.

WILE, PETER, RR 3, Bridgewater, Nova Scotia, CANADA B4V 2W2, Phone: 902-543-1373
Specialties: Collector-grade one-of-a-kind file-worked folders. **Patterns:** Folders or fixed blades of his design or to customers specs. **Technical:** Grinds ATS-34, carbon and stainless Damascus. Does intricate filework on blades, spines and liners. Carves. Prefers natural handle materials. Does own heat treating. **Prices:** $350 to $2000; some to $4000. **Remarks:** Part-time maker; sold first knife in 1985; doing business as Wile Knives. **Mark:** Wile

WILKINS, MITCHELL, 15523 Ralson Chapel Rd, Montgomery, TX 77316, Phone: 409-588-2696

WILLEY, W. G., R. D. 1, Box 235-B, Greenwood, DE 19950, Phone: 302-349-4070
Specialties: Fancy working straight knives. **Patterns:** Small game knives, Bowies and throwing knives. **Technical:** Grinds 440C and 154CM. **Prices:** $225 to $600; some to $1500. **Remarks:** Part-time maker; first knife sold in 1975. Owns retail store. **Mark:** Last name inside map logo.

WILLIAM E, STAPLETON, Buffalo 'B' Forge, 5425 Country Ln, Merritt Island, FL 32953
Specialties: Classic and traditional knives of my design and customer spec. **Patterns:** Hunters and using knives. **Technical:** Forges, 01 and L-6 Damascus, cable Damascus and 5160; stock removal on request. **Prices:** $150 to $1000. **Remarks:** Part-time maker, first knife sold 1990. Doing business as Buffalo "B" Forge. **Mark:** Anvil with S initial in center of anvil.

WILLIAMS, A. L., 4950 Lake Pierce Dr, Lake Wales, FL 33853, Phone: 941-439-1906

WILLIAMS, MICHAEL L., Rt. 4, PO Box 64-1, Broken Bow, OK 74728, Phone: 405-494-6326
Specialties: Plain to fancy working and dress knives. **Patterns:** Hunters, Bowies, camp knives and others. **Technical:** Forges 1084, L6, 52100 and pattern-welded steel. **Prices:** $295 and up. **Remarks:** Part-time maker; first knife sold in 1989. ABS Mastersmith. **Mark:** Williams.

WILLIAMS, JASON L., PO Box 67, Wyoming, RI 02898, Phone: 401-539-8353, Fax: 401-539-0252
Specialties: Fancy & high tech folders of his design, co-inventor of the Axis Lock. **Patterns:** Fighters, locking folders, automatics and fancy pocket knives. **Technical:** Forges Damascus and other steels by request. Uses exotic handle materials and precious metals. Offers inlaid spines and gemstone thumb knobs. **Prices:** $1000 and up. **Remarks:** Full-time maker; first knife sold in 1989. **Mark:** First and last initials on pivot.

WILLIAMS JR., RICHARD, 1440 Nancy Circle, Morristown, TN 37814, Phone: 615-581-0059
Specialties: Working and using straight knives of his design or to customer specs. **Patterns:** Hunters, dirks and utility/camp knives. **Technical:** Forges 5160 and uses file steel. Hand-finish is standard; offers filework. **Prices:** $80 to $180; some to $250. **Remarks:** Spare-time maker; first knife sold in 1985. **Mark:** Last initial or full initials.

WILLIAMSON, TONY, Rt. 3, Box 503, Siler City, NC 27344, Phone: 919-663-3551
Specialties: Flint knapping—knives made of obsidian flakes and flint with wood, antler or bone for handles. **Patterns:** Skinners, daggers and flake knives. **Technical:** Blades have width/thickness ratio of at least 4 to 1. Hafts with methods available to prehistoric man. **Prices:** $58 to $160. **Remarks:** Student of Errett Callahan. **Mark:** Initials and number code to identify year and number of knives made.

WILLIS, BILL, RT 7 Box 7549, Ava, MO 65608, Phone: 417-683-4326
Specialties: Forged blades, Damascus & carbon steel. **Patterns:** Cable, random or ladder lamented. **Technical:** Professionally heat treated blades. **Prices:** $75 to $600. **Remarks:** Lifetime guarantee on all blades against breakage. **Mark:** WF. **Other:** All work done by myself; including leather work.

WILLSON, WAYNE O, 11403 Sunflower Ln, Fairfax, VA 22030-6031, Phone: 703-278-8000

WILSON, JAMES R, PO Box 1285, Westcliffe, CO 81252, Phone: 719-331-4995
Specialties: Collectible, traditional functional knives. **Patterns:** Bowies, fighters, hunters, skinners and folders. **Technical:** Forges 5160, 1095 & my own Damascus. **Prices:** $150 to $1000. **Remarks:** Limited production fine knives; first knife sold in 1994. **Mark:** J and last name.

WILSON, MIKE, 1416 McDonald Rd, Hayesville, NC 28904, Phone: 828-389-8145
Specialties: Fancy working and using straight knives of his design or to customer specs, folders. **Patterns:** Hunters, Bowies, utility knives, gut hooks, skinners, fighters and miniatures. **Technical:** Hollow-grinds 440C, L-6, 01 and D2. Mirror finishes are standard. Offers filework. **Prices:** $50 to $600. **Remarks:** Full-time maker; first knife sold in 1985. **Mark:** Last name.

WILSON, RON, 2639 Greenwood ave, Morro Bay, CA 93442, Phone: 805-772-3381
Specialties: Classic and fantasy straight knives of his design. **Patterns:** Daggers, fighters, swords and axes—mostly all miniatures. **Technical:** Forges and grinds Damascus and various tool steels; grinds meteorite. Uses gold, precious stones and exotic woods. **Prices:** Vary. **Remarks:** Part-time maker; first knife sold in 1995. **Mark:** Stamped first and last initials.

WILSON, PHILIP C., Seamount Knifeworks, PO Box 846, Mountain Ranch, CA 95246, Phone: 209-754-1990
Specialties: Working knives; emphasis on salt water fillet knives and utility hunters of his design. **Patterns:** Fishing knives, hunters, kitchen knives. **Technical:** Grinds CPM S-30V, CPM10V, S-90V and 154CM. Heat-treats and Rockwell tests all blades. **Prices:** Start at $280. **Remarks:** First knife sold in 1985. Doing business as Sea-Mount Knife Works. **Mark:** Signature.

WILSON, R. W., PO Box 2012, Weirton, WV 26062, Phone: 304-723-2771
Specialties: Working straight knives; period pieces. **Patterns:** Bowies, tomahawks and patch knives. **Prices:** $85 to $175; some to $1000. **Technical:** Grinds 440C; scrimshaws. **Remarks:** Part-time maker; first knife sold in 1966. Knife maker supplier. Offers free knife-making lessons. **Mark:** Name in tomahawk.

WILSON, JAMES G., PO Box 4024, Estes Park, CO 80517, Phone: 303-586-3944
Specialties: Bronze Age knives; Medieval and Scottish-styles; tomahawks. **Patterns:** Bronze knives, daggers, swords, spears and battle axes; 12-inch steel Misericorde daggers, sgian dubhs, "his and her" skinners, bird and fish knives, capers, boots and daggers. **Technical:** Casts bronze; grinds D2, 440C and ATS-34. **Prices:** $49 to $400; some to $1300. **Remarks:** Part-time maker; first knife sold in 1975. **Mark:** WilsonHawk.

WILSON, JON J., 1826 Ruby St, Johnstown, PA 15902, Phone: 814-266-6410
Specialties: Miniatures & full size. **Patterns:** Bowies, daggers and hunters. **Technical:** Grinds Damascus, 440C and O1. Scrimshaws and carves. **Prices:** $75 to $500; some higher. **Remarks:** Full-time maker; first knife sold in 1988. **Mark:** First and middle initials, last name.

WILSON (SEE SIMONELLA, GIANLUIGI)

WILSON, III, GEORGE H., 150-6 Dreiser Loop #6-B, Bronx, NY 10475

WIMPFF, CHRISTIAN, PO Box 700526, 70574 Stuttgart 70, GERMANY, Phone: 711 7206 749, Fax: 711 7206 749
Specialties: High-tech folders of his design. **Patterns:** Boots, locking folders and liners locks. **Technical:** Grinds CPM-T-440V, ATS-34 and Schneider stainless Damascus. Offers meteorite bolsters and blades. **Prices:** $1000 to $2800; some to $4000. **Remarks:** Full-time maker; first knife sold in 1984. **Mark:** First initial, last name.

WINBERG, DOUGLAS R., 19720 Hiway 78, Ramona, CA 92076, Phone: 760-788-8304

WINGO, PERRY, 22 55th St, Gulfport, MS 39507, Phone: 228-863-3193
Specialties: Traditional working straight knives. **Patterns:** Hunters, skinners, Bowies and fishing knives. **Technical:** Grinds 440C. **Prices:** $75 to $1000. **Remarks:** Full-time maker; first knife sold in 1988. **Mark:** Last name.

WINGO, GARY, 240 Ogeechee, Ramona, OK 74061, Phone: 918-536-1067
Specialties: Folder specialist. Steel 44OC, D2, others on request. Handle bone-stag, others on request. **Patterns:** Trapper 3-blade stockman, 4-blade congress, single- and 2-blade barlows. **Prices:** 150 to $400. **Mark:** First knife sold 1994. Steer head with Wingo Knives or Straight line Wingo Knives.

WINKLER, DANIEL, PO Box 2166, Blowing Rock, NC 28605, Phone: 828-295-9156, Fax: 828-295-0673
Specialties: Forged cutlery styled in the tradition of an era past. **Patterns:** Fixed blades, friction folders, axes/tomahawks and war clubs. **Technical:** Forges and grinds carbon steels and his own Damascus. **Prices:** $200 to $4000. **Remarks:** Full-time maker since 1988. Exclusively offers leatherwork by Karen Shook. **Mark:** Initials connected. **Other:** ABS MasterSmith; Knifemakers Guild voting member.

WINN, TRAVIS A., 558 E. 3065 S., Salt Lake City, UT 84106, Phone: 801-467-5957
Specialties: Fancy working knives and knives to customer specs. **Patterns:** Hunters, fighters, boots, Bowies and fancy daggers, some miniatures, tantos and fantasy knives. **Technical:** Grinds D2 and 440C. Embellishes. **Prices:** $125 to $500; some higher. **Remarks:** Part-time maker; first knife sold in 1976. **Mark:** TRAV stylized.

WINSTON, DAVID, 1671 Red Holly St, Starkville, MS 39759, Phone: 601-323-1028
Specialties: Fancy and traditional knives of his design and to customer specs. **Patterns:** Bowies, daggers, hunters, boot knives and folders. **Technical:** Grinds 440C, ATS-34 and D2. Offers filework; heat-treats. **Prices:** $40 to $750; some higher. **Remarks:** Part-time maker; first knife sold in 1984. Offers lifetime sharpening for original owner. **Mark:** Last name.

WINTER, GEORGE, 5940 Martin Hwy, Union City, TN 38261

WIRTZ, ACHIM, Mittelstrasse 58, Wuerselen, D-52146, GERMANY, Phone: 0049-2405-2587
Specialties: Period pieces, Scandinavian and middle east style knives. **Technical:** Forges 5160, and own Damascus. Makes wootz and mokume gane. **Prices:** Start at $50. **Remarks:** Spare-time maker. First knife sold in 1997. **Mark:** Stylized initials.

WISE, DONALD, 304 Bexhill Rd, St. Leonardo-On-Sea, East Sussex, TN3 8AL, ENGLAND
Specialties: Fancy and embellished working straight knives to customer specs. **Patterns:** Hunters, Bowies and daggers. **Technical:** Grinds Sandvik 12C27, D2 D3 and O1. Scrimshaws. **Prices:** $110 to $300; some to $500. **Remarks:** Full-time maker; first knife sold in 1983. **Mark:** KNIFECRAFT.

WITSAMAN, EARL, 3957 Redwing Circle, Stow, OH 44224, Phone: 330-688-4208
Specialties: Straight and fantasy miniatures. **Patterns:** Wide variety—Randalls to D-guard Bowies. **Technical:** Grinds O1, 440C and 300 stainless; buys Damascus; highly detailed work. **Prices:** $85 to $300. **Remarks:** Part-time maker; first knife sold in 1974. **Mark:** Initials.

custom knifemakers

WOLF, BILL, 4618 N. 79th Ave, Phoenix, AZ 85033, Phone: 623-846-3585, Fax: 623-846-3585
Specialties: Investor-grade folders and straight knives. **Patterns:** Lockback, slip joint and side lock interframes. **Technical:** Grinds ATS-34 and 440C. **Prices:** $400 to $1800. **Remarks:** Full-time maker; first knife sold in 1989. **Mark:** Name.

WOLF JR., WILLIAM LYNN, 4006 Frank Rd, Lagrange, TX 78945, Phone: 409-247-4626

WOOD, WILLIAM W., PO Box 606, Seymour, TX 76380, Phone: 817-888-5832
Specialties: Exotic working knives with Middle-East flavor. **Patterns:** Fighters, boots and some utility knives. **Technical:** Grinds D2 and 440C; buys Damascus. Prefers hand-rubbed satin finishes; uses only natural handle materials. **Prices:** $300 to $600; some to $2000. **Remarks:** Full-time maker; first knife sold in 1977. **Mark:** Name, city and state.

WOOD, WEBSTER, 22041 Shelton Trail, Atlanta, MI 49709, Phone: 989-785-2996
Specialties: Work mainly in stainless; art knives, Bowies, hunters and folders. **Remarks:** Full-time maker; first knife sold in 1980. Guild member since 1984. All engraving done by maker. **Mark:** Initials inside shield and name.

WOOD, OWEN DALE, PO Box 515, Honeydew 2040 (Transvaal), SOUTH AFRICA, Phone: 011-958-1789
Specialties: Fancy working knives. **Patterns:** Hunters and fighters; variety of big knives; sword canes. **Technical:** Forges and grinds 440C, 154CM and his own Damascus. Uses rare African handle materials. **Prices:** $280 to $450; some to $3000. **Remarks:** Full-time maker; first knife sold in 1976. **Mark:** Initials.

WOOD, LARRY B., 6945 Fishburg Rd, Huber Heights, OH 45424, Phone: 513-233-6751
Specialties: Fancy working knives of his design. **Patterns:** Hunters, buckskinners, Bowies, tomahawks, locking folders and Damascus miniatures. **Technical:** Forges 1095, file steel and his own Damascus. **Prices:** $125 to $500; some to $2000. **Remarks:** Full-time maker; first knife sold in 1974. Doing business as Wood's Metal Studios. **Mark:** Variations of last name, sometimes with blacksmith logo.

WOOD, ALAN, Greenfield Villa, Greenhead, Carlisle, CA6 7HH, ENGLAND, Phone: 016977-47303
Specialties: High-tech working straight knives of his design. **Patterns:** Hunters, utility/camp and woodcraft knives. **Technical:** Grinds Sandvik 12C27, D2 and O1. Blades are cryogenic treated. **Prices:** $150 to $400; some to $750. **Remarks:** Full-time maker; first knife sold in 1979. **Mark:** First initial, last name and country.

WOODARD, WILEY, 4527 Jim Mitchell W., Colleyville, TX 76034
Specialties: Straight knives, Damascus carbon and stainless, all natural material.

WOODCOCK, DENNIS "WOODY", PO Box 416, Nehalem, OR 97131, Phone: 503-368-7511
Specialties: Working knives. **Patterns:** Hunters, Bowies, skinners, hunters. **Technical:** Grinds ATS-34, D2, 440C, 440V. Offers filework; makes sheaths. **Prices:** $50 to $500. **Remarks:** Full-time maker; first knife sold in 1982. Doing business as Woody's Custom Knives. **Mark:** Nickname, last name, city, state.

WOODIWISS, DORREN, PO Box 396, Thompson Falls, MT 59873-0396, Phone: 406-827-0079

WOODWARD, WILEY, 4517 Jim Mitchell W, Colleyville, TX 76034, Phone: 817-267-3277

WOOTTON, RANDY, 83 Lafayette 254, Stamps, AR 71860, Phone: 870-533-2472

WORTHEN, BILL, 200 E 3rd, Little Rock, AR 72201-1608, Phone: 501-324-9351

WRIGHT, RICHARD S., PO Box 201, 111 Hilltop Dr, Carolina, RI 02812, Phone: 401-364-3579
Specialties: Bolster release switchblades. **Patterns:** Folding fighters, gents pocket knives, one-of-a-kind high-grade automatics. **Technical:** Reforges and grinds various makers Damascus. Uses a variety of tool steels. Uses natural handle material such as ivory & pearl, extensive filework on most knives. **Prices:** $2000 and up. **Remarks:** Part-time knife maker with background as a gunsmith. Made first folder in 1991. **Mark:** RSW on blade, all folders are serial numbered.

WRIGHT, L. T., 1523 Pershing Ave, Steubenville, OH 43952, Phone: 740-282-4947
Specialties: Distressed finish on blades, filework. **Patterns:** Drop point hunters, patch, lil skinner. **Technical:** Grinds 440C, saw blade steel. **Prices:** $15-$500. **Remarks:** Part-time makers. First knives sold in 2002. **Mark:** First and middle initial & last name.

WRIGHT, KEVIN, 671 Leland Valley Rd. W, Quilcene, WA 98376-9517, Phone: 360-765-3589
Specialties: Fancy working or collector knives to customer specs. **Patterns:** Hunters, boots, buckskinners, miniatures. **Technical:** Forges and grinds L6, 1095, 440C and his own Damascus. **Prices:** $75 to $500; some to $2000. **Remarks:** Part-time maker; first knife sold in 1978. **Mark:** Last initial in anvil.

WRIGHT, TIMOTHY, PO Box 3746, Sedona, AZ 86340, Phone: 928-282-4180
Specialties: High-tech folders and working knives. **Patterns:** Interframe locking folders, non-inlaid folders, straight hunters and kitchen knives. **Technical:** Grinds BG-42, AEB-L, K190 and Cowry X; works with new steels. All folders can disassemble and are furnished with tools. **Prices:** $150 to $1800; some to $3000. **Remarks:** Full-time maker; first knife sold in 1975. **Mark:** Last name and type of steel used.

WUERTZ, TRAVIS, 2487 E. Hwy 287, Casa Grande, AZ 85222, Phone: 520-723-4432

WYATT, WILLIAM R., Box 237, Rainelle, WV 25962, Phone: 304-438-5494
Specialties: Classic and working knives of all designs. **Patterns:** Hunters and utility knives. **Technical:** Forges and grinds saw blades, files and rasps. Prefers stag handles. **Prices:** $45 to $95; some to $350. **Remarks:** Part-time maker; first knife sold in 1990. **Mark:** Last name in star with knife logo.

WYMAN, MARC L., 5320 SW 28th Terrace, Ft Lauderdale, FL 33312, Phone: 954-985-3863, Fax: 954-964-4418
Remarks: Part-time maker.

y

YASHINSKI, JOHN L., 207 N Platt, PO Box 1284, Red Lodge, MT 59068, Phone: 406-446-3916
Specialties: Native American Beaded sheathes. **Prices:** Vary.

YEATES, JOE A., 730 Saddlewood Circle, Spring, TX 77381, Phone: 281-367-2765
Specialties: Bowies and period pieces. **Patterns:** Bowies, toothpicks and combat knives. **Technical:** Grinds 440C, D2 and ATS-34. **Prices:** $400 to $2000; some to $2500. **Remarks:** Full-time maker; first knife sold in 1975. **Mark:** Last initial within outline of Texas; or last initial.

YESKOO, RICHARD C., 76 Beekman Rd, Summit, NJ 07901

YORK, DAVID C., PO Box 3166, Chino Valley, AZ 86323, Phone: 928-636-1709
Specialties: Working straight knives and folders. **Patterns:** Prefers small hunters and skinners; locking folders. **Technical:** Grinds D2 and 440C; buys Damascus. **Prices:** $75 to $300; some to $600. **Remarks:** Part-time maker; first knife sold in 1975. **Mark:** Last name.

YOSHIHARA, YOSHINDO, 8-17-11 Takasago, Katsushi, Tokyo, JAPAN

YOSHIKAZU, KAMADA, 540-3 Kaisaki Niuta-cho, Tokushima, JAPAN, Phone: 0886-44-2319

YOSHIO, MAEDA, 3-12-11 Chuo-cho tamashima Kurashiki-City, Okayama, JAPAN, Phone: 086-525-2375

YOUNG, GEORGE, 713 Pinoak Dr, Kokomo, IN 46901, Phone: 765-457-8893
Specialties: Fancy/embellished and traditional straight knives and folders of his design and to customer specs. **Patterns:** Hunters, fillet/camp knives and locking folders. **Technical:** Grinds 440C, CPM440V, and Stellite 6K. Fancy ivory, black pearl and stag for handles. Filework—all Stellite construction (6K and 25 alloys). Offers engraving. **Prices:** $350 to $750; some $1500 to $3000. **Remarks:** Full-time maker; first knife sold in 1954. Doing business as Young's Knives. **Mark:** Last name integral inside Bowie.

YOUNG, RAYMOND L., Cutler/Bladesmith, 2922 Hwy 188E, Mt Ida, AR 71957, Phone: 870-867-3947
Specialties: Cutler-Bladesmith, Sharpening service. **Patterns:** Hunter, skinners, fighters, no guard, no ricasso, chef tools. **Technical:** Edge tempered 1095, 516C, Mosiac handles, water buffalo and exotic woods. **Prices:** $100 and up. **Remarks:** Federal contractor since 1995. Surgical steel sharpening. **Mark:** R/.

YOUNG, BUD, Box 336, Port Hardy, BC, CANADA V0N 2P0, Phone: 250-949-6478
Specialties: Fixed blade, working knives, some fancy. **Patterns:** Drop-points to skinners. **Technical:** Hollow or flat grind, 5160, 440-C, mostly ATS-34, satin finish. **Prices:** $150 to $500 CDN. **Remarks:** Spare-time maker; making knives since 1962; first knife sold in 1985. **Mark:** Name. **Other:** Not taking orders at this time, sell as produced.

YOUNG, CLIFF, Fuente De La Cibeles No. 5, Atascadero, San Miguel De Allende, GTO., MEXICO, Phone: 37700, Fax: 011-52-415-2-57-11 **Specialties:** Working knives. **Patterns:** Hunters, fighters and fishing knives. **Technical:** Grinds all; offers D2, 440C and 154CM. **Prices:** Start at $250. **Remarks:** Part-time maker; first knife sold in 1980. **Mark:** Name.

YOUNG, ERROL, 4826 Storey Land, Alton, IL 62002, Phone: 618-466-4707
Specialties: Traditional working straight knives and folders. **Patterns:** Wide range, including tantos, Bowies, miniatures and multi-blade folders. **Technical:** Grinds D2, 440C and ATS-34. **Prices:** $75 to $650; some to $800. **Remarks:** Part-time maker; first knife sold in 1987. **Mark:** Last name with arrow.

YOUNG, PAUL A., 168 Elk Ridge Rd, Boone, NC 28607, Phone: 704-264-7048
Specialties: Working straight knives and folders of his design or to customer specs; some art knives. **Patterns:** Small boot knives, skinners, 18th-century period pieces and folders. **Technical:** Forges O1 and file steels. Full-time embellisher—engraves and scrimshaws. Prefers floral designs; any design accepted. Does not engrave hardened metals. **Prices:** Determined by type and design. **Remarks:** Full-time maker; first knife sold in 1978. **Mark:** Initials in logo.

YURCO, MIKE, PO Box 712, Canfield, OH 44406, Phone: 330-533-4928
Specialties: Working straight knives. **Patterns:** Hunters, utility knives, Bowies and fighters, push knives, claws and other hideouts. **Technical:** Grinds 440C, ATS-34 and 154CM; likes mirror and satin finishes. **Prices:** $20 to $500. **Remarks:** Part-time maker; first knife sold in 1983. **Mark:** Name, steel, serial number.

Z

ZACCAGNINO JR., DON, 2256 Bacom Point Rd, Pahokee, FL 33476-2622, Phone: 407-924-7844
Specialties: Working knives and some period pieces of their designs. **Patterns:** Heavy-duty hunters, axes and Bowies; a line of light-weight hunters, fillets and personal knives. **Technical:** Grinds 440C and 17-4 PH—highly finished in complex handle and blade treatments. **Prices:** $165 to $500; some to $2500. **Remarks:** Part-time maker; first knife sold in 1969 by Don Zaccagnino Sr. **Mark:** ZACK, city and state inside oval.

ZAHM, KURT, 488 Rio Casa, Indialantic, FL 32903, Phone: 407-777-4860
Specialties: Working straight knives of his design or to customer specs. **Patterns:** Daggers, fancy fighters, Bowies, hunters and utility knives. **Technical:** Grinds D2, 440C; likes filework. **Prices:** $75 to $1000. **Remarks:** Part-time maker; first knife sold in 1985. **Mark:** Last name.

ZAKABI, CARL S., PO Box 893161, Mililani Town, HI 96789-0161, Phone: 808-626-2181
Specialties: Working and using straight knives of his design. **Patterns:** Fighters, hunters and utility/camp knives. **Technical:** Grinds 440C and ATS-34. **Prices:** $55 to $200. **Remarks:** Spare-time maker; first knife sold in 1988. Doing business as Zakabi's Knifeworks. **Mark:** Last name and state.

ZAKHAROV, CARLOS, R. Pernambuco175, Rio Comprido Jacarei, SP-12305-340, BRAZIL, Phone: 55 12 3958 4021, Fax: 55 12 3958 4103
Specialties: Using straight knives of his design. **Patterns:** Hunters, kitchen, utility/camp and barbecue knives. **Technical:** Grinds his own

"secret steel." **Prices:** $30 to $200. **Remarks:** Full-time maker. **Mark:** Arkhip Special Knives.

ZBORIL, TERRY, RT 4 Box 318, Caldwell, TX 77836, Phone: 979-535-4157
Specialties: ABS Journey man smith.

ZEMBKO III, JOHN, 140 Wilks Pond Rd, Berlin, CT 06037, Phone: 860-828-3503
Specialties: Working knives of his design or to customer specs. **Patterns:** Likes to use stabilized high-figured woods. **Technical:** Grinds ATS-34, A-2, D-2; forges O-1, 1095; grinds Damasteel. **Prices:** $50 to $400; some higher. **Remarks:** First knife sold in 1987. **Mark:** Name.

ZEMITIS, JOE, 14 Currawong Rd, Cardiff Hts., 2285 Newcastle, AUSTRALIA, Phone: 0249549907
Specialties: Traditional working straight knives. **Patterns:** Hunters, Bowies, tantos, fighters and camp knives. **Technical:** Grinds O1, D2, W2 and 440C; makes his own Damascus. Embellishes; offers engraving and scrimshaw. **Prices:** $150 to $3000. **Remarks:** Full-time maker; first knife sold in 1983. **Mark:** First initial, last name and country, or last name.

ZIMA, MICHAEL F., 732 State St, Ft. Morgan, CO 80701, Phone: 970-867-6078
Specialties: Working straight knives and folders. **Patterns:** Hunters; utility, locking and slip-joint folders. **Technical:** Grinds D-2, 440C, ATS-34, and Specialty Damascus. **Prices:** $150 to $300; some higher. **Remarks:** Full-time maker; first knife sold in 1982. **Mark:** Last name.

ZINKER, BRAD, BZ Knives, 1591 NW 17 St, Homestead, FL 33030, Phone: 305-216-0404
Specialties: Fillets, folders & hunters. **Technical:** Uses ATS-34 and stainless Damascus. **Prices:** $200-$600. **Remarks:** Voting member of Knifemakers Guild & Florida Knifemakers Association. **Mark:** Offset connected initials BZ.

ZIRBES, RICHARD, Neustrasse 15, D-54526 Niederkail, GERMANY, Phone: 0049 6575 1371
Specialties: Fancy embellished knives with engraving and self-made scrimshaw (scrimshaw made by maker). High-tech working knives and high-tech hunters, boots, fighters and folders. All knives made by hand. **Patterns:** Boots, fighters, folders, hunters. **Technical:** I use only the best steels for blade material like CPM-T 440V, CPM-T 420V, ATS-34, D2, C440, stainless Damascus or steel according to customer's desire. **Prices:** Working knives & hunters: $200 to $600. Fancy embellished knives with engraving and/or scrimshaw: $800 to $3000. **Remarks:** Part-time maker; first knife sold in 1991. Member of the German Knife Maker Guild. **Mark:** Zirbes or R. Zirbes.

ZOWADA, TIM, 4509 E. Bear River Rd, Boyne Falls, MI 49713, Phone: 231-348-5446
Specialties: Working knives, some fancy. **Patterns:** Hunters, camp knives, boots, swords, fighters, tantos and locking folders. **Technical:** Forges O2, L6, W2 and his own Damascus. **Prices:** $150 to $1000; some to $5000. **Remarks:** Full-time maker; first knife sold in 1980.

ZSCHERNY, MICHAEL, 1840 Rock Island Dr, Ely, IA 52227, Phone: 319-848-3629
Specialties: Quality folding knives. **Patterns:** Liner-lock and lock-back folders in titanium, working straight knives. **Technical:** Grinds 440 and commercial Damascus, prefers natural materials such as pearls and ivory. **Prices:** Starting at $200. **Remarks:** Full-time maker, first knife sold in 1978. **Mark:** Last name, city and state; folders, last name with stars inside folding knife.

ak

Barlow, Jana Poirier	Anchorage
Brennan, Judson	Delta Junction
Breuer, Lonnie	Wasilla
Broome, Thomas A.	Kenai
Cannon, Raymond W.	Homer
Cawthorne, Christopher A.	Wrangell
Chamberlin, John A.	Anchorage
Clark, Peter	Anchorage
Dempsey, Gordon S.	N. Kenai
Dufour, Arthur J.	Anchorage
England, Virgil	Anchorage
Flint, Robert	Anchorage
Gouker, Gary B.	Sitka
Grebe, Gordon S.	Anchor Point
Hibben, Westley G.	Anchorage
Kommer, Russ	Anchorage
Lance, Bill	Eagle River
Little, Jimmy L.	Wasilla
Malaby, Raymond J	Juneau
McFarlin, Eric E.	Kodiak
McIntosh, David L.	Haines
Mirabile, David	Juneau
Parrish III, Gordon A.	North Pole
Schmoker, Randy	Slana
Shore, John I.	Anchorage
Stegall, Keith	Anchorage
Trujillo, Adam	Anchorage
Trujillo, Miranda	Anchorage
Trujillo, Thomas A.	Anchorage
Van Cleve, Steve	Sutton
Whipple, Wesley A.	Kodiak
Whitman, Jim	Chugiak

al

Andress, Ronnie	Satsuma
Batson, James	Madison
Bowles, Chris	Reform
Bullard, Bill	Andalusia
Coffman, Danny	Jacksonville
Conn Jr., C.T.	Attalla
Connell, Steve	Adamsville
Cutchin, Roy D.	Seale
Daniels, Alex	Town Creek
Di Marzo, Richard	Birmingham
Durham, Kenneth	Cherokee
Elrod, Roger R.	Enterprise
Fikes, Jimmy L.	Jasper
Fogg, Don	Jasper
Fowler, Ricky & Susan	Silverhill
Fronefield, Daniel	Hampton Cove
Gilbreath, Randall	Dora
Green, Mark	Graysville
Hammond, Jim	Arab
Hodge, J.B.	Huntsville
Howard, Durvyn M.	Hokes Bluff
Howell, Len	Opelika
Howell, Ted	Wetumpka
Huckabee, Dale	Maylene
Hulsey, Hoyt	Attalla
Madison II, Billy D.	Remlap
McCullough, Jerry	Georgiana
Militano, Tom	Jacksonville
Monk, Nathan P.	Cullman
Morris, C.H.	Frisco City
Pardue, Melvin M.	Repton
Roe Jr., Fred D.	Huntsville
Russell, Tom	Jacksonville
Sandlin, Larry	Adamsville
Sinyard, Cleston S.	Elberta
Thomas, David E.	Lillian
Watson, Billy	Deatsville

ar

A.G., Russell	Lowell
Alexander, Jered	Dierks
Anders, David	Center Ridge
Anders, Jerome	Center Ridge
Ardwin, Corey	North Little Rock
Barnes, Eric	Mountain View
Barnes Jr., Cecil C.	Center Ridge
Brown, Jim	Little Rock
Browning, Steven W.	Benton
Bullard, Tom	Flippin
Burnett, Max	Paris
Cabe, Jerry (Buddy)	Hattieville
Connelley, Larry	Little Rock
Cook, James R.	Nashville
Copeland, Thom	Nashville
Crawford, Pat & Wes	West Memphis
Crowell, James L.	Mtn. View
Dozier, Bob	Springdale
Duvall, Fred	Benton
Echols, Roger	Nashville
Edge, Tommy	Cash
Ferguson, Lee	Hindsville
Fisk, Jerry	Lockesburg
Fitch, John S.	Clinton
Flournoy, Joe	El Dorado
Foster, Ronnie E.	Morrilton
Foster, Timothy L.	El Dorado
Frizzell, Ted	West Fork
Gadberry, Emmet	Hattieville
Greenaway, Don	Fayetteville
Hartgrove, Wm. Anthony	Eagle River
Herring, Morris	Dyer
Lane, Ben	North Little Rock
Lawrence, Alton	De Queen
Livesay, Newt	Siloam Springs
Martin, Bruce E.	Prescott
Martin, Hal W.	Morrilton
Massey, Roger	Texarkana
Newton, Ron	London
O'Dell, Clyde	Camden
Olive, Michael E.	Leslie
Passmore, Jimmy D.	Hoxie
Perry, Jim	Hope
Perry, John	Mayflower
Peterson, Lloyd (Pete) C.	Clinton
Polk, Clifton	Van Buren
Quattlebaum, Craig	Searcy
Ramey, Marshall F.	West Helena
Red, Vernon	Conway
Remington, David W.	Gentry
Rowe, Kenny	Hope
Sisemore, Charles Russel	Mena
Smoker, Ray	Searcy
Solomon, Marvin	Paron
Stanley, John	Crossett
Stout, Charles	Gillham
Sweaza, Dennis	Austin
Townsend, Allen Mark	Texarkana
Tycer, Art	Paron
Walker, Jim	Morrilton
Ward, Chuck	Benton
Waters, Herman Harold	Magnolia
Waters, Lu	Magnolia
White, Bryce	Little Rock
Wootton, Randy	Stamps
Worthen, Bill	Little Rock
Young, Raymond L.	Mt. Ida

az

Ammons, David C.	Tucson
Bennett, Glen C.	Tucson
Birdwell, Ira Lee	Bagdad
Boye, David	Dolan Springs
Bryan, Tom	Gilbert
Cheatham, Bill	Laveen
Choate, Milton	Somerton
Dodd, Robert F.	Camp Verde
Evans, Vincent K. & Grace	Show Low
Fuegen, Larry	Prescott
Goo, Tai	Tucson
Guignard, Gib	Quartzsite
Gundersen, D.F. "Doc"	Tempe
Hancock, Tim	Scottsdale
Hankins, R.	Tempe
Hoel, Steve	Pine
Holder, D'Alton	Peoria
Hull, Michael J.	Cottonwood
Karp, Bob	Phoenix
Kelley, Thomas P.	Cave Creek
Kopp, Todd M.	Apache Jct.
Lampson, Frank G.	Rimrock
Lee, Randy	St. Johns
Lively, Tim and Marian	Tucson
McFall, Ken	Lakeside
McFarlin, J.W.	Lake Havasu City
Murray, Bill	Green Valley
Newhall, Tom	Tucson
Norris, Don	Tucson
Purvis, Bob & Ellen	Tucson
Rybar Jr., Raymond B.	Phoenix
Snare, Michael	Phoenix
Tamboli, Michael	Glendale
Torgeson, Samuel L.	Sedona
Weiler, Donald E.	Yuma
Weiss, Charles L.	Phoenix
Wolf, Bill	Phoenix
Wright, Timothy	Sedona
Wuertz, Travis	Casa Grande
York, David C.	Chino Valley

ca

Abegg, Arnie	Huntington Beach
Abernathy, Paul J.	Eureka
Adkins, Richard L.	Mission Viejo
Aldrete, Bob	Lomita
Barnes, Gregory	Altadena
Barron, Brian	San Mateo
Benson, Don	Escalon
Berger, Max A.	Carmichael
Biggers, Gary	Ventura
Blum, Chuck	Brea
Bost, Roger E.	Palos Verdes
Boyd, Francis	Berkeley
Brack, Douglas D.	Camirillo
Breshears, Clint	Manhattan Beach
Brooks, Buzz	Los Angles
Browne, Rick	Upland
Brunetta, David	Laguna Beach
Butler, Bart	Ramona
Cabrera, Sergio B.	Harbor City
Cantrell, Kitty D.	Ramona
Chelquist, Cliff	Arroyo Grande
Clark, R.W.	Corona
Cohen, Terry A.	Laytonville
Comus, Steve	Anaheim
Connolly, James	Oroville
Davis, Charlie	Santee
Davisson, Cole	Hemet
De Maria Jr., Angelo	Carmel Valley
Dion, Greg	Oxnard
Dixon Jr., Ira E.	Ventura
Doolittle, Mike	Novato
Driscoll, Mark	La Mesa
Dugan, Brad M.	San Marcos
Eaton, Al	Clayton
Ellis, Dave/ABS Mastersmith	Vista
Ellis, William Dean	Fresno
Emerson, Ernest R.	Torrance
English, Jim	Jamul
Essegian, Richard	Fresno
Felix, Alexander	Torrance
Ferguson, Jim	Temecula
Fisher, Theo (Ted)	Montague
Flores, Henry	Santa Clara
Forrest, Brian	Descanso
Foster, Burt	Moreno Valley
Fox, Jack L.	Citrus Heights
Fraley, D. B.	Dixon
Francis, Vance	Alpine
Fred, Reed Wyle	Sacramento
Freer, Ralph	Seal Beach
Fulton, Mickey	Willows
Gamble, Frank	Fremont
Gofourth, Jim	Santa Paula
Golding, Robin	Lathrop
Green, Russ	Lakewood
Guarnera, Anthony R.	Quartzhill
Guidry, Bruce	Murrieta
Hall, Jeff	Los Alamitos
Hardy, Scott	Placerville
Harris, Jay	Redwood City
Hartsfield, Phill	Newport Beach
Hayes, Dolores	Los Angeles

Helton, Roy	San Diego
Hermes, Dana E.	Fremont
Herndon, Wm. R. "Bill"	Acton
Hink III, Les	Stockton
Hockenbary, Warren E.	San Pedro
Hogstrom, Anders T.	Belmont
Holden, Larry	Ridgecrest
Hoy, Ken	North Fork
Humenick, Roy	Rescue
Jacks, Jim	Covina
Jackson, David	Lemoore
Jensen, John Lewis	Pasadena
Johnson, Randy	Turlock
Jones, Curtis J.	Palmdale
Jurgens, John	Torrence
Kazsuk, David	Perris
Keyes, Dan	Chino
Koster, Steven C.	Hunting Beach
Kreibich, Donald L.	San Jose
Lang, Bud	Orange
Larson, Richard	Turlock
Leland, Steve	Fairfax
Likarich, Steve	Colfax
Lockett, Sterling	Burbank
Loveless, R.W.	Riverside
Luchini, Bob	Palo Alto
Mackie, John	Whittier
Mallett, John	Ontario
Manabe, Michael K.	San Diego
Martin, Jim	Oxnard
Massey, Ron	Joshua Tree
Mata, Leonard	San Deigo
Maxwell, Don	Fresno
McAbee, William	Colfax
McClure, Michael	Menlo Park
McGrath, Patrick T.	Westchester
Melin, Gordon C.	Whittier
Meloy, Sean	Lemon Grove
Montano, Gus A.	San Diego
Morgan, Jeff	Santee
Moses, Steven	Santa Ana
Mosier, Richard	Rolling Hills Est
Mountain Home Knives	Jamul
Naten, Greg	Bakersfield
Orton, Richard	La Verne
Osborne, Donald H.	Clovis
Packard, Bob	Elverta
Padilla, Gary	Auburn
Pendleton, Lloyd	Volcano
Penfold, Mick	Vacaville
Perry, Chris	Fresno
Pfanenstiel, Dan	Modesto
Phillips, Randy	Ontario
Pitt, David F.	Anderson
Posner, Barry E.	N. Hollywood
Richard, Ron	Fremont
Richards Jr., Alvin C.	Fortuna
Rinaldi, T.H.	Winchester
Rodebaugh, James L.	Oak Hills
Rozas, Clark D.	Wilmington
St. Cyr, H. Red	Wilmington
Scarrow, Wil	Lakewood
Schmitz, Raymond E.	Valley Center
Schroen, Karl	Sebastopol
Sibrian, Aaron	Ventura
Sjostrand, Kevin	Visalia
Slobodian, Scott	San Andreas
Sornberger, Jim	Volcano
Stapel, Chuck	Glendale
Stapel, Craig	Glendale
Steinberg, Al	Laguna Woods
Stimps, Jason M.	Orange
Stockwell, Walter	Redwood City
Stover, Howard	Pasadena
Strider, Mick	Oceanside
Taylor, Scott	Gardena
Terrill, Stephen	Lindsay
Tingle, Dennis P.	Jackson
Vagnino, Michael	Visalia
Van Riper, James N.	Citrus Heights
Ward, Ken	Weed
Warren, Al	Roseville
Watanabe, Wayne	Montebello
Weinstock, Robert	San Francisco

Wilson, Philip C.	Mountain Ranch
Wilson, Ron	Morro Bay
Winberg, Douglas R.	Ramona

co

Anderson, Mel	Cedaredge
Appleton, Ray	Byers
Barrett, Cecil Terry	Colorado Springs
Booco, Gordon	Hayden
Brandon, Matthew	Denver
Brock, Kenneth L.	Allenspark
Campbell, Dick	Conifer
Davis, Don	Loveland
Dawson, Barry	Durango
Dawson, Lynn	Durango
Delong, Dick	Aurora
Dennehy, Dan	Del Norte
Dill, Robert	Loveland
Ewing, Wyman	Pueblo
High, Tom	Alamosa
Hockensmith, Dan	Berthoud
Hodgson, Richard J.	Boulder
Hughes, Ed	Grand Junction
Inman III, Paul R.	Glenwood Springs
Irie, Michael L.	Colorado Springs
Kitsmiller, Jerry	Montrose
Leck, Dal	Hayden
Lewis, Steve	Woodland Park
Lyons, William R.	Ft. Collins
Miller, Hanford J.	Cowdrey
Miller, M.A.	Northglenn
Mitchell, Wm. Dean	Lamar
Nolen, R.D. and Steve	Estes Park
Olson, Wayne C.	Bailey
Ott, Fred	Durango
Owens, John	Nathrop
Roberts, Chuck	Golden
Rollert, Steve	Keenesburg
Ronzio, N. Jack	Fruita
Sanders, Bill	Mancos
Thompson, Lloyd	Pagosa Springs
Tollefson, Barry A.	Gunnison
Topliss, M.W. "Ike"	Montrose
Vunk, Robert	Colorado Springs
Watson, Bert	Westminster
Wilson, James G.	Estes Park
Wilson, James R.	Westcliffe
Zima, Michael F.	Ft. Morgan

ct

Barnes, William	Wallingford
Buebendorf, Robert E.	Monroe
Chapo, William G.	Wilton
Framski, Walter P.	Prospect
Jean, Gerry	Manchester
Lepore, Michael J.	Bethany
Martin, Randall J.	Middletown
Padgett Jr., Edwin L.	New London
Pankiewicz, Philip R.	Lebanon
Plunkett, Richard	West Cornwall
Putnam, Donald S.	Wethersfield
Rainville, Richard	Salem
Turecek, Jim	Ansonia
Zembko III, John	Berlin

de

Antonio JR., William J.	Newark
Daland, B. Macgregor	Harbeson
Schneider, Karl A.	Newark
Willey, W.G.	Greenwood

fl

Adams, Les	Hialeah
Angell, Jon	Hawthorne
Atkinson, Dick	Wausau
Bacon, David R.	Bradenton
Barry III, James J.	West Palm Beach
Bartrug, Hugh E.	St. Petersburg
Beers, Ray	Lake Wales
Benjamin Jr., George	Kissimmee
Birnbaum, Edwin	Miami

Blackton, Andrew E.	Bayonet Point
Bosworth, Dean	Key Largo
Bradley, John	Pomona Park
Bray Jr., W. Lowell	New Port Richey
Brown, Harold E.	Arcadia
Butler, John	Havana
Chase, Alex	Deland
Cole, Dave	Satellite Beach
Cooper, Todd A.	Crystal River
Davenport, Jack	Dade City
Dietzel, Bill	Middleburg
Doggett, Bob	Brandon
Dotson, Tracy	Baker
Ellerbe, W.B.	Geneva
Enos III, Thomas M.	Orlando
Essman, Justus P.	St. Petersburg
Fagan, James A.	Lake Worth
Ferrara, Thomas	Naples
Ferris, Bill	Palm Beach Garden
Fowler, Charles R.	Ft . McCoy
Gamble, Roger	St. Petersburg
Garner Jr., William O.	Pensacola
Gibson Sr., James Hoot	Bunnell
Goers, Bruce	Lakeland
Griffin Jr., Howard A.	Davie
Grospitch, Ernie	Orlando
Harris, Ralph Dewey	Brandon
Heitler, Henry	Tampa
Hennon, Robert	Ft. Walton Beach
Hodge III, John	Palatka
Hoffman, Kevin L.	Orlando
Holland, John H.	Titusville
Hughes, Dan	West Palm Beach
Humphreys, Joel	Bowling Green
Hunter, Richard D.	Alachua
Hytovick, Joe "Hy"	Dunnellon
Jernigan, Steve	Milton
Johanning Custom Knives, Tom	Sarasota
Johnson, Durrell Carmon	Sparr
Johnson, John R.	Plant City
Kelly, Lance	Edgewater
King, Bill	Tampa
Klingbeil, Russell K.	Oviedo
Krapp, Denny	Apopka
Levengood, Bill	Tampa
Leverett, Ken	Lithia
Lewis, Mike	Debary
Long, Glenn A.	Dunnellon
Lovestrand, Schuyler	Vero Beach
Lozier, Don	Ocklawaha
Lunn, Gail	St. Petersburg
Lunn, Larry A.	St. Petersburg
Lyle III, Ernest L.	Chiefland
McDonald, Robert J.	Loxahatchee
Miller, Ronald T.	Largo
Mink, Dan	Crystal Beach
Newton, Larry	Jacksonville
Ochs, Charles F.	Largo
Owens, Donald	Melbourne
Parker, Cliff	Zephyrhills
Pendray, Alfred H.	Williston
Piergallini, Daniel E.	Plant City
Randall Made Knives	Orlando
Roberts, E. Ray	Monticello
Robinson III, Rex R.	Leesburg
Rodkey, Dan	Hudson
Rogers, Rodney	Wildwood
Ross, Gregg	Lake Worth
Russ, Ron	Williston
Schlomer, James E.	Kissimmee
Schwarzer, Stephen	Pomona Park
Selvidio, Ralph	Crystal River
Simons, Bill	Lakeland
Smart, Steaten	Tavares
Smith, Bobbie D.	Bonifay
Smith, Michael J.	Brandon
Smith, W.M.	Bonifay
Stapleton, William E.	Merritt Island
Stephan, Daniel	Valrico
Stidham, Rhett & Janie	Roseland
Stipes, Dwight	Palm City
Straight, Kenneth J.	Largo
Sweder, Joram	Ocala
Turnbull, Ralph A.	Spring Hill
Vogt, Donald J.	Tampa

Waldrop, Mark	Summerfield
Wallace, Roger L.	Tampa
Watson, Tom	Panama City
Weiland Jr., J. Reese	Riverview
Wicker, Donnie R.	Panama City
William, E. Stapleton	Merritt Island
Williams, A. L.	Lake Wales
Wyman, Marc L.	Ft. Lauderdale
Zaccagnino Jr., Don	Pahokee
Zahm, Kurt	Indialantic
Zinker, Brad	Homestead

ga

Arrowood, Dale	Sharpsburg
Ashworth, Boyd	Powder Springs
Barker, Robert G.	Bishop
Bentley, C. L.	Albany
Bish, Hal	Jonesboro
Black, Scott	Covington
Bradley, Dennis	Blairsville
Buckner, Jimmie H.	Putney
Carey Jr., Charles W.	Griffin
Cash, Terry	Canton
Chamblin, Joel	Concord
Cofer, Ron	Loganville
Cole, Welborn I.	Atlanta
Coughlin, Michael M.	Winder
Crockford, Jack	Chamblee
Davis, Steve	Powder Springs
Dempsey, David	Macon
Dunn, Charles K.	Shiloh
Feigin, B.	Marietta
Frost, Dewayne	Barnesville
Gaines, Buddy	Commerce
Glover, Warren D.	Cleveland
Greene, David	Covington
Halligan, Ed	Sharpsburg
Hardy, Douglas E.	Franklin
Harmon, Jay	Woodstock
Hawkins, Rade	Fayetteville
Haynie, Charles	Toccoa
Hensley, Wayne	Conyers
Hinson and Son, R.	Columbus
Hossom, Jerry	Duluth
Hyde, Jimmy	Ellenwood
Johnson, Harold "Harry" C.	Trion
Jones, Franklin (Frank) W.	Columbus
Kimsey, Kevin	Cartersville
King, Fred	Cartersville
Landers, John	Newnan
Lonewolf, J. Aguirre	Demorest
McGill, John	Blairsville
McLendon, Hubert W.	Waco
Mitchell, James A.	Columbus
Moncus, Michael Steven	Smithville
Moore, Bill	Albany
Parks, John	Jefferson
Poole, Marvin O.	Commerce
Poole, Steve L.	Stockbridge
Powell, Robert Clark	Smarr
Poythress, John	Swainsboro
Prater, Mike	Flintstone
Price, Timmy	Blairsville
Ragsdale, James D.	Lithonia
Rogers Jr., Robert P.	Acworth
Roghmans, Mark	Lagrange
Rosenfeld, Bob	Hoschton
Scofield, Everett	Chickamauga
Sculley, Peter E.	Rising Fawn
Smith Jr., James B. "Red"	Morven
Snell, Jerry L.	Fayetteville
Snow, Bill	Columbus
Sowell, Bill	Macon
Stafford, Richard	Warner Robins
Thompson, Kenneth	Duluth
Tomey, Kathleen	Macon
Walters, A.F.	Tyty
Washburn Jr., Robert Lee	Adrian
Werner Jr., William A.	Marietta
Whetsell, Alex	Sharpsburg
White, Lou	Ranger
Whittaker, Randy	Cummings

hi

Bucholz, Mark A.	Holualoa
Dolan, Robert L.	Kula
Fujisaka, Stanley	Kaneohe
Gibo, George	Hilo
Guild, Don	Paia
Lui, Ronald M.	Honolulu
Mann, Tim	Honokaa
Mayo Jr., Tom	Waialua
Mitsuyuki, Ross	Waipahu
Onion, Kenneth J.	Kaneohe
Zakabi, Carl S.	Mililani Town

ia

Brooker, Dennis	Derby
Brower, Max	Boone
Clark, Howard F.	Runnells
Cockerham, Lloyd	Denham Springs
Helscher, John W.	Washington
Lainson, Tony	Council Bluffs
Miller, James P.	Fairbank
Thie, Brian	Sperry
Trindle, Barry	Earlham
Westberg, Larry	Algona
Zscherny, Michael	Ely

id

Alderman, Robert	Sagle
Alverson, Tim (R.v.)	Peck
Andrews, Don	Coeur D'alene
Burke, Bill	Salmon
Eddy, Hugh E.	Caldwell
Hawk, Grant and Gavin	Idaho City
Hogan, Thomas R.	Boise
Horton, Scot	Buhl
Howe, Tori	Athol
Kranning, Terry L.	Pocatello
Mann, Michael L.	Spirit Lake
Metz, Greg T.	Cascade
Mullin, Steve	Sandpoint
Nealey, Ivan F. (Frank)	Mt. Home
Patton, Dick & Rob	Garden City
Quarton, Barr	McCall
Reeve, Chris	Boise
Rohn, Fred	Coeur D'Alene
Roy, Robert F.	Bayview
Sawby, Scott	Sandpoint
Schultz, Robert W.	Cocolalla
Selent, Chuck	Bonners Ferry
Sparks, Bernard	Dingle
Spragg, Wayne E.	Ashton
Steiger, Monte L.	Genesee
Towell, Dwight L.	Midvale

il

Abbott, William M.	Chandlerville
Bloomer, Alan T.	Maquon
Caudell, Richard M.	Lawrenceville
Cook, Louise	Ozark
Cook, Mike	Ozark
Detmer, Phillip	Breese
Dicristofano, Anthony P.	Northlake
Eaker, Allen L.	Paris
Hawes, Chuck	Weldon
Hill, Rick	Maryville
James, Peter	Hoffman Estates
Knuth, Joseph E.	Rockford
Kovar, Eugene	Evergreen Park
Lang, Kurt	McHenry
Leone, Nick	Pontoon Beach
Markley, Ken	Sparta
Meier, Daryl	Carbondale
Millard, Fred G.	Chicago
Myers, Paul	Wood River
Nevling, Mark	Hume
Nowland, Rick	Waltonville
Poag, James	Grayville
Potocki, Roger	Goreville
Pritchard, Ron	Dixon
Rados, Jerry F.	Grant Park

Rossdeutscher, Robert N.	Arlington Hts
Rzewnicki, Gerald	Elizabeth
Schneider, Craig M.	Seymour
Smale, Charles J.	Waukegan
Smith, John M.	Centralia
Steinbrecher, Mark W.	Glenview
Thomas, Bob G.	Thebes
Todd, Richard C.	Chambersburg
Tompkins, Dan	Peotone
Veit, Michael	Lasalle
Voss, Ben	Galesburg
Werth, George W.	Poplar Grove
West, Charles A.	Centralia
Wheeler, Robert	Bradley
White, Robert J.	Gilson
White Jr., Robert J. Butch	Gilson
Young, Errol	Alton

in

Ball, Ken	Mooresville
Barrett, Rick L. (Toshi Hisa)	Goshen
Bose, Reese	Shelburn
Bose, Tony	Shelburn
Chaffee, Jeff L.	Morris
Claiborne, Jeff	Franklin
Damlovac, Sava	Indianapolis
Darby, Jed	Greensburg
Fitzgerald, Dennis M.	Ft. Wayne
Fraps, John	Indianapolis
Hunt, Maurice	Avon
Imel, Billy Mace	New Castle
Johnson, C.E. Gene	Portage
Kain, Charles	Indianapolis
Keeslar, Steven C.	Hamilton
Keeton, William L.	Laconia
Kinker, Mike	Greensburg
Largin, Kelgin Knives	Metamora
Mayville, Oscar L.	Marengo
Minnick, Jim	Middletown
Oliver, Todd D.	Spencer
Parsons, Michael R.	Indianapolis
Quakenbush, Thomas C.	Ft. Wayne
Robertson, Leo D.	Indianapolis
Rubley, James A.	Angola
Shostle, Ben	Muncie
Smock, Timothy E.	Marion
Snyder, Michael Tom	Zionsville
Stover, Terry "Lee"	Kokomo
Thayer, Danny O.	Romney
Welch, William H.	Kimmell
Young, George	Kokomo

ks

Bradburn, Gary	Wichita
Chard, Gordon R.	Iola
Courtney, Eldon	Wichita
Craig, Roger L.	Topeka
Culver, Steve	Meriden
Darpinian, Dave	Olathe
Dawkins, Dudley L.	Topeka
Dugger, Dave	Westwood
George, Les	Wichita
Greene, Steve	Rossville
Hegwald, J.l.	Humboldt
Herman, Tim	Overland Park
King, Jason M.	Eskridge
King Jr., Harvey G.	Eskridge
Kraft, Steve	Abilene
Lamb, Curtis J.	Ottawa
Magee, Jim	Salina
Petersen, Dan L.	Topeka

ky

Addison, Kyle A.	Murray
Barr, A.T.	Nicholasville
Baskett, Lee Gene	Eastview
Baumgardner, Ed	Glendale
Bodner, Gerald "Jerry"	Louisville
Bybee, Barry J.	Cadiz
Carson, Harold J. "Kit"	Vine Grove
Clay, J.D.	Greenup

Coil, Jimmie J.	Owensboro
Downing, Larry	Bremen
Dunn, Steve	Smiths Grove
Edwards, Mitch	Glasgow
Finch, Ricky D.	West Liberty
Fister, Jim	Simpsonville
France, Dan	Cawood
Frederick, Aaron	West Liberty
Gevedon, Hanners (Hank)	Crab Orchard
Greco, John	Greensburg
Hibben, Daryl	Lagrange
Hibben, Gil	Lagrange
Hibben, Joleen	Lagrange
Hoke, Thomas M.	Lagrange
Holbrook, H.I.	Olive Hill
Howser, John C.	Frankfort
Keeslar, Joseph F.	Almo
Lott, Sherry	Greensburg
Miller, Don	Lexington
Mize, Richard	Lawrenceburg
Obenauf, Mike	Vine Grove
Pease, W.D.	Ewing
Pierce, Harold L.	Louisville
Pulliam, Morris C.	Shelbyville
Rigney Jr., Willie	Bronston
Smith, Gregory H.	Louisville
Smith, John W.	West Liberty
Vowell, Donald J.	Mayfield
Walker III, John Wade	Paintlick
Wallingford Jr., Charles W.	Union

la

Barker, Reggie	Springhill
Blaum, Roy	Covington
Caldwell, Bill	West Monroe
Calvert Jr., Robert W. (Bob)	Rayville
Capdepon, Randy	Carencro
Capdepon, Robert	Carencro
Chauvin, John	Scott
Culpepper, John	Monroe
Dake, C.M.	New Orleans
Dake, Mary H.	New Orleans
Diebel, Chuck	Broussard
Durio, Fred	Opelousas
Elkins, R. Van	Bonita
Faucheaux, Howard J.	Loreauville
Fontenot, Gerald J.	Mamou
Forstall, Al	Pearl River
Gorenflo, Gabe	Baton Rouge
Gorenflo, James T. (JT)	Baton Rouge
Graffeo, Anthony I.	Chalmette
Holmes, Robert	Baton Rouge
Ki, Shiva	Baton Rouge
Laurent, Kermit	Laplace
Leonard, Randy Joe	Sarepta
Mitchell, Max, Dean and Ben	Leesville
Phillips, Dennis	Independence
Potier, Timothy F.	Oberlin
Primos, Terry	Shreveport
Provenzano, Joseph D.	Chalmette
Randall Jr., James W.	Keithville
Randow, Ralph	Pineville
Reggio Jr., Sidney J.	Sun
Roath, Dean	Baton Rouge
Sanders, Michael M.	Ponchatoula
Tilton, John	Iowa
Trisler, Kenneth W.	Rayville
Wiggins, Horace	Mansfield

ma

Aoun, Charles	Wakefield
Daconceicao, John M.	Rehoboth
Dailey, G.E.	Seekonk
Entin, Robert	Boston
Frankl, John M.	Cambridge
Gaudette, Linden L.	Wilbraham
Grossman, Stewart	Clinton
Hinman, Ted	Watertown
Jarvis, Paul M.	Cambridge
Khalsa, Jot Singh	Millis
Kubasek, John A.	Easthampton
Lapen, Charles	W. Brookfield

Laramie, Mark	Fitchburg
Little, Larry	Spencer
McLuin, Tom	Dracut
Moore, Michael Robert	Lowell
Olofson, Chris	Cambridge
Rebello, Indian George	New Bedford
Reed, Dave	Brimfield
Richter, Scott	S. Boston
Rizzi, Russell J.	Ashfield
Siska, Jim	Westfield
Smith, J.D.	S. Boston
Stoddard's, Inc., Copley Place	Boston
Szarek, Mark G.	Revere

md

Bagley, R. Keith	White Plains
Barnes, Aubrey G.	Hagerstown
Barnes, Gary L.	New Windsor
Beers, Ray	Monkton
Bouse, D. Michael	Waldorf
Cohen, N.J. (Norm)	Baltimore
Dement, Larry	Prince Fredrick
Freiling, Albert J.	Finksburg
Fuller, Jack A.	New Market
Hart, Bill	Pasadena
Hendrickson, E. Jay	Frederick
Hendrickson, Shawn	Knoxville
Hudson, C. Robbin	Rock Hall
Hurt, William R.	Frederick
Kreh, Lefty	Cockeysville
Kretsinger Jr., Philip W.	Boonsboro
McCarley, John	Taneytown
McGowan, Frank E.	Sykesville
Merchant, Ted	White Hall
Moran Jr., Wm. F.	Braddock Heights
Nicholson, R. Kent	Phoenix
O'Ceilaghan, Michael	Baltimore
Rhodes, James D.	Hagerstown
St. Clair, Thomas K.	Monrovia
Sentz, Mark C.	Taneytown
Smit, Glenn	Aberdeen
Sontheimer, G. Douglas	Potomac
Spickler, Gregory Noble	Sharpsburg
Walker, Bill	Stevensville

me

Coombs Jr., Lamont	Bucksport
Corrigan, David P.	Bingham
Courtois, Bryan	Saco
Gray, Daniel	Brownville
Hillman, Charles	Friendship
Kravitt, Chris	Ellsworth
Lawler, Tim	Grand Ledge
Leavitt Jr., Earl F.	E. Boothbay
Oyster, Lowell R.	Corinth
Sharrigan, Mudd	Wiscasset

mi

Ackerson, Robin E.	Buchanan
Andrews, Eric	Grand Ledge
Behnke, William	Lake City
Bethke, Lora Sue	Grand Haven
Booth, Philip W.	Ithaca
Bruner, Rick	Jenison
Buckbee, Donald M.	Grayling
Canoy, Andrew B.	Hubbard Lake
Carlisle, Frank	Detroit
Carr, Tim	Muskegon
Carroll, Chad	Grant
Cashen, Kevin R.	Hubbardston
Cook, Mike A.	Portland
Costello, Dr. Timothy L.	Farmington Hills
Cousino, George	Onsted
Cowles, Don	Royal Oak
Dilluvio, Frank J.	Warren
Ealy, Delbert	Indian River
Erickson, Walter E.	Atlanta
Gordon, Larry B.	Farmington Hills
Gottage, Dante	Clinton Twp.
Gottage, Judy	Clinton Twp.
Harm, Paul W.	Attica

Hartman, Arlan (Lanny)	N. Muskegon
Hughes, Daryle	Nunica
Kalfayan, Edward N.	Ferndale
Krause, Roy W.	St. Clair Shores
Lankton, Scott	Ann Arbor
Leach, Mike J.	Swartz Creek
Lucie, James R.	Fruitport
Mankel, Kenneth	Cannonsburg
Mills, Louis G.	Ann Arbor
Nix, Robert T.	Wayne
Noren, Douglas E.	Springlake
Parker, Robert Nelson	Rapid City
Repke, Mike	Bay City
Rydbom, Jeff	Annandale
Sakmar, Mike	Rochester
Serven, Jim	Fostoria
Sigman, James P.	North Adams
Tally, Grant	Flat Rock
Van Eizenga, Jerry W.	Nunica
Vasquez, Johnny David	Wyandotte
Viste, James	Detroit
White, Richard T.	Grosse Pointe Farms
Whittaker, Wayne	Metamore
Whitworth, Ken J.	Sterling Heights
Wood, Webster	Atlanta
Zowada, Tim	Boyne Falls

mn

Fiorini, Bill	Dakota
Goltz, Warren L.	Ada
Griffin, Thomas J.	Windom
Hagen, Philip L.	Pelican Rapids
Hansen, Robert W.	Cambridge
Janiga, Matthew A.	Andover
Johnson, R.B.	Clearwater
Knipschield, Terry	Rochester
Maines, Jay	Wyoming
Shadley, Eugene W.	Bovey
Steffen, Chuck	St. Michael
Voorhies, Les	Faribault

mo

Ames, Mickey L.	Monett
Andrews II, E. R. (Russ)	Sugar Creek
Bolton, Charles B.	Jonesburg
Burrows, Stephen R.	Kansas City
Conner, Allen L.	Fulton
Cover, Raymond A.	Mineral Point
Cox, Colin J.	Raymore
Davis, W.C.	Raymore
Dippold, Al	Perryville
Driskill, Beryl	Braggadocio
Duvall, Larry E.	Gallatin
Ehrenberger, Daniel Robert	Shelbyville
Engle, William	Boonville
Hanson III, Don L.	Success
Harris, Jeffery A.	St. Louis
Harrison, James	St. Louis
Harrison, Jim (Seamus)	St. Louis
Jones, John A.	Holden
Kinnikin, Todd	House Springs
Knickmeyer, Hank	Cedar Hill
Knickmeyer, Kurt	Cedar Hill
Marks, Chris	Ava
Martin, Tony	Arcadia
Mason, Bill	Excelsior Springs
McCrackin, Kevin	House Springs
McCrackin and Son, V.J.	House Springs
McDermott, Michael	Defiance
McKiernan, Stan	Vandalia
Miller, Bob	Oakville
Muller, Jody & Pat	Pittsburg
Newcomb, Corbin	Moberly
Pryor, Stephen L.	Boss
Ramsey, Richard A.	Neosho
Rardon, A.D.	Polo
Rardon, Archie F.	Polo
Rice, Stephen E.	St. Louis
Riepe, Richard A.	Harrisonville
Scroggs, James A.	Warrensburg
Shelton, Paul S.	Rolla
Sonntag, Douglas W.	Nixa

Steketee, Craig A.	Billings
Stewart, Edward L.	Mexico
Stormer, Bob	St. Peters
Warden, Roy A.	Union
Weddle Jr., Del	St. Joseph
Willis, Bill	Ava

ms

Black, Scott	Picayune
Boleware, David	Carson
Davis, Jesse W.	Sarah
Evans, Bruce A.	Booneville
Lamey, Robert M.	Biloxi
Lebatard, Paul M.	Vancleave
Roberts, Michael	Clinton
Robinson, Chuck	Picayune
Skow, H. A. "Tex"	Senatobia
Taylor, Billy	Petal
Vandeventer, Terry L.	Terry
Wehner, Rudy	Collins
Wingo, Perry	Gulfport
Winston, David	Starkville

mt

Barnes, Jack	Whitefish
Barnes, Wendell	Missoula
Barth, J. D.	Alberton
Beam, John R.	Kalispell
Beaty, Robert B.	Missoula
Becker, Steve	Conrad
Bizzell, Robert	Butte
Boxer, Bo	Whitefish
Brooks, Steve R.	Walkerville
Caffrey, Edward J.	Great Falls
Carlisle, Jeff	Simms
Christensen, Jon P.	Shepherd
Colter, Wade	Colstrip
Conklin, George L.	Ft. Benton
Crowder, Robert	Thompson Falls
Dunkerley, Rick	Lincoln
Eaton, Rick	Shepherd
Ellefson, Joel	Manhattan
Fassio, Melvin G.	Lolo
Forthofer, Pete	Whitefish
Gallagher, Barry	Lewistown
Harkins, J.A.	Conner
Hill, Howard E.	Polson
Hintz, Gerald M.	Helena
Hollar, Bob	Great Falls
Hulett, Steve	West Yellowstone
Kajin, Al	Forsyth
Kauffman, Dave	Montana City
Kraft, Elmer	Big Arm
Luman, James R.	Anaconda
McGuane IV, Thomas F.	Bozeman
Mortenson, Ed	Darby
Moyer, Russ	Havre
Munroe, Deryk C.	Bozeman
Nedved, Dan	Kalispell
Patrick, Willard C.	Helena,
Peele, Bryan	Thompson Falls
Peterson, Eldon G.	Whitefish
Piorek, James S.	Rexford
Pursley, Aaron	Big Sandy
Robinson, Robert W.	Polson
Rodewald, Gary	Hamilton
Ruana Knife Works	Bonner
Schirmer, Mike	Twin Bridges
Schmidt, Rick	Whitefish
Simonich, Rob	Clancy
Smallwood, Wayne	Kalispell
Smith, Josh	Frenchtown
Sweeney, Coltin D.	Missoula
Taylor, Shane	Miles City
Thill, Jim	Missoula
Weinand, Gerome M.	Missoula
Woodiwiss, Dorren	Thompson Falls
Yashinski, John L.	Red Lodge

nc

Baker, Herb	Eden

Bauchop, Peter	Cary
Britton, Tim	Winston-salem
Busfield, John	Roanoke Rapids
Chastain, Wade	Horse Shoe
Clark, Dave	Andrews
Coltrain, Larry D.	Buxton
Comar, Roger N.	Marion
Daniel, Travis E.	Chocowinity
Drew, Gerald	Asheville
Edwards, Fain E.	Topton
Fox, Paul	Claremont
Gaddy, Gary Lee	Washington
Goguen, Scott	Newport
Greene, Chris	Shelby
Gross, W.W.	Archdale
Gurganus, Carol	Colerain
Gurganus, Melvin H.	Colerain
Guthrie, George B.	Bassemer City
Hazen, Mark	Charlotte
Kearney, Jarod	Brown Summit
Livingston, Robert C.	Murphy
Maynard, William N.	Fayetteville
McDonald, Robin J.	Fayetteville
McLurkin, Andrew	Raleigh
McNabb, Tommy	Winston-Salem
McRae, J. Michael	Mint Hill
Norris, Mike	Albermarle
Parrish, Robert	Weaverville
Patrick, Chuck	Brasstown
Patrick, Peggy	Brasstown
Patterson, Alan W.	Hayesville
Popp Sr., Steve	Fayetteville
Scholl, Tim	Angier
Simmons, H.R.	Aurora
Snody, Mike	Liberty
Sprouse, Terry	Asheville
Sterling, Murray	Mount Airy
Summers, Arthur L.	Concord
Sutton, S. Russell	New Bern
Vail, Dave	Hampstead
Van Hoy, Ed & Tanya	Candor
Wagaman, John K.	Fayetteville
Walker, Don	Burnsville
Warren, Daniel	Canton
Whitley, L. Wayne	Chocowinity
Williamson, Tony	Siler City
Wilson, Mike	Hayesville
Winkler, Daniel	Blowing Rock
Young, Paul A.	Boone

nd

Keidel, Gene W. and Scott J.	Dickinson
Paulicheck, Garth	Williston
Pitman, David	Williston

ne

Jensen Jr., Carl A.	Blair
Jokerst, Charles	Omaha
Mosier, Joshua J.	Edgar
Robbins, Howard P.	Elkhorn
Schepers, George B.	Shelton
Suedmeier, Harlan	Nebraska City
Syslo, Chuck	Omaha
Tiensvold, Alan L.	Rushville
Tiensvold, Jason	Rushville
Till, Calvin E. and Ruth	Chadron

nh

Classic Cutlery	Franklin
Ellis, Willy B.	Litchfield
Gunn, Nelson L.	Epping
Hill, Steve E.	Goshen
Hitchmough, Howard	Peterborough
MacDonald, John	Raymond
McGovern, Jim	Portsmouth
Philippe, D. A.	Cornish
Saindon, R. Bill	Goshen

nj

Eden, Thomas	Cranbury

Grussenmeyer, Paul G.	Cherry Hill
Licata, Steven	Clifton
Little, Guy A.	Oakhurst
McCallen Jr., Howard H.	So Seaside Park
Nelson, Bob	Sparta
Phillips, Jim	Williamstown
Polkowski, Al	Chester
Pressburger, Ramon	Howell
Quick, Mike	Kearny
Schilling, Ellen	Hamilton Square
Sheets, Steven William	Mendham
Slee, Fred	Morganville
Viele, H.J.	Westwood
Yeskoo, Richard C.	Summit

nm

Beckett, Norman L.	Farmington
Black, Tom	Albuquerque
Cherry, Frank J.	Albuquerque
Coleman, Keith E.	Albuquerque
Cordova, Joseph G.	Peralta
Cumming, R.J.	Cedar Crest
Digangi, Joseph M.	Santa Cruz
Duran, Jerry T.	Albuquerque
Dyess, Eddie	Roswell
Fisher, Jay	Clouis
Goode, Bear	Navajo Dam
Gunter, Brad	Tijeras
Hethcoat, Don	Clovis
Hurst, Gerard T.	Albuquerque
Jones, Bob	Albuquerque
Kimberley, Richard L.	Santa Fe
Lewis, Tom R.	Carlsbad
MacDonald, David	Los Lunas
McBurnette, Harvey	Eagle Nest
Rogers, Richard	Magdalena
Schaller, Anthony Brett	Albuquerque
Stalcup, Eddie	Gallup
Terzuola, Robert	Santa Fe
Trujillo, Albert MB	Bosque Farms
Walker, Michael L.	Rancho De Taos
Ware, Tommy	Datil
Wescott, Cody	Las Cruces

nv

Barnett, Van	Reno
Beasley, Geneo	Wadsworth
Blanchard, G.R. (Gary)	Las Vegas
Cameron, Ron G.	Logandale
Defeo, Robert A.	Henderson
Dellana,	Reno
Duff, Bill	Reno
George, Tom	Henderson
Hrisoulas, Jim	Las Vegas
Mount, Don	Las Vegas
Nishiuchi, Melvin S.	Las Vegas
Norton, Don	Las Vegas
Thomas, Devin	Panaca
Tracy, Bud	Reno
Washburn, Arthur D.	Pioche

ny

Baker, Wild Bill	Boiceville
Champagne, Paul	Mechanicville
Cute, Thomas	Cortland
Davis, Barry L.	Castleton
Farr, Dan	Rochester
Faust, Dick	Rochester
Hobart, Gene	Windsor
Isgro, Jeffery	West Babylon
Johnston, Dr. Robt.	Rochester
Levin, Jack	Brooklyn
Loos, Henry C.	New Hyde Park
Ludwig, Richard O.	Maspeth
Maragni, Dan	Georgetown
McCornock, Craig	Willow
Meerdink, Kurt	Barryville
Meshejian, Mardi	E. Northport
Page, Reginald	Groveland
Palazzo, Tom	Bayside
Pattay, Rudy	Long Beach

Peterson, Karen	Brooklyn
Phillips, Scott C.	Gouverneur
Rachlin, Leslie S.	Elmira
Rappazzo, Richard	Cohoes
Rotella, Richard A.	Niagara Falls
Scheid, Maggie	Rochester
Schippnick, Jim	Sanborn
Schlueter, David	Syracuse
Serafen, Steven E.	New Berlin
Smith, Lenard C.	Valley Cottage
Smith, Raymond L.	Erin
Summers, Dan	Whitney Pt.
Szilaski, Joseph	Wappingers Falls
Turanski, Ted	Lansing
Turner, Kevin	Montrose
Wilson III, George H.	Bronx

oh

Babcock, Raymond G.	Vincent
Bailey, Ryan	Galena
Bendik, John	Olmsted Falls
Busse, Jerry	Wauseon
Click, Joe	Swanton
Collins, Harold	West Union
Collins, Lynn M.	Elyria
Coppins, Daniel	Cambridge
Cottrill, James I.	Columbus
Downing, Tom	Cuyaho Falls
Downs, James F.	Londonderry
Etzler, John	Grafton
Foster, R.I. (Bob)	Mansfield
Francis, John D.	Ft. Loramie
Franklin, Mike	Aberdeen
Geisler, Gary R.	Clarksville
Gittinger, Raymond	Tiffin
Glover, Ron	Mason
Greiner, Richard	Green Springs
Guess, Raymond L.	Mechanicstown
Hinderer, Rick	Wooster
Hudson, Anthony B.	Midland
Imboden II, Howard L.	Dayton
Jones, Roger Mudbone	Waverly
Kiefer, Tony	Pataskala
Koval, Michael T.	New Albany
Kubaiko, Hank	Beach City
Longworth, Dave	Hamersville
Loro, Gene	Crooksville
Maienknecht, Stanley	Sardis
McDonald, Rich	Columbiana
McGroder, Patrick J.	Madison
Mercer, Mike	Lebanon
Messer, David T.	Dayton
Moore, Marve	Xenia
Morgan, Tom	Beloit
Oakes, Winston	Dayton
Ralph, Darrel	Galena
Rose, Derek W.	Gallipolis
Salley, John D.	Tipp City
Scrimshaw by Lynn Benade	Beachwood
Shinosky, Andy	Canfield
Shoemaker, Carroll	Northup
Shoemaker, Scott	Miamisburg
Spinale, Richard	Lorain
Stevens, Barry B.	Cridersville
Stoddart, W.B. Bill	Forest Park
Strong, Scott	Beavercreek
Summers, Dennis K.	Springfield
Thomas, Kim	Seville
Thourot, Michael W.	Napoleon
Tindera, George	Brunswick
Votaw, David P.	Pioneer
Ward, J.J.	Waverly
Warther, Dale	Dover
Witsaman, Earl	Stow
Wood, Larry B.	Huber Heights
Wright, L.T.	Steubenville
Yurco, Mike	Canfield

ok

Baker, Ray	Sapulpa
Barngrover, Jerry	Afton
Brown, Troy L.	Park Hill
Burke, Dan	Edmond
Crenshaw, Al	Eufaula
Darby, David T.	Cookson
Dill, Dave	Bethany
Englebretson, George	Oklahoma City
Fletcher, Michael J.	Tulsa
Gepner, Don	Norman
Griffith, Lynn	Glenpool
Johns, Rob	Enid
Kennedy Jr., Bill	Yukon
Kirk, Ray	Tahlequah
Lairson Sr., Jerry	Ringold
Martin, John Alexander	Luther
Miller, Michael E.	Wagoner
Sanders, A.A.	Norman
Spivey, Jefferson	Yukon
Williams, Michael L.	Broken Bow
Wingo, Gary	Ramona

or

Bell, Michael	Coquille
Bochman, Bruce	Grants Pass
Brandt, Martin W.	Springfield
Buchman, Bill	Bend
Buchner, Bill	Idleyld Park
Clark, Nate	Yoncalla
Coon, Raymond C.	Gresham
Corrado, Jim	Glide
Davis, Terry	Sumpter
Dowell, T.M.	Bend
Ferdinand, Don	Shady Cove
Fox, Wendell	Springfield
Frank, Heinrich H.	Seal Rock
Goddard, Wayne	Eugene
Harsey, William H.	Creswell
Hergert, Bob	Port Orford
Hilker, Thomas N.	Williams
Horn, Jess	Eugene
Huey, Steve	Eugene
Kelley, Gary	Aloha
Lake, Ron	Eugene
Lindsay, Chris A.	Bend
Little, Gary M.	Broadbent
Lockett, Lowell C.	North Bend
Lum, Robert W.	Eugene
Martin, Gene	Williams
Martin, Walter E.	Williams
Miller, Michael K.	Sweet Home
Olson, Darrold E.	Springfield
Osterman, Daniel E.	Junction City
Rider, David M.	Eugene
Schoeningh, Mike	North Powder
Schrader, Robert	Bend
Sevey Custom Knife	Gold Beach
Sheehy, Thomas J.	Portland
Shoger, Mark O.	Beaverton
Smith, Rick	Rogue River
Stover, James K.	Lakeview
Thompson, Leon	Gaston
Thompson, Tommy	Portland
Vallotton, Butch and Arey	Oakland
Vallotton, Rainy D.	Umpqua
Vallotton, Shawn	Oakland
Vallotton, Thomas	Oakland
Veatch, Richard	Springfield
Wahlster, Mark David	Silverton
Woodcock, Dennis "Woody"	Nehalem

pa

Amor Jr., Miguel	Lancaster
Anderson, Gary D.	Spring Grove
Anderson, Tom	Manchester
Appleby, Robert	Shickshinny
Besedick, Frank E.	Ruffsdale
Candrella, Joe	Warminster
Chavar, Edward V.	Bethlehem
Clark, D.E. (Lucky)	Mineral Point
Corkum, Steve	Littlestown
D'andrea, John	East Stroudsberg
Darby, Rick	Levittown
Evans, Ronald B.	Middleton
Frey Jr., W. Frederick	Milton
Goldberg, David	Blue Bell
Goodling, Rodney W.	York Springs
Gottschalk, Gregory J.	Carnegie
Heinz, John	Upper Black Eddy
Hudson, Rob	Northumberland
Malloy, Joe	Freeland
Marlowe, Donald	Dover
Mensch, Larry C.	Milton
Milford, Brian A.	Knox
Miller, Rick	Rockwood
Moore, Ted	Elizabethtown
Morett, Donald	Lancaster
Navagato, Angelo	Camp Hill
Nealy, Bud	Stroudsburg
Neilson, J.	Wyalusing
Nott, Ron P.	Summerdale
Ogden, Bill	Avis
Ortega, Ben M.	Wyoming
Parker, J.E.	Clarion
Rupert, Bob	Clinton
Scimio, Bill	Spruce Creek
Sinclair, J.E.	Pittsburgh
Steigerwalt, Ken	Orangeville
Stroyan, Eric	Dalton
Valois, A. Daniel	Lehighton
Vaughan, Ian	Manheim
Whittaker, Robert E.	Mill Creek
Wilson, Jon J.	Johnstown

ri

Bardsley, Norman P.	Pawtucket
Burak, Chet	E. Providence
Dickison, Scott S.	Portsmouth
Lambert, Ronald S.	Johnston
McHenry, William James	Wyoming
Olszewski, Stephen	Coventry
Potter, Frank	Middletown
Williams, Jason L.	Wyoming
Wright, Richard S.	Carolina

sc

Barefoot, Joe W.	Liberty
Beatty, Gordon H.	Seneca
Branton, Robert	Awendaw
Brend, Walter	Walterboro
Bridwell, Richard A.	Taylors
Campbell, Courtnay M.	Columbia
Cannady, Daniel L.	Allendale
Cox, Sam	Gaffney
Defreest, William G.	Barnwell
Denning, Geno	Gaston
Easler Jr., Russell O.	Woodruff
Fecas, Stephen J.	Anderson
Gainey, Hal	Greenwood
Gaston, Ron	Woodruff
George, Harry	Aiken
Gregory, Michael	Belton
Hendrix, Jerry	Clinton
Hendrix, Wayne	Allendale
Herron, George	Springfield
Kaufman, Scott	Anderson
Kay, J. Wallace	Liberty
Kessler, Ralph A.	Fountain Inn
Knight, Jason	Harleyville
Langley, Gene H.	Florence
Lewis, K.J.	Lugoff
Lutz, Greg	Greenwood
Majer, Mike	Hilton Head
Manley, David W.	Central
McManus, Danny	Taylors
Montjoy, Claude	Clinton
Odom, Vic	North
Page, Larry	Aiken
Parler, Thomas O.	Charleston
Peagler, Russ	Moncks Corner
Perry, Johnny	Spartanburg
Reed, John M.	Goose Creek
Reeves, Winfred M.	West Union
Sears, Mick	Sumter
Thomas, Rocky	Moncks Corner
Tyser, Ross	Spartanburg
Whitmire, Earl T.	Rock Hill

sd

Boysen, Raymond A.	Rapid City
Ferrier, Gregory K.	Rapid City
Sarvis, Randall J.	Fort Pierre
Thomsen, Loyd W.	Oelrichs

tn

Bailey, Joseph D.	Nashville
Baker, Vance	Riceville
Breed, Kim	Clarksville
Broyles-Sebenick, Lisa	Chattanooga
Byrd, Wesley L.	Evensville
Canter, Ronald E.	Jackson
Casteel, Dianna	Monteagle
Casteel, Douglas	Monteagle
Centofante, Frank	Madisonville
Claiborne, Ron	Knox
Clay, Wayne	Pelham
Conley, Bob	Jonesboro
Coogan, Robert	Smithville
Copeland, George Steve	Alpine
Corby, Harold	Johnson City
Dickerson, Gordon S.	Hohenwald
Elder Jr., Perry B.	Clarksville
Ewing, John H.	Clinton
Harley, Larry W.	Bristol
Heflin, Christopher M.	Nashville
Hurst, Jeff	Rutledge
Johnson, David A.	Pleasant Shade
Johnson, Ryan M.	Hixson
Keeler, Robert	Memphis
King, Herman	Millington
Levine, Bob	Tullahoma
Marshall, Stephen R.	Mt. Juliet
McAdams, Dennis	Chattanooga
McCarty, Harry	Blaine
McDonald, W.J. "Jerry"	Germantown
McNeil, Jimmy	Memphis
Moulton, Dusty	Loudon
Raley, R. Wayne	Collierville
Ramey, Larry	Chapmansboro
Rollick, Walter D.	Maryville
Ryder, Ben M.	Copperhill
Sampson, Lynn	Jonesborough
Smith, Newman L.	Gatlinburg
Taylor, C. Gray	Fall Branch
Two Knife Guys	Chattanooga
Vanderford, Carl G.	Columbia
Walker, John W.	Bon Aqua
Ward, W.C.	Clinton
Williams Jr., Richard	Morristown
Winter, George	Union City

tx

Adams, William D.	Burton
Alexander, Eugene	Ganado
Allen, Mike "Whiskers"	Malakoff
Ashby, Douglas	Dallas
Bailey, Kirby C.	Lytle
Barnes, Marlen R.	Atlanta
Barr, Judson C.	Irving
Batts, Keith	Hooks
Benfield Jr., Robert O.	Forney
Blasingame, Robert	Kilgore
Blum, Kenneth	Brenham
Boatright, Basel	New Braunfels
Bradshaw, Bailey	Dallas
Bratcher, Brett	Plantersville
Brightwell, Mark	Leander
Broadwell, David	Wichita Falls
Brooks, Michael	Lubbock
Bullard, Randall	Canyon
Burden, James	Burkburnett
Cairnes Jr., Carroll B.	Palacios
Callahan, F. Terry	Boerne
Cannon, Dan	Dallas
Carpenter, Ronald W.	Jasper
Carter, Fred	Wichita Falls
Champion, Robert	Amarillo
Chase, John E.	Aledo
Churchman, T.W.	San Antonio

Clark, Roger	Rockdale
Cole, James M.	Bartonville
Connor, John W.	Odessa
Connor, Michael	Winters
Cosgrove, Charles G.	Arlington
Costa, Scott	Spicewood
Crain, Jack W.	Granbury
Darcey, Chester L.	College Station
Davis, Vernon M.	Waco
Dean, Harvey J.	Rockdale
Dietz, Howard	New Braunfels
Dominy, Chuck	Colleyville
Dyer, David	Granbury
Edwards, Lynn	W. Columbia
Eldridge, Allan	Ft. Worth
Elishewitz, Allen	New Braunfels
Epting, Richard	College Station
Eriksen, James Thorlief	Garland
Evans, Carlton	Aledo
Fant Jr., George	Atlanta
Ferguson, Jim	San Angelo
Fortune Products, Inc.	Marble Falls
Foster, Al	Magnolia
Foster, Norvell C.	San Antonio
Fowler, Jerry	Hutto
Fritz, Jesse	Slaton
Fuller, Bruce A.	Baytown
Gardner, Rob	Port Aransas
Garner, Larry W.	Tyler
Gault, Clay	Lexington
Glasscock, John	Cypress
Goytia, Enrique	El Paso
Graham, Gordon	New Boston
Green, Bill	Garland
Griffin, Rendon and Mark	Houston
Hamlet Jr., Johnny	Clute
Hand, Bill	Spearman
Hawkins, Buddy	Texarkana
Hayes, Scotty	Texarkana
Haynes, Jerry	San Antonio
Hays, Mark	Austin
Hearn, Terry L.	Lufkin
Hemperley, Glen	Spring
Hesser, David	Dripping Springs
House, Lawrence	Canyon Lake
Howell, Jason G.	Lake Jackson
Howell, Robert L.	Kilgore
Hudson, Robert	Humble
Hughes, Bill	Texarkana
Hughes, Lawrence	Plainview
Jackson, Charlton R.	San Antonio
Jaksik Jr., Michael	Fredericksburg
Johnson, Gorden W.	Houston
Johnson, Ruffin	Houston
Kerby, Marlin W.	Brashear
Kern, R. W.	San Antonio
Kious, Joe	Kerrville
Knipstein, R.C. (Joe)	Arlington
Ladd, Jim S.	Deer Park
Ladd, Jimmie Lee	Deer Park
Lambert, Jarrell D.	Granado
Laplante, Brett	McKinney
Laughlin, Don	Vidor
Lay, L.J.	Burkburnett
Leblanc, John	Winnsboro
Lemcke, Jim L.	Houston
Lister Jr., Weldon E.	Boerne
Locke, Keith	Watauga
Luchak, Bob	Channelview
Luckett, Bill	Weatherford
Marshall, Glenn	Mason
Martin, Michael W.	Beckville
McConnell Jr., Loyd A.	Odessa
Mellard, J. R.	Houston
Merz III, Robert L.	Katy
Miller, R.D.	Dallas
Moore, James B.	Ft. Stockton
Neely, Greg	Bellaire
Nelson, Dr. Carl	Texarkana
Obrien, George	Katy
Odgen, Randy W.	Houston
Ogletree Jr., Ben R.	Livingston
Oliver, Anthony Craig	Ft. Worth
Osborne, Michael	New Braunfels

Osborne, Warren	Waxahachie
Overeynder, T.R.	Arlington
Ownby, John C.	Plano
Pate, Lloyd D.	Georgetown
Patterson, Pat	Barksdale
Pierce, Randall	Arlington
Pollock, Wallace J.	Cedar Park
Polzien, Don	Lubbock
Powell, James	Texarkana
Pugh, Jim	Azle
Ray, Alan W.	Lovelady
Richardson Jr., Percy	Hemphill
Roberts, Jack	Houston
Robinson, Charles (Dickie)	Vega
Rogers, Charles W	Douglass
Ruple, William H.	Charlotte
Ruth, Michael G	Texarkana
Scott, Al	Harper
Self, Ernie	Dripping Springs
Shipley, Steven A.	Richardson
Sims, Bob	Meridian
Sloan, Shane	Newcastle
Smart, Steve	Melissa
Stokes, Ed	Hockley
Stone, Jerry	Lytle
Stout, Johnny	New Braunfels
Theis, Terry	Harper
Thuesen, Ed	Damon
Thuesen, Kevin	Houston
Treiber, Leon	Ingram
Turcotte, Larry	Pampa
Watson, Daniel	Driftwood
Watt III, Freddie	Big Spring
Watts, Wally	Gatesville
West, Pat	Charlotte
White, Dale	Sweetwater
Whitley, Weldon G.	Odessa
Wilcher, Wendell L.	Palestine
Wilkins, Mitchell	Montgomery
Wolf Jr., William Lynn	Lagrange
Wood, William W.	Seymour
Woodard, Wiley	Colleyville
Woodward, Wiley	Colleyville
Yeates, Joe A.	Spring
Zboril, Terry	Caldwell

ut

Allred, Bruce F.	Layton
Baum, Rick	Lehi
Black, Earl	Salt Lake City
Ence, Jim	Richfield
Ennis, Ray	Ogden
Erickson, L.M.	Liberty
Hatch, Ken	La-Point
Hunter, Hyrum	Aurora
Johnson, Steven R.	Manti
Maxfield, Lynn	Layton
Nielson, Jeff V.	Monroe
Nunn, Gregory	Castle Valley
Palmer, Taylor	Blanding
Peterson, Chris	Salina
Rapp, Steven J.	Midvale
Strickland, Dale	Monroe
Velarde, Ricardo	Park City
Warenski, Buster	Richfield
Winn, Travis A.	Salt Lake City

va

Arbuckle, James M.	Yorktown
Ballew, Dale	Bowling Green
Barber, Robert E.	Charlottesville
Batley, Mark S.	Wake
Batson, Richard G.	Rixeyville
Beverly II, Larry H.	Spotsylvania
Callahan, Errett	Lynchburg
Catoe, David R.	Norfolk
Chamberlain, Charles R.	Barren Springs
Compton, William E.	Sterling
Conkey, Tom	Nokesville
Davidson, Edmund	Goshen
Douglas, John J.	Lynch Station
Frazier, Ron	Powhatan

Harris, Cass	Bluemont
Hawk, Jack L.	Ceres
Hawk, Joey K.	Ceres
Hedrick, Don	Newport News
Hendricks, Samuel J.	Maurertown
Holloway, Paul	Norfolk
Jones, Barry M. and Phillip G.	Danville
Jones, Enoch	Warrenton
Kellogg, Brian R.	New Market
McCoun, Mark	Dewitt
Metheny, H.A. "Whitey"	Spotsylvania
Murski, Ray	Reston
Norfleet, Ross W.	Richmond
Parks, Blane C.	Woodbridge
Pawlowski, John R.	Newport News
Richter, John C.	Chesapeake
Ryan, C.O.	Yorktown
Tomes, P. J.	Shipman
White, Gene E.	Alexandria
Willson, Wayne O.	Fairfax

vt

Haggerty, George S.	Jacksonville
Kelso, Jim	Worcester

wa

Amoureux, A.W.	Northport
Baldwin, Phillip	Snohomish
Begg, Todd M.	Spanaway
Ber, Dave	San Juan Island
Berglin, Bruce D.	Mount Vernon
Bloomquist, R. Gordon	Olympia
Boguszewski, Phil	Lakewood
Boyer, Mark	Bothell
Bromley, Peter	Spokane
Brothers, Robert L.	Colville
Brown, Dennis G.	Shoreline
Brunckhorst, Lyle	Bothell
Bump, Bruce D.	Walla Walla
Butler, John R.	Shoreline
Chamberlain, John B.	Wenatchee
Chamberlain, Jon A.	E. Wenatchee
Conti, Jeffrey D.	Port Orchard
Crain, Frank	Spokane
Crossman, Daniel C.	Blakely Island
Crowthers, Mark F.	Rolling Bay
D'Angelo, Laurence	Vancouver
Davis, John	Selah
Diskin, Matt	Freeland
Ferry, Tom	Auburn
Frey, Steve	Snohomish
Gallagher, Sean	Monroe
Goertz, Paul S.	Renton
Gray, Bob	Spokane
Greenfield, G.O.	Everett
Hansen, Lonnie	Spanaway
Higgins, J.P. Dr.	Coupeville
House, Gary	Ephrata
Hurst, Cole	E. Wenatchee
Leet, Larry W.	Burien
Mosser, Gary E.	Kirkland
O'Malley, Daniel	Seattle
Park, Valerie	Seattle
Sanderson, Ray	Yakima
Schempp, Ed	Ephrata
Schempp, Martin	Ephrata
Smith, D. Noel	Poulsbo
Stegner, Wilbur G.	Rochester
Swyhart, Art	Klickitat
Wright, Kevin	Quilcene

wi

Bostwick, Chris T.	Burlington
Brandsey, Edward P.	Milton
Bruner Jr., Fred, Bruner Blades	Fall Creek
Delarosa, Jim	Mukwonago
Garrity, Timothy P.	Waukesha
Genske, Jay	Fond Du Lac
Haines, Jeff, Haines Custom Knives	Wauzeka
Hembrook Knives	Neosho
Johnson, Richard	Germantown

Kanter, Michael	New Berlin
Kohls, Jerry	Princeton
Kolitz, Robert	Beaver Dam
Lary, Ed	Mosinee
Lerch, Matthew	Sussex
Maestri, Peter A.	Spring Green
Martin, Peter	Waterford
Nelson, Ken	Pittsville
Niemuth, Troy	Sheboygan
Ponzio, Doug	Pleasant Prairie
R. Boyes Knives	Menomonee Falls
Revishvili, Zaza	Madison
Ricke, Dave	West Bend
Rochford, Michael R.	Dresser
Schrap, Robert G.	Wauwatosa
Wattelet, Michael A.	Minocqua

wv

Bowen, Tilton	Baker
Carnahan, Charles A	Green Spring
Dent, Douglas M.	S. Charleston
Derr, Herbert	St. Albans
Drost, Jason D.	French Creek
Drost, Michael B.	French Creek
Elliott, Jerry	Charleston
Jeffries, Robert W.	Red House
Liegey, Kenneth R.	Millwood
Maynard, Larry Joe	Crab Orchard
McConnell, Charles R.	Wellsburg
Morris, Eric	Beckley
Pickens, Selbert	Liberty
Reynolds, Dave	Harrisville
Shaver II, James R.	Parkersburg
Sigman, Corbet R.	Liberty
Small, Ed	Keyser
Straight, Don	Points
Tokar, Daniel	Shepherdstown
Wilson, R.W.	Weirton
Wyatt, William R.	Rainelle

wy

Alexander, Darrel	Ten Sleep
Ankrom, W.E.	Cody
Archer, Ray & Terri	Medicine Bow
Banks, David L.	Riverton
Bartlow, John	Sheridan
Bennett, Brett C.	Cheyenne
Draper, Audra	Riverton
Draper, Mike	Riverton
Fowler, Ed A.	Riverton
Friedly, Dennis E.	Cody
Justice, Shane	Sheridan
Kilby, Keith	Cody
Kinkade, Jacob	Carpenter
Rexroat, Kirk	Wright
Reynolds, John C.	Gillette
Ross, Stephen	Evanston
Walker, George A.	Alpine

argentina

Ayarragaray, Cristian L.	(3100)
	Parana-Entre Rios
Bertolami, Juan Carlos	Neuquen
Kehiayan, Alfredo	Buenos Aires
Rho, Nestor Lorenzo	Buenos Aires

australia

Bennett, Peter	Engadine N.S.W. 2233
Crawley, Bruce R.	Croydon 3136 Victoria
Cross, Robert	Tamworth 2340
Del Raso, Peter	Mt. Waverly, Victoria, 3149
Gerus, Gerry	Qld. 4870
Giljevic, Branko	N.S.W.
Green, William (Bill)	View Bank Vic.
Harvey, Max	Perth 6155
Husiak, Myron	Victoria
Jones, John	Manly West, Qld 4179
K B S, Knives	Vic 3450
Maisey, Alan	Vincentia 2540
Rowe, Stewart G.	Brisbane 4306
Tasman, Kerley	Western Australia
Zemitis, Joe	2285 Newcastle

belgium

Dox, Jan	B 2900 Schoten
Monteiro, Victor	1360 Maleves Ste Marie

brazil

Bodolay, Antal	Belo Horizonte MG-31730-700
Bossaerts, Carl	14051-110, Ribeirao Preto
Campos, Ivan	Tatui, SP
De Castro, Marco A. M.	Sao Paulo
Dorneles, Luciano Oliverira	Nova Petropolis, RS
Gaeta, Angelo	SP-17201-310
Gaeta, Roberto	05351 Sao Paulo
Garcia, Mario Eiras	Sao Paulo SP-05516-070
Ikoma, Flavio Yuji, R. Manoel R. Teixeira	SP-19031-220
Lala, Paulo Ricardo P. and Lala, Roberto P.	SP-19031-260
Neto Jr., Nelson and De Carvalho, Henrique M.	SP-12900-000
Paulo, Fernandes R.	Sao Paulo
Petean, Francisco and Mauricio	SP-16200-000
Ricardo Romano, Bernardes	Itajuba MG
Rosa, Pedro Gullherme Teles	SP-19065-410
Sfreddo, Rodrito Menezes	Nova Petropolis, RS
Villa, Luiz	Sao Paulo, SP-04537-081
Villar, Ricardo	SP-07600-000
Zakharov, Carlos	SP-12305-340

canada

Arnold, Joe	London, Ont.
Beauchamp, Gaetan	Stoneham, PQ
Beets, Marty	Williams Lake, BC
Bell, Donald	Bedford, Nova Scotia
Berg, Lothar	Kitchener, Ont.
Bold, Stu	Sarnia, Ont.
Boos, Ralph	Edmonton, Alberta
Bourbeau, Jean Yves	Ile Perrot, Quebec
Bradford, Garrick	Kitchener, Ont.
Dallyn, Kelly	Calgary AB
DeBraga, Jose C.	Aux Lievres Quebec
Deringer, Christoph	Sherbrooke, Quebec
Diotte, Jeff	LaSalle, Ont.
Doiron, Donald	Messines PQ
Doussot, Laurent	Montreal, Quebec
Downie, James T.	Port Franks, Ont.
Dublin, Dennis	Enderby, BC
Freeman, John	Cambridge, Ont.
Frigault, Rick	Niagara Falls Ont.
Garvock, Mark W.	Balderson, Ont.
Gilbert, Chantal	Quebec City, Quebec
Grenier, Roger	Saint Jovite, Que.
Harildstad, Matt	Edmonton, AB, T5T 2M8
Haslinger, Thomas	Calgar,y AB
Hayes, Wally	Orleans, Ont.
Hofer, Louis	Rose Prairie, BC
Hoffmann, Uwe H.	Vancouver, BC
Jobin, Jacques	Levis, Quebec
Kaczor, Tom	Upper London, Ont.
Lay, R. J. (Bob)	Falkland, BC
Leber, Heinz	Hudson's Hope, BC
Lightfoot, Greg	Kitscoty, AB
Linklater, Steve	Aurora, Ont.
Loerchner, Wolfgang	Bayfield, Ont.
Lyttle, Brian	High River, AB
Maneker, Kenneth	Galiano Island, B.C.
Martin, Robb	Elmira, Ontario
Marzitelli, Peter	Langley, BC
Massey, Al	Mount Uniacke, Nova Scotia
McKenzie, David Brian	Campbell River B.
Olson, Rod	High River, AB
Patrick, Bob	S. Surrey, B.C.
Pepiot, Stephan	Winnipeg, Man.
Piesner, Dean	St. Jacobs, Ont.
Pugh, Vernon	Saskatoon, SK
Roberts, George A.	Whitehorse, YT
Ross, Tim	Thunder Bay, ONT
St. Amour, Murray	Pembroke, Ont.
Schoenfeld, Matthew A.	Galiano Island, B.C.
Stancer, Chuck	Calgary, AB
Storch, Ed	Alberta, T0B 2W0

Stuart, Steve — Gores Landing, Ont.
Sunderland, Richard — Quathiaski Cove, BC
Tichbourne, George — Mississauga, Ont.
Tighe, Brian — Ridgeville, Ont.
Toner, Roger — Pickering, Ont.
Treml, Glenn — Thunder Bay, Ont.
Trudel, Paul — Ottawa, Ont.
Whitenect, Jody — Nova Scotia
Wile, Peter — Bridgewater, Nova Scotia
Young, Bud — Port Hardy, BC

denmark

Andersen, Henrik Lefolii — 3480, Fredensborg
Anso, Jens — 116, 8472 Sporvp
Carlsson, Marc Bjorn — 1112 Copenhagen K
Dyrnoe, Per — DK 3400 Hilleroed
Henriksen, Hans J. — DK 3200 Helsinge
Strande, Poul — Dastrup 4130 Viby Sj.
Vensild, Henrik — DK-8963 Auning

france

Bennica, Charles — 34190 Moules et Baucels
Bertholus, Bernard — Antibes
Chauzy, Alain — 21140 Seur-en-Auxios
Doursin, Gerard — Pernes les Fontaines
Ganster, Jean-Pierre — F-67000 Strasbourg
Graveline, Pascal and Isabelle — 29350 Moelan-Sur-Mer
Headrick, Gary — Juan Les Pins
Madrulli, Mme Joelle — Salon De Provence
Reverdy, Pierre — Romans
Thevenot, Jean-Paul — Dijon
Viallon, Henri — Thiers

germany

Balbach, Markus — 35789 Weilmunster-Laubuseschbach/TS.
Becker, Franz — 84533, Marktl/Inn
Boehlke, Guenter — 56412 Grossholbach
Borger, Wolf — 76676 Graben-Neudorf
Dell, Wolfgang — D-73277 Owen-Teck
Faust, Joachim — 95497 Goldkronach
Fruhmann, Ludwig — 84489 Burghausen
Greiss, Jockl — 73252, Gutenberg
Hehn, Richard Karl — 55444 Dorrebach
Herbst, Peter — 91207 Lauf A.D. Pegn.
Joehnk, Bernd — 24148 Kiel
Kaluza, Werner — 90441 Nurnberg
Kressler, D.F. — Odetzhausen
Neuhaeusler, Erwin — 86179 Augsburg
Rankl, Christian — 81476 Munchen
Rinkes, Siegfried — Markterlbach
Selzam, Frank — Bad Koenigshofen
Steinau, Jurgen — Berlin 0-1162
Tritz, Jean Jose — 20255 Hamburg
Wimpff, Christian — 70574 Stuttgart 70
Wirtz, Achim — D-52146
Zirbes, Richard — D-54526 Niederkail

greece

Filippou, Ioannis-Minas — Athens 17122

israel

Shadmot, Boaz — Arava

italy

Albericci, Emilio — 24100, Bergamo
Ameri, Mauro — 16010 Genova
Ballestra, Santino — 18039 Ventimiglia (IM)
Bertuzzi, Ettore — 24068 Seriate (Bergamo)
Bonassi, Franco — Pordenone 33170
Extreme Ratio S.A.S. — 59100 Prato
Fogarizzu, Boiteddu — 07016 Pattada
Giagu, Salvatore and Deroma Maria Rosaria — 07016 Pattada (SS)
Pachi, Francesco — 17046 Sassello (SV)
Scordia, Paolo — Roma
Simonella, Gianluigi — 33085 Maniago
Toich, Nevio — Vincenza
Tschager, Reinhard — I-39100 Bolzano

japan

Aida, Yoshihito — Itabashi-ku, Tokyo 175-0094
Akahori, Yoichiro — 426-0006
Carter, Murray M. — Kumamoto
Ebisu, Hidesaku — Hiroshima City
Fujikawa, Shun — Osaka 597 0062
Fukuta, Tak — Seki-City, Gifu-Pref
Hara, Kouji — Gifu-Pref. 501-32
Hirayama, Harumi — Saitama Pref. 335-0001
Hiroto, Fujihara — Hiroshima
Isao, Ohbuchi — Fukuoka
Ishihara, Hank — Chiba Pref.
Kagawa, Koichi — Kanagawa
Kanda, Michio — Yamaguchi 746 0033
Kanki, Iwao — HYOUGO
Kansei, Matsuno — Gitu-city
Kato, Kiyoshi — Tokyo 152
Kato, Shinichi — Moriyama-Ku, Nagoya, Aichi
Katsumaro, Shishido — Hiroshima
Kawasaki, Akihisa — Kobe
Keisuke, Gotoh — Ohita
Koyama, Captain Bunshichi — Nagoya City 453-0817
Kozai, Shingo — Kamoto Kumamoto
Mae, Takao — Toyonaka, Osaka
Makoto, Kunitomo — Hiroshima
Matsusaki, Takeshi — Nagasaki
Michinaka, Toshiaki — Tottori 680-0947
Micho, Kanda — Yamaguchi
Okaysu, Kazou — Tokyo
Ryuichi, Kuki — Saitama
Sakakibara, Masaki — Tokyo 156-0054
Shikayama, Toshiaki — Saitama 342-0057
Sugihara, Keidoh — Osaka, F596-0042
Sugiyama, Eddy K. — Ohita
Takahashi, Kaoru — Kamoto, Kumamoto
Takahashi, Masao — Gunma 371 0047
Terauchi, Toshiyuki — Fujita-Cho Gobo-Shi
Toshifumi, Kuramoto — Fukuoka
Uchida, Chimata — Kumamoto
Uekama, Nobuyuki — Tokyo
Wada, Yasutaka — Nara Prefect 631-0044
Waters, Glenn — Hirosaki City 036-8183
Yoshihara, Yoshindo — Tokyo
Yoshikazu, Kamada — Tokushima
Yoshio, Maeda — Okayama

mexico

Scheurer, Alfredo E. Faes — C.P. 16010
Young, Cliff — San Miguel De Allende, GTO.

netherlands

Van De Manakker, Thijs — 5759 px Helenaveen
Van Den Elsen, Gert — 5012 AJ Tilburg
Van Eldik, Frans — 3632bt Loenen
Van Rijswijk, Aad — 3132 AA Vlaardingen
Van Schaik, Bastiaan — Amsterdam

new zealand

Gerner, Thomas — Walpole
Pennington, C.A. — Kainga Christchurch 8009
Reddiex, Bill — Palmerston North
Ross, D.L. — Dunedin

norway

Bache-Wiig, Tom — Eivindvik
Holum, Morten — Oslo
Jorgensen, Gerd — N-3262 Larvik
Momcilovic, Gunnar — N-30055 Krokstadelva
Sellevold, Harald — N5834 Bergen
Vistnes, Tor — N6930 Svelgen

russia

Kharlamov, Yuri — 300007

saudi arabia

Kadasah, Ahmed Bin — Jeddah 21441

singapore

Tay, Larry C-G — Singapore 9145

slovakia

Bojtos, Arpa D. — 98403 Lucenec

slovakia

Pulis, Vladimir — 96 701 Kremnica

south africa

Bauchop, Robert — Kwazulu-Natal 4278
Beukes, Tinus — Vereeniging 1939
Bezuidenhout, Buzz — Malvern, Queensburgh, Natal 4093
Boardman, Guy — New Germany 3619
Brown, Rob E. — Port Elizabeth
Burger, Fred — Kwa-Zulu Natal
Burger, Pon — Bulawayo
De Villiers, Andre & Kirsten — Cascades 3202
Dickerson, Gavin — Petit 1512
Fellows, Mike — Velddrie 7365
Grey, Piet — Naboomspruit 0560
Harvey, Heather — Belfast 1100
Harvey, Kevin — Belfast 1100
Horn, Des — 7700 Cape Town
Kojetin, W. — Germiston 1401
La Grange, Fanie — Selborne, Bellville 7530
Lancaster, C.G. — Free State
Liebenberg, Andre — Bordeauxrandburg 2196
Mackrill, Stephen — Johannesburg
Nelson, Tom — Gauteng
Pienaar, Conrad — Bloemfontein 9300
Rietveld, Bertie — Magaliesburg 1791
Russell, Mick — Port Elizabeth 6070
Schoeman, Corrie — Danhof 9310
Shoebotham, Heather — Belfast 1100
Smit, Corn — Zimbabwe
Theuns Prinsloo Knives — Bethlehem, 9700
Watson, Peter — La Hoff 2570
Wood, Owen Dale — Honeydew 2040 (Transvaal)

sweden

Bergh, Roger — 83070 NRA
Billgren, Per — S81576 Soderfors
Eklund, Maihkel — S-820 41 Farila
Embretsen, Kaj — S-82821 Edsbyn
Johansson, Anders — S-772 40 Grangesberg
Lundstrom, Jan-Ake — 66010 Dals-Langed
Nilsson, Johnny Walker —
Nordell, Ingemar — 82041 Färila
Persson, Conny — 820 50 Loos
Ryberg, Gote — S-562 00 Norrahammar
Vogt, Patrik — S-30270 Halmstad

switzerland

Gagstaetter, Peter — 9306 Freidorf TG
Roulin, Charles — 1233 Geneva
Soppera, Arthur — CH-8038 Zurich

united kingdom

Boden, Harry — Derbyshire DE4 2AJ
Elliott, Marcus — Llandudno Gwynedd
Farid R., Mehr — Kent
Hague, Geoff — Wilton Marlborough, Wiltshire
Harrington, Roger — East Sussex
Heasman, H.G. — Llandudno
Henry & Son, Peter — Wokingham, Berkshire
Horne, Grace — Sheffield Britian
Jackson, Jim — Chapel Row Bucklebury RG7 6PU
Jones, Charles Anthony — N. Devon E31 4AL
Lamprey, Mike — Devon EX38 7BX
Maxen, Mick — Hatfield, Herts
Morris, Darrell Price — Devon
Wardell, Mick — N. Devon EX39 3BU
Wise, Donald — East Sussex, TN3 8AL
Wood, Alan — Carlisle, CA6 7HH

uruguay

Gonzalez, Leonardo Williams — CP 20000
Symonds, Alberto E. — Montevideo 11300

knifemakers membership lists

Not all knifemakers are organization-types, but those listed here are in good standing with these organizations.

the knifemakers' guild

2004 voting membership

a   Les Adams, Yoshihito Aida, Mike "Whiskers" Allen, Michael Anderson, W.E. Ankrom, Joe Arnold, Boyd Ashworth, Dick Atkinson

b   Joseph D. Bailey, Santino Ballestra, Norman Bardsley, Van Barnett, A.T. Barr, James J. Barry III, John Bartlow, Gene Baskett, James Batson, Gaetan Beauchamp, Norman Beckett, Raymond Beers, Charlie Bennica, Tom Black, Andrew Blackton, Gary Blanchard, Alan T. Bloomer, Arpad Bojtos, Phillip Booth, Wolf Borger, Tony Bose, Dennis Bradley, Edward Brandsey, W. Lowell Bray Jr., Clint Breshears, Tim Britton, David Broadwell, David Brown, Harold Brown, Rick Browne, Jimmie Buckner, R.D. "Dan" Burke, John Busfield

c   Bill Caldwell, Errett Callahan, Ron Cameron, Daniel Cannady, Ronald Canter, Robert Capdepon, Harold J. "Kit" Carson, Fred Carter, Dianna Casteel, Douglas Casteel, Frank Centofante, Jeffrey Chaffee, Joel Chamblin, William Chapo, Alex Chase, Edward Chavar, William Cheatham, Howard F. Clark, Wayne Clay, Lowell Cobb, Keith Coleman, Vernon Coleman, Blackie Collins, Bob Conley, Gerald Corbit, Harold Corby, Joe Cordova, Jim Corrado, George Cousino, Raymond Cover, Colin Cox, Pat & Wes Crawford, Dan Cruze, Roy Cutchin

d   George E. Dailey, Charles M. Dake, Alex Daniels, Jack Davenport, Edmund Davidson, Barry Davis, Terry A. Davis, Vernon M. Davis, W.C. Davis, Harvey Dean, Robert DeFeo, Dellana, Dan Dennehy, Herbert Derr, Howard Dietz, William Dietzel, Robert Dill, Frank Dilluvio, Allen Dippold, David Dodds, T.M. Dowell, Larry Downing, Tom Downing, Bob Dozier, Bill Duff, Melvin Dunn, Steve Dunn, Jerry Duran, Fred Durio, Dwayne Dushane

e   Russell & Paula K. Easler, Rick Eaton, Allen Elishewitz, Jim Elliott, David Ellis, Kaj Embretsen, Ernest Emerson, Jim Ence, Virgil England, William Engle, James T. Eriksen

f   Howard Faucheaux, Stephen Fecas, Lee Ferguson, Bill Fiorini, Jay Fisher, Jerry Fisk, Joe Flournoy, Pete Forthofer, Paul Fox, Derek Fraley, Henry Frank, Michael H. Franklin, Ron Frazier, Aaron Frederick, Ralph Freer, Dennis Friedly, Daniel Fronefield, Larry Fuegen, Shun Fujikawa, Stanley Fujisaka, Tak Fukuta, Bruce Fuller, Shiro Furukawa

g   Frank Gamble, Roger Gamble, William O. Garner Jr., Ron Gaston, Clay Gault, James "Hoot" Gibson Sr., Warren Glover, Stefan Gobec, Bruce Goers, David Goldberg, Warren Goltz, Greg Gottschalk, Roger M. Green, Jockl Greiss, Carol Gurganus, Melvin Gurganus, Kenneth Guth

h   Philip L. "Doc" Hagen, Geoffrey Hague, Ed Halligan & Son, Tomonori Hamada, Jim Hammond, James E. Hand, M.D., Shaun Hansen, Kouji Hara, J.A. Harkins, Larry Harley, Ralph D. Harris, Rade Hawkins, Richard Hehn, Henry Heitler, Earl Jay Hendrickson, Wayne Hendrix, Wayne G. Hensley, Peter Herbst, Tim Herman, George Herron, Don Hethcoat, Gil Hibben, Howard Hill, Steve E. Hill, R. Hinson & Son, Harumi Hirayama, Howard Hitchmough, Steve Hoel, Kevin Hoffman, D'Alton Holder, Jess Horn, Jerry Hossum, Durvyn Howard, Jeff Howlett, Daryle Hughes, Roy Humenick, Joel Humphreys, Gerald Hurst, Joseph Hytovick

i   Billy Mace Imel, Michael Irie

j   Jason Jacks, Jim Jacks, Paul Jarvis, John Jensen, Steve Jernigan, Tom Johanning, Brad Johnson, Ronald Johnson, Ruffin Johnson, Steven R. Johnson, W.C. Johnson, Enoch D. Jones, Robert Jones

k   Edward N. Kalfayan, William Keeton, Bill Keller, Bill Kennedy Jr., Jot Singh Khalsa, Bill King, Russell Klingbeil, Terry Knipschield, R.C. Knipstein, Mick Koval, Roy W. Krause, D.F. Kressler, John Kubasek

l   Ron Lake, Ken Largin, Kermit Laurent, Mike Leach, William Letcher, Matthew J. Lerch, Bill Levengood, Yakov Levin, Bob Levine, Tom Lewis, Greg Lightfoot, Steve Linklater, Wolfgang Loerchner, Juan A. Lonewolf, R.W. Loveless, Schuyler Lovestrand, Don Lozier, Robert Lum, Larry Lunn, Ernest Lyle

m   Joe Malloy, Dan Maragni, Peter Martin, Randall J. Martin, Roger Massey, Charles McConnell, Loyd McConnell, Richard McDonald, Robert J. McDonald, W. J. McDonald, Ken McFall, Frank McGowan, Thomas McGuane, W.J. McHenry, Tommy McNabb, Kurt Meerdink, Mike Mercer, Ted Merchant, Robert L. Merz III, Toshiaki Michinaka, James P. Miller, Steve Miller, Louis Mills, Dan Mink, Jim Minnick, Gunnar Momcilovic, Sidney "Pete" Moon, James B. Moore, Jeff Morgan, C.H. Morris, Dusty Moulton

n   Bud Nealy, Corbin Newcomb, Larry Newton, Ron Newton, R.D. & Steve Nolen, Ingemar Nordell, Ross Norfleet, Rick Nowland

o   Charles Ochs, Ben R. Ogletree Jr., Raymond Frank Oldham, Warren Osborne, T.R. Overeynder, John Owens

p   Francesco Pachi, Larry Page, Robert Papp, Joseph Pardue, Melvin Pardue, Robert Patton, W.D. Pease, Alfred Pendray, John L. Perry, Eldon Peterson, Kenneth Pfeiffer, Daniel Piergallini, David Pitt, Leon & Tracy Pittman, Al Polkowski, Joe Prince, Jim Pugh, Morris Pulliam

r   Jerry Rados, James D. Ragsdale, Steven Rapp, Chris Reeve, John Reynolds, Ron Richard, David Ricke, Bertie Rietveld, Willie Rigney, Dean Roath, Howard Robbins, Rex Robinson III, Fred Roe, Richard Rogers, Charles Roulin, Ron Russ, A.G. Russell

s   Masaki Sakakibara, Mike Sakmar, Hiroyuki Sakurai, John Salley, Scott Sawby, Michael Schirmer, Maurice & Alan Schrock, Mark C. Sentz, Yoshinori Seto, Eugene W. Shadley, John I. Shore, Bill Simons, R.J. Sims, Cleston Sinyard, Jim Siska, Fred Slee, Scott Slobodian, J.D. Smith, John W. Smith, Michael J. Smith, Ralph Smith, Jerry Snell, Marvin Solomon, Arthur Soppera, Jim Sornberger, Ken Steigerwalt, Jurgen Steinau, Daniel Stephan, Murray Sterling, Barry B. Stevens, Johnny Stout, Keidoh Sugihara, Arthur L. Summers, Russ Sutton, Charles Syslo, Joseph Szilaski

t Grant Tally, Robert Terzuola, Leon Thompson, Brian Tighe, P.J. Tomes, Dan Tompkins, John E. Toner, Bobby L. Toole, Dwight Towell, Leon Treiber, Barry Trindle, Reinhard Tschager, Jim Turecek, Ralph Turnbull

v Michael Vagnino, Frans Van Eldik, Edward T. Van Hoy, Aad Van Rijswijk, Michael Veit, Ricardo Velarde, Howard Viele, Donald Vogt

w James Walker, John W. Walker, George Walker, Michael Walker, Charles S. Ward, Tommy Ware, Buster Warenski, Daniel Warren, Dale Warther, Thomas J. Watson, Charles Weeber, John S. Weever, Reese Weiland, Robert Weinstock, Charles L. Weiss, Weldon Whitley, Wayne Whittaker, Donnie R. Wicker, R.W. Wilson, Daniel Winkler, Earl Witsaman, Frank Wojtinowski, William Wolf, Owen Wood, Webster Wood, Tim Wright

y Joe Yeates, Yoshindo Yoshihara, George Young, Mike Yurco

z Brad Zinker

american bladesmith society

a Robin E. Ackerson, Lonnie Adams, Kyle A. Addison, Charles L. Adkins, Anthony "Tony" Aiken, Yoichiro Akahori, Douglas A. Alcorn, David Alexander, Mike Alexander, Eugene Alexander, Daniel Allison, Chris Amos, David Anders, Jerome Anders, Gary D. Anderson, Ronnie A. Andress Sr, E. R. (Russ) Andrews II, James M Arbuckle, Doug Asay, Boyd Ashworth, Ron Austin

b David R. Bacon, Robert Keith Bagley, Marion Bagwell, Brent Bailey, Larry Bailey, Bruce Baker, David Baker, Stephen A. Baker, Randall Baltimore, Dwayne Bandy, Mark D. Banfield, David L. Banks, Robert G. Barker, Reggie Barker, Aubrey G. Barnes Sr., Cecil C. Barnes Jr., Gary Barnes, Marlen R. Barnes, Van Barnett Barnett International, Judson C. Barr, Nyla Barrett, Rick L. Barrett, Michael Barton, Hugh E. Bartrug, Paul C. Basch, Nat Bassett, James L. Batson, R. Keith Batts, Michael R. Bauer, Rick Baum, Dale Baxter, Geneo Beasley, Jim Beaty, Robert B. Beaty, Steve Becker, Bill Behnke, Don Bell, John Bendik, Robert O. Benfield Jr., George Benjamin Jr., Brett Bennett, Rae Bennett, Bruce D. Berglin, Brent Beshara, Chris Bethke, Lora Sue Bethke, Gary Biggers, Ira Lee Birdwell, Hal Bish, William M. Bisher, Jason Bivens, Robert Bizzell, Scott Black, Randy Blair, Dennis Blankenheim, Robert Blasingame, R. Gordon Bloomquist, Josh Blount, Otto Bluntzer, David Bolton, David Boone, Roger E. Bost, Raymond A. Boysen, Bailey Bradshaw, Sanford (Sandy) Bragman, Martin W. Brandt, Robert Branton, Brett Bratcher, W. Lowell Bray Jr., Steven Brazeale, Charles D. Breme, Arthur Britton, Peter Bromley, Charles E. Brooks, Christopher Brown, Dennis G. Brown, Mark D. Brown, Rusty Brown, Troy L. Brown, Steven W. Browning, C. Lyle Brunckhorst, Aldo Bruno, Jimmie H. Buckner, Nick Bugliarello-Wondrich, Bruce D. Bump, Larry Bundrick, Bill Burke, Paul A. Burke, Stephen R. Burrows, John Butler, John R. Butler, Wesley L. Byrd

c Jerry (Buddy) Cabe, Sergio B. Cabrera, Ed Caffrey, Larry Cain, F. Terry Callahan, Robt W. Calvert Jr., Craig Camerer, Ron Cameron, Courtnay M. Campbell, Dan Cannon, Andrew B. Canoy, Jeff Carlisle, Chris Carlson, Eric R. Carlson, William Carnahan, Ronald W. Carpenter, James V. Carriger, Chad Carroll, George Carter, Murray M. Carter, Shayne Carter, Terry Cash, Kevin R. Cashen, P. Richard Chastain, Milton Choate, Jon Christensen, Howard F. Clark, Jim Clary, Joe Click, Russell Coats, Charles Cole, Frank Coleman, Wade Colter, Larry D. Coltrain, Roger N. Comar, Roger Combs, Wm. E. (Bill) Compton, Larry Connelley, John W. Connor, Michael Connor, Charles W. Cook, III, James R. Cook, Robert Cook, James Roscoe Cooper, Jr., Ted Cooper, Joseph G. Cordova, David P. Corrigan, Dr. Timothy L. Costello, William Courtney, Collin Cousino, Gregory G. Covington, Monty L. Crain, Dawnavan M. Crawford, George Crews, Jim Crowell, Peter J. Crowl, Steve Culver, George Cummings, Kelly C. Cupples, John A. Czekala

d George E. Dailey, Mary H. Dake, B. MacGregor Daland, Kelly Dallyn, Sava Damlovac, Alex Daniels, David T. Darby, Chester L. Darcey, David Darpinian, Jim Davidson, Richard T. Davies, Barry Davis, John Davis, Patricia D. Davis, Dudley L. Dawkins, Michael de Gruchy, Angelo De Maria Jr., Harvey J. Dean, Anthony Del Giorno, Josse Delage, Clark B. DeLong, William Derby, Christoph Deringer, Dennis E. Des Jardins, Chuck Diebel, Bill Dietzel, Eric Dincauze, Jason Dingledine, Al Dippold, Matt Diskin, Michael Distin, Luciano Dorneles, Patrick J. Downey, Audra L. Draper, Mike Draper, Joseph D. Drouin, Paul Dubro, Ron Duncan, Calvin Duniphan, Rick Dunkerley, Steve Dunn, Eric Durbin, Kenneth Durham, Fred Durio, David Dyer

e Rick Eaton, Roger Echols, Mike Edelman, Thomas Eden, Gregory K. Edmonson, Randel Edmonson, Mitch Edwards, Lynn Edwards, Joe E. Eggleston, Daniel Robert Ehrenberger, Fred Eisen, Perry B. Elder Jr., Allen Elishewitz, R. Van Elkins, Rickie Ellington, Gordon Elliott, Carroll Ellis, Darren Ellis, Dave Ellis, Roger R. Elrod, Kaj Embretsen, Edward Engarto, Al Engelsman, Richard Epting, David Etchieson, Bruce E. Evans, Greg Evans, Ronald B. Evans, Vincent K. Evans, Wyman Ewing

f John E. Faltay, George Fant Jr., Daniel Farr, Alexander Felix, Gregory K. Ferrier, Robert Thomas Ferry III, Michael J. Filarski, Steve Filicietti, Ioannis-Minas Filippou, Jack Fincher, John Fincher, Ray Fincher, Perry Fink, Sean W. Finlayson, William Fiorini, Jerry Fisk, James O. Fister, John S. Fitch, Dawn Fitch, Mike Fletcher, Joe Flournoy, Charles Fogarty, Don Fogg, Stanley Fortenberry, Burt Foster, Edward K. Foster, Norvell C. Foster, Ronnie E. Foster, Timothy L. Foster, C. Ronnie Fowler, Ed Fowler, Jerry Fowler, Kevin Fox, Walter P. Framski, John M. Frankl, John R. Fraps, Aaron Frederick, Steve Freund, Steve Frey, Rolf Friberg, Rob Fritchen, Daniel Fronefield, Dewayne Frost, Larry D. Fuegen, Bruce A. Fuller, Jack A. Fuller, Richard Furrer

g Barry Gallagher, Jacques Gallant, Jesse Gambee, Tommy Gann, Tommy Gann, Rodney Gappelberg, Jim L. Gardner, Robert J. Gardner, Larry W. Garner, Mike Garner, Timothy P. Garrity, Mark W. Garvock, Bert Gaston, Brett Gatlin, Darrell Geisler, Thomas Gerner, James Gibson, Fabio Giordani, Joel Gist, Kevin Gitlin, Gary Gloden, Wayne Goddard, Jim Gofourth, Scott K. Goguen, David Goldberg, Rodney W. Goodling, Tim Gordon, Thomas L. Gore, Gabe

Gorenflo, James T. Gorenflo, Greg Gottschalk, Rayne Gough, Edward Graham, Paul J. Granger, Daniel Gray, Don Greenaway, Jerry Louis Grice, Michael S. Griffin, Larry Groth, Anthony R. Guarnera, Bruce Guidry, Christian Guier, Tom & Gwen Guinn, Garry Gunderson, Johan Gustafsson

h Cyrus Haghjoo, Ed Halligan, N. Pete Hamilton, Timothy J. Hancock, Bill Hand, Don L. Hanson III, Douglas E. Hardy, Larry Harley, Sewell C. Harlin, Paul W. Harm, Brent Harper-Murray, Cass Harris, Jeffrey A. Harris, Tedd Harris, Bill Hart, Sammy Harthman, Heather Harvey, Kevin Harvey, Robert Hatcher, Buddy Hawkins, Rade Hawkins, Rodney Hawkins, Wally Hayes, Charlie E. Haynes, Gary Headrick, Kelly Healy, Chad Heddin, Dion Hedges, Win Heger, Daniel Heiner, John Heinz, E. Jay Hendrickson, Bill Herndon, Harold Herron, Don Hethcoat, Jim B. Hill, John M. Hill, Amy Hinchman, Vance W. Hinds, Donald R. Hinton, Dan Hockensmith, Dr. Georg Hoellwarth, William G. Hoffman, Thomas R. Hogan, Troy Holland, Michael Honey, Un Pyo Hong, John F. Hood, John Horrigan, Robert M. Horrigan, Lawrence House, Gary House, Michael Houston, Jason G Howell, F. Charles Hubbard, Dale Huckabee, Gov. Mike Huckabee, C. Robbin Hudson, Anthony B. Hudson, Bill Hughes, Daryle Hughes, Tony Hughes, Brad Humelsine, Maurice Hunt, Raymon E. Hunt, Richard D. Hunter, K. Scott Hurst, William R. Hurt, David H. Hwang, Joe Hytovick

i Gary Iames, Hisayuki Ishida

j David Jackson, Jim L. Jackson, Chuck Jahnke, Jr., Karl H. Jakubik, Melvin Jennings Jr., John Lewis Jensen, Mel "Buz" Johns, David A. Johnson, John R. Johnson, Ray Johnson, Thomas Johnson, Clayton W. Johnston, Dr. Robt. Johnston, William Johnston, Chris E. Jones, Enoch Jones, Franklin W. Jones, John Jones, Roger W. Jones, William Burton Jones, Terry J. Jordan, Shane Justice

k Charles Kain, Al J. Kajin, Gus Kalanzis, Barry Kane, David Kazsuk, Jarod Kearney, Robert Keeler, Joseph F. Keeslar, Steven C. Keeslar, Jerry Keesling, Dale Kempf, Larry Kempf, R. W. Kern, Joe Kertzman, Lawrence Keyes, Charles M. Kilbourn, Jr., Keith Kilby, Nicholas Kimball, Richard L. Kimberley, Herman King, David R. King, Fred J. King, Harvey G. King Jr., Kenneth King, Frederick D. Kingery, Donald E. Kinkade, Ray Kirk, Todd Kirk, John Kish, Brad Kliensmid, Russell K. Klingbeil, Hank Knickmeyer, Kurt Knickmeyer, Jason Knight, Steven C. Koster, Bob Kramer, Lefty Kreh, Phil Kretsinger

l Simon Labonti, Jerry Lairson Sr., Curtis J. Lamb, J. D. Lambert, Robert M. Lamey, Leonard D. Landrum, Warren H. Lange, Paul Lansingh, Rodney Lappe, Kermit J. Laurent, Alton Lawrence, Randell Ledbetter, Denis H. LeFranc, Jim L. Lemcke, Jack H. Leverett Jr., Wayne Levin, Bernard Levine, Steve Lewis, Tom Lewis, John J. Lima, Lindy Lippert, Guy A. Little, Tim Lively, Keith Locke, Lowell C. Lockett , Anthony P. Lombardo, Phillip Long, Jonathan A. Loose, Eugene Loro, Jim Lott, Sherry Lott, Jim Lovelace, Ryan Lovell, Steven Lubecki, Bob Luchini, James R. Lucie, James R. Luman, William R. Lyons

m John Mackie, Madame Joelle Madrulli, Takao Mae, Mike Majer, Raymond J. Malaby, John Mallett, Bob Mancuso, Kenneth Mankel, Matt Manley, James Maples, Dan Maragni, Ken Markley, J. Chris Marks, Stephen R. Marshall, Tony Martin, John Alexander Martin, Hal W. Martin, Alan R. Massey, Roger D. Massey, Mick Maxen,

Lynn McBee, Daniel McBrearty, Howard H. McCallen Jr, Michael McClure, Sandy McClure, Frederick L. McCoy, Kevin McCrackin, Victor J. McCrackin, Richard McDonald, Robert J. McDonald, Robin J. McDonald, Frank McGowan, Donald McGrath, Patrick T. McGrath, Eric McHugh, Don McIntosh, Neil H. McKee, Tim McKeen, David Brian McKenzie, Hubert W. McLendon, Tommy McNabb, J. Michael McRae, David L. Meacham, Maxie Mehaffey, J. R. Mellard, Walter Merrin, Mardi Meshejian, Ged Messinger, D. Gregg Metheny, Dan Michaelis, Tracy Mickley, Gary Middleton, Bob Miller, Hanford J. Miller, Michael Mills, David Mirabile, Wm. Dean Mitchell , Jim Molinare, Michael Steven Moncus, Charlie Monroe, Keith Montgomery, Lynn Paul Moore, Marve Moore, Michael Robert Moore, Shawn Robert Moore, William F Moran Jr., Jim Moyer, Russell A. Moyer, James W. Mueller, Jody Muller, Deryk C. Munroe, Jim Mutchler, Ron Myers

n Ryuji Nagoaka, Evan Nappen, Maj. Kendall Nash, Angelo Navagato, Bob Neal, Darby Neaves, Gregory T. Neely, Thomas Conor Neely, James Neilson, Bill Nelson, Lars Nelson, Mark Nevling, Corbin Newcomb, Ron Newton, Tania Nezrick, John Nicoll, Marshall Noble, Douglas E. Noren, H.B. Norris, Paul T. Norris, William North, Vic Nowlan

o Charles F. Ochs III, Julia O'Day, Clyde O'Dell, Vic Odom, Michael O'Herron, Hiroaki Ohta, Michael E. Olive, Todd D. Oliver, Joe Olson, Kent Olson, Richard O'Neill, Robert J. O'Neill, Rich Orton, Philip D. Osattin, Donald H. Osborne, Warren Osborne, Fred Ott, Mac Overton, Donald Owens

p Anthony P. Palermo, Rik Palm, Paul Papich, Ralph Pardington, Cliff Parker, Earl Parker, John Parks, Jimmy D. Passmore, Rob Patton, Jerome Paul, Gary Payton, Michael Peck, Alfred Pendray, Christopher A. Pennington, Johnny Perry, John L. Perry, Conny Persson, Dan L. Petersen, Lloyd Pete C. Peterson, Dan Pfanenstiel, Jim Phillips, Benjamin P. Piccola, Ray Pieper III, Diane Pierce, Dean Piesner, Dietrich Podmajersky, Dietmar Pohl, Clifton Polk, Rusty Polk, Jon R. "Pop" Poplawski, Timothy Potier, Dwight Povistak, James Powell, Robert Clark Powell, Jake Powning, Houston Price, Terry Primos, Jeff Prough, Gerald Puckett, Martin Pullen

q Thomas C. Quakenbush

r Michael Rader, John R. Radford Jr., R. Wayne Raley, Darrel Ralph, Richard A. Ramsey, Gary Randall, James W. Randall Jr., David L. Randolph, Ralph Randow, Mike Reagan, George R. Rebello, Lee Reeves, Roland R. "Rollie" Remmel, Zaza Revishvili, Kirk Rexroat, Scott Reyburn, John Reynolds, Linden W. Rhea, Jim Rice, Stephen E. Rice, Alvin C. Richards Jr., James Richardson, David M. Rider, Richard A. Riepe, Dennis Riley, E. Ray Roberts, Jim Roberts, Don Robertson, Leo D. Robertson, Charles R. Robinson, Michael Rochford, James L. Rodebaugh, James R. Rodebaugh, Gary Rodewald, Charles W. Rogers, Richard Rogers, Willis "Joe" Romero, Frederick Rommel, Troy Ronning, N. Jack Ronzio, Steven Roos, Doun T. Rose, Robert Rosenfeld, Robert N. Rossdeutscher, George R. Roth, Charles Roulin, Kenny Rowe, Clark D. Rozas, Ronald S. Russ, Michael G. Ruth, Michael G. Ruth Jr., Brad Rutherford, Tim Ryan, Wm. Mike Ryan, Raymond B. Rybar Jr., Gerald Rzewnicki

s David Sacks, William Sahli, Ken Sands, Paul Sarganis, Charles R. Sauer, James P. Saviano, Ed Schempp, Ellen Schilling, Tim Scholl, Robert Schrader, Stephen C.

directory

Schwarzer, James A. Scroggs, Bert Seale, Turner C. Seale, Jr., David D. Seaton, Steve Seib, Mark C. Sentz, Jimmy Seymour, Rodrigo Menezes Sfreddo, Steve Shackleford, Gary Shaw, James F. Shull, Robert Shyan-Norwalt, Ken Simmons, Brad Singley, Cleston S. Sinyard, Charles Russel Sisemore, Charles J. Smale, Charles Moran Smale, Carel Smith, Clifford Lee Smith, Corey Smith, J.D. Smith, Joshua J. Smith, Lenard C. Smith, Raymond L. Smith, Timothy E. Smock, Michael Tom Snyder, Max Soaper, John E. Soares, Arthur Soppera, Bill Sowell, Randy Spanjer Sr., David R. Sparling, H. Red St. Cyr, Chuck Stancer, Craig Steketee, Daniel Stephan, Tim Stevens, Edward L. Stewart, Rhett & Janie Stidham, Jason M. Stimps, Walter Stockwell, J.B. Stoner, Bob Stormer, Mike Stott, Charles Stout, John K. Stout Jr., Johnny L. Stout, Howard Stover, John Strohecker, Robert E. Stumphy Jr., Harlan Suedmeier, Wayne Suhrbier, Alan L. Sullivan, Fred Suran, Tony Swatton, John Switzer, John D. Switzer, Arthur Swyhart, Mark G. Szarek, Joseph Szilaski

t Scott Taylor, Shane Taylor, Danny O. Thayer, Jean-Paul Thevenot, Brian Thie, David E. Thomas, Devin Thomas, Guy Thomas, Scott Thomas, Hubert Thomason, Robert Thomason, Kinzea L. Thompson, Alan L. Tiensvold, Jason Tiensvold, John Tilton, George Tindera, Dennis Tingle, Dennis P. Tingle, Brion Tomberlin, P. J. Tomes, Kathleen

C. Tomey, Mark Torvinen, Lincoln Tracy, Joe E. Travieso III, James J. Treacy, Craig Triplett, Kenneth W Trisler, James Turpin, Ross Tyser

v Michael V. Vagnino, Jr, , Butch Vallotton, Steve Van Cleve, Jerry W. Van Eizenga, Terry L. Vandeventer, Robert Vardaman, Chris Vidito, Michael Viehman, Gustavo Colodetti Vilal, Ricardo Vilar, Mace Vitale, Patrik Vogt, Bruce Voyles

w Steve "Doc" Wacholz, Lawrence M. Wadler, Adam Waldon, Bill Walker, Don Walker, James L. Walker, Carl D. Ward, Jr., Ken Warner, Robert Lee Washburn Jr., Herman Harold Waters, Lu Waters, Robert Weber, Charles G. Weeber, Fred Weisenborn, Ronald Welling, Eddie Wells, Gary Wendell, Elsie Westlake, Jim Weyer, Nick Wheeler, Wesley Whipple, John Paul White, Lou White, Richard T. White, L. Wayne Whitley, Randy Whittaker, Timothy L. Wiggins, William Burton Wiggins, Jr., Scott Wiley, Dave Wilkes, Craig Wilkins, A. L. Williams, Charles E. Williams, Linda Williams, Michael L. Williams, Edward Wilson, George H. Wilson III, Jeff Wilson, Daniel Winkler, Randy Winsor, George Winter, Ronald E. Woodruff, Steve Woods, Bill Worthen, Terry Wright, Derrick Wulf

z Mark D. Zalesky, Kenneth Zarifes, Matthew Zboray, Terry Zboril, Karl Zimmerman

miniature knifemaker's society

Paul Abernathy, Joel Axenroth, Blade Magazine, Dennis Blaine, Gerald Bodner, Gary Bradburn, Brock Custom Knives, Ivan Campos, Mitzi Cater, Don Cowles, Creations Yvon Vachon, Dennis Cutburth, David Davis, Robert Davis, Gary Denms, Dennis Des Jardins, Eisenberg Jay Publishers, Allen Eldridge, Peter Flores, David Fusco, Eric Gillard, Wayne Goddard, Larah Gray, Gary Greyraven, Tom & Gwen Guinn, Karl Hallberg, Ralph Harris, Richard Heise, Laura Hessler, Wayne Hensley, Tom Hetmanski, Howard Hosick, Albert Izuka, Garry Kelley, Knife World Publishers, R F Koebbeman, Terry Kranning, Gary Lack, John LeBlanc, Mike Lee, Les Levinson, Jack Lewis, Mike Ley, Ken Liegey, Henry Loos, Jim Martin, Howard Maxwell, McMullen & Yee Publishing, Ken McFall, Mal Mele, Paul Meyers, Toshiaki Michinaka, Allen G Miller, Wayne & June Morrison, Mullinnix & Co, National Knife Collectors Assoc., Allen Olsen, Charles Ostendorf, Mike Pazos, Jim Pear, Gordon Pivonka, Jim Pivonka, Prof. Knifemakers Assoc, Jim Pugh, Roy Quincy, John Rakusan, A D Rardon, Dawin Richards, Stephen Ricketts, Mark Rogers, Alex Rose, Hank Rummell, Helen Rummell, Sheffield Knifemakers Supply, Sporting Blades, Harry Stalter, Udo Stegemann, Mike Tamboli, Hank Rummell, Paul Wardian, Ken Warner, Michael Wattelet, Ken Wichard Jr. Charles Weiss, Jim Whitehead, Steve Witham, Shirley Whitt, G T Williams, Ron Wilson, Dennis Windmiller, Carol Winold, Earl Witsaman, James Woods

professional knifemaker's association

Mike "Whiskers" Allen, John Anthon, Ray Archer, Eddie Baca, Cecil Barret, John Bartlow, Paul Basch, Brett Bennett, Nico Bernard, Phillip Booth, Kenneth Brock, Craig Camerer, Tim Cameron, Rod Carter, Jeff Chaffee, Roger Craig, Bob Cumming, Dave Darpinian, Michael Donato, Mike Draper, Audra Draper, Ray Ennis, Jim Eriksen, Jack Feder, John Fraps, Bob Glassman, Sal Glesser, John Greco, Jim Griksen, John Harbuck, Marge Hartman, Mike Henry, Gary Hicks, Guy Hielscher, Howard Hitchmough, Terrill Hoffman, Robert Hunter, Mike Irie, Donald Jones, Jot Singh Khalsa, Harvey King, Jason King, Steve Kraft, Jim Largent, Jim Lemcke (Texas Knifemakers Supply), WSSI (Mike Ludeman), Jim Magee, Daniel May, Jerry McClure, Mac McLaughlin, Larry McLaughlin, Clayton Miller, Mark Molnar, Ty Montell, Mike Mooney, NC Tool Company, Bill Noehren , Steve Nolen, Rick Nowland, Fred Ott, Dick Patton, Rob Patton, PKA, Pop Knives, Dennis Riley, Rocky Mountain Blade Collectors, Steve Rollert, Clint Sampson, Charles Sauer, Jerry Schroeder, Craig Steketee, Joe Stetter, Big Mike Taylor, Bob Terzuola, Loyd Thomsen , James Thrash, Ed Thuesen, Chuck Trice, Louis Vallet, Louis Vinquist, Bill Waldrup, Tommy Ware, David Wattenberg, Joe Wheeler, Dan Wittman, Owen Wood, Mike Zima, Daniel Zvonek

state/regional associations

alaska knifemakers association

A.W. Amoureux, John Arnold, Bud Aufdermauer, Robert Ball, J.D. Biggs, Lonnie Breuer, Tom Broome, Mark Bucholz, Irvin Campbell, Virgil Campbell, Raymond Cannon, Christopher Cawthorne, John Chamberlin, Bill Chatwood, George Cubic, Bob Cunningham, Gordon S. Dempsey, J.L. Devoll, James Dick, Art Dufour, Alan Eaker, Norm Grant, Gordon Grebe, Dave Highers, Alex Hunt, Dwight Jenkins, Hank Kubaiko, Bill Lance, Bob Levine, Michael Miller, John Palowski, Gordon Parrish, Mark W. Phillips, Frank Pratt, Guy Recknagle, Ron Robertson, Steve Robertson, Red Rowell, Dave Smith, Roger E. Smith, Gary R. Stafford, Keith Stegall, Wilbur Stegner, Norm Story, Robert D. Shaw, Thomas Trujillo, Ulys Whalen, Jim Whitman, Bob Willis

arizona knifemakers association

D. "Butch" Beaver, Bill Cheatham, Dan Dagget, Tom Edwards, Anthony Goddard, Steve Hoel, Ken McFall, Milford Oliver, Jerry Poletis, Merle Poteet, Mike Quinn, Elmer Sams, Jim Sornberger, Glen Stockton, Bruce Thompson, Sandy Tudor, Charles Weiss

arkansas knifemakers association

David Anders, Auston Baggs, Don Bailey, Reggie Barker, Marlen R. Barnes, Paul Charles Basch, Lora Sue Bethke, James Black, R.P. Black, Joel Bradford, Gary Braswell, Paul Brown, Shawn Brown, Troy L. Brown, Jim Butler, Buddy Cabe, Allen Conner, James Cook, Thom Copeland, Gary L. Crowder, Jim Crowell, David T Darby, Fred Duvall, Rodger Echols, David Etchieson, Lee Ferguson, Jerry Fisk, John Fitch, Joe & Gwen Flournoy, Dewayne Forrester, John Fortenbury, Ronnie Foster, Tim Foster, Emmet Gadberry, Larry Garner, Ed Gentis, Paul Giller, James T. Gilmore, Terry Glassco, D.R. (Rick) Gregg, Lynn Griffith, Arthur J. Gunn, Jr., David Gunnell, Morris Herring, Don "Possum" Hicks, Jim Howington, B. R. Hughes, Ray Kirk, Douglas Knight, Lile Handmade Knives, Jerry Lairson Sr., Claude Lambert, Alton Lawrence, Jim Lemcke, Michael H. Lewis, Willard Long, Dr. Jim Lucie, Hal W Martin, Tony Martin, Roger D. Massey, Douglas Mays, Howard McCallen Jr., Jerry McClure, John McKeehan, Joe McVay, Bart Messina, Thomas V. Militano, Jim Moore, Jody Muller, Greg Neely, Ron Newton, Douglas Noren, Keith Page, Jimmy Passmore, John Perry, Lloyd "Pete" Peterson, Cliff Polk, Terry Primos, Paul E Pyle Jr, Ted Quandt, Vernon Red, Tim Richardson, Dennis Riley, Terry Roberts, Charles R. Robinson, Kenny Rowe, Ken Sharp, Terry Shurtleff, Roy Slaughter, Joe D. Smith, Marvin Solomon, Hoy Spear, Charles Stout, Arthur Tycer, Ross Tyser, James Walker, Chuck Ward, Herman Waters, Bryce White, Tillmon T Whitley III, Mike Williams, Rick Wilson, Terry Wright, Ray Young

australian knifemakers guild inc.

Peter Bald, Wayne Barrett, Peter Bennett, Wayne Bennett, Wally Bidgood, David Brodziak, Neil Charity, Terry Cox, Bruce Crawley, Mark Crowley, Steve Dawson, Malcolm Day, Peter Del Raso, John Dennis, Michael Fechner, Steve Filicietti, Barry Gardner, Thomas Gerner, Branko Giljevic, Eric Gillard, Peter Gordon, Stephen Gregory-Jones, Ben Hall, Mal Hannan, Lloyd Harding, Rod Harris, Glen Henke, Michael Hunt, Robert Hunt, Myron Husiak, John Jones, Simeon Jurkijevic, Wolf Kahrau, Peter Kandavnieks, Peter Kenny, Tasman Kerley, John Kilby, Murray Lanthois, Anthony Leroy, Greg Lyell, Paul Maffi,

Maurice McCarthy, Shawn McIntyre, Ray Mende, Dave Myhill, Adam Parker, John Pattison, Mike Petersen, Murray Shanaughan, Kurt Simmonds, Jim Steele, Rod Stines, David Strickland, Kelvin Thomas, Doug Timbs, Hardy Wangemann, Brendon Ware, Glen Waters, Bob Wilhelm, Joe Zemitis

california knifemakers association

Arnie Abegg, George J. Antinarelli, Elmer Art, Gregory Barnes, Mary Michael Barnes, Hunter Baskins, Gary Biggers, Roger Bost, Clint Breshears, Buzz Brooks, Steven E. Bunyea, Peter Carey, Joe Caswell, Frank Clay, Richard Clow, T.C. Collins, Richard Corbaley, Stephanie Engnath, Alex Felix, Jim Ferguson, Dave Flowers, Logwood Gion, Peter Gion, Joseph Girtner, Tony Gonzales, Russ Green, Tony Guarnera, Bruce Guidry, Dolores Hayes, Bill Herndon, Neal A. Hodges, Richard Hull, Jim Jacks, Lawrence Johnson, David Kazsuk, James P. Kelley, Richard D. Keyes, Michael P. Klein, Steven Koster, John Kray, Bud Lang, Tomas N. Lewis, R.W. Loveless, John Mackie, Thomas Markey, James K. Mattis, Toni S. Mattis, Patrick T. McGrath, Larry McLean, Jim Merritt, Greg Miller, Walt Modest, Russ Moody, Emil Morgan, Gerald Morgan, Mike Murphy, Thomas Orth, Tom Paar, Daniel Pearlman, Mel Peters, Barry Evan Posner, John Radovich, James L. Rodebaugh, Clark D. Rozas, Ron Ruppe, Brian Saffran, Red St. Cyr, James Stankovich, Bill Stroman, Tony Swatton, Gary Tamms, James P. Tarozon, Scott Taylor, Tru-Grit Inc., Tommy Voss, Jessie C. Ward, Wayne Watanabe, Charles Weiss, Steven A. Williams, Harlan M. Willson, Steve Wolf, Barry B. Wood

canadian knifemakers guild

Gaetan Beauchamp, Shawn Belanger, Don Bell, Brent Beshara, Dave Bolton, Conrad Bondu, Darren Chard, Garry Churchill, Guillaume J. Cote, Christoph Deringer, Jeff Diotte, Randy Doucette, Jim Downie, John Dorrell, Eric Elson, Lloyd Fairbairn, Paul-Aime Fortier, Rick Frigault, John Freeman, Mark Garvock, Brian Gilbert, Murray Haday, Tom Hart, Thomas Haslinger, Ian Hubel, Paul Johnston (London, Ont.), Paul Johnston (Smith Falls, Ont.), Jason Kilcup, Kirby Lambert, Greg Lightfoot, Jodi Link, Wolfgang Loerchner, Mel Long, Brian Lyttle, David Macdonald, Michael Mason, Alan Massey, Leigh Maulson, James McGowan, Edward McRae, Mike Mossington, Sean O'Hare, Rod Olson, Neil Ostroff, Ron Post, George Roberts, Brian Russell, Murray St. Armour, Michael Sheppard, Corey Smith, David Smith, Jerry Smith, Walt Stockdale, Matt Stocker, Ed Storch, Steve Stuart, George Tichbourne, Brian Tighe, Robert Tremblay, Glenn Treml, Steve Vanderkloff, James Wade, Bud Weston, Peter Wile

florida knifemaker's association

Dick Atkinson, Albert F. "Barney" Barnett, James J. Barry III, Howard Bishop, Andy Blackton, Stephen A. Bloom, Dean Bosworth, John Boyce, W. Lowell Bray Jr., Harold Brown, Douglas Buck, Dave Burns, Patrick Burris, Norman J. Caesar, Peter Channell, Mark Clark, Lowell Cobb, David Cole, Mark Condron, William (Bill) Corker, Ralph L. D'Elia, Jack Davenport, Kevin Davey, J.D. Davis, Kenny Davis, Bill Dietzel, Bob Doggett, William B. Douglas, John B. Durham, Jim Elliot, Tom M. Enos, Bob Ferring, Todd Fischer, Mike Fisher, Ricky Fowler, Mark Frank, Roger Gamble, Tony Garcia, John Gawrowski, James "Hoot" Gibson, Pedro Gonzalez, Ernie Grospitch, Pete Hamilton, Dewey Harris, Henry Heitler, David Helton, Phillip Holstein,

John Hodge, Kevin Hoffman, Edward O. Holloway, Joel Humphreys, Joe Hytovick, Tom Johanning, Raymond C. Johnson II, Paul S. Kent, Bill King, F.D. Kingery, Russ Klingbeil, John E. Klingensmith, William S. Letcher, Bill Levengood, Tim Logan, Glenn A. Long, Gail Lunn, Larry Lunn, Ernie Lyle, Bob Mancuso, Randy Mason, R.J. McDonald, Faustina Mead, Maxie Mehaffey, Dennis G. Meredith, Steve Miller, Dan Mink, Steven Morefield, Martin L. "Les" Murphy, Toby Nipper, Cliff Parker, L.D. (Larry) Patterson, James Perry, Dan Piergallini, Martin Prudente, Carlo Raineri, Ron Russ, Rusty Sauls, Dennis J. Savage, David Semones, Ann Sheffield, Brad Shepherd, Bill Simons, Stephen J. Smith, Kent Swicegood, Louis M. Vallet, Donald Vogt, Roger L. Wallace, Tom Watson, Andrew M. Wilson, Stan Wilson, Hugh E. Wright III, Brad Zinker

knifemakers' guild of southern africa

Jeff Angelo, George Baartman, Francois Basson, Rob Bauchop, George Beechey, Arno Bernard, Buzz Bezuidenhout, Chris Booysen, Ian Bottomley, Peet Bronkhorst, Rob Brown, Fred Burger, Sharon Burger, William Burger, Larry Connelly, Z. Andre de Beer, Andre de Villiers, Melodie de Witt, Gavin Dickerson, Roy H. Dunseith, Leigh Fogarty, Andrew Frankland, Ettore Gianferrari, Stan Gordon, Nick Grabe, John Grey, Piet Grey, Heather Harvey, Kevin Harvey, Dries Hattingh, Gawie Herbst, Thinus Herbst, Greg Hesslewood, Des Horn, Billy Kojetin, Mark Kretschmer, Fanie La Grange, Steven Lewis, Garry Lombard, Steve Lombard, Ken Madden, Edward Mitchell, Gunther Muller, Tom Nelson, Jan Olivier, Christo Ooosthuizen, Cedric Pannell, Willie Paulsen, Nico Pelzer, Conrad Pienaar, David Pienaar, Jan Potgieter, Lourens Prinsloo, Theuns Prinsloo, Hilton Purvis, Derek Rausch, Chris Reeve, Bertie Rietveld, Dean Riley, John Robertson, Corrie Schoeman, Eddie Scott, Mike Skellern, Toi Skellern, Carel Smith, Ken Smythe, Graham Sparks, Andre E. Thorburn, Fanie Van Der Linde, Johan van der Merwe, Van van der Merwe, Marius Van der Vyver, Louis Van der Walt, Cor Van Ellinkhuijzen, Danie Van Wyk, Ben Venter, Willie Venter, Gert Vermaak, Rene Vermeulen, Erich Vosloo, Desmond Waldeck, John Wilmot, Wollie Wolfaardt, Owen Wood

midwest knifemakers association

E.R. Andrews III, Frank Berlin, Charles Bolton, Tony Cates, Mike Chesterman, Ron Duncan, Larry Duvall, Bobby Eades, Jackie Emanuel, James Haynes, John Jones, Mickey Koval, Ron Lichlyter, George Martoncik, Gene Millard, William Miller, Corbin Newcomb, Chris Owen, A.D. Rardon, Archie Rardon, Max Smith, Ed Stewart, Charles Syslo, Melvin Williams

montana knifemaker's association

Bill Amoureux, Wendell Barnes, James Barth, Bob Beaty, Brett C. Bennett, Arno & Zine Bernard, Robert Bizzell, Peter Bromley, Bruce Bump, Ed Caffrey, C Camper, John Christensen, Roger Clark, Jack Cory, Bob Crowder, Roger Dole, Rick Dunkerley, Mel Fassio, Tom Ferry, Gary Flohr, Vern Ford, Barry Gallagher, Doc Hagen, Ted Harris, Thomas Haslinger, Sam & Joy Henson, Gerald Hintz, Tori Howe, Al Inman, Dan Kendrick, Doug Klaudt, Mel Long, James Luman, Mike Mann, Jody Martin, Neil McKee, Larry McLaughlin, Mac & Nancy McLaughlin, Gerald Morgan, Ed Mortenson, Deryk Munroe, Dan Nedved, Joe Olson, Daniel O'Malley, Patton Knives, Eldon Peterson, Jim Raymond,

Lori Ristinen, James Rodebaugh, Gary Rodewald, Gordon St. Clair, Andy Sarcinella, Charles Sauer, Dean Schroeder, Art Swyhart, Shane Taylor, Jim Thill, Frank Towsley, Bill Waldrup, Michael Wattelet, Darlene & Gerome Weinand, Daniel Westlind, Nick Wheeler, Michael Young, Fred Zaloudek

new england bladesmiths guild

Phillip Baldwin, Gary Barnes, Paul Champagne, Jimmy Fikes, Don Fogg, Larry Fuegen, Rob Hudson, Midk Langley, Louis Mills, Dan Maragni, Jim Schmidt, Wayne Valachovic and Tim Zowada

north carolina custom knifemakers' guild

Mark Amon, Marion Bagwell, Herbert M. Baker, Robert E. Barber, Dr. James Batson, Wayne Bernauer, William M. Bisher, Dave Breme, Tim Britton, John (Jack) H. Busfield, E. Gene Calloway, Terry Cash, R. C. Chopra, Thomas Clegg, Joe Corbin, Harry Cosgrove, Robert (Bob) J. Cumming, Travis Daniel, Rob Davis, Geno Denning, Dexter Ewing, Brent Fisher, Charles F. Fogarty, Don Fogg, Alan Folts, Norman A. Gervais, Nelson Gimbert, Scott Goguen, Mark Gottesman, Ed Halligan, Koji Hara, Mark Hazen, George Herron, Daniel C. Hilgenberg, Terrill Hoffman, Stacey Holt, B.R. Hughes, Jack Hyer, Steve James, Dan Johnson, Tommy Johnson, Barry & Phillip Jones, Tony Kelly, Robert Knight, Ben Lumpkin, Lavra Marshall, Tom Matthews, Andrew McLurkin, Tommy McNabb, J. Michael McRae, Charlie & Maureen Monroe, Bill Moran, Ron Newton, Victor L. Odom Jr., Charles Ostendorf, Bill Pate, James Poplin, Harry S. Powell, John W. Poythress, M. Perry Price, Darrel Ralph, Bruce M. Ryan, Robert J. Schmidt, Tim & Kathy Scholl, Danks Seel, Daryl Shelby, Rodney N. Shelton, J. Wayne Short, Harland & Karen Simmons, Ken & Nancy Simmons, Johnnie Sorrell, Chuck Staples, Murray Sterling, Carl Strickland, Russ Sutton, Kathleen Tomey, Bruce Turner, Kaiji & Miki Uchida, Dave Vail, Edward & Tanya VanHoy, Wayne Whitley, James A. Williams, Daniel Winkler, Rob Wotzak

ohio knifemakers association

Raymond Babcock, Van Barnett, Harold A. Collins, Larry Detty, Tom Downing, Jim Downs, Patty Ferrier, Jeff Flannery, James Fray, Bob Foster, Raymond Guess, Scott Hamrie, Rick Hinderer, Curtis Hurley, Ed Kalfayan, Michael Koval, Judy Koval, Larry Lunn, Stanley Maienknecht, Dave Marlott, Mike Mercer, David Morton, Patrick McGroder, Charles Pratt, Darrel Ralph, Roy Roddy, Carroll Shoemaker, John Smith, Clifton Smith, Art Summers, Jan Summers, Donald Tess, Dale Warther, John Wallingford, Earl Witsaman, Joanne Yurco, Mike Yurco

south carolina association of knifemakers

Bobby Branton, Gordo Brooks, Daniel L. Cannady, Thomas H. Clegg, John Conn, Geno Denning, Charlie Douan, Jerry G. Hendrix, Wayne Hendrix, George H. Herron, T.J. Hucks, Johnny Johnson, Lonnie Jones, Jason Knight, Col. Thomas D. Kreger, Gene Langley, Eddie Lee, David Manley, William (Bill) Massey, David McFalls, Claude Montjoy, Larry Page, Ricky Rankin, John (Mickey) Reed, Gene Scaffe, Mick Sears, Ralph Smith, S. David Stroud, Robert Stuckey, Rocky Thomas, Woodrow W. Walker, Charlie Webb, Thomas H. Westwood

tennessee knifemakers association

John Bartlow, Doug Casteel, Harold Crisp, Larry Harley, John W. Walker, Harold Woodward, Harold Wright

knife photo index

knives 2004

etchers/carvers

Burke, Dan, 144
Dippold, Al, 143
Dunkerley, Rick, 141
Cha, Back Cover
Fellows, Mike, 143
Fuegen, Larry, 142
Gallagher, Barry, 140
Goo, Tai, 141
Grussenmeyer, Paul, 144
Hansen, Sharla, 144

Hansen, Shaun, 144
Higgins, J.P., 144
Hirayama, Harumi, 141
Hoffman, Kevin, 143
Jernigan, Steve, 142
Jones, Roger "Mudbone",
 108
Lerch, Matthew, 141
Lunn, Gail, 141
Lunn, Larry, 142

McConnell, Loyd, 144
McNabb, Tommy, 144
McRae, Mike, 143
Minnick, Jim, 171
Muller, Jody, 142
Muller, Pat, 142
Norris, Don, 143
Olszewski, Stephen, 140
Palmer, Taylor, 140
Pendleton, Lloyd, 141

Saindon, Bill, 143
Slobodian, Scott, 142
Stephan, Daniel, 144
Sterling, Tom, 144
Szilaski, Joseph, 141
Vogt, Donald, 142
Wright, Richard, 142

engravers

Amatori, Francesco, 169
Bates, Billy, 168, 169
Clayton, Mark, 169
Dailey, George, 170
Davidson, Jere, 171
Dunn, Steve, 168
Eaton, Rick, 167
Foster, Norvell, 168
Frank, H.H., 167
Hands, Barry Lee, 168
Herman, Tim, 171
Johns, Bill, 169

Khalsa, Jot Singh, 170
Limings, Harry, 158, 171
Lunn, Gail, 170
Lytton, Simon, 97, 135
McArdle, Tom, 113
Meyer, Chris, 147, 151, 170,
 171
Minnick, Joyce, 171
Moulton, Dusty, 170, Back
 Cover
Nilsson, Jonny Walker, 170
Nott, Ron, 89, 147

Pachi, Mirella, Back Cover
Parsons, Michael, 166
Patterson, Tom, 94
Rho, Nestor Lorenzo, 169
Rudolph, Gil, 168
Shaw, Bruce, 73, 82, 166,
 168
Shostle, Ben, 167
Smith, Everett "Smitty", 169
Stepanian, Amayak, 167
Tippetts, Colten, 167
Van Eldik, Frans, 166

Van Hoy, Tanya, 122
Van Wyk, Helene, 122
Volgger, M., 167
Warenski, Buster, 86
Warenski, Julie, 86, 96, 98,
 135, 157, 167, 169, 171
Warren, Kenneth, 112
Waters, Glenn, 170
White, Jim, 131
Whitehead, Jim, 98

knifemakers

Allred, Bruce, 71, 104
Anders, David, 78, 92, 95,
 110
Anders, Jerome, 59, 88
Anderson, Tom, 59, 65
Ankrom, W.E., 133
Appleby, Robert, 97, 152
Appleton, Ron, 64
Atkinson, Dick, 131
Barker, Reggie, 74, 90, 109
Barnes, Wendell, 80, 115
Barr, A.T., 153, 168
Barth, J.D., 73, 83
Baumgardner, Ed, 106
Beaty, Robert, 58, 70, 104,
 114, 154
Begg, Todd, 67, 72, 104,
 159
Behnke, Bill, 75
Bennett, Brett, 106
Bennica, Charles, 63, 125
Berger, Max, 118
Bernard, Arno, 129
Bertholus, Bernard, 74, 82
Bertuzzi, Etore, 98, 146
Best, Ronald, 108
Bethke, Lora Sue, 96, 125

Boguszewski, Phil, 69
Booco, Gordon, 71, 104,
 120, 136
Booth, Philip, 60, 67, Front
 Cover
Bose, Reese, 64
Bowles, Chris, 83
Boyes, Tom, 76
Bradshaw, Bailey, 136
Brandsey, Edward, Front
 Cover
Breed, Kim, 105
Brend, Walter, 173, 176
Browne, Richard, 138
Bucholz, Mark, 64
Bump, Bruce, 156
Burger, William, 131
Burke, Dan, 63, 135, 159
Buxton, Bill, 156
Caffrey, Ed, 73
Callahan, Errett, 118
Camerer, Craig, 90
Cannady, Daniel, 75
Carter, Fred, 125, 133
Carter, Murray, 174
Cashen, Kevin, 153
Choate, Milton, 147

Christensen, Jon, 72, 91,
 109, 116
Claiborne, Jeff, 66, 113
Colter, Wade, 62, 84, 149
Cook, James, 71, 93
Corbit, Gerald, 80, 151, 158,
 171
Cordova, Joe, 91, 146, 150
Courtois, Bryan, 87
Crawford, Pat, 66
Crowder, Gary, 60
Crowell, Jim, 91
Dailey, George, 36, 135, 138
Darcey, Chester, 74, 91
Davidson, Edmund, 27, 98,
 107, 131, 171
Davis, Barry, 134
Dean, Harvey, 83, 95, 117
Dellana, 136
Denig, H., 167
Deringer, Christoph, 136
Dippold, Al, 81, 97, 137
Diskin, Matt, 153
Dodd, Robert, 70
Doggett, Bob, 108, 156, 167
Dole, Roger, 69

Dorneles, Luciano
 Oliveira, 96
Downing, Larry, 109, 131
Downs, Jim, 157
Dozier, Bob, 182, 185
Draper, Audra, 121, 124,
 151
Draper, Melissa, 151
Draper, Mike, 151, 154
Driscoll, Jeffrey, 72
Duff, Bill, 62
Duff, William, 87, 105
Dugdale, Daniel, 61
Duncan, Brad, 64, 67, Front
 Cover
Dunkerley, Rick, 81, 146
Dunn, Steve, 91
Duran, Jerry, 75, 115
Durham, Ken, 132, 133
Eaton, Rick, 159
Eggerling, Robert, 67, 69,
 80, 83, 85, 111, 119, 137,
 142, 148, 150, 153, 156,
 157, 158, 159, 170, 171
Ehlers, Paul, 119
Elishewitz, Allen, 182, 183,
 187

leatherworkers/sheathmakers

scrimshanders

sporting cutlers

The firms listed here are special in the sense that they make or market special kinds of knives made in facilities they own or control either in the U.S. or overseas. Or they are special because they make knives of unique design or function. The second phone number listed is the fax number.

A.G. RUSSELL KNIVES INC
1920 North 26th St
Lowell, AR 72745-8489
479-631-0130 800-255-9034
749-631-8493
ag@agrussell.com
www.agrussell.com
The oldest knife mail-order company, highest quality. Free catalog available. In these catalogs you will find the newest and the best. If you like knives, this catalog is a must.

AHERN GROUP, THE/EXECUTIVE EDGE
3462 Cascade Ive Drive
Buford, GA 30519
678-482-8116 or 800-334-3790
6784829421; 800-334-3790
tahern@bellsouth.net
www.executiveedge.com
Pen style shirt pocket knives ideal for carry or gift giving. Several sizes and style available.

AL MAR KNIVES
PO Box 2295
Tualatin, OR 97062-2295
503-670-9080; 503-639-4789
www.almarknives.com
Featuring our ultralight™ series of knives. Sere 2000™ Shirke, Sere™, Operator™, Nomad™, and Ultralight series™.

ALCAS COMPANY
1116 E State St
Olean, NY 14760
716-372-3111; 716-373-6155
twarner@kabar.com
www.cutco.com
Household cutlery / sport knives.

ANZA KNIVES
C Davis
PO Box 710806
Santee, CA 92072
619-561-9445
619-390-6283
sales@anzaknives.com
www.anzaknives.com

B&D TRADING CO.
3935 Fair Hill Rd.
Fair Oaks, CA 95628

BARTEAUX MACHETES, INC.
1916 SE 50th St.
Portland, OR 97215
503-233-5880
barteaux@machete.com
www.machete.com
Manufacture of machetes, saws, garden tools.

BEAR MGC CUTLERY
1111 Bear Blvd. SW
Jacksonville, AL 36265
256-435-2227; 256-435-9348
Lockback, commemorative, multi tools, high tech & hunting knives.

BECK'S CUTLERY & SPECIALTIES
McGregor Village Center
107 Edinburgh South Dr
Cary, NC 27511
919-460-0203
919-460-7772
beckscutlery@mindspring.com
www.beckscutlery.com

BENCHMADE KNIFE CO. INC.
300 Beaver Creek Rd.
Oregon City, OR 97045
503-655-6004; 503-655-6223
info@benchmade.com
www.benchmade.com
Sports, utility, law enforcement, military, gift and semi custom.

BERETTA U.S.A. CORP.
17601 Beretta Dr.
Accokeek, MD 20607
800-528-7453
www.berettausa.com
Full range of hunting & specialty knives.

BLACKJACK KNIVES
PO Box 3
Greenville, WV 24945

BLUE GRASS CUTLERY CORP
20 E Seventh St PO Box 156
Manchester, OH 45144
937-549-2602; 937-549-2709 or 2603
sales@bluegrasscutlery.com
www.bluegrasscutlery.com
Manufacturer of Winchester Knives, John Primble Knives and many contract lines.

BOKER USA INC
1550 Balsam St
Lakewood, CO 802014-5917
303-462-0662
303-462-0668
sales@bokerusa.com
www.bokerusa.com
Wide range of fixed blade and folding knives for hunting, military, tactical and general use.

BROWNING
One Browning Pl
Morgan, Ut 84050
801-876-2711; 801-876-3331
www.browning.com
Outdoor hunting & shooting products.

BUCK KNIVES INC
1900 Weld Blvd.
El Cajon, CA 92020
800-735-2825; 619-562-2285
www.buckknives.com
Sports cutlery.

BULLDOG BRAND KNIVES
PO Box 23852
Chattanooga, TN 37422
423-894-5102
423-892-9165
Fixed blade and folding knives for hunting and general use.

BUSSE COMBAT KNIFE CO.
11651 CO Rd 12
Wauseon, OH 43567
419-923-6471; 419-923-2337
www.bussecombat.com
Simple & very strong straight knife designs for tactical & expedition use.

CAMILLUS CUTLERY CO.
54 Main St.
Camillus, NY 13031
315-672-8111; 315-672-8832
customerservice@camillusknives.com
www.camillusknives.com

CAS IBERIA INC
650 Industrial Blvd.
Sale Creek, TN 37373
423-332-4700
423-332-7248
www.casiberia.com
Extensive variety of fixed-blade and folding knives for hunting, diving, camping, military and general use.

CASE CUTLERY
W R & Sons
Owens Way
Bradford, PA 16701
800-523-6350; 814-368-1736
consumer-relations@wrcase.com
www.wrcase.com
Folding pocket knives.

CHICAGO CUTLERY CO.
9234 W Belmont Ave
Franklin Park, IL 60131
847-678-8600
www.chicagocutlery.com
Sport & utility knives.

CHRIS REEVE KNIVES
11624 W President Dr.No.B
Boise, ID 83713
208-375-0367
208-375-0368
crknifo@chrisreeve.com
www.chrisreeve.com
Makers of one-piece range of fixed blades, sebenza and mnand folding knives.

COAST CUTLERY CO
2045 SE Ankeny St
Portland, OR 97214
800-426-5858 or 503-234-4545

503-234-4422
www.coastcutlery.com
Variety of fixed-blade and folding knives and multi-tools for hunting, camping and general use.

COLD STEEL INC
3036 Seaborg Ave. Suite A
Ventura, CA 93003
800-255-4716 or 805-650-8481
805-642-9727
art@coldsteel.com
www.coldsteel.com
Wide variety of folding lockbacks and fixed-blade hunting, fishing and neck knives, as well as bowies, kukris, tantos, throwing knives and kitchen knives.

COLONIAL CUTLERY INTERNATIONAL
K.M. Paolantonio
P.O. Box 960
North Scituate, RI 02857
866-421-6500
401-421-6500
colonialcutlery@aol.com
Custom design, sport and camp knives.

COLUMBIA RIVER KNIFE & TOOL
9720 SW Hillman Ct.
Wilsonville, OR 97070
800-891-3100
503-682-9680
info@crkt.com
www.crkt.com
Complete line of sport, work and tactical knives.

CRAWFORD KNIVES
205 N Center
West Memphis, AR 72301
870-732-2452
Folding knives for tactical and general use.

CRIPPLE CREEK KNIVES
Rt. 1, Box 501B
Oldfort, TN 37362

DAVID BOYE KNIVES
PO Box 1238
Dolan Springs, AZ 86441
800-853-1617 or 520-767-4273
520-767-3030
www.boyeknives.com
Semi-production fixed-blade and folding knives for hunting and general use.

DELTA Z KNIVES, INC
PO Box 1112
Studio City, CA 91614
818-786-9488
818-787-8560
sales@deltaz-knives.com
www.deltaz-knives.com
Wide range of folders and fixed-blade designs.

DUNN KNIVES
Steve Greene
PO Box 204
Rosville, KS 66533
785-584-6856
785-584-6856

EMERSON KNIVES, INC.
PO Box 4180
Torrance, CA 90510-4180
310-212-7455
310-212-7289
www.emersonknives.com
Hard use tactical knives; folding & fixed blades

FALLKNIVEN AB
Havrevagen 10
S-96142 Boden
SWEDEN
46-92154422
46-92154433
info@fallkniven.se
www.fallkniven.com
High quality stainless knives.

FROG TOOL CO
PO Box 600
Getzville, NY 14068-0600
716-877-2200; 716-877-2591
gatco@buffnet.net
www.frogtool.net
Precision multi tools

FROST CUTLERY CO
PO Box 22636
Chattanooga, TN 37422
800-251-7768 or423-894-6079
423-894-9576
www.frostcutleryco.com
Wide range of fixed-blade and folding knives with a multitude of handle materials.

GATCO SHARPENERS
PO Box 600
Getzville, NY 14068
716-877-2200; 716-877-2591
gatcosharpeners.com
Precision sharpening systems, diamond sharpening systems, ceramic sharpening systems, carbide sharpening systems, natural Arkansas stones.

GENUINE ISSUE INC.
949 Middle Country Rd.
Selden, NY 11784
631-696-3802; 631-696-3803
gicutlery@aol.com
Antique knives, swords.

GERBER LEGENDARY BLADES
14200 SW 72Nd Ave.
Portland, OR 97223
503-639-6161
www.gerberblades.com
Knives, multi-tools, axes, saws, outdoor products.

GIGAND USA
701 Penhoun Ave
Secaucus, NJ 07094
201-583-5968
Imports designed by Fred C.

GROHMANN KNIVES LTD.
PO Box 40
Pictou Nova Scotia B0K 1H0
CANADA
888-756-4837 OR 902-485-4224
902-485-5872
Fixed-blade belt knives for hunting and fishing, folding pocketknives for hunting and general use.

GT KNIVES
7734 Arjons Dr.
San Diego, CA 92126
858-530-8766; 858-530-8798
gtknives@gtknives.com
www.gtknives.com
Law enforcement & military automatic knives.

GUTMANN CUTLERY INC
PO Box 2219
Bellingham, WA 98227
800-288-5379
Junglee knives, Smith & Wesson tools and optics, Walther knives and optics.

H&B FORGE CO.
235 Geisinger Rd.
Shiloh, OH 44878
419-895-1856
Tomahawks & throwing knives.

HISTORIC EDGED WEAPONRY
1021 Saddlebrook Dr
Hendersonville, NC 28739
828-692-0323
828-692-0600
histwpn@bellsouth.net
Antique knives from around the world; importer of puukko and other knives from Norway, Sweden, Finland and Lapland.

HONEYCUTT MARKETING, INC., DAN
3165 C-4 S Campbell
Springfield, MO 65807
417-886-2288; 417-887-2635
ozk_knife_gun@hotmail.com
All kinds of cutlery, military, Randalls.

IMPERIAL SCHRADE CORP.
7 Schrade Ct.
Ellenville, NY 12428
800-2-Schrade
www.schradeknives.com

JOY ENTERPRISES-FURY CUTLERY
1104 53rd Court South

West Palm Beach, FL 33407
800-500-3879 or 561-863-3205
561-863-3277
mail@joyenterprises.com
www.joyenterprises.com; www.furycutlery.com
Extensive variety of fixed-blade and folding knives for hunting, fishing, diving, camping, military and general use; novelty key-ring knives.

KA-BAR KNIVES INC
1125 E State St
Olean, NY 14760
800-282-0130
www.info@ka-bar.com

KATZ KNIVES, INC.
PO Box 730
Chandler, AZ 85224-0730
480-786-9334; 480-786-9338
katzkn@aol.com
www.katzknives.com

KELLAM KNIVES CO.
902 S Dixie Hwy
Lantana, FL 33462
800-390-6918; 561-588-3185; 561-588-3186
info@kellamknives.com
www.kellamknives.com
Largest selection of Finnish knives; handmade & production.

KERSHAW/KAI CUTLERY CO.
25300 SW Parkway
Wilsonville, OR 97070

MESSEV KLOTZLI
Hohengasse E Ch 3400
Burgdorf
SWITZERLAND
(34) 422-2378
(34) 422-7693
info@klotzli.com
www.klotzli.com
High-tech folding knives for tactical and general use.

KNIFEWARE INC
PO Box 3
Greenville, WV 24945

KNIGHTS EDGE LTD.
5696 N Northwest Highway
Chicago, IL 60646-6136
773-775-3888
773-775-3339
sales@knightsedge.com
www.knightsedge.com
Medieval weaponry, swords, suits of armor, katanas, daggers.

KNIVES OF ALASKA, INC.
Charles Or Jody
3100 Airport Dr
Denison, TX 75020 8623
903-786-7366, 800-752-0980; 903-786-7371
info@knivesofalaska.com
www.knivesofalaska.com
High quality hunting & outdoorsmen's knives.

KUTMASTER KNIVES
Div Of Utica Cutlery Co
820 Noyes St
Utica, NY 13502
315-733-4663; 315-733-6602
www.kutmaster.com
Manufacturer and importer of pocket, lockback, tool knives and multi-purpose tools

LAKOTA
620 E Monroe
Riverton, WY 24945
307-856-6559
307-856-1840
AUS 8-A high-carbon stainless steel blades.

LEATHERMAN TOOL GROUP, INC.
PO Box 20595
Portland, OR 97294
503-253-7826; 503-253-7830
mktg@leatherman.com
www.leatherman.com
Multi-tools

LONE WOLF KNIVES
Doug Hutchens
17400 SW Upper Boones Ferry Rd Suite 240
Portland, OR 97224

503-431-6777

MARBLE'S OUTDOORS
420 Industrial Park
Gladstone, MI 49837
906-428-3710; 906-428-3711
marble@up.net
www.marblesoutdoors.com

MASTERS OF DEFENSE KNIFE CO
256 A Industrial Park Dr
Waynesville, NC 28786
828-452-4158
828-452-7327
info@mastersofdefense.com
www.mastersofdefense.com
Fixed-Blade and folding knives for tactical and general use.

MEYERCO MANUFACTURING
4481 Exchange Service Dr
Dallas, TX 75236
214-467-8949
214-467-9241
www.meyercousa.com
Folding tactical,rescue and speed-assisted pocketknives; fixed-balde hunting and fishing designs; multi-function camping tools and machetes.

MCCANN INDUSTRIES
132 S 162nd PO Box 641
Spanaway, WA 98387
253-537-6919; 253-537-6993
McCann.machine@worldnet.att.net
www.mccannindustries.com

MICRO TECHNOLOGY
932 36th Ct. SW
Vero Beach, Fl 32968
772-569-3058
772-569-7632
sales@microtechknives.com
www.microtechknives.com
Manufacturers of the highest quality production knives.

MORTY THE KNIFE MAN, INC.
4 Manorhaven Blvd
Pt. Washington, NY 11050
516-767-2357; 516-767-7058

MUSEUM REPLICAS LTD.
PO Box 840 Dept PQ
Conyers, GA 30012
800-883-8838
www.museumreplicas.com
Historically accurate & battle-ready swords & daggers.

MYERCHIN MARINE CLASSICS
14185 Regina Dr Ste G
Rancho Cucamonga, CA 91739
909-463-6741; 909-463-6751
myerchin@myerchin.com
www.myerchin.com
Rigging/ Police knives.

NATIONAL KNIFE DISTRIBUTORS
PO Box 188
Forest City, NC 28043
800-447-4342 or 828-245-4321
828-245-5121
Benchmark pocketknives from Solingen, Germany.

NORMARK CORP
10395 Yellow Circle Dr
Minnetonka, MN 55343
800-874-4451
612-933-0046
Hunting knives, game shears and skinning ax.

ONTARIO KNIFE CO.
26 Empire St
Franklinville, NY 14737
800-222-5233; 800-299-2618
salesokc@aol.com
www.ontarioknife.com
Fixed blades, tactical folders, military & hunting knives, machetes.

OUTDOOR EDGE CUTLERY CORP.
4699 Nautilus Ct. S
Boulder, CO 80301
800-447-EDGE
303-530-7020
outdooredge@plinet.com
www.outdooredge.com

Sporting Cutlers, continued

PARAGON CUTLERY CO.
2015 Asheville Hwy.
Hendersonville, NC 28791
828-697-8833; 828-697-5005
www.paragonweb.com
Knifemaking furnaces.

PILTDOWN PRODUCTIONS
Errett Callahan
2 Fredonia Ave.
Lynchburg, VA 24503

QUEEN CUTLERY COMPANY
PO Box 500
Franklinville, NY 14737
800-222-5233; 800-299-2618
salesokc@aol.com
www.queencutlery.com
Pocket knives, collectibles, Schatt & Morgan, Robeson, club knives.

QUIKUT
PO Box 29
Airport Industial Park
Walnut Ridge, AR 72476
870-886-6774
870-886-9162

RANDALL MADE KNIVES
PO Box 1988
Orlando, FL 32802-1988
407-855-8075
407-855-9054
grandall@randallknives.com
www.randallknives.com
Handmade fixed-blade knives for hunting, fishing, diving, military and general use.

REMINGTON ARMS CO., INC.
870 Remington Drive
P.O. Box 700
Madison, NC 27025

RICHARTZ USA
1825 Walnut Hill Lane Suite 120
Irving, TX 78038
800-859-2029
972-331-2566
info@richartz.com
www.richartz.com
German-made, multi-balde folding knives for hunting, camping and general use.

ROUND EYE KNIFE & TOOL
PO Box 818
Sagel, ID 83860
208-265-8858
208-263-0848
roundeye@nidlink.com
www.roundeye.com
Folding and fixed-blade knives for hunting and general use.

SANTA FE STONEWORKS
3790 Cerrillos Rd.
Santa Fe, NM 87507
800-257-7625; 505-471-0036
knives@rt66.com
www.santafestoneworks.com
Gem stone handles.

SARCO CUTLERY LLC
449 Lane Dr
Florence, AL 35630
256-766-8099

256-766-7246
sarcoknives@earthlink.net
www.sarcoknives.com
Fixed-blade camping knife.

SOG SPECIALTY KNIVES & TOOLS, INC.
6521 212th St. S.W.
Lynwood, WA 98036
425-771-7689
425-771-7681
info@sofknives.com
www.sogknives.com
ARC-LOCK advantage, automatic tools. Specialized fixed blades, folding knives, multi-tools.

SPYDERCO, INC.
PO Box 800
Golden, CO 80402-0800
800-525-7770; 303-278-2229
sales@spyderco.com
www.spyderco.com
Knives and sharpeners

SWISS ARMY BRANDS INC.
PO Box 874
One Research Dr
Shelton, CT 06484-0874
800-243-4045
800-243-4006
www.swissarmy.com
Folding multi-blade designs and multi-tools for hunting, fishing, camping, hiking, golfing and general use. One of the original brands (Victorinox) of Swiss Army Knives.

TAYLOR CUTLERY
1736 N Eastman Rd
PO Box 1638
Kingsport, TN 37662-1638
800-251-0254 or 423-247-2406
423-247-5371
taylor@preferred.com
www.taylorcutlery.com
Fixed-blade and folding knives for tactical, rescue, hunting and general use.

TIGERSHARP TECHNOLOGIES
1002 N Central Expwy Suite 499
Richardson, TX 75080
469-916-2861
972-907-0716
claudettehead@hotmail.com

TIMBERLINE KNIVES
PO Box 600
Getzville, NY 14068-0600
716-877-2200; 716-877-2591
gatco@buffnet.net; timberlineknives.com
High Technology production knives for professionals, sporting, tradesmen & kitchen use.

TINIVES
1725 Smith Rd
Fortson, GA 31808
888-537-9991
706-322-9892
info@tinives.com
www.tinives.com
High-tech folding knives for tactical, law enforcement and general use.

TRU-BALANCE KNIFE CO.
PO Box 140555
Grand Rapids, MI 49514

TURNER, P.J., KNIFE MFG., INC.
PO Box 1549
Afton, WY 83110
307-885-0611
pjtkm@silverstar.com
www.eknife.net

UTICA CUTLERY CO
820 Noyes St
Utica, NY 13503-1537
800-888-4223
315-733-6602
sales@kutmaster.com
Wide range of folding and fixed-blade designs, multi-tools and steak knives.

WARNER, K.
PO Box 3
Greenville, WV 24945
304-832-6878

WENGER NORTH AMERICA
15 Corporate Dr
Orangeburg, NY 10962
800-431-2996 or 845-365-3500
845-365-3558
www.wengerna.com
One of the official makers of folding multi-blade Swiss Army knives.

WILD BOAR BLADES
1701 Broadway Pmb 282
Vancouver, WA 98666
888-735-8483 or 360-735-0570
360-735-0390
Wild Boar Blades is pleased to carry a full line of Kopormed knives and kitchenware imported from Poland.

WILLIAM HENRY FINE KNIVES
2125 Delaware Ave Suite C
Santa Cruz, CA 95060
831-454-9409
831-454-9309
www.williamhenryknives.com
Semi-custom folding knives for hunting and general use; some limited editions.

WORLD SURVIVAL INSTITUTE
C Janowsky
PO Box 394
Tok, AK 99780
907-883-4243

WUU JAU CO INC
2600 S Kelly Ave
Edmond, OK 73013
800-722-5760 or 405-359-5031
877-256-4337 or 405-340-5965
www.wuujau.com
Wide variety of imported fixed-blade and folding knives for hunting, fishing, camping, and general use.

WYOMING KNIFE CORP.
101 Commerce Dr.
Ft. Collins, CO 80524

XIKAR INC
PO Box 025757
Kansas City, MO 64102
888-266-1193
info@xikar.com
www.xikar.com

importers & foreign cutlers

A. G. RUSSELL KNIVES INC
1920 North 26th St
Lowell, AR 72745-8489
479-631-0130; 800-255-9034
479-631-8493
ag@agrussell.com
www.agrussell.com
The oldest knnife mail-order company, highest quality. Free catalog available. In these catalogs you will find the newest and the best. If you like knives, this catalog is a must.

ADAMS INTERNATIONAL KNIFEWORKS
8710 Rosewood Hills
Edwardsville, IL 62025

AITOR-BERRIZARGO S.L.
P.I. Eitua PO Box 26
48240 Berriz Vizcaya
SPAIN
946826599
94602250226
info@aitor.com
www.aitor.com
Sporting knives.

ATLANTA CUTLERY CORP.
2143 Gees Mill Rd.
Box 839Fd
Conyers, GA 30207
770-922-3700

770-388-0246
www.atlantacutlery.com

BAILEY'S
PO Box 550
Laytonville, CA 95454

BELTRAME, FRANCESCO
Flli Beltrame F&C SNA
Via Dei Fabbri AS/3
33085 Maniago PN
ITALY
switches@iol.it
www.italianstiletto.com

Importers & Foreign Cutlers, continued

BOKER USA, INC.
1550 Balsam St.
Lakewood, CO 80214-5917
303-462-0662
303-462-0668
sales@bokerusa.com
www.bokerusa.com
Ceramic blades.

CAMPOS, IVAN DE ALMEIDA
Custom And Old Knives Trader
R. Stelio M. Loureiro, 206
CENTRO, TATUI
BRAZIL

C.A.S. IBERIA, INC.
650 Industrial Blvd.
Sale Creek, TN 37373
423-332-4700
423-332-7248
cas@casiberia.com
www.casiberia.com
Paul Chen/Hanwei Swords, Muela, Ajtor, Replica weaponry.

CATOCTIN CUTLERY
PO Box 188
Smithsburg, MD 21783

CLASSIC INDUSTRIES
1325 Howard Ave., Suite 408
Burlingame, CA 94010

COAST CUTLERY CO.
2045 Se Ankeny St.
Portland, OR 97214

COLUMBIA PRODUCTS CO.
PO Box 1333
Sialkot 51310
PAKISTAN

COLUMBIA PRODUCTS INT'L
PO Box 8243
New York, NY 10116-8243
201-854-3054
201-854-7058
nycolumbia@aol.com
http://columbiaproducts.homestead.com/cat/html
Pocket, hunting knives and swords.

COMPASS INDUSTRIES, INC.
104 E. 25th St.
New York, NY 10010

CONAZ COLTELLERIE
Dei F.Lli Consigli-Scarperia
Via G. Giordani, 20
50038 SCARPERIA (FIRENZE)
ITALY
conaz@dada.it
www.conaz.com

CONSOLIDATED CUTLERY CO., INC.
696 Nw Sharpe St.
Port St. Lucie, FL 34983

CRAZY CROW TRADING POST
PO Box 847 Dept 96
Pottsboro, TX 75020
903-786-2287
903-786-9059
info@crazycrow.com
www.crazycrow.com
Solingen blades, knife making parts & supplies.

DER FLEISSIGEN BEAVER
(The Busy Beaver)
Harvey Silk
PO BOX 1166
64343 GRIESHEIM
GERMANY
4961552231
49 6155 2433
Der.Biber@t-online.de

EMPIRE CUTLERY CORP.
12 Kruger Ct.
Clifton, NJ 07013

EXTREME RATIO SAS
Mauro Chiostri
Maurizio Castrat, Viale
Montegrappa 298
59100 Prato
ITALY
0039 0574 58 4639

0039 0574 581312
chios@iol.it
www.extremaratio.com
Tactical & military knives manufacturing.

FALLKNIVEN AB
Havrevagen 10
S-96142 Boden
SWEDEN
46 92154422
4692154433
info@fallkniven.se
www.fallkniven.com
High quality knives.

FREDIANI COLTELLI FINLANDESI
Via Lago Maggiore 41
I-21038 Leggiuno
ITALY

GIESSER MESSERFABRIK GMBH, JOHANNES
Raiffeisenstr 15
D-71349 Winnenden,
GERMANY
49-7195-18080
49-7195-64466
info@giesser.de
www.giesser.de
Professional butchers and chef's knives.

HIMALAYAN IMPORTS
3495 Lake Side Dr
Reno, NV 89509
775-825-2279
himimp@aol.com
httpillmembers.aol.com/himinp/index.html

IVAN DE ALMEIDA CAMPOS-KNIFE DEALER
R. Xi De Agosto
107, Centro, Tatui, Sp 18270
BRAZIL
55-15-2518092
55-15-251-4896
campos@bitweb.com.br
Custom knives from all Brazilian knifemakers.

JOY ENTERPRISES
1104-53Rd Court
South West Palm Beach, FL 33407
561-863-3205/800-500-3879
561-863-3277
mail@joyenterprises.com
www.joyenterprises.com
Fury™, Mustang™, Hawg Knives, Muela.

KELLAM KNIVES CO.
902 S Dixie Hwy
Lantana, FL 33462
561-588-3185; 800-390-6918
561-588-3186
info@kellamknives.com
www.kellamknives.com
Knives from Finland; own line of knives.

KNIFE IMPORTERS, INC.
PO Box 1000
Manchaca, TX 78652
800-561-5301
800-266-2373
Wholesale only.

KNIGHTS EDGE
5696 N Northwest Hwy
Chicago, IL 60646
773-775-3888
773-775-3339
Exclusive designers of our Rittersteel, Stagesteel and Valiant Arms lines of weaponry.

LEISURE PRODUCTS CORP.
PO Box 1171
Sialkot-51310
PAKISTAN

L. C. RISTINEN
Suomi Shop
17533 Co Hwy 38
Frazee MN 56544
218-538-6633
icrist@scta.net
Scandinavian cutlery custom antique.

LINDER, CARL NACHF.
Erholungstr. 10
42699 Solingen
GERMANY
212 330856
212 337104

info@linder.de
www.linder.de

MARTTIINI KNIVES
PO Box 44 (Marttiinintie 3)
96101 Rovaniemi
FINLAND

MATTHEWS CUTLERY
4401 Sentry Dr., Suite K
Tucker, GA 30084

MESSER KLÖTZLI
PO Box 104
Hohengasse 3, Ch-3402 Burgdorf
SWITZERLAND
034 422 2378
034 422 7693
info@klotzli.com
www.klotzli.com

MURAKAMI, ICHIRO
Knife Collectors Assn. Japan
Tokuda Nishi 4 Chome, 76 Banchi, Ginancho
HASHIMAGUN, GIFU
JAPAN
81 58 274 1960
81 58 273 7369
www.gix.orjp/~n-resin/

MUSEUM REPLICAS LIMITED
2147 Gees Mill Rd., Box 840 Pq
Conyers, GA 30012
800-883-8838
www.museumreplicas.com

NICHOLS CO.
PO Box 473, #5 The Green
Woodstock, VT 05091
802-457-3970
802-457-2051
janjesse@sover.net
Import & distribute knives from EKA (Sweden), Helle (Norway), Brusletto (Norway), Roselli (Finland). Also market Zippo products and Snow & Neally axes.

NORMARK CORP.
Craig Weber
10395 Yellow Circle Drive
Minnetonka, MN 55343

PRO CUT
9718 Washburn Rd
Downey, CA 90241
562-803-8778
562-803-4261
sales@procutdist.com
Wholesale only. Full service distributor of domestic & imported brand name cutlery. Exlusive US importer for both Marto Swords and Battle Ready Valiant Armory edged weapons.

PRODUCTORS AITOR, S.A.
Izelaieta 17
48260 Ermua
SPAIN
943-170850
943-170001
info@aitor.com
Sporting knives.

SCANDIA INTERNATIONAL INC.
5475 W Inscription Canyon Dr
Prescott, AZ 86305
928-442-0140
928-442-0342
frosts@cableone.net
www.frosts-scandia.com
Frosts Knives of Sweden.

STAR SALES CO., INC.
1803 N. Central St., PO Box 1503
Knoxville, TN 37901

SVORD KNIVES
Smith Rd., Rd 2
Waiuku, South Auckland
NEW ZEALAND

SWISS ARMY BRANDS LTD.
The Forschner Group, Inc.
One Research Drive
Shelton, CT 06484
203-929-6391
203-929-3786
www.swissarmy.com

Importers & Foreign Cutlers, continued

TAYLOR CUTLERY
PO Box 1638
1736 N. Eastman Rd.
Kingsport, TN 37662
*Colman Knives along with Smith & Wesson,
Cuttin Horse, John Deere, Zoland knives.*

UNITED CUTLERY CORP.
1425 United Blvd.
Sevierville, TN 37876
865-428-2532
865-428-2267
order@unitedcutlery.com
www.unitedcutlery.com
*Harley-Davidson™, Colt™, Stanley™ hunting,
camping, fishing, collectible & fantasy knives.*

UNIVERSAL AGENCIES INC
4690 S Old Peachtree Rd., Ste C

Norcross, GA 30071-1517
678-969-9147; 678-969-9148
678-969-9169
info@uai.org
www.knifesupplies.com; www.thunderforged.com;
www.uai.org
*Serving the cutlery industry with the finest
selection of India Stag, Buffalo Horn,
Thunderforged ⁸ Damascus. Mother of Pearl,
Knife Kits and more.*

VALOR CORP.
1001 Sawgrass Corp Pkwy
Sunrise, FL 33323-2811
954-377-4925
954-377-4941
www.valorcorp.com
Wide variety of imported & domestic knives.

WENGER N. A.
15 Corporate Dr.

Orangeburg, NY 10962
800-431-2996
www.wengerna.com
Swiss Army™ Knives.

WILD BOAR BLADES
1701 Broadway, Suite 282
Vancouver, WA 98663
888-735-8483; 360-735-0570
360-735-0390
usakopro@aol.com
www.wildboarblades.com
*Wild Boar Blades is plesed to carry a full line of
Kopromed knives and kitchenware imported
from Poland.*

ZWILLING J.A.
Henckels Inc
171 Saw Mill River Rd
Hawthorne, NY 10532

knifemaking supplies

AFRICAN IMPORT CO.
Alan Zanotti
20 Braunecker Rd.
Plymouth, MA 02360
508-746-8552
508-746-0404
Ivory.

ALASKAN ANTLERCRAFT & IVORY
Roland And Kathy Quimby
Box 3175-Rb
Casa Grande, AZ 85222

AMERICAN SIEPMANN CORP.
65 Pixley Industrial Parkway
Rochester, NY 14624
585-247-1640
585-247-1883
www.siepmann.com
*CNC blade grinding equipment, grinding
wheels, production blade grinding services.*

ANCHORAGE CUTLERY
Greg Gritten
801 Airport Hts #351
Anchorage, AK 99508
907-277-5843
cutlery@artic.net
www.anchoragecutlery.com
*Custom knife making supplies; ivory,
gemstones, antler, horn, bone.*

ART JEWEL ENTERPRISES, LTD.
460 Randy Rd.
Carol Stream, IL 60188

ATLANTA CUTLERY CORP.
2147 Gees Mill Rd., Box 839Xe
Conyers, GA 30012
800-883-0300

BATAVIA ENGINEERING
PO Box 53
Magaliesburg, 1791
SOUTH AFRICA
27-14-5771294
bertie@batavia.co.za
www.batavia.co.za
*Contact wheels for belt grinders and surface
grinders; damascus and mokume.*

BILL'S CUSTOM CASES
PO Box 2
Dunsmuir, CA 96025
530-467-3783
530-467-3903
billscustomcases@sisqtel.net
Knife cases.

BOONE TRADING CO., INC.
PO Box 669
Brinnon, WA 98320
800-423-1945
www.boonetrading.com
Ivory of all types, bone, horns.

BORGER, WOLF
Benzstrasse 8
76676 Graben-Neudorf
GERMANY
wolf@messerschmied.de
www.messerschmied.de

BOYE KNIVES
PO Box 1238
Dolan Springs, AZ 86441
800-853-1617
520-767-3030
boye@ctaz.com
www.boyeknives.com
Dendritic steel and Dendritic cobalt.

BRONK'S KNIFEWORKS
C. Lyle Brunckhorst
23706 7th Ave SE
Country Village, Suite B
Bothell, WA 98021
425-402-3484
bronks@net-tech.com
www.bronksknifeworks.com
Damascus steel.

CHRISTOPHER MFG., E.
PO Box 685
Union City, TN 38281

CRAZY CROW TRADING POST
PO Box 847 Dept. 96
Pottsboro TX 75076
903-786-2287
903-786-9059
info@crazycrow.com
www.crazycrow.com
Solingen blades, knive making parts & supplies.

CUSTOM FURNACES
PO Box 353
Randvaal, 1873
SOUTH AFRICA
27 16 365-5723
27 16 365-5738
johnlee@custom.co.za
Furnaces for hardening & tempering of knives.

CUSTOM KRAFT
PO Box 2337
Riverview, FL 33568
813-671-0661
727-595-0378
RWPHIL413@earthlink.net
www.rwcustomknives.com
*Specialize in precision screws and hardware for
folders. Also carrying gemstones and
cabochons for inlay work. Catalog available.*

CUTLERY SPECIALTIES
Dennis Blaine
22 Morris Ln.
Great Neck, NY 11024-1707
516-829-5899 800-229-5530
516-773-8076
dennis13@aol.com
www.restorationproduct.com

*US agent/distributor for Renaissance-wax/
polish and other restoration products. Dealer in
medium to high end custo made knives, Antique
knives and hard to find knives and extraordinary
cutlery.*

DAMASCUS-USA CHARLTON LTD
149 Deans Farm Rd.
Tyner, NC 27980-9718
252-221-2010
252/221/2010
damascususa@inteliport.com

DAN'S WHETSTONE CO., INC.
130 Timbs Place
Hot Springs, AR 71913
501-767-1616
501-767-9598
questions@danswhetstone.com
www.danswhetstone.com
Produce natural abrasive stone products.

DIAMOND MACHINING TECHNOLOGY, INC.
85 Hayes Memorial Dr.
Marlborough, MA 01752
800-481-5944
508-485-3924
dmtsharp@dmtsharp.com
www.dmtsharp.com
Knife and tool sharpeners.

DIXIE GUN WORKS, INC.
PO Box 130
Union City, TN 38281
731-885-0700; 731-885-0440 or 800-238-6785
info@dixiegun.com
www.dixiegun.com
Knive and knifemaking supplies.

E CHRISTOPHER MANUFACTURING
PO Box 685
Union City, TN 38281
731-885-0374
731-885-0440
*Solingen blades from Germany (ground and
polished).*

EZE-LAP DIAMOND PRODUCTS
3572 Arrowhead Dr.
Carson City, NV 89706
775-888-9500
775-888-9555
sales@eze-lap.com
www.eze-lap.com
Diamond coated sharpening tools.

FIELDS, DONALD
790 Tamerlane St
Deltona, FL 32725
386-532-9070
donaldfields@aol.com
Mammoth ivory, fossil walrus ivory, bone, etc.

FLITZ INTERNATIONAL, LTD.
821 Mohr Ave.
Waterford, WI 53185
800-558-8611
262-534-2991
info@flitz.com
www.flitz.com
Metal polish, buffing pads, wax.

Knifemaking Supplies, continued

FORTUNE PRODUCTS, INC.
205 Hickory Creek Rd
Marble Falls, TX 78654
830-693-6111
830-693-6394
www.accusharp.com
AccuSharp knife sharpeners.

GILMER WOOD CO.
2211 Nw St. Helens Rd.
Portland, OR 97210
503-274-1271
www.gilmerwood.com

GOLDEN AGE ARMS CO.
115 E. High St.
PO Box 366
Ashley, OH 43003

GRS CORP.
D.J. Glaser
PO Box 1153
900 Overlander St
Emporia, KS 66801
620-343-1084 800-835-3519
620-343-9640
glendo@glendo.com
www.glendo.com
*Engraving, Equipment, Tool Sharpener, Books/
Videos.*

HALPERN TITANIUM INC.
Les And Marianne Halpern
Po Box 214
Three Rivers, MA 01080
413-283-8627
413-289-2372
les@halperntitanium.com
*Titanium, carbon fiber, G-10, fasteners; CNC
milling.*

HARMON, JOE T.
8014 Fisher Drive
Jonesboro, GA 30236

HAWKINS CUSTOM KNIVES & SUPPLIES
110 Buckeye Rd.
Fayetteville, GA 30214
770-964-1177
770-306-2877
radeh@bellsouth.net
www.radehawkinscustomknives.com
All styles.

HAYDU, THOMAS G.
Tomway Products
750 E Sahara Ave
Las Vegas, NV
888 4 Tomway
702-366-0626
tom@tomway.com

HILTARY DIAMOND INDUSTRIES
7117 Third Ave.
Scottsdale, AZ 85251
480-945-0700 480-994-5752
480-945-3333
usgrc@qwest.net
www.bigbrainsdont.com

HOUSE OF TOOLS LTD.
#136, 8228 Macleod Tr. S.E.
Calgary, AB Canada
T2H 2B8

HOV KNIVES & SUPPLIES
Box 8005
S-700 08 Orebro
SWEDEN

INDIAN JEWELERS SUPPLY CO.
601 E Coal Ave
Gallup, NM 87301
505-722-4451
888-722-4172
www.ijsinc.com
Gems, metals, tools.

INTERAMCO INC.
5210 Exchange Dr.
Flint, MI 48507
810-732-8181
810-732-6116
solutions@interamco.com
Knife grinding and polishing.

JANTZ SUPPLY
PO Box 584-K4
Davis, OK 73030-0584
800-351-8900
580-369-3082
jantz@brightok.net
www.knifemaking.com
*Pre shaped blades, kit knives, complete
knifemaking supply line.*

JOHNSON, R.B.
I.B.S. Int'L. Folder Supplies
Box 11
Clearwater, MN 55320
320-558-6128
320-558-6128
hclark@radiks.net
www.customknives.com/r.b.johnson
Threaded pivot pins, screws, taps, etc.

JOHNSON WOOD PRODUCTS
34968 Crystal Rd.
Strawberry Point, IA 52076

K&G FINISHING SUPPLIES
PO Box 458
Lakeside, AZ 85929
928-537-8877
928-537-8066
www.knifeandgun.com
Full sevice supplies.

KOVAL KNIVES, INC.
5819 Zarley St.
New Albany, OH 43054
614-855-0777
614-855-0945
koval@kovalknives.com
www.kovalknives.com
Knifemaking supplies & equipment.

LINDER-SOLINGEN KNIFE PARTS
4401 Sentry Dr., Suite K
Tucker, GA 30084

LITTLE GIANT POWER HAMMER
420 4th Corso
Nebraska City, NE 68410

LIVESEY, NEWT
3306 S Dogwood St
Siloam Springs, AR 72761
479-549-3356
479-549-3357
Newt@Livesay.com
www.newt.livesay.com
*Combat utility knives, titanium knives, hunting
knives, custom orders, Kydex™ sheaths,
Kydex™ and steel supplies.*

LOHMAN CO., FRED
3405 N.E. Broadway
Portland, OR 97232

MARKING METHODS, INC.
Katie Yamane
301 S. Raymond Ave.
Alhambra, CA 91803-1531
626-282-8823
626-576-7564
sales@markingmethods.com
www.markingmethods.com
Knife etching equipment & service.

MASECRAFT SUPPLY CO.
254 Amity St
Meriden, CT 06450
203-238-3049
203-238-2373
masecraft.supply@snet.net
*Natural & specialty synthetic handle materials &
more.*

MEIER STEEL
Daryl Meier
75 Forge Rd.
Carbondale, IL 62901

MOTHER OF PEARL CO.
Joe Culpepper
PO Box 445, 293 Belden Cir
Franklin, NC 28734
828-524-6842
828-369-7809
www.knifehandles.com; www.stingrayproducts.com
Mother of pearl, bone, abalone, stingray.

NICHOLAS EQUIPMENT CO.
730 E. Washington St.

Sandusky, OH 44870

NICO BERNARD
PO Box 5151
Nelspruit1200
SOUTH AFRICA
011-2713-7440099
011-2713-7440099
bernardn@iafrica.com

OREGON ABRASIVE & MFG. CO.
12345 Ne Sliderberg Rd
Brush Prairie, WA 98606
360-892-1142
360-892-3025
Tripel grit 3 stone sharpening system.

OSO FAMOSO
Box 654
Ben Lomond,CA 95005
831-336-2343
oso@osofamoso.com
www.osofamoso.com
Mammoth ivory bark.

OZARK KNIFE & GUN
3165 C-4 S. Campbell
Springfield, MO 65807
417-886-CUTT
417-887-2635
ozk_knife_gun@hotmail.com
Randall and custom folders.

PAPAI, ABE
5013 N. 800 E.
New Carlisle,IN 46552

PARAGON INDUSTRIES, INC.
2011 South Town East Blvd.
Mesquite, TX 75149-1122
972-288-7557
800-876-4328
paragonind@worldnet.att.net
www.paragonweb.com
Heat treating furnaces for knife makers.

POPLIN, JAMES/POP KNIVES & SUPPLIES
103 Oak St.
Washington, GA 30673

PUGH, JIM
PO Box 711
Azle, TX 76098
817-444-2679
817-444-5455
*Rosewood ebony Micarta blocks-handle rivets
for Kydex sheath, 0-80 screws for folders.*

RADOS, JERRY
PO Box 531
7523E 5000 N. Rd.
Rant Park, IL 60940
815-472-3350
815-472-3944
rados@favoravi.com
Damascus steel.

REACTIVE METALS STUDIO, INC.
PO Box 890
Clarkdale, AZ 86324
928-634-3434
928-634-6734
reactive@commspeed.net
www.reactivemetals.com

REPRODUCTION BLADES
17485 Sw Pheasant Ln.
Beaverton, OR 97006
503-649-7867
Period knife blades for hobbyists & re-enactors.

RIVERSIDE KNIFE & FORGE SUPPLY
201M W Stillwell
Dequeen, AR 71832
870-642-7643/870-642-4023
uncleal@ipa.net
www.riversidemachine.net

ROCKY MOUNTAIN KNIVES
George L. Conklin
PO Box 902, 615 Franklin
Ft. Benton, MT 59442
406-622-3410
bbgrus@ttc-cmc.net
Working knives.

RUMMELL, HANK
10 Paradise Lane
Warwick, NY 10990

Knifemaking Supplies, continued

MIKE SAKMAR
2470 Melvin
Rochester, MI 48307
248-852-6775
248-852-8544
Mokume bar stock. Retail & Wholesale.

SANDPAPER, INC. OF ILLINOIS
270 Eisenhower Ln. N., Unit 5B
Lombard, IL 60148
630-629-3320
630-629-3324
www.sandpaperinc.com
Abrasive belts, rolls, sheets & discs.

SCHEP'S FORGE
PO Box 395
Shelton, NE 68876-0395

SENTRY SOLUTIONS LTD
111 Sugar Hill Rd
PO Box 130
Contoocook, NH 03229-0130
603-746-5687; 800-546-8049
603-746-5847
knives2002@sentrysolutions.com
www.sentrysolutions.com
Knife care products.

SHEFFIELD KNIFEMAKERS SUPPLY, INC.
PO Box 741107
Orange City, FL 32774-1107
386-775-6453
386-774-5754
www.sheffieldsupply.com

SHINING WAVE METALS
PO Box 563
Snohomish, WA 98290-0563
425-334-5569
425-334-5569
phb@u.washington.edu
A full line of Mokune-Gane in precious and non-precious metals for knifemakers, jewelers and other artists.

SMITH ABRASIVES, INC.
1700 Sleepy Valley Rd.
Hot Springs, AR 71901

SMITH WHETSTONE, INC.
1700 Sleepy Valley Rd.
Hot Springs, AR 71901

SMOLEN FORGE, INC.
Nick Smolen

S1735 Vang Rd
Westby, WA 54667
608-634-3569
608-634-3869
www.smolenforge.com
Damascus billets & blanks, Mokume gane billets.

SOSTER SVENSTRUP BYVEJ 16
Dastrup 4130 Viby Sj
Denmark

STAMASCUS KNIFEWORKS INC
Mike Norris
2115 W. Main St.
Albermarle, NC 28001
704-982-8445
Blade Steels.

STOVER, JEFF
PO Box 43
Torrance, CA 90507
310-532-2166
edgedealer@aol.com
Fine custom knives- top makers.

TEXAS KNIFEMAKERS SUPPLY
10649 Haddington, Suite 180
Houston, TX 77043

TRU-GRIT, INC.
760 E. Francis St. #N
Ontario, CA 91761
909-923-4116 800-532-3336
909-923-9932
trugrit@aol.com
www.trugrit.com
The latest in Norton and 3/M ceramic grinding belts. Also Super Flex, Trizact, Norax and Micron belts to 3000 grit. All of the popular belt grinders. Buffers and variable speed motors. ATS-34, 440C, BG-42, CPM S-30V, 416 and Damascus steel.

UNIVERSAL AGENCIES INC
4690 S Old Peachtree Rd. Ste C
Norcross, GA 30071-1517
678-969-9147; 678-969-9148
678-969-9169
info@uai.org
www.knifesupplies.com, www.thunderforged.com;
www.uai.org
Serving the cutlery industry with the finest selection of India Stag, Buffalo Horn, Thunderforged™ Damascus. Mother of Pearl, Knife Kits and more.

WASHITA MOUNTAIN WHETSTONE CO.
PO Box 20378
Hot Springs, AR 71903
501-525-3914
501-525-0816
wmw@hsnp

WEILAND J REESE
PO Box 2337
Riverview, FL 33568
813-671-0661
727-595-0378
rwphil413@earthlink.net
www.rwcustomknives.com
Folders, straight knives etc.

WILD WOODS
Jim Fray
PO Box 104
Monclova, OH 43542
419-866-0435

WILSON, R.W.
113 Kent Way
Weirton, WV 26062

WOOD CARVERS SUPPLY, INC.
PO Box 7500-K
Englewood, FL 34295-7500
800-284-6229
941-698-0329
www.woocarverssupply.com
Over 2,000 unique wood carving tools.

WOOD STABILIZING SPECIALITS INT'L
Mike & Cara Ludemann
2940 Fayette Ave
Ionia, IA 50645
641-435-4746
641-435-4759
Mike@Stabilizedwood.com
www.stabilizedwood.com
Processor of acrylic impregnated materials.

WYVERN INDUSTRIES
PO Box 1564
Shady Cove, OR 97539-1564

ZOWADA CUSTOM KNIVES
Tim Zowada
4509 E. Bear River Rd.
Boyne Falls, MI 49713
231-348-5416
knifeguy@nmo.net
www.tzknives.com
Damascus, pocket knives, swords, Lower case gothic tz logo.

mail order sales

A. G. RUSSELL KNIVES INC
1920 North 26th St
Lowell, AR 72745-8489
479-631-0130
479-631-8493
ag@agrussell.com
www.agrussell.com
The oldest knife mail-order company, highest quality. Free catalog available. In these catalogs you will find the newest and the best. If you like knives, this catalog is a must.

ADAMS BILL
PO Box 666
Conyers, GA 31078
912-836-4195

ARIZONA CUSTOM KNIVES
Jay And Karen Sadow
8617 E. Clydesdale
Scottsdale, AZ 85258
480-951-0699
sharptalk@aol.com
www.arizonacustomknives.com
Color catalog $5 U.S. / $7 Foreign.

ATLANTA CUTLERY CORP.
2147 Gees Mill Rd., Box 839Dy
Conyers, GA 30012
800-883-0300
www.atlantacutlery.com
Special knives & cutting tools.

ATLANTIC BLADESMITHS/PETER STEBBINS
50 Mill Rd

Littleton MA 01460
978-952-6448
j.galt1100@verizon.ent
www.atlanticbladesmiths.com
Sell, trade, buy; carefully selected handcrafted, benchmade and factory knives.

BALLARD CUTLERY
1495 Brummel Ave.
Elk Grove Village, IL 60007

BECK'S CUTLERY SPECIALTIES
Macgregor Village #109
107 Edinburgh S
Cary, NC 27511
919-460-0203
www.beckscutlery.com
Knives.

BLUE RIDGE KNIVES
166 Adwolfe Rd
Marion, VA 24354-6664
276-783-6143
276-783-9298
www.blueridgeknives.com
Wholesale distributor of knives.

BOB NEAL CUSTOM KNIVES
PO Box 20923
Atlanta, GA 30320
770-914-7794
770-914-7796
bob@bobnealcustomknives.com
www.bobnealcustomknives.com
Exclusive limited edition custom knives-sets & single.

BOONE TRADING CO., INC.
PO Box 669
Brinnon, WA 98320
800-423-1945
www.boonetrading.com
Ivory scrimshaw horns.

CARMEL CUTLERY
Dolores & 6th; PO Box 1346
Carmel, CA 93921
831-624-6699
831-624-6780
ccutlery@ix.netcom.com
www.carmelcutlery.com
Quality custom and a variety of production pocket knives, swords; kitchen cutlery; personal grooming items.

CORRADO CUTLERY
Otto Pomper
1630 Payne St
Chicago, IL 60602
847-329-9770
847-329-9770
www.corradocutlery.com
Knives, Nippers, Scissors, Gifts, Optical Goods.

CREATIVE SALES & MFG.
Box 111
Whitefish, MT 59937
406-849-5174
406-849-5130
www.creativesales.com

Mail Order Sales, continued

CUTLERY SHOPPE
357 Steelhead Way
Boise, ID 83704
800-231-1272
208-672-8588
www.cutleryshoppe.com
Discount pricing on top quality brands.

CUTTING EDGE, THE
1920 North 26Th St
Lowell, AR 72745-8489
479-631-0055
479-631-8734
editor@cuttingedge.com
www.cuttingedge.com
After-market knives since 1968. We offer about 1,000 individual knives for sale each month. Subscription by first class mail, in U.S. $20 per year, Canada or Mexico by air mail, $25 per year. All overseas by air mail, $40 per year. The oldest and the most experienced in the business of buying and selling knives. We buy collections of any size, take knives on consignment. Every month there are 4-8 pages in color featuring the work of top makers.

DENTON, J.W.
102 N. Main St., Box 429
Hiawassee, GA 30546
706-896-2292
706-896-1212
jwdenton@alltel.net
Loveless knives.

DUNN KNIVES INC.
PO Box 204
Rossville KS 66533
785-584-6856
785-584-6856

EDGE CO. KNIVES
17 Kit St
Keene, NH 03431-7125
603-357-9390
edgeco.com

FAZALARE, ROY
PO Box 1335
Agoura Hills, CA 91376
818-879-6161 after 7pm
ourfaz@aol.com
Handmade multiblades; older case; Fight'n Rooster; Bulldog brand & Cripple Creek.

FROST CUTLERY CO.
PO Box 22636
Chattanooga, TN 37422

GENUINE ISSUE, INC.
949 Middle Country Rd.
Selden, NY 11784
516-696-3802
516-696-3803
g.l._cutlery.com
All knives.

GODWIN, INC., G. GEDNEY
2139 Welsh Valley Rd.
Valley Forge, PA 19481
610-783-0670
610-783-6083
www.gggodwin.com
18th century reproductions.

GUILD KNIVES
320 Paani Place 1A
Paia HI 96779
808-877-3109
808-877-3524
donguild@aol.com
www.donguild1@aol.com
Purveyor of Custom Art Knives.

HAWTHORN GALLERIES, INC.
PO Box 6071
Branson, MO 65616
417-335-2170
417-335-2011
hg_inc@hotmail.com

HERITAGE ANTIQUE KNIVES
Bruce Voyles
PO Box 22171
Chattanooga, TN 37422

423-894-8319
423-892-7254
bruce@jbrucevoyles.com
www.jbrucevoyles.com
Knives, knife auctions.

HOUSE OF TOOLS LTD.
#136, 8228 Macleod Tr. Se
Calgary, Alberta, Canada
T2H 2B8

HUNTER SERVICES
Fred Hunter
PO Box 14241
Parkville, MD 64152

JENCO SALES, INC.
PO Box 1000
Manchaca, TX 78652
800-531-5301
800-266-2373
jencosales@sbcglobal.net
Wholsale only.

KELLAM KNIVES CO.
902 S Dixie Hwy
Lantana, FL 33462
561-588-3185; 800-390-6918
561-588-3186
info@kellamknives.com
www.kellamknives.com
Largest selection of Finnish knives; own line of folders and fixed blades.

KNIFEART.COM
13301 Pompano Dr
Little Rock AR 72211
501-221-1010
501-221-2695
www.knifeart.com
Large internet seller of custom knives & upscale production knives.

KNIFE IMPORTERS, INC.
PO Box 1000
Manchaca, TX 78652

KNIFEMASTERS CUSTOM KNIVES/J&S FEDER
PO Box 208
Westport, CT 06881
(203) 226-5211
(203) 226-5312
Investment grade custom knives.

KNIVES PLUS
2467 I 40 West
Amarillo TX 79109
800-687-6202
Retail cutlery and cutlery accessories since 1987.

KRIS CUTLERY
PO Box 133 KN
Pinole, CA 94564
510-223-8968
kriscutlery@attbl.com
www.kriscutlery.com
Japanese, medieval, Chinese & Philippine.

LDC CUSTOM KNIVES
PO Box 20923
Atlanta, GA 30320
770-914-7794
770-914-7796
bob@bobnealcustomknives.com
Exclusive limited edition custom knives - sets & single.

LES COUTEAUX CHOISSIS DE ROBERTS
Ron Roberts
PO Box 273
Mifflin, PA 17058

LONE STAR WHOLESALE
PO Box 587
Amarillo TxX79105
806-356-9540
806-359-1603
Wholesale only; major brands and accessories.

MATTHEWS CUTLERY
4401 Sentry Dr., Suite K
Tucker, GA 30084

MORTY THE KNIFE MAN, INC.
4 Manorhaven Blvd.
Port Washington, NY 11050

MUSEUM REPLICAS LTD.
2143 Gees Mill Rd., Box 840Pq
Conyers, GA 30207
800-883-8838
www.museumreplicas.com
Historically accurate and battle ready swords & daggers.

NORDIC KNIVES
1634Cz Copenhagen Dr.
Solvang, CA 93463
805-688-3612
info@nordicknives.com
www.nordicknives.com
Custom and Randall knives.

PARKER'S KNIFE COLLECTOR SERVICE
6715 Heritage Business Court
Chattanooga, TN 37422
423-892-0448
423-892-0448
bbknife@bellsouth.net

PEN AND THE SWORD LTD., THE
PO Box 290741
Brooklyn, NY 11229 0741
(718) 382-4847
(718) 376-5745
info@pensword.com
Custom folding knives, engraving, scrimshaw, Case knives, English fruit knives, antique pocket knives.

PLAZA CUTLERY, INC.
3333 S. Bristol St., Suite 2060South Coast Plaza
Costa Mesa, CA 92626
714-549-3932
plazacutlery@earthlink.net
www.plazacutlery.com
Largest selection of knives on the west coast. Custom makers from beginners to the best. All customs, reeves, randalls & others available online by phone.

ROBERTSON'S CUSTOM CUTLERY
PO Box 1367
Evans,GA 30809-1367
706-650-0252
706-860-1623
customknives@comcast.net
www.robertsoncustomcutlery.com
Limited edition exclusive designs, Vanguard knivesand world class custom knives.

ROBINSON, ROBERT W.
1569 N. Finley Pt.
Polson, MT 59860

SHAW, GARY
24 Central Ave.
Ridgefield Park, NJ 07660
201-641-8801
201-641-0872
gshaw@carroll.com
Investment grade custom knives.

SMOKY MOUNTAIN KNIFE WORKS
2320 Winfield Dunn Pkwy
Sevierville, TN 37876
865-453-5871; 800-251-9306
info@smkw.com
www.eknifeworks.com
The world's largest knife showplace, catalog and website.

STIDHAM'S KNIVES
PO Box 570
Roseland, FL 32957-0570
772-589-0618
772-589-3162
rstidham@gate.net
www.randallknifesociety.com
Randall, Loveless, Scagel, custom and antique knives.

STODDARD'S, INC.
Copley Place 25
100 Huntington Ave.
Boston, MA 02116
617-536-8688
617-536-8689
Cutlery (Kitchen, pocket knives, Randall-made knives, custom knives, scissors & manicure tools) Binoculars, lwo vision aids, personal care items (hair brushes, manicure sets mirrors).

directory

appraisers

A.G. Russell Knives inc, 1920 North 26th St, Lowell, AR, 72745-8489, 800-255-9034 479-631-0130, 479-631-8493, ag@agrussell.com, www.agrussell.com

Levine, Bernard, PO Box 2404, Eugene, OR, 97402, 541-484-0294, brlevine@ix.netcom.com

Vallini, Massimo, Via G. Bruno 7, 20154 Milano, ITALY, 02-33614751, massimo_vallini@yahoo.it, Knife expert

custom grinders

Cooper, Jim, 1221 Cook Pl., Ramona, CA, 92065-3214, 760-789-1097, (760) 788-7992, jamcooper@aol.com

High, Tom, Rocky Mountain Scrimshaw & Arts, 5474 S. 112.8 Rd., Alamosa, CO, 81101, www.rockymountainscrimshaw.com

McGowan Manufacturing Company, 25 Michigan St, Hutchinson, MN, 55350, 800-342-4810, (320) 587-7966, info@mcgowanmfg.com, www.mcgowanmfg.com

McLuin, Tom, 36 Fourth St., Dracut, MA, 01826, 978-957-4899, tmcluin@attbi.com, www.people.ne.mediaone.net/tmcluin

Peele, Bryan, The Elk Rack, 215 Ferry St. P.O. Box 1363, Thompson Falls, MT, 59873

Schlott, Harald, Zingster Str. 26, 13051 Berlin, GERMANY, 049 030 9293346, harald.schlott@T-online

Wilson, R.W., PO Box 2012, Weirton, WV, 26062

custom handles

Eccentric Endeavors, Michel Santos and Peggy Quinn, P.O. Box 97, Douglas Flat, CA, 95229

Genske, Jay, 283 Doty St, Fond du Lac, WI, 54935, 920-921-8019/Cell Phone 920-579-0144, jaygenske@hotmail.com

Grussenmeyer, Paul G., 310 Kresson Rd, Cherry Hill, NJ, 08034, 856-428-1088, 856-428-8997, pgrussentne@comcast.net, www.pgcarvings.com

High, Tom, Rocky Mountain Scrimshaw & Arts, 5474 S. 112.8 Rd., Alamosa, CO, 81101, www.rockymountainscrimshaw.com

Holden, Larry, PO Box 2017, Ridgecrest, CA, 93556-2017, lardog44@yahoo.com

Holland, Dennis K., 4908-17th Pl., Lubbock, TX, 79416

Imboden II, Howard L., HI II Originals, 620 Deauville Dr., Dayton, OH, 45429

Kelso, Jim, 577 Collar Hill Rd, Worcester, VT, 05682, 802-229-4254, (802) 223-0595

Knack, Gary, 309 Wightman, Ashland, OR, 97520

Krogman, Pam, 838 Merlarkkey St., Winnemucca, NV, 89445

Marlatt, David, 67622 Oldham Rd., Cambridge, OH, 43725, 740-432-7549

Mead, Dennis, 2250 E. Mercury St., Inverness, FL, 34453- 0514

Miller, Robert, 216 Seminole Ave., Ormond Beach, FL, 32176

Myers, Ron, 6202 Marglenn Ave., Baltimore, MD, 21206, 410-866-6914

Saggio, Joe, 1450 Broadview Ave. #12, Columbus, OH, 43212, jvsag@webtv.net, www.j.v.saggio@worldnet.att.net

Schlott, Harald, Zingster Str. 26, 13051 Berlin, GERMANY, 049 030 9293346, harald.schlott@T-online

Snell, Barry A., 4801 96th St. N., St. Petersburg, FL, 33708- 3740

Vallotton, A., 621 Fawn Ridge Dr., Oakland, OR, 97462

Watson, Silvia, 350 Jennifer Lane, Driftwood, TX, 78619

Williams, Gary, (Garbo), PO Box 210, Glendale, KY, 42740-2010

display cases

Bill's Custom Cases, PO Box 2, Dunsmuir, CA, 96025, 530-467-3783, 530-467-3903, billscases@sisqtel.net

Brooker, Dennis, Rt. 1, Box 12A, Derby, IA, 50068

Chas Clements' Custom Leathercraft, Chas, 1741 Dallas St., Aurora, CO, 80010-2018, 303-364-0403, gryphons@home.net

Gimbert, Nelson, PO Box 787, Clemmons, NC, 27012

Haydu, Thomas G., Tomway Products, 750 E Sahara Ave, Las Vegas, NV, 89104, 8884 Tomway, (702) 366-0626, tom@tomway.com, tomway.com

McLean, Lawrence, 18361 Larkstone Circle, Huntington Beach, CA, 92646, 714-848-5779, lmclean@socal.rr.com

Miller, Michael K., M&M Kustom Krafts, 28510 Santiam Highway, Sweet Home, OR, 97386

Miller, Robert, PO Box 2722, Ormond Beach, FL, 32176

Retichek, Joseph L., W9377 Co. TK. D, Beaver Dam, WI, 53916

Robbins, Wayne, 11520 Inverway, Belvidere, IL, 61008

S&D Enterprises, 20 East Seventh St, Manchester, OH, 45144, 937-549-2602, 937-549-2602, sales@s-denterprises.com, www.s-denterprises.com

Schlott, Harald, Zingster Str. 26, ^305^ Berlin, GERMANY, 049 030 9293346, harald.schlott@T-online.de

engravers

Adlam, Tim, 1705 Witzel Ave., Oshkosh, WI, 54902, 920-235-4589, 920-235-4589

Alfano, Sam, 36180 Henry Gaines Rd., Pearl River, LA, 70452

Allard, Gary, 2395 Battlefield Rd., Fishers Hill, VA, 22626,

Allred, Scott, 2403 Lansing Blvd., Wichita Falls, TX

Alpen, Ralph, 7 Bentley Rd., West Grove, PA, 19390

Baron, David, Baron Technolog Inc, 62 Spring Hill Rd., Trumbull, CT, 06611, 203-452-0515, bti@baronengraving.com, www.baronengraving.com

Bates, Billy, 2302 Winthrop Dr. SW, Decatur, AL, 35603

Bettenhausen, Merle L., 17358 Ottawa, Tinley Park, IL, 60477

Blair, Jim, PO Box 64, 59 Mesa Verde, Glenrock, WY, 82637, 307-463-8115, jblairengrav@msn.com

Bonshire, Benita, 1121 Burlington, Muncie, IN, 47302

Boster, A.D., 3744 Pleasant Hill Dr., Gainesville, GA, 30504

Brooker, Dennis B., Rt. 1 Box 12A, Derby, IA, 50068

Bryan, Bridges Engraving CO, PO Box 24254, Tempe, AZ, 85282

Churchill, Winston G., RFD Box 29B, Proctorsville, VT, 05153

Collins, David, Rt. 2 Box 425, Monroe, VA, 24574

Collins, Michael, Rt. 3075, Batesville Rd., Woodstock, GA, 30188

Cupp, Alana, PO Box 207, Annabella, UT, 84711

Dashwood, Jim, 255 Barkham Rd., Wokingham, Berkshire RG11 4BY, ENGLAND

Davidson, Jere, 6023 Goode Rd, Goode, VA, 24556, 540-587-7695, JereDavidson@centralva.net

Dean, Bruce, 13 Tressider Ave., Haberfield, N.S.W. 2045, AUSTRALIA

DeLorge, Ed, 6734 W Main St, Houma, LA, 70360, 504-223-0206

Dickson, John W., PO Box 49914, Sarasota, FL, 34230

Dolbare, Elizabeth, PO Box 502, Dubois, WY, 82513-0502

Downing, Jim, PO Box 4224, Springfield, MO, 65808, 417-865-5953, www.thegunengraver.com

Drain, Mark, SE 3211 Kamilche Pt. Rd., Shelton, WA, 98584

Duarte, Carlos, 108 Church St., Rossville, CA, 95678

Dubben, Michael, 414 S. Fares Ave., Evansville, IN, 47714

Dubber, Michael W., 8205 Heather Pl, Evansville, IN, 47710-4919

Eklund, Maihkel, Föne 1111, S-82041 Färila, SWEDEN, www.art-knives.com

Eldridge, Allan, 1424 Kansas Lane, Gallatin, TN, 37066

Engel, Terry (Flowers), PO Box 96, Midland, OR, 97634

Eyster, Ken, Heritage Gunsmiths inc, 6441 Bishop Rd, Centerburg, OH, 43011

Flannery, Jeff, Flannery Engraving Co., 11034 Riddles Run Rd., Union, KY, 41091, engraving@fuse.net, http://home.fuse.net/engraving

Foster, Norvell, Foster Interprises, PO Box 200343, San Antonio, TX, 78220

Fountain Products, 492 Prospect Ave., West Springfield, MA, 01089

Gipe, Sandi, Rt. 2, Box 1090A, Kendrick, ID, 83537

Glimm, Jerome C., 19 S. Maryland, Conrad, MT, 59425

Gournet, Geoffroy, 820 Paxinosa Ave., Easton, PA, 18042, 610-559-0710, www.geoffroygournet.com

Hands, Barry Lee, 26192 E. Shore Rte., Bigfork, MT, 59911

Harrington, Fred A., Winter: 3725 Citrus, Summer: 2107 W Frances Rd Mt Morris MI 48458-8215, St. James City, FL, 33956, Winter: 239-283-0721 Summer: 810-686-3008

Henderson, Fred D., 569 Santa Barbara Dr., Forest Park, GA, 30297, 770-968-4866

Hendricks, Frank, 396 Bluff Trail, Dripping Springs, TX, 78620, 512-858-7828

Holder, Pat, 7148 W. Country Gables Dr., Peoria, AZ, 85381

Hudson, Tommy, 1181 E 22nd St. Suite #18, Marysville, CA, 95901, 530-681-6531, twhunson@attbi.com, www.picturetrail.com/tommyhudson

Ingle, Ralph W., 151 Callan Dr., Rossville, GA, 30741, 706-858-0641, riengraver@aol.com, Photographer

Johns, Bill, 610 Yellowstone Ave, Cody, WY, 82414, 307-587-5090

Kelly, Lance, 1723 Willow Oak Dr., Edgewater, FL, 32132

Kelso, Jim, RD 1, Box 5300, Worcester, VT, 05682

Koevenig, Eugene and Eve, Koevenig's Engraving Service, Rabbit Gulch, Box 55, Hill City, SD, 57745-0055

Kostelnik, Joe and Patty, RD #4, Box 323, Greensburg, PA, 15601

Kudlas, John M., 55280 Silverwolf Dr, Barnes, WI, 54873, 715-795-2031, jkudlas@cheqnet.net, scrimshander

Limings Jr., Harry, 959 County Rd. 170, Marengo, OH, 43334- 9625

Lindsay, Steve, 3714 West Cedar Hills Drive, Kearney, NE, 68847

Lyttle, Brian, Box 5697, High River AB CANADA, T1V 1M7

Lytton, Simon M., 19 Pinewood Gardens, Hemel Hempstead, Herts. HP1 1TN, ENGLAND

McCombs, Leo, 1862 White Cemetery Rd., Patriot, OH, 45658

McDonald, Dennis, 8359 Brady St., Peosta, IA, 52068

McKenzie, Lynton, 6940 N Alvernon Way, Tucson, AZ, 85718

Meyer, Chris, 39 Bergen Ave., Wantage, NJ, 07461, 973-875-6299

Minnick, Joyce, 144 N. 7th St., Middletown, IN, 47356

Morgan, Tandie, PO Box 693, 30700 Hwy. 97, Nucla, CO, 81424

Morton, David A., 1110 W. 21st St., Lorain, OH, 44052

Moschetti, Mitch, 1435 S. Elizabeth, Denver, CO, 80210

Moulton, Dusty, 135 Hillview Ln, Loudon, TN, 37774, 865-408-9779

Nelida, Toniutti, via G. Pasconi 29/c, Maniago 33085 (PN), ITALY

Nott, Ron, Box 281, Summerdale, PA, 17093

Parsons, Michael R., McKee Knives, 7042 McFarland Rd, Indianapolis, IN, 46227, 317-784-7943

Patterson, W.H., PO Drawer DK, College Station, TX, 77841

Peri, Valerio, Via Meucci 12, Gardone V.T. 25063, ITALY

Pilkington Jr., Scott, PO Box 97, Monteagle, TN, 37356, 931-924-3400, scott@pilkguns.com, www.pilkguns.com

Poag, James, RR1, Box 212A, Grayville, IL, 62844

Potts, Wayne, 912 Poplar St., Denver, CO, 80220

Rabeno, Martin, Spook Hollow Trading Co., 92 Spook Hole Rd., Ellenville, NY, 12428

Raftis, Andrew, 2743 N. Sheffield, Chicago, IL, 60614

Roberts, J.J., 7808 Lake Dr., Manassas, VA, 20111, 703-330-0448, jjrengraver@aolc.om, www.angelfire.com/va2/engraver

Robidoux, Roland J., DMR Fine Engraving, 25 N. Federal Hwy. Studio 5, Dania, FL, 33004

Robyn, Jon, Ground Floor, 30 E. 81st St., New York, NY, 10028

Rosser, Bob, Hand Engraving, 1824 29th Ave. South, Suite 214, Birmingham, AL, 35209, www.hand-engravers.com

Rudolph, Gil, 20922 Oak Pass Ave, Tehachapi, CA, 93561, 661-822-4949, www.gtraks@csurfers.net

Rundell, Joe, 6198 W. Frances Rd., Clio, MI, 48420

Schickl, L., Ottingweg 497, A-5580 Tamsweg, AUSTRIA, 0043 6474 8583

Schlott, Harald, Zingster Str. 26, 13051 Berlin, GERMANY, 049 030 9293346, harald.schlott@T-online

Schönert, Elke, 18 Lansdowne Pl., Central, Port Elizabeth, SOUTH AFRICA

Shaw, Bruce, PO Box 545, Pacific Grove, CA, 93950, 831-646-1937, 831-644-0941

Shostle, Ben, 1121 Burlington, Muncie, IN, 47302

Sinclair, W.P., The Orchard, Church Lane, Fovant, Wiltshire SP3 5LA, ENGLAND, 44 1722 714692, wsinclair@clara.net

Smith, Ron, 5869 Straley, Ft. Worth, TX, 76114

Smitty's Engraving, 800N Anderson Rd, Choctaw, OK, 73020, 405-769-3031, www.smittys-engraving.us

Spode, Peter, Tresaith Newland, Malvern, Worcestershire WR13 5AY, ENGLAND

Steduto, Giovanni, Gardone, V.T., ITALY

Swartley, Robert D., 2800 Pine St., Napa, CA, 94558, Engraver

Takeuchi, Shigetoshi, 21-14-1-Chome kamimuneoka Shiki shi, 353 Saitama, JAPAN

Theis, Terry, 21452 FM 2093, Harper, TX, 78631, 830-864-4438

Valade, Robert B., 931 3rd Ave., Seaside, OR, 97138, 503-738-7672, (503) 738-7672

Waldrop, Mark, 14562 SE 1st Ave. Rd., Summerfield, FL, 34491

Wallace, Terry, 385 San Marino, Vallejo, CA, 94589

Warenski, Julie, 590 East 500 N., Richfield, UT, 84701

Warren, Kenneth W., PO Box 2842, Wenatchee, WA, 98807-2842, 509-663-6123, (509) 663-6123

Whitehead, James D., 204 Cappucino Way, Sacramento, CA, 95838

Whitmore, Jerry, 1740 Churchill Dr., Oakland, OR, 97462

Williams, Gary, 221 Autumn Way, Elizabeth, KY, 42701

Winn, Travis A., 558 E. 3065 S., Salt Lake City, UT, 84106

Wood, Mel, PO Box 1255, Sierra Vista, AZ, 85636

Zietz, Dennis, 5906 40th Ave., Kenosha, WI, 53144

etchers

Baron Technology Inc., David Baron, 62 Spring Hill Rd., Trumbull, CT, 06611

Fountain Products, 492 Prospect Ave., West Springfield, MA, 01089

Hayes, Dolores, P.O. Box 41405, Los Angeles, CA, 90041

Holland, Dennis, 4908 17th Pl., Lubbock, TX, 79416

Kelso, Jim, RD1, Box 5300, Worcester, VT, 05682

Larstein, Francine, Francine Etchings & Etched Knives, 800-557-1525, 831-684-1949, francine@francinetchings.com, www.francineetchings.com

Lefaucheux, Jean-Victor, Saint-Denis-Le-Ferment, 27140 Gisors, FRANCE

Leibowitz, Leonard, 1025 Murrayhill Ave., Pittsburgh, PA, 15217

Mead, Faustina L., 2550 E. Mercury St., Inverness, FL, 34453-0514, 352-344-4751, scrimsha@infi.net, www.scrimshaw-by-faustina.com

Myers, Ron, 6202 Marglenn Ave., Baltimore, MD, 21206

Schlott, Harald, Zingster Str. 26, 13051 Berlin, GERMANY, 049 030 9293346, harald.schlott@T-online.de

Vallotton, A., Northwest Knife Supply, 621 Fawn Ridge Dr., Oakland, OR, 97462

Watson, Silvia, 350 Jennifer Lane, Driftwood, TX, 78619

heat treaters

Aoun, Charles, Galeb Knives, 69 Nahant St, Wakefield, MA, 01880, 781-224-3353, (781) 224-3353

Bay State Metal Treating Co, 6 Jefferson Ave, Woburn, MA, 01801

Paul, Bos Heat Treating, Shop:1900 Weld Blvd, El Cajon, CA, 92020, 619-562-2370 / 619-445-4740 Home, PaulBos@BuckKnives.com

Holt, B.R., 1238 Birchwood Drive, Sunnyvale, CA, 94089

Metal Treating Bodycote Inc, 710 Burns St, Cincinnati, OH, 45204

O&W Heat Treat inc, One Bidwell Rd, South Windsor, CT, 06074, 860-528-9239, (860) 291-9939, owht1@aol.com

Progressive Heat Treating Co, 2802 Charles City Rd, Richmond, VA, 23231, 804-545-0010, 804-545-0012

Texas Heat Treating Inc, 303 Texas Ave, Round Rock, TX, 78664

Texas Knifemakers Supply, 10649 Haddington Suite 180, Houston, TX, 77043

The Tinker Ship, 1120 Helen, Deer Park, TX, 77536

Valley Metal Treating Inc, 355 S East End Ave, Pomona, CA, 91766

Wilson, R.W., PO Box 2012, Weirton, WV, 26062

leather workers

Chas, Clements' Custom Leathercraft, 1741 Dallas St, Aurora, CO, 80010-2018

Congdon, David, 1063 Whitchurch Ct., Wheaton, IL, 60187

Cooper, Harold, 136 Winding Way, Frankfort, KY, 40601

Cooper, Jim, 1221 Cook Pl., Ramona, CA, 92065-3214, 760-789-1097, 760-788-7992, jamcooper@aol.com

Cow Catcher Leatherworks, 3006 Industral Dr, Raleigh, NC, 27609

Cubic, George, GC Custom Leather Co., 10561 E. Deerfield Pl., Tucson, AZ, 85749, 520-760-0695, gcubic@aol.com

Dawkins, Dudley, 221 N. Broadmoor, Topeka, KS, 66606-1254, 785-235-0468, dawkind1@junocom, ABS member/knifemaker forges straight knives

Evans, Scott V, Edge Works Mfg, 1171 Halltown Rd, Jacksonville, NC, 28546, 910-455-9834, (910) 346-5660, edgeworks@coastalnet.com, www.tacticalholsters.com

Genske, Jay, 283 Doty St, Fond du Lac, WI, 54935, 920-921-8019/Cell Phone 920-579-0144, jaygenske@hotmail.com, Custom Grinder, Custom Handle Artisan

Hawk, Ken, Rt. 1, Box 770, Ceres, VA, 24318-9630

Hendryx Design, Scott, 5997 Smokey Way, Boise, ID, 83714, 208-377-8044, (208) 377-2601

Homyk, David N., 8047 Carriage Ln., Wichita Falls, TX, 76306

John R., Stumpf, John's Custom Leather, 523 S Liberty St, Blairsville, PA, 15717

K & J Leatherworks, PO Box 609, Watford, ON, N0M 2S0, CANADA

Kravitt, Chris, HC 31 Box 6484, Rt 200, Ellsworth, ME, 04605-9805, 207-584-3000, 207-584-3000, sheathmkr@aol.com, www.treestumpteather.com, Reference: Tree Stump Leather

Larson, Richard, 549 E. Hawkeye, Turlock, CA, 95380

Layton, Jim, 2710 Gilbert Avenue, Portsmouth, OH, 45662

Lee, Randy, PO Box 1873, St. Johns, AZ, 85936, 928-337-2594, 928-337-5002, www.randyleeknives.com

Mason, Arne, 258 Wimer St., Ashland, OR, 97520, 541-482-2260, (541) 482-7785, www.arnemason.com

McGowan, Liz, 12629 Howard Lodge Dr., Sykesville, MD, 21784, 410-489-4323

Metheny, H.A. Whitey, 7750 Waterford Dr., Spotsylvania, VA, 22553

Miller, Michael K., 28510 Santiam Highway, Sweet Home, OR, 97386

Mobley, Martha, 240 Alapaha River Road, Chula, GA, 31733

Morrissey, Martin, 4578 Stephens Rd., Blairsville, GA, 30512

Niedenthal, John Andre, Beadwork & Buckskin, Studio 3955 NW 103 Dr., Coral Springs, FL, 33065-1551, 954-345-0447, a_niedenthal@hotmail.com

Neilson, Tess, RR2 Box 16, Wyalusing, PA, 18853, 570-746-4944, www.mountainhollow.net, doing business as Neilson's Mountain Hollow

Parsons, Michael R., McKee Knives, 7042 McFarland Rd, Indianapolis, IN, 46227, 317-784-7943

Poag, James H., RR #1 Box 212A, Grayville, IL, 62844

Rowe, Kenny, 1406 W. Ave. C, Hope, AR, 71801, 870-777-8216, (870) 777-2974, rowesleather@yahoo.com, www.knifeart.com or www.theedgeequipment.com

Ruiz Industries, 1513 Gardena Ave, Glendale, CA, 91204

Schrap, Robert G., 7024 W. Wells St., Wauwatosa, WI, 53213-3717, 414-771-6472, (414) 479-9765, knifesheaths@aol.com, www.customsheaths.com

Strahin, Robert, 401 Center St., Elkins, WV, 26241

Stuart, V. Pat, Rt. 1, Box 447-S, Greenville, VA, 24440

Tierney, Mike, 447 Rivercrest Dr., Woodstock ON CANADA, N4S 5W5

Todd, Ed, Red's Custom Leather, 9 Woodlawn Rd, Putnam Valley, NY, 10579, 845-528-3783

Turner, Kevin, 17 Hunt Ave., Montrose, NY, 10548

Velasquez, Gil, 7120 Madera Dr., Goleta, CA, 93117

Walker, John, 17 Laber Circle, Little Rock, AR, 72209

Watson, Bill, #1 Presidio, Wimberly, TX, 78676

Whinnery, Walt, 1947 Meadow Creek Dr., Louisville, KY, 40218

Williams, Sherman A., 1709 Wallace St., Simi Valley, CA, 93065

photographers

Alfano, Sam, 36180 Henery Gaines Rd., Pearl River, LA, 70452

Allen, John, Studio One, 3823 Pleasant Valley Blvd., Rockford, IL, 61114

Berisford, Bob, 505 West Adams St., Jacksonville, FL, 32202

Bilal, Mustafa, Turk's Head Productions, 908 NW 50th St., Seattle, WA, 98107-3634, 206-782-4164, (206) 783-5677, turksheadp@aol.com, www.turkshead.com

Bogaerts, Jan, Regenweg 14, 5757 Pl., Liessel, HOLLAND

Box Photography, Doug, 1804 W Main St, Brenham, TX, 77833-3420

Brown, Tom, 6048 Grants Ferry Rd., Brandon, MS, 39042- 8136

Buffaloe, Edwin, 104 W. Applegate, Austin, TX, 78753

Butman, Steve, PO Box 5106, Abilene, TX, 79608

Calidonna, Greg, 205 Helmwood Dr., Elizabethtown, KY, 42701

Campbell, Jim, 7935 Ranch Rd., Port Richey, FL, 34668

Courtice, Bill, PO Box 1776, Duarte, CA, 91010-4776

Crosby, Doug, RFD 1, Box 1111, Stockton Springs, ME, 04981

Danko, Michael, 3030 Jane Street, Pittsburgh, PA, 15203

Davis, Marshall B., PO Box 3048, Austin, TX, 78764

Dikeman, Lawrence, 17571 Parkplace Cir, Spring Lake, MI, 49456-9148

Durant, Ross, 316 E. 1st Ave., Vancouver BC CANADA, V5T 1A9

Earley, Don, 1241 Ft. Bragg Rd., Fayetteville, NC, 28305

Ehrlich, Linn M., 2643 N. Clybourn Ave., Chicago, IL, 60614

Ellison, Troy, PO Box 94393, Lubbock, TX, 79493, tellison@hiplains.net

Etzler, John, 11200 N. Island Rd., Grafton, OH, 44044

Fahrner, Dave, 1623 Arnold St., Pittsburgh, PA, 15205

Faul, Jan W., 903 Girard St. NE, Rr. Washington, DC, 20017

Fedorak, Allan, 28 W. Nicola St., Amloops BC CANADA, V2C 1J6

Forster, Jenny, 534 Nantucket Way, Island Lake, IL, 60042, www.thesilkca.msn.com

Fox, Daniel, Lumina Studios, 6773 Industrial Parkway, Cleveland, OH, 44070, 440-734-2118, (440) 734-3542, lumina@en.com

Gardner, Chuck, 116 Quincy Ave., Oak Ridge, TN, 37830

Gawryla, Don, 1105 Greenlawn Dr., Pittsburgh, PA, 15220

Goffe Photographic Associates, 3108 Monte Vista Blvd NE, Albuquerque, NM, 87106

Graham, James, 7434 E Northwest Hwy, Dallas, TX, 75231, jags2dos@onramp.net

Graley, Gary W., RR2 Box 556, Gillett, PA, 16925

Griggs, Dennis, 118 Pleasant Pt Rd, Topsham, ME, 04086, 207-725-5689

Hanusin, John, Reames-Hanusin Studio, PO Box 931, Northbrook, IL, 60065 0931

Hardy, Scott, 639 Myrtle Ave., Placerville, CA, 95667

Hodge, Tom, 7175 S US Hwy 1 Lot 36, Titusville, FL, 32780-8172

Holter, Wayne V., 125 Lakin Ave., Boonsboro, MD, 21713

Ingle, Ralph W., 151 Callan Dr., Rossville, GA, 30741, 706-858-0641, riengraver@aol.com, Photographer

Kelley, Gary, 17485 SW Pheasant Lane, Aloha, OR, 97006

Kerns, Bob, 18723 Birdseye Dr., Germantown, MD, 20874

LaFleur, Gordon, 111 Hirst, Box 1209, Parksville BC CANADA, V0R 270

Lautman, Andy, 4906 41st N.W., Washington, DC, 20016

Lear, Dale, 11342 State Route 588, Rio Grande, OH, 45674, 740-245-5007, dalelear@yahoo.com

LeBlanc, Paul, No. 3 Meadowbrook Cir., Melissa, TX, 75454

Lenz Photography, 939 S 48t St. Suite 206, Tempe, AZ, 85281

Lester, Dean, 2801 Junipero Ave Suite 212, Long Beach, CA, 90806-2140

Leviton, David A., A Studio on the Move, PO Box 2871, Silverdale, WA, 98383, 360-697-3452

Long, Gary W., 3556 Miller's Crossroad Rd., Hillsboro, TN, 37342

Long, Jerry, 402 E. Gladden Dr., Farmington, NM, 87401

Lum, Billy, 16307 Evening Star Ct., Crosby, TX, 77532

McCollum, Tom, PO Box 933, Lilburn, GA, 30226

Moake, Jim, 18 Council Ave., Aurora, IL, 60504

Moya Inc., 4212 S. Dixie Hwy., West Palm Beach, FL, 33405

Norman's Studio, 322 S. 2nd St, Vivian, LA, 71082

Owens, William T., Box 99, Williamsburg, WV, 24991

Palmer Studio, 2008 Airport Blvd, Mobile, AL, 36606

Parker, T.C., 1720 Pacific, Las Vegas, NV, 89104

Parsons, 15 South Mission, Suite 3, Wenatchee, WA, 98801

Payne, Robert G., PO. Box 141471, Austin, TX, 78714

Petertson Photography, Kent, 230 Polk St, Eugene, OR, 97402, kdp@pond.net, www.pond.net/kdp

Pigott, John, 231 Heidelberg Drive, Loveland, OH, 45140, 513-683-4875

Point Seven, 810 Seneca St., Toledo, OH, 43608

Rasmussen, Eric L., 1121 Eliason, Brigham City, UT, 84302

Rhoades, Cynthia J., Box 195, Clearmont, WY, 82835

Rice, Tim, 310 Wisconsin Ave., Whitefish, MT, 59937

Richardson, Kerry, 2520 Mimosa St., Santa Rosa, CA, 95405, 707-575-1875, kerry@sonic.net, www.sonic.net/~kerry

Ross, Bill, 28364 S. Western Ave. Suite 464, Rancho Palos Verdes, CA, 90275

Rubicam, Stephen, 14 Atlantic Ave., Boothbay Harbor, ME, 04538-1202

Rush, John D., 2313 Maysel, Bloomington, IL, 61701

Schreiber, Roger, 429 Boren Ave. N., Seattle, WA, 98109

Semmer, Charles, 7885 Cyd Dr., Denver, CO, 80221

Silver Images Photography, 2412 N Keystone, Flagstaff, AZ, 86004

Slobodian, Scott, 4101 River Ridge Dr., PO Box 1498, San Andreas, CA, 95249, 209-286-1980, (209) 286-1982, www.slobodianswords.com

Smith, Earl W., 5121 Southminster Rd., Columbus, OH, 43221

Smith, Randall, 1720 Oneco Ave., Winter Park, FL, 32789

Storm Photo, 334 Wall St, Kingston, NY, 12401

Surles, Mark, PO Box 147, Falcon, NC, 28342

Third Eye Photos, 140 E Sixth Ave, Helena, MT, 59601

Thurber, David, PO Box 1006, Visalia, CA, 93279

Tighe, Brian, RR 1, Ridgeville ON CANADA, L0S 1M0, 905-892-2734, www.ckg.org

Towell, Steven L., 3720 N.W. 32nd Ave., Camas, WA, 98607

Troutman, Harry, 107 Oxford Dr., Lititz, PA, 17543

Valley Photo, 2100 Arizona Ave, Yuma, AZ, 85364

Vara, Lauren, 4412 Waples Rd., Granbury, TX, 76049

Verno, Jay, Verno Studio, 3030 Jane St, Pittsburgh, PA, 15203

Wells, Carlene L., 1060 S. Main Sp. 52, Colville, WA, 99114

Weyer International, 2740 Nebraska Ave, Toledo, OH, 43607, 800-448-8424, (419) 534-2697, law-weyerinternational@msn.com

Wise, Harriet, 242 Dill Ave., Frederick, MD, 21701

Worley, Holly, 6360 W David Dr, Littleton, CO, 80128-5708

scrimshanders

Adlam, Tim, 1705 Witzel Ave., Oshkosh, WI, 54902, 920-235-4589, (920) 234-4589

Anderson, Terry Jack, 10076 Birnamwoods Way, Riverton, UT, 84065-9073

Bailey, Mary W., 3213 Jonesboro Dr., Nashville, TN, 37214, mbscrim@aol.com

Baker, Duane, 2145 Alum Creek Dr., Cambridge Park Apt. #10, Columbus, OH, 43207

Barndt, Kristen A., RR3, Box 72, Kunkletown, PA, 18058, 610-381-4048, kris@kabstudio.com, www.kabstudio.com

Barrows, Miles, 524 Parsons Ave., Chillicothe, OH, 45601

Brady, Sandra, PO Box 104, Monclova, OH, 43542, 419-866-0435, (419) 867-0656, sandyscrim@hotmail.com

Beauchamp, Gaetan, 125 de la Riviere, Stoneham , PQ, G0A 4P0, CANADA, 418-848-1914, (418) 848-6859

Bellet, Connie, PO Box 151, , Palermo, ME, 04354 0151, 207-993-2327, phwhitehawk@gwl.net

Benade, Lynn, 2610 Buckhurst Dr, Beachwood, OH, 44122, 216-464-0777, llbnc17@aol.com

Bonshire, Benita, 1121 Burlington Dr., Muncie, IN, 47302

Boone Trading Co Inc, PO Box 669, Brinnon, WA, 98320, 800-423-1945, ww.boonetrading.com

Bryan, Bob, 1120 Oak Hill Rd., Carthage, MO, 64836

Byrne, Mary Gregg, 1018 15th St., Bellingham, WA, 98225-6604

Cable, Jerry, 332 Main St., Mt. Pleasant, PA, 15666

Caudill, Lyle, 7626 Lyons Rd., Georgetown, OH, 45121

Cole, Gary, PO Box 668, Naalehu, HI, 96772, 808-929-9775, 808-929-7371

Collins, Michael, Rt. 3075, Batesville Rd., Woodstock, GA, 30188

Conover, Juanita Rae, PO Box 70442, Eugene, OR, 97401, 541-747-1726 or 543-4851, juanitaraeconover@yahoo.com

Courtnage, Elaine, Box 473, Big Sandy, MT, 59520

Cover Jr., Raymond A., Rt. 1, Box 194, Mineral Point, MO, 63660

Cox, J. Andy, 116 Robin Hood Lane, Gaffney, SC, 29340

Davenport, Susan, 36842 Center Ave., Dade City, FL, 33525

Dietrich, Roni, Wild Horse Studio, 1257 Cottage Dr, Harrisburg, PA, 17112, 717-469-0587, ronimd@aol

DiMarzo, Richard, 2357 Center Place, Birmingham, AL, 35205

Dolbare, Elizabeth, PO Box 502, Dubois, WY, 82513-0502

Downing, Jim, PO Box 4224, Springfield, MO, 65808, 417-865-5953, www.thegunengraver.com

Eklund, Maihkel, Föne 1111, S-82041 Färila, SWEDEN, +46 6512 4192, maihkel.eklund@swipnet.se, www.art-knives.com

Eldridge, Allan, 1424 Kansas Lane, Gallatin, TN, 37066

Evans, Rick M., 2717 Arrowhead Dr., Abilene, TX, 79606

Fields, Donald, 790 Tamerlane St, Deltona, FL, 32725, 386-532-9070, donaldfields@aol.com

Fisk, Dale, Box 252, Council, ID, 83612, dafisk@ctcweb.net

Foster, Norvell , Foster Interprises, PO Box 200343, San Antonio, TX, 78220

Fountain Products, 492 Prospect Ave., West Springfield, MA, 01089

Gill, Scott, 925 N. Armstrong St., Kokomo, IN, 46901

Halligan, Ed, 14 Meadow Way, Sharpsburg, GA, 30277, ehkiss@bellsouth.net

Hands, Barry Lee, 26192 East Shore Route, Bigfork, MT, 59911

Hargraves Sr., Charles, RR 3 Bancroft, Ontario CANADA, K0L 1C0

Harless, Star, c/o Arrow Forge, P.O. Box 845, Stoneville, NC, 27048-0845

Harrington, Fred A., Summer: 2107 W Frances Rd., Mt Morris MI 48458 8215 Winter: 3725 Citrus, St. James City, FL, 33956, Winter 239-283-0721, Summer 810-686-3008

Hielscher, Vickie, 6550 Otoe Rd, P.O. Box 992, Alliance, NE, 69301, 308-762-4318, hielscher@premaonline.com

High, Tom, 5474 S. 112.8 Rd., Alamosa, CO, 81101, 719-589-2108, scrimshaw@vanion.com, www.rockymountainscrimshaw.com

Himmelheber, David R., 11289 40th St. N., Royal Palm Beach, FL, 33411

Holland, Dennis K., 4908-17th Place, Lubbock, TX, 79416

Imboden II, Howard L., 620 Deauville Dr., Dayton, OH, 45429, 937-439-1536, Guards by the Last Wax Technic

Johnson, Corinne, W3565 Lockington, Mindora, WI, 54644

Johnston, Kathy, W. 1134 Providence, Spokane, WA, 99205

Karst-Stone, Linda , 402 Hwy. 27 E., Ingram, TX, 78025-3317, 830-896-4678, 830-896-4678, karstone@ktc.com

Kelso, Jim, RD 1, Box 5300, Worcester, VT, 05682

Kirk, Susan B., 1340 Freeland Rd., Merrill, MI, 48637

Koevenig, Eugene and Eve, Koevenig's Engraving Service, Rabbit Gulch, Box 55, Hill City, SD, 57745-0055

Kostelnik, Joe and Patty, RD #4, Box 323, Greensburg, PA, 15601

Kudlas, John M., 55280 Silverwolf Dr, Barnes, WI, 54873, 715-795-2031, jkudlas@cheqnet.net, scrimshander

Lemen, Pam, 3434 N. Iroquois Ave., Tucson, AZ, 85705

Martin, Diane, 28220 N. Lake Dr., Waterford, WI, 53185

McDonald, René Cosimini-, 14730 61 Court N., Loxahatchee, FL, 33470

McFadden, Berni, 2547 E Dalton Ave, Dalton Gardens, ID, 83815-9631

McGowan, Frank, 12629 Howard Lodge Dr., Sykesville, MD, 21784

McGrath, Gayle, PMB 232 15201 N Cleveland Ave, N Ft Myers, FL, 33903

McLaran, Lou, 603 Powers St., Waco, TX, 76705

McWilliams, Carole, PO Box 693, Bayfield, CO, 81122

Mead, Faustina L., 2550 E. Mercury St., Inverness, FL, 34453-0514, 352-344-4751, scrimsha@infi.net, www.scrimshaw-by-faustina.com

Mitchell, James, 1026 7th Ave., Columbus, GA, 31901

Moore, James B., 1707 N. Gillis, Stockton, TX, 79735

Ochonicky, Michelle Mike, Stone Hollow Studio, 31 High Trail, Eureka, MO, 63025, 636-938-9570, www.bestofmissourihands.com

Ochs, Belle, 124 Emerald Lane, Largo, FL, 33771, 727-530-3826, chuckandbelle@juno.com, www.oxforge.com

Pachi, Mirella, Via Pometta 1, 17046 Sassello (SV), ITALY, 019 720086, www.pachi-knives.com

Parish, Vaughn, 103 Cross St., Monaca, PA, 15061

Peterson, Lou, 514 S. Jackson St., Gardner, IL, 60424

Poag, James H., RR #1 Box 212A, Grayville, IL, 62844

Polk, Trena, 4625 Webber Creek Rd., Van Buren, AR, 72956

Purvis, Hilton, PO Box 371, Noordhoek, 7979, SOUTH AFFRIC, 27-21-789114, hiltonp@relkomsa.net, www.kgsa.co.za/member/hiltonpurvis

Ramsey, Richard , 8525 Trout Farm Rd, Neosho, MO, 64850

Ristinen, Lori, 14245 County Hwy 45, Menahga, MN, 56464, 218-538-6608, lori@loriristinen.com

Roberts, J.J., 7808 Lake Dr., Manassas, VA, 22111

Rudolph, Gil, 20922 Oak Pass Ave, Tehachapi, CA, 93561, 661-822-4949, www.gtraks@csurfers.net

Rundell, Joe, 6198 W. Frances Rd., Clio, MI, 48420

Saggio, Joe, 1450 Broadview Ave. #12, Columbus, OH, 43212, jvsag@webtv.net, www.j.v.saggio@worldnet.att.net

Sahlin, Viveca, Konstvaktarevagem 9, S-772 40 Grangesberg, SWEDEN, 46 240 23204, www.scrimart.use

Satre, Robert, 518 3rd Ave. NW, Weyburn SK CANADA, S4H 1R1

Schickl, L., Ottingweg 497, A-5580 Tamsweg, AUSTRIA, 0043 6474 8583, Scrimshander

Schlott, Harald, Zingster Str. 26, 13051 Berlin, 929 33 46, GERMANY

Schulenburg, E.W., 25 North Hill St., Carrollton, GA, 30117

Schwallie, Patricia, 4614 Old Spartanburg Rd. Apt. 47, Taylors, SC, 29687

Selent, Chuck, PO Box 1207, Bonners Ferry, ID, 83805

Semich, Alice, 10037 Roanoke Dr., Murfreesboro, TN, 37129

Shostle, Ben, 1121 Burlington, Muncie, IN, 47302

Sinclair, W.P., 3, The Pippins, Warminster, Wiltshire BA12 8TH, ENGLAND

Smith, Peggy, 676 Glades Rd., #3, Gatlinburg, TN, 37738

Smith, Ron, 5869 Straley, Ft. Worth, TX, 76114

Stahl, John, Images In Ivory, 2049 Windsor Rd., Baldwin, NY, 11510, 516-223-5007

Steigerwalt, Jim, RD#3, Sunbury, PA, 17801, imivory@msn.com, www.imagesinivory.org

Stuart, Stephen, 15815 Acorn Circle, Tavares, FL, 32778, 352-343-8423, (352) 343-8916, inkscratch@aol.com

Talley, Mary Austin, 2499 Countrywood Parkway, Cordova, TN, 38018

Thompson, Larry D., 23040 Ave. 197, Strathmore, CA, 93267

Tong, Jill, PO Box 572, Tombstone, AZ, 85638

Toniutti, Nelida, Via G. Pascoli, 33085 Maniago-PN, ITALY

Tucker, Steve, 3518 W. Linwood, Turlock, CA, 95380

Tyser, Ross, 1015 Hardee Court, Spartanburg, SC, 29303

Velasquez, Gil, Art of Scrimshaw, 7120 Madera Dr., Goleta, CA, 93117

Warren, Al, 1423 Santa Fe Circle, Roseville, CA, 95678, 916-257-5904, al@warrenknives.com, www.warrenknives.com

Williams, Gary, (Garbo), PO Box 210, Glendale, KY, 42740-0210

Winn, Travis A., 558 E. 3065 S., Salt Lake City, UT, 84106

Young, Mary, 4826 Storeyland Dr., Alton, IL, 62002

Zima, Russell, 7291 Ruth Way, Denver, CO, 80221

other

Robertson, Kathy, Impress by Design, PO Box 1367, Evans, GA, 30809-1367, 706-650-0982, (706) 860-1623, impressbydesign@comcast.net, Advertising/graphic designer

Rudolph, Gil, 20922 Oak Pass Ave, Tehachapi, CA, 93561, 661-822-4949, www.gtraks@csurfers.net, Firearms engraver

organizations & publications

organizations

AMERICAN BLADESMITH SOCIETY
c/o Jim Batson; PO Box 977; Peralta, NM 87042

AMERICAN KNIFE & TOOL INSTITUTE*
Dave Kowalski, Comm. Coordinator; AKTI, Dept BL2; PO Box 432; Iola WI 54945-0432; 715-445-3781; 715-445-5228; communications@akti.org; www.akti.org

AMERICAN KNIFE THROWERS ALLIANCE
c/o Bobby Branton; 4976 Seewee Rd.; Awendaw, SC 29429

ART KNIFE COLLECTOR'S ASSOCIATION
c/o Mitch Weiss, Pres.; 2211 Lee Road, Suite 104; Winter Park, FL 32789

AUSTRALIAN KNIFEMAKERS GUILD INC.
PO Box 659; Belgrave 3160; Victoria, AUSTRALIA

CALIFORNIA KNIFEMAKERS ASSOCIATION
c/o Clint Breshears, Membership Chairman; 1261 Keats St.; Manhattan Beach CA 90266

CANADIAN KNIFEMAKERS GUILD
c/o Peter Wile; RR # 3; Bridgewater N.S.; B4V 2W2; 902-543-1373; www.ckg.org

JAPANESE SWORD SOCIETY OF THE U.S.
PO Box 712; Breckenridge, TX 76424

KNIFE COLLECTORS CLUB INC, THE
1920 N 26th St.; Lowell AR 72745; 479-631-0055; 479-631-8734; ag@agrussell.com Web:www.club@k-c.com
The oldest and largest association of knife collectors. Issues limited edition knives, both handmade and highest quality production, in very limited numbers. The very earliest was the CM-1, Kentucky Rifle.

KNIFE WORLD
PO Box 3395; Knoxville, TN 37927

KNIFEMAKERS GUILD
c/o Al Pendray, President; 13950 N.E. 20th St.; Williston FL 32696; 352-528-6124; 352-528-6124; bpendray@aol.com

KNIFEMAKERS GUILD OF SOUTHERN AFRICA, THE
c/o Carel Smith; PO Box 1744; Delmars 2210; SOUTH AFRICA; carelsmith@therugby.co.za Web:www.kgsa.co.za

MONTANA KNIFEMAKERS' ASSOCIATION, THE
14440 Harpers Bridge Rd.; Missoula, MT 59808; 406-543-0845
Annual book of custom knife makers' works and directory of knife making supplies; $19.99

NATIONAL KNIFE COLLECTORS ASSOC.
PO Box 21070; Chattanooga, TN 37424; 423-892-5007; 423-899-9456; nkca@aol.com Web: nationalknive.org

NEO-TRIBAL METALSMITHS
PO Box 44095; Tucson, AZ 85773-4095

NEW ENGLAND CUSTOM KNIFE ASSOCIATION
George R. Rebello, President; 686 Main Rd.; Brownville, ME 04414; Web:www.kinvesby.com/necka.html

NORTH CAROLINA CUSTOM KNIFEMAKERS GUILD
c/o Tommy McNabb, Pres.; 4015 Brownsboro Rd.; Winston-Salem, NC 27106; tommy@tmcnabb.com; Web:www.nckniveguild.org

PROFESSIONAL KNIFEMAKERS ASSOCIATION
2905 N. Montana Ave., Ste. 30027; Helena, MT 59601

UNITED KINGDOM BLADE ASSOCIATION (UKBA)
PO Box 1; Brampton, CA67GD; ENGLAND

publications

BLADE
700 E. State St., Iola, WI 54990-0001; 715-445-2214; www.blademag.com
The world's No. 1 knife magazine.

CUTTING EDGE, The
1920 N 26th St.; Lowell AR 72745; 479-631-0055; 479-631-8734; buyer@cuttingedge.com
After-market knives since 1968. We offer about 1,000 individual knives each month. Subscription by first class mail, in U.S. $20 per year, Canada or Mexico by air mail, $25 per year. All overseas by air mail, $40 per year. The oldest and the most experienced in the business of buying and selling knives. We buy collections of any size, take knives on consignment or we will trade. Every month there are eight pages in color featuring the work of top makers.

KNIVES ILLUSTRATED
265 S. Anita Dr., Ste. 120; Orange, CA 92868; 714-939-9991 knivesillustrated@yahoo.com Web:www.knivesillustrated.com
All encompassing publication focusing on factory knives, new handmades, shows and industry news.

RESOURCE GUIDE AND NEWSLETTER / AUTOMATIC KNIVES
2269 Chestnut St., Suite 212; San Francisco, CA 94123; 415-731-0210; Web:www.thenewsletter.com

TACTICAL KNIVES
Harris Publications; 1115 Broadway; New York, NY 10010

TRIBAL NOW!
Neo-Tribal Metalsmiths; P.O. Box 44095; Tucson, AZ 85733-4095

WEYER INTERNATIONAL BOOK DIVISION
2740 Nebraska Ave.; Toledo, OH 43607-3245

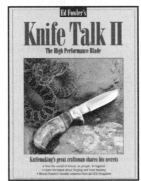
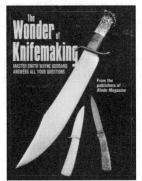